# The Cathedrals of England

MIDLAND, EASTERN AND NORTHERN ENGLAND

BY NIKOLAUS PEVSNER AND PRISCILLA METCALF

WITH CONTRIBUTIONS BY VARIOUS HANDS

VIKING

VIKING

Penguin Books Ltd, Harmondsworth, Middlesex, England
Viking Penguin Inc., 40 West 23rd Street, New York, New York 10010, U.S.A.
Penguin Books Australia Ltd, Ringwood, Victoria, Australia
Penguin Books Canada Ltd, 2801 John Street, Markham, Ontario, Canada L3R 1B4
Penguin Books (N.Z.) Ltd, 182–190 Wairau Road, Auckland 10, New Zealand

First published 1985

Designed by Gerald Cinamon

Typeset in 9/11 Aldus
by Rowland Phototypesetting Ltd, Bury St Edmunds, Suffolk, England
Printed in Great Britain by
Balding & Mansell Ltd, Wisbech, Cambs, England

*Frontispiece: Ely Cathedral, the Octagon, interior*

*British Library Cataloguing in Publication Data*

Pevsner, Nikolaus
    The cathedrals of England: Midland, Eastern
    and Northern England.
    1. Cathedrals—England
    I. Title   II. Metcalf, Priscilla
    726'.6'0942   NA5461

ISBN 0-670-80125-9

*Library of Congress Catalog Card Number*
    84-51886

Dedicated by the compiler
to Nikolaus Pevsner
1902–83

LECTOR
SI MONUMENTUM REQUIRIS
CIRCUMSPICE

Newcastle-upon-Tyne

Carlisle

Durham

Middlesbrough

Ripon  York

Lancaster

Bradford  Leeds

Blackburn  Wakefield

Salford  Manchester

Liverpool  Sheffield

Chester  Lincoln

Southwell

Derby  Nottingham

Shrewsbury  Lichfield  Leicester  Norwich

Peterborough

Birmingham  Coventry  Ely

Worcester  Northampton  Bury St Edmunds

Hereford

Gloucester  St Albans  Chelmsford

Brentwood

Oxford  London

Rochester

Bristol  Guildford  Canterbury

Wells  Winchester

Salisbury  Chichester  Arundel

Portsmouth

Exeter

Truro  Plymouth

| 0 | | 50 | | 100 miles |
|---|---|---|---|---|
| 0 | 50 | 100 | 150 km | |

# Contents

# Foreword

'Pevsner's cathedral descriptions' are among the most brilliant parts of his *Buildings of England* series – not only the big set-pieces on Ely Octagon, the spatial experiments at Bristol and Wells, the Lincoln 'crazy vaults', but the whole sustained disciplined coverage of these for the most part marvellous buildings. Many people have wished that his descriptions could be brought together, revised where required by increase in knowledge since they were first published in that series between 1951 and 1974. When Sir Nikolaus asked me to do this, he thought the book should be more than a gathering of updated B of E texts: dealing as it does with only one building-type, it could be moulded a little by the compiler. Much is just as it was, but wherever seemed useful I have altered wording, rearranged paragraphs, woven in new matter and removed obsolete matter, inserted cross-references, improved sign-posting and placed buildings and furnishings more specifically in their settings, rewritten texts originally written before the series got into its stride (e.g. Exeter, Southwark Anglican), edited contributions from other scholars and offered a few small thoughts of my own: e.g. on Chichester crossing tower, Durham kitchen vault, the Ely Octagon restorations, Liverpool nave bridge, St Paul's dome, Worcester nave pavement, attitudes to monuments in Westminster Abbey, the Victorian naves at Bristol and Southwark, and, here and there, on historicism in the Middle Ages. (Sir Nikolaus's views on historicism or revivalism, as I have pointed out in the General Introduction, were far from monolithic.) In smaller matters, the Glossary looks askance at one or two accepted terms used in the text (spherical triangle, syncopated arcading). But it has all been to the one end of making this the architectural description of the species English Cathedral that Sir Nikolaus had in mind. It is a pleasure to present it in this new context and demonstrate again how there was always the appreciative eye and word for quality, how even amid the austerest prose such phrases as 'that irresistible *excelsior*' (as at Worcester) arose. Whether I have done too little or too much is for readers to judge: young ones may think the former, elders the latter. The revision of well-known texts, like the restoration of well-loved cathedrals, invites infinite fuss.

Part of the fascination of such buildings lies in the fact that each one is different. Yet they can be roughly grouped as follows (fuller definitions are given in the General Introduction): medieval cathedral churches, former abbey churches, and former collegiate churches; enlarged parish churches, medieval and later; the one C17 cathedral church built as such; Victorian buildings of the revived Roman Catholic Church; and new buildings of the past hundred years. At present England has sixty-one cathedrals, nineteen Catholic and forty-two Anglican. (For the following cathedrals, see the B of E *London* volumes: Russian Orthodox, Paddington; Ukrainian-in-exile, Westminster; Greek Orthodox, Camberwell (by Oldrid Scott, Waterhouse and Belcher respectively). For Welsh, Scottish and Irish cathedrals, see the B of W, B of S, and B of I series.) To the sixty-one English cathedrals we add Westminster Abbey: in its special role as coronation church, sometime royal burial church, and independent 'Royal Peculiar', it has had much architectural, sculptural and decorative influence on some of the medieval cathedrals. We leave out Bath Abbey, which since the C12 has been only nominally part of a bishop's title (see Wells), and also great churches like Beverley and Selby that are not seats of diocesan bishops: church-administrative history, not church-architectural history, dictates our subject. One might have made this book 'Pevsner's Great Churches' and omitted the so-called parish-church cathedrals, thus inviting problems of how many ruined abbey churches to include and evading the architectural problems of the working diocesan church. At first Sir Nikolaus himself wondered whether our inclusion of Westminster Abbey might be inconsistent, but subsequently he agreed with an early version of this foreword. One can but observe that a country tolerant of Royal Peculiars may not mind inconsistency too much. And the entirely consistent architectural historian may not exist. So we can display the virtuosity of his description of Westminster Abbey among its peers, making the number of our entries sixty-two. And a mixed lot they are.

As they would have made too huge a single volume, the book is in two volumes, divided geographically by an imaginary line from the mouth of the River Severn to the mouth of the River Blackwater – that is, keeping Oxford, St Albans and the small cathedrals of Essex south of it and the Three Choirs cathedrals of Gloucester, Hereford and Worcester and the cathedrals of East Anglia north of it. Each entry concentrates on the main vessel, with cloister, chapter house, library and closely attached buildings only. Details of precinct or close, and of detached deaneries and bishops' palaces, are omitted except in summaries of surroundings. Important as such related buildings often are – e.g. the Castle at Durham – their inclusion would have meant a less concentrated and unbearably bulky text. Like the rest of the cathedral town, these can be found in the relevant B of E volume. Gold and silver plate, with a very few exceptions, joins the list of mobile items excluded, though new treasuries for displaying diocesan plate are mentioned. With the exception of a few large tapestries, textiles are omitted (banners, frontals, vestments, kneelers). Also omitted are bells, books (and candles), but important chandeliers are in. Chests, tables and chairs are out save for a few very old and interesting ones.

Sir Nikolaus's prescription for the B of E volumes was this: after library research by an assistant for printed sources to fortify his own knowledgeable observation, he made his own notes on the spot and wrote his description at the end of the same day, later checking details against photographs or local knowledge. Sometimes he added brief contributions from other scholars' research, but without undertaking deeper research himself. The aim was to attend mostly to features one can see (e.g. referring only occasionally to timber roofs hidden by vaults), and on the whole to be selective – the most significant and justifiable departure from that rule here being David O'Connor's survey of all the York glass. It should be added that the Leverhulme Trust funded initial research for a number of B of E volumes.

Authors of the original texts, where not Pevsner, are named at the head of the entry. As time and the county series went on, Sir Nikolaus called in younger scholars to take on part of the load, some of whom produced cathedral descriptions that now appear here. John Newman (Canterbury and Rochester), the late David Verey (Gloucester) and Alexandra Wedgwood (Birmingham St Chad's) have revised their own texts, with suggestions and additions from me. John Hutchinson, who had a hand in the original text on York Minster, revised it in accord with the latest restoration work there, and he also revised Ripon with some additions from me. I have revised the late Ian Nairn's texts on Chichester, Guildford and Arundel, with help from specialists. Anthony Quiney rewrote Truro, George McHardy rewrote Brentwood, and Philip M. Draper of Bristol contributed the new entry on Clifton, all with insertions by me. I have been able to use and slightly revise David Lloyd's entries on Portsmouth and Elizabeth Williamson's recent revisions of Durham, Southwell, Derby, Leicester and Nottingham, and am grateful to them. Bridget Cherry's advice and moral support from the Buildings of England office have been indispensable throughout. She and John Newman have both kindly read and commented on the General Introduction. Most of all I thank the copy editor Judith Wardman, the picture editor Susan Rose-Smith and especially Catriona Luckhurst for their help on this unusually complicated book.

Many scholars have helped. One most useful was George McHardy, who went round nineteen major cathedrals as well as many smaller ones for us, checking the old text 'on site' with a diligent eye. Michael Swanton sent much useful matter on Exeter, and I am grateful to Michael Laithwaite for checking monuments there. From historians of art and architecture we had Sir John Summerson's comments on St Paul's and the two Liverpool texts, John

Maddison's on Lichfield and Chester, Eric Fernie's on Norwich, and Peter Draper's on Lincoln; also from Thomas Cocke on C17 and C18 restorations, Jane Geddes on medieval ironwork, Michael Gillingham on organ cases, J. Mordaunt Crook on the Victorian decoration of St Paul's and the restoration of Salisbury chapter house, Julian Munby on Chichester and Oxford, Jeffrey West on Chichester, and on stained glass Martin Harrison and David O'Connor most liberally, on Catholic furnishings Roderick O'Donnell most lavishly, and miscellaneous observations on a number of cathedrals from Peter Howell, John Martin Robinson, Christopher Wilson, Andor Gomme and David Palliser. Members of the staff of the Victoria and Albert Museum patiently answered questions. This book is a splendid example of the scholarly community's willingness to help; for any mistakes in my use of it, of course, they are not to blame. Indeed the British Archaeological Association's recent conference publications on the English cathedrals (see Recent Literature) show a resurgence of the keenest interest in medieval art and architecture among young scholars since the C19 – now with an added sense of the C19.

We particularly thank the Deans of Chichester, Ely, St Paul's and Salisbury for answering questions; Monsignor Canon Bartlett for reading the text on Westminster Cathedral; and Dean Emeritus Holderness of Lichfield and Canon Lowther Clarke of Chichester for writing to us earlier with information. We are much indebted to reports on the furnishings of Chester and York published by the late Canon Addleshaw; and Canon Ingram Hill has been most helpful to me about Canterbury. Among cathedral archivists and librarians, L. S. Colchester at Wells has been wonderfully informative and helpful, and Mrs Audrey Erskine at Exeter most kindly went over my text, as did N. H. MacMichael our text on Westminster Abbey, where too the late librarian Howard Nixon so kindly answered questions.

Peter Burman, Secretary to the Cathedrals Advisory Commission for England, kindly informed the cathedral architects about this book. I am especially anxious to mention the cathedral architects or, as sometimes entitled, surveyors of the fabrics of these great and often awkward buildings, especially those who, when they heard of the book, immediately volunteered help and subsequently put up with many questions: Stephen Dykes Bower, a thesaurus of lore on many fabrics, particularly at Westminster Abbey, as well as Peter Foster, his successor there; Bernard Ashwell on Worcester and Gloucester; Alan Rome on Peterborough, Salisbury and others; John Phillips on Westminster Cathedral and Truro; and on Derby and Portsmouth Anthony New of Seely & Paget, who also shared much information he was about to publish in a cathedrals book of his own; also Mrs Corinne Bennett most minutely on Winchester; Ian Curry most fully on Durham restorations; and subsequently Peter Miller on Ely, Peter Gundry on Exeter, Charles Brown on Lichfield and Coventry, Ronald Sims on Chester, Southwark, Southwell and Newcastle, Keith Darby of Feilden & Mawson on Norwich – and from there particularly, for information sent over many years, Arthur B. Whittingham, the former cathedral architect, now its archaeological consultant. For the historian, a word with the learned architect to dean and chapter can be so rewarding; present restorations become more comprehensible the more one understands the nature of the site, the stone, the client, the craftsmen – and the restorations done before. Gerald Cobb's recent book on the 'forgotten centuries' since the Reformation shows, for one group of cathedrals, what a complex matter is that intermittently continuous performance, restoration.

Among the archaeologists, Warwick Rodwell has most generously summarized the excavations at Wells, so has Derek Phillips with John Hutchinson for York, and Tim Tatton-Brown has most fully answered many questions on Canterbury. For Winchester, although Martin Biddle unfortunately had no time to revise his own brief report of 1966 in B of E *Hampshire* for us, the Biddles' detailed reports will be found in the relevant periodicals and in their own final publication, and no doubt this will be the case with their excavation at St Albans. Cathedral archaeology really needs a book to itself, as well as continual progress reports, and we cannot do it full justice here. On the whole, let me say most emphatically, the willingness of so many people – historians, librarians, architects, archaeologists – to help us is a recognition of Sir Nikolaus's national influence in urging official help to the causes they are engaged in. Many have told me how much they owe to him.

It would have been tempting to add more items of literary interest, and a few could not be resisted, e.g. the epitaphs of Jane Austen at Winchester and Richard Jefferies at Salisbury. For an obscure reference naming the designer of Charlotte Yonge's memorial at Winchester we are indebted to the County Archivist Miss Margaret Cash and the Winchester Archivist Mr A. P. Whitaker. And, in time to correct old notions about Donne's monument in St Paul's, Professor Emeritus Kathleen Tillotson directed me to Dame Helen Gardner's conclusions on the matter. Architectural historians need friends in other disciplines; some of them are aware that they need us. Tempting too to extend our musical references, but organs or at any rate their cases are more our business than organists, save those known also as composers who received memorable memorials. One can never forget that the performance of cathedral music is one of the greatest arts of England.

Old hands among B of E readers will recall that the sequence of description is seldom that of the visitor starting at the west door. We begin more often though not invariably with the earliest surviving part of the building, often though not always the east end. Exteriors usually though not always precede interiors, and those are followed in varying sequence by cloisters etc. and furnishings; the place of the chapter house in the text sequence is especially variable. So the framework is flexible and sign-posted by headings, and individual lists of contents indicating chronology have been supplied for the more complex cathedrals. 'Furnishings' include fixtures and fittings, sometimes with monuments and/or stained glass separately. While the glass is treated as furnishing, window tracery is usually described as part of the architectural exterior. Architectural sculpture, including bosses and capitals *in situ*, is described with the architecture, but movable statues are with furnishings. It may be found that since we went to press even quite big fittings have mysteriously moved about in keeping with new liturgical ways. Visitors will understand that not every corner of a cathedral described here is always open to the public, though a quiet word to a verger may help. These are busy working buildings that must occasionally be closed to sightseers, in part and for short periods.

It is good to be allowed so many illustrations. A few have been chosen from antiquarian motives, to show features since altered or no longer in place, e.g. the screens at Hereford and Birmingham, and pre-war views of St Paul's. Some of our antiquarian views were engraved in the early C 19 for John Britton's *Cathedral Antiquities* volumes, with their pre-Victorian flavour. For medieval cathedral plans we have been able to use the fine set published in the *Builder* during 1891–3, from an unbound set in the library of the Society of Antiquaries. Both our Glossary and Recent Literature sections have short introductions added for the use of those seeking more help on terminology and bibliography than we have space for.

May I add appreciation for British Rail, by which comfortable day trips to all the English cathedrals are and always should be possible. The writing of the B of E series had to depend for county coverage on a motor car. For the more single-minded journeys in aid of this book, only trains would do. And for the modern pilgrim, an unpackaged tour on foot from the station to each great focal building should be a ritual part of the visit. In the larger cathedrals in the 1980s bookshops, plumbing, even sometimes feeding (in season) for visitors have arrived since I first went round in the 1950s. One has heard from Sir Nikolaus's old students about the rigorous all-day cathedral tours he led them on. With this book we can sample the splendid rigours of his descriptions, and compare one cathedral with another, at our own speed. For me it has been rather like restoring a cathedral.

Westminster, 1983                     PRISCILLA METCALF

# General Introduction

The begetter of this book began his *Outline of European Architecture* in the 1940s, when so much European architecture was under stress, by discriminating: 'A bicycle shed is a building; Lincoln Cathedral is a piece of architecture.' A cathedral is more indeed than 'a building'. More too than a work of art, very much more than a museum of works of art. Churchmen quickly remind us of its purpose as centre of worship and generator of prayer for a widespread diocese. Such a fabric is more than a setting for ritual observance and religious experience, more than a seat of administration, more than a teaching place, more than a concert hall. Ministered to by centuries of clergy and craftsmen, the medieval fabrics are mosaics of communal memory, memorials to English men and women's own pasts. These fabrics can be dated, as if by tree-rings or geological strata, by their layers of architectural styles. Pioneering structurally they were, often it seems blindly bold, rearing high vaults on huge piers over shallow foundations before pumps able to remove deeper ground-water were invented. Crypts and undercrofts, we shall find, were only partly if at all underground. In the engineering sense, most cathedrals were more complex than most castles. We try to know what all the functions performed in cathedrals were, so that we may understand all that the masons and carpenters were up to. More bequests endowing altars and chantries meant more east-end expansion, more elaborate processions needed wider ambulatories, new shrines meant practical arrangements for channelling pilgrims in and out, the monks' choir must be separated from the laymen's nave, and there seem to have been at various periods special uses for galleries and porches and cloisters. A medieval cathedral can be seen as an arena for the continuous performance, centuries deep, of functions formed and re-formed for the glory of God and of the Church by human hopes and skills and energies, an arena cherished with stubborn devotion, however vandalized by time and wars and good intentions. Sometimes a shell, sometimes a dynamo, decaying and reviving, decaying and reviving, a cathedral is a record of human aspirations. Its layers of architecture are part of the record, supplementing the often fragmentary written record.

Just before the Reformation, England had – besides many great non-diocesan churches – seventeen cathedral churches. That is, it had two archbishops and fifteen bishops under Rome. Nine of the cathedrals had been run from the start by secular canons under statutes that went on after the Reformation – the so-called Old Foundations: Chichester, Exeter, Hereford, Lichfield, Lincoln, London St Paul's, Salisbury, Wells, York. And there were eight monastic cathedrals, reconstituted at the Reformation with secular canons under new statutes – the New Foundations: Canterbury, Carlisle, Durham, Ely, Norwich, Rochester, Winchester, Worcester. (The fuller history of these dioceses' shifting seats and boundaries, of course, is not so tidy.)

To these cathedrals Henry VIII added six old abbey churches: Bristol, Chester, Gloucester, Oxford, Peterborough and, as cathedral of Middlesex, Westminster. Westminster's cathedral status proved to be temporary, so then there were twenty-two Anglican cathedrals. Much later, two more pre-Reformation monastic churches were made cathedrals, St Albans in 1877 and St Saviour's (former priory church of St Mary Overie) Southwark in 1905, both after post-Reformation use as parish churches. Three medieval collegiate churches (big parish churches served by colleges of canons and so having large eastern arms), Ripon, Manchester and Southwell, became cathedrals in 1836, 1847 and 1884 respectively. (Ripon in the C 7, like Coventry in the C 12, had been briefly the seat of a bishop.) Manchester, less cathedral-like than the other two, is sometimes listed with the Anglican 'parish-church cathedrals' – Birmingham, Blackburn, Bradford, Bury St Edmunds, Chelmsford, Coventry, Derby, Leicester, Newcastle, Portsmouth, Sheffield, Wakefield – large town churches consecrated as cathedrals between 1882 and 1927. Entirely new Anglican cathedral churches have been built during the past century at Truro, Liverpool and Guildford, and at Coventry to replace the bombed medieval church there. Which in all comes to forty-two Anglican cathedrals in England today, including the seats of the two archbishops at Canterbury and York. Our forty-third Anglican entry is Westminster Abbey, with its considerable influence on the architecture of some of the others and its peculiar status as, in a way, a national cathedral (see also the Foreword above).

Of Roman Catholic cathedrals today in England there are nineteen, with some changes since thirteen were authorized in 1850. Besides the two metropolitan cathedrals at Westminster and Liverpool, these are at Arundel, Birmingham, Brentwood, Bristol (Clifton), Lancaster, Leeds, London (Southwark), Middlesbrough, Newcastle, Northampton, Norwich, Nottingham, Plymouth, Portsmouth, Salford, Sheffield and Shrewsbury. A number of them were envisaged as, necessarily modest, cathedrals even before 1850, the initial architectural impetus coming from *Pugin*. Two of the architecturally most exciting departures of the past century in cathedral design have been the two metropolitan cathedrals. The irony will of course strike the thoughtful reader, that every medieval church was built under Rome. The post-Fire St Paul's in the City of London was the first Anglican cathedral built as such. All the present-day Catholic cathedrals are 'R.C. new series'.

To summarize the sixty-two structures in a different way, we now have twenty-six mainly medieval large complicated buildings, *Wren's* large c 17 building, two mainly c 18 buildings of parish-church size (Birmingham, Derby), ten parish-size mixtures of many periods c 12–20, fourteen equally modest buildings of the early c 19 to early c 20, and finally nine of more distinct cathedral character built during the past century that form a striking series, proceeding from extreme revived medievalism through degrees of dilution to extreme modernism: Arundel (R.C.), Norwich (R.C.), Truro (Angl.), Westminster (R.C.), Liverpool (Angl.), Guildford (Angl.), Coventry (Angl.), Liverpool (R.C.) and Clifton (R.C.). The long course of cathedral time in this country runs from 602, when St Augustine consecrated his cathedral at Canterbury, on to 1973, when Clifton Cathedral was consecrated at Bristol: almost fourteen centuries so far.

Before the Christian era, a number of present-day cathedral sites were under Roman occupation of one sort or another. Part of a Roman fortress has been found under the crossing at York. A well-shaft under Southwark (Angl.) Cathedral has yielded Roman sculpture, not necessarily *in situ*. At Chichester the mosaic floor of a Roman house can be seen below the south choir aisle. A Roman villa lies under Southwell. At Chester, Exeter, Gloucester, Lincoln and others, remains of the Roman town have been found round about. But pre-Christian religious use of these sites is harder to prove. Wren's workmen digging the foundations of St Paul's turned up evidence of pottery kilns and a cemetery, but no legendary temple to Diana. But Augustine in 602, according to Bede, was rehallowing a church built for Roman Christians, and recent excavation south of the crypt at Canterbury found remains of what may have been a pre-Christian Roman temple there. At St Albans there are strong traditions of a Roman Christian shrine to St Alban, England's first Christian martyr, on the site of his martyrdom in Verulamium's extramural cemetery on the hill – somewhere under the present cathedral. And a similar cemetery outside the town walls is thought to lie under Bristol Cathedral. Excavating under a working cathedral is obviously difficult, especially when money is needed to keep it standing. Only dire need for major work on the tower foundations at York presented that great opportunity.

So to the architecture and appurtenances of Christianity. First, SAXON remains. Little is left of the cathedrals' pre-Conquest predecessors. An evocative and very early

survival is Wilfrid's crypt at Ripon of *c.* 670, a little earlier than his crypt at Hexham. Such a crypt with its narrow vaulted gangways reflected the Early Christian catacombs at Rome. From the other end of the pre-Conquest period, four centuries after Wilfrid, dark monastic passages survive at Westminster Abbey (south-east of the main cloisters, especially the east–west passage to the Little Cloister) that still give a sense of the very early Middle Ages. Of excavated remains requiring more trained imaginations to decipher, considerable traces of Saxon churches have recently been found near their successors at Winchester, Exeter and Wells (and may be present at e.g. Rochester and Worcester), with axial siting of separate churches as is known to have been the case at Canterbury. At Peterborough outlines of a Saxon church can be seen under the south transept, and at Southwell a possibly Saxon pavement is under the north transept. At St Albans in the Norman transept Saxon material was re-used (triforium colonnettes), as Roman bricks were re-used in the tower. Inevitably there survive from this period, followed by so much rebuilding, more mobile carvings than static buildings. Some remarkably sophisticated c 7 sculpture from Reculver in Kent is in the crypt at Canterbury. At Norwich the Bishop's Throne, three times moved about East Anglia, is now recognized as of the c 7. (The c 13 throne at Canterbury, perhaps also a fragmentary c 13 stone seat at Ely, must have been modelled on more ancient seats.) There is a late c 7 cross shaft and base at Ely. The so-called Hedda Stone at Peterborough, thought to be a shrine-cover, is of *c.* 800, and the battered font at Wells is now believed to be of similar date. A carved roundel of Christ at Gloucester of *c.* 950 is, like the Reculver carvings, of European importance. Durham has carvings of the early or mid-c 11, found under the chapter house. Bristol has a magnificent relief of *c.* 1050, a Harrowing of Hell scene, probably from a cemetery chapel on the abbey site. A lesser survival is a small relief of an angel at Manchester, thought to come from an earlier church on the site.

It is of psychological interest that, after the Norman Conquest, special reverence was shown for the remains of pre-Conquest saints upon their reburial in new Norman churches – as it were striking retrospective Anglo-Saxon attitudes out of anxiety to root the English Church in St Augustine's mission from Rome rather than in a transplant from Normandy. Examples of the translation of saints' bones to new shrines were at Ely (St Etheldreda) and Winchester (St Swithun), and of bishops at Wells (retrospective effigies *c.* 1200, now recumbent but possibly made to stand in the main reredos), at Hereford (the rigidly uniform ready-made series of posthumous effigies lining the early c 14 pilgrim route), at Ely (retrospective painted portraits, now vanished, on former screen-walls behind the choir stalls when at the crossing) and at Winchester (bone-chests on the presbytery screens). Such warmed-over memorials conferred credibility on their successors.

In the first thirty years after the NORMAN Conquest, i.e. before 1100, major building or rebuilding was energetically begun at (chronologically) Canterbury, Lincoln, Old Sarum (see under Salisbury), Rochester, St Albans, Winchester, York, Ely, Worcester, London St Paul's, Gloucester, Chichester, Chester, Durham and Norwich; and during the next half-century at Hereford, Southwell, Peterborough, Carlisle and Oxford. Today the most telling Norman remains are the gigantic choir and nave at Durham, the crypts of Worcester, Gloucester and Canterbury, the transepts of Winchester (north), Ely, St Albans, Hereford (south), Chester (north) and Peterborough, and the naves of Rochester, St Albans (north-east), Ely, Gloucester, Chichester, Southwell and Oxford, all with changes to windows which by enlarging the light-source altered the overall effect. Also there are the chapter-house entrance remains at Winchester and the lower walls of Worcester chapter house; the central towers of St Albans and Norwich (the latter with later spire), and the mighty side towers at Exeter (two) and Rochester (one). A type of 'westwork' consisting of a single narthex-tower flanked by west transepts, a Germanic formation, is represented in this country by Ely, and in a sense even earlier at Lincoln; Hereford had one until 1786. At Wells the initial layout of c. 1190 may at first have intended such a formation instead of the screen as built with the eventual pair of towers. The first of the Norman screen fronts with, originally, five stepped arched recesses, was that of Lincoln, later imitated at Bury St Edmunds Abbey; on the origins of the single recess at Tewkesbury, see Lincoln, and on the c 13 development of three niches, see Peterborough. No Norman east end survived later rebuilding in any English cathedral. At Peterborough and Winchester the curve of the central apse can be detected, and the presumed plan of side apses is marked in the floor; see also the former Norman work marked on our plans of Ely, Lichfield, St Albans, and the excavations at York. At Canterbury, Norwich and Gloucester surviving north-east and south-east chapels (see also *Chapels* below) reflect the radiating-chapel type of east end, apparently first built in England at Battle Abbey. A feature of Norman monastic planning was the choir run through the crossing, as can still be seen at e.g. Gloucester, Winchester, Norwich and St Albans – as if chanting below and bellringing above ought to soar together up the central tower as up a chimney. Structural design was empirical: Winchester's new tower promptly fell in 1107; Durham's pioneering rib-vaults over the choir had to be rebuilt in the c 13 (but the original aisle vaults remain); Worcester's early c 12 chapter house had to be partly reshaped in the c 14; flying buttresses had to be added to Southwark's c 13 choir in the c 14. Meanwhile, certain formations such as

the alternating octagonal and circular piers probably already present in the early Norman choir at Canterbury appeared at Peterborough (presbytery and transepts) and Oxford (nave), and then in the new choir (begun 1175) at Canterbury, from which their use spread to Lincoln and Southwark. In the half-century after 1150 tentative transitional work, between Romanesque and Gothic, was appearing at Bristol (chapter-house vestibule), in work of the 1170s at Ripon, and in west bays at Worcester after damage in 1175. But by 1200 great Gothic works were already in full swing at Canterbury, Wells and Lincoln.

Norman architectural carvings include, pre-eminently, the tympanum over the Prior's Door at Ely of c. 1135, and the c 12 reliefs on Lincoln west front. As for more mobile work, furnishings (so aptly in French *les mobiliers*) in their several categories are summarized later in this introduction, but even a quick survey of Norman architecture should sample the flavour of such fittings as these: the pair of stone reliefs from a screen of c. 1125–30 at Chichester, both majestic and poignant; the grand black marble fonts of c. 1140–50 at Winchester and Lincoln; the marble effigies of c 12 abbots and bishops at Peterborough, Salisbury and Exeter; and the turned-wood throne-like chair of c. 1200 at Hereford and the door-knocker or sanctuary ring at Durham – the former one of the most important pieces of medieval furniture in Britain, the latter one of the great examples of European metalwork. In a sense, Norman art in England culminated in the monumental stained-glass ancestor figures at Canterbury: although presiding over an early Gothic rebuilding, they are Romanesque in spirit – and, as Sir Nikolaus said of Durham, spirit is what counts.

The Gothic style arrived in England from France c. 1175 at Canterbury in the idiom of the c 12 Île de France, while Cistercian Gothic arrived in the northern abbeys (see Ripon). From Canterbury it went to Wells mixed with West Country influences shared with, e.g., Worcester's west nave bays. At Wells this assimilated style is still visible in the transepts and nave, begun before 1200. Meanwhile Gothic also went from Canterbury to Lincoln, from c. 1190, in the hands of one superlative individual artist, in the east transepts and as continued from c. 1200 in St Hugh's Choir, though the strangely planned east end does not survive. Late in the c 12 also came Portsmouth chancel, and the Chichester retrochoir was begun. So by 1200 England, long before Germany and Spain, had begun to make out of French Gothic its own native style.

The fully assimilated style called EARLY ENGLISH was in force by the first decade of the c 13. Soon after 1200 Winchester retrochoir was begun, subsequently influencing Southwark retrochoir, begun after 1212, and the Salisbury east end, started in 1220. There began a series of rectangular east ends, opening out the darker Norman apsed formation, and some, as apparently at Winchester, intended to house saints' shrines. New work at Rochester was vaulted by 1214, at Worcester begun in 1224, at Southwell and Ely by 1234, and from 1242 Durham's great Chapel of the Nine Altars was added to the old east end like the crossing of a T, as was then being done at Fountains Abbey. Yet in 1220 a polygonal-apsed Lady Chapel was added to the Norman church at Westminster Abbey; this chapel (probably heightened) survived the ambitious rebuilding of the church from 1245 until finally it was replaced by the Henry VII Chapel in the c 16. The plan of that c 13 chapel may well have influenced Gloucester's c 13 Lady Chapel (rebuilt) and very likely the plan of Lichfield's Lady Chapel a century later. (Further on eastward extension, and on the east end as feretory, see *Chapels* below.)

The purest Early English work is to be found at Salisbury, with its entirely rectangular plan, its lancet windows, its cool dark accents of Purbeck marble, as already used at Canterbury and Lincoln. On the Englishness of such black or grey minor shafting – a draughtsman's linear emphasis little used in France – see Canterbury (William of Sens's choir), Lincoln (St Hugh's interior) and Salisbury (interior); and, for pre-Canterbury examples, Rochester chapter house. But Salisbury's east-transept formation – i.e. with a second set east of the main transept producing what might be called a cross-of-Lorraine plan – stemmed ultimately from the third church at Cluny. This plan, adding elbow-room and light at the high altar, first appeared in England in the Canterbury choir of *c.* 1100 and subsequently in Roger's choir of *c.* 1160 at York, but more emphatically in the Canterbury rebuilding begun in 1175 and then at Lincoln from 1192 (also in the 1190s intended at Hereford, only realized there *c.* 1300), and in the 1220s at Salisbury, Worcester and Rochester. These of the fifty years after 1175 all made full-height east crossings. (Side bays that look like east transepts on plan, but lower than the main vessel and not producing a proper crossing, occur later at Exeter and Wells, not really east transepts except on plan; quite the reverse was to happen at York in the 1390s with the heightening of a pair of aisle bays that project like east transepts in elevation but not on plan.)

A characteristic element of Early English work was the disciplined vitality of the so-called stiff-leaf decoration of capitals and mouldings that had developed out of Norman crocketed work, until more naturalistic foliage ornament began to replace it in the 1270s. Surviving stained glass most typically Early English, sub-fusc in tone and filling lancets free of tracery, is the grisaille glass at Salisbury and in the north transept at York; on reasons for introducing grisaille glass, i.e. more light at less expense and the possible influence from Cistercian monks' austere churches, see the introduction to York glass. The glowing colour of the late c 12/early c 13 glass at Canterbury made a church darker, gloriously so. A stain that would produce bright yellow came into use, probably from the Arab world, only in the c 14.

Tracery had already appeared at the heads of openings, both of windows and of gallery arches, by the mid-c 13. At first it was of the transitional, pierced-solid kind called plate tracery. Early examples of that are in Winchester retrochoir, and there was blank plate tracery in the Great Hall at Winchester by 1236. Plate tracery appeared in the Salisbury transepts, on the chapter-house staircase at Wells and in the north transept gallery at York. But it was soon superseded by the lighter openwork of bar tracery introduced from France, first used at Reims *c.* 1210–20, and in England especially at Westminster Abbey. There, with the most whole-hearted use of French c 13 cathedral forms in England, rebuilding was begun in 1245, and the eastern arm, transepts and chapter house were complete by 1255. Its openwork tracery of foiled circles, also known as geometrical tracery, gave the name often used for that developed c 13 style called Geometrical in England. A few great circular windows had already been begun in this country: in the late c 12 east transepts at Canterbury, in the Lincoln transepts by 1220 (north, Dean's Eye; the flowing tracery of the Bishop's Eye on the south is early c 14); in the York south transept the rose of 1220–55; and the rose-windows in both Westminster transepts were originally part of the 1245–55 programme. In fact, as Sir Nikolaus pointed out, the original north rose at Westminster (later much renewed) was apparently so close to the roses of the Paris transepts, begun only in 1258, that a common pattern, now missing, must be deduced. But unlike certain French cathedrals, no medieval English cathedral was given a west rose-window. Old St Paul's extension of 1256–80 had a great east rose, but how soon Durham's east-end (Nine Altars) rose existed, before *Wyatt*, is not clear. (The east round window at Oxford is of course c 19.)

As windows were enlarged and vaults heightened, more supports were needed: there are modest flying buttresses on the Trinity Chapel extension of *c.* 1180 at Canterbury, but the first spectacular tiers of them appeared at Westminster Abbey, supporting the tallest vessel in England (eastern arm; those of the nave of course date from its c 14–16 completion; prominent flying buttresses for the c 13 chapter house there were added in the c 14). Internal diagonal buttresses at Gloucester were inserted to reinforce the central tower. Meanwhile, as at St Paul's, when new east ends were built, they were given great east windows: under the rose at St Paul's were seven lights, the rose as it were forming their upper tracery (as e.g. in Notre Dame south transept). In the north of England came the eight-light window at Lincoln (Angel Choir), *c.* 1275, and at Ripon seven lights, *c.* 1290, and the great six-light north window of the late 1280s in Durham's Nine Altars Chapel, followed in the early C14 by the nine-light east window at Carlisle. Exeter's great east window of the 1290s was partly rebuilt in 1389–90 with nine lights; its great west window of the 1340s (much renewed) has nine. Deftly handled development can be seen in Exeter's other window traceries from the 1290s on, in the same vein as court work in London (below).

By the mid-C13 the rib-vault type initiated c. 1100 at Durham had received a new member, the tierceron rib, one pair to each half-bay in Lincoln nave, presumably soon after 1233, and in Ely presbytery between 1234 and 1252, in both places allied with a transverse ridge rib taken only partway across. The next step, at Westminster c. 1253 in the first nave bays past the crossing (i.e. part of the original building programme to buttress the central tower), took the ridge rib all the way across, as was done thereafter in the rest of that nave. Further playing with the tierceron idea ensued at Exeter late in the C13, first in the Lady Chapel with two pairs of tierceron ribs to each half-bay, and then three pairs each in the presbytery and so right through the cathedral, producing a forest of branches with the vaulting-shafts that supported all these new ribs. An apotheosis of tiercerons formed part of the timber lantern of the Octagon at Ely. The next and smaller element was the lierne rib, from which networks of ribs could be built up (see further below).

At west ends the C13 continued the English fashion for screen fronts. The Norman stepped niches of Lincoln and Bury St Edmunds Abbey became three huge equal niches at Peterborough, while at Wells and Salisbury ranks of sculpture provided showcases of biblical figures (see *Architectural sculpture* below). Inside, some of the best C13 sculpture in England remains *in situ* in the Westminster south transept, censing angels in spandrels below the rose-window; and in the Angel Choir at Lincoln, angels in spandrels again; winged creatures suiting such triangular fields just as flying victories had fitted those of Roman triumphal arches. Late in the century came the superb foliage carvings in Southwell chapter house, and some lovely, similar, but simpler foliage in the Lincoln cloisters. Fine C13 sculpture no longer in place includes the figure now in Winchester retrochoir, without attributes but thought to represent the Church or the Synagogue; the damaged Christ in Majesty re-used in Worcester refectory; and the seated Christ now at Swynnerton but probably made for Lichfield's west gable. C13 decorative painting miraculously survives on the nave ceiling at Peterborough. C13 architectural painting is best represented by the series of Crucifixion scenes on the northeast nave piers at St Albans, also by various elongated figures at Westminster, e.g. in the south transept. C13 panel painting of high quality is represented by retable

panels of European importance now in the ambulatory at Westminster.

Sir Nikolaus's readers know that he constantly spoke from a European point of view that embraced England. 'The architecture of England between 1250 and 1350 was, although the English do not know it, the most forward, the most important, and the most inspired in Europe', he said in his *Outline*; since he first wrote that, they have learnt to know it. The century 1250–1350 produced, first, the growing assurance of C13 English work we have just seen, followed by a new handling of architectural space, at Bristol and Wells and Ely, which Sir Nikolaus especially enjoyed describing and was the first to celebrate for English readers as it deserved, and, third, the work at London and Gloucester that announced a vigorously native English style that was to persist to the end of the Middle Ages. That is, the period 1250–1350 contained these major developments: the matured stage of Early English style sometimes called Geometrical, the excitement of the Decorated style, and the first stage of the Perpendicular.

The so-called DECORATED style was more than a matter of decoration. The introduction to B of E *North Somerset and Bristol* (1958) put it thus: 'Architecture is the art of shaping space for utilitarian as well as emotional purposes. No style has ever existed in architecture that was not primarily concerned with space. And in space also 1300 was the moment of a great change in England, a change of international importance. C13 space had possessed the same clarity as C13 decoration. Now space began to flow, unexpected interpenetrations were sought, and thus effects obtained which must have been as disquieting to some and as thrilling to others as were the spatial innovations of C20 architecture when first they were seen.' In fact, 'designers turned away from . . . harmoniousness and regularity in pursuit of a new ideal of complexity, intricacy, perhaps even perversity. It was an attitude familiar to those who have experienced the revulsion from Impressionism to Post-Impressionism, an attitude comparable also to that of the Mannerists about 1520 towards the High Renaissance. No more calm perfection; let us have imperfection provided it is not calm.' Goodbye Salisbury, welcome Bristol and Wells. Immediately after 1300, the new east ends of Wells and Bristol were 'leading for England and for Europe . . . the composition of Lady Chapel and retrochoir at Wells and of chancel, chancel aisles, and Lady Chapel at Bristol and also the sensational strainer arches at Wells, all this is conceived in terms of open spaces merging with each other and of surprising and not easily understood vistas, diagonally through space. The arrangement of the piers in the Wells retrochoir seems at first as arbitrary as the arrangement of the bridges and transverse little vaults of the chancel aisles at Bristol. The very fact that both Wells and Bristol here worked in terms of the ''hall'', the room with nave and aisles of equal height [as had indeed been done in Winchester and Salisbury retrochoirs in a simpler way], is telling enough. For this became the *leitmotif* of the most creative Late Gothic style on the Continent, the German *Sondergotik*. English *Sondergotik*, already with all the characteristics of an anti-classic style, is 150 years older.' The next tremendous step, in the 1320s, was the making of diagonal vistas with the Octagon at Ely.

Already in the 1290s the vocabulary of the just-emerging Decorated style had been enriched by the new pageantry and power of the court of Edward I, and from *c.* 1290 there was a recognizable court style, notably in the series of Eleanor Crosses set up along the route of his queen's funeral journey from Lincolnshire to London, and also in certain tombs. The wide-arch-flanked-by-narrow-arches of the Crouchback tomb at Westminster († 1296) and the tomb at Ely of Bishop William of Louth (latinized as Luda; † 1299) soon appeared at Bristol (Berkeley Chapel entrance, Lady Chapel reredos). A little flying-ribs motif that appeared first, so far as we now know, at Lincoln (Easter Sepulchre, pulpitum passage vault), on a slightly larger scale at Bristol and then in Southwell pulpitum may reflect some vanished spirited work on one of the Eleanor Crosses, of which only three now remain. Some fifty years after the flying ribs at Lincoln and Bristol, the motif appeared at Prague Cathedral (sacristy and porch): proof of the impact of English design abroad in the c 14. The immensely popular motif of the ogee arch, composed of two S-curves meeting at an acute angle, first appeared in the decoration of the Eleanor Crosses and on Crouchback's tomb, and then gradually, sinuously spread about the country, to the Norwich cloisters, to the window tracery of Wells chapter house, to the Exeter throne canopy, and traceries and canopies all over England. For canopies, ogee arches developed three-dimensionally to become 'nodding ogees'. The most inventive handling of the ogee now surviving is that burst of elegant playful fantasy, the sedilia canopy at Exeter of *c.* 1320. We can only guess what was lost of such work in England to the vandals of the 1540s and 1640s, and indeed of later times. A small element already mentioned is the lierne or short linking rib (first used in St Stephen's lower chapel, Westminster Palace). With it net-like vaults could be built up that were medieval equivalents of small domes: Wells Lady Chapel has a most fascinating example, the range of its ambiguities suggesting comparison to the earlier Southwell chapter-house vault and even to the later Durham monks' kitchen vault. These were only a few of the elements exploited by the Decorated style's space-handlers. The most glorious enclosure and exposure of space in the early c 14 was of course the pyrotechnical Ely Octagon, perhaps the most marvellous example of co-operation between mason and carpenter of the entire Middle Ages.

The royal palace at Westminster contained seeds of both Dec and Perp. St Stephen's Lower Chapel and part of the shell of the Upper Chapel were built 1292–7; the Upper Chapel was completed in 1320–6 and 1331–48, served as the House of Commons from 1547, and was burnt in 1834. St Stephen's Chapel and the chapter house and cloisters added in 1332 to the old St Paul's Cathedral, burnt in 1666, are the most important offstage characters in the story of English Gothic. If it were not for Hollar's c 17 engravings of St Paul's before the Great Fire, and for drawings made by various early c 19 artists of the ruins of the Houses of Parliament immediately after the fire of 1834, London's rightful place in the history of the PERPENDICULAR style would not be known. The Lower Chapel of St Stephen's with its lierne vaults still exists. But the vanished Upper Chapel with its descending mullions (vertical mouldings taken down the wall below an opening) was the key monument. How much did that continue the style of York nave, begun in 1291? The interior of York nave, reflecting the style the French call Rayonnant, used descending mullions to unify clerestory with triforium (as had been done at St-Denis and Clermont-Ferrand), and in that insistence upon verticals York nave must be called proto-Perp. In the chapter house and cloisters of St Paul's as recorded by Hollar, mullions were carried down over the wall-face and the window tracery was rectilinear: inevitable human response in the 1330s to bursts of curvaceous fancy in the 1320s. The West Country was the next receptacle of these new ideas after London, not only in the great east window of Wells presbytery, glazed before 1339, with its 'verticals standing hard on arches or pushing up against arches' (B of E *North Somerset*), but more especially in the south transept at Gloucester, begun in 1331, with its four-centred arches, its panelling and, in its great south window, mullions running straight up to the arch.

The subsequent encasing of the Norman eastern arm at Gloucester was intended to honour the burial there of Edward II. Much of the grandest cathedral work in the Perp style encased or rebuilt Norman work. The uncompromising verticality of the one reinforced that of the other. The eastern arms at Gloucester (1337–67) and Norwich (1362–9, 1472–99) and the naves of Winchester (*c.* 1345–66, *c.* 1394–1404) and Norwich (1464–72) all show their Norman bones through the new framework. At Canterbury demolition of Lanfranc's nave left the old pier and wall foundations, so the c 11 plan still dictated the c 14/15 plan, though not of course the tremendous elevation reared upon it.

The completion or rebuilding of great naves raises the matter of HISTORICISM, or revivalism, in the Middle Ages, i.e. the question of style-consistency in big complex buildings not finished all at one go but carried on or reconstructed by later generations. First, as to the matter of the long sides of an internal space such as a nave: to make the north side of Chester nave of *c.* 1490 match (but for a few details) the south side begun *c.* 1360 can be called 'self-conscious conservatism . . . typically English' (B of E *Cheshire*), and to leave the north side of St Albans nave in its Norman state opposite the early C 14 south side (omitting for the moment the matter of the C 13 west bays) can mean 'conflict' and 'no peace for the eye' (B of E *Hertfordshire*). But consider: (1) the St Albans south arcade fell down and had to be replaced, and rebuilding *à la normande* in the C 14 was very much less likely than Chester's rebuilding *à la* 1360 in 1490; and (2) the alternative, a C 14 rebuilding of the Norman north piers *à la* C 14, would have meant the loss of their precious paintings and of a unique sense of the original building embedded there: that consideration should mitigate our sense of 'conflict' between the opposing elevations as they stand. In long buildings such as these, the style of spaces added east or west is a different matter, whether we call it historicism or conservatism, affection for the past, or 'keeping in keeping', or tact. For a new age to continue the same style farther east or west in such buildings, the case may be that of *Ramsey*'s regard in Lichfield presbytery for the parts east and west of it so that he unified the whole building (a point which our new text stresses more than B of E *Staffordshire*). Deliberate continuity of design at York from the nave rebuilding, begun 1291, to the rebuilding of the eastern arm, begun 1361, is called unusual for the Middle Ages (B of E *Yorkshire: York and the East Riding*), though of course style-consistency westwards was a feature of Westminster Abbey because of the ceremonial and iconographical character peculiar to that church. The whole matter of expecting the styles of successive stages of a complex building to evolve in an organic way, of being surprised if consistency with earlier stages was preferred to development, reflects the outlook of architectural historians trained to believe in Progress as a biological growth – the organic view of history. In the end, rising above this, Pevsner concludes that the homogeneity of Westminster Abbey is admirable.

The issue of historicism diverted us from the progress of the Perp style. One Perp invention was the FAN-VAULT, first developed on a minor scale in the West Country in the 1350s, at Hereford (chapter house, ruined) and at Gloucester (east cloister walk). Both can be attributed to one man (called *Thomas of Cambridge*, after a hamlet near Gloucester), though exact dates and sequence are unclear. The single 360° cone formerly in Hereford chapter house seems clearly derived from the cluster of ribs in Wells chapter house of half a century before. The Gloucester half-cones were, perhaps, immediately adapted from the Hereford cone. Yet the series of rib-clusters vaulting Exeter Cathedral from end to end could have suggested Gloucester's half-cones first – and this man *Thomas*, known to have worked at both Hereford and Gloucester, is thought to have been familiar with Exeter as well. It was only in the middle of the next century that the fan-vault developed on a larger scale, as at Sherborne Abbey and, in eastern England, in Canterbury Lady Chapel, completed after 1468. (Construction of the little fan-vaulted Stanbury Chapel at Hereford of *c.* 1480 was, incidentally, overseen by a brother of Archbishop Morton of Canterbury.) At King's College Chapel, Cambridge, preparations for fan-vaulting, only carried out in 1512–15, were in hand by the 1480s. At the end of the C 15 (between 1496 and 1508) the fan-vaulted retrochoir or New Building went up at Peterborough. By then many fan-vaults had been made in England. A final metamorphosis came in the Henry VII Chapel at Westminster during 1503–9, though only after intermediate experiments had taken place at Oxford, at the Divinity School by 1483 and in the present cathedral by 1503, and on a lesser scale at Winchester in the south-east (Langton) chapel between 1493 and 1500; and mildly reflected in Prince Arthur's Chantry at Worcester from 1504.

Next TOWERS, the first visible feature of an English medieval great church, some spired and some not. A crossing tower usually reflects an initially Norman plan; surviving Norman towers are at Norwich and St Albans. The earliest surviving spire is Oxford's of the C 13 (Rochester's being of 1904). The tallest spire in England now is Salisbury's at 404 ft (begun 1334), outdone for two centuries by that of Old St Paul's at 489 ft (1315) until it was hit by lightning in 1561. Of other ambitious early C 14 spires, the one on Lincoln's central tower was blown down in 1548; the west towers there were spired from the C 15 until 1807. Lichfield's three towers were spired in the 1320s and, though the central tower fell in the Civil War and there has been much rebuilding since, three spires still stand, the only triple set until *Pearson* emulated Lincoln's medieval skyline at Truro. In the C 15 the present spire at Norwich was built to replace one hit by lightning in 1463. Chichester's C 15 spire collapsed in 1861 and was rebuilt. The spire, the most poignantly symbolic part of a cathedral, is also its most vulnerable member. Of unspired towers, the tallest was Canterbury's Bell Harry (1490s) at 250 ft until *Sir Giles Scott*'s tower at Liverpool reached 330 ft. One of the mightiest is at Durham, rebuilt in the C 15; the C 12–13 west towers there once had C 14 spires. Three noble central towers are those at Hereford (early C 14), Wells (1315–22 and 1440) and, perhaps, the noblest, Worcester (1357–74); and one of the most elegant is at Gloucester (*c.* 1450) with its open coronet. Ely's great C 14 timber lantern is unique anywhere; the C 15 stone lantern or crown at Newcastle (Angl.) is one of a series with Continental connections. York's great keep-like central tower and beautiful west towers were finished in the 1470s.

Among the parish churches made cathedrals in the past century are three dramatically tall early C 15 spires, the one surviving beside the new Coventry Cathedral and those on Wakefield and Sheffield cathedrals. Spires were to be revived in the C 19 by the Catholic architects *Pugin* and *Hansom* (see below).

An important auxiliary to great churches is the CHAPTER HOUSE, often, though not always, east of the east cloister walk, and in England often, though not always, of centralized polygonal form. The Continent had centralized churches, baptisteries, treasuries, but not, for some reason, centralized chapter houses. One of the oldest English examples is the very early C 12 chapter house at Worcester, originally circular, with central pier and ten vaulting-compartments; it became structurally necessary to make it ten-sided in the C 14. (Hereford's former C 14 chapter house was ten-sided, and one wonders what shape its C 12 predecessor had.) Lincoln's chapter house, begun *c.* 1220, is ten-sided; the one built soon after at Beverley was eight-sided, now gone. Lichfield's elongated octagon, which dates from *c.* 1240, is said to have been so designed for its larger chapter when allied with Coventry. The first with the structural assurance to fill each side almost entirely with window was at Westminster (octagonal), laid out by 1249 and in use by 1257; the big flying buttresses had to be added in the C 14. The octagon at Wells was laid out by *c.* 1250, when the undercroft was built (main chapter room completed *c.* 1306). Salisbury's (octagonal) was being built from *c.* 1279. All these had the central pier. Then, before *c.* 1290, two octagonal chapter houses were contrived without central piers: York's with its timber ceiling and Southwell's stone-vaulted on a smaller scale; and subsequently, in the early C 14, at London St Paul's. There were also rectangular chapter houses (some with apsed east wall) at Bristol, Canterbury, Chester, Durham, Gloucester and Oxford. One would like to know more about the acoustics of these talking-houses, especially at Westminster, where the first House of Commons sat for a while. Those with the more considerable vestibules (e.g. York, Lichfield, Chester, Salisbury, Westminster) will have had more privacy for their discussions than those opening directly off the cloisters (Oxford, Worcester). A room with related functions but separate from the chapter house, at least in the later Middle Ages, was the CONSISTORY COURT. At Lincoln this was held in the south-west nave chapel, at Wells in a chapel off the east cloister. At Norwich the originally Norman Bauchun Chapel was refitted for the purpose *c.* 1500 with vault-bosses illustrating Chaucer's *Man of Law's Tale*. (Chester retains in its south-west nave chapel a unique early C 17 set of consistory-court furniture: one wonders what the medieval precedents were.)

It was by no means only the great monastic churches that had the quadrangle of covered passages called CLOIS-

TERS. These were generally though not always fitted into the angle between nave and transept, more often on the south, sometimes on the north. Sometimes there was no fourth walk next to the nave (but at Wells it is now known that one was originally intended, with open space between it and the nave wall, as imitated at Salisbury). Chichester's irregular layout embracing the transept was unique. In general, the east walk, as most essential for circulation, was built first (e.g. at Westminster and Norwich). At the monastic churches, the monks were usually housed and fed in ranges alongside and over the cloister walks (but see Worcester). When fully glazed the walks themselves may have served for studying and teaching (e.g. carrels at Gloucester and Worcester); now when we see the walks without their glass we think of them as out-of-doors. The main surviving medieval cloisters (many replacing Norman ones) are, with later interferences and additions, at: Lincoln, C 13 (and C 17); Westminster, C 13–14; Salisbury, C 13; Norwich, C 13–15; Gloucester, C 14; Canterbury, C 14–15; Worcester, C 14–15; Chichester, *c.* 1400; Hereford, early C 15; Wells, C 15–16; Durham, C 15; Chester, early C 16; and there are more partial remains at Bristol, Ely and Oxford. The prior's, abbot's or bishop's doorway from the cloister to the nave aisle, often but not invariably from the east walk, was given architectural and sculptural importance.

Upstairs the east cloister range of a monastic cathedral generally contained the monks' dormitory, but from the C 15 at Wells (full length of the range) and Salisbury (half the length) that space contained the cathedral LIBRARY; only after the Reformation did the corresponding space at Westminster become the library (when Camden was librarian and writing his *Britannia* there). At Gloucester (north side) and at Winchester (south side) the library is over the slype or east–west passage against the transept. At Hereford the famous chained library is now in a former sacristy over the north transept east aisle, and at Lichfield it is over the chapter house (but the library over the chapter house at Ripon was originally the Lady Chapel). Cathedral and abbey libraries were centres of medieval learning, as well as repositories of archives that help us to read medieval architecture.

Surviving monastic quarters, e.g. dormitories and refectories, are only briefly summarized in the text, e.g. for Canterbury, Durham, Gloucester, Chester, Westminster and Worcester. But we must single out one fascinating structure, another centralized space, at Durham: the octagonal C 14 KITCHEN with its possibly Islamic-influenced stone vault, also possibly influenced by the circle-enclosing ribs of the C 13 Nine Altars vault nearby. (The probably C 14 stone kitchen at Glastonbury, with its truncated-pyramid roof, is described in B of E *South and West Somerset*.) On the other hand, the timber roof of the late

C13 bishop's kitchen at Chichester (its central lantern-opening now closed) rests on the earliest known hammerbeams. So, by c. 1290, cathedral builders' techniques were such that comparatively small octagonal spaces could be roofed without a central pier, as proved in York and Southwell chapter houses, and an open central lantern could rest upon either stone vaults or wooden hammerbeams: the way towards conception of the Ely Octagon in the 1320s was ready.

To return to the main vessel of a cathedral, it has many CHAPELS. As we have seen, these could be not only little auxiliary spaces but extensions of the main vessel. Those extending the basic plan eastwards include the Trinity Chapel at Canterbury and the very different Nine Altars Chapel at Durham, as well as numerous mostly square-ended Lady Chapels, as at Bristol, Chester, Chichester, Exeter, Gloucester, Hereford, Salisbury, Wells and Winchester, and the polygonal-apsed chapel at Lichfield; and east of the northern arm at Bristol (Elder Lady Chapel), Canterbury, Ely and Peterborough (now gone) – the last two probably influenced in that position by a former north-east chapel at Lincoln. North-east and south-east apsidal chapels of oddly imperfect orientation (ENE and ESE respectively) had been part of the early Norman work at Canterbury and Norwich (also at Gloucester, but NE and SE respectively there); a pair of slightly later counterparts in that regard are at Sens. Indeed, Westminster Abbey's four mid-C13 apsidal chapels also have no unambiguously eastern walls for altars. Between those two pairs at Westminster, and pre-dating them, was the early C13 polygonally apsed Lady Chapel replaced in the early C16 by Henry VII's bigger chapel intended as both Lady Chapel and burial chapel for himself. In that dual role, on the brink of the Reformation, it was the culmination of English cathedral chapels. The chapel as saint's-shrine-container had been elaborated long before, primarily at Canterbury for Becket's shrine and at Westminster for St Edward the Confessor's shrine, the latter both saintly and royal (see *Shrines* below). Henry VII intended his own burial chapel to have similar importance, but it was a more secular sort of importance (as emphasized by the mercantile air of the figures carved upon the walls). Although initially he had intended it to be a burial chapel for the saintly Henry VI, the age of pilgrimage to shrines was over.

Side chapels visible as such externally include the Berkeley Chapel at Bristol, part of the late C13/early C14 reconstruction of the east end, and interesting for its vestibule vault (see flying ribs, above) and for the first of those, apparently Islamic-influenced, concave-framed niche openings. The Zouche Chapel at York was probably part of the C14–15 rebuilding of the eastern arm and contains rare contemporary cupboards. Rectangular spaces at the east end of the aisles were often annexed by bishops for their own burial chapels, as at Ely at the end of the C15. Winchester has the outstanding series of bishops' chantries (i.e. enclosures within larger open spaces for the chanting of memorial masses): six from 1366 to 1555, from nearly the beginning to beyond the end of the Perp style. Prince Arthur's Chantry at Worcester, begun shortly after Henry VII's Chapel at Westminster, was in a sense a try-out for the latter's sculptural decoration. Indeed, Henry VII meant his own tomb-enclosure to stand like a chantry in the centre of his chapel at Westminster, not at its east end as decided by his successor. St Anselm's Chapel at Chester is an interesting example of a Norman abbot's chapel altered in the early C17. And finally, two-storey chapels at Westminster are those of Henry V and Abbot Islip, with the tomb downstairs and a chantry chapel for celebration of masses upstairs. The most ancient two-storey chapel in England was the bishop's chapel at Hereford, begun 1095, but little of it is left. (Bishops' chapels, e.g. at Ely, Wells and Durham, are only summarily mentioned in our text, as parts of their palaces, for which see the relevant B of E volume.) The most important English two-storey chapel no longer exists as such, St Stephen's in the Palace of Westminster, already described, influenced in this respect by the Sainte Chapelle in Paris.

Here we should mention the accompanying parish church that often stood near, attached to or even separately inside a great monastic church – to keep the neighbours out of the monks' way. Of those alongside, St Margaret's Westminster and St Nicholas Rochester still stand. St Augustine the Less at Bristol and St Michael at Worcester are gone, as is St Mary Major at Exeter, where an early predecessor may have been the original Saxon cathedral. The present cathedral at Bury St Edmunds was once the parish church nearest the great abbey. Until the early C19 at Southwark a C14–15 church of St Mary Magdalene stood attached to the south-east choir-transept angle, demolished but recorded by Gwilt and so by Dollman (see London, Southwark, Angl.). At Chester it was only from the 1530s (until 1881) that the south transept itself served as a screened-off parish church; and there have been other such arrangements. The Lady Chapel at Ely owes its survival to such post-Reformation use, and the Lady Chapel at St Albans owes its life to use as a grammar school.

ARCHITECTURAL SCULPTURE. The display of sculpture on the C13 west front at Wells, despite centuries of wear and tear, becomes with the latest conservation work much more rewarding to study than it was. So Sir Nikolaus's judgements of 1958 can be tempered a little. The quality of the figures on Exeter's C14–15 west front is also becoming clearer. The C14 motif of cross-legged kings there also appears on Lincoln and Lichfield west fronts, the latter inevitably much restored owing to the nature of the stone.

Sculpture on porches, e.g. Lincoln's Judgement Porch, has also suffered wear and tear, as have other outdoor figures of quality, such as one on the south side of the choir at Lichfield. We have mentioned various figures now *ex situ*, such as the late C 13 Christ at Swynnerton, probably from Lichfield's west front. Of interior figures surviving *ex situ*, the loveliest is the half-length Virgin and Child of *c*. 1500 at Winchester (now presbytery), one supposes made for the Lady Chapel altered in the late C 15. (Distinctions between architectural sculpture and furnishing sculpture inside a medieval cathedral alive with carved walls and fittings need not be too rigorous.) More strictly architectural sculpture inside and *in situ* remains at Westminster Abbey, almost three centuries apart: of the C 13 in the ambulatory chapels (fragmentary), on the south transept south wall, and in the chapter house; while for early C 16 sculpture the Henry VII Chapel is the *locus classicus* in England. And there is the C 13 work at Lincoln (St Hugh's Choir, Angel Choir) and, considerably restored, at Worcester (east transepts, choir triforium). Lincoln also has gorgeous decorative carving on the gateways to the choir aisles. Every medieval cathedral has its carved bosses – of stone or wood depending on the vaulting material – fastened like brooches at the joins of the vaulting-ribs, and often much larger than they appear from the floor. The nave vault at Norwich, for example, has a lavish display of them. In positions near enough to be closely inspected, bosses were elaborately carved, e.g. in Norwich cloisters, one under the pulpitum at York, and the central boss of the Wells Lady Chapel vault. A set of C 15 wooden bosses displayed at Southwark show how they 'plugged in' to the vaulting system. Much of both decorative and figure sculpture in great medieval churches was concentrated on prominent fixtures such as pulpitum and reredos, and this brings us to furnishings.

MEDIEVAL FURNISHINGS. Of these only a precious residue has survived. (A few have been briefly referred to above with the architecture.) Cathedral furnishings add immeasurably to, much more often than they detract from, cathedral architecture. The longer the period when layers of fittings were being deposited, the more evocative the resulting mixture, especially where post-Reformation fittings of quality have accrued since. Within a few square yards at Chichester, for example, are a Roman mosaic floor, powerful Romanesque reliefs, C 14 misericords, C 18 brass chandeliers, windows by the C 19 *Kempe* and the C 20 *Chagall*, and a C 20 tapestry by *Piper*. The more fortunate parish churches contain such multiple textures on a lesser scale. The nearest secular comparison, of shorter time-span, is of course with the English country house that has kept its contents.

The PULPITUM (originally meaning 'raised platform', from the same word-source as 'pulpit') was the prominent partition between nave and choir. Unlike the wooden rood screen of a parish church (e.g. Manchester Cathedral's handsome one of *c*. 1500) this barrier in the bigger churches was usually of stone, one bay deep and roofed, with a little east–west vaulted passage through the centre, and sometimes enclosing a staircase. Since at least the C 14, organs have often been put on top. Medieval pulpitums, with later alterations, exist at a number of cathedrals. Rochester's has C 13 remains amid the *Scott* and *Pearson* work. Of the early C 14: Lincoln, the most elaborately and beautifully carved of all; also Southwell, nearly as much so; Exeter, partly opened up in the C 19; and, of the C 14 much restored, Wells and St Albans. Of the C 15: Canterbury and York, both with statues of kings, Norwich, Ripon and Chichester, this last three-arched like Exeter's but now lacking the veranda and rear-enclosure dimension. On trends towards transparency in later screens, see *Victorian furnishings* below.

In the case of the medieval REREDOS, it is easy to single out the most precious survival, the Neville Screen at Durham. London work of the 1370s, it has been attributed to *Henry Yevele*. The slim verticals of its canopy supports can be seen as development, probably from Exeter's now-vanished reredos of the 1320s, for which the accompanying sedilia are evidence (see below). The multiple tabernacles of Durham's screen, still semi-transparent, became a century later the tall solid wall of niches of the Winchester reredos and St Albans reredos, both of the 1480s (today with Victorian figures). In the C 14 an ensemble of such pieces as the Neville Screen included one or more sets of priests' seats or SEDILIA (in Saxon times combined with the bishop's throne when that stood east of the high altar; see below). The glorious set of three seats at Exeter, along with a surviving canopy fragment in a north chapel there, suggest the quality of excitement that the Exeter reredos must have had. To compare such heaped-up fantastic canopies with the austere unambiguous character of the Aquablanca tomb at Hereford, of fifty years before, is to see the difference between the C 13 and the early C 14.

The next most prominent fixture to the high altar was the bishop's THRONE. As demonstrated at Norwich, this anciently stood at the east of the apse behind and above the altar. A curved wooden bench at Winchester may have been part of the priests' seating beside the throne in the Norman apse there. When east ends became rectangular, and perhaps also for acoustical reasons, the throne was placed nearer the choir, on the south side. Post-Conquest religious ceremonial seats surviving in England represent more than one type, all with Continental connections: the C 13 marble throne at Canterbury is in the Saxon tradition of those at Hexham and Norwich (and its own predecessor 'formed out of a single stone'); the turned-wood chair of *c*. 1200 at Hereford is a Romanesque royal or episcopal seat; and the originally painted wood-panelled coronation chair enclosing its symbolic stone at Westminster is a Gothic royal seat. Early in the c 14 improved woodcarving techniques produced the matchless Exeter throne canopy, unique in Europe – elaboration of the canopy taking over from that of the seat itself. Hereford's must have come soon after. Later in the c 14, not content with the possibilities of canopies, the bishop of Durham placed his seat on top of his own tomb, at the side of the presbytery but emulating the old altitude of Saxon bishops and so looking down his nose upon both high altar and choir.

Some two centuries of glorious woodcarving are represented in the sets of medieval CHOIR STALLS surviving in English cathedrals, with their canopies supported on slender shafts and their bench-end figures and misericords under the seats (see below). Chronologically the stalls range mainly between early c 14 and early c 16, with later interferences, at: (c 14) Winchester, Hereford, Chichester, Wells, Ely, Gloucester, Lincoln, Worcester, Chester; (c 15) Carlisle, Norwich, Ripon; (early c 16) Manchester, Westminster (Henry VII), Bristol, Oxford. Rochester has remains of c 13 stalls, without misericords. Exeter has the earliest complete set of MISERICORDS, of the c 13 but long since departed from their original stalls. After them come the misericords at Salisbury. The Ely stalls are thought to be by the master of the Octagon lantern, *William Hurley*. The stalls of Chester, Lincoln (altered) and York (burnt) may have been from the workshop of the later c 14 master carpenter *Hugh Herland*. The stalls dating either side of 1500 at Ripon and Manchester, and also Beverley, are attributed to *William Brownfleet* of Ripon. The misericord, by the way, was a little shelf on the underside of the upturned seat, against which the occupier could lean while standing during long services (some London bus-shelters have similar mercies). The subject-matter of those little carvings – far from authority's eye, like the loftier vault-bosses – could be delightfully irreverent and undidactic, often inspired by folklore, and more often secular than biblical. Also, a unique piece of woodcarving must be mentioned, the c 14 pyx canopy at Wells.

Medieval FONTS, some also with elaborate canopies (e.g. at Bradford and Newcastle), usually stood in the nave near the north or west entrance door, baptism being the believer's way in, though fonts, like lecterns and pulpits, have long since become the most mobile of furnishings. The tub-shaped stone font at Wells may be much older than the present cathedral; much of its decoration has been chiselled off. That shape, with arcaded saints round it, was continued e.g. in the c 12 font at Hereford. Such tubs may originally have stood directly on the floor for adult baptism. A large ribbed tub of the c 12 is at Ripon. A c 12 font made of lead is now in Gloucester Cathedral, with arcaded saints and scrolls from the same mould as others in that

region. The black Tournai marble fonts at Lincoln and Winchester, of the mid-c 12, are of international quality and grandeur. Peterborough's font-bowl, possibly of local marble, with undulating rim, is of the c 13. As for Perp fonts, Norwich has a sumptuous though time-worn 'Seven Sacraments' one, octagonal with attached figures; c 15 octagonal fonts at Newcastle and Ripon have concave sides with shields.

Medieval LECTERNS and PULPITS. Three fine brass eagle lecterns of East Anglian provenance and dating from around 1500 are at Newcastle (Angl.), Peterborough and Southwell, and there is a similar one at Exeter. The presence of near-relations not only in many parishes but also as far off as Italy (Urbino Cathedral, St Mark's Venice) suggests an active export trade from East Anglia. But the handsome brass pelican lectern in Norwich Cathedral, of the late c 15 except for lower figures added in the early c 19, is thought to be Flemish. A magnificent late c 15 Flemish brass lectern, now in New York and previously at Oscott College, was for a while in St Chad's Cathedral at Birmingham, where the Flemish c 16 carved wood pulpit given with it survives without canopy. (We can also mention here the rare c 15 brass chandelier, possibly Flemish, in the Berkeley Chapel of Bristol Cathedral. On memorial brasses, see *Monuments* below.) A few stone reading desks survive. A built-in stone lectern is part of the c 14 screen between north transept and eastern aisle at Gloucester, apparently for taking attendance as monks filed past into the choir. And a refectory pulpit – for edifying readings during meals – is part of the c 13 wall structure within the north range of the cloister at Chester. A small canopied stone relief of the New Jerusalem, now on a windowsill at Worcester, may come from a c 14 or c 15 pulpit: it was incorporated in a pulpit made in 1642 to replace one broken up by soldiers. Four carved wooden pulpits survive in cathedrals from the years around and after 1500, the earliest probably that in Winchester choir, followed by one made for the Henry VII Chapel and now in the nave at Westminster; and two Flemish pulpits, one already mentioned in St Chad's Birmingham and one at Carlisle acquired in the c 20. Wells has a monumental c 16 nave pulpit of stone, given in the 1540s and surprisingly Renaissance in character.

Much screenwork of stone or wood survives in the cathedrals, and much more must have existed. Some of the handsomest and oldest screens are of IRONWORK, one of the earliest crafts. For c 13 ironwork see Chichester (some of it now in the Victoria and Albert Museum), also work of the 1290s at Westminster, Lincoln and Winchester, perhaps all of it by *Thomas of Leighton*. The c 14 west choir gates at Canterbury in an Islamic pattern were emulated in smoother c 19 work in the north and south gates there. At Wells the sturdy Bekynton Chantry screen is a rarity of the c 15. Henry V's Chantry gates at Westminster show early use of iron tracery, by *Roger Johnson*. The iron screen of Duke Humphrey's c 15 tomb at St Albans, sometimes called c 13, may be contemporary with the tomb. In a number of cathedrals, early ironwork remains as scrollwork on medieval wooden doors, e.g. on the west doors at Lichfield.

One of the most glorious of English medieval arts was that of STAINED GLASS, and a surprising amount has survived the slings and arrows of centuries. York Minster has the most complete collection from all periods since the c 12; our description has its own introduction after the other York furnishings. Canterbury is especially important for glass of the c 12–13; indeed, for the grandeur of the c 12 ancestor figures originally enthroned around the eastern clerestories, it is unparalleled. Some precious c 13 medallions remain in Hereford Lady Chapel; there is fine c 13 glass in the Dean's Eye (north transept) at Lincoln, and some late c 13 glass remaining on Wells chapter-house staircase and at Exeter. Early c 14 glass of high quality, dating both before and after the coming of silver-stain for making yellow, survives at Wells; precious fragments from Ely Lady Chapel are similar to work at York, and there is fine tracery glass in Oxford's St Lucy Chapel. Iconoclasts often missed the glass in the upper traceries. The largest spread of c 14 glass fills the great east window at Gloucester, where the canted-in side panels of glass fit into the canted-out spurs of the presbytery side-walls as if set by a jeweller – a lovely piece of precision engineering to combat wind pressure. The mason-in-charge is thought to have been that same *Thomas of Cambridge* who apparently designed the first fan-vaults: if so, one of the most fertile minds of that fertile time.

Medieval WALL PAINTING and PANEL PAINTING. Inner surfaces between and above the windows were also rich with colour. Only a little survives in proportion to what was. Important c 12 wall paintings survive in two chapels at Canterbury, walled off until the c 19. Norwich nave vault has faded remains of late c 12 painting, and there is c 13–14 work in the ambulatory. On the west wall of Rochester nave are some late c 12 sketches for a programme of decoration, and there is c 13 painting as well. At Winchester, work of great quality in the little Holy Sepulchre Chapel of *c.* 1200, north of the crossing, has scenes, found under later work, that are still fresh in colour and related in style to the c 12 Winchester Bible. Also at Winchester there are mid-c 13 vault paintings in the north-east chapel and early c 16 paintings in the Lady Chapel similar to work in Eton College Chapel. St Albans has an unusual amount of surviving c 13–16 wall decoration and, pre-eminently, the c 13 Crucifixion scenes on the north-eastern nave piers. Westminster has a striking series of elongated figures of the late c 13/early c 14, the earlier ones on the south wall of the south transept and in

St Faith's Chapel behind it, the later ones on the sedilia facing both sanctuary and ambulatory. Lichfield has recently revealed work of *c.* 1400 in the south choir aisle, also a small c 14 Crucifixion in a niche. And Exeter has early c 16 wall paintings in north transept and retrochoir. Two especially fine painted timber ceilings remain: on a large scale, the Peterborough c 13 nave ceiling, one of the most important medieval painted ceilings in Europe, and, on a smaller scale, that of the early c 16 prior's room at Carlisle. There are traces of early c 16 decoration on the vaults at Chichester (Lady Chapel) by *Lambert Bernard*, which must originally have been more delightful than his panels (transepts) with portrait medallions of bishops and kings, rightly compared by Ian Nairn to cigarette cards. Of valuable panel painting, retable panels now in the ambulatory at Westminster are, as already said, among the finest of the c 13 in Europe; and at Norwich in St Saviour's and St Luke's Chapels, panels of the late c 14/early c 15 are of high quality and interest. A rare late c 14 royal portrait hangs on a nave pier at Westminster, representing Richard II, and apparently his votive gift to St Edward's shrine.

Medieval PAVEMENTS. The finest spreads of c 13 floor tiles in England are in Winchester retrochoir and in Westminster chapter house. Many related tile designs can be seen in the British Museum. Also of the c 13, and far more rare and sumptuous, are the inlaid pavements, one formerly surrounding the shrine of St Thomas à Becket in Trinity Chapel at Canterbury, and at Westminster the sanctuary pavement with remains of the shrine pavement east of it. The Westminster pavements are known to have been made by Roman craftsmen, the *Cosmati*, brought here for the purpose. Less is known of the origins of the Canterbury workmen, though a pink marble used is thought to be Mediterranean. The most-used floors and steps in such buildings will have been repaved many times for safety's sake; there is fine c 18 paving at York, and some of the handsomest pavements now are Victorian (see below).

Which brings us to the SHRINES, miracle-working saints' tombs that brought pilgrims and revenue to many cathedrals. The tomb itself, in every case, survives only in fragments or not at all. Their gold and jewelled ornaments invited pillage, not only after the Reformation but before. The c 15 watching lofts at St Albans and Oxford were pieces of furniture installed to ensure security. At Canterbury in the c 12 and c 13 watching chambers were contrived in the building itself to overlook Becket's tomb both before and after it was moved from temporary accommodation in the crypt to the Trinity Chapel built for it. The shrine itself, by *Walter of Colchester*, is gone; marks in the elaborate pavement show where it stood. The architectural form of east ends could be dictated by prudent entrepreneurial placing of shrines, as was possibly the case with the c 13 retrochoir at Winchester (St Swithun) and Old St

Paul's (St Erkenwald). The acquisition of a miracle-making martyr at Rochester provided funds for C 13 rebuilding of the east end and may have dictated the size of the east transepts there. At Hereford, when Bishop Cantilupe was canonized in the early C 14, his tomb, now in the north transept, was moved to the Lady Chapel and the choir aisles were embellished as pilgrim routes in and out. The holiest spot for a shrine was behind the main altar in the space called the feretory, e.g. St Edward the Confessor's at Westminster at the heart of Henry III's new east end: here only the C 13 base is original. At St Albans what remains is the very early C 14 base, reconstructed from two thousand fragments in the C 19; and St Frideswide's shrine at Oxford and St Werburgh's at Chester were also reconstructed in the C 19. There also survive little portable shrines, one of the C 13 of Limoges enamel being now kept in the library at Hereford. (Late C 13 enamelling on copper plates sheathing an effigy in St Edmund's Chapel at Westminster is thought to have been done at Limoges, a more unusual import than a tiny portable shrine.)

Medieval MONUMENTS. Royal tombs were also worth having. At Westminster, still with their effigies, are those of (feretory) Henry III, Eleanor of Castile, Edward III, Richard II and his queen, the figures of gilt bronze, also Philippa's of marble, and Henry V (restored); and (Henry VII Chapel) the effigies of Henry VII and his queen, of gilt bronze, and those of Elizabeth I and Mary of Scots, of marble, as well as some chests without effigies and the tombs of numerous relations. The sculptors included the late C 13 *William Torel*, the early C 16 *Torrigiani*, and the early C 17 *Maximilian Colt*. (Here, for the sake of mentioning the royal effigies at Westminster together, we have trespassed on our post-medieval summary.) At Winchester the supposed tomb of William II, a plain low gabled chest, may be that of Henry of Blois. William's uncle, Duke Robert of Normandy, is buried at Gloucester, with a C 12 wooden effigy of great interest. King John's C 13 marble effigy at Worcester is of high quality. One of the first and most beautiful effigies of alabaster is Edward II's, of the early C 14, at Gloucester. At Canterbury the stiff copper-gilt effigy of the Black Prince contrasts with the elaborate alabaster figures of Henry IV and his queen. A study of tomb sculpture is essential to the history of dress, ecclesiastical, secular and military. For details of armour, note e.g. Duke Robert's at Gloucester, probably mid-C 12, and William Longespée's of the early or mid-C 13 at Salisbury, also the mid- or late C 15 armour of Robert Lord Hungerford there. And details of C 13 armour have been revealed on Wells west front. Canterbury and York have their series of archbishops' tombs, as other medieval cathedrals have their tombs of bishops, rewarding not only as records of episcopal dress but, like the tombs of all the well-buried, for their architectural and sculptural features.

One marvellous tomb is that of Bishop Bridport († 1262) at Salisbury, with its shrine-like canopy and its bar tracery following the new Westminster style. Two tombs commemorating deaths of the 1530s, yet without a hint of the Renaissance detail which had started to creep into English decorative carving in the 1520s, Bishop Sherbourne's at Chichester and Archbishop Warham's at Canterbury, show how a death-date is no indicator of the date of an artist's commission; the latter tomb is known to have been made in 1507, long before Warham died in 1532. Caution is also wise in case of over-eager C 19 restorations of tombs, e.g. of the Fitzalan tomb in Chichester nave and the Courtenay tomb in Exeter south transept; pre-Victorian engravings of tomb sculpture can be helpful. Another warning: medieval tombs have endured a deal of moving about from one part of a cathedral to another, with separations of chests from canopies etc., ever since the Reformation.

In a special category was the flat memorial BRASS, either a cut-out figure indented in a stone slab or an engraved sheet, the latter an imported Continental type. Many were lost, robbed for the material; others were turned over and re-used. At Hereford by 1717 there remained 170 indents of lost brasses, though a few fine brasses still remain there, the best being that of Bishop Trillek, mid-C 14. At Canterbury there are now no brasses at all, only indents. Exeter has two fine brasses, both C 15, of special interest for Canon Langton's vestments and Sir Peter Courtenay's armour. The epitome of the successful merchant's memorial is the great Thornton double brass of the early C 15, now in Newcastle (Angl.) Cathedral, of the incised-sheet type, probably Flemish. One of the biggest and most interesting brasses in England is that of Bishop Wyvil or Wyville at Salisbury, adapting a theme from tales of chivalry to the celebration of a triumphant lawsuit and unique in showing the weapons peculiar to trial by combat (north-east transept, with facsimile in the nave for brass-rubbers).

Medieval master CRAFTSMEN designed furnishings as well as architecture. *Henry Yevele*, to whom many buildings are attributed, produced tomb-chests for Westminster Abbey; *William Hurley* apparently designed both the great timber lantern at Ely and the stalls below; and *Hugh Herland*, whose celebrated timber roof at Westminster Hall rested on Yevele's walls, is thought to have supplied choir stalls to three northern cathedrals. One marvels at the travels of some of these men, who also had to visit quarries and forests to select their materials. Perhaps master painters and sculptors travelled less when cathedral and monastic libraries were so rich in illustrated manuscripts to copy. Yet models as portable as illuminated manuscripts, embroidered vestments and imported woven silks, and small metalwork such as miniature shrines, carried patterns along clerical and commercial routes inside and outside the country. And craftsmen themselves going from one job to another carried ideas in their heads and their sketchbooks. There is no room in such a rapid survey as this introduction to characterize the known medieval craftsmen-designers of architecture and furnishings referred to in the text, for whom see the index under: Alexander, Attegrene, Bertie, Beverley, Brownfleet, Cambridge, Canterbury, Clyve, Colchester, Everard, Farleigh, Gloucester, Hedon, Herland, Hoo, Hoton, Hurley, Joy, Lesyngham, Lewyn, Lock, Luve, Mapilton, Montacute, Noiers, Norreys, Orchard, Patrington, Ramsey, Reyns, Roger, Sens, Smythe, Sponlee, Wastell, William, Witney, Wodehirst, Woodruff, Wynford, Yevele; and of course Mr Harvey's biographical dictionary. Next we proceed to the domain of Mr Colvin (for both, see Recent Literature) and after.

## Cathedrals after the Reformation

Except for the rebuilding of Old St Paul's after the Great Fire (and one new parish church later to become a cathedral, *Archer*'s St Philip's Birmingham), no new cathedral was built in England after the Reformation until *Pugin*'s C 19 Catholic cathedrals. Apart from St Paul's, the architectural works of deans and chapters between C 16 and C 19 consisted of rebuilding, repairing and adorning the medieval fabrics, especially after the two periods of vandalism in the 1540s and 1640s. Of the twenty-two cathedral structures of Elizabeth's reign all but Salisbury (1220) had been begun between the 1070s and the 1180s. So looking after them was no new exercise, although some generations were readier to ignore the need than others, and both the spiritual and the social incentives had altered. Political, religious, art-historical and social changes had coincided in the Reformation with the end of the Gothic style and the rise of Renaissance classicism and the gradual change from craftsmen-designers to architects. Shifts in architectural attitudes to cathedrals in the four centuries since the Reformation are best illustrated by noting what succeeding architects did with them.

If inevitably at first no cathedrals were built, a great burst of sumptuous house-building for the new men of the day was inevitably followed by sumptuous tomb-making for the same clients. Between the 1530s and the 1630s the principal additions inside English cathedrals were the monuments of Elizabethan and Jacobean peers, politicians and merchants, in lavish but limited variation on a few newly learned classical themes (see the preface to Westminster Abbey furnishings), followed in the early C 17 by the more truly classical sculpture of *Nicholas Stone* and *Hubert Le Sueur*, both at Westminster, and the former also

at St Paul's, Southwark and Portsmouth, the latter at Winchester. Meanwhile, the battered and partly emptied cathedrals themselves increasingly needed attention. In the 1630s it was part of Archbishop Laud's policy to urge restoration and adornment, particularly at St Paul's and Winchester, where the work was encouraged by Charles I and designed by the King's Surveyor, *Inigo Jones*. Both for Jones's new pulpitum at Winchester and for his new west portico at St Paul's, there was no question of reviving medieval style: both must be utterly classical. Yet at Winchester the new ceiling inserted in the crossing tower in 1635, with the king's portrait on the main boss above Jones's pulpitum, was a neo-medieval wooden fan-vault; and his encasing of the Norman parts of St Paul's was tactfully, minimally Tuscan, nearest classical mode to Romanesque: seeds of Anglo-Gothic attitudes for the next hundred years. Reverence for medieval forms was not dead. Furnishings of the 1630s also survive at Oxford (pulpit with ogee-ribbed open canopy, glass by the *Van Linge* family) and at Chester (consistory-court furniture, redecoration of St Anselm's Chapel).

Even in the second hiatus, during Civil War and Commonwealth, when more battering and emptying of cathedrals took place, there was recording of cathedrals, e.g. in the engravings of Hollar and the writings of Dugdale and others. After the restoration of the monarchy and the established Church, the shoring-up and renovating of old churches began again. And then one of the landmarks of English architecture, its first Protestant-built cathedral, was in effect brought about by the destruction of its predecessor in the Great Fire of London in 1666. With all of the new St Paul's classical elements, its dome and its orders, *Christopher Wren* fused Gothic elements, such as the long-naved cruciform plan, in an Anglican synthesis. In details of plan there is likeness to Lincoln (placing of nave chapels) and Ely (enlarged crossing). At both Lincoln and Ely, Wren acted as consultant for rebuilding works, of north cloister and library at the former, of the north transept's north-west corner at the latter: for both, a Tuscan round-arched simplicity was thought to be the right note in the context, though a doorway at Ely was French in inspiration *via* a design of his own for St Mary-le-Bow. At Salisbury Wren supervised strengthening of the tower. At Westminster, where London smoke was already damaging stonework, he was in charge of restoration, assisted by *William Dickinson*; their work on the north transept was later redone by *Scott* and *Pearson*. Wren gave his views on Gothic, at Salisbury in 1668 praising its proportions and freedom from over-ornamentation and making only structural criticisms; at Westminster in 1713 reporting in a similarly businesslike and objective way: Gothic was an interesting practical problem.

In the early c 18, after Wren's death, *Nicholas Hawksmoor* designed Westminster's west towers, which Abbot Islip had not managed to complete. Hawksmoor had been in charge of repairing original medieval work at Beverley, but was also interested in recreating Gothic skylines as he had done at All Souls College, Oxford. His church tower for St George-in-the-East (initially designed for St Alphege Greenwich) seems to have been inspired by the Ely Octagon lantern (pre-*Essex*; see below). In silhouette his Westminster towers are spirited approximations of medieval towers. Yet he cared about the preservation of Gothic buildings 'Martyr'd by Neglect' (see St Albans).

Even before the Great Fire created new opportunities for craftsmen, the Restoration stimulated church arts: great brass lecterns made in London in the early 1660s by *William Burroughs* are at Canterbury, Lincoln, Wells and Queen's College Chapel at Oxford. But in the late c 17/ early c 18 the furnishing of St Paul's and the City churches stimulated the decorative crafts more than at any time since the high Middle Ages. Sculptors such as *Grinling Gibbons, Edward Pierce* and *Jonathan Maine* worked both in stone and in wood: St Paul's is a *locus classicus* for their work, as only a few City churches still are. *Jean Tijou*'s masterly ironwork, of European quality, at St Paul's and Hampton Court is echoed at Derby and Birmingham by that of *Robert Bakewell*. A majestic Corinthian throne canopy at Canterbury was designed probably by *Hawksmoor* in his most superbly classical manner. But he rebuilt the medieval pulpitum at Westminster in his own Gothic (rebuilt in the 1830s by *Blore* in *his* Gothic, still with inner-passage vault in *Henry Keene*'s late c 18 Gothic). The nave face of this pulpitum holds two niches where the medieval side altars will have been, which, after Hawksmoor's work, were immediately filled by *William Kent*'s Newton and Stanhope monuments (executed by *Rysbrack*), not at all Gothic. But Kent designed a pulpitum himself for Gloucester Cathedral that was a variation on Exeter's c 14 pulpitum in his own furniture-designer's Gothic, later replaced. York Minster in the 1730s was entirely repaved in black and white marble (the black, or some of it, was really deep blue) in a bold classical-key design by *Lord Burlington* in association with Kent; this paving remains in the nave. In this period *James Gibbs* (architect of St Martin-in-the-Fields in London and of the main body of the present cathedral at Derby) tactfully used the round arch at Lincoln in interior screen-walls under the Norman west towers; that is, approximating a Norman arch as Jones and Wren had done. Gibbs, incidentally, also designed memorial sculpture: his Craggs monument at Westminster precedes Kent's Shakespeare figure there in adopting the artificial bent-knee pose from the antique (but the elaborately negligent knee had already appeared in England in the paintings of Hilliard and Oliver). As for

c 17–18 stained-glass design, it became more and more like contemporary painting (as tapestry design was also doing): see the Nineveh window of the 1630s by *Van Linge* at Oxford, and much c 18 work by *William Peckitt* of York, especially at York.

In the mid-c 18 architects began to take Gothic more seriously and cathedrals began to be recognized as sources of styles to be used elsewhere, while to a few deans their restoration became intellectually interesting. Both Ely and Lincoln owe much to intelligent restoration by the architect *James Essex*. Even so, in restoring the exterior of the Octagon lantern at Ely, he seems to have misread existing remains of its appearance and turned it into a not very exciting work of masonry rather than the triumph of carpentry suggested in early c 18 engraved views, which *Scott* later had the good sense to follow in his own restoration. At Carlisle in 1765 the bishop, happening to be President of the Society of Antiquaries and keenly interested in medieval architecture, had his nephew *Thomas Pitt* design new choir furnishings, of which only fragments survived Victorian disapproval. In the late 1780s began the cathedral restorations of *James Wyatt*. Quantitatively these pale beside *Scott*'s (below): Wyatt worked on or was consulted at Lichfield, Salisbury, Hereford, Durham, Ely and also Westminster Abbey. He is worst remembered for his tidying of the nave and destruction of glass at Salisbury and for his proposal to demolish the galilee at Durham. But he has been unjustly maligned for his work on Hereford nave after the west tower fell: there he was self-effacing. His Gothic fantasizing on cathedral themes was done for country houses.

By the second quarter of the c 19 designs for renovation of cathedrals by men like *Salvin* and *Ferrey* and *Blore* were serious antiquarian exercises. As late as the 1820s the ages-old tradition of a cathedral's master mason designing his own work had been maintained at Exeter by *John Kendall*, but by then that was unusual. Increasingly in the c 19 the relative responsibilities of master masons, clerks of the works, architects or surveyors to deans and chapters, and consultant architects from London or from other cathedrals varied from one cathedral to another (see e.g. *Durham* and *Worcester*).

Which brings us to the cathedral restorations of *George Gilbert Scott* (knighted in 1872) at Chester, Chichester, Durham, Ely, Exeter, Gloucester, Hereford, Lichfield, Oxford, Ripon, Rochester, St Albans, Salisbury, Winchester, Worcester and also Westminster Abbey (not counting all his other ecclesiastical work). There are two reasons why Scott's church restorations are better regarded than they were, apart from the usual pendulum-swing in such matters: recent research has found evidence for the previous existence of some of his more daring conceits, e.g. Chester's south-east chapel roof (though hardly as high as he made it); and a sober realism about weathering stonework and the results of neglect accepts that much now stands that, but for him, would have fallen. It is also right, in all cases of amendment to fabric or lack of same, to consider what the client – deans and chapters, and sometimes lay committees – wanted done or not done, and could afford.

Another endlessly debatable consideration is the old matter of tact in adding new work to existing fabric, illustrated by the naves of *Street* at Bristol and *Blomfield* at Southwark. Quite apart from the superior quality of both new and old at Bristol, the problem was the same: how to design a modern introduction to old work of great interest without upstaging it. Both men, it may be thought, achieved this successfully. The other principal Victorian figure in cathedral works was *John Loughborough Pearson*, the architect of Truro and restoring architect at Peterborough, Westminster Abbey and Lincoln. Controversies during the two stages of his work at Peterborough illustrated the gathering forces of lay opinion anxious to defend historic buildings from change and even destruction. The founding of the Society for the Preservation of Ancient Buildings by William Morris in 1877 was set off in opposition to Scott's doings at Tewkesbury. The ageing of physical structures coincided with all the other stresses and strains affecting the Victorian Church. One angry voice, for example, was that of the Rev. J. C. Cox, LL.D., F.S.A., addressing the Royal Archaeological Institute's summer meeting at Dorchester in 1897 on 'The Treatment of Our Cathedral Churches in the Victorian Age', and 'an attack it is intended to be', admitting that the fabrics were in better repair than in 1837 or even 1867, but mourning 'irreparable destruction of much that is ancient'. Perhaps he was thinking of Scott's brand-new east end at Oxford, though there we now know that the previously Perp window had already been redone in 1853. Dr Cox deplored 'the playing at parish church with the whole of the cathedral . . . and hence endeavouring to obliterate the proper division between quire and nave' (i.e. presumably he disliked the transparency of Scott's screens), and he objected to the 'undue giving way to the rage for gigantic organ effects' and 'the pervading influence of sound', perhaps referring to the immense organ of which the case remains in Worcester south transept.

There is now more appreciation for VICTORIAN CATHEDRAL FURNISHINGS than there was, one barometer being regard for *Scott*'s choir screens. Instead of the solid walls of medieval pulpitums or their c 18 or early c 19 replacements, a new semi-transparency between choir and nave was indeed wanted by Victorian chapters. So Scott seems to have worked up his designs from medieval wooden rood screens and iron chantry screens. His first cathedral screen is at Ely (1851), and he followed its type in designs for Lichfield, Hereford, Worcester and, with simpler elements, Salisbury. (In the mid-c 20 those for Hereford and Salisbury were dispensed with.) At Winchester and Chester in the 1870s he took as his point of departure the carved-wood canopies of the return stalls against the screen. But Durham posed difficulties for a screen-designer in the extreme majesty of its architecture and in the, to him unsympathetic, c 17 Gothic of its choir stalls, and the screen there has less character than most of Scott's furnishings. Other Victorian work of great quality appears in splendid pavements designed by Scott (Durham, Worcester, Gloucester, Oxford) and *Pearson* (Bristol, Peterborough, Truro). The bold key pattern at Worcester, although Scott claimed he was inspired by the marble floor at Amiens, is much closer to the Burlington–Kent paving at York, an c 18 source that a high Victorian might not rush to claim. Scott at Durham and Pearson were obviously influenced by the c 13 Cosmati pavements at Westminster.

Three Victorian furnishings of unusual quality were shown in the 1862 Exhibition in London: Scott's Hereford screen, made by the Coventry metalworker *Skidmore*; Scott's great rood cross formerly at Chester (q.v.); and Gloucester's most spirited of eagle lecterns, designed by the young *J. F. Bentley*. Victorian stained glass is particularly well represented at Lincoln and Ely. Bradford and Peterborough have very early examples of glass made by Morris & Co., early enough to include designs by *Rossetti* as well as by *Webb* and *Morris*. At Oxford there is even an early *Burne-Jones* window designed before he worked for Morris & Co., but the Burne-Jones windows Oxford is best known for were for Morris's firm in the 1870s. These have a lyrical quality. In the 1880s Burne-Jones and Morris produced exciting windows for St Philip's Birmingham (not then a cathedral): windows more like brass bands in their splendour, perhaps not entirely suited to Archer's cool c 18 interior. A later, twilit Burne-Jones window is at Norwich (north transept).

When in the 1870s it was proposed to have a whole new cathedral built at Truro in Cornwall, many voices within the Anglican Church protested that 'another cathedral from an English architect' was impossible (Dean Goodwin of Ely, quoted by Owen Chadwick). But Truro and three more Anglican cathedrals by English architects were indeed to be built by the 1960s, charting the final stages of Gothic tradition in England: complete absorption at Truro culminating in Gothic apotheosis at Liverpool, followed by dilution at Guildford and rethinking at Coventry. The progress of Roman Catholic handling of the Gothic tradition in c 19–20 England, to provide the new cathedrals needed, went a little differently.

Although the Catholic Emancipation Act was passed by Parliament in 1829, there were officially no Catholic cathedrals until the hierarchy was restored in 1850. But the young *A. W. N. Pugin* had cathedrals in mind when he designed St George Southwark in 1838–9, St Chad Birmingham in 1839, and St Barnabas Nottingham in 1841; and in 1850, when they became cathedrals, his somewhat smaller St Mary Newcastle, also designed in 1841, was made the fourth of his cathedrals in England. They are much less complex than the old medieval fabrics, more on a scale with the Anglican 'parish-church cathedrals' (see below). Nevertheless, Pugin was intensely conscious that he was designing the first new English cathedrals in the Gothic style since the Reformation. (For Truro, after St Paul's, was to be only the second Anglican cathedral in England built new.) In spite of the needs of large congregations, and the resources of a very few rich patrons, Pugin was never able to build on the scale his Church was later able to afford for Bentley at Westminster. Nor are most of the beautiful fittings Pugin designed still in place. But the 'R.C. new series' cathedrals started worthily with him, and the Catholic Gothic tradition was continued by his son and by architects such as *Hadfield* and the *Hansom* family. At Norwich the grand church (only recently made a cathedral but designed on a modest-cathedral scale) by the sons of Sir Gilbert Scott actually owes more to Scott's last achievement in St Mary's Cathedral at Edinburgh.

The Roman Catholic break with English Gothic tradition was made in 1894 at Westminster. It was felt that Gothic should not be used so near Westminster Abbey, and *John Francis Bentley* made masterly use of Byzantine and Italian inspiration instead. Westminster Cathedral is rich in fittings and in handsome marbles; only the mosaic wall-coverings are weak. The next time a Catholic metropolitan cathedral was to be built, in the 1930s at Liverpool, the Church went architecturally to the opposite extreme, commissioning *Lutyens*'s vast classical design that was meant to outdo St Paul's if not St Peter's. But it was too vast, and only the crypt was built. Now *Gibberd*'s bold centralized design has been built upon that crypt, in fine contrast to *Sir Giles Scott*'s Anglican cathedral. And a quite different, equally non-traditional, smaller cathedral has been built at Clifton, Bristol. The Catholic hierarchy abandoned the Gothic tradition sooner than the Anglican hierarchy did.

Meanwhile, with the growth of urban populations between the 1880s and the 1960s, deans and architects pursued various stratagems for turning certain large parish churches into small cathedrals by extension of existing spaces. Medieval cathedrals of course had incessant additions but to fabrics already elaborate, especially east of the crossing. Extension of parish-church cathedrals has had to be mainly eastward, where the site has allowed it, for bigger choirs and new ambulatories and vestries (as variously at Chelmsford, Derby and Wakefield), some-

times also creating transepts and crossing where none were before (Blackburn, Bury). Portsmouth was extended westward, but dramatic plans for still more extension were abandoned. Sometimes the site was so cramped by other buildings, as at Leicester and Newcastle, that rearrangements and elaborate refitting were concentrated within existing chancels. Some Roman Catholic cathedrals have cleared space by rejecting fine original fittings, as at Birmingham and Sheffield. Bold action at Brentwood switched orientation of the whole church through 90°, as was for a time intended at Sheffield's Anglican cathedral, and Northampton has twice had its orientation switched through 180°. The greatness of great churches built from the start as such is a matter of scale and eludes these scaled-up churches. But the interest of their histories can be respected where the evidences have not been lost in the enlarging process.

A seasoned medieval master mason, presumably consulting other specialists such as the water-carpenter or the roof-carpenter, during his lifetime might himself design bridges and towers and halls and cathedrals or parts thereof. So in the C 20, the architect who acted as consultant for the external design of Battersea Power Station and collaborated on the design of Waterloo Bridge designed the Anglican cathedral at Liverpool. And the architect of the Catholic cathedral there also designed passenger terminals for Heathrow Airport and planned Harlow New Town. Some techniques and some materials and many secular building-types have changed or evolved since the Middle Ages, along with human (or inhuman) ideas about scale. The cathedral is an old building-type, despite new ideas about the performance of its functions. And cathedrals are still patrons of the decorative arts. Certain cathedrals are especially distinguished for their C 20 furnishings, in new cathedrals especially Coventry and Liverpool R.C., in old cathedrals especially Chichester, also Salisbury and Manchester.

It is right that we should mention the restorative crafts of conservation work now being employed in the never-ending care of ageing fabrics. During the war of 1939–45 Coventry, Exeter, Manchester and, in London, St Paul's and Southwark R.C. cathedrals and Westminster Abbey suffered direct hits, as did the precincts of Canterbury and Norwich, and there was lesser damage to the Anglican cathedrals at Liverpool and Birmingham. New enemies are traffic vibration and oil-burning pollution of the air. An old enemy is lack of money for conservation. It is usual to reflect that cathedrals remind us of the transience of human life and the durability of human institutions. May the fabrics we celebrate endure.

PRISCILLA METCALF

# The Cathedrals of England

MIDLAND, EASTERN AND NORTHERN ENGLAND

# Birmingham

## CATHEDRAL CHURCH OF ST PHILIP *Anglican*

(Based on B of E *Warwickshire*, 1966, by N P and Alexandra Wedgwood, revised, with information from Sewter 1974–5, Beard 1981, and George McHardy.)

Cathedral since 1905. Built 1710–15, tower finished 1725. Designed 1709 by *Thomas Archer*, the first of his outstanding churches (cf. St Paul's Deptford and St John's Smith Square, London). Archer came of a local family of Warwickshire gentry, a circumstance to which he must at least partly have owed this commission.

In character and quality St Philip's and its immediate surroundings have no parallel in Birmingham's history: this was the one C 18 development which managed to keep industry at a distance. The church still stands in its own square. Though the contemporary town houses have now all been demolished and most of the green walks have been encroached upon, enough remains to give a dignified and worthy setting to this sophisticated and elegant building. It is in fact of far more than local importance. This was the first English church since St Paul's Covent Garden to be designed by an architect who had seen for himself many major Continental buildings, for Wren knew at first hand only Paris, whereas Archer travelled for four years on the Continent, from 1689 to 1693. He no doubt knew Rome, which to him meant Bernini and, even more, Borromini; and he may have been to Austria. His style represents an original and entirely personal reworking of what he had seen, which of course also included works by Wren, Hawksmoor and Vanbrugh. The result is a most subtle example of the elusive English Baroque. Yet still it is mainly a single-celled parish church. What Archer might have done if asked, like Wren, to design an Anglican cathedral remains a question.

The builder was *Francis Smith* of Warwick, the mason *Joseph Pedley* of Warwick, and the stone came from quarries on Archer's brother's estate at Umberslade. It did not weather well, and various parts of the exterior have had to

2. BIRMINGHAM (ANGL.) Designed 1709 by Thomas Archer. View from the south

1. BIRMINGHAM (ANGL.)
Ascension window, 1884, by Edward Burne-Jones

be refaced (1864, 1911, 1958, 1980) in the Hollington reddish sandstone also used on Hereford and Coventry cathedrals. In plan, the building forms a rectangle with E and W projections for chancel and tower (the chancel altered and deepened by *J. A. Chatwin*, 1883–4). At each end the aisles extend farther than the nave, forming vestries (since 1884) on each side of the chancel and vestibules with staircases to the gallery on each side of the tower.

## EXTERIOR

It is the external elevations, and in particular the W end and the tower, that reveal the subtlety and interest of Archer's design. The lower stage of the tower, which projects in the middle of the W front, has a large round-headed W window and a curved pediment, between coupled Doric pilasters. Above, the tower stands free, and all sides are treated identically. The bell-stage has concave sides, inspired probably by Wren's St Vedast, and large round-headed windows between broad diagonal piers faced with twin Corinthian pilasters. These support pairs of scrolled brackets at the octagonal attic stage. Above is a leaded dome and an open colonnaded lantern to ball and weathervane. To either side of the tower are the enclosed porches, flanked by Doric pilasters and with a complicated surround to the doorways – pedimental sections of cornice on splayed triglyphs over polygonal jambs – and elaborately framed oval cartouches above. The inspiration for this kind of detail is obviously Borromini. More complicated the corresponding doorways at the E end. In the side elevations the bays with round-headed windows are divided by Doric pilasters, which support an entablature with frieze, and parapet and urns above. Everywhere there is horizontal banding. The C19 chancel keeps to the same basic design.

## INTERIOR

The C18 plasterwork is by *Richard Huss* of Derby and is austere with no frills, white with the slightest touch of gold. The nave has five-bay arcades with square fluted piers, set on a high base, and round-headed arches. The arcades are stately, and there has been some attempt to integrate the galleries, though they block the aisle windows awkwardly, but their simple oak-panelled fronts are inserted between the piers and do not cut across the arcade. The ceiling is coved. In the C19 restoration the W gallery was removed and the arch from the nave into the tower was opened up to provide a baptistery.

To eastward there is a most effective change from the plain but light and spacious nave to the rich and grand chancel. Chatwin could rise to an occasion more than adequately, particularly when he was working within the framework of a better architect's design and with sufficient

money. The present chancel is, in fact, developed from the earlier arrangement, which also used Corinthian columns. Now the E end has a slightly projecting straight-ended centre framed by Corinthian pilasters and by apsidal curves either side. The chancel is divided into bays by three pairs of free-standing Corinthian columns on high bases, with a coffered ceiling above.

## FURNISHINGS

ORGAN CASE of 1715, by *Thomas Schwarbrick* of Warwick, with pretty putti heads. – Near it at the E end of the N gallery an ORGAN CASE of similar date from St Chrysostom, Hockley. – COMMUNION RAIL, wrought iron, similar to the work of *Jean Tijou* or his pupil *Robert Bakewell* of Derby (cf. Queen's College Chapel, Oxford). – STAINED GLASS. The E and W windows are by *Sir Edward Burne-Jones* and made by *William Morris*. Burne-Jones is always linear, but here his designs are taut and dramatic, and also the colour is vibrant and exciting. The green and red Last Judgement, dating from 1889, glows from the dark W tower, and the mostly red and blue Ascension, of 1884, with the Crucifixion to the S and the Nativity to the N, both of 1887, shout triumphantly from behind the altar. One verdict is that this glass is superbly right for this building. But Dr Sewter has pointed out that one can see it quite differently, Archer's geometry demanding instead an even diffusion of light, whereas Burne-Jones and Morris considered the architecture an unavoidable monstrosity and the character of Archer's volumes of no importance. The windows they regarded as their greatest achievement. Burne-Jones, incidentally, was born in Birmingham and baptized in this church.

MONUMENTS. Rebecca †1781 and William Grice †1790, by *William Thompson*, plain (N aisle). – Dr Rogers †1804, by *Peter Rouw the Younger* (N aisle). – Mrs Outram †1810, by *Westmacott* (W end of nave, S side). – Moses Haughton †1804, by *Peter Rouw the Younger*, marble wall-monument with medallion portrait in slight relief (W end of N aisle). – Edmund Outram †1821, by *William Hollins*, severely Greek (W end of N aisle). – Rev. John George Breay †1839, by *Peter Hollins*, also a marble monument with medallion portrait (tower). – Edward Wilkes †1835, by *Peter Hollins*, a lady and an urn (S aisle). – David Owen †1823 and Mary †1831, by *William Hollins*, a well-draped urn (SW porch). – John Heap and William Badger †1833, the base of a fluted column, intended for the town hall, during the building of which these two were killed (churchyard). – Bishop Gore, bronze by *Stirling Lee*, 1914 (churchyard).

In Birmingham as in Bristol and Liverpool the Anglican and the Roman Catholic cathedrals are at opposite poles of architectural style. In power of first impression (w fronts), while Pugin's church (see below) was conceived from the first as a small cathedral and Archer's church was not, St Philip's undoubtedly has the greater presence, however one feels about style.

For the neighbourhood of St Philip's (Colmore Row, Temple Row etc.) and the surrounding redevelopment of Inner Birmingham, see the latest edition of B of E *Warwickshire*.

# Birmingham

## Cathedral Church of St Chad  *Roman Catholic*

(Based on the entry in B of E *Warwickshire*, 1966, by Alexandra Wedgwood, revised by her, with additions by Roderick O'Donnell.)

Cathedral since 1850, although envisaged as such from 1839. This was one of *A. W. N. Pugin*'s earliest and most important commissions. He chose to use red brick, perhaps because the material was so eminently suitable for its site, screwed into the side of the hill, dominating all the then surrounding two-storey dwellings of the densely built gunmakers' quarter. But today the surroundings have changed dramatically. Gone are many little buildings that housed the factories and men of the C19 gun trade, gone too is the Bishop's House by Pugin of 1839–41, of red brick, diagonally opposite the cathedral and making a counterpoint to it (a sad loss to road-building in 1960). Large glass and concrete towers are now sited on either side of the Snow Hill Ringway and the St Chad's Circus Ringway, and the most direct approach to the cathedral is *via* a green tile-lined subway. Yet St Chad's still holds its own, just. Whatever Pugin's reasons for choosing brick, he chose a style to match his material, that of C14 Baltic Germany, where brick facing and two w towers with spires are common features.

The history of the cathedral began at a meeting of the Catholics of Birmingham in January 1834, when the resolution was passed 'That it appears to this meeting highly desirable that a commodious and splendid Catholic Church be erected in the town of Birmingham'. Thomas Rickman was engaged as architect and he prepared designs. There were, however, differences of opinion over the site, and the scheme was dropped. In 1839 it was revived by Bishop Walsh, who on his own initiative decided to build a cathedral on the site of an existing church of St Chad (although the territorial see could be officially established only in 1850). Pugin was called in to advise, coming to Birmingham on 28 February, and his diary entry for 1 March reads 'with the Bishop'. Presumably he quickly disposed of

Rickman's designs, one of which, now in the R.I.B.A. Drawings Collection, has a rapid pencil sketch on it, certainly in Pugin's hand, in which he succinctly demonstrated the difference between Rickman's Gothic box and a building constructed on medieval principles. No time was wasted; the drawings were immediately prepared, the foundation stone was laid on 29 October 1839, and the building was consecrated on 21 June 1841, though one of the w towers was not complete until 1856. The design clearly belongs to Pugin's early period and has considerable stylistic similarities, particularly in plan and treatment of light and space, with his St Marie's Derby and two unexecuted designs, the one for St Marie's Manchester and the first design for St George's Southwark. The unhappy reordering of St Chad's in 1967 was the work of the Liverpool firm of *Weightman & Bullen*.

### EXTERIOR

Excellent composition of the N side, with chapels and transepts climbing up the hill, also the triangular excrescence with big doors (for coffins), which forms an entrance lobby to the crypt. The addition of 1933 by *S. Pugin Powell*, a N W chapel with octagonal end, is less sensitive. The s side is covered by later additions, including the adjoining Cathedral House, by *Harrison & Cox*, which seems to be just another office block. The w front is not effective as a whole; in particular the sculpture has not been integrated into the design. But there were splendid and typical details, like the decorative ironwork on the w doors, now removed. And the needle-sharp w spires have all the confidence and precision of the Early Victorian Birmingham metalwork trades.

### INTERIOR

The immediate impression is one of space and light, which, when analysed, is conveyed by most economical means. The six-bay arcades of stone piers with clustered shafts, which carry almost no weight, stretch up to the light roof with its rather thin construction. There is a continuous roof slope over nave and aisles. While it is not a hall-church, the general design is similar and again reminds one of C14 Germany. The roof itself, steeply pitched, is most effectively painted with a broad pattern. The tall two-light windows of the N and s walls contribute to the effect. There is also a w gallery, which Pugin would not have tolerated later in his life. The E end consists of a short chancel, with an apsidal end and three two-light windows, plus another s window pierced later, a small N chapel and s vestries. No projecting transepts, but the roof is hipped laterally to give the effect of a crossing. (On the effect upon the whole space of the recent removal of Pugin's screen, see *Furnishings* below.) There is a small square projection from the middle of the N wall, containing baptistery and stairs down to the crypt.

CRYPT (not open to the public). The sloping site gave Pugin the opportunity to build a crypt, at first intended for

3 and 4. BIRMINGHAM (R.C.)
Designed 1839 by A. W. N. Pugin.
(*below*) View from the north-east in 1961.
(*right*) Interior in 1941, with Pugin's screen

parish schools. As built, however, it consists of a series of tunnel-vaulted chapels or oratories and burial chambers, some with original mural decorations, obviously Pugin's own pattern. Easternmost chapel with a chancel arch of roll mouldings supported on chunky Romanesque columns. In this way Pugin intended to suggest, as in an actual medieval building, the development of the cathedral between the Romanesque and Gothic periods.

FURNISHINGS

*Pugin*, with the sixteenth Earl of Shrewsbury and his close friends and colleagues *John Hardman Sr* and *Jr*, the Birmingham metalwork and stained-glass manufacturers, filled the church with furniture designed by Pugin and usually made by the Hardman firm, except for some Continental antiques and a few works from other firms. When consecrated, the cathedral's most striking feature was Pugin's rood screen, the gift of the Hardmans, incorporating medieval figures and bosses, painted and decorated, with a massive Crucifixus attended by Our Lady and St John. This screen was always controversial – attempts being made to have it removed before the cathedral was opened – but although it was moved slightly forward in 1854 and some of the work was removed to increase visibility, it survived until 1967, when it was demolished, save for parts re-erected in the Anglican church of Holy Trinity, Reading, and the Crucifixus, which, still in Catholic hands, could well be re-erected here (as was done at Pugin's cathedral at Nottingham). Without the screen, we totally lose Pugin's intended drama of the nave space revealing the chancel as a giant reliquary, that is, for relics of the C7 Bishop of Mercia, St Chad (in Catholic hands since the Reformation; see also Lichfield), housed in the gilt feretory above the high-altar reredos. Pugin's HIGH ALTAR survived the reordering of the 1960s: carved stone painted and gilded, with wooden baldacchino and side curtains, and carved frontal as in the 1840s.

The PULPIT, probably from the abbey of St Gertrude, Louvain, was made in a Brabant workshop *c.* 1520. Hexagonal with concave sides, niches containing statues of four Fathers of the Church, intricate carving and dark wood. Now without its canopy. (A magnificent late C15 brass lectern from Louvain was briefly here – like the pulpit a gift from the Earl of Shrewsbury – before being placed in the chapel of Oscott College, whence since to the Cloisters, New York.)

The N aisle has some good early *Hardman* STAINED GLASS, the Fitzherbert-Brockles window of 1851 with figures of St Francis and St Thomas (next to the baptistery) and the Glassworkers' window of 1853, with figures of St Luke painting the Virgin, and St Andrew of Crete. The latter window was the gift of the glassworkers in the

Hardman works, and the individually identifiable donors are shown in various stages of designing, painting and firing glass. – In the s aisle the only early Hardman window is that to George Waring, who died during a service in the church in 1844. – The transepts have the finest glass: N window, 1865, life and martyrdom of St Thomas à Becket, and s window, 1868, Immaculate Conception of the Virgin in memory of John Hardman Jr (who can be seen at bottom l.), in technique, drawing and colouring typical of Hardman's nephew *John Hardman Powell*, Pugin's son-in-law and only pupil, at the height of his powers. – In the N transept, TOMB of Bishop Walsh, a work shown at the 1851 Exhibition, designed by *Pugin* and carved in *Myers'* workshop: the figure holds a model of the church; original railings gone.

At the E end, the three apse windows by *Warrington*, 1841, also given by the Earl of Shrewsbury, their rich yellow tones contrasting with the blues and reds of the C19 Hardman glass in the cathedral. – s choir window by *Hardman*, 1847. – Pugin's floor-level here, and encaustic tiles throughout most of the building, went in the destruction of 1967, as did Victorian wall stencilling and texts, and many statues. However, the roof STENCILLING and PAINTING of the wall-shafts were renewed sympathetically. – STALLS from the church of St Maria im Capitol, Cologne, survive in part, but with insensitive modern reading desks. The BISHOP'S THRONE has lost its openwork spire by *Pugin*.

The altar in the NE LADY CHAPEL, decorated in the 1840s (*Pugin's* drawing dated 1840), preserves most fully the feeling of Pugin's church. Reredos and screen survive, as do brasses to members of the Hardman family. – STATUE of Virgin and Child, probably C15 German, given by Pugin in 1841 and painted to his specifications. – WINDOWS by *Hardman* and *Warrington*. – The BAPTISTERY, screened, has its original glass and encaustic flooring, but the Pugin font has been removed and replaced by a deliberately crude monolith in the aisle. – Sebastian Pugin Powell's careful if unexciting 1930s-Gothic CHAPEL OF ST EDWARD has typical *Hardman* glass of that period, carefully drawn, illustrating the preservation of St Chad's relics.

On the cathedral's surroundings and the Birmingham motorscape, see the latest edition of B of E *Warwickshire*.

# Blackburn

CATHEDRAL CHURCH OF ST MARY  *Anglican*

(Based on B of E *North Lancashire*, 1969, revised, with information from Michael Gillingham, Anthony New and A. C. Sewter.)

Cathedral since 1926. There are records of a pre-Conquest and a medieval church here, but the existing parish church was rebuilt 1820–6 by *John Palmer*, burned in 1831 and reconstructed in consultation with *Thomas Rickman*. High three-light Dec windows with a transom, buttresses between. Clerestory. The w tower looks later but isn't. The nave piers are tall and round, with four thin attached shafts. Tierceron-star vaults of plaster. The w wall has a nice composition of three ogee arches, the middle one for the entrance, the others crowning vaulted niches.

*W. A. Forsyth* converted the church to cathedral use from 1933, keeping the w tower and nave, and adding an e end with transepts in a conventional, simplified Gothic. But his intended octagonal lantern tower proved too costly. *Lawrence King* in 1961 added the corona over the crossing, its pinnacles and long spire bringing in a modern element.

STALLS, N transept aisles. Eight, with C15 MISERI-CORDS thought to come from Whalley Abbey (Remnant 1969): Adam and Eve's Temptation, fox preaching to geese, a fine angel with scroll etc. – ORGAN CASE by *Walker*, spread out like an ironmongery display, console with italic script (Gillingham). – STAINED GLASS. N transept N window: Flemish, C18. Some *Morris* glass in the transepts: Sewter records three *Burne-Jones* figures in the E clerestory, three more in store. – Recent fittings by *John Hayward*: wrought-iron figure of Christ the Worker (w wall), glass panels of lantern (crossing), bronze font-cover (s transept).

Sloping churchyard with trees and fine cast-iron GATE of *c.* 1825 towards Church Street at the NW, probably designed by *Palmer*. The cathedral lies immediately opposite the station square and, viewed from the railway station, competes with the Palace Theatre's irresponsible curligigs.

Further on surroundings, see the latest edition of B of E *North Lancashire*.

# Bradford

CATHEDRAL CHURCH OF ST PETER *Anglican*

(Based on B of E *Yorkshire: The West Riding*, 1967, revised, with information from Michael Gillingham, Anthony New and A. C. Sewter.)

Cathedral since 1919, after being the parish church for many centuries, with more architectural evidence than appears outside. Impressively placed on rising ground above the centre of the modern city. The exterior is very Yorkshire in character, of millstone grit, with a sturdy Perp w tower built, it is said, in 1493–1508 (six-light window, twin two-light bell-openings, battlements, eight pinnacles), and a low embattled body with Perp windows dating

from *c.* 1430–58. Until 1724 the roof was thatched (New). All but one wall of the Bolling Chapel of 1615 (s choir aisle) was pulled down to make way for the C20 enlargements: are we back in the Victorian Age that so little respect is shown to the C17? In fact, this church has been a continual palimpsest. Reconstruction of 1832–3 (s aisle, s clerestory, s porch) by *John Clark* was partly remodelled in work of the 1890s, and shallow transepts were added in 1899 by *T. H. & F. Healey*. To the N of the w tower the Song Room was added in 1951–4 by *Sir Edward Maufe*. Then followed his new E end: lantern tower, choir and aisles, sanctuary, and Lady Chapel (1958–63), as well as his s vestry (1959), chapter house with St Aidan Chapel under, and s E porch of 1963–5.

The interior of the nave is still dominated by the activity of the C14–15 after a fire of 1327. Of the earlier building, work of *c.* 1200 is said to survive in the E piers of the s arcade, but with early C14 caps. The other piers of the eight-bay arcades are of deeply undulating section with four shafts connected by hollows and plain caps. Arches with typical moulding of two sunk quadrants, as also in the w bay added when the C15–16 w tower was built to connect it with the older nave. The transeptal additions of 1899 did not imply a crossing between them: Maufe placed his lantern tower over his choir one bay further E. He admirably arranged that the early *Morris* glass of the former great E window, newly reset in his polygonal apse (see *Furnishings* below), should be seen from the nave over the stone screen between choir and Lady Chapel (one more thoughtful example of his care for interior spaces; cf. Guildford).

FURNISHINGS

FONT COVER. A spectacular Late Gothic piece, tall, with tall spire and a filigree of buttresses and tracery (cf. St John's Halifax). – SCULPTURE, N aisle. Small square Anglo-Saxon piece with irregular interlace. Probably from a C10 cross. – At the w end of the nave, ungainly ORGAN CASE on stilts, in the cinema style, by *Maufe*: an isolated box of pipes separated from the console of the organ farther E (a separation unacceptable to the organ purist: Gillingham). – STAINED GLASS. The E window of 1864 when first installed had seven lights, the overall design by *William Morris* with panels by *Rossetti* (Christ in Majesty), *Webb* (Agnus Dei), also *Ford Madox Brown*, *Burne-Jones*, *Marshall* and *Morris*. Before tactful restoration as three windows in 1964, this glass had been ruthlessly hacked out, with some loss of borders, now repaired. Five excess angels were presented to the Whitworth Art Gallery at the University of Manchester (Sewter).

For Victorian and post-Victorian Bradford, see the latest edition of B of E *Yorkshire: The West Riding*.

# Bury St Edmunds

CATHEDRAL CHURCH OF ST JAMES  *Anglican*

(Based on B of E *Suffolk*, 1974, revised, with information from S. E. Dykes Bower and George McHardy.)

Cathedral since 1914. The w front of this former parish church is flush with the pavement at the narrow end of Angel Hill, facing the flank of the Athenaeum, while the body of the church stands within the abbey precinct. The powerful Benedictine abbey of St Edmundsbury, once one of England's richest monasteries, is now in ruins. Remains of the w front of the former abbey church, with later houses embedded in the eroded flint rubble, stand S E of the present cathedral. Just s of the cathedral's w front and still intact is the free-standing gatehouse called the Norman Gate, with original ground-level restored: a splendid piece of proudly decorated architecture built between 1120 and 1148 as gateway to the abbey church, and later serving as bell-tower to St James's. (A second gatehouse, the abbey's C 14 Great Gate, stands farther N facing the open space of Angel Hill.) The ground s of the cathedral, between the Norman Gate and the ruins, is not officially part of the cathedral precinct and consists of a civic grass-plot with sculpture by *Elisabeth Frink* and, beyond, an overgrown churchyard extending to the sister parish church of St Mary's. N E of the cathedral the multiple park-like setting for surviving fragments of the once extensive abbey layout is maintained by the Department of the Environment. The whole area, therefore, being under a complex of caretakers, is not concentrated on setting off the cathedral.

St James's was first built to replace a C 11 basilica of St Denis, demolished for extension of the abbey's w front in the C 12. But no traces of the C 12–15 parish church are now visible. The St James's that survived into our own time, consisting of a nine-bay nave and a lower-roofed chancel, was built chiefly during *c.* 1510–30, and completed under Edward VI, who gave £200 towards it. The designer of the nave is thought to have been *John Wastell* († 1515), a native of Bury, designer of the vaults and w window of King's College Chapel, Cambridge, of Bell Harry, the central tower at Canterbury Cathedral, and probably of the retrochoir or New Building at Peterborough Cathedral. St James's C 16 chancel replaced one of *c.* 1400 (noted in excavations by Dr Ralegh Radford) and was itself rebuilt during 1865–9 by *Gilbert Scott*, who also rebuilt the nave roof. Scott's chancel, adequate for a parish church but too small for cathedral use, has been enlarged since 1960 to create transepts and crossing (with a future crossing tower), a new taller chancel, and a new N cloister with administrative wing, all by *S. E. Dykes Bower*, in progress.

The original C 16 w front is stone-faced with embattled aisles, and a gable by *Scott*. Original transomed seven-light

w window below (compare Wastell's w window at King's) and original transomed five-light aisle w windows. Ornamented base and buttresses, tall niches l. and r. of the central doorway. The side windows all three-light and transomed, with double the number of clerestory windows. The s side is stone-faced, with some flintwork on the new transept and chancel. Very tall arcades inside, the piers of lozenge shape with four thin shafts and four broad diagonal hollows, with capitals only for the shafts towards the arch openings, and shafts towards the nave rising right up to the roof. The nave roof that existed before Scott replaced it was of shallow pitch and divided by ribs into panels. When it became unsafe the church authorities resolved to replace it with a high-pitched hammerbeam roof to rival the famous C 15 roof of St Mary's next door, and would not agree to *Scott*'s first design for a low-pitched roof like its predecessor. So he was forced to design the present roof against his better judgement, handsome though it is (information via Mr Dykes Bower from undated guide to Bury by W. S. Spanton). The angels now felicitously repainted.

The work carried out after 1960 began with the erection of a new porch at the N W corner of the nave with a room over it to house the cathedral library. Eight (out of a future twelve) bays of the cloisters were then built along the N side of the nave, where the lower level of the ground enabled this to be kept below the sill-level of the aisle windows. The new choir, with its flanking chapels, started from the E end and was finished in 1967, after which the crossing and transepts were undertaken to join the choir with the nave.

For reasons of cost it has not as yet been possible to raise the tower above the ridge line of the roofs, or, internally, to face in stone, above the four arches of the crossing, the walls of what will eventually be the lantern. In the N transept too the three arches that will open into a gallery remain temporarily blocked up until the three bays of the cloister that will pass below it (cf. the Muniment Room at Westminster Abbey over part of the E cloister) can be built. The brick wall of the N aisle of the new choir is also temporary, until an arcade of four arches can be built to open into an outer N aisle giving entrance to a future sacristy and chair store, beyond which will be vestries etc. at ground-level and, at first-floor-level, a Lady Chapel, chapter house and song school. The Lady Chapel as planned will be identical in size with the former chancel, designed by Scott, so that its oak roof, stalls and E window, with fine *Hardman* glass, can be re-used there.

The ultimate scheme comprises, within the space bounded on the N side by the high medieval wall of the monastic bowling green, a complete four-sided cloister connecting under cover all the buildings that a modern cathedral needs. (Model and drawings are shown in the cathedral.)

FURNISHINGS

FONT designed by *Scott*, 1870. Cover designed by *F. E. Howard* (co-author with Crossley of *English Church Woodwork*), c. 1914. Later decoration of font and cover by *Dykes Bower*. – THRONE also by *Howard*. – PULPIT designed by *Scott* and made by *Kett*. – PAINTINGS. In the S chapel a German 'Selbdritt' of c. 1500 with two small demi-figures in the predella. – 'The face of Jesus wiped by Veronica', c. 1560, attributed to *Luis de Morales*, on loan from Horham Church. – STAINED GLASS (some in store). S nave aisle, first from the W. Good Flemish early c 16 glass, e.g. story of Susanna, Tree of Jesse. – Much of the c 19 glass is by *Clayton & Bell*, e.g. S aisle, another Tree of Jesse, 1898. – The W window a Last Judgement by *Hardman*. – The E windows of the new sanctuary are fine early work by *Kempe*, 1867–74, made for the side windows of Scott's chancel, with new glass at the base of these taller lights by *Dykes Bower*. – S transept S, c. 1847 by *Warrington*. – MONUMENTS, W wall S, James Reynolds, Chief Justice of the Exchequer, †1738. White and black marble. Seated frontally in robe and wig. And W wall N, his wife †1736. No figure (by his order or hers?). Sarcophagus with obelisk and urns. – Outside, W front, IRONWORK, c 19? Nice fleur-de-lys bootscrapers, and railings.

For the great abbey's remains, the sister church of St Mary, the uneven square called Angel Hill and the town of Bury St Edmunds, see the latest edition of B of E *Suffolk*.


# Carlisle

## CATHEDRAL CHURCH OF THE HOLY AND UNDIVIDED TRINITY  *Anglican*

(Based on B of E *Cumberland and Westmorland*, 1967, revised, with information from Thomas Cocke, S. E. Dykes Bower, Anthony New, David O'Connor and J. T. Smith.)

Plan, Fig. 5, from the *Builder*, 1893, by C. J. Ferguson and F. S. Bedford. (The nave bays demolished in 1645–52 and the parish church on their site 1870–1954 are not shown.)

INTRODUCTION

The cathedral is evidence of Carlisle's place on the ancient Anglo-Scottish battle-line and, perhaps twice over, witness to the uses of old structures as quarries. In the c 12 Hadrian's Wall allegedly was pillaged of stone to build the nave, which in turn during siege in the c 17 was robbed for the building of defensive walls again. Carlisle was a Roman civil settlement, Luguvalium, which developed above a fort occupied from the Flavian period until its abandonment when Hadrian's Wall was built. The wall runs through the northern suburbs of the present town. In the c 10 and c 11 the town was Scottish. Rufus recaptured it in 1092, and Henry II gave it its first charter in 1158. Already in about 1102 Henry I had granted a site at Carlisle for the foundation of a religious establishment. Building may not have been begun until Ranulph de Meschines had left Carlisle and Henry had taken over. He established Augustinian Canons. The church was under construction in 1130. Then, in 1133, Henry made the town the see of a bishop. These years probably are the time of intense building. For the chancel all we have is 1246 as the date for a gift of 20 marks by Henry III to the building work. Then follows the fire of 1292, which made much rebuilding necessary. Work on this, according to gifts of money, still went on in 1354, 1356 and 1362. Six bays of the nave were demolished between 1645 and 1652 by the Scots. (On a c 15 misericord in the choir, W end N side, a man being swallowed by a dragon wears the kilt.)

A major restoration (at any rate internally), with extensive refitting of the choir, took place in 1765 under Bishop Lyttelton to Gothic designs by his young nephew *Thomas Pitt*, later Lord Camelford. The bishop, who was President of the Society of Antiquaries at the time, was unusually knowledgeable in such matters (he wrote the first account of Romanesque as a separate style), and the fragmentary remains of this work are evidence of advanced Gothic Revival taste in the mid-c 18 (Cocke). During 1853–7 there was restoration by *Ewan Christian*. The c 20, under *S. E. Dykes Bower* and others, has had to do considerable rescue work. This, as at Lichfield and Chester, has been partly a matter of the poor weathering quality of local red sandstones used originally (apart from the dark grey stone which may have come from Hadrian's Wall). As Clifton-Taylor (1972) points out, Cumberland does afford red sandstones of good quality, but they are less accessible than stone used that required only a five-mile river journey. The cathedral from its original Norman W front to the E end was 315 ft long – longer than Ripon, shorter than Chester.

It is at once evident that the nave survives only as a stump. It originally had eight bays; now there are only two. In the C17 five bays were wholly destroyed and a rough new W wall was built within the sixth bay. On the N side the Norman aisle and Norman clerestory windows survive, shafted, with scallop capitals and decorated arches. On the S side only the clerestory windows are Norman, but on the other hand the transept has its E and W clerestory still Norman and a little on the S side at gable-level too. Otherwise the S transept front is all of the 1850s. It must formerly have been quite different, as here the cloister adjoined. In the E bay of the aisle is still the blocked

Norman chancel and chancel aisle had been together and add a new N aisle. The irregularity that this leads to inside will be pointed out later. Strickland's work on the transept has neither a W nor an E clerestory. The N front has a large window in Early Dec forms but so handled that it may well be of after 1660. The same will thus apply to the round window over, with its seven circles.

The chancel is preserved in its full length and is quite a spectacular piece. It is confusing only at first that it patently belongs to two styles, E.E. and Dec. The N and S walls of the aisles are E.E. The system is pairs of lancets and blank arches l. and r., shafts with shaft-rings, and canted buttresses. But the E bay is different and has a two-light window with cusped and enriched Y-tracery. It is the same

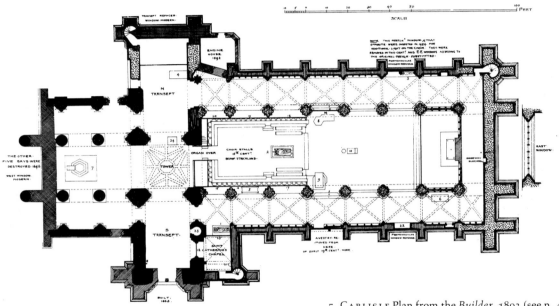

5. CARLISLE Plan from the *Builder*, 1893 (see p. 41)

doorway into this. Long after the nave had been demolished, in 1870, a parish church of St Mary was built in its stead, but this in its turn was pulled down in 1954. (In fact the nave appears to have been parochial since the Middle Ages, which is presumably why the dean and chapter were not responsible for rebuilding it.) When this Victorian parish church was begun, the present W end of the stump of the nave was given a new W window designed by *Ewan Christian*. The N transept is largely a late medieval rebuilding. It is attributed to Bishop Strickland (1400–19), who also built the present crossing tower. The crossing tower has Perp bell-openings and battlements and a higher, square stair-turret. The odd wall extending N from its N E corner is explained by the fact that, when the chancel was rebuilt, it was decided to make it as wide as the

round the corner to the E, and the main E window is a gorgeous display of flowing tracery, 51 ft high, of nine lights, divided 4 – 1 – 4, with the middle light expanding into a bulbous shape with internal tracery and the side parts developing tracery of the type with leaves off a stem. Big buttresses l. and r. with statues in two tiers on its upper parts. Above the E window a window in the form of a spherical triangle with three spherical triangles set in and on the gable a display of pinnacles. This is from the restoration of the 1850s. The side walls of the aisles differ in so far as on the N side all is as described above, but on the S side work must have proceeded more slowly, and funds may have run out. So the shafting stops, and the fenestration is simply chamfered lancets in stepped groups of three. The remains of a vaulted building are those of a sacristy.

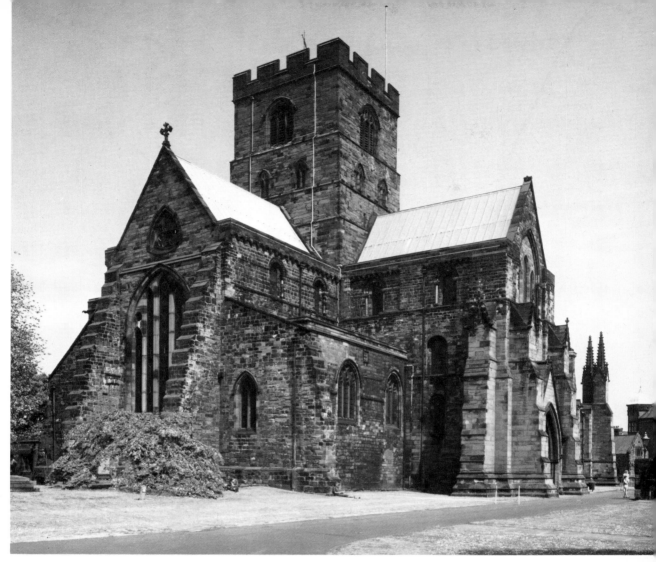

6. CARLISLE Remains of the C12 nave: view from the south-west

The simplified type continues to the E chapel of the S transept, which was founded by a rich citizen, John de Capella. One would be inclined to date the shafted windows *c.* 1220–50 and the simpler *c.* 1250–80. On the N side there is no such chapel: instead there is a large, Perp four-light window. The chancel clerestory is again entirely Dec. The tracery patterns differ considerably, but reticulation occurs several times.

### INTERIOR

For a reconstruction of the Norman cathedral we have not much to go by. Of the E end all that is known is a length of wall curving in the place where the Norman apse would have been, if the chancel was of two bays. Maybe there were side apses too, as at Durham. We are on safe ground only at the crossing. The W and E arches have no responds, but those of the N and S arches are triple and have scalloped capitals of a broad and elementary kind which suggests an early C12 date. The responds are not high and are continued by Perp responds, but it is likely that the capitals were originally high up and later re-set (yet J. T. Smith points out that these capitals are at exactly the same height as the moulded string facing the nave and might be part of the same scheme). The arches to the S chancel aisle and to the N and S nave aisles have the same responds and similar capitals. But it is very noticeable that the face towards the nave aisles themselves has smaller scallops, a little more decorated, a sign that the nave was built after the E parts.

7. CARLISLE East end, with C14 window

Of the Norman transepts little else appears on the N side, more on the S. In the E wall, to the r. of the arch into the chancel aisle, remains the arch into a former Norman E chapel. The chapel which is there now is, as has already been said, of the late C13. It has a rib-vault of elegantly thin ribs, standing on corbels. Three of these have stiff-leaf, one a human demi-figure. One corbel starts with a roguish knot. In the N transept of the E chapel only the blocked arch survives. It has, like that of the S transept, an outer band of zigzag. The opening into the chancel, which – as will be remembered – is wider than the Norman chancel had been, is pushed to the N. The S transept W wall is

44

8. CARLISLE The C12 nave from the south transept

Norman throughout. It has plain windows and a clerestory with the stepped tripartite arrangement so typical of the Norman style. In the s wall something similar must have been done, but only the easternmost and westernmost shafts remain. The upper part of the crossing has leaf capitals, many-moulded arches, and, set in the N arch, a Perp traceried arch with glazing grooves originally for a window. Tierceron-star crossing vault.

Of the nave there are only two bays. They have enormous, but not high, round piers, about 6 ft 6 in. in diameter, and round arches of two slight chamfers, a late C 12 characteristic. The capitals are round and many-scalloped on the s side, plain on the N side. In the aisles are triple responds. But no cross arches are preserved. The gallery has un-subdivided plain single-step openings, the clerestory the tripartite arrangement as in the transept. Shafts, starting above the arcade capitals, led up to the principal roof-beams, but are now truncated (but J. T. Smith sees no sign of this in the masonry of triforium and clerestory).

That the chancel belongs to two periods is as obvious inside as outside. Of *c.* 1220–50 are the blank arcading of the aisle walls, cinquefoiled with small dogtooth on the N but not the s, and the shafted lancets. However, the E bay does not partake of this arrangement. The bay is narrower, and the blank arcading has thick Dec capitals. So one must assume that this bay is a C 14 addition, and Mr Bulman has made the convincing suggestion that the masonry of the lower courses of the E wall is E.E. and that it represented a chancel projecting a little beyond the chancel aisles. That would explain the narrowness of the bay. The arcade piers may all be of after the fire of 1292, and also the vaults of the aisles, though they still look C 13. (G. H. Cook suggested that arches and aisles were pre-1292, but new piers inserted after, by underpinning.) The spectacular E window (see *Exterior* above) is of course of the early C 14.

The piers have eight strong shafts, the diagonal ones keeled, or rather filleted. There are deep continuous hollows between the shafts. The capitals are bands of knobbly leaves, and in them are small figures illustrating the labours of the months: January as Janus with two heads feasting, February warming himself by a fire, March digging, April pruning, May offering a branch, June hawking, July mowing, August working in the fields, September reaping, October harvesting grapes, November sowing, December killing an ox. All this is of delightful workmanship. Arches of many mouldings with prominent dogtooth. Hoodmould with small nailhead. That gives a date not later than the early C 14. The arch into the N transept from the aisle is of the same kind, and to its N, visible from the aisle, is the springing of a second such arch, proof that at that time the plan was to scrap the existing transept and build a new one with an E aisle. This was not done, and so, as we have seen, it was in the end left to Bishop Strickland

10. CARLISLE Capital, early C 14. Owl attacking an animal

to build a very simple transept. To go back to the chancel 'nave', the gallery has three small two-light openings per bay with reticulation units. The clerestory is still tripartite, but very bare. The semicircular chancel ceiling dates from *c.* 1530. Of the original timber vault some members were removed in the C 18, and what look like hammerbeams are sawn-off tie-beams (New). A plaster quadripartite vault was inserted under the Tudor vault in 1765 (Cocke). The plaster vault was removed in 1856–7 and the old curved-panelled ceiling was decorated with stars on a blue sky by *Owen Jones*; *Dykes Bower* had it repainted 1970.

### FURNISHINGS, E TO W

Monuments are described separately below. STAINED GLASS. In the main E window by *Hardman*, 1861, but in the top tracery some original mid-C 14 glass, including York-style Doom with seated Christ at the very top, much restored *c.* 1857 by *William Wailes*. – E window of s aisle by *Wailes*. – PULPIT. 1559, of wood. From St Andrew's, Antwerp, but bought for Carlisle in the mid-C 20 from Cockayne Hatley Church, Bedfordshire, to which much Belgian church woodwork was brought by Lord Brownlow's son in the 1820s (a somewhat parallel case to that of Flemish C 16 glass in Lichfield Lady Chapel). Very rich foot with brackets ending in claws. Brackets for the pulpit proper too. They are human figures enclosed in strapwork. Fluted angle colonnettes and little pedimented aedicules with the statuettes of the four Evangelists. – BISHOP'S THRONE. By *Street*, *c.* 1880. – By the same, at the same time, the REREDOS, now hidden. – STALLS. Of *c.* 1400 (under Bishop Strickland, 1399–1413), but the canopies

9. CARLISLE Chancel, mostly after 1292, with C 15 brass

11. CARLISLE Choir stalls, *c.* 1400–after 1430

said to be by Prior Haythwaite, i.e. after 1430. High canopies originally with many statuettes, the arms of the stalls with figure and leaf work, the ends with blank tracery and poppyheads. A delightful variety of MISERICORDS, forty-six, including on the N side monsters, birds, the Coronation of the Virgin, angels making music, and on the S side angels, monsters, a boar killing a man, a mermaid. They are all full of life, even if they are not high art. These occur in time between the late C14 sets at Worcester and Chester cathedrals and the late C15–early C16 sets at Ripon and Manchester, and perhaps nearest in date to the westernmost misericords at Norwich of *c.* 1420. – Lower stalls by *Nicholson*, extended 1976 by *Dykes Bower*. – On

the upper stall backs (aisles) are PAINTINGS, rows of stories from the life of St Augustine (S) and St Cuthbert and St Anthony (N) and also the twelve Apostles (N). They are all of *c.* 1500 (with monogram of Prior Gondiber, 1484–1507) and all bad, considering what the Netherlands or France or Germany did in that line of work. The Cuthbert stories are directly derived from a Durham manuscript in the British Museum (Add. 39943). – From Bishop Lyttelton's restoration of 1765: DOORS to the bishop's and dean's stalls, the upper part of the ORGAN GALLERY, and also PANELLING to the N wall of the N transept, fragments of the complete scheme designed by *Thomas Pitt*, much of it ejected in 1856 by Ewan Christian

(Colvin, Cocke, Dykes Bower). – SCREEN to the N aisle, of wood, given by Prior Salkeld after he had become dean in 1541. This is an uncommonly complete example of English Early Renaissance decoration, with all the typical motifs, profile heads in medallions and lozenges, dolphins, and also balusters instead of mullions. – SCREENS to the E chapel of the S transept. With close panels of Flamboyant tracery, inspired by French and Scottish rather than English work. Similar to the Aberdeen and Hexham screens. The date is *c.* 1500, here again with Gondiber's initials. – SCULPTURE. In this chapel a Nottingham alabaster panel of the Crucifixion. – In the N transept FONT. 1890 by *Sir Arthur Blomfield*. Gothic, with a boldly ogee-curved outline and three seated bronze figures. – STAINED GLASS. In the N transept N, *c.* (†) 1858 by *Hardman*. – w window *c.* (†) 1870.

12. CARLISLE Dean Salkeld's screen (detail), after 1541

MONUMENTS, E TO W

*Chancel*   Large worn BRASS in the centre of the choir floor. Bishop Bell † 1496. With figure and triple canopy. Made in London.

*North chancel aisle*   Marble effigy of a bishop; early C14 and very good. It cannot be Bishop Barrow, who died in 1429. The effigy lies on a plain tomb-chest with thinly outlined large quatrefoils. – Double tomb recess with a segmental arch starting on short vertical pieces. The arch aggressively decorated with thorns or short branch stumps (probably damaged) in three orders and two different directions. One recess is empty; under the other an excellent effigy of a bishop, mid-C13, the same type as those at Ely of the 1250s. Pointed trefoiled canopy and originally shafts l. and r. One stiff-leaf capital survives.

*South chancel aisle*   Bishop John Wareing Bardsley. By *Andrea Carlo Lucchesi*, 1906. Strange bronze tablet, the forms as if cut out in leather. Similar to Gilbert, but all is broader and balder. – Bishop Waldegrave, by *John Adams-Acton*, 1872. White and asleep. – Bishop Robinson † 1616. Brass tablet with kneeling figure and many inscriptions, as it was often done in those years, e.g. 'Deadly feude extinct'. Also one Greek inscription. This brass is a contemporary copy of the one to him in the chapel of Queen's College, Oxford. – Dean Close. By *Armstead*, 1885. White, under a wooden canopy. – Bishop Goodwin † 1891. Bronze effigy by *Hamo Thornycroft*.

*North transept*   Prior Senhouse, *c.* 1510–20. Plain black slab on a tomb-chest with shields in quatrefoils. – J. R. Graham † 1830. Standing mourning female figure bent over an urn. – Hugh James † 1817. By *Regnart*, and exceptionally busy. Two small allegorical figures l. and r. of a short sarcophagus. Urn on the top. – Tablet to John Johnson † 1792 by *Nollekens*, 1800.

*South transept*   In the w wall a stone block has a runic

inscription: 'Tolfihu wrote these runes on this stone' – a very remarkable proof of how long runes were still current; for the wall is of course C12. – Thomas Sheffield. Roundel by *George Nelson*, 1856. Seated figure, reading – a Flaxman motif. – Robert Anderson † 1833. With profile portrait. By *David Dunbar Sr.* – Also by *Dunbar*, sleeping figure of the artist's infant daughter † 1825. – On the E wall marble bust of George Moore † 1876, textile manufacturer and philanthropist.

Outside, at the E end of the s clerestory, the C20 has added a carved head-stop, with police helmet, to commemorate a local constable killed in the line of duty.

CLOISTER, CHAPTER HOUSE ETC., REMAINS

Not much is left, but a certain amount can be pieced together. s of the s transept is a path with a low wall on the E, a high wall on the w. This path represents the E range of the cloister, i.e. the UNDERCROFT of the dormitory. This was vaulted, as the springers show. The ribs were single-chamfered. The doorways in the W and, in line, in the E wall are of the mid or later C 13; one led into the chapter-house vestibule, the other into the CHAPTER HOUSE itself. This was, as the start of the wall N of the doorway proves, octagonal. The vestibule doorway has a *trumeau*, and the twin arches sit in a super-arch in the way Y-tracery is formed. The chapter-house doorway is single.

The upper storey of the E range containing the dormitory is gone, except for one small lancet visible in the E wall of the refectory, which was as usual in the S range, also on the first floor. On the ground floor in the S E corner is the doorway to a passage leading S out of the cloister, and to its l., the doorway to the dormitory day stair. The S view of the refectory range here is quite irregular and picturesque with a small turret. The REFECTORY (now the library) stands to its full height. It was built in the early C 14 and remodelled by Prior Gondiber, i.e. *c.* 1500. The corbels to the N show where the cloister roof was. The refectory undercroft is vaulted, and dates from the early C 14 entirely. It is a beautiful room, only very recently cleared of rubbish and restored to its full dignity. It has a row of very low octagonal piers along its longitudinal axis and vaults with hollow-chamfered ribs. The difference in moulding marks the difference between the C 13 and the late C 15. The refectory has to the W a large Perp window, to the S also large Perp windows, but their tracery all Victorian, and to the N small two-light windows entirely Dec (one reticulation unit). In the S wall of the refectory is the reading pulpit, a delightful piece with original Perp tracery to the S (a window, smaller than the others) and to the N as well. In the W wall are two hatches, no doubt to the former kitchen. From the corner of the refectory the walls of the W range can just be seen for a few inches. The rest is missing. The porch is Victorian.

The customary name for the precinct here is the Abbey, and it merges with the few remains of the claustral part. It is entered from the W through a GATEHOUSE of 1527 (inscription of Prior Slee). This has to E and W a triple-chamfered round arch and midway between the two a division between pedestrian and carriage entrance. Both parts of the gatehouse are tunnel-vaulted. Above the E arch is a typical early C 16 window with uncusped lights. As one enters, to the S is the REGISTRY, a pretty, single-storey, three-bay building dated 1699. Doorway with open curly pediment, moulded surrounds to doorway and windows. Opposite is No. 2 CANONRY, Early Georgian, of five bays, with broad rustication round the doorway. What does the framing round the staircase window at the back signify? A mullioned and transomed window? It cannot of course be earlier than the demolition of the nave in, as we have seen, the C 17.

Next on the S side, with its back to West Walls, the former PRIOR'S LODGING, now Deanery. It consists of a pele tower of *c.* 1510–20, a hall range on the W, and another addition on the E. The tower has a basement, tunnel-vaulted and provided with five mighty, single-chamfered, closely set transverse arches. The room above has an oriel to the N and one to the S. Both have charming moulded transverse arches inside. The ceiling has splendid moulded beams, in one direction very prettily arched. The handsome painted ceiling-decoration, reclaimed in the 1970s from centuries of smoke and a layer of Victorian varnish, consists of birds, roses, scallop-shells and lettered scrolls. It is here that Prior Senhouse recorded himself as the builder: 'Simon Senhus sette thys roofe and scallope here'. The staircases are partly in the thickness of the wall, and partly spiral. The range to the r. contained the hall, and the room following that must have been the kitchen. Its enormous fireplace is still there. The main staircase of the house now is of the later C 17, with dumb-bell balusters used upside down. The range has to the outside a blank, vertically placed oval with a coat of arms – a shape that fits a late C 17 date. The l. range has an Early Georgian front. A THIRD CANONRY S of the E end of the cathedral is of *c.* 1700, seven bays, with segmental-headed windows. String-course (later?) of bricks sticking out triangularly. The great iron GATES by the E end of the cathedral are of 1930, by *John F. Matthew*.

Further on the precinct and on the buildings of Carlisle, see the latest edition of B of E *Cumberland and Westmorland*.

# Chester

CATHEDRAL CHURCH OF CHRIST
AND THE BLESSED VIRGIN MARY   *Anglican*

(Based on B of E *Cheshire*, 1971, revised, with information from Thomas Cocke, Mr Ganz, Michael Gillingham, Peter Howell, John Maddison, David Palliser and Ronald Sims.)

Chronology (for text sequence, see the contents list below): (Abbey from 1092.) *Late c 11–early c 12*: N transept, N choir pier bases, N W tower (internally), monastic remains. *c. 1200*: N transept E chapel, now sacristy. *Mid-c 13 to c. 1280*: chapter house and vestibule; Lady Chapel. *Late c 13–early c 14*: new sanctuary and choir; crossing; refectory. *Mid-c 14*: new S transept. *Late c 14*: rebuilding of nave S side. *Late c 15*: rebuilding of nave N side, central tower. *Early c 16*: W front, S W porch, S W tower; central tower completed; chapel at E end of N choir aisle; cloister walks rebuilt. *Early c 17*: fittings, consistory court. St Anselm's Chapel etc.

Plan, Fig. 14, from the *Builder*, 1893, by Roland Paul; since then, C 12 arch on E side of N transept opened up, 1929.

Some references (see Recent Literature): Addleshaw 1971; Belcher 1970; Bennett n.d.; Bony 1979; P. Eames 1977; Harvey 1978; Maddison 1978; Remnant 1969.

## INTRODUCTION

The former abbey church sits on St Werburgh's Mount just up the slope from Eastgate Street and with Northgate Street immediately before it, that is, in the centre of the busy town. Yet on E and N the cathedral is set in a small secluded precinct next to the ancient city wall, overlooked by the pleasant wall-walk preserved in the C 18 as a promenade on medieval and Roman foundations. Permission to cut through the wall for the Kaleyard Gate at the N E corner of the abbey precinct was granted by Edward I in 1275. The abbey gatehouse W of it may be of similar date. Chester was near the front lines of the king's Welsh campaign. From older wars, remains of the Roman legionary fortress within the city walls have continued to be unearthed, for example S W of the cathedral, wherever commercial redevelopment has allowed archaeological excavation.

Nearer to the River Dee the church of St John Baptist, originally a Saxon foundation, was briefly a cathedral at the end of the C 11, and nominally retained joint rank with Lichfield and Coventry until the Reformation. Meanwhile on St Werburgh's Mount, where an establishment of secular canons had existed probably from the C 9, a Benedictine abbey of St Werburgh was founded in 1092 by Hugh Lupus, Earl of Chester, nephew of William the Conqueror and forebear of the Dukes of Westminster. In 1541 Henry VIII raised the abbey to cathedral rank.

With its length of 371 ft, Chester Cathedral is not long as major abbeys or indeed cathedrals go. (Yet from inside the W door, higher than the nave floor as it is, there is a first sensation of length.) It is built of soft red local sandstone, of a variety tending to crumble, so that Gilbert Scott found the building in 1868 'like a mouldering sandstone cliff'. And so here, as with the similar stones of Lichfield and Worcester and Carlisle, restoration never ends. From some angles the church is impressive indeed, although for the architectural scholar it is an extremely confusing building, partly because little documentary evidence has come down to us, even more because the whole series of C 19–20 restorations has made the exterior what it is now, and often it is difficult to determine whether the restorers – *Thomas Harrison*, 1818–20, *Richard Charles Hussey*, 1843–64, *Sir George Gilbert Scott*, 1868–76, *Sir Arthur William Blomfield*, 1882–94, *Charles James Blomfield*, 1900–2, *Sir Giles Gilbert Scott*, from 1908, etc. – reproduced what had been there before (supposing it was still deducible) or followed their own hunches.

## EXTERIOR

This tour is topographical, starting at the E end, which is the Lady Chapel, a beautiful vessel of *c.* 1260–80 with side windows of three stepped lancets and an E window of five stepped lancets. The stonework is all *Hussey* and *Scott* (especially the high-pitched roof and gable are Scott's own), but for a lancet-style building genuineness of surface is not so necessary. Between 1525 and 1537 the two choir aisles were extended to flank the two W bays of the Lady Chapel (Addleshaw 1971), and that is the date of the N choir aisle's E window (St Werburgh's Chapel). But on the S side we find *Scott's* daring conceit, for which he said he had evidence: the S aisle now ends in a polygonal apse covered by an absurdly high polygonal roof, reaching right up into the clerestory. One cannot check now, but perhaps Scott's design was not all wishful thinking: there is now held to be reason to suppose that the original C 13 S E chapel had a conical stone roof, if hardly as tall as Scott's (Maddison, acknowledging the research of Dr Virginia Jansen). The choir clerestory is Scott's but faithfully reproduced two original windows that then survived, as earlier views show. The windows are Dec, of four lights. The main E window is by *Hussey*; the pinnacles are by *Scott*. The aisle windows on the other hand have geometrical tracery of late C 13 character, but those on the N side are by *Hussey*, those on the S by *Scott*. Hussey seems to have decided in favour of them on the strength of surviving minor internal features with geometrical details.

The S transept has Dec aisle and Perp clerestory windows, confirmed by early views as faithful to the originals (Maddison). The great S window anyway is of 1887, by *Blomfield*. The S end of the transept was repaired by *Harrison* during his restoration of 1818–20, and the squat corner turrets etc. are his. The flying buttresses here and on the nave are *Scott's* entirely. On the S wall of the transept, at a nice height which makes them easily seen, is a

13. CHESTER View from the south-east

row of figural corbels, and among them Gladstone and Disraeli can be recognized, reflecting the politics of the period of Scott's restoration. The s doorway to the w aisle is by *Giles Scott*.

The crossing tower is Perp, but the top with embattled corner turrets is by *Scott* (his intervening pinnacles were removed in 1911 and after; a spire design by him was never executed). The nave again has Dec aisle and Perp clerestory windows, the former by *Hussey*. So to the s w porch, the stump of a s w tower, and the w front. All this is work of the early c 16, thoroughly restored and perhaps embellished by *Scott*. The s w porch (just E of the s w

tower; not to be confused with the entrance to the s transept) is of two storeys. The inner doorway is intact; so are the vaulting-shafts in the corners. But the fan-vault is by Scott's son, *G. G. Jr*. The over-decorated upper floor, except perhaps for the two two-light windows, is by *Sir G. G.*

The w front is a mixture. On the lower level work is palpably original, the recessing of the doorway, some of the niche-work of the recess (but probably not the larger outer niches), and the delightful frieze of little angels and yet littler people in the frieze above the doorway culminating in the Assumption of the Virgin. The eight-light window is also basically original, but battlements, pediment and turrets are by *Scott*. The w front is unfortunate in that the N W tower – a Norman tower, as we shall see inside – is totally hidden by Barclays Bank, formerly the King's School, replacing the Bishop's Palace, originally the Abbot's Lodgings. So nearly one-third of the façade is missing.

The N views are more complex. Part of the Lady Chapel is hidden by the late Perp Chapel of St Werburgh at the E end of the N choir aisle. And the main vessel of the church

cannot be isolated from the monastic ranges around the cloisters: we cannot see that the N transept is still Norman. What we see there is the exterior of the chapter house, an exquisite exterior of long slender lancets of about 1250–60, on the N side two, three, and three and a blank, and the E side a curious system of lancets set in a system of giant blank lancet arches. This is largely due to *Blomfield* (though Addleshaw only mentions work by him on the N side, w gable and roof). The lower building N of the chapter

14. CHESTER Plan from the *Builder*, 1893 (see p. 51)

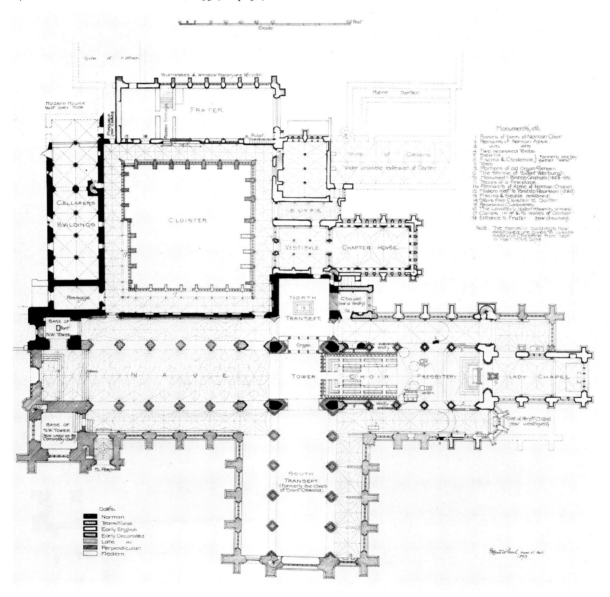

house was the warming room (now Song School), all externally not original. Of the great refectory on the N side of the cloisters the E window of reticulated tracery is by *Giles Scott*, 1913, replacing something quite different; the N side windows are mostly Dec, but towards the W end Perp. To see more one must stand in the cloister garth: then the N side of the nave can be seen, with Perp half-windows. On the E side it is at once clear that the dormitory is gone entirely which either ran along the upper floor of the E range or, as Sir Harold Brakspear considered, E from the N E corner. On the N side of the cloister appears the S wall of the refectory: at the E end of this wall the five close Dec windows lighting the staircase to the reading pulpit inside. The high Norman walling at the S W corner of the cloisters belongs to St Anselm's Chapel. For the interiors of all this, see *Cloister ranges* below.

## INTERIOR

Norman work appears in three places: the N transept, the N W tower, and the cloister ranges (see below). The first two will be described now out of topographical order. The church was no doubt begun in 1092, and again no doubt at the E end. That at least was the overwhelmingly general custom. The E end is supposed to have had an apsed choir. The choir aisles ended in apses too, and their outline is marked in the floor. How long building took is uncertain, but the details of the NORTH TRANSEPT do not look later than *c.* 1100 or so. In the E wall is the opening to a chapel formerly also apsed. The opening, which is surprisingly decayed for indoor work, has sturdy Early Norman details. Triple responds, two-scallop(?) capitals, two-step arch. The

15. CHESTER North transept, east side, *c.* 1100

chapel itself – to anticipate – was replaced *c.* 1200 by a straight-ended one of two bays. Vaulting-shafts with rings, capitals stiff-leaf as well as Late Norman; rib-vault. The E wall, however, has the three stepped lancets of the Lady Chapel, i.e. – if original – it is a later C 13 alteration, and the piscina also is later C 13 with its pointed-trefoiled head and its stiff-leaf capitals. Another such piscina is in the E wall of the transept between the openings into the chapel and the choir aisle, and this is cut into a wall-pier of the choir type (see below). The fragments S of this pier may have belonged to a screen. From the chapel an arch opens to the S into the N choir aisle. It is a later (*c.* 1300) alteration, as it cuts into the architecture of the chapel. This arch has two head-stops. Back in the transept again, above the Norman arch into the chapel (now a sacristy) is a low triforium of six openings: short columns with plain Early Norman single-scallop capitals and unmoulded arches. Above that is the Perp parapet with quatrefoils of open-work and the clerestory corresponding to that in the S transept (below). In the W wall are some small blocked Norman windows at triforium level. The W clerestory windows are Perp again, but of a different pattern. In the N wall is a small E. E. doorway. The big N window is by *Scott*. Excellent timber ceiling of *c.* 1520 with many bosses.

If one enters the N choir aisle for a moment, one sees at once in the first bay on the r. the circular base of a round pier and also a mighty round scalloped capital upside down. So the choir, e.g. like St John's Chester and Hereford Cathedral, had round piers.

Now the NORTH-WEST TOWER, only visible inside. This also is Norman, but about forty or fifty years later than the transept, i.e. therefore of the mid-C 12, though the arches are still merely stepped. But among the shafts of the arches to S and E are keeled ones, and the capitals have many small scallops. (It may be worth mentioning, though, that these two previously blocked arches were opened up by *Blomfield* in 1885 when the tower bay became the baptistery.) A window in the N wall was placed high up because of the cloister. In the adjoining W bay of the N aisle is another such window, blocked.

For the rest of the interior, chronology continues at the E end, and then we proceed topographically. Chronologically the latest item so far has been the E chapel of the N transept, i.e. a job of *c.* 1200 (and, outside the main vessel, the chapter house of *c.* 1250–60). Nothing is preserved in the church itself between *c.* 1200 and the Lady Chapel of *c.* 1260–80. The chapel is of three bays with a rib-vault with longitudinal ridge ribs and also short transverse ones caught up by a pair of tiercerons in the N and S cells of each bay. Three big bosses of the Trinity, the Virgin and Child, and the Murder of St Thomas à Becket, and also smaller bosses. The vaulting-shafts are tripartite, the front ones with fillets. Thick leaf capitals. Are sedilia and piscina to be

16. CHESTER Choir, *c.* 1260–*c.* 1320

trusted? The piscina is of two lights, the sedilia have only a pendant instead of a mid-shaft. The N choir aisle ends in the Chapel of St Werburgh, an early C16 addition (see *Exterior*, Lady Chapel, above). (On the shrine itself, see *Furnishings*, Lady Chapel.) Vault of two bays with tierceron stars.

Precise dating of the CHOIR is a complicated matter. Evidence of halting progress is probably to be explained by the intermittent demand for workmen generated by Edward I's Welsh campaigns of 1277, 1282 and 1294. Maddison, on the basis of pier sections and arch profiles, distinguishes five separate building periods between *c.* 1260 and *c.* 1320 for the whole eastern arm. The presumed employment here of Burgundian and/or Savoyard crafts-men and engineers, brought to England to work on the royal castles, has been noted by recent scholars (listed in Bony 1979).

Choir and sanctuary combined make five bays, three-storeyed in elevation. Strong piers of four major and four minor shafts connected by small hollows. The shafts have small fillets, finer on the N, broader on the s side. The bases and the capitals are still in the E.E. tradition. Moulded arches, on the N side with dominant rolls, on the s side with dominant hollows. The E arch is not wholly original. Vaulting-shafts start in the spandrels of the arcade. They stand on corbel figures, larger on the s than on the N side. A triforium follows of four small openings per bay, consist-ing of shafts carrying depressed trefoiled arches, which may betray Burgundian influence (Bony). In the NE bay the details of the arches are a little more complicated, and altogether it is likely that the N preceded the s side. (Maddison suggests: first two N bays, then two s bays, remaining bays at one go.) The clerestory is Dec, and it is said (see *Exterior* above) that two of the windows are original. The vault of the choir has diagonal and both longitudinal and transverse ridge ribs: this vault is of timber and by *Scott*, with painted decoration by *Clayton & Bell*. The sedilia are lusciously Dec and very largely by *Scott*. The original parts can easily be recognized, and they include three-dimensional ogee arches. The back towards the aisle consists of long thin panels separated by vertical leaf strips, also only very scantily original. The sedilia came from St John's Church, but at an early date. The CHOIR AISLES have tripartite vaulting-shafts with a fillet, as in the Lady Chapel. The vaults are again *Scott*'s. In the s aisle (all now a separate chapel entered only from the s transept) are two large genuine recesses, cusped, and still without ogees, and at the start of Scott's apse a Perp image niche. In the s aisle apse are sedilia and piscina with simple geometrical tracery; and in the E bay of the N aisle is another piscina with such tracery – justifying *Hussey*'s geometrical windows. (On remains of C11–12 piers in the N choir aisle, see Norman work above.)

17. CHESTER Corbel in the choir, *c.* 1300

The CROSSING piers continue from the choir into the early C14. Typical mouldings. The lantern stage has two large blank arches to each side, a wall-passage, and a longitudinal and a transverse arch rising from the middle of each lantern wall. They differ in their section. The decor-ation of the ceiling is by *G. G. Pace*.

The SOUTH TRANSEPT takes us up to *c.* 1340 (Maddison puts much of it a generation later). It has the unusual length of five bays – exactly like the choir except for being two-storeyed. From the 1530s until 1881 this was the parish church of St Oswald, earlier accommodated first in the nave s aisle and then in a detached chapel nearby: like other medieval abbeys, St Werburgh had its attendant parish. The parishioners had their separate entrance in the s door to the w aisle, and the whole transept was screened off from the crossing. The transept has both E and W aisles. The vault in the s bay of the E aisle is the only genuinely medieval rib-vault in the transept. It is of diagonal ribs and tiercerons, with both longitudinal and transverse ridge ribs, and has bosses. Also in the s wall a sedile and a piscina. The stone vaults of the other three bays of the E aisle by *A. W. Blomfield*, 1883; in the N bay, however, a genuine vaulting springer, and it is remarkable that Blomfield did not continue from it. He thought he knew better. He also incidentally did not continue Scott's choir aisle ribs. The transept's main centre vault is of timber, the w aisle vaults of stone, both by the younger *Blomfield*, 1900–2. The s transept 'nave' piers are like those of the choir, except that here vaulting-shafts start from the ground. The capitals have individual ornamental motifs, and those of the s wall leaf-bands. Are these latter to be trusted? Perp clerestory with wall-passage. Parapets of openwork quatrefoils. *A. W. Blomfield*'s Dec s window replaced a big Perp window (Maddison 1978).

The most remarkable thing about the NAVE is that between the s side, which continues direct from the s transept, starting, say, about 1360, and the N side, which at first sight is identical with the s side, there should be well over a hundred years. The latter work was done by Abbot Ripley (1485–93): the capital of the w respond has his monogram. This self-conscious conservatism or, as it were, historicism is something typically English. The same case exists at Westminster Abbey and at Beverley Minster (yet consider the case of St Albans). Only the pier bases are Perp on the N, while they are Dec on the s, and the s capitals have individual fleurons etc., but whole leaf-bands on the N. The E bays adjoining the crossing differ from all the others on both sides. They have continuous mouldings of three sunk convex curves and should probably be explained as a necessary buttressing for the crossing when it was being built. In the nave, like the s transept but unlike the choir, there is no triforium. The clerestory is Perp, and the parapet after that first E bay changes to bareness. The lierne vault is of timber and by *Scott*. The w wall has high blank arcading below which cannot be later than c. 1300 if it is original. Above it is the huge eight-light Perp w window. The s aisle has window surrounds which are original and Dec, justifying the Dec c 19 aisle windows which *Hussey* introduced. The stone vaults of the aisles are *Scott*'s again. Access to the s w tower is by a panelled arch. The rise in floor-level at the w end of the nave is due to a rise in ground-level, not to any crypt or previous building. On the baptistery, see N W *tower* above.

## FURNISHINGS, E TO W, AND N BEFORE S

*Lady Chapel* Stained glass by *Wailes*, 1859. Medallions *à la* c 13 (clear-glass fields inserted 1960). ST WERBURGH'S SHRINE. Stone, Dec, two bays by one, much restored by *Blomfield*, 1889, after fragments of the original had been found as rubble when the arch at the w end of the N nave aisle was opened up. The shrine's lower part, since the Dissolution, had served in the choir as base to the Bishop's Throne. Maddison (1978) notes similarities in design with the s transept aisles, especially in the shrine gables and those of the transept windows. On the upper stage, several statuettes of kings and saints. – MONUMENT. Archdeacon Wrangham, a brass cross; 1846 by *Hardman* to design by *Pugin* (Addleshaw).

*North choir chapel* STAINED GLASS. E window by *A. & M. O'Connor*, 1857, one large pictorial representation of the Nativity. – MONUMENTS. Bishop Graham, 1867. Designed by *Kelly & Edwards*. Recumbent effigy and Gothic architectural surround. – William Bispham † 1685. Brass plate and stone surround with short columns and an open scrolly segmental pediment.

*Choir and Sanctuary* REREDOS mosaic of the Last Supper and FLOOR PAVEMENT of incised marbles, both designed by *Clayton & Bell*. (On lectern designed to stand here, see *Nave* below.) ALTAR TABLE of woods from Palestine designed by *Scott*, executed by *Farmer & Brindley* with plant carvings by *G. F. Armitage*. STALLS. One of the finest sets in the country. In Cheshire only Nantwich can compare in quality, in the rest of the North of England only Manchester. (But the Manchester stalls, in type associated rather with Ripon and Beverley, are of the early c 16.) Those at Nantwich and Chester are both late c 14, but not alike in detail. Chester's are in a class by themselves, though their system of tabernacles was taken over from Lincoln (where later partly restored), and both shared traits of London court style with York (burnt early c 19): on the possible responsibility of *Hugh Herland*, see Harvey 1978. The Chester stalls have powerfully carved ends, some original and some Victorian. Among the former the dean's stall shows the Tree of Jesse, as does an end on the N side as well. Musical angels added to canopies in 1876. Carvings on the arm-rests are worth inspecting, but the greatest wealth is in the MISERICORDS. Here only a few can be singled out (a cathedral booklet lists them all). From the dean's stall (s side N w end) s and then E: Coronation of the Virgin; Sir Gawain and the portcullis falling on his horse; a monster killing a knight; unicorn, virgin and knight; wrestlers; a man leading a lion; sow and litter; Virgin and Child; quarrelling couple; Reynard the fox; Samson and the lion. – From the vice-dean's stall (N side s w end) first N and then E: pelican; knight on horseback; angels with Instruments of the Passion; life of St Werburgh; woman beating her husband; fox shamming dead; the ascent of Alexander; angel with harp; Tristram and Iseult; tiger hunt; stag hunt; and other scenes just as aesthetically rewarding, e.g. the two herons on the N side.

18. CHESTER
Choir stalls, bench end, north side, east end, *c.* 1380

Four on the N side are by *Scott*'s carvers, Nos. 7–10 from the w gateway; No. 5, inscribed 'League of Nations to the Rescue', was made in 1919 by *G. F. Armitage*, who had been one of those young carvers in 1876. Scott placed the stalls in their present position, *Hussey* having moved them farther w. For Scott's screen behind the w return stalls, see *Crossing* below. – Behind the stalls backing on to the w bays of both choir aisles and visible from there: STONE SCREEN-WALLS from the former pulpitum, of the C14 according to Paul's plan of 1893 but according to Addleshaw part of *Hussey*'s w face added to it in 1846; set up here in 1875. They are high and have blank single-light panels with crocketed ogee arches. – BISHOP'S THRONE.

1876, by *Farmer & Brindley* to *Scott*'s design. – STAINED GLASS. E by *Heaton, Butler & Bayne*, 1884, Presentation of Christ in the Temple. – CANDLESTICKS. By *Censore*, a Bolognese gun-founder who lived in Rome and died in 1622. – LECTERN. A wooden eagle on a stem with wooden figurines. First half of the C17 (perhaps part of Bishop Bridgeman's fittings).

*North choir aisle*    (For E chapel, see after *Lady Chapel* above; and for pieces of former pulpitum, see *Choir* above.) The open STONE SCREEN like that of a chantry is by *Hussey*, also a corresponding one on the s aisle. – IRON GATE from Guadalajara in Spain, 1558: cherubim with (?) 'Mexican'-style headdresses. When the C19 donor, the first Duke of Westminster, bought the gates (also in s choir aisle) Christie's attributed them to Alonso Berruguete (Addleshaw 1971). – STAINED GLASS. The four first on the N side from the E by *Wailes*; the first three 1859, the fourth 1853. – Then a good *Heaton, Butler & Bayne*, 1863, and the westernmost *Clayton & Bell*, 1863. – MONUMENTS. Tablet to Bishop Jacobson, 1887. Portrait relief, signed by *Boehm*; the design by *Blomfield*. – George Travis † 1797 by *Joseph Turner*, architect. With portrait in an oval. By the entrance to the Lady Chapel, a brass to the Rev. Mascie Domville Taylor † 1845. By *Hardman* and based on a design by *Pugin* (Addleshaw 1971; see Pugin's *Apology*, 1847, Pl. vi, x). At the w end of the N wall are brasses, one above the other, to Dean J. S. Howson and to James Frater, clerk of works, both of whom played so considerable a part in Scott's restoration of the cathedral.

*South choir aisle*    The apse (Chapel of St Erasmus) has STAINED GLASS by *Clayton & Bell*, 1872, and below good MOSAICS designed by *Clayton* and made by *Salviati*, 1879. – FRESCO PAINTING also by *Clayton & Bell*, 1874. – Floor of Minton TILES, 1874, reproducing medieval tiles found on site during Scott's rebuilding of the apse. – Mahogany ALTAR RAILS designed by *Pace*, 1968, with brass panels from *Skidmore*'s high-altar rails of 1876. – The other STAINED GLASS is as follows: the first from the E, Resurrection window (Anson memorial), 1850, executed by *Hardman* to a design of *Pugin*'s cartoonist *Oliphant* (Harrison). Then two by *Wailes*, 1852. – IRON GATE, Spanish, 1558 (see N *choir aisle*). – MONUMENTS. Black tomb-chest with quatrefoil decoration and small painted figures between. C13 or early C14. The reference to the Emperor Henry IV is erroneous. – Bust of Thomas Brassey. The Italian Quattrocento design by *Blomfield*, 1882, the bust made before 1877 by *Wagmüller*. – Bishop Peploe † 1752. Very fine architecture and decoration. – Three painted-wood tablets by the *Randle Holme* family of arms painters: to Robert Bennet † 1614 (flat strapwork), John Leche † 1639 and Katharine Wynne † 1698 (both heraldic).

*Crossing*    In 1844 after the pulpitum was removed from the E to the w tower arch by *Hussey*, a new organ was placed on it, then the largest English cathedral organ except York's. When the stone pulpitum was removed in 1875 (for its remains, see above), the organ was rebuilt and placed at the entrance to the N transept, its oak case carved by *Farmer & Brindley* and its loft on Italian marble columns both designed by *Scott* (slightly altered by *Pace*). Scott provided the present open wooden choir SCREEN, inspired by the medieval stalls, and made by *Farmer & Brindley*, 1876, with metal gates by *Skidmore*. Over the gateway arch of the screen and Scott's central traceried tabernacle stood a small detached CHOIR ORGAN, 1876–1910 (now on the s side of the choir), replaced in 1913 by the present rood designed by *Giles Scott* and carved by *Ferdinand Stuflesser*. PAVEMENT designed by *Gilbert Scott*. (A great cross which Scott designed to hang overhead was transferred in 1921 to the church at Dunham-on-the-Hill, N W of Chester: a treasure lost to the cathedral, typical Skidmore work, typical Scott design, and typical High Victorian elaboration, it would be an ornament to any exhibition of Victorian art.)

*North transept* STAINED GLASS. The two clerestory E windows by *Wailes*, 1853. – MONUMENTS. One to the C 17 Bishop Pearson. Designed by *A. W. Blomfield*, carved by *Thomas Earp*, 1864. – On the N wall, Samuel Peploe, c. 1784, by *Nollekens* (putto before an obelisk), and Lt L. W. Halsted † 1829, by *Thomas Kelly* (with a pyramid and some heavy Grecian decoration). – On the w wall: Edward Massy † 1836. In a Gothic surround, but the representation curiously Baroque. He lies on a couch, an angel above him in a cloud. – Col. T. G. Egerton † 1855. Signed by *Thomas Bedford* of Oxford Street, London. The Colonel reclines; mourners stand by him. – Henry Trowbridge Moor † 1837. Large Gothic tablet with a gable at the top.

*South transept* Stone SCREEN between E transept aisle and s choir aisle. Only partly old. – REREDOS in the second chapel from the N by *Kempe*, 1906. – STAINED GLASS. The great s window by *Heaton, Butler & Bayne*, 1886, 'The Triumph of Faith', design exhibited Royal Academy 1888. – In the E aisle the first from the N also by them, 1876. Then three by *Kempe*, 1890, 1892, 1902, and at the s end by *Clayton & Bell*, 1890. – On the w side the first from the N by *Powell*, 1892, and the second by *Kempe*, 1904. – MONUMENTS. George Ogden † 1788 by *Hayward*. Kneeling female figure leaning on a rock, an anchor in front of it. – John Phillips Buchanan † 1815 at Waterloo. Dramatic trophy with a big Grecian helmet. – First Duke of Westminster † 1899. Designed by *C. J. Blomfield* (shown Royal Academy 1901), recumbent effigy by *Pomeroy*, 1902. – Also monument to Sarah Jervis † 1748, signed by *Daniel Sephton* of Manchester.

*Nave* FONT s of the w door. Black marble, a big baluster carrying a big bowl, 1687. (For font under N W

tower, see N *aisle* below.) – WEST DOOR. Traceried, much restored. – Lectern, with eagle and evangelists, by *Skidmore*, 1876, to *Scott's* design, originally standing in the choir on a circular paved space designed for it by *Clayton & Bell*. – PULPIT. Stone, designed by *Hussey*, 1846, carved by *Henry Frith*. – PANELS fronting the clergy stalls were formerly part of Bishop Bridgeman's choir pulpit of 1637, reset by *Pace*. – STAINED GLASS. The w window by *W. T. Carter Shapland*, 1961. With large single figures and strong colours. A work that will please many but can also please the few. – MONUMENTS. Gothic standing monument to Col. Roger Barnston of 1838 by *John Blayney*. – Bishop Stratford † 1707. Large tablet with above the inscription three putto-heads and at the top a bust. – Bishop Hall † 1668. Noble black and white marble tablet with open scrolly pediment. No figures. – Edmund Entwisle, 1712. With two putto-heads and garland. – John and Thomas Wainwright † 1686 and 1720, signed by *George Berkeley* (the later bishop, who probably composed the epitaph) and by *William Kent*, but lovably rustic in the execution. Two cherubs hold the inscription plate over which hangs a fat garland. It really looks 1670 rather than 1720. – Robert Bickerstaff † 1841. By *Blayney*. Weeping willow over an urn. – Mrs Dod, 1723. Oval medallion with frontal bust. – Dean Smith † 1787. By *Banks*. Mourning female figure by an urn. – Sir William Mainwaring, 1671. Large tablet with twisted columns and a segmental pediment; two putti squeezed in.

*North aisle* On the wall MOSAICS. Stories in large figures, 1883–6. Designed by *Clayton*, executed by *Burke & Co.* and set in stonework designed by *Blomfield*. – The MOSAIC FLOOR in the tower bay was designed by *Dean Howson* and made by *Burke & Co.*, 1885. – FONT, procured from Venice as C 5, now regarded as C 19 pastiche of Early Christian work, installed 1885 on legs designed by *Blomfield*. – STAINED GLASS. A series by *Heaton, Butler & Bayne*, 1890.

*South aisle* STAINED GLASS. Slade window by *Wailes*, 1862, one of a pair of which the other was destroyed in the last war. – Under the s w tower the complete C 17 furnishings of the CONSISTORY COURT fitted up in 1636 (though some of the fittings, e.g. the great table, may be earlier, Addleshaw says). Entered through a screen with contemporary overthrow. There is a wooden enclosure with a bench round, raised on the side with canopied chancellor's throne, and an oddly raised corner seat.

## CLOISTER RANGES

A Norman cloister and Norman domestic quarters must of course have existed, and there is quite some evidence of them. (On the present cloister walks, see below.) The earliest is the UNDERCROFT of the w range, groin-vaulted

19. CHESTER Chapter-house vestibule, early C13

in two naves with short round piers with round scalloped capitals – early C12 (called Cellarers' Buildings on the plan; now partly cathedral shop). The ABBOT'S PASSAGE to its S, i.e. in the SW corner (next to the NW tower), came later, say c. 1150. It is not bonded in, i.e. was an afterthought. It has two bays of rib-vaulting, the ribs of a later profile than those of the tower (half-roll and two small half-hollows). Above the passage is the C12 CHAPEL OF ST ANSELM, originally part of the abbot's lodging and later private chapel of the bishop's palace. (It is now approached from NW of the cathedral.) This also is not bonded into the early C12 NW tower's N wall, and it obscures the tower's N window. The wall supports for the original transverse arches of the chapel have volute and scallop capitals. But the delight now is the early C17 CEILING and FITTINGS inserted for Bishop Bridgeman (1619–44). In the two W bays panelled plaster was laid over the Norman vaults, while the E bay (over the cloister walk) has a lovely flat plaster ceiling with E window of similar date. Also C17, screen, altar rails, strap-topped doors.

St Anselm's Chapel originally adjoined the Abbot's Lodging, which was above the W range of the cloister (see *Undercroft* above) and later extended westward (see below) – a late medieval development often to be found. The W face of the E wall of the original lodging can still be seen from outside.

20. CHESTER Refectory pulpit stair, late C13

The whole s wall of the cloister, i.e. the N wall of the nave N aisle, is Norman too. It has two sets of three blank arches with patterned shafts. E of them is the major doorway from church to cloister, and this is the only example of Latest Norman in the cathedral. Three orders of columns, waterleaf capitals, as they are characteristic of say *c*. 1175–90, moulded arch, the outer order with a kind of intermittent corn-cob motif. The contrast between this Latest Norman and the Earliest E.E. of the N transept E chapel is telling.

In the w walk N of the undercroft is another passage with a Norman doorway. Inside is the springing of a Norman rib-vault, and in the E range, near the s end, is a blocked perfectly simple Norman doorway. Much rebuilding of the ranges round the cloister took place in the C13. The best start is with the CHAPTER HOUSE. Its front is entirely by *Hussey*, but the VESTIBULE is genuine and memorable as one of the earliest cases of piers running into vaults without any intervening capitals. The piers have bundles of eight attached shafts, and the ribs do not strictly continue them, but break up each shaft into a triple rib. There are no bosses. The chapter house is the aesthetic climax of the cathedral, a wonderfully noble room, vaulted with rib-vaults, including ridge ribs. The vaulting-shafts are triple, the middle one polygonal. They stand on stiff-leaf corbels and have stiff-leaf capitals. The windows are slim lancets, as we have already seen. There are inside boldly detached shafts with rings repeating the forms of the windows. The proportions are admirable. The wall to the vestibule is in the usual way divided into a portal and two two-light windows over (quatrefoil in the spandrels). – CUPBOARD, wooden doors with iron scrollwork of c. 1294 in later frame (P. Eames 1977, No. 22). – STAINED GLASS. The E window by *Heaton, Butler & Bayne*, 1872. – LECTERN. 1846, by *Hussey*, who also put in the fireplace.

N of the chapter house is the SLYPE, formerly to the monastic infirmary. This is E.E. too. Its doorway has detached shafts. The vault is of four bays and has diagonal as well as ridge ribs.

The WARMING ROOM, now Song School, with two large former fireplaces, is N of the slype. It is of four by two bays and it has single-chamfered ribs. The piers are octagonal. Taking up a little of the oblong space of this room is the DAY STAIR to the former dormitory, opened handsomely to the E walk by a big quatrefoil in a circle. E.E. also is the doorway into the warming room, in the NE corner. It has a cinquecusped head.

More E.E. work in the N walk. In the N range of course is the refectory (see below). Its doorway has two orders and a cusped arch. E of this is the LAVATORIUM, of three arches. The cloister vault interferes with it and other features with a ruthlessness now hard to understand.

The CLOISTER WALKS were in fact rebuilt about 1525–30. Proof of the date in the initials of an abbot of 1527–9 and the arms of Cardinal Wolsey. The s walk was rebuilt again by *Scott*, 1871–2 on the pattern of the s half of the w walk, i.e. with detached piers forming niches, or CARRELS, i.e. reading spaces set aside. The vaults have diagonal and ridge ribs, all hollow-chamfered, and bosses. They stand on wall corbels which look earlier than Perp in the E walk and which stand on big figures in the N and w ranges. The cloister windows are all Perp and of the same design except in the NE and NW corners. In the NE corner are the earliest-looking corbels; yet the window pattern as such is not earlier than the other. Much STAINED GLASS of the 1920s by *F. C. Eden, A. K. Nicholson, Trena Mary Cox* and *G. P. Gamon*.

In conclusion the REFECTORY (called Frater on the plan). This is basically Norman – cf. the inside of the main doorway – but its present appearance is late C13 to early C14. The windows, as has already been said, are largely Dec, and the E window, of 1913, is by *Giles Scott*, who restored the refectory and other of the monastic parts. The roof is by *F. H. Crossley*, 1939. What can only be seen from the cloister garth is a set of five small, closely set windows in the s wall near the E end. They are cinquecusped, and their very raw ogee tops cannot be trusted. Their function is to light the steps which run up in the wall to the READING PULPIT. The stair is in the thickness of the wall, and the arches to the room itself are pointed-trefoiled. The pulpit projects triangularly on a big corbel with three bands of stiff-leaf. The whole ensemble – in spite of the ogee detail just mentioned – is decidedly pre-ogee, say c. 1290. So incidentally are the wall-shafts between the Dec windows.

Beside the w front of the cathedral on the site of the Bishop's Palace (Abbot's Lodgings), Barclays Bank in the s wing, 1877, of the former King's School building by *Sir A. W. Blomfield*, the w wing, 1879, now the Choir School. Adjoining them the ABBEY GATEWAY. It has continuous chamfers, the outer ones enclosing the carriage as well as the pedestrian entrance. Three-bay vault with both diagonal and ridge ribs all of one chamfer, and excellent bosses. Maddison points out that its great segmental relieving arch is like that of the Queen's Gate at Caernarvon, and its mouldings are like those of the cathedral's w choir piers, so the date of the licence to crenellate the abbey walls, c. 1377, seems far too late.

The free-standing bell-tower of 1973, SE of the cathedral, has a concrete frame under its slate cladding, despite its apparent derivation from the forms of timber construction. Designed by *George Pace* and, according to his successor, Ronald Sims, based unspecifically on medieval bell-houses in Essex and Scandinavia. In its upright angularity next to the warm red mother-building it has the air of an Anglican folly.

Further on surroundings, city walls and Chester itself, see the latest edition of B of E *Cheshire*.

## Coventry

CATHEDRAL CHURCH OF ST MICHAEL  *Anglican*

(Based on B of E *Warwickshire*, 1966, revised, with information from Charles Brown and George McHardy and Anthony New.)

Cathedral since 1918. Until 1940 this was the medieval building of Coventry's prime parish church. From far off the cathedral is still signalled by St Michael's medieval spire – with Holy Trinity's and Greyfriars', one of Coventry's famous trio of spires. On 14 November 1940, along with much of the centre of the city, the cathedral, except for the spire, was largely destroyed by fire bombs.

A competition for a new building was held in 1951 and won by (*Sir*) *Basil Spence*. The principal features of his design had come to him when he first visited the site: the placing N–S and the use of the ruin of the old church as a forecourt. The design, when made known, was blamed by the moderns as not modern enough, by the traditionalists as too modern, by the man in the street as jazzy. Those

21. COVENTRY New cathedral, 1951–62, designed by Sir Basil Spence, and ruins of the C15 cathedral

initial controversies are over now that the building has been complete for some years (consecration: 1962), but some still maintain that Sir Basil's brief was wrong and that a church in the mid-C20 ought to be planned not like one of the past, but in accordance with what calls itself the Liturgical Movement, that is, like the 'theatre in the round' with the altar in the centre and the faithful all turned towards it (cf. Liverpool R. C. Cathedral below). This is arguable – objections have e.g. been raised on the grounds that what is good for a parish church is not necessarily good for a cathedral – but has nothing to do with the architectural appreciation to which we must now proceed.

The new cathedral is small – only 270 ft long – but Sir Basil managed to make it appear large. It is built of red Hollington sandstone – the traditional local material – and is entered from the E (ritually S) or the S (ritually W). To the S remain the outer walls of the church of St Michael and to their W its steeple, 295 ft high. St Michael, with a floor area of 24,000 sq. ft, was one of the largest English parish churches.

## THE MEDIEVAL CHURCH

One should first tarry in the forecourt and examine what survives after 1940 of this splendid old parish church. The oldest surviving part is the S porch. This is late C13, with moulded capitals and a broadly trefoil-cusped arch. Possibly also as early or earlier are the curious lengths of bare wall between steeple and nave. Below the N transept is a rib-vaulted crypt of c. 1300, of two by three bays; to the E a later extension. The rest is all Perp but stretches from 1371 into the early C16. In 1371 the steeple was begun. It was not completed until the 1430s at the earliest. It has a large W window, then two stages with tall one- and two-light windows with concave-sided or ogee-sided crocketed gables – the composition is very handsomely varied – then the bell-openings, two tall twins with transoms and flanked by statues, and then battlements and an octagonal storey – an afterthought no doubt to make the steeple yet higher – with two-light transomed windows and battlements, and finally the banded spire rising effortlessly, supported (so it seems to the eye) by slim flying buttresses. Ruskin wrote of it, passionate geologist that he was, that 'the sand of Coventry' binds itself 'into stone which can be built half-way to the sky' (1874). Inside, the tower is now open right up to a lierne vault just below the octagonal stage.

As one stands inside the ruins, one will notice at once the great and undeniably painful anomaly of the church. The nave was considerably wider than the steeple. To its N there is enough space for a whole porch and portal with a lierne vault inside. The reason is that the steeple was built to stand w of the C13 (or C12) nave. The widening of the nave is part of a somewhat later and even more ambitious building programme. When the wealthy of Coventry embarked on it we do not know, but there is reason to assume a date near the completion of the spire. Work started with the chancel and proceeded quickly. The chancel has a polygonal apse, a rarity in England (cf. Lichfield), and especially at so late a date. With its decorated battlements and pinnacles it now stands higher than the rest of the walls. The windows are of four lights with ample panel tracery. The subsidiary rooms at the foot date from 1885. As one turns N or S, one first sees the seven-light chancel aisle E windows (N four plus four intersecting, S three plus one plus three) and then the large N and S windows, the latter now entirely without mullions and tracery. But from about midway to the w one does not see outer walls of the aisles any longer; for late in the C15 and early in the C16, chapels were added E as well as w of the porches. The E window of the SE chapel and two windows of the N chancel aisle have pretty quatrefoils in the tracery (more of these at St John's Coventry). In the SW chapel two C18 monuments, calcined but once of good quality: Dame Mary Bridgeman † 1701, and Mrs Eliza Samwell † 1724, portrait busts with flanking columns carrying open segmental pediments.

On the wall over the site of the high altar the words 'FATHER FORGIVE' have been inscribed. It must be hard for anyone too young to remember the church to visualize the scale and character of the old interior – or indeed to imagine the scale and character of one night's destruction. The piers are marked in the ground. Only one pier stands fully: in the SE chapel. But in this state, like the arena of a martyrdom, this bare space open to the sky is deeply moving. And then, already under a new canopy, one descends twenty steps into the porch of the new cathedral, prepared for whatever spiritual impact may come.

THE NEW CATHEDRAL

*Exterior*

The survival of the steeple was an untold boon to competitors for the new building; for the C20 style has not been able to create anything anywhere both as elegant and as powerful as a late medieval steeple. But the relation between the walls of the church and the new building was all Sir Basil Spence's. The motif of his design which has hit his many imitators most forcibly is the saw-tooth walls N and S (we use the ritual directions). The sharp rhythm of almost completely bare rose sandstone walls pointing half-w and each section rising along the skyline towards the w, and equally completely grid walls of concrete and glass pointing half-E and thus throwing their coloured light towards the altar establishes at once a poignancy which will be found in many other places and ways. The E wall is entirely bare, except for a row of nine oblongs, a large cross in relief, and the batter of the angle buttresses. The Lady Chapel N and S walls have a rather smaller rhythm of long and short oblong windows and small square windows. To the S near the E end projects the GUILD CHAPEL with its glazed walls and slate fins, to the N near the w end the dodecagonal CHAPEL OF UNITY with its deep, battered slate buttresses and irregularly detailed slit windows. Opposite it the S wall curves outward gently and has a bold stone grid of a different pattern from that of the windows. Behind this is the font. Finally the PORCH. It is open to N and S (again ritually speaking). The main entrance, unless one passes through the Perp forecourt, is from the S, where a flight of steps leads up to it. Here to the r. is *Epstein*'s St Michael and Lucifer, one of his last works (cf. his massive earlier work recently placed in the ruins; see below). It is large, of bronze, and the two figures are kept entirely separate. St Michael hovers over Lucifer, but Lucifer, although reclining, reclines nowhere. It is a sentimental piece, its expressionism more in feature and gesture than in emotional intensity of forms. In Sir Basil Spence's taste it marks the one extreme. The other we shall find later, and the two never in the cathedral reach a full reconciliation. Similarly the porch itself differs in style from the rest of the church. Its design was in fact revised at the end, and as it was finally built, it is closer to the University of Sussex than to the saw-tooth walls of Coventry. Earlier Spence was sharp, later Spence (under Le Corbusier's influence: Maisons Jaoul) is more massive. The piers of the porch are circular and extremely high. They are sheer, except that very convincingly just under the top they stop and disclose the much thinner gauge of concrete doing the real carrying job. Canopies jut out or grasp out to N, S and w.

Having the steeple of St Michael, the new cathedral needed no beacon of its own. But some vertical accent on the flattish roof seemed to be called for, and so Sir Basil decided on a flèche. This also went through a number of phases. It ended up as a tall, transparent space-frame, looking – in spite of *Geoffrey Clarke*'s thorny, abstract cross, so amazingly lowered into position by an R.A.F.

22. COVENTRY The nave.
Tapestry designed by Graham Sutherland, 1952

helicopter – like a piece of television apparatus. One could imagine that Sir Basil himself might later have wished to change this flèche.

## Interior and furnishings

At Coventry the distinction between architectural description and description of the furnishings loses its sense. The two are too much part of one conception. What has been made for, and gone into, the cathedral between the laying of the foundation stone in 1956 and the consecration in 1962 is what the architect wanted and went where he wanted it. Some later additions are mentioned at the end of this description.

One enters through doors that are part of a w wall almost completely of glass. The WEST WINDOW above is engraved with saints and angels by *John Hutton*, long gaunt figures more stylized than Epstein's St Michael, but in the Expressionist way telling their story by intensified gesture and tense drapery. Henry Moore's wartime drawings are evidently the source of style.

Our first impression of the interior, in looking through the glass wall or passing through the doors, is undeniably Gothic. This is due to four causes: the proportions, the existence of nave and aisles, the slenderness of the piers, and the semblance of a ribbed vault. As for proportion, it is not only a matter of width to height of nave, although that matters greatly, but also of length to both of them, i.e. the uninterrupted vista along many piers to a distant altar-wall. There is in fact no altar-wall, as there is no vault, but the mind interprets the visual data that way. The piers are cruciform, set diagonally, and taper outward as they rise. They could be slenderer yet at the bottom, and once again Sir Basil decided to demonstrate this structural fact by giving them a girth of much smaller section. The engineers building train sheds for railway stations had done that for nearly a hundred years. From the piers issue concrete ribs creating a vaulting grid of folded square panels filled in with wooden slats in two directions, an exciting pattern of exactly the same fighting energy as the saw-tooth walls. In fact all this has nothing to do with vaulting the building in the Gothic sense. Piers and ribs form a canopy from w end to altar space and keep detached from the real concrete roof. This is not easily noticed, and those who ask for structural truth will not be satisfied with the very narrow gap between walls and canopy. It is only when one looks back from the Lady Chapel that one realizes that a man can stand upright between the two.

Next to the piers and vaults the side walls speak most powerfully. Owing to the saw-tooth plan one sees only walls and no windows, except for the one behind the font, and the walls are sheer, except for *Ralph Beyer's* monumental inscriptions. The walls are harled, to use the Scottish term for a Scottish architect's choice, i.e. roughcast a whitish grey, i.e. not made to look precious. The large inscription tablets are done in a script of Roman capitals very much with the carver's irregularities; for there is no machine transmission here. The sculptor who designed them cut them himself. They are of biblical passages, and most are illustrated by a simple symbol: a key, a chalice, the sun. *Ralph Beyer* also designed the dedication inscription for the floor at the w end, and this is carried out in brass letters, three feet high. The floor is of white and black marble and might compete unfavourably with the greys above, if it were not for the permanently set rows of stacking chairs (designed by *Russell, Hodgson & Leigh*).

But before the inscriptions can be read and the visitor proceeds towards the chancel, there is a double halt, almost immediately after the entry. On the s is the baptistery, on the N the access to the Chapel of Unity. The BAPTISTERY curves out very gently to hold the FONT, which is an enormous raw boulder brought from Bethlehem, another of those poignant ideas in which Sir Basil's mind was so fertile. The concave wall is a three-dimensional stone grid filled entirely by STAINED GLASS designed by *John Piper* and made by *Patrick Reyntiens*. It is among the best English glass of the c 20, entirely abstract, but its colours expressing a perfectly convincingly presented message. The message is *per aspera ad astra*, to a sun-like yellow with actually a white centre, from dark blue at the top, dark red, blue and green along the sides, a dark green lower down, and a busier mixture of colours down below, where we are. The detail is largely organized in forms parallel to those of the grid, which results in a sense of order and direction and so finally in repose.

Opposite is the one long stretch of bare wall simply at r. angles to the entry wall. The access to the CHAPEL OF UNITY is low and flanked by two areas of absolutely plain clear glass, release from the intensity of the interior mood of the cathedral. The passage leading to the chapel is funnel-shaped, functionally appropriate and at the same time in accordance with the *leitmotif* of diagonals which runs throughout the building (except for the porch). After the flanking areas of clear glass, the chapel is mysterious, more concentratedly perhaps than any other part of the building. What Sir Basil has done is to alternate round the room between angular stretches of high walling, each taking in an angle of the dodecagon, and deep funnel-shaped recesses like the jambs of windows in a keep, ending (on the outer surface of what seem buttresses externally) with irregularly shaped small panels of coloured glass all the way up. The glass, again entirely abstract, is by *Margaret Traherne*. But in order not to keep the chapel too much in darkness unfiltered light was needed, and this Sir Basil provided by the thinnest slits all the way up

23. COVENTRY Baptistery. Stained glass by John Piper and Patrick Reyntiens

between walls and recesses. The floor mosaic is by *Einar Forseth*. (The inclusion of a chapel with the theme of religious unity – an ecumenical milestone in modern cathedral design – was the idea of the provost 1933–58, the Very Rev. R. T. Howard.)

As one returns to the nave and proceeds eastward, one first becomes aware of the STAINED GLASS of the aisle windows, each 80 ft high. The windows, as has already been said, all face diagonally towards the altar, and they are seen only as one looks back in bay after bay. There are ten of them, i.e. five pairs, and they were designed and made by *Lawrence Lee*, *Geoffrey Clarke* and *Keith New*. They are all one in style, even if individually distinguishable. They are essentially abstract, and whereas John Piper's is

mostly rectilinear and, whatever its colour coherence, self-contained in each of the panels, these can only be read as a whole each, and they are, some aggressively diagonal and criss-cross in pattern, some rounder and weightier. Also in some of them objects can be discovered, while others keep away entirely from representation. From the w, the first l. (*K. New*) and r. (*K. New*) with much yellow are restless and full of conflict, the second l. (*L. Lee*) introduces more red, in the second r. (*L. Lee*) flowers are distinguishable. The third l. (*G. Clarke*) is quite different, with larger areas of rounded form, whereas the third r. (*K. New*), with much red, is still restless. Then number four l. (*G. Clarke*) introduces deep blue, and number four r. (*G. Clarke*) is the darkest of them all. Finally, five l. (by all three of the artists) returns to the yellow of the beginning but now in a more controlled composition, and five r. (*L. Lee*) is also pale and one of the most harmonious. That the progress is meant to be towards the divine will be patent from this inadequate description. (They have been given labels: Beginnings at the w end, then Conflict, Struggle, Maturity, and finally Realization, casting light towards the altar.) If the description remains inadequate, that is due to a certain extent to the essentials of so-called Abstract Expressionism. Its message can be strong but not explicit. One can enthuse, but not formulate precisely.

The chancel begins with PULPIT and LECTERN, designed by Sir Basil. The lectern is given, as a book-rest, an eagle (the traditional motif) modelled brilliantly by *Elisabeth Frink* and carried out in bronze. Against the E walls of the aisles stand the ORGAN pipes, in Sir Basil's own ingenious arrangement, a complete success as the subsidiary *point de vue* for the aisles. Meanwhile in the centre the CHOIR STALLS insist on attention. Sir Basil accepted the Gothic principle of canopies and the most prominent canopy for the bishop's throne, but interpreted them in terms of slender-membered three-pointed stars, their tips or some of their tips carrying the centre of the next star. Each star is somewhat like the Mercedes trade-mark interpreted three-dimensionally. The whole is an intricate, ever-changing pattern, reminding everybody, especially from a distance, of birds in flight. In themselves they are exhilarating, but as part of the total vista towards the E wall they may be too insistent.

The ALTAR, a long, heavy piece with short legs and massive top, stands free. On the altar the cross, by *Geoffrey Clarke*, an abstract interpretation in gilded silver, both of the Cross and the agonized pain of the Crucified. The large ceramic candlesticks l. and r. are by *Hans Coper*. To approach the Lady Chapel one goes through a low passage on the l. with, by one's side, some STAINED GLASS saints – in design, colour and technique unlike other glass in the cathedral – by *Einar Forseth*.

The LADY CHAPEL is divided off from the retrochoir by an iron screen of, as it were, vertical propeller blades (McHardy). The chapel, and of course the whole cathedral, is dominated by *Graham Sutherland*'s TAPESTRY, made in France by *Pinton Frères* at Felletin. Designed 1952 (even before the foundation stone was laid). It is 75½ ft high ('the largest tapestry in the world') and cost £17,500, a very reasonable sum. It is undoubtedly the climax of the building, and was meant from the beginning to fulfil that function. Not only its scale and the size of the figure of Christ, but also the colouring have no peer. Everything visible ahead as one progresses was muted in colour, to enhance the effect of the intensity of the green background of the tapestry. It is a nature-green, very full and rich, and very pure, neither yellowy nor blueish. Against it Christ

seated in a white garment with yellow lights against a dun-coloured *mandorla*. He is seated frontally and his hands are raised – a figure obviously inspired by Early Christian mosaics, yet not imitating them. The *mandorla* has a frame of golden yellow, as if it were brass, and this metallic frame extends, as for the wings of a polyptych, to frame the symbols of the four Evangelists. They are, against the directness of representation in the Christ, disturbed, thorny beings and have reds and purples and browns. The frame also extends above as if intended to secure the whole of the figure-work to the walls and roof. At the top are rays, between Christ's feet stands a tiny man. Below this are the chalice and the serpent of eternity, and right below, ash-grey, like a predella, is Christ crucified, again thorny and fierce. The tapestry receives full light, as high and narrow clear glass windows, again not at once visible, are to its l. and r. The tapestry has come in for much criticism. One of the two most important arguments is that the design was not made with a view to the tapestry-making technique, but that is hardly convincing; for where the size is as great as it is here, the individual square which is the maker's unit need no longer tell in the whole. (Still, this is less textile design than mural-painting design; cf. e.g. the late C15 tapestry in St Mary's Hall, Coventry.) The other crucial criticism of the tapestry is that it is corny and too obvious, i.e. too directly representational.

Now this criticism is one which runs parallel to one raised against Sir Basil Spence as well, and to answer it we ought now to see the two last parts not yet looked at. One is the CHAPEL OF CHRIST THE SERVANT or GUILDS CHAPEL, the Cinderella of the cathedral, with its even light and its lack of atmosphere – in spite of the Crown of Thorns hanging in the middle, by *Geoffrey Clarke*. (Yet this even light must have been intended, for with it comes a view of the workaday world of trades outside, i.e. the life-blood of Coventry and its guilds for which the chapel is named.)

The other is the CHAPEL OF CHRIST IN GETHSEMANE, the smallest in the cathedral. There are only a few benches in it, for intimate devotion, and the feeling is one of being in a cave. On the back wall in ceramics the large, consciously Byzantine angel of Gethsemane and a panel of the sleeping disciples by *Steven Sykes*. The entrance side is a screen with a large wrought-iron Crown of Thorns designed by Sir Basil himself. So here we are back at the criticism of the furnishings and the building as corny.

What is meant by that? That it appeals to all? For it does. Still today, as in 1964 when this was first written, thousands go on pilgrimage and queue outside to be let in. Do they come to pray in the house of God that was bombed and rebuilt? No – they come to admire a work of architecture and works of art. And many of them still are

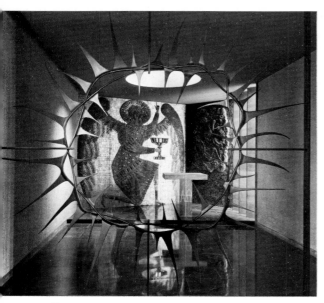

24. COVENTRY
Chapel of Gethsemane, with Crown of Thorns

the same people who in 1952 called the design 'this un-usually ugly factory . . .. resembling a cockroach . . . the gasholder on one side and the glorified dustbin on the other . . . an utter monstrosity . . . a concrete disgrace.' These were the people who wanted their cathedrals still imi-tation-Gothic or imitation-Early Christian. (The most recent 'new cathedral' in England then was Guildford, q.v. in the companion volume.) Could Sir Basil Spence have convinced them so spectacularly if he had not thought from the beginning in terms of a building conducive to worship? Had he been entirely uncompromising, he would not only have had no chance of winning the competition and building the building, he would also have had no chance of winning those for whom he built. And to think of them in the first place surely is true, spiritual, functional-ism.

At the same time there is of course a danger to aesthetic values nowadays in thinking exclusively of pleasing the consumer. We all know what happens in show business, where that is the sole consideration. The letter from which I have just quoted shows that this was not Sir Basil's attitude. He visualized something fully to satisfy himself and yet capable of convincing worshippers at large. And satisfying himself implied of course satisfying other mod-ern architects, critics of architecture, and those laymen susceptible to architecture in the C20. In this also, at least in my opinion, he succeeded. Even internationally speak-ing, the cathedral acts with a high emotive power. (On its power to 'send' us, see also Liverpool's Anglican cathedral,

below.) And it has moreover plenty of subtleties which can be appreciated coolly – such as the walls of the Chapel of Unity, the position and shape of the baptistery, the inter-locking of old and new building.

Not that a building on this scale can hope to silence all criticism. Criticism from those in whom religious emo-tions do not exist can perhaps be neglected. But those also who insist on a church being a church and who are more-over sympathetic to Sir Basil's modes of expression are left in doubt on certain major points. I can only sum up my own. They are these. If the rib-vault is not a rib-vault but a canopy, it ought to have been separated more demon-stratively from the walls. If the stained glass of the aisles was intended to throw all light on to the altar, it ought not to have been given the clear glass wall at the w end as a competitor. w in the cathedral is s, and so on a fine day light streams in from the entrance, and silences the stained glass of the aisles. The form of the flèche is perhaps not a major point. But it does not seem to participate in the mood of the rest of the building.

A last major point, however, is the furnishings. The canopies of the choir stalls tend to interfere with the fullness of the impact of the tapestry. And, more subtly, the process of appreciating Geoffrey Clarke and the process of appreciating Epstein are so different that one may not find it easy to apply both of them in the same building. One can fully understand Sir Basil's intention. Here, he felt from the start, is the C20 cathedral. It must not be an architect's drawingboard job, it must be alive like its medieval predecessors. And they, at the time when they were the centre of spiritual life, were cram-full of orna-ments and fitments, nor was there one man to impose his style or taste on them (though bishops such as Stapledon at Exeter and Cosin at Durham did their best). So let this new building's contents also be representative of the good things going on now, the easier ones and the hard ones, provided once again they would – in Sir Basil's conviction – have a chance of conveying their message.

This is as far as one can go, or at least as I can go. The same arguments might have been used and the result might have been an aesthetic nonentity or an aesthetic disaster. If that is not so, if the cathedral as a whole and with what it contains has become a contribution to English C20 art, this is due to the genuine humility, the resource-fulness and the imagination of its begetter. By abandoning all period forms without abandoning what might be called a Gothic spirit, this cathedral can please the many, while by subtleties of design it pleases the few. And it has inter-national validity – there can be no doubt.

Four works of art have been added since the 1960s. In the ruins, former s choir aisle: Epstein's massive 'Ecce Homo' of 1935. – New 's' aisle, near the baptistery: wooden cross with intaglio carving, by Jundrich Severa. – Same aisle, 'E' end: abstract metal sculpture, 'The Plumbline and the City', by *Clarke Fitz-Gerald*. – Lady Chapel: sculpture in polyester resin of Our Lady by *John Bridgeman*.

For the surrounding pre-war remains and post-war redevelopment of Coventry, see the latest edition of B of E *Warwickshire*.

## Derby

<small>CATHEDRAL CHURCH OF ALL SAINTS</small> *Anglican*

(Based on B of E *Derbyshire*, 1978, as revised by Elizabeth Williamson, further revised, with information from George McHardy and Anthony New.)

Cathedral since 1927. Until then the chief parish church of the town, with a pre-Conquest collegiate foundation. The w tower of *c.* 1520–32 is one of the biggest Perp towers in England, testifying to the town's trading prosperity. The rest of the church was rebuilt 1723–5 (over older burial vaults: see Cavendish monuments below) to a design by *James Gibbs*, by then known for his London churches (St Mary-le-Strand and, just begun, St Martin-in-the-Fields). His design for All Saints is illustrated in his *A Book of Architecture* (1728). The builders were *William* (†1724) and *Francis Smith* of Warwick, who also built St Philip's Birmingham (q.v.). There was restoration work in 1873–4 by *J. Young*, who discarded some of Gibbs's furnishings; in 1904–5 by *Temple Moore*; and in 1928 by *Sir Ninian Comper*. With a view to adapting the church to cathedral functions, Comper in 1939 made plans, revised in the early 1950s, for a large overpowering extension of choir and sanctuary raised above ancillary rooms; followed by completely new and more sympathetic plans by *Sebastian Comper* in 1954 and 1958, finally accepted and work begun in 1967, completed 1972 after his retirement in 1969 by *Anthony New* of Seely & Paget Partnership.

Both the C16 and the C18 parts are of high quality. The tower, replacing one demolished *c.* 1475, was begun by 1520. The mason first mentioned in 1527 was *John Otes*, who had worked under Wastell at King's College, Cambridge. (For Wastell, see Canterbury, Peterborough and Bury St Edmunds.) In outline it is tall, square, broad and stately, the one powerful accent in the skyline of Derby. It has three tall storeys, all highly decorated with friezes, canopies etc. The buttresses nearly meet at the angles. The ground floor has a big w door, the second stage large blank three-light windows with four-centred tops and blank decorative niches. The bell-openings on the third stage are equally large, of four lights with panelled tracery. The top of the tower has ornamented battlements, and very big pinnacles.

The body of the church appears low compared with the C16 work – intentionally so. 'The plainness of the Building makes it less expensive and renders it more suitable to the old steeple', Gibbs said. The exterior is a combination of the first design for St Mary-le-Strand and an early, rejected design for St Martin's. It spreads out broadly in only one storey of large round-headed windows, and is crowned by a balustrade. Door and window surrounds show a surfeit of Gibbs's favourite motif of intermittent rustication. As the windows are all separated from each other by coupled pilasters, the rhythm of the sides is comfortably unhurried. Gibbs's church had a rectangular E end with a big pediment across nave and aisles and a Venetian window. The window was removed when the C20 E extension was built. The two-bay-long retrochoir follows the C18 elevation, without Gibbs's rustication, and ends in a shallow V-shaped apse. Underneath, the Chapter Room, Song School etc. present a plain façade to Full Street.

The INTERIOR also appears broad and relatively low. It is designed on the same principle as Gibbs's St Martin-in-the-Fields. Nave and aisles are separated by Tuscan columns on tall pedestals (to allow for box pews). The aisles are groin-vaulted, the nave tunnel-vaulted. The arcade arches cut into the tunnel-vault. The vaults are rather poorly decorated with panels. The C20 retrochoir has a plain groin-vault and a minimum of ornamentation. It is tactful but dull. The whole interior was given a new colour scheme of mauvish-grey, white and gold by *Anthony New*, 1972.

FURNISHINGS

PULPIT, given 1876. With tester on two columns, 1945 by *Sir Ninian Comper*. – BALUSTER FONT in Pentelicon marble, made in 1974 to a design in *Gibbs's A Book of Architecture* (1728). – BALDACCHINO by *Sebastian Comper*, of Early Christian type but strictly classical: canopy on Corinthian columns. – In the chancel, SEDILIA, 1941 by *Sir Ninian Comper*; CANONS' STALLS, reconstructed 1972 from choir stalls of 1894 by *Temple Moore*. – On the s the C17 CORPORATION PEW with wrought-iron mace and sword stands (see below), typical of a civic church; on the N the COUNTY COUNCIL PEW with wrought-iron symbols of local government by *New*, 1972. – PANELLING and raised seat in the N chancel chapel (consistory court), C17. – WEST GALLERY. 1732–3, on fluted Ionic columns, extended over the aisles in 1841. The old centre part curves back gracefully and carries the organ, by *Compton*, 1939; case by *Sebastian Comper*, 1963. – BISHOP'S THRONE. C18; from Constantinople; acquired in the 1920s. – CUPBOARD at the w end of the N aisle. Early C18, richly carved, Flemish. – CHANCEL SCREEN. The most important possession of the cathedral. Wrought ironwork by

*Robert Bakewell*, the brilliant local smith who died in 1752. Side sections by him considerably altered. The screens to the chancel chapels were assembled *c.* 1900. Also by *Bakewell* the COMMUNION RAILS, the STANDS for mace and sword belonging to the Corporation Pew (see above), the SUPPORT of the altar table in the s chapel, the RAILS to Thomas Chambers's monument (see below) at the E end of the N aisle, and the W gates outside the church. – STAINED GLASS. (From the E window, now in store: Crucifixion by *Clayton & Bell*, 1863, in memory of the Prince Consort: surprisingly vigorous for its date; strong colours, good faces.) E windows of both aisles 1967, designed by *Ceri Richards* and made by *Patrick Reyntiens*, representing All Souls (N) and All Saints (S). Vivid blues and yellows in conflict with the later colour scheme.

MONUMENTS. Alabaster slab to Sub-Dean Lawe, *c.* 1480; incised figure surrounded by architecture with smaller decorative figures; the workmanship mediocre (N chancel chapel). – Timber monument with decayed timber effigy, small figures of mourners, and fragment of a gisant or cadaver below (perhaps Sub-Dean Johnson, *c.* 1527; S aisle). – Elizabeth Countess of Shrewsbury † 1607, better known as Bess of Hardwick. Standing wall-monument, designed by *John Smythson*. In 1601 it was finished 'and wanteth nothing but setting up'. Recumbent effigy of alabaster, not especially good. Black columns to the l. and r., and between them a shallow coffered arch. Back wall with inscription and strapwork cartouche. Above the entablature two obelisks and a tall central achievement. The monument stands in the s chancel chapel, which was the Cavendish Chapel. In the middle stood until 1876 the monument to the second Earl of Devonshire († 1628) by *Edward Marshall*. In the (pre-Gibbs) vault beneath the chapel over forty members of the family were buried between 1607 and 1848 (see the mounted coffin plates): access staircase at E end of S aisle. – Richard Croshawe † 1631, erected 1636, wall-monument with kneeling figure (N aisle). – William Allestry † 1655, and two wives † 1638 and 1674, wall-monument with sarcophagus inscribed to the first wife's 'Beautiful Dust', i.e. the monument erected between 1638 and 1655. No effigies (N aisle). – Sir William Wheler † 1666, large wall-monument with two busts high up (N aisle). – Thomas Chambers † 1726, and his wife † 1735, by *Roubiliac*, a tripartite composition with the centre filled by the inscription below a pediment; in the sides two fine busts in circular niches. – Sarah Ballidon † 1736, wall-monument to a design in Gibbs's *Book of Architecture* (1728). – Caroline Countess of Bessborough † 1760, daughter of the third Duke of Devonshire, by *Rysbrack*. Standing wall-monument; seated allegorical figure with bust behind to her l. on a bracket, the whole against a black pyramid. – William Ponsonby Earl of Bessborough † 1793, by *Nollekens*, wall-monument with

bust above a sarcophagus. – Richard Bateman † 1821, signed by *Chantrey* (who was born on the Derbyshire border), 1822, wall-monument with weeping seated female by an urn. – Mary Elizabeth Chichester † 1830, by *Sir R. Westmacott*, small wall-monument with reclining figure on a couch in a gently recessed oval panel. – Innumerable minor wall-tablets. The following two are signed: Thomas Swanwick † 1814, by *James Sherwood* of Derby. – John Hope † 1819, by *Joseph Hall the Younger* of Derby.

The impulse to rebuild All Saints' Church was part of the C18 surge of local energies that made the Silk Mill on the nearby riverbank the earliest factory in England. Although a London architect was sent for to design the new church and the builders were Warwick men, Derby craftsmen were then producing superb ironwork, silks and porcelains. For merchants' houses still standing in the streets near the cathedral, despite the C19 railway age and C20 clearances, see the latest edition of B of E *Derbyshire*.

# Durham

CATHEDRAL CHURCH OF CHRIST
AND THE BLESSED MARY THE VIRGIN    *Anglican*

(Based on B of E *County Durham*, 1983, mainly as revised by Elizabeth Williamson with information from Bridget Cherry, Ian Curry, Ian Doyle, Jane Geddes, Katharine Galbraith, Roger Norris, Martin Snape, Christopher Wilson, Richard Halsey, Jill Allibone, and Richard Benny of Donald Insall & Associates, and further slightly revised, also with information from S. E. Dykes Bower.)

Plan, Fig. 26, from the *Builder*, 1893, by C. C. Hodges.

Some references (see Recent Literature): principally papers in B.A.A. (1977) 1980; also Bony 1979.

Durham is one of the great experiences of Europe to the eyes of those who appreciate architecture, and to the minds of those who understand architecture. The group of cathedral, castle and monastery on the rock can only be compared to Avignon and Prague, and (by circumstance and planning) the old town has hardly been spoilt and is to almost the same degree the visual foil to the monuments that it must have been two and five hundred years ago. The River Wear forms so close a loop that the town is surrounded by it on three sides. On the land side the two medieval bridges are a bare 900 ft from each other. The position was ideal for a fortress, and it is ideal for the picture of a town. For a cathedral it is as unusual as for a monastery.

The combination of the three at Durham has its historical reasons. The position of the shrine of St Cuthbert in the North and near the Scottish border was an exposed one. To guard the land and to guard the shrine was so much the same that as early as the C11 the bishop was also earl. Nearly all the temporal privileges which in other counties belonged to the king, in the County Palatine were the bishop's. He had his own Parliament (Durham sent no representatives to London) and his own coinage, his subjects were bidden to do military service under him, not under the king, and licences 'to crenellate', that is to build castles, were granted by him. His position was in fact like that of the great episcopal rulers of Germany rather than that of the other English bishops. Moreover, ever since Anglo-Saxon times the religious community of Durham (as of Lindisfarne and many others) had been one of monks under a bishop. So, when the Normans reformed the see, Durham became one of the monastic cathedrals of England, as were Canterbury, Ely and several others, a complete anomaly from the point of view of Continental episcopal organization, but one familiar in England. Hence the unforgettable group of ecclesiastic, military and domestic buildings at Durham. Avignon and Prague have been mentioned, but what distinguishes Durham visually from them is again something exceedingly English. The pictures of the buildings on the hill which one remembers all have foregrounds of green. The most moving one, from the Prebends' Bridge, in fact shows the cathedral rising straight above the tops of the venerable trees up the steep bank, as if it were the vision of a Caspar David Friedrich or Schinkel. Verdure mellows what would otherwise be too domineering, domineering the castle, domineering the site of the cathedral, domineering the architecture of the cathedral, and domineering inside the cathedral the throne of the bishop raised higher than the shrine of the saint.

The relics of St Cuthbert were brought from Lindisfarne after Danish raids to Chester-le-Street in 883 and thence in 995 to Durham, where they rested for three years in a temporary church, probably of timber. A stone church, the ALBA ECCLESIA or 'the larger church', was consecrated by Bishop Aldhun in 998 and demolished by Bishop de St-Calais in 1093. No structural remains have yet been identified. The fullest description of it is the eye-witness account written down in the late C12, which tells of two stone towers with bronze pinnacles, one at the W end and one over the choir. From this, it has been accepted that the church was cruciform with a crossing tower (cf. Norton, Co. Durham, and many Continental parallels). The W tower, left unfinished by Aldhun, was completed and dedicated by his successor, Eadmund, between 1021 and 1042. W. H. St John Hope, in a fundamental paper published in 1909, deduced the plan and location of the White Church from excavations in the SW corner of the cloister garth and detailed inspection of the claustral buildings. Some of the claustral buildings, planned in relation to the White Church at various times between 1071 and 1091, still survive (see *Cloister* below): the W, N and E walls of the 'prison' and most of the E wall of the prior's hall undercroft are pre-1083 (perhaps even pre-1071, as Mr Markuson suggests). Important evidence is, of course, the pre-Norman sculpture uncovered mostly from the foundations of the chapter-house apse during the 1874 excavations and now on display in the Monks' Dormitory (see *Cloister* below).

The chronicle of Symeon of Durham, written c. 1105, and continued at various times during the C12, tells us most of what we know about the Norman church. Bishop Walcher, who had begun in the 1070s to rebuild the monastery for the Benedictine community he planned to introduce, was murdered in 1080. William de St-Calais introduced the Benedictines, continued the monastery, and in 1092 decided to build a new church. He laid the foundation stone on 11 August 1093. William of St-Calais or St Carileph, as they anglicized his name here, was a Frenchman; he had been a secular priest at Rouen, and then became a monk at St-Calais in Maine and abbot of St-Vincent at Le Mans. William the Conqueror called him to Durham in 1080. In 1088 he had to flee the land and spent three years in Normandy before returning. He must have been familiar with the great abbeys of Normandy, St-Étienne and the Trinité at Caen and Jumièges, as well as much in other parts of France. Yet his building was not French, nor indeed entirely Normandy-Norman. It had from the beginning Anglo-Norman features, which is perhaps not to be wondered at, as Durham came late among the great cathedrals and abbeys of William's new kingdom. Canterbury and St Augustine's at Canterbury, Battle, Old Sarum, St Albans, Winchester, Lincoln, Ely, Worcester, London, Gloucester, Rochester, Chester, all had been begun before Durham. He must have had plenty of funds

accumulated, for building went on so rapidly that by the time he had been dead three years and a successor was at last appointed (that is in 1099), this successor, Ranulph Flambard, known in political history more than in architectural history, found the church 'usque navem . . . jam factam'. So by then choir, transepts and crossing, and as much of the nave as had to be put up to help abut the crossing, were already complete. It will be shown below that five years later the choir must also have been vaulted. The nave was built by Flambard gradually as offerings accrued. The continuator of Symeon, our chief source, tells us that he erected 'navem circumdatis parietibus usque testudinem' of Durham. The 'testudo', i.e. the vault, was put on between Flambard's death in 1128 and 1133.

Additions to the church began early: the galilee was finished by 1189, the w towers in the early c 13. A new E work, the Nine Altars transept, and new main choir vault to replace the old one full of 'fissures and cracks' was decided on in 1235 and begun in 1242. Building took forty years, as long as all of the c 12 work. The last major medieval work was the building of the top stage of the tower, struck by lightning in 1429 and again in 1459. Not begun before 1464, it was being finished in 1487–8. On the uses of the late-medieval cathedral buildings there survives the c 16 *Rites of Durham*, written down by an ex-monk just after the Reformation (Surtees Society, 1903).

Although ecclesiastical art declined in England after the Reformation, the c 17 saw its revival in County Durham in the activities of that remarkable man John Cosin († 1672). After graduating from Cambridge in 1610 he became secretary to John Overall, Bishop of Lichfield, who with Lancelot Andrewes was an early exponent of the revival of the 'beauty of holiness'. (Cosin's monument to Overall is in the ambulatory at Norwich.) Cosin came to Durham in 1623 to be chaplain to Laud's follower Bishop Neile; in 1633 he became Master of Peterhouse, Cambridge, and in 1640 Dean of Peterborough; he fled to France in 1643 and returned in 1660, when he was made Bishop of Durham. A High Church man to whom ritual pomp and circumstance meant much, Cosin commissioned for many churches in his diocese furnishings in which medieval forms were consciously revived. At the cathedral the piled-up canopy of his font cover (1663) emphasizes the font's liturgical significance as its late Perp models did (cf. Newcastle), and his choir stalls (1665) may imitate those destroyed by Scots in the 1650s. Yet their carving is Baroque, Carolean. This hybrid Gothic revival celebrated the restoration of church and monarchy.

26. DURHAM Plan from the *Builder*, 1893 (see p. 71)

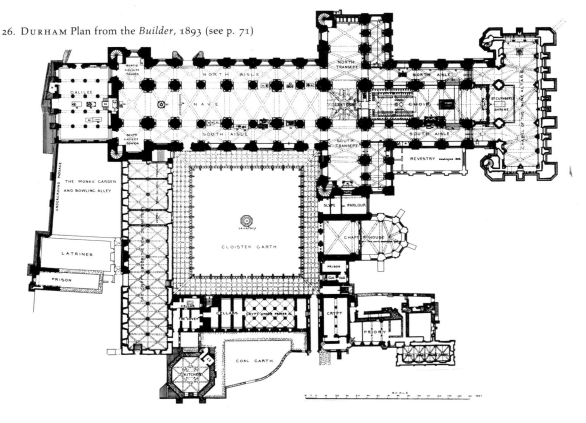

Attention to the fabric waned for some time. There was a thorough and thoroughly insensitive c 18 restoration. *Mylne* reported on the fabric in 1777 but a local architect, *John Wooler*, was employed as consultant, with *George Nicholson* as site architect and Thomas Hogg as financial clerk of works. Their worst crime was to cure the deep erosion of the stone by chipping away the surface to a depth of on average two inches, which reduced of course the dimensions of all features and flattened the mouldings. Wooler also suggested rebuilding the porch without its upper chamber, and the parapets and the upper parts of the turrets of the Nine Altars and of the N transept, all of which was done during the next twenty years (and is described in the text below). Mr *Morpeth* replaced Nicholson in 1793, with *Wyatt* appointed consultant in 1794. Wyatt's designs for a number of devastating 'improvements', including a Fonthill-like spire for the tower and demolition of the galilee (he got as far as removing the roof coverings), for a carriage sweep, were successfully combated by the London Society of Antiquaries. His major work, at the E end, was finished in 1798. Morpeth replaced the nave roof with one of lower pitch, and substituted slate for lead on the roofs. The old medieval revestry s of the choir went in 1801–2: the aim seems to have been to purify the Norman cathedral of all later accretions. *William Atkinson* and the famous plasterer *Bernasconi* in 1804–9 repaired the tower with Parker's cement whose 'Brown Tint adds highly to the sublimity of the Building'.

The next main phase of the restoration began in 1827 with the refacing in fine sandstone ashlar of most of the s front by *Bonomi* and his mason *Thomas Jackson*. Throughout the s front and s gable of the Nine Altars (1827), the s choir clerestory (1830) and the s transept gable (1835), Bonomi made a conscious effort to reproduce the original mouldings and capitals. In 1839 Thomas's son *George Jackson* became clerk of works and was required to work with the consultant architect, *Anthony Salvin*, who had been appointed by the chapter in 1834. Salvin, however, did not work on the cathedral itself until 1843, when he repaired the dormitory undercroft. It was Jackson's successor, *George Pickering*, who in 1843 finished the refacing of the choir s front by replacing the aisle windows to the original designs recorded by Jackson. Only the hoodmoulds, running below instead of piercing the string-course, were different. Salvin was less circumspect with replacing the choir N aisle windows for which he borrowed 'superior' Dec designs in 1848. With Salvin's approval all the other originally Norman windows were restored to their Norman form by Pickering in 1847–50 and (N transept E aisle windows) 1850–7.

Meanwhile in 1844–7 drastic measures were being taken inside to purify the cathedral of post-medieval accretions. Firstly, in 1844 Cosin's stalls were pushed back between the piers to make more room for seating in the choir. Then, in Wyatt's spirit, in order to restore 'the original uninterrupted view of the whole length of the Cathedral' the feretory screen, partitions in the choir and transept aisles, the font and canopy were moved and the reredos of Bishop Langley's altar was taken from in front of the W portal, where doors were hung instead. The restored Neville screen became the *point de vue* when Cosin's choir screen ('after designs wholly inappropriate to a place of worship') and the organ were dismantled in 1847. Pickering may have been to blame: Salvin's name is directly linked only with the new neo-Norman pulpit (1845), font (1846) and altar rails (1849).

In 1858 *E. R. Robson* was appointed clerk of works and *Sir G. G. Scott* consulted about the tower. Together they restored it (1858–61), thickening the facing and heightening the battlements. (Their removal of cement and restoration of mouldings was done so well, few now realize it was restored at all, Mr Dykes Bower points out.) Like Wyatt, Scott seemed to think an extra accent was necessary, but his proposal for a lantern based on that of St Nicholas, Newcastle, was rejected on structural grounds. The N side of the galilee was restored to the good antiquarian designs of *E. R. Robson* (who had restored the w side in 1863) by *C. Hodgson Fowler*, who succeeded Robson in 1864, and became architect to the Dean and Chapter in 1885. Fowler, Scott's former pupil, probably should be credited with some of Scott's 1870–5 restoration and refurbishment of the choir. Most criticized of this scheme has been Scott's choir screen, which, however, without dominating the E–W vista gave it the necessary punctuation and a sense of scale, with more simplicity than many of his screens, to suit this mighty setting (see *Furnishings*, crossing, below).

The cloisters had been repaired *c.* 1763–77 while Thomas Hogg was clerk of works. Who it was who designed the rather bleak tracery is not known. Other monastic buildings were restored and altered during the c 19: *P. C. Hardwick* in 1849–53 converted the dormitory into Dean and Chapter Library; *Salvin* put new windows and a new s portal in the refectory in 1858; and *Hodgson Fowler* in 1892 rebuilt the chapter house, which had had minor repairs in 1858.

The c 20 work has in general been more discreet. *Sir Mervyn Macartney*, who took over as cathedral architect from 1910 to 1920, made major repairs to the vault in 1915. *W. D. Caröe*, brought in as consultant in 1913–15, repaired the crossing tower in 1922 and designed the Durham Light Infantry Chapel in 1924. The w towers were repaired in 1930 by *R. A. Cordingley*, cathedral architect *c.* 1928–35. He was succeeded as resident architect until 1969 by his partner *D. McIntyre*. *Stephen Dykes Bower* was occasionally consulted after 1938, on the Prior Castell clock for example. More than any other of the C 20 architects mentioned, *George Pace*, consultant from 1955 to 1975, has left his mark in characteristic furnishings and some restoration (e.g. in the dormitory undercroft, the so-called Spendement). *Ian Curry* was appointed his successor in 1976.

For those who like such comparisons, Durham is about as long as York and Lincoln, a bit longer than Norwich and Peterborough, but shorter than Canterbury.

As for its character, there are cathedrals which remain in one's memory as a procession of architecture through the ages (Canterbury, for instance), and there are others which, whatever later centuries may have added to them, are essentially of one period. Thus it is at Lincoln, thus at Durham. Nothing of Durham Cathedral is earlier than 1093, and with the exception of visually so separate a part as the Nine Altars, with the exception of the great W, N and S windows, and with the exception of the tops of all the towers, nothing essential to the general impression is later than the late C 12. Most of what makes Durham Durham is of the short space of time between 1093 and 1133, and of that phase, the phase of Vézelay and Laach, it is one of the most perfect and also historically most interesting buildings in Europe. Of its aesthetic perfection more will be said later; as for its historical significance, an introductory remark must be made now.

Durham, as far as can be ascertained, possessed the earliest rib-vaults ever ventured upon in the West. (This is not the place to discuss the priority of Durham or Lombardy. In any case the early rib-vaults of Lombardy are low and heavy, they lie on low naves and have broad ribs of plain rectangular section. They don't aspire to the effect of effortless growth heralded in the Durham vaults.) Now rib-vaults are supposed by the layman to be one of the hallmarks of the Gothic style, but the Gothic style was created over thirty years later than the closing of the first vaults at Durham, and it was created in France, at St-Denis. What is the essential function of the rib-vault? Aesthetically it completes a process which can also be watched in Gothic walls. It is the process by which the inert masses of masonry which constitute a building are made for the eye to disappear. We follow the long shafts up a Gothic wall and see the tall openings of arcades and windows and overlook what is left of solid walls. But a vault must remain completely solid. It cannot be made transparent. So the ribs allow us to go on seeing vigorous, slender lines of action and forget the massive surfaces between. A tunnel-vault or even a groined vault are mass lying heavily on the walls. A rib-vault seems always far lighter, and as a rule really is. For as a rule the transverse arches and the ribs are built separately on their own centering, and the cells are then filled in with less substantial masonry. That is also the case at Durham, and it is almost certain that here this system, which is the constructional foundation of Gothic masons,

was invented. John Bilson (*Archaeological Journal*, 1922) wrote this: 'In the course of the repairs of 1915, when the plastering of the cells was stripped, it became possible to ascertain the thickness of the cells in certain places, and the manner of their construction. In the eastern bays their thickness may reach 20 inches or more. I measured it as 18 inches in three places in the second and third bays from the crossing. In the western bays the thickness is less, varying from 12 to 16 inches, and averaging about 14 inches. The cells are built of coursed rubble, with stones of irregular length up to about 18 inches, and generally from 2½ to 3 inches thick on the soffit, with some thicker courses (about 4 inches) in the lower parts of the cells. Between the tops of the diagonal and transverse ribs and the cell, there is always a wide joint (of 2 inches or so) which received the boards of the centering on which the cells were built, and some fragments of oak boards were found in the course of the repairs.

These observations refer to the nave, vaulted *c.* 1130, and not to the earlier choir. But John Bilson proved beyond doubt that the choir also was rib-vaulted from the beginning, that is *c.* 1104, as indeed the choir aisles still are. The designer of the Durham choir was thus probably as great a technical inventor as he was an architect. The evidence of the building suggests it was only the vault of the choir that was planned from the beginning; the transepts were not originally intended to be vaulted. Professor Bony has suggested that the N transept received its vault *c.* 1110, the S transept and nave vaults followed by 1130, giving Durham the distinction of being the first major English church to be covered entirely with a stone vault ('Le premier projet de Durham' in *Urbanisme et architecture, Études . . . en honneur de P. Lavedan*, Paris, 1954).

But to call Durham Cathedral a Gothic building because it is the first to use Gothic methods and a Gothic motif, the rib-vault, would be manifestly wrong. In spirit Durham is still entirely Romanesque, and it is spirit that determines architecture, not technique.

THE NORMAN CHURCH: EXTERIOR

Durham Cathedral on its rock is so overwhelming an apparition that no one will regret the time spent on obtaining the best general views of the whole building before studying its details (prefaced for railway travellers by a privileged moving panorama from high ground). The best views are, in my opinion, from Prebends' Bridge to see the towers above the trees, from South Street to see the W front dead on, from Gilesgate to see the whole N side above the town, from the S end of Church Street for the corresponding view from the S, and from Palace Green to get a close yet complete picture. It is here that we shall begin to examine the exterior.

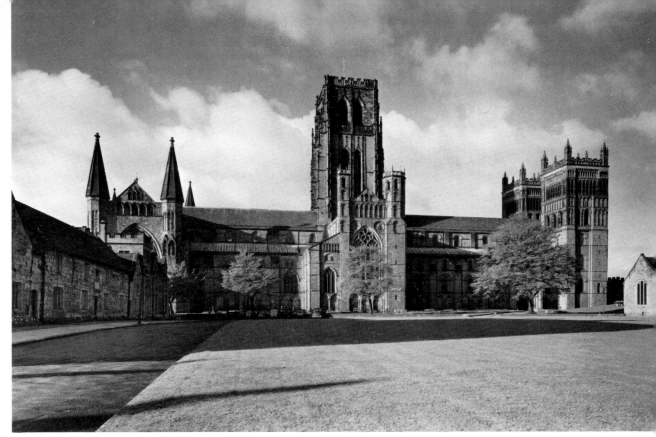

27. DURHAM View from the north

Medieval churches were usually started at the E end. Durham was no exception. But the E end was altered in the C13. So we shall open the book of the cathedral at the junction between that 'novum opus' and the original work and then follow it to the W (taking N and S sides together, which will be tiresome to the visitor) and end by the galilee, before turning to the Gothic E end.

The CHOIR is divided into bays by broad flat buttresses. The thin string-courses separating the storeys from each other are taken round the buttresses. The ground floor has large blank arcades, two for each interior bay. The outer and inner orders rest on columns with cushion capitals (the most elementary form the Romanesque style had conceived) but have arches with quite articulated mouldings, although restorations have made the detail of most of these unreliable. (But see those on the side within the masons' yard.) The arches stand on a plinth with a square chamfered projection, which continues across the buttresses – an unusual form of plinth occurring inside the building as well. Every one of the aisle windows above this dado is a different pattern. Those on the S side were restored in 1843 by *Pickering* from *Jackson*'s drawings of the original designs of c. 1438–9 by *William Chaumere* and *Bell*. On the

N side the windows were renewed by *Salvin* in 1848, using as models examples from well-known churches (Holbeach and Sleaford, Lincs; Boughton Aluph, Kent). Above these windows those of the gallery are of the earliest design again, very small twins each in a larger blank arched panel and the two together in a joint panel with a depressed rounded arch, all very primitive-looking. Perhaps the smallness of these windows and the amount of solid wall left finds its explanation in the thought that the temerity of the vaulting inside called for the greatest solidity of abutment. On the S side the tympanum of these gallery panels has flat lozenge decoration, the earliest piece of geometrical surface decoration in the cathedral, but mostly refaced in new stone in 1843. As to its date, this question must be postponed for a short while. The clerestory has one sizeable window per bay, with nook-shafts and a moulded arch. They were restored in 1830 (S) by *Bonomi*, 1847–50 (N) by *Pickering*. Only the easternmost bays on each side, which belong with the Nine Altars transept, are different: double lancets with Y-tracery and nook-shafts in the clerestory, a more pointed relieving arch over the gallery windows, and a dado cut down to accommodate a large C13 aisle window. Beneath it some of the grotesque corbel heads from the corbel table which finished the elevation. The earlier roofs were higher than they are now, as can be seen from their waterline against the crossing tower.

The present CROSSING TOWER (218 ft high) is Norman only in its crossing piers and arches: everything above clerestory parapet level is now C15. How high it went up beyond that, no one can say. That a tower existed from the C13 if not earlier is known from medieval references. (The chronicle attributes the great tower to Prior Darlington 1258–72 and 1286–90: it was altered in 1430–7 after being struck by lightning.) About 1465 a new crossing tower was begun. It is of two stages, the higher one being an addition of *c*. 1483–90, and faced with different stone by *Scott* and *E. R. Robson* in 1858–61, to replace *William Atkinson*'s Roman cement of 1804–9. (More refacing by *W. D. Caröe* in 1921–3.) Two of the masons are probably known by name. The master mason to the cathedral in the 1480s was *Thomas Barton*. He was succeeded in 1488 by *John Bell Jr.* The lower stage has on each side two very long two-light windows with one transom each and simple Perp tracery. They are set close together. Above them is a broad band of panelled crenellations meant to be the crowning motif of the tower. At this level, part of the medieval roof structure survives. Then, when the top stage was put on, the same kind of window was used, but not so long. The real battlements are pierced, and slightly heightened in 1858–61. The tower is strengthened by set-back buttresses, decorated with three tiers of statues under canopies and with pinnacles at first parapet level. It is a sound and robust design, even if out of keeping with the Norman work. It adds a decisive accent in a place where William de St-Calais and his great mason would not have wanted it. But the Perp style adored big and tall single towers, be they at the w end of a parish church as at Boston or Louth, or above the crossing of a cathedral like Bell Harry at Canterbury or our Durham tower.

The TRANSEPTS on their E sides now give the most complete picture of the character of the earliest work, strong and forbidding, though a little mellowed by the beautiful, almost Pentelic light brown of the stone. The system is almost the same as in the choir, except in the E aisle, where instead of Dec windows there are large Norman ones with nook-shafts, renewed 1843 (N), 1856–7 (S), and the dado has only one arch per bay. Neither of the transept fronts is in its pristine state. On the N side, under Prior Fossor (1341–74), a very large Dec window of six lights was put in, plus one for the aisle. The date seems to be *c*. 1360, and it is, therefore, interesting to note that in the two vertical bars to the l. and r. of the big five-plus-one lobed star a first sign of Perp feeling appears. This transitional type can be seen as an amalgam of the Perp lozenge pattern pioneered by Ramsey (Old St Paul's cloister, London, 1332) and the Dec star pattern he used in the provinces

(e.g. Lichfield, 1337). In the spandrels two roundels carved originally with two monks: an early example of the use of figures to decorate an English Romanesque building; now with C18 figures of a prior and Bishop Hugh of le Puiset from his seal. On the S side the monastic buildings abut against the transept. The disposition must, therefore, be different. The first floor is now blocked by the Song School (see *Cloister* below), but inside the transept a very large centrally placed blocked Norman window can be recognized. Above it is a large Perp window of six lights, probably put in between 1420 and 1440. The aisle S window is restored Norman, which returns us to the other Norman evidence. At the top of the aisle ends of both transepts is a blank arcade of intersecting arches. In the N transept 'nave' end, above the Fossor window, the same arcaded motif is used. The gable above was rebuilt in C13 style by *Nicholson*, who replaced the raised lattice pattern in 1780–94. On the S side the decoration of the gable (restored by *Bonomi* in 1835) with two rows of arcading, one intersecting, is a little different, and an unprecedented all-over lozenge pattern, large and more distinctive than above the gallery windows, appears. Both the transepts have flanking turrets decorated with blank arcading. Those at the w ends, housing spiral staircases, are bigger and end in octagonal tops.

We must now proceed to the NAVE. But before doing so it is well to recall that the church had been finished as far as the nave between 1093 and 1099 and that by 1128 Flambard had finished it up to the vault, which was put on between 1128 and 1133 (see *Introduction*). Flambard's mason was content to follow in William de St-Calais's footsteps. The ground-floor arcades are unchanged, and the aisle windows unchanged. (All the windows were restored to their Norman form in 1847–50 by *Pickering*, who removed the Perp tracery.) Only above these, for the gallery, he permitted himself one large window with nook-shafts instead of the two minute ones, and only here on the S side and on both sides in the clerestory did he begin to use what was to become the standard motif of C12 decoration in England, the zigzag. (On its earliest appearance at Durham, see *Interior*.) Both sides of the nave are identical, though they have lost much of their character due to the N side being dressed back two inches in the 1780–90 restoration and the S side being thoroughly refaced in 1847–50 by *Pickering*.

On the N side near the w end of the nave, in the place usual for the principal porches of English churches, is the main PORTAL, probably totally renewed, with its five orders of shafts projecting in front of the wall, replacing a simple arch. The capitals of a design not otherwise occurring in the cathedral or the county are therefore probably completely fictitious: they are cushion capitals, the upper segment decorated by curved rows of beading, the receding part below closely fluted. Along the entablature a frieze of anthemion. Every other order has a frieze of grouped

zigzags. The Perp-style surround is certainly C18, probably to *Nicholson*'s design, with polygonal turrets and an
ogee arch within the gable, all decorated by blank panelling. Inside, traces of the windows that lit the chamber over
the original two-storey porch. Affixed to the oaken door of
this portal is the celebrated C12 SANCTUARY RING (replica
on the door, original in the treasury), one of the greatest
examples of the power which the Romanesque style could

28. DURHAM Door-knocker, C12.
Original in the treasury, replica on the north door

achieve by stylization. It stands in the front rank of
metalwork of the century, together with the Brunswick
Lion. The different way in which hair and flesh are interpreted in terms of parallel lines should be noted. The fleshy
nose is a system of convex flutings, like rope, the wildly
flickering curls of incised lines. The eyes were of course of
coloured enamel. Representations (1180) on stone fragments in Canterbury Cathedral and on the feet of the
Milan candlestick of *c*. 1200 are closest stylistically. There
were two or more bronze rings on the w door, replaced by
Puiset when he built the galilee. On the door itself stumps
of hinges and traces of the original scrolled ironwork.

The WEST TOWERS were probably begun together with
the nave. They have nothing of the slightly more ornate
character which we find in the upper parts of the nave. This
is, however, present in the GREAT WEST PORTAL, now
blocked by the galilee. It will therefore be referred to under
*Interior*. But it must already here be said that, though it is
ornate, its ornateness is also essentially obtained by a
multiplication of zigzags. The towers have three Norman
stages; only on one does zigzag occur in the windows. The
broad stair-turrets are completely plain, opened only in the
narrowest slits. Between the towers and above the w
doorway is a huge containing arch and there is internal
evidence for a multiple arrangement of Norman windows,
possibly two tiers each of three windows. But this was
replaced by Prior Fossor (1341–74) with a huge seven-light
window still entirely in the Dec style. The tracery cannot
easily be described. Above this runs a narrow Norman
blank arcade in which jambs and arches are all one display
of zigzag. Above this the Norman style is replaced by E.E.,
though when these additions were made is not known. The
forms are early C13 anyway, and go with similar work at
Darlington, Hartlepool, Gateshead, and Sherburn Hospital. The tower tops and the gable have lancet and round-
headed windows and blank shafted arcades. On the towers
there are four tiers, two high, two low. The pierced battlemented parapets with their pinnacles were added about
1801, apparently to *Nicholson & Wooler*'s design. Up to
the Commonwealth the w towers had lead spires (an odd
idea to the present admirer of the cathedral). They were
probably put on in the C14. But the C13 upper stage of the
s w tower internally has triangular squinches as if a stone
spire were intended (Mr Curry). And it must not be
forgotten that, to reconstruct in one's mind a Norman
cathedral, one must think in terms, if not of spires, of
pyramid roofs on w towers and crossing tower. What
makes an even approximate reconstruction impossible,
however, is the fact that, quite apart from the roofs, we do
not know at all how high St-Calais and Flambard wanted
their towers and in what relation of height they wanted
them to each other.

*The Galilee: exterior*

The galilee at the w end is Bishop le Puiset's chief contribution to the cathedral. (His name is sometimes anglicized to
Pudsey.) Its purpose remains obscure. That it was called
'the galilee' and had an altar of the Blessed Virgin is certain
from a charter datable to 1174–89. But by the C14, the
Bishop's Consistory Court was regularly held there, an
arrangement which continued until 1796. We are told, and
evidence has confirmed it, that he began building at the E
end, the more obvious site. Presumably the monks thought
this too near their shrine, so Le Puiset went to the w end

instead, so close to the ravine that he could not have a W entrance. The story that St Cuthbert was such a misogynist that he was disgusted at the idea of admitting women to the E end of the church probably covers a more serious dispute between monks and bishop. It is true though that a line in grey local marble in the floor of the nave just W of the main N portal bay marks how far women were allowed to penetrate into the church. The building was probably inspired by the grand porches of Burgundian churches, no doubt familiar to Le Puiset. While housing a Lady altar (perhaps for the women banned from the church proper), it probably served a number of other purposes, e.g. for gathering processions (see the C16 'Rites') and for ecclesiastical business, probably conducted previously in the bishop's palace, then the castle. (Before 1069 the bishop's house stood on the site of the galilee.) Its part-secular nature may explain its aisled hall form with no reasonable central space for main or Lady altar, as the W door occupied the central aisle.

Its general appearance can only be appreciated from the other side of the river and that can never have been otherwise. The chapel consists of nave and inner and outer aisles, all embattled at a later date. The five parts step down gently in two stages, though, despite conflicting evidence, it seems likely that the roof-line was originally gabled towards the W. Now, the whole galilee is not high and so, seen from the W, appears to the eye no more than an offering at the feet of the cathedral. Of Le Puiset's exterior only the patterning of the W front and the N doorway remain. Against the W front's substructure a tier of blank corbel-like arches, then a tier of blank intersected arches, and then a large lozenge pattern, different from the earlier lozenges in that these were slightly raised scales or tiles, whereas Le Puiset's is a diagonal trellis of thick rope (best seen inside a little chamber in the W wall of the galilee, with access from the galilee). N doorway unblocked and externally redone in 1866 by *E. R. Robson* and *C. Hodgson Fowler*, who renovated the whole N wall. Three orders with zigzag and crenellation motifs in the arches, nothing like as rich as Le Puiset's portals at the castle and in the cloister. *Hodgson Fowler* renewed and modified the C14 N windows. S ones renewed C19 (by *Bonomi*?). Main W windows replaced in the early C15: depressed pointed heads, one transom each and minimum Perp panel tracery.

### The Chapel of the Nine Altars: exterior

Now to the E end, the great 'novum opus' of the cathedral, the EAST TRANSEPT or Chapel of the Nine Altars. It replaced the apsidal E end of St-Calais's church and was planned, it seems, as early as 1235, when an indulgence was granted for contributions to the 'novum opus . . . apud orientalem ecclesiae partem', and begun in 1242 ('Anno Domini MCCXLII incepit Thomas Prior novam fabricam ecclesiae') by Thomas de Melsanby, the then prior. In 1253 the High Altar and five unspecified altars 'in fronte Dunelmensis ecclesiae' were dedicated and the transept was in a state which made it possible for the monks to move in ('Eodem anno intraverunt monachi novum chorum'), possibly while the high altar was moved to allow the old and new work to be joined up, but at that time the chapel may have had only a temporary and comparatively low roof. Or the choir may have been revaulted by then and so classed as new. The S altars of the Nine Altars were dedicated in 1274, but it was not yet complete in 1279, when the last indulgence tried to procure donations 'ad reparacionem novae fabricae Dunelmensis ecclesiae celerius consummandam'.

The conception of an E end stretching out to the N and S just like a transept is most unusual. The form and dimensions of the Nine Altars were taken from the E end of Fountains Abbey in the West Riding, completed by an abbot who ruled from 1220 to 1247. This is a North Country parallel, and, although much has been made of the fact that in 1235 the Bishop of Durham was Richard Poore, who as Bishop of Salisbury had begun the cathedral there, there really are no architectural relations between Salisbury and Durham. (Elias de Derham, who was in charge of building-funds at Salisbury Cathedral 1220–45, is not relevant either: his name was de Dereham, not Durham; he did not accompany Bishop Poore to the North, and only came once, as a witness in 1229.)

The Nine Altars, especially in the interior (see below), is essentially of the northern school. The show front is the E side, and this unfortunately has been greatly interfered with. *Wyatt* restored it with much licence, omitting the canopies with colossal heads of St-Calais and Flambard from the central buttresses and renewing the rose-window, rather thin but roughly like the C15 one already there. So we do not know at all what the great architect's original design was. One has to be careful not to use the present-day term 'architect' too freely in dealing with the master masons of the Middle Ages. In the case of the Nine Altars it is known that at that time one *Richard of Farnham* was 'architector novae fabricae', but whether this means he designed as well as supervised the work is open to speculation. The E end is divided into three times three parts. The angles and the two main inner divisions are marked by broad and strong buttresses, the angles being in addition crowned by turrets. The turrets, of course, repeat at the N W and S W angles of the transept. Their detail is far from reliable: the N turrets are due to *Wooler & George Nicholson c.* 1780; the S E turret is probably by *Morpeth* to Wyatt's design replacing a lead spirelet; the S W one by *Bonomi*, 1828, to a slightly more elaborate design than the original. The three outer bays of the E front on the l. and the r. have three long double-nook-shafted lancet windows, each with smaller single shafted lancets above. The windows are separated by buttresses not as heavy as those making the main division. The centre, instead of the buttresses, has projected uprights, set back only at sill and plinth level, which form hoods to the three main lancets, giving them deep shadow. Above that is the rose-window. The s front of the Nine Altars is divided into two bays by a heavy middle buttress. Each bay has two tiers of two lancet windows (provided with delicate Perp tracery from 1416 to 1446 and restored by *Bonomi* in 1827), a curiously even composition without any gradation to a climax. The master who, after all this had been done or begun, designed the N front must have felt that.

The N front had been started in a similar way as that on the s; see the foundations of the central buttress, like all the N buttresses slightly narrower than the s ones. But the new master (aware no doubt of the glorious E window of the Angel Choir at Lincoln put in about 1275) decided to give the Nine Altars another such window, far larger than any Durham (or the whole North) had seen before. The JOSEPH WINDOW is of six lights, with a three-light intersecting pattern as the main feature and with eleven foiled circles to enliven the spaces between the main intersecting bars. Lincoln also operates entirely with such simple forms, but the motif of intersection is more characteristic of the late than of the high Early English style. It marks the very moment when England left the French pattern of Amiens and set out on her own voyage of discoveries which led her so far away from France and to all the enchantments of the Dec style. The Nine Altars is a very early example of this, and the interior will show how conscious the designer was of its importance. It is less classical than the Westminster–Lincoln system of tracery, as it makes the positions and sizes of the foiled circles a little less logical. At Lincoln you could not alter any size or any location without upsetting the whole composition; here richness begins to have precedence over clarity. The parallels are mostly with buildings of the 1280s and 1290s (St Etheldreda, Holborn, London; Exeter Cathedral Lady Chapel). The fact that the wealthy and ostentatious Bishop Bek (1284–1310) was buried at the foot of it inside (his was the first burial allowed inside the cathedral: presumably it was exceptional munificence that earned him this privilege) suggests a date in the late 1280s. The many hollow chamfers on the jambs support this. Related to the Joseph window, the Y-tracery in the w wall clerestory of the Nine Altars and the intersecting tracery in the E bays of the choir aisles (q.v.).

## THE NORMAN CHURCH: INTERIOR

The character of the work at Durham changed so little between its inception in 1093 and the completion of the nave in 1133 that the visitor, after entering the church by the N portal and sitting down in the nave to abandon himself to his first impressions, can be certain that it is essentially at the design of the first great master that he is looking.

The impression is overpowering. The forms which surround him are domineering to the utmost, without, however, being brutal. The force of the impact is conducted with a supreme mastery. The size of Durham is not greater than that of our other Norman cathedrals. The nave is 201 ft long by 39 ft wide and 73 ft high. That compares, for instance, with the 248 by 40 by 72 ft of Ely or the 174 by 34 by 68 ft of Gloucester. Yet the effect is quite different. That has chiefly two reasons: one the design and proportions of the elevations, the other the shape of the chief members used. As for the elevation, it consists of nave arcade, gallery and clerestory, as in nearly all major Norman churches of England and Normandy. But it could be interpreted in two ways in the direction from w to E, and in two ways in the direction from floor to roof. Concerning the first, all piers could be identical or nearly so as at St-Étienne in Caen and Ely, in which case a rapid and uninterrupted progress towards the altar is symbolized, or they could be of alternating shapes, every second subordinate. This was done in Normandy at Jumièges, c. 1035–65, and it is done at Durham, whose compound piers alternate with circular ones. In this case progress towards the E is slower, every two bays being felt as one square major bay. One is inclined to halt in the middle of each of these major bays and take them in centrally. This experience can be had at Jumièges as at Durham, but whereas at Jumièges the subordinate columns are indeed subordinate, at Durham they are given an enormity of size which in the end remains a distinctive feature of the whole cathedral. These columns or round piers are 27 ft high and nearly 7 ft in diameter. The monument to James Britton in the nave, with the deceased reclining comfortably on a mattress on which he has placed an open book, could be put inside one of the piers, and if he had a self-fuelling lamp he could continue reading and musing in that circular cell. Moreover, the piers are patterned in nobly scaled grooved designs. So everything is done to give them the utmost importance, and it is the mighty impact of the piers from left and right which makes one feel so utterly overwhelmed. But there is nothing savage in this attack. The proportions are actually handled with a sense of balance rarely achieved in the Norman style. One has to study the elevation to appreciate that. At Ely arcade and gallery are nearly of the same height. Hence the same sense of uniform movement which is present in the w–E direction prevails in the upward movement as well. At Gloucester, on the other hand, the gallery is so low and its openings are so small that its effect on the eye is hardly more than that of a band above the arcade. At

Durham the gallery is neither too large nor too small. It is there in its own right, yet can never compete with the cyclopic arcade. The actual proportion of gallery to arcade is 2:5. Niceness of proportion is so rarely aimed at in early medieval buildings on such a large scale that, if one has not been to Durham for a long time and has only seen the cathedral in the meantime in occasional postcards or illustrations, one is every time shocked by the sheer bigness of everything, starting from the blank arcading along the outer walls of the aisles, which is no more than an enrichment of the dado of the walls and yet has colonnettes of more than the height of a man.

The nave, where most visitors will experience their first impressions of the interior design, is not the earliest part of the Norman church. That was begun at the E end, as has been said before, and here then must our detailed examination start. William de St-Calais's CHOIR was built with a large apse terminating the choir 'nave' and two subsidiary apses (encased in square walls) terminating the choir aisles, a type of E end usual in Normandy, not unusual in Norman England, and common in France during the C 11. The foundation of the apse at Durham has been excavated and can be seen (trapdoor in the feretory behind the high altar). The apses and the choir with its aisles were complete by 1104, when the shrine of St Cuthbert was transferred to the new church. The choir is not as easily seen as the nave, because of the stalls, organ, bishop's throne etc. The system is two double bays E of the crossing, and then originally a long piece of solid wall behind which lay the aisle apses with their thick E walls. At the E end of that wall the main apse followed. The aisles have the blank arcading already referred to. It has coupled colonnettes with cushion capitals (one or two fluted or scalloped, N aisle) and intersected arches of quite a multiform moulding, a surprisingly early occurrence of the Norman motif of intersecting arches and altogether of a certain *finesse* of detailing. The aisle windows are C 19 (see *Exterior*), the easternmost bay belongs to the Nine Altars (see below). The vaulting of the aisles is done by means of cross-ribs, the earliest surviving ribs in the cathedral. The European importance of these ribs has already been discussed. Their mouldings again are remarkably refined. They and the transverse arches rest on tripartite shafts against the outer walls and against the main piers.

These piers, to say it again, alternate between compound and circular. The two circular piers on each side are spiral-grooved on a wonderfully bold scale. The painting of Romanesque piers in spiral, lozenge, geometrical and other patterns was of course not at all unusual. Notre-Dame-la-Grande at Poitiers has preserved a specially complete display of marble-painted piers. Other examples are St-Savin, also in Poitou, and St Maria im Capitol at Cologne. But to do the same thing sculpturally may well have been an

30. DURHAM Europe's first rib-vault, *c.* 1095–*c.* 1100. Choir aisle

innovation of the great Durham designer, who was so clearly out to combine force and splendour. The innovation caught on at once in Britain, and examples are found as far N as Dunfermline and as far S as Norwich and Waltham Abbey near London, apart from Selby and the crypt at York Minster. On a smaller scale than Durham, the columns in the C 11 crypts of St Peter Utrecht and St Lebuinus Deventer are carved with spiral patterns, as are the columns of the still earlier crypt at Repton. The undercroft piers of the dormitory of Christ Church Canterbury, which are carved with geometric patterns in relief, may also be earlier than Durham. But to do the same thing on such a huge scale, and to do it by emphatic grooving instead of projecting bands, appears to have been an innovation. The only slight disappointment in the original design at Durham is the way in which at the back, towards the aisles, the cylindrical piers suddenly become tripartite to hold arches and ribs of the aisle vaults, an indication perhaps of how new the idea of diagonal ribs altogether was. On the possible genesis of spiral designs in the twisted (salomonic) columns of the saint's shrine in Old St Peter's, Rome, see Norwich, Nave, below.

29. DURHAM Choir, late C 11 with mid-C 13 revaulting

The circular piers have low circular capitals in which the plain segments characteristic of block capitals are simply multiplied. Multi-scalloped capitals are a later stage than that of the E end. Their bases have a double hollow (double talus), the most Norman of all early Norman base mouldings, a trifle old-fashioned maybe in the last decade of the C11 though they also occur in the North c. 1080 at Richmond Castle, North Yorkshire. The superordinate piers are really large chunks of solid wall enriched by three groups of three demi-shafts. The middle ones go right up to the vault, the others support the arcade arches, which are of two orders. Both these and the gallery arches have unusually refined mouldings for their date, arguably the starting point of the English taste for complex profiles. They combine both soffit rolls (a motif favoured in the buildings of the Saxo-Norman overlap period, see e.g. Bosham, Sussex) with the more orthodox Norman hollow chamfer and angle roll. The capitals are single-scalloped, an elementary form of scalloping developed immediately from the block capital. (In the Winchester transept of the 1070s both forms occur side by side.) The gallery has a twin opening under one containing arch for each arch of the arcade below. The capitals are again single-scalloped. The gallery can be used, although its outer windows are very small. The visitor will notice that it is crossed by transverse arches. These have neither decoration nor adornment, but are part of the provisions regarded as necessary by the architect who planned to give the Durham chancel its vaults. It must be repeated again that there was, as far as we know, no precedent whatever for the rib-vaulting of naves. The earliest nave vaults belong to France and the C11. They are all tunnel-vaulted. The more difficult task of groin-vaulting, where the weight of the vault is carried by four corner points instead of the whole side wall, as in the case of tunnel-vaults, had only been faced at the end of the C11 in the Rhineland (Speyer) and also in Normandy. But Durham is not later than these and yet adds the refinement of ribs.

As to accurate dates, if the beginning at Durham was in 1093 and the whole choir was complete by 1104, the aisle vaults (which remain) must certainly belong to about 1095 and the original main vault to c. 1103–4. The latter date is confirmed by a legend re-told soon after, according to which St Cuthbert one night, immediately before the date assigned to the solemn transfer of his shrine, was so perturbed by the remaining muddle of wooden centerings inside that he came along and knocked down thoroughly but gently 'materia lignorum quae recentem presbiterii testudinem sustruebat' (William of Malmesbury). These choir main vaults were replaced by new ones in the C13 (see below), because they were already in 1235 'plenae fissuris et rimis'. This perhaps is additional confirmation of their experimental character. The existence of Norman

vaults prior to the present ones can be deduced as well as seen. The deduction, carried out in a masterly fashion by Bilson, can point to the fact that to the l. and r. of the triple shafts of the main pier which were to support the triple transverse arch there rises from the recessed gallery sill yet one more shaft on each side. What can they have been meant to perform? Moreover, between the two gallery openings, i.e. above each circular pier, there rise from the same level another three shafts. The only explanation is that the middle one of these was intended to carry a subordinate transverse arch, whereas the lateral ones together with the lateral shafts of the compound piers were supports of ribs. As a confirmation of this, Bilson could point to marks on the clerestory wall facing the chancel, which were left by the original vault close to the present vault when it was hacked down in the C13. These marks are unmistakable, and they give a shape of vault identical with that of the N transept.

The CROSSING rests on four arches each carried on three big demi-shafts like the transverse arches of the chancel. In addition there is in each corner one more shaft reaching right up into the tower masonry. This was probably meant to help in carrying the beams of a ceiling inside the tower. With the addition of the C15 lantern tower the ceiling was removed and the whole height of 155 ft opened. The C15 design has at its foot a gallery on corbels, then a zone of tall, slim, twin two-light windows with transoms and Perp tracery. The vault is star-shaped with tiercerons and liernes. The wonderful thing about this tower is the suddenness with which its quite un-Norman height meets the eye, after one has felt, in Norman terms, the nave itself to be so splendidly high.

The TRANSEPTS were perhaps still in progress at the time of the translation in 1104. Their aisled E side indeed appears as a continuation of the system of the chancel, but various details indicate that they belong to a different building phase. One is the change in the type of pier plinth. In the choir the piers rest on a stepped plinth; in the transepts and nave the plinth has a projecting chamfered band (the same profile as that of the cathedral's external plinth). The piers of transepts and nave are also of slightly different dimensions from those in the choir. A more noticeable difference is that when the outer circular pier was reached on the s side a broad horizontal zigzag pattern was substituted for the spiral pattern used so far. It seems to be the earliest instance in England of the later ubiquitous use of zigzags. The N and s transepts have identical gallery arrangements, but these differ in a significant way from those of the choir. The furthermost N and s bays on the E side have a pair of shafts reaching from the gallery sill up to the vault without any capitals and without any function. There are no corresponding shafts on the w side. The shafts suggest that when they were built a stone vault was not

intended. There are other indications pointing in the same direction. On the E side between the gallery openings above the inner circular piers there are two demi-shafts instead of the three in the choir. In the choir they supported transverse arch and ribs. Here they were meant to support ribs only. That would result in a composition of two cross-ribbed bays without transverse arch between, a somewhat unsatisfactory arrangement but one which was indeed executed and continued in the nave. Then we come to the clerestory. This differs in the transepts from the choir and in both from each other. In the choir there simply was one window with solid wall to the l. and r. In the N transept there is the much more handsome arrangement of a tripartite stepped group of arches with the window in the higher middle one and with a wall-passage. This composition appears a little earlier in the N transept of Winchester. In the s transept at Durham we find a much odder arrangement, though most of the openings are now blocked. On the w, where it survives intact in the s w bay, it can be seen more clearly than the E side. There is also a tripartite composition without shafts. But the side arches are as high as the middle arch, and that makes vaulting impossible. The vaults, as finally put on, indeed cut into the side arches.

Professor Bony puts forward a further argument: the tripartite clerestory of the transepts is designed, as in other unvaulted Anglo-Norman buildings, in conjunction with a passage within the thickness of the wall, but this hollow wall construction does not occur in the choir, where, as we have seen, it can be plausibly argued that vaults were intended from the beginning. Taken together, the evidence all suggests that construction of the transepts was from the first planned differently from that of the choir and that the anomalies in the upper parts reflect not a last-minute failure of nerve but a bold decision to add a stone vault where one had not originally been intended. The addition of the vaults helped to unify the otherwise irregular features of the transepts. The w elevations in particular are much cruder and heavier in all their details than the work elsewhere. Perhaps this phase coincides with the difficult period when the bishopric was vacant for three years (1096–9) and money was short. Then, perhaps with the election of Flambard in 1099, things changed again. The N transept received its tripartite clerestory and then, later, its vaults, and after this work had been completed the s transept was also vaulted, in disregard of the timid clerestory design. And as the year 1110 was probably now reached, the ribs, unlike those of the N transept, were adorned with zigzag work.

The zigzag became the one distinguishing feature of the NAVE. The blank arcades of the outer aisle walls indeed continue so unchanged right round the church that perhaps their outer walls had already been set out to a height of ten feet or so in the very early days. In addition the eastern-most parts of the newer arcades and galleries must have been started; for they are a necessary abutment of the w crossing arch and the crossing tower. In fact we find the very first gallery openings almost identical with the E parts, but with no zigzag as in the other bays of the nave. It is quite instructive to trace the joint between the old and the new work in detail. The most interesting thing is that there are no vaulting-shafts at all between the twin openings of the galleries and there is a clerestory passage. This suggests, as in the transepts, that a vault was not at first intended. The vault was put on last, after 1128, not on shafts but simply on corbels in the spandrels between the gallery openings. The nave vaults are like those of the inner bays of the transepts, i.e. oblong and cross-ribbed with transverse arches struck only above the main piers and not above the circular subordinate piers. Such oblong rib-vaults may be evolutionarily particularly interesting, as the High Gothic style of the c 13 used them as sexpartite vaults, but they are visually not as satisfactory as those of the chancel must have been. The vaults call for transverse supports on both sides. As it is, they seem to limp or sag a little where the arches are lacking. In the detail the zigzag now appears everywhere; in the aisle vaults and the main vault, in the arcade arches and gallery arches, and in the clerestory. Other modifications of the original scheme (to which however, by and large, the c 12 architect remained remarkably faithful) are no doubt improvements. He introduced two more and equally successful patterns for the circular piers, one of lozenges, the other of close vertical flutings, and he did not stick to the back of his circular piers tripartite bits for the support of the aisle vaults, but, on the contrary, made the wall supports of these vaults also semicircular or rather segmental.

Finally, the c 12 master introduced two more new features, and these are of special interest, considering the date of the vaults (the nave was completed in 1128 and vaulted between 1128 and 1133). Inside the galleries, the transverse arches are no longer semicircles as in the chancel but quarter-circles, and a quarter-circle struck from the clerestory wall to the outer aisle wall buttresses the outward pressure of the upper walls and had been used in this way by the French already in the c 11 to abut tunnel-vaults (Nevers, Clermont-Ferrand etc.) Secondly, the transverse arches across the nave itself (and this influences its appearance considerably) are pointed and no longer semicircular. This also has of course its technical advantages. The thrust of a heavy vault will be carried down more safely along the steeper curve of a pointed arch than along the flatter curve of a semicircle. This again was understood in France at the same time or probably a little earlier (at Cluny in the new building begun in 1089 and then at Autun, also in Burgundy). But Durham is certainly amongst the earliest building making use of pointed arches for rib-vaults.

32. DURHAM Doorway, later C 12, from east cloister walk to nave (see *Cloister*)

The w end of the nave is disturbed a little in its elevation by the two towers. They need strong corner supports, and so instead of a further pair of circular piers, as one would expect them, the superordinate, compound piers are here repeated, and in the vaults two oblong bays appear with a proper transverse arch between. In the vaulted chambers beneath the towers the staircases are an ugly, unintegrated interference (as the exceptionally large ones are in the w corners of the transept). The w wall must be imagined with the big original WEST PORTAL. This has, facing the nave, only one order of columns and one zigzag frieze in the arch, but in addition an outer frieze of foliage embracing medallions with animals and monsters, an innovation for Durham. The outer, originally exterior side of this portal is much grander. It must be mentioned in conjunction with the galilee. But Durham is exceptionally well-endowed with rich PORTALS; there is one on the N side and two on the S. Unlike many in smaller churches, they have no tympana, but two of them have richly ornamented orders of arches. The two S ones lead from the S aisle to the cloister and these have now to be examined (for the exterior of both, see *Cloister* below). The more easterly one is interesting as the earliest of the Durham portals. It probably belongs to the work complete by 1104. The order of columns here has capitals different from nearly all others at Durham, except those in the castle chapel, but similar to late C 11 capitals in other places in England. They have the crudest of volutes and just a few lancet-like leaves rising up to them. The arch is moulded like the blank arches of the walls. The S W portal, most unusually, is more lavishly decorated on the inside than the outside (perhaps it had already been realized that the sandstone was vulnerable to weathering). It has three orders of columns, the outer ones decorated with zigzag, the inner with a lozenge pattern and a tiny leaf design in each lozenge, a playful small-scale repetition of the grooving of the cylindrical piers. The capitals are of interlaced foliage. The arches have zigzag but also figure (monsters etc.) and foliage sculpture, in roundels along the labels of both S portals. Similar figures occur again in lozenges along the label of the N door, which has, for the first time in an English Romanesque cathedral portal, shafts enriched with figural designs enclosed in beaded roundels connected by beaded straps (on the N doorway, see also *Exterior*, nave, above). The appearance of foliage and figures in the portals is characteristic of the tendency to increased luxury and ornament noticeable in other major churches during the C 12.

*The Galilee: interior*

The buildings for which Bishop Hugh of le Puiset or Pudsey (1153–95) was responsible are very different in character from the earlier work. It was he as we have seen who, about 1170–80, placed in front of the w portal the galilee. The galilee is still Norman in style, but late Norman with some Transitional motifs (flattened attic bases, waterleaf capitals, keeled arch mouldings) ultimately of French (Gothic) derivation. One can well understand that the bishop in his late years showed so much appreciation of the arriving Gothic style. In the galilee all is lightness. Its nave is four bays long and divided from the inner aisles and then from the outer aisles by thin coupled but detached shafts of Purbeck marble (the only occurrence of this southern material at Durham) carrying waterleaf capitals and arches elaborately enriched by zigzag. The capitals and rolls flanked by chevron are close to those in Newcastle Keep chapel (1172–7) and seem to originate at York (cf., for roll mouldings with chevron, the minster crypt arches; for identical waterleaf capitals, fragments in the Yorkshire Museum, in the minster, and in St Michael Spurriergate). The pairs of shafts placed at right angles to the main direction of the galilee were later found too flimsy a support, and early in the C 15 (apparently) they were strengthened by two sandstone shafts for each pair, with capitals remarkably faithfully copied from the old ones. The idea seems to have been taken from the great hall at Bishop Auckland, where the piers looked from the beginning like the present ones in the galilee. (Richard Halsey believes the sandstone shafts to be contemporary with the marble ones, principally because it is doubtful if C 15 masons would have copied the C 12 work exactly, but also because 41 fothers (40 tons) 'lapidem emptis pro columnis Galileae' is more likely to refer to Langley's buttressing of the w front, 'columnis' here meaning piers; and because more quatrefoil than double shafts were used structurally, e.g. at York in the minster crypt and in St Michael Spurriergate.) The sandstone shafts are, at any rate, undoubtedly second thoughts but may date from the change of site from E to w (see *Exterior*). Above the arcades on the inner aisles blocked windows which may never have been open: there is no trace of them on the outer face of the walls. Even if originally open they can never have admitted much light. They had no nookshafts but roll mouldings all round (cf. the chapter house below).

The main WEST PORTAL of the cathedral can here be admired in its size and details. It has four (originally five) orders and generous zigzag ornamentation, with again a label of medallions with leaves. Le Puiset's mason created arched niches on either side of the door c. 1175. The N one, of C 13 date, was opened as a door, like the S one, when Bishop Langley blocked the main portal early in the C 15 in order to erect an altar and a monument to himself there (see *Furnishings* below). The timber roofs are also no doubt of his time. The windows are all of later centuries (see *Exterior*). With their mostly clear glass they make Le Puiset's room much too light. One feels in it as though

34. DURHAM Nine Altars Chapel, 1242–c. 1290, looking north

outdoors, an impression certainly misleading. (In this compare also Bristol chapter house, in our companion volume.)

### The Chapel of the Nine Altars: interior

After the completion of the galilee nothing major was done to the interior for sixty years at least, though Le Puiset 'beautified' the chancel with a new gold and silver shrine for Bede, whose bones he separated from Cuthbert's, with stained glass and possibly a nave screen (i.e. a pulpitum). Possible survivals from such a screen are two carved panels now in the library: the two slabs divided into two registers, on one side the Noli Me Tangere, on the other the Transfiguration and Agony, in a soft, sensitive version of the French damp-fold style introduced to England c. 1135. (As the only other subjects from Durham showing this style, a manuscript and Le Puiset's seal, date from his episcopacy, he presumably introduced the style to Durham.) Then the decision was taken to replace the c 11 apses of the church by a far more ambitious and spacious E end. The old E end had allowed for three altars in the three apses. Now, behind the remaining high altar, another nine were to be accommodated.

The peculiar conception of an E transept has been commented on above (see *Exterior*, on the source at Fountains Abbey). We must now describe it and try to analyse its aesthetic effect. If that of the Norman cathedral is essentially one of colossal forces held in balance, the Nine Altars neither operates with forces of such weight nor wants to achieve balance. The effect aimed at is one of sustainedly stressed verticals at the expense of the horizontals, and one of forces compressed into shafts of extreme slenderness. The ground falls away sharply at the E end, so rather than go to the expense of building a substructure or crypt up to the level of the choir, the designer (as has been said, probably *Richard of Farnham*) constructed the floor lower than that of the choir aisles and even lower than the choir and the feretory behind. The feretory, i.e. the space behind the altar where the shrine was going to repose, is at choir level and thus a good 5 ft 9 in. above the new transept. The transept and the easternmost bays of the chancel aisles which had to be adapted to connect the old work with the new continue the blank arcading introduced by William de St-Calais's mason. But instead of coupled colonnettes, these are now single, and they are in addition slimmer and taller and made of grey Frosterley marble (the Durham substitute for Purbeck) to emphasize their linear thinness. This is symptomatic. On a large scale it is taken up by the very tall lancet windows of the transept, by the extreme multiplication of shafts between them, and by making every second in each cluster of shafts of Frosterley so as to stress once more the thin uprightness of them.

The E side of the Nine Altars is divided into nine bays inside, as outside, and each has a tall lancet surmounted by another at clerestory level. The bays are separated by substantial compound responds which project sufficiently to allow for a wall-passage at sill-level of the lower as well as the upper tier, characteristic of the northern school (e.g. Hexham and especially Tynemouth, with whose elevation Durham has much in common and which is probably the major source of the Durham design). The responds are of nine shafts plus two on each side which are the nook-shafts of the adjoining windows. The three middle bays, of a width exactly corresponding to the Norman nave, are treated as a unity, as they are in the exterior. This is done by giving the responds between the three middle windows only five shafts each, but those flanking the middle bays thirteen each. The dominance of this centre of the E wall is yet further stressed by the rose-window above. We can well believe that a round window has always existed in this place. (Glass for a 'round window' was bought in 1359–61.) Such a window, it is true, has never been a favourite with the British, but it could be seen, for example, at Lincoln (N transept, c. 1225). As we see it, it is entirely *Wyatt's*, though he seems to have followed the outline of the then-existing c 15 tracery quite faithfully.

So much for the general composition of the E wall. The S wall is simpler but in harmony. The same wall-arcading is followed by the same two tiers of lancets, though they are here indeed of Yorkshire slenderness. Curiously enough there are not three or five but four of them. The four are grouped in two pairs with a big central respond corresponding to the outer buttress occupying the middle, i.e. the remains of a scheme to provide a massive central group of vaulting-shafts: only some of its coursed core was built. At the level of the lower window heads a single spindly shaft takes over and receives the fifth rib of the S vault compartment. The tracery, as has already been said, is c 15, restored quite accurately by *Bonomi* in 1827.

In detail the blank arcades have lively stiff-leaf capitals and carry trefoil-headed arches. In the spandrels are head-stops (as far as one can still see exceedingly well carved), and above these pierced elongated quatrefoils. The forms almost crowd each other out, with a tendency to overdo things which can often be noticed in the E.E. style. Higher up the heads of the principal tier of windows are enriched by dogtooth, friezes of separated stylized flowers, and head-stops. Finally the vaults are reached. They are set out in an interesting way. The outer bays are quadripartite and relatively narrow. The next bays of the vaults comprise two of the elevation. The designer here had a difficult problem. He had taken the exact dimensions of the plan of the Nine Altars transept at Fountains, but the proportions of the nave and aisles in the two c 12 buildings were quite different, so in the second and fourth bays he was forced to

35. DURHAM Ring boss and rib-vault, *c.* 1280–90. Nine Altars Chapel

have the transverse arch, springing from the pier at the junction of the transept and outer choir aisle wall, cutting quite arbitrarily across his quadripartite vault. He chose not to conceal this, but to clarify the structure by intersecting the mouldings of the ribs and those of the transverse arch, possibly to suggest, together with great clusters of shafts almost like crossing piers, a kind of E crossing, unlike the Fountains arrangement. This centre has a vault of a form invented, it seems, by the Durham architect. From the main piers in the corners spring eight instead of four ribs. They slightly diverge so that in the centre the eight are just far enough from each other to contain a large ring. Carved into the mouldings of this ring are the seated figures of the four Evangelists, pieces of exquisite carving, clearly of the same style as the bosses of the Angel Choir at Lincoln, begun in 1256 and completed about 1280. The foliage and figures in the other bosses are of the same style and the same quality. One should have a good field-glass ready to examine them and wait for a sunny morning.

From Lincoln also may have come the idea of a large window for the N façade. The Joseph window is without any doubt the finest piece of Gothic design at Durham,

possibly not part of the original design but a development of about a decade later, see the capitals of the inner jambs of the N window which seem to be *in situ* and clearly belong with the adjacent E and W walls, not the present window. If so, the original scheme for the N window was different to that of the S, where the comparable capitals are at a lower level. The composition need not be described again (see *Exterior* above), but what strikes one immediately when looking N is the tremendous and at first inexplicable depth of the intersecting tracery. The tracery is duplicated in two layers to allow for a wall-passage to pass through as, for instance, in the Angel Choir clerestory at Lincoln. The mullions and the main intersecting arches are inside as well as outside the wall-passage, the trefoiled and cinquefoiled circles are only in the outer wall. The effect is one of breath-taking vigour and splendour.

Only when the Chapel of the Nine Altars was nearing completion was the joining up with the Norman work carried out. It was a bigger job than had probably at first been contemplated. The Norman choir main vaults, it will be remembered, had as early as 1235 been badly cracked. They were now taken down and rebuilt in the style of the

36. DURHAM Double tracery, north window, *c.* 1280–90. Nine Altars Chapel

mature c 13, with transverse arches and ribs richly decorated. The cushion capitals of the Norman vaulting-shafts at the same time were recarved *in situ* with thick foliage, and little, rather ugly, Frosterley shafts were added high up for the wall ribs. Between the last Norman pier and the main apse there had been a broad strip of bare wall which was demolished together with all three apses. The blank area each side, created by the removal of a Norman transverse arch abutting the last pier, must have looked too solid to the Gothic builders, and so shafts, again alternately of sandstone and Frosterley marble, were placed in front of it. Beyond them another bay of the arcade was opened and thus the Nine Altars reached. The new bay is rather makeshift in its composition, a none too happy compromise between what the old style necessitated and the new style demanded. The elevation of arcade, gallery, clerestory is kept. But the arcade has most oddly shaped arches

starting with a vertical piece and then breaking round into the curve. The gallery has a wide tripartite opening with steeply pointed arches which, in order to have a containing arch like the Norman work, are placed beneath a depressed arch, the only motif of the c 13 at Durham to compare immediately with Salisbury. The clerestory has two shafted lancet windows with a shaft between, but they are not placed centrally above the gallery. And the vault is sexpartite with the transverse rib running almost horizontally along the N–S ridge.

However, these discrepancies are remedied by a display of decoration so luxuriant that it clearly shows the mood of the end of the century and the approaching Dec style. Foliage in the blank arcading on the ground-floor level had been entirely of stiff-leaf type. These capitals indeed must have been carved shortly after the beginning of the work, i.e. *c.* 1250. The capitals of the arches between chancel

37. D U R H A M North gallery, rebuilt sanctuary bay, *c.* 1250–80

aisles and E transept, on the other hand, bring in beasts, birds, harpies and other monstrous combinations of man and beast. They go closely with those in York N transept, whence the sculptors probably came after that building was finished in the early 1250s. Also associated is the N porch at Bridlington. This style is introduced with the main piers terminating the choir arcade, i.e. built only after the demolition of the Norman apse. The capitals of the N and S piers differ notably: on the S pier one capital per shaft, on the N a continuous abacus. There are clear indications of changes of plan during construction of these piers, stone rather than marble shafts becoming predominant here. The shafts along the blank piece of wall to the N and S of the altar space rest on demi-figures. They end in capitals again with human and animal forms as well as foliage, and carry trefoiled arches under steep crocketed gables. In other capitals one can see a fight between a lion and a gryphon, and a fox stealing geese. Even the string-courses below the gallery and below the clerestory have their leaves and beasts and birds and little men. And so it goes on into the gallery capitals and the clerestory capitals. The very lintel in the clerestory which connects the shaft between the twin openings with the outer wall has figure carving. Finally high up, on each side of the E end of the chancel, are two much larger figures of angels. They are again of the very best quality and clearly derived from the Angel Choir at Lincoln. One hesitates to date them and the capitals with their rich fauna before 1280.

## FURNISHINGS, W TO E

### Galilee

WALL PAINTINGS. A king and a bishop, perhaps St Oswald and St Cuthbert, on the jambs of the arched recess N of the former portal, and decorations with painted hangings against the back wall of the recess. These are extremely valuable survivals of Bishop Le Puiset's time, c. 1175–85. The bold leaf-frieze on the soffit of the arch also deserves study. The dominant colours are yellow, red, green and blue. Above the recess, the remains of a later, huge painting of the Coronation of the Virgin (?), with a mitred figure at the lower r.; and, on the wall above the arcade immediately to the S, a late C 13 or early C 14 series of scenes including the Crucifixion, and spirited depictions of apostles undergoing martyrdom. Remains of colour on the arcades themselves include, on the second from the S, painted chevrons, in red outline. All over the chevron mouldings and round the capitals of the w door much white base with red-line foliage, presumably of c. 1430, contemporary with Langley's chantry chapel (see below). Over the door, an inscription, possibly original C 15 script. Hanging in the l. recess a wooden CROSS by George Pace, 1967. In the central recess, a TRIPTYCH of the Crucifixion with Christ carrying the Cross and the Virgin mourning Christ, said to be Westphalian, c. 1500, given in 1935.

STAINED GLASS. An important collection of medieval fragments, incorporating remnants of the late medieval glazing of the cathedral and panels purchased by the Dean and Chapter set in clear glass (not, visually, an entirely satisfactory method) to George Pace's designs by the Dean and Chapter's glaziers, 1956 and 1971. Unfortunately several panels are set inside-out. Characteristic and pleasing leading designs in the clear glass here and in the rest of the cathedral. – S wall (from E to W). Three windows containing thirty panels of mainly C 14–16 fragments of York provenance, purchased in 1962. In the fourth, panels by C. E. Kempe from Warwick Priory. – W wall (from S to N). Panels by Pugin (1842), from Ackworth Grange, Yorkshire, with, in the second row, Sacrament of Marriage (c. 1435), archbishop saint (c. 1340) and C 17 armorial with medieval fragments. Above, in the central light are C 15 and C 19 armorials with medieval fragments. – Nineteen panels, mainly fragments, with in the second row a C 15 armorial of Percy/Warren between two C 14 armorials of Greystock (Fitzwilliam), all brought in except for, above the transom, remnants of a Benedictine saint and Bede (c. 1430–40) between late C 14 foliage from the great W Jesse window. In the tracery, composite figures and fragments of the C 15. – In the centre window, eighteen panels of fragments, mainly C 14 and C 15, much of it originally in the Chapel of the Nine Altars; set before 1950, redesigned in 1963. In the tracery lights substantial remains of New Testament scenes including the Flight into Egypt and Virgin and Child, part of Langley's glazing scheme. – In the fourth window, mainly early C 16 Flemish roundels below the transom (one dated 1529), with a C 15 French angel and inscriptions from England in the central light. Above are a Chalice and Host (C 14 grisaille) and composite Crucifixion (both C 15, the latter from the S choir aisle) between more foliage from the great W Jesse window. In the tracery, composite figures and fragments, C 15, inserted before 1950 from various windows in the cathedral. – Filling the fifth window, more glass by Pugin from Ackworth Grange. – N wall. Abstract design commemorating Bede by Alan Younger (1973). N E window with figures of saints by Kempe from Jarrow.

MONUMENTS. Bishop Langley (1406–37) blocked the W portal of the cathedral. He wished to place a new altar here, and his own tomb (1429–35). It is an impressive composition, with the very large tomb-chest, without an effigy, in the middle and steps to the l. and r. leading up to the altar. A wooden reredos stood behind it until the W door was reopened in 1846. Two bays of the central aisle were enclosed by stone screens to form his chantry chapel. Of this, a simply-detailed four-centred doorway of Teesdale marble (cf. tomb-chest and refectory lavatorium) survives, now in the refectory undercroft. – The Venerable Bede: also a plain big tomb-chest with black marble top: no effigy. His bones were brought to Durham in 1020 and transferred to the galilee in 1370; the traditional Latin epitaph, which translated reads 'In this tomb are the bones of the Venerable Bede', was carved for Cosin and re-used in 1831. – In the s recess behind, a quotation from Bede's Latin commentary on the Apocalypse with an English translation, designed by *George Pace*, 1970–1, as a memorial to Dean Alington † 1955. Gilded aluminium letters in an irregular arrangement on an oak screen: sculptor *Frank Roper*. Associated ledger by *Pace*, 1958.

*Nave and aisles* FONT. 1663. A beautifully simple, yet elegant example of the baluster type, white marble with a gadrooned bowl. (*Salvin*'s Norman-style font took its place from 1846 until 1935, according to Dr Allibone.) – The FONT CANOPY is one of the most gorgeous of the many pieces of elaborate woodwork made for Bishop Cosin during the eleven years that he held the see of Durham. It stands more than 40 ft high and is at the base about 9 ft across. It is octagonal, with fluted composite columns, an acanthus frieze, and a cartouche with a pendant on each side at ground-floor level. That kind of post-Restoration, classical decoration goes well with the shape of the font itself. But above, between the next tier of unfluted baluster-like columns, Gothic tracery and Gothic crocketed gables appear, and from there it goes on entirely Gothic with a tall traceried canopy crowned by a crocketed spire. The canopy is almost exactly like the subsidiary canopies on the screen at Sedgefield, Co. Durham, in form, but this is more Baroque, with flickering movement in the carving of the crockets etc. – Beneath the canopy flanking the font, tall wrought-iron CANDLESTICKS by *George Pace*. – ORGAN CASE, at the w end of the s aisle. Made in 1683 for one of the first of the Father Smith instruments, removed from its original position to the choir in 1847, dismantled in 1876 and what remained re-assembled as adequately as could still be done in 1903. The rest forms part of the screen at Roxwell, Essex. These parts are wholly in the Baroque vein with no more of Cosin's Gothic reminiscences. Scrolly pediments, thick garlands, terms ending in the heads of young angels the size of live young girls or boys. Enormous mitres as finials. The bottom half includes parts of Cosin's choir screen. – The N and S DOORS towards the w end are contemporary with the completion of the nave and roof: 1128–33 (information from Dr Geddes). Each leaf simply made with three wedged ledges which slot along grooves at the back of the door. Towards the cloister the s door has a splendid display of ironwork of 1175–1200 comprising C-hinges and straps with palmette terminals – a bold geometric design unique in England, though palmettes and lozenges are found on doors in central

France (Neuvy-St-Sépulchre, Liginiac etc.). – SANCTUARY RING. Replica on N door outside: see *Exterior*, nave, main N portal, above. – WALL PAINTINGS. At the w end of the N aisle, a large panel of diaper pattern, probably C14. C12 decorative painting in blank arcading at the E end of the s aisle, repainted in one bay. Small-size ashlar imitated by painted joints, and in the middle of each stone a many-petalled flower. A frieze of scrolly tendrils with small crocket-like leaves above. The colours are buff, black, red and pink. On an adjacent column are painted chevrons, like those carved into the piers of the nave arcades. – OFFER-TORY BOX, N door. 1964 by *Pace*.

STAINED GLASS. Nave. In the great w window a Tree of Jesse, uncommonly good, by *Clayton & Bell*, 1867, in C14 style. – In the N w window St Cuthbert, in the s w window St Oswald, both quite obviously by *Hugh Easton*. – N aisle (w to E). First window also by *Easton*, 1948, an Airman over Durham, painfully obtrusive. – Third window by *Clayton & Bell*, 1881. – Easternmost, Good Shepherd by *William Wailes*, 1868. – The rest clear, leaded to *Pace*'s designs in 1965. – s aisle (w to E). – Six windows (the High Priest Coifi, St Paulinus, St Aidan, St Cuthbert, Benedict Biscop, Venerable Bede) by *Clayton & Bell*, mainly 1875.

MONUMENTS. In 1417 the Nevilles were allowed to make a chantry chapel between two bays near the E end of the s nave aisle. Slight indications of the enclosing screenwork remain, together with the aumbry for the chantry altar. The bodies of Ralph Lord Neville † 1367, and his wife, originally buried centrally at the E end of the nave, now lie under the second arch of the s arcade. Alabaster, hopelessly badly preserved. Ralph's part in the victory of 1346 at Neville's Cross earned him the honour of being the first layman granted burial inside the cathedral. – In the third arcade bay, John Lord Neville † 1388, and his wife, also alabaster, on a fine tomb-chest with shields and mutilated but still elegant figures of mourners. The grief-stricken posture of a male mourner on the w side is exceptional in English tomb sculpture. As with the Hatfield tomb and throne (see *Choir* below) there are connections with Yorkshire (the tomb of Thomas de Ingleby † c. 1369 is of the same workmanship) which, comparing it with the metropolitan style of Neville's screen, suggest the tomb was ordered after his impeachment in 1376 and his disappearance from court. – MINERS' MEMORIAL (s aisle). Made up by *Donald McIntyre* in 1947 of four cherubs from Cosin's screen and of fragments from a Baroque (Spanish?) altar used as an overmantel at Ranside Hall. Big twisted columns and instruments of the Passion. – Sir George Wheler † 1724 (s aisle). Standing wall-monument with bust against a reredos background; not big. – James Britton, by *Charles R. Smith*, 1839, comfortably semi-reclining on a mattress rolled up to support his elbow, a scheme usual about 1700 but unusual in the C19.

38. DURHAM Font cover, *c*. 1663. West end of nave

*Crossing and transepts* A PULPIT given to the cathedral by Bishop Crewe (1674–1721) was replaced in 1876 by one by *Sir George Gilbert Scott*, designed ill-advisedly in the Italian Cosmati style of the Shrine of the Confessor at Westminster Abbey, though at the time thought aesthetically perfect. – The LECTERN opposite the pulpit is still more recent. It was designed by *D. McIntyre* about 1940 in the style of 1700. Octagonal tester on eight Corinthian columns. Not raised off the floor.

CHOIR SCREEN also by *Scott* (1870–6). With its three wide arches and its polished Frosterley marble columns just as much out of sympathy with the C 12 as with the C 13 cathedral; at least it punctuates the vista *Salvin* (or *Pickering*) had unwisely opened too completely. (Scott's contemporary screens at Chester and Winchester were inspired by the medieval stalls, but he could not be expected to be inspired by Cosin's stalls, then, although he did restore them. Fragments of Cosin's choir screen have been re-used in the cathedral – see the following – and the castle, and parts of the return choir stalls in St Cuthbert, Farne Inner.)

SCREENS to the chancel aisles. Cosin work: round arches decorated with a species of nailhead (Cosin's lozenge). Cusped spandrels between fluted pilasters supporting an acanthus frieze. – CLOCK. Originally erected by Prior Castell (1494–1519), rebuilt and much altered by Dean Hunt in 1630, taken down by Salvin, and reconstructed in 1938 by *S. Dykes Bower* in the s transept with as much of the woodwork as could be collected. A huge contraption in a mixed Gothic and Jacobean style; presumably Dean Hunt, when he re-used the Perp polygonal turrets at the corners of his openwork dome with its pinnacles, thought already in terms of a revival. After all, Hunt was a contemporary of Cosin, and the pinnacles are almost exactly like those used on Cosin's screens at Brancepeth and Sedgefield. The doors below are painted with a pretty church interior with little figures, no doubt by a Dutchman. – DURHAM LIGHT INFANTRY CHAPEL. Fitted in 1924 by *W. D. Caröe*. Altar and panelling much altered since, and screen inscribed with battle honours.

STAINED GLASS. s transept E wall (from N to s). Bishop Richard of Bury by *Clayton & Bell*. – Second window, C 15 armorial of Cheney, beneath a fine mid-C 14 figure of St Leonard, – s wall. Te Deum window by *Clayton & Bell*, 1869. – Four composite restored figures of c. 1430–40 survive in the tracery. – w wall. Superbly decorative Moses window in the Egyptian style by *Henry Holiday*, 1895–6. – N transept E wall (from s to N). Christ and mainly northern saints perhaps by *Clayton & Bell*, c. 1897. – St Gregory by *Clayton & Bell*, c. 1887. – St Nicholas, 1899. – N wall (from E to w). Passion scenes perhaps by *Clayton & Bell*. – In the N window Arma Christi with angels and St Cuthbert and the Virgin and Child flanked by the Four Doctors of the Church above, by *Clayton & Bell*,

1875. – w wall. One window by *Hugh Easton*.

MONUMENTS. In the N transept E aisle Matthew Woodifield †1826, a very self-assertive Grecian monument of white marble; aedicule with absurdly short Greek Doric columns on a big plinth. Entablature above with segmental top and acroteria, a large bath sarcophagus with ball finial on top. – In the s transept, Bishop Shute Barrington †1826, by *Chantrey*, 1830, a standing wall-monument of white marble, with the kneeling figure of the Bishop in profile.

*Choir* REREDOS (NEVILLE SCREEN). Largely paid for by John Lord Neville and made in London of 'frenche peere', i.e., in this case, Caen stone. Funds were collected between 1372 and 1376, and it was consecrated in 1380. Even deprived of its bright paint and 107 alabaster figures, it remains precious. Although Perp in style, it lacks (apart from the ends facing the aisles) the rectangularity typical of large-scale Perp from the beginning (e.g. Gloucester s transept, begun c. 1330). Here, indeed, the verticals are emphasized to the almost complete exclusion of the horizontals. Five major and four subordinate spire-like canopies tower above the low wall which visually shuts off the choir from St Cuthbert's Shrine in both a novel and influential way. The only access now is through doors in the later side walls. Not surprisingly, in this design there is little scope for Perp tracery, except in the door jambs. The canopies are like those of other luxurious Perp pieces, for example wooden font covers and choir stalls and, in stone, chantries like those of Beaufort and Waynflete at Winchester or Alcock at Ely. The skyline is as spiky as that of Edward II's monument, the Exeter sedilia, and other such masterpieces of the Dec style, though less crowded and more clearly articulated at the cost of some hardness and dryness. More obviously Perp, the rectangular units towards the aisles. The details are all based on London prototypes of a generation earlier (Old St Paul's cloister, begun 1332; w porch St Stephen's Chapel, Westminster, 1340s), suggesting that the designer was a member of the Royal Works: *Henry Yevele* is the obvious candidate. Neville was a member of Edward III's inner circle. It is the only surviving example of this type of low-wall-plus-canopies reredos, of which there were early C 14 examples at Exeter and Peterborough. Restored in 1846. – SEDILIA. Erected together with the screen. Four seats on each side. The sedilia at Selby Abbey appear to be from the same hand.

CHOIR STALLS. 1665, that is under Cosin. Restored to their original appearance by *Scott* in the 1870s, after the canopies had been cut up and set back between the piers in the 1840s. Cosin's style is unmistakable. Only the close ornamentation of the stall ends is surprising; otherwise there are the long, thin Ionic columns and the high Gothic canopies and the backs with Gothic tracery and cherubs'

39. DURHAM Neville Screen, 1372–80. Perhaps by Henry Yevele

heads tipping the cusps (cf. Hatfield tomb, below). The first stalls on the l. and r. are distinguished by backs with thick garlands. The carver is said to have been *John Clement*. The stall fronts are panelled, with lozenges and blind tracery alternating; to the ends poppyhead finials and a combination of arabesques, swags and modified strapwork. Misericords with fruit swags pendant from masks (all different) on the canons' stalls. – One STALL FRONT made up of parts of the same (Spanish?) altar which provided parts of the Miners' Memorial. – Eight PRIE-DIEU with a very thick, oversized acanthus frieze. – ALTAR. Beneath Scott's movable table, Dean Hunt's small (6 ft 6 in. wide, only 3 ft high) altar of *c.* 1626. Pink marble, six pillars inlaid with black (Frosterley?) marble and on each broken marble dowels with some chisel marks where some decoration, probably cherubs' heads, was attached. – COMMUNION RAIL with fine pierced acanthus work, 1940, in the style of 1700. By *W. Hollis*. – PROCESSIONAL CROSS. Silver head by *Henry Wilson*, 1917. – Marble PAVEMENT by *Scott*, 1870–5. – Movable CHOIR PULPIT. Made up of Cosinesque traceried panels with cherubs' heads in upper tier. Balustrade by *Pace*, 1964. – PARCLOSE SCREENS to the aisles. Again Cosin work, the lowest parts remarkably exact in the imitation of Perp screen tracery. In this case one is tempted to believe that the Bishop insisted on the actual copying of some surviving screen. Usual canopies above. – PRAYER DESK. Also Cosin work, formerly under the crossing, now in the s choir aisle. – (*Scott's* metal LECTERN made by *Skidmore*, laboriously ornate and highly dangerous to the reader's shins, and its matching altar book stand have been removed to the refectory.)

STAINED GLASS. Chancel s aisle. In the second window from the E a pleasing kaleidoscope of medieval fragments, mainly remnants of Bishop Langley's reglazing of the Chapel of the Nine Altars, *c.* 1420–30, including fragments of large-scale figures, canopies, border motifs, and inscriptions. – BISHOP'S THRONE. This forms part of the funeral monument which Bishop Hatfield erected for himself (see below). – MONUMENTS. Bishop Beaumont † 1333. Matrix in front of the sanctuary step, the brass a copy of 1951. – Bishop Hatfield, who died in 1381, built a deep wide arch over his tomb, and, on the platform above, a new bishop's throne backed by a stone screen, with provision for imagery. The monks gave their assent for it in 1363. As a composition it is unique; as a work of art it lacks imagination. Perp style with a heavy admixture of Dec. Many of its features suggest a Yorkshire-trained designer, most specifically in the panelling of the back and sides of the throne and the canopy over the seat (from York Lady Chapel wall panelling and E front respectively). The lower stage rather solid, heavy and old-fashioned, encrusted with diapered surfaces, heavy foliage and shields. On the walls panelling, with rather archaic ogee-trefoil

heads. Under the segmental arch (cusped, with angels at the tips of the cusps flying upside down), a vault with deeply undercut foliage bosses (cf. Beverley high altar screen, *c.* 1334). Alabaster effigy on a tomb-chest. Up to the platform a staircase with a balustrade with C17 acanthus work, the gate at its foot with Bishop Crewe's arms (1674–1721). The balustrade of the platform itself is earlier, with balusters between fluted dwarf pilasters. Much painting and gilding was done in 1933–6, but there are fragmentary original paintings of angels on the walls at the E and W ends, those at the w holding Hatfield's soul in a napkin, originally beneath a Majesty (as shown in an C18 drawing in the British Museum). – Bishop Skirlaw † 1403. Of his chantry chapel built in the N chancel aisle in 1398–1403 by *Thomas Hyndley* and *John Piercebridge* only a bench along the wall with a display of heraldic shields remains. – Bishop Lightfoot † 1889. Recumbent effigy of white marble, by *Sir E. Boehm*, on a tomb-chest under one of the Cosin screens. – Sixth Marquess of Londonderry †1915, and his wife †1919. Bronze relief with kneeling figures by *Tweed* (N chancel aisle).

*Feretory* Wooden SCREEN behind the feretory. The original parts Marian, but mostly a reconstruction of 1934, in the main from the parts that survived the 1844 dismantling. Cresting copied from a pre-1847 drawing. – TESTER over St Cuthbert's tomb, elaborately gilded, by *Sir Ninian Comper* and of 1949. – STATUE of St Cuthbert with the head of St Oswald (still buried with him) in his hand. It comes from the central tower; C15.

*Nine Altars* SCULPTURE. C13 cross head with stiff-leaf decoration; on one side the Crucifixion, on the other Christ in Majesty (brought from Low Middleton Hall in 1938). – STAINED GLASS. E wall. Southernmost window by *Bell* of Bristol, 1865. – The rest by *Clayton & Bell* in a C13 style, the central E lancets and the rose of 1877. – N wall. Joseph window by *Clayton & Bell*, 1877. – MONUMENTS. Six foliated slabs. – Tablet to Dean Spencer Cowper † 1774. Unsigned but exceedingly delicately done. Probably not a provincial workshop production. – Emily Cadogan, *c.* 1830. Sentimental tablet by *Joseph Gott*. – Bishop Van Mildert † 1836. White statue on a circular base, seated (cf. Nollekens' Bishop Trevor at Bishop Auckland), unlike Chantrey's more fashionable kneeling Bishop Barrington. Carved by *John Gibson* in Rome.

THE CLOISTER AND RELATED BUILDINGS

Bishop Walcher (1071–80), we are told by Symeon, 'coepit aedificare habitacula monachorum'. It is part of the buildings in the SE corner of the cloister that seem to pre-date 1083, when, under William de St-Calais, the monks moved in, and to be related to the smaller cloister deduced by W. H. St John Hope. The E range was, of course, the logical place to start building, as it provided the two main necessities: a dormitory for the monks and a chapter house for business. In its present size the CLOISTER belongs, however, to the great Norman building period of the cathedral. Apparently begun at the same time as the nave and built parallel with it, it has undergone many changes and is more profitably described topographically. The cloister arcades themselves, rebuilt by *Thomas Mapilton* (1409–12) and *Thomas Hyndley* (1412–19) with money from Bishops Skirlaw and Langley, were completed in 1419. The tracery of the three-light openings is an odd, somewhat bleak invention of *c.* 1763–77. C 15 timber ceilings with shields on the bosses by *John Rasyn* and *John Wadley*, 1409–19, much restored in 1828 and 1907. In the N walk, peg marks on the wall of carrels and cupboards. In the centre of the garth the Teesdale marble basin from the refectory lavatorium, an octagonal building originally projecting into the garth from the s cloister walk near the w corner.

The cloister is entered from the nave by one of two PORTALS (for their inside faces, see *Interior*, nave). The one to the w is of the time of the lower stages of the nave (but q.v.), with three plain orders of shafts with block capitals. A comparison with the E doorway, clearly of Le Puiset's time (cf. the castle doorway), is illuminating. Le Puiset's doorway also has three orders of shafts, but the capitals are either scalloped with beading or of the waterleaf type. The arches are ornamented with rope and battlement friezes in the highest relief. A frieze of small petalled flowers also occurs, and an odd sawn-off branch motif in the outer order (cf. the early C 13 tomb niches in Carlisle Cathedral, N chancel aisle). Zigzag is used only for minor purposes. The tendency to luxury and rather ostentatious display which had come into the Norman style in its latest stages is at once evident (see Fig. 32 on p. 87).

First, we examine the CHAPTER HOUSE in the centre of the EAST RANGE. It has, as was usual, a central entrance flanked by two windows. These have twin openings with continuous outer mouldings. All the arches here are enriched by zigzag in the style characteristic of the last stage in the building of the nave. The chapter house was indeed completed by Bishop Rufus, i.e. between 1133 and 1141. (Excavations in 1874 revealed part of the E wall of a shorter, square-ended chapter house of before 1083, judging from sculpture found in the foundations of the later apse and now in the dormitory.) Decorating the walls, arcades of intersected arches with a zigzag frieze running above them. The same elevation is used for the slype (q.v.). This is a rib-vaulted room of ample and satisfying proportions. It has two square bays and an apse of equal width. The transverse arches rest on triple shafts, the ribs on corbels, as in the cathedral. The ribs are accompanied by fine zigzag friezes. Their roll mouldings (and the diagonal ribs in the straight bays) are keeled, puzzling because keeling is usual-

ly considered a Transitional innovation (see e.g. galilee arches). However, keeled billet mouldings occur in a purely Romanesque context at Cérisy-la-Forêt, and original pieces re-used in the reconstructed vault and the removed keystone show this detail to be authentic. The E end was pulled down in 1796, but rebuilt close to the original plan in 1895 by *C. Hodgson Fowler*. Only the setting-out of the apse ribs was not copied (the keystone is nearer the transverse rib than before; see the original keystone in the refectory undercroft) and windows were put in where there were C 14 replacements for which there was no authority. The apse ribs rest on corbels carved with foliate scrolls, dragons etc. carried by atlantes, the originals of which are now set in the N wall. The atlantes are a motif unique in England. Though probably not a direct source, contemporary work in North Italy of the style of Niccolò is similar in its massiveness, and examples in the South of France are comparable. Tall C 15 w window, of five lights, with a fine two-centred arch. On the inner face of the portal, charming capitals with fantastic creatures (e.g. mermaid, centaur) of the same workmanship as the doors at the w end of the nave. Bishop's seat partly original. – STAINED GLASS. E end by *Hugh Easton*, more sensitive than his windows in the church. Figures of bishops, Norman to C 13, buried under the floor (see tomb slabs). – w wall. Two windows with strangely mutilated panels by *Pugin* (1842) from Ackworth Grange (cf. galilee) and C 15 fragments and quarries, some with birds and heraldry.

On the N side of the chapter house, the tunnel-vaulted SLYPE, its walls decorated like those of the chapter house. Above it the former library (now SONG SCHOOL), begun in 1414–15. Five-light depressed pointed E and N windows of that date, probably altered by *Bonomi* in 1836. The walls of the three chambers (the first two now a vestry) to the s of the chapter house are older (see masonry exposed to the cloister, very different from neighbouring C 12 parts). In the first one, visible only from the inside, a triangular-headed window, cut into when the chapter house was built, dated to Walcher's time by comparison to one shown in Buck's drawing of Jarrow. The s w room, which could be bolted, was the PRISON, with a food hatch blocked very early when the cemetery passage to the s was constructed. Right in the corner, the UNDERCROFT of the original dormitory (later made into the Prior's Hall, now Deanery). This has two tunnel-vaulted aisles divided by arches on very short unmoulded piers, similar to those in the REFECTORY UNDERCROFT that also seems to precede the main works begun in 1093. It lies in the SOUTH RANGE of the cloister (as usual in Benedictine monasteries) and has rude groined vaults on piers only 3 ft high and tiny windows to the s with their heads cut out of stone, more Saxon- than Norman-looking. At the w end, two tunnel-vaulted bays, one at the E end, and E of that, also contemporary, the

PASSAGE with short unmoulded wall arcades and a tunnel-vault. In a projection on the N side of the westernmost bay the doorway to the original stairs to the refectory was found during repairs in 1961. Connected with the early cloister, it was superseded by a doorway further W when the cloister was extended c. 1140–93. The original steps are hardly worn.

In 1961 the medieval floor level of the REFECTORY was found, with E dais and glazed tiles probably laid by Prior Castell in 1518, in association with the stone wall-benches and panelling, a large open hearth, and above the dais steps (S wall) the jambs of, probably, a large oriel of c. 1500 (*Archaeological Journal*, 123, 1966). The refectory was converted in 1684 into the DEAN AND CHAPTER LI-BRARY, with a floor at a higher level. The high and low book-presses, i.e. dwarf bookcases with desks for standing readers, very much like those in contemporary Oxford and Cambridge libraries, remain. The outer doorway is re-strainedly classical with Tuscan pilasters. Walls ashlar-faced, inside with E and W niches. *Salvin* replaced the C17 windows with Perp ones in 1858. Concealed by panelling on the E wall, an important Romanesque WALL PAINTING found in 1962: unidentified figure scene. Oak STANDARD LAMPS by *Pace*, 1963. At the W end, the LOFT (formerly the dining room of the canon's house that filled the end of the adjacent dormitory until 1849). Lined with bolection-moulded panelling and incorporating the library stair with heavy twisted balusters. Wooden ELECTROLIERS by *Pace*, 1965. Either side of the entrance, BUSTS, one of G. Waddington by *J. E. Jones*, 1858, the other of S. W. Gilly by *J. G. Lough*, 1857.

In the SW corner of the cloister are two straight-headed doorways of C14 form which connect with the KITCHEN (now Muniment Room), in its way one of the most re-markable monastic buildings of England and comparable only with the kitchen at Glastonbury of roughly the same date. Ingeniously designed by *John Lewyn* and built in 1366–74. The building is octagonal, made square outside by having four big storerooms behind fireplaces in the four corners. Above them under the lean-to roofs a mass of rubble that must buttress the vault. The louver is carried on broad ribs arranged so that they form a perfect eight-cornered star. Ribs are thrown from corner one to four and six, two to five and seven, three to six and eight, four to seven (and one), and five to eight (and two). By doing this a smaller octagon is left in the middle at the intersection of the ribs, which carried the louver and carries a modern replica of the C18 lantern. This delightful method of vaulting has no parallel in England and may either be John Lewyn's invention or have been inspired by Mohammedan vaults in Spain (mosque, Cordova). By travel or by clients' travel the master mason of the Middle Ages could possess wide international knowledge. (But perhaps too, with such

forms in mind, was Lewyn not also taking further the diverging ribs-enclosing-a-circle of the Nine Altars centre vault?) In a kitchen, of course, a stone vault was particularly valuable because fireproof.

The DORMITORY, filling all of the WEST RANGE, is one of the most impressive parts of the monastic buildings of Durham. 194 ft long and 39 ft wide, it was built by Bishop Skirlaw in 1398–1404, apparently on the site of the previous dormitory but not on the site of the original one (q.v.). The move from the S range may have been made before the C13 (the likely date of the present undercroft) as suggested by the Norman door at the W end, fragments of Norman work in the middle of the W wall, and the substantial C12 substructure of a reredorter out on the W precipice above the river (cf. placing of the dormitory at Worcester, though there the dormitory was end-on to the river). The construction in the C12 of the new cathedral further N and of the chapter house cut off direct access from the old dormitory to the cathedral. The contractors of the new one were *John Middleton* until 1400, then *Peter Dryng*. *Ellis Harpour* was the carpenter of the big solid timber roof, cusped along the underside of its ridge-beam. Very rough for its date (cf. Westminster Hall). The windows are tall, two-light and Perp with two-centred heads. Below, double the number of small straight-headed windows corresponding to the monks' cubicles. *P. C. Hardwick* restored it in 1849–53 to house the modern books of the Dean and Chapter Library in specially designed bookcases. It also houses a collection of pre-Norman sculpture and casts, including pieces found under the chapter-house apse. Note especially four complete CROSS HEADS of c. 1000–80; also fragments of a GRAVE COVER of 998–1080 etc.

The DORMITORY UNDERCROFT is divided along the middle into twelve bays by short circular piers with heavy, simply chamfered arches and ribs. The northern bay forms the SPENDEMENT, still with its medieval iron grille to the original cathedral treasury in the W section. Restored by *Salvin* and converted with a theatrical touch in 1971–3 by *G. G. Pace* to house the most precious manuscripts and books. The remainder was the WARMING HOUSE and (S) the GREAT CELLAR. Restored by *Salvin* and converted into (S three bays) the bookshop, restaurant (by *Pace*, 1974–5) and (central four bays) cathedral treasury (by *Curry*, 1977–8). Details of the objects displayed (including plate and the relics of St Cuthbert) can be found in the treasury catalogue.

Around to the NW between the dormitory and the sheer drop to the river (and just S of the galilee), part of the castle's OUTER BAILEY WALL with a tower into which the STABLES and the MONKS' PRISON were fitted later. (There is a contemporary intra-mural passage in the wall immediately to the N which was cut off when the galilee was built.) In the lofts of the stables small windows, which

40. DURHAM Monks' kitchen roof, 1366–74. By John Lewyn

prove beyond doubt that we have here the remains of the monks' REREDORTER, probably using drains associated with the defences. The windows gave light to the individual seats. 23 ft below the stables, the monks' prison, a tunnel-vaulted chamber with large blank arcades, obviously not in their original state. The room, rarely entered, remains one of the most moving evocations of the early monastery as known to us from the Rites of Durham.

For more detailed description of the monastic buildings, the Deanery, the College and the Castle etc., see the latest edition of B of E *County Durham*.

# Ely

CATHEDRAL CHURCH
OF THE HOLY TRINITY   *Anglican*

(Based on B of E *Cambridgeshire*, 1970, further revised, with information from the Dean and from Thomas Cocke, Michael Gillingham, Martin Harrison, Peter Miller, Jeffrey West and John Wilton-Ely.)

Plan, Fig. 42, from the *Builder*, 1892, by Roland Paul. (Presbytery vaults: transverse ridge ribs should be shown stopped short as in Lincoln nave, Fig. 98.)

Some recent references (see Recent Literature): Bony 1979; Cherry 1978; Clifton-Taylor 1972; Cobb 1980;

Cocke 1975; Colvin 1978; Draper, Coldstream, Fletcher, Cocke, Keen *et al.* in B.A.A. 1979; Harvey 1978; Whittingham 1980.

## INTRODUCTION

Ely is a small town, still entirely dominated by the cathedral, and when in the Middle Ages the monastic precinct was complete, the town cannot have been more than a fringe around it, as still on the s side. On the N the width is two or three streets, on the E one and the back lanes down to the river, and only on the w is something like a town of independent existence, centred rather on the parish church. But as one approaches Ely, preferably on foot or on a bicycle, or perhaps in an open car, the cathedral dominates the picture for miles around. It lies raised on an eminence 68 ft above the flat fenland: 'a flatt of many miles . . . while Ely Minster is in one's view', wrote Celia Fiennes, who disliked the C 17 mud and damp of the place but was impressed by this 'curious pile of building'. From everywhere it offers an outline different from that of any other English cathedral. Instead of two front towers and square crossing tower, as one expects after seeing Canterbury and York, Lincoln and Durham, Ely has only one tower at the w end, and, in the place of a normal crossing tower, that curious corona, the Octagon. The w tower rises very high and broad, accompanied on the s by a lower extension, the surviving wing of the w transept. And the Octagon in its stone-built parts appears from a distance rather broad and spreading than tall, with eight big crocketed stone pinnacles surrounding the base of the timber lantern, which again has its own square-topped finials – from a distance quite a light and fanciful crowning. From dead-on N or s, the length of the building dominates – a typically English characteristic – but from the w and E the most curious groups of crags of varying heights and shapes result.

Yet Ely Cathedral must be seen not only as architecturally unique, but also in its geographical region of eastern England sharing certain features: in the C 12 with Peterborough and Norwich, in the C 13 with Lincoln, in the C 14 with all three. There were also, through the first Norman abbot, architectural relations with Winchester.

When the Normans arrived in the C 11, Ely had already a long history. St Etheldreda in 673 founded a minster here. The monastery was sacked by the Danes in 870, and reconsecrated a hundred years later, in 970, by Ethelwold, Bishop of Winchester. In the last Saxon century it was as powerful as Canterbury and Glastonbury. After the Conquest, in 1081, Simeon was made abbot, a kinsman of William the Conqueror, and a brother of Bishop Walkelin of Winchester. He had been Prior of Winchester before he was transferred to Ely. He started rebuilding in 1083 and

died in 1093. He seems to have begun, as was usual, at the E end, and he had got as far as the beginning of the transepts and crossing when he died. The translation of the relics of St Etheldreda took place in 1106. By then no doubt the E end was complete. In 1109 Ely was made the see of a bishop, but the monastery, under a prior, carried on – under the typically English arrangement of the monastic cathedral, as it existed also at Canterbury, Durham and so on. In the course of the C 12 building went on, along the nave and to the w end with its strange w tower, w crossing, w transepts and w porch. Those parts, except for the tower top, seem to have been complete by the early years of the C 13. Immediately after, it seems, Bishop Eustace began to remodel the w porch or galilee. The *Liber Eliensis* (British Library, Harley 258) says that he built it 'a fundamento versus occidentem sumptibus suis'. However, the side walls probably existed already in the Norman building, and the front and interior must have been finished later in the C 13.

But before that happened, the Norman chancel – as in nearly all English cathedrals and major monastic churches – proved inadequate and was enlarged. The apse was pulled down, and the chancel and its aisles lengthened and finished straight, without apses or ambulatory at the E end. The work was begun under Bishop Northwold in 1234 and dedicated by him in 1252. The church must now have seemed complete, and nothing was indeed done for two generations. (But a chapel in London built by a bishop of Ely, St Etheldreda's, Holborn – an important little building of the late 1280s erected by Bishop Kirkby († 1290), though some less persuasively place it in the 1290s – was related to the London court style and not to any previous or contemporary work at Ely.) Then, when John of Hotham had been made bishop (1316), John of Crauden prior (1321), and Alan of Walsingham sacrist (1321), it was felt that a proper Lady Chapel was desirable, and in 1321 the foundation stone was laid, oddly enough, for an almost separate building to the NE of the N transept and to the N of the chancel. While the position somewhat resembles that of certain chapter houses (Chester, Wells, York), the placing is more like that of Peterborough's late C 13 Lady Chapel (demolished), only set farther from the main vessel. Both these Lady Chapels were the same length, 100 ft, though Ely's was made wider. (Lincoln's N chapel of the NE transept may have been a Lady Chapel.) But then came a catastrophe.

On 22 February 1322 the Norman crossing tower collapsed, damaging in its fall the Norman bays of the chancel. The energy which would otherwise have been devoted to the Lady Chapel was at once diverted to the crossing, and – to a most unusual design of which much will have to be said later – the crossing tower was rebuilt from 1322 to 1328. It was made larger than before and given an octagonal shape.

41. ELY View from the south-east *c.* 1870

Between 1328 and 1342 the stone octagon was crowned by an octagonal lantern of timber. Meanwhile the bays immediately E of the crossing were rebuilt, and the Lady Chapel carried on probably when the masons were free after completion of those bays, say about 1337. It is by no means certain that work on the Lady Chapel was entirely

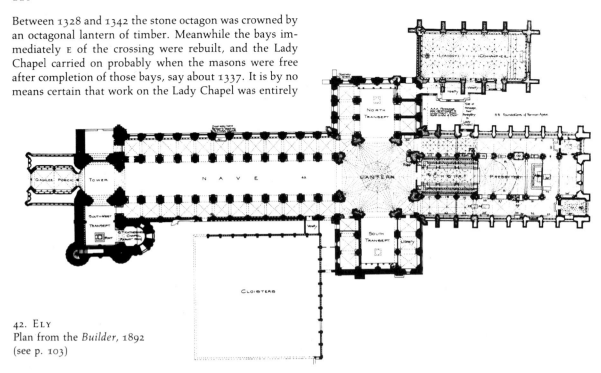

42. ELY
Plan from the *Builder*, 1892
(see p. 103)

suspended while the Octagon was being built; separate crews may have worked concurrently. The altar in the Lady Chapel was dedicated in 1353, when the E and W windows had yet to be finished but the whole chapel and its carvings were otherwise ready. Comparative analyses of documents and building work at Ely and Norwich by Harvey, Coldstream, Whittingham and Fernie have somewhat clarified the travels of masons in East Anglia, especially of the two *Ramseys*, *John* and *William*, and the elder and younger *John Attegrene*, as well as mason-decorators from Lincoln.

After the Black Death little architectural work was done at Ely. Only fitments and furnishings kept extending, the most sumptuous being the chantry chapels of Bishops Alcock and West. (But for that of Stanley, Bishop of Ely 1506–15, see Manchester.) Of the principal shrine of Ely, that of St Etheldreda, only a few fragments survived the fury of the iconoclasts. The monastery was dissolved in 1539. A dean replaced the prior, canons the monks. The cloister was pulled down and much of the monastic buildings. The use of the Lady Chapel from 1566 as a parish church ensured its survival. Of the fabric of the church the N arm of the W transept had collapsed in the C 15. Rebuilding was begun but no progress made.

For the work of restoration carried out by those more recent generations who cared for an ancient building for the sake of its aesthetic, historical and sentimental (and sometimes religious) associations, two names must be mentioned: *James Essex* – friend of Horace Walpole, Thomas Gray and William Cole – who began work in 1757, and (*Sir*) *George Gilbert Scott* who started in 1847. But first, earlier careful work on the transepts should be mentioned, by Wren's mason *Robert Grumbold* of Cambridge. In 1696–8 he buttressed the S W corner of the S transept, which suffered from the loss of the cloisters, and in 1699, after collapse of the N W corner of the N transept, he rebuilt almost exactly, with the exceptions noted below. *Essex* restored the E end to the vertical *c.* 1757, reconstructed the lantern in 1758 and the presbytery roof in 1768, and removed the choir from the crossing to the E end in 1771–2; tribute should also be paid to Bishop Mawson, who instigated this restoration and to James Bentham, the cathedral's historian, who also acted as clerk of works (Cocke). In 1796 *James Wyatt* made a survey of the W end, and during 1800–2, in consultation with him, *John Thomas Groves* repaired the W front and *Bernasconi* embellished the galilee. *Blore* made some improvements in 1840–1 and 1844. In 1845 *George Basevi*, while inspecting the W tower, fell to his death through the floor of the belfry (brass in N choir aisle). From 1847 *Scott* was busy blotting out most of what Essex, in particular, had done. He moved the choir stalls to their present place, added the present choir screen, and restored the lantern of the Octagon to its presumed original external appearance. Dean Peacock (1839–58) and Dean Goodwin (1858–69) were both keenly interested in the restoration, especially the latter, who had been one of the founders of the Cambridge Camden Society. The cathedral suffered no damage from the Second World War. But when *Stephen Dykes Bower* was called in after the war, he found what Scott had found a century before him, and doubtless what Essex had found a century before Scott, that the enemy within the Octagon lantern was death-watch beetle (*R.I.B.A. Journal* report, September 1952), since vanquished, it is hoped.

Now to summarize Ely's architectural styles. Inside and out, so far as the early stages are concerned, Ely represents, in terms of the highest architectural quality, a complete synopsis of the development of the Norman and Transitional styles from 1083 into the early c13. Then came the galilee porch w of the w tower in a pure E.E. style, followed more luxuriantly by the new E end of 1234–52, a by-product of developments in the Lincoln workshops. And finally Ely's period of great Dec magnificence in the 1320s–40s produced Octagon, Lady Chapel and choir. As John Harvey has pointed out, the great lantern and the Lady Chapel stand on the brink of the Perp style. But for a study of developed Perp, Ely is useless. Its architecture, both despite and because of post-medieval restorations, has remained as it stood in 1350.

The cathedral is faced entirely with ashlar of Barnack limestone from the quarries near Peterborough, whose monks owned them and allowed Ely and other monasteries quarrying rights. The inside of the Octagon and the Lady Chapel are said to be of Weldon or Clipsham limestone, while the Lady Chapel carvings and the Alcock Chapel are in local clunch (chalk). Mr Clifton-Taylor says the Octagon lantern, 'although in wood covered externally with lead, is markedly lithic in character', that is, especially the timber vaulting inside; yet we shall see how its outer design (except between 1758 and 1863) was controlled by the great timber posts of its frame.

The dimensions of the cathedral are as follows: 537 ft long overall, 199 ft wide at the main transepts, height of w tower 215 ft, height of Octagon 170½ ft, outside height of nave 105 ft, inside 86 ft.

## EXTERIOR

A detailed examination of the exterior should start at the SOUTH TRANSEPT; for Simeon's abbey church was begun in the usual way from the E end. This, the chancel, with apse and straight-headed chancel aisles, exists no longer. But by the time of the translation of St Etheldreda, in 1106, the ground floor of the transepts had probably already been started. It contains, externally as internally, the most ancient features of the church. It comes out three bays beyond the aisle walls and is provided with E and W aisles – both motifs taken over by Simeon from his brother Walkelin's new cathedral at Winchester, which had been begun in 1079. Externally the w wall of the s transept – visible, above the remains of the E cloister wall, only from the present Bishop's Garden – has three ground-floor windows, with just one roll moulding along jambs and arch, but with no shafts or billet decoration. At the height of the springing of the window arches and running right round them is a frieze or string-course chip-carved with small saltire crosses. The same motif occurs in the contemporary blocked doorway from the transept into the cloister (see *Cloister* below). The string-course at the ground level of the upper floor consists of two rows of tiny raised triangles. The upper windows are Perp. On the E side the corresponding features are altered (the ground floor has late c13 geometrical tracery), but on the s side more elements can be observed which belong to the earliest of the building. The ground floor here is disturbed by the former monastic structures (cf. below under *Precinct*), but a blocked, undecorated Norman doorway can be recognized and one (restored and apparently altered) early window. Above, the aisle fronts have single windows made into a tripartite motif by narrower blank arcades to the l. and r. The same motif is used twice in the front of the transept-nave, with a broad flat buttress between. Above that, there is a billet frieze; then follows a blind arcade and above – by now clearly a later stage – windows surrounded by billet friezes and with double shafting. Yet higher up one can just recognize the remains of another blank arcade. But this was replaced in the c15 by a low, broad, simple Perp window. To the l. and r. of the transept-nave rise two turrets. The clerestory on the E and w sides has again the tripartite window surrounds, but now all outlined by billet decoration.

We must now cross the church and emerge outside the NORTH TRANSEPT to study the differences between the two, which indicate a slightly later date for the N transept. On the N front the dividing buttress is no longer entirely flat, but has two shafts at the angles and higher up consists of a group of three shafts. The billet friezes which on the s side appear only higher up form here the sill-line of the ground-floor windows, and these windows have nook-shafts. Only on the E side, where work seems to have begun and where the ground-floor windows unfortunately are a later insertion, are the tripartite windows on the gallery-level without billet frieze and with only single nook-shafts. Above them is a corbel table, as also at the same level on the w side (where the gallery windows are Perp). The battlements on top of the gallery wall on the w side are of course also later. The clerestory is identical with that of the s transept. The N front at that level has a blank arcade and

above it two tall Perp windows. The turrets are not identical with those on the s side either.

In 1699 the N W corner of the N transept collapsed. The
N W turret was rebuilt, the Norman window at the W end of
the N front received new mullions, and a new doorway was
put in below it. The work was carried out by *Robert
Grumbold*, Wren's mason at Trinity Library, and *Wren*
himself was consulted on it. The window design is indeed a
repetition of that of Trinity Library, Cambridge, and the
doorway with its concave jambs and arch moulding and its
banded rustication comes immediately from St Mary-le-
Bow, and less directly from such French designs as that of
Mansart's Hôtel de Conti in Paris of *c.* 1645. Was it not, as
Cocke (1979) suggests, a case of Tuscan being thought the
proper modern C 17 equivalent to Romanesque? The classical C 17 grotesque masks on the rebuilt turret have as
much vigour as medieval ones on the N E turret.

The elements established in the course of completing the
transepts were then taken over for the NAVE, and no
innovations were introduced. A billet frieze runs at the
level of the aisle windows, also billet surrounds the tripartite groups of the clerestory windows. The blank arcading
on the s side is rather a part of the decoration of the cloister
than of the nave (see *Cloister* below, also for the carved
doorways from cloister to nave). The gallery windows are
Perp on both sides. The N aisle was apparently recased in
1662 when the remains of a C 14–15 parish church abutting
on it were removed (Cocke 1979).

The WEST END, with its remaining s wing and mighty W
tower, is not dated or precisely datable, but it seems to have
followed the completion of the nave after a short interval.
It forms a W transept, of which the N half has never been
rebuilt since its collapse in the C 15 and the s half has one E
chapel, which was ruinous in 1764 and rebuilt in 1848. The
splendour of this W end's broad-chested appearance when
its N wing was still standing may have been matched by
Bury St Edmunds (where hardly anything of all this now
remains above ground), and preceded by Winchester (W
front rebuilt).

The country where the conception of the W transept and
gigantic W tower was at home is Germany, but no immediate sources for the type of Ely have yet been found. Two
things especially are not German: the duplication of the
polygonal (to be more precise: decagonal) turrets at the
ends of the transept – in Germany there was usually one on
each side against the middle of the transept N and s ends –
and the clothing of all the walls, except for the plinth, in tier
after tier of blank arcading. This of course was the Englishman's favourite motif, used *ad nauseam* in many
cathedrals, particularly in the C 12–13, though wholly
successfully at Ely. The success here is due to a wide variety
of sizes and forms, which give a clear account of building
history, as follows.

The lowest tier of blank arches is plain and narrow, the
second introduces the remarkable enrichment of arcading
in two layers immediately behind each other so that only
the back layer can strictly be called blank. The third tier is
larger and contains windows. They have a tripartite stepped setting, and the wall above them is entirely diapered.
Above this follows a small tier of blank trefoil-headed
arches, and above them the Gothic motif of the pointed
arch is reached. There are here again windows, and they are
again arranged in tripartite stepped groups. The nook-
shafts have a series of shaft-rings, and there are sunk
quatrefoils in circles in the spandrels above. A corbel table
and late battlements end the composition. In the angle-
turrets on the s W and s E and on the E side of the transept –
where, incidentally, in a very English way, the apsed chapel
projects with its own horizontal divisions, regardless of
those of the transept – the motifs are identical or similar.
The turrets rise three stages higher, and there is no essential change in their details, except for one remarkable
conceit, impossible in any country but England. All the
way up the turrets, shafts are carried not at the angles but
in the middle of the sides. In the lowest stage of the turrets
above the battlements of the transepts these shafts are not
attached to the wall but run in front of blank arches behind
them. The big W tower also must have been continued
quickly; for right up to the stage of the quatrefoils above
the bell-openings and the corbel table above the quatrefoils
stylistic material still remains the same, although here also
decoration is used rather more sparingly. About 1200 the
W tower was ready. It received a stone spire *c.* 1230 (the
*Liber Eliensis* says explicitly 'ab opere coementario').
Then, during the later C 14, the spire was replaced by a tall
octagon storey (post-dating the central Octagon at the
main crossing, below) with large windows enriched by
tracery still in the Dec tradition and yet taller polygonal
angle pinnacles. This octagon carried a slender lead spire
which was taken down only in 1801.

The next part of the building to be erected was the W
porch or GALILEE in its present form; for a porch, very
probably two-storeyed, seems to have been built at once, in
the way to be seen to this day for instance at St Pantaleon at
Cologne – one of the component parts of what in Germany
is called a *Westwerk*. The whole W group at Ely is indeed
such a 'westwork'. In its present form the galilee is a
puzzling structure. Its date is known but seems to fit it only
partially. As has already been said, it is recorded as the
work of Bishop Eustace, who died in 1215. Now the
cladding of the N and s wall may well be as early as that – cf.
the four tiers of plain blank arcades in the E.E. style, with
no more complications than pointed trefoils in the spandrels. The angles have thin keeled shafts ending in thin
pinnacles and dogtooth between the shafts. But the W front
and also the interior, which, being open to the outside, may

be considered in our present context, are two generations later in style. In the interior the walls have tall arcading in two layers, the front layer starting from a lower plinth, the back layer from what is known as a bench table. Their interlocking is most effective. The motif derives from the choir aisle at Lincoln. Above these arcades runs an upper wall arcade, detached from the wall, and this has the same elaborate stepping and cusping (groups of five arches) as the clerestory in the work of *c.* 1250 (see *Presbytery* below). The porch is vaulted, the earliest major vaulting at Ely: two bays with finely detailed thin ribs and transverse arches no wider than the ribs. The inner portal need not be considered too seriously. It is virtually new work of *Scott*. And the outer portal also in its most surprising motif is not original, the pierced vesica in the tracery flanked by two 'mouchettes'. This, if old, would only be early C14. But it is a fanciful reconstruction by *Bernasconi*, working here 1801–2. The outer portal had, according to C18 engravings, two tall arches with a shaft between (a *trumeau*) and a solid tympanum decorated by a blank sexfoiled vesica. Above the portal is a fine group of three tall lancet windows, shafted, with shaft-rings, and dogtooth decoration, and these could again well belong to the early C13. Their nearest parallel is the E end of the retrochoir. The room behind these windows was (according to the VCH) originally open to the W crossing. About 1500 it was connected by a gallery to the Bishop's Palace (then S W of the W front, see *Precinct* below). The room is now without a roof: removed 1801–2 under *Wyatt*; *Essex* had recommended removal of the whole galilee.

The PRESBYTERY (former retrochoir) was added to the Norman chancel by Bishop Northwold in 1234–52. Its E end is intact, with its beautiful group of three tall lancets on the ground floor shafted and decorated by dogtooth and the two upper tiers of five stepped lancets above. The top tier gives light to the roof above the vaults. In the spandrels above the windows are sunk quatrefoils, sexfoils etc., and the gable is decorated rather fussily with two elongated sexfoils and a larger elongated cusped quatrefoil. Also, for the sake of the same odd *horror vacui*, the group of five upper lancet arches is continued towards the flanking turrets of the retrochoir end by half-arches, a motif that appears equally illogically and distressingly at Wells and Salisbury. At the angles of the aisles are also turrets. The N aisle E end shows the C13 design on the gallery floor; on the ground floor the E windows are altered. On the N and S sides, owing to early C14 alterations (see below), less can be seen of Hugh de Northwold's design. It should be examined on the S side. Here, though the aisle windows are all C14, the gallery windows are preserved in bays four and five from the W, twin lancet openings with vertical rows of crockets outside the nook-shafts. These two bays appear now as a screen, because the gallery behind was taken out

*c.* 1366–73 (Draper) in order to give better light to the Shrine of St Etheldreda: i.e. the internal gallery openings were glazed and the gallery roof removed, on both N and S, in Northwold's two W bays. The C13 clerestory has stepped groups of three lancets under an arch, with dogtooth decoration, and the bays are here separated by flying buttresses.

The early C14 has in these parts caused much adjustment. When the Norman crossing tower had fallen in 1322 and was replaced by the OCTAGON (1322–42), one bay each of the transept aisles, the nave aisles, and the chancel aisles was cut out for the widening from the former square to the new polygonal shape. That led to the arrangement with a pair of flying buttresses meeting in front of a very large Dec window set diagonally in each of the four shorter sides of the Octagon. Above these and the roofs of transepts, nave and chancel is a low arched wall-passage, and then the pierced balustrade and the big stone pinnacles of the Octagon. (Apparently no pinnacles at that level survived into the C18; those restored or intended there by Essex, shown in Bentham's engravings of 1771, had gone by the mid-C19, and the present ones are *Scott's*, added after he had finished restoring the lantern.) Above rises the extremely elegant timber lantern, renewed by *Scott* (who also restored flying struts removed by Essex) and more recently strengthened by *Dykes Bower*. The lantern's finials are more than pretty fanciful cresting. These eight post-like square-topped pinnacles of lead-sheathed timber rise from (as it were, out of) the eight main posts of the lantern's frame, as if to proclaim the nature of the frame's wooden skeleton and the boldness needed even to get the material for it: this open countryside lacked great oaks 'for the huge beams required . . . which had to be sought far and wide, found with much difficulty, bought at great price, and carried to Ely by land and water' (Monk of Ely, *Anglia Sacra*, quoted in Salzman 1967). Scott went by the Browne Willis view of 1730 in restoring these finial-posts, whereas *Essex* in 1758 had clothed the main posts with conventional buttresses ending in pointed pinnacles of no post-like character whatever, i.e. he imitated masonry. Perhaps we should bless Scott for giving us back more nearly the look of the great carpenter Hurley's lantern. At least, no big work on it is recorded between C14 and C18. (Its various stages C18–C20 are illustrated in Cobb 1980 and in Cocke 1975 and 1979; but with Dr Cocke's statement that Essex's lantern was closer to the presumed medieval original than Scott's one must respectfully disagree.) On sources of the Octagon idea and further on its structure, see *Interior* below, pp. 117–20.

As soon, it seems, as the masonry of the Octagon was complete, the Norman bays E of it, which had fallen under the weight of the collapsing crossing tower, were rebuilt (*c.* 1330–5). The windows are Dec in all three storeys,

44. ELY The Octagon, 1322–42, exterior

broad, of four lights and with flowing tracery. In the clerestory the jambs and arches have fleuron decoration, and at the top, below the parapet, is another frieze with fleuron or square leaf motifs. On the N side and most of the S side the flying buttresses were at the same time re-done. These bays are now the choir.

There is now only one more part of the exterior to be examined, the LADY CHAPEL begun in 1321. Perhaps actual building only went on during c. 1335–53 or, possibly more likely, continuously from the 1320s. Occupied as a parish church 1566–c 20. It is an almost free-standing rectangle of 100 ft by 46 ft with a seven-light E window and eight-light W window, and tall four-light N and S windows.

These are entirely in the flowing Dec style, except for the E window, where in the rather wilful, not to say ugly, development out of the singled-out middle light into the top of the arch head, the Perp is heralded, in feeling if not in actual motifs. (This window was the gift of Bishop Barnet and was made between 1371 and 1375. VCH) The windows have embattled transoms and the roof-pitch is comparatively low. Below the W window runs a row of eight broad ogee-headed niches with brackets for statues, and above the W and E windows is another, of nine rising niches squeezed in between window and embattled gable, and also provided with brackets for statues. These top niches are all ogee-headed.

The NAVE of Ely is Early Norman still, though it can hardly have been begun before *c.* 1110, Early Norman in its inexorably uniform rhythm and its absence of all light relief. As one sees it coming in from the w, it seems immensely high, immensely long, and uncomfortably narrow in relation to the other two dimensions, moving, but grim and gaunt with its seemingly endless repetition of the same shafts from floor to ceiling, the same large bare arcade openings, and the same gallery openings gaping nearly as wide. Even the clerestory is not much less tall. (The proportions of arcade, gallery and clerestory are 6:5:4.) Subdivisions one cannot see from the entrances, variations of dimensions are not at once noticed, and subtler modifications less still. With the shafts marking the division from bay to bay like huge masts, and the sturdy but also far from short shafts of arcades and gallery looking like so many poles, the general impression is, in spite of the massive stone blocks, oddly oaken. A contributing factor perhaps is the relation of void to solid, so astounding for a stone building of so early a date. The Gothic builders of France fifty years later certainly did not go beyond the transparency of Ely.

To appreciate the details of the nave, however, one has to see it in its position in the building history of the cathedral, and that, for us, begins first with one vestige of the Norman E end, then with the transepts. Simeon's cathedral was no doubt started at the E end. The beginning dates from 1083, and the first consecration took place in 1106. We do not know how much was done then, whether the chancel only, or the transepts, the crossing tower and the E end of the nave as well. We can only go by the evidence surviving in the building. From the Norman apse all that survives is the pair of piers, or rather remains of two responds each with mast-like shaft, to l. and r. of the site of the springing of the apse, between the present choir and presbytery (see the plan, Fig. 42). The existence of an apse has been proved by excavation, and it has also been shown that it was very soon replaced by a square E end, as the English liked it (Southwell, Romsey). These former responds, now bonded into later piers, were rectangular on their inner sides, each with attached cylindrical shaft running straight up from floor to (former) ceiling. So that motif existed from the beginning, as indeed it had existed already at Jumièges (1040–67).

Apart from that pair of responds, the SOUTH TRANSEPT is the oldest existing part of the cathedral. The w windows and the ground floor of the s side have already been mentioned (see *Exterior* above). Now the interior disposition must be studied, and in doing so it must not be forgotten that the first of its former four bays was cut out when the Octagon replaced the square Norman crossing tower. So what the Norman crossing piers were like we

cannot say. The remaining three bays have aisles on both sides just as at Winchester, which was undoubtedly Simeon's example. The arcades are arranged with a kind of alternation of supports. Starting from the s wall and following w or E arcade there is first a circular pier, then a composite pier, and then again a circular pier, although this is now halved at its meeting with the Octagon piers. The composite pier is of an odd design, flat towards the transept nave (where one might expect a shaft to go up to the ceiling, as indeed it does at Winchester – against a similarly flat background) and with three stepped attached shafts carrying the plain one-stepped, unchamfered and unmoulded arches. The capitals of the circular and the composite piers are of the characteristically Early Norman variety with stunted volutes at the angles (this has no parallel at Winchester), and on the E side there are in addition flatly carved thin tendrils or scrolls to decorate the surfaces of the capitals, and also affronted birds and beasts. The E and w aisles are vaulted, with groined vaults not too precisely set out. The E aisle (also of the N transept) was divided by low walls into chapels, the w aisle, in the same way as at Winchester, by a wall closing the arcade, was made into a sacristy. At the sill-level of the gallery floor appears the first billet frieze in the cathedral. The gallery openings are about as large as those of the arcade, but they are subdivided into two openings above each one of the arcades. The shafts between the twin openings are thin and straight like sturdy staves. The gallery was evidently built a little later than the arcade. The arches now have two roll mouldings, and the sub-arches one. (In the w wall they have in addition an odd kind of fillet.) The alternation of supports is between the composite piers and the circular piers with their thin attached shafts in the main directions. Most capitals are of the plain block or cushion type, except for two at the E wall close to the N end. (These, and some similar ones in the N transept gallery, are block capitals decorated with foliage, in a style closer to that of the cloister doorways (below) than to the ground-floor capitals. Professor Zarnecki suggests that these gallery capitals were carved *in situ* when the scaffolding was in place for the building of the central tower.) The clerestory has the same motif as Winchester: an inner wall-passage in front of the windows with a tripartite stepped group of arches for each bay: narrow–wide–narrow, and low–taller–low. Block capitals repeat here throughout, as they do at Winchester.

Now for the s wall. This is probably not in its original state. The wall space of the nave is divided in the middle by a three-shaft wall-pier with one of the early carved capitals. But narrowly in front of this and the wall runs an arcade of six arches on circular piers, and above these small blank arcading of intersecting arches. They carry an open passageway or balcony from w gallery to E gallery. Intersecting arches seem to appear at Ely only in the second third of the

45. ELY Looking from the C 14 crossing into the late C 11/early C 12 south transept

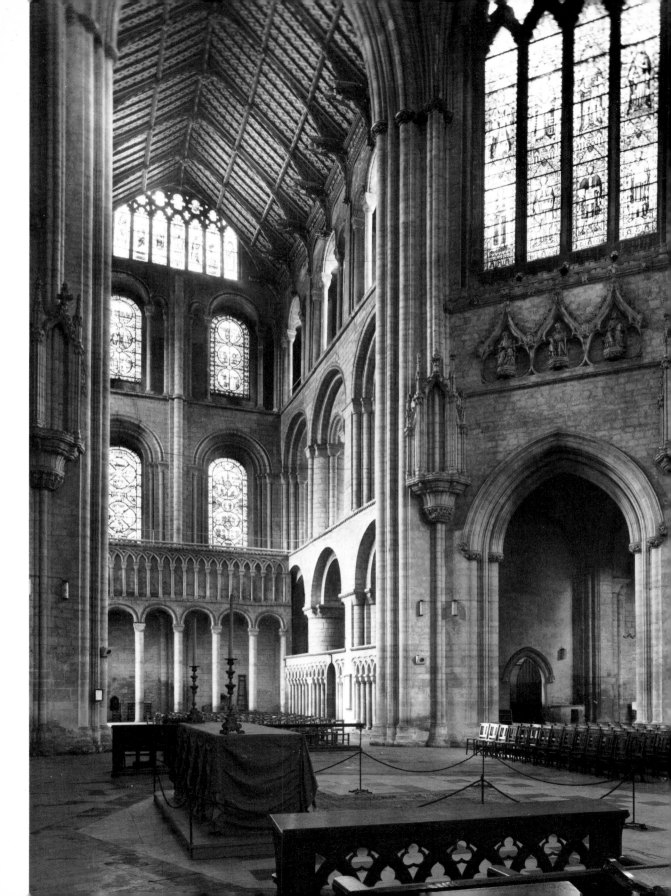

C 12, although they are present at Durham before 1100, and so one may presume that the original plan was for a balcony the width of one whole bay, exactly as it still exists at Winchester. Whether this was ever built or not cannot be said. Intersecting arches also are the decoration of the screen dividing the sacristies from the transept nave. This was no doubt brought here from somewhere else, perhaps from the N W transept when this was demolished. As the demolition is attributed to the C 14, the DOORWAY now leading into the vestries from the nave aisle would confirm this assumption. It is clearly of the C 14 and has two good large head-stops at the ends of the hoodmould (cf. Octagon). Above the balcony the s wall of the transept nave goes on with a tall shaft rising as high as to touch the sill of the Perp window in the gable, that is in the C 12 probably rising right up to the ceiling. The present R O O F is a fine hammerbeam roof of the C 15 with angels as supporters of the hammerbeam.

The NORTH TRANSEPT must have been begun a little later than its companion. They differ from each other in many remarkable, if on the whole minor, ways. First of all,

both have alternating supports, but the relation on the N side is rather illogically reversed. Starting again from the outer wall, that is this time from the N, the first pier is composite and the second circular. That may have been done with a view to the broad balcony across the N end, but it must have led to trouble at the Norman crossing; for while the pier leaning against the Octagon is now composite, the half-pier against the Norman crossing must have been semicircular. There are other differences too. The capitals on the ground floor have volutes only on the E side, where also the gallery windows seemed earlier than the others (see *Exterior* above). On the w side they are block-shaped. The w aisle has a stone seat running along its w wall and was perhaps used as a vestibule for pilgrims (VCH). To return to the arcade, the piers of the N transept, as against those on the s side, have demi-shafts to the nave which run right up to the ceiling, marking the division into bays much more clearly than in the s transept. The arcade arches are like those in the s transept. The gallery and clerestory also are not altered. The N wall is similar, too, but the narrow balcony, replacing also what was, or was meant to be, a

46. ELY Nave, early C 12, looking west

wider one, is different. It here consists of alternating narrower and wider arches, the wider arches being taller also, that is a motif similar to that of the clerestory. The capitals are still of the block kind. This balcony must have been put in almost immediately after the completion of the transept, though not as part of its design; for the balcony cuts into the arcade arches. The ROOF of the N transept is similar to that of the other transept.

The NAVE is twelve bays long from the E face of the W tower to the Octagon, and was therefore originally thirteen to the Norman crossing – a length excessive even in England, yet cf. Norwich and Winchester with fourteen. Its general character has already been described (opening paragraph on *Interior* above). If we reckon that it was begun in 1110 or even a little earlier, it must either have been built very quickly or with a surprising and rare faith in the original plan. For except for the billet frieze at the gallery sill there is virtually no decoration at all in the nave. Capitals are still block-shaped; even the usual scalloping is not (or hardly) done. Shaft after shaft runs right up to the ceiling – a cambered ceiling, in its present form of the C 19 – regardless of the fact that in the arcade as well as the gallery alternation of supports is not given up. There is a curious lack of decision in the design here, a wavering between the two chief types of Norman elevation – one-bayed and double-bayed. At Ely the main effect is entirely of uniform bays, as the shafts are identical, whether they stand against piers with five stepped shafts towards the arches or with one fat segmental less-than-demi-pier. The former motif comes straight from the transept galleries, the latter is a none too happy innovation of the designer of the nave. In the gallery the alternation is between five stepped shafts towards the arches and less-than-demi-piers with one shaft added in the middle, again not a happy invention. In the aisles there are more original features, especially the blank arcading all along the outer walls. This is again quite plain, but in various places above it, and below the sill-line of the aisle windows, a broad zigzag frieze appears. There is some of it to the l. and r. of the Prior's Door (see below under *Cloister*) and more towards the W end. (It also existed in the N aisle, but was there hacked off, except in the easternmost bay.) The aisle windows on the S side start higher up than on the N side because the N walk of the cloister had to find place beneath. A few more indications of later date towards the W end have to be added. The arcade arches have three instead of two roll mouldings towards the nave and the transverse arches across the aisles two instead of none. In the clerestory scalloped capitals begin to appear, and in the westernmost bay of the S aisle two tiers of blank arches, the upper ones being interlaced. That leads direct to the W transept.

Otherwise there is so much difference between the ground floor of the WEST TRANSEPT and the nave that work must have been interrupted, probably during the troubled years of Stephen. The very arch out of the nave into the transept and the corresponding one into the E chapel of the transept are thickly decorated with row upon row of zigzag – in a style quite alien to that of the nave, and with a feeling for show absent from Ely until then (in spite of the Prior's Door). The apsed chapel (St Catharine's) also has zigzag round the windows, intersecting arches in the upper tier of its blank wall-arcading, and scalloped capitals, though no ribs in the vault yet. How much of this is a correct representation of the original state cannot now be known. The chapel was in ruins early in the C 19, and rebuilt in 1848. Higher up in the E wall, capitals are of the many-scalloped and even the waterleaf varieties.

The W and S walls of the W transept are as illuminating from inside as they are from outside. Again the tiers of decorative arcades above each other afford a sequence of historical phases in quick succession, starting with plain blank arches as in the nave aisles, going on to a zigzag frieze, to interlaced arches, to arches in two layers behind each other, to trefoil-headed arches, and then, yet higher up, notably in the crossing of the W transept, to pointed arches and shafts with several shaft-rings. The crossing was in fact strengthened inside when the octagonal lantern was put on in the C 14. The present crossing piers and arches belong entirely to that period, but above the arches are the pointed ones of c. 1200 with a kind of spiky crenellation in three dimensions (similar to some in the infirmary; see *Precinct* below). To the l. and r. of the crossing arches are two vesica-shaped sunk medallions. They also appear on the E side of the arch facing the nave.

The GALILEE interior is described with its exterior (above).

Next the C 13 eastern extension of six bays, i.e. the bays behind the present high altar plus the four bays of the present PRESBYTERY, originally the retrochoir when the high altar was farther W. (For about a century between Essex and Scott both choir and presbytery were here, with the high altar against the E wall; for the C 14 bays where the choir now is, see *Choir* below.) Bishop Hugh of Northwold added this extension to the Norman eastern arm during 1234–52, apparently especially for the grander siting of St Etheldreda's Shrine. These dates thus lie exactly between the completion of the Lincoln nave and the beginning of the retrochoir or Angel Choir there, and Ely's new E end is indeed the missing link between the two. Of its stylistic connection with Lincoln there can be no doubt. The piers are the same as one of several types in Lincoln nave, with a circular core and eight detached Purbeck shafts around, tied together by a band of shaft-rings. The capitals are the same, of Purbeck marble, with sumptuous stiff-leaf decoration. The arch mouldings, however, are yet more finely split up, and the bit of dogtooth enrichment is lacking at Lincoln. The pointed sunk trefoils in the spandrels foretell the trefoils in the Angel Choir spandrels, and the brackets

supporting the vaulting-shafts are as big and fully decorated as in the Angel Choir, at least in the w bays of
Northwold's retrochoir, where the shrine stood. Here they
are as gloriously profuse in their stiff-leaf crockets as any
in England. Further E they are simpler and oddly denuded,
the surface rather like a dry fir-tree's when one has
chopped off all the branches. The shafts are tripartite, as at
Lincoln nave, and carry a vault, also exactly as at Lincoln
nave. It was there put in shortly after 1233; that is exactly
when building began at Ely. The vault at Ely, like the nave
vault at Lincoln, consists of transverse arches as thin as the
diagonal ribs, ridge ribs along the ridge, shortened or cut
off ridge ribs at r. angles, and one pair each of tierceron ribs
in each cell of the vault. The effect is palm-like but not as
tropical as at Exeter (after 1275), where tiercerons are
multiplied. But the palm effect certainly confuses the logic
of the vault. We do not see it any longer as bay following
bay, but as sprouting wall-shaft following sprouting wall-
shaft. The result is that at the E end we are left with the
unsatisfactory feature of what seems to be a half-bay.
Bosses run all along the longitudinal ridge ribs and also
stress the ends of the transverse ridge ribs. They are mostly
of stiff-leaf; but there is also a beautifully tender little
Coronation of the Virgin above the altar, a seated figure of
St Etheldreda above her shrine, and a seated figure of a
monk (?) holding a church and keys.

So far the presbytery gallery and clerestory have not yet
been looked at in detail. The gallery is as copiously decorated as that of the Angel Choir was to be, though no figure
sculpture is introduced anywhere. The motif of twin openings is taken over from Norman Ely and also from Lincoln
nave. The dividing colonnette is a thin quatrefoil Purbeck
shaft. The sub-arches are trefoiled, and in the spandrel
appears no bar tracery yet (as at the Angel Choir) but still
only a sunk pointed quatrefoil with big flat sprays of
stiff-leaf r. and l. The surrounding main arch rests on three
shafts separated by vertical bands of crocketing (as in the
Angel Choir) – a most lively motif. Finally in the spandrels
of the main arches are again sunk pointed quatrefoils. (As
noted outside, in 1366–73 the two gallery bays nearest the
present choir were unroofed and their inner openings
glazed, to throw more light on the shrine.) The clerestory
has no bar tracery yet either, but instead the charming
motif of a group of tall stepped lancet openings of the
wall-passage, again with Purbeck shafts, shaft-rings and
dogtooth, and with elaborately cusped or foiled arches – a
motif we have already found inside the galilee.

The E end also uses Purbeck shafts and dogtooth to
enrich the beautiful group of three big lancets, and the five
smaller lancets above have a screen of cusped or foiled
stepped arches in front, the immediate continuation of the
clerestory. Finally the aisle vaults. These, being amongst
the earliest work, have no tiercerons, just the straightforward ribs and transverse arches, like the galilee vault. For
the N E and S E chapels, see *Monuments*, E end, below.

The OCTAGON (exterior, p. 110): the masonry crossing
structure and the space it encloses, roofed by timberwork
vaults and lantern. In February 1322 the Norman crossing
tower fell down (with damage also E of the crossing; see
below on rebuilding of three bays now the choir). The
member of the chapter in charge of building work was the
sacrist, and to this post *Alan of Walsingham* had been
promoted one year before. When the disaster happened he
was so overwhelmed that, the chronicle tells us, he did not
at first know 'where to turn or what to do'. But then he
collected himself, had stones and timber cleared out of the
church and 'had the place excavated where the new tower
was to be constructed, measuring it out with architectural
skill in eight parts, in which eight stone columns were to be
erected to support the whole building'.

As the idea of a wide octagonal crossing is the greatest
individual achievement of architectural genius at Ely
Cathedral, it must be emphasized as strongly as possible
that according to the evidence of this source, the Monk of
Ely who wrote in the later C 14, the idea of the Octagon was
not the mason's but the sacrist's. Alan of Walsingham, it is
true, was an artist as well; he first appears at Ely in 1314, as
a monk and goldsmith. It has lately become fashionable to
minimize the role played by the layman in architectural
invention in the Middle Ages, but there is nothing in this
great spatial idea that would not have been possible for an
amateur. (It throws an odd sidelight on one stage of
research into medieval architecture that the late G. G.
Coulton and his school, in spite of the documents quoted,
refused to accept the creative contribution of Alan of
Walsingham because they were irritated by the C 19 notion
of medieval churchmen as actual designers of churches – a
romantic conception that indeed died hard: the relevant
volume of *Cambridge County Geographies*, 1909, even
had it that Alan carved the figure reliefs on the Octagon's
great corbels.) But what Lord Burlington could do in the
C 18, Alan could do in the C 14.

Had he any 'exemplar'? Octagonal towers or top stages
of towers existed of course even in the C 11 and C 12: at
Jumièges in Normandy, St Germans in Cornwall, Swaff-
ham Prior in Cambridgeshire; Ely itself may have had an
octagonal lantern on its Norman crossing tower (the one on
the w tower is later C 14) and Peterborough was given one
c. 1325. But these could not have fired Alan's spatial
conception. Possible precedents abroad are the hexagonal
C 13 crossing of the cathedral at Siena and the crossing of
Arnolfo di Cambio's Florence Cathedral. Alan may have
known Italy or he may not. We have too little information
about his life to say anything about that. In any case the
Siena crossing is rather crooked and unimpressive and
Arnolfo's was not yet built in Alan's time and would have

47. ELY Presbytery, 1234–52, looking north-east

to have been made known to him on paper. The Florence crossing has certainly more of the spirit of Ely. Yet it seems unnecessary to seek foreign sources. In England certain centrally planned religious auxiliary buildings, then recently built, were structurally venturesome in a relevant way. The wooden octagonal vault of York chapter house of before *c.* 1300 covered a 59-ft span without any central pier. On a lesser scale, the Bishop's Palace kitchen at Chichester was roofed *c.* 1300 by the use of the hammer-beam principle to cover the central void (Fletcher 1979). Such work may have been a springboard for the leap at Ely.

Even if Alan of Walsingham knew or imagined such a precedent himself, he still needed someone to work it out. The temptation for historians to throw out the baby with the bath-water has been great both ways. The Octagon contains so much ingenuity in the details, it would be just as interesting to know who the structural designer was (who, in London c 20 terms, the Ove Arup was) as to know who had the initial idea. The answer which the Sacrist's Rolls gives us is more tantalizing than enlightening. Under Edw. II 17 we find just one entry: 'Item dat. cuidam de Londonia ad ordinand novum opus 3/4.' *Ordinare* in medieval documents means almost without exception to design or lay out. On the other hand 3*s*. 4*d*. is not much for the visit of a distinguished mason for such a purpose. And if he who came was a distinguished mason, say the King's Mason from London, would not Alan have mentioned his name in the roll? The date fits, and it is tempting to assume a visit of a consultant de Londonia, before the Ely masons, first a *John Cementarius* and then *John Attegrene*, were left to the execution of the great work. The style of the Octagon allows, as far as I can see, for no attribution to one particular London mason. (For attribution of the timber-work overhead, see below.)

And now, having said so much historically about the Octagon, it is time to enter and enjoy it. It is a delight from beginning to end for anyone who feels for space as strongly as for construction. For the basic emotion created by the Octagon as one approaches it along the nave is one of spaciousness, a relief, a deep breath after the oppressive narrowness of the Norman work. Then follows, as one tries to account for that sudden widening of one's lungs, the next moment's feeling, a feeling of surprise. Its immediate cause is that light falls in from large windows diagonally – a deviation unheard of in great church crossings of the West. The rhythm of the Octagon as one takes it in, once one has reached its centre, is an alternation of immensely tall arches in the main directions and of a three-tier arrangement in the diagonals, consisting of arches of arcade height, a kind of blind triforium above, and the large 'clerestory' windows. The arches, the tall ones too, have capitals only to some of their jamb mouldings. Hoodmoulds rest on excellently carved head-stops. The blind triforium consists

in each diagonal of three ogee niches of odd trefoil shape, filled by seated Victorian figures. The windows have rather gross and heavy flowing tracery.

Of special ingenuity are the shafts in the eight angles which carry the vault. They are hard to describe. They start as one tripartite shaft in each angle, until, a little above the springing of the diagonal arches, they are met by a kind of corbelled-out lantern shapes. These odd lanterns or triple niches rest on corbels carved with eight stories from the life of St Etheldreda. They are worth a close examination with field glasses, as relatively untouched English narrative sculpture of *c.* 1325. Then the lantern or niche corbels out and rises into a complex nodding ogee arch with crockets and pinnacles. The canopies are also worth close study. They are tripartite with flanking buttress shafts and buttress shafts between the parts. The outer parts have little flying buttresses rising to the centre part, rather as in the Hawton Easter Sepulchre in Notts, but wrapped round. The brackets on which the canopies stand have undulating embattled tops. Now, if one looks into each lantern, one sees that the triple shaft which had started at the bottom goes on rising, unconcerned by the corbel and the crocketed gable which it seems to penetrate. It continues behind and above them until it reaches its final capital, where the ribs of the vault spring.

The vault is of wood, of the tierceron kind, and shoots up with its palm-branches from each of the eight angles to one side of the eight-sided lantern balancing on the vault. It seems a miraculous feat, though in fact the lantern is of timber and hence not as heavy as if it were of stone (even so, the whole wooden superstructure of the Octagon weighs over 450 tons); and the lantern does not really stand on the vaulting-ribs, but on a magnificent sturdy timber construction behind the vaults. (See the little wooden model kept in the s transept; there is a tradition in the cathedral that 'it was made by [or for] Mr Essex': information from Mr Miller.) A word must be said about this construction, as it can be seen if one climbs into the lantern and on to the roofs. From the angles of the masonry octagon, reinforced by the heavy weight of their big stone pinnacles and supported by flying buttresses, jut out horizontal beams realizing – for the first time on such a scale – the principal of the hammerbeam (already worked out in little, e.g. in the aforementioned kitchen roof at Chichester). In addition, from somewhat lower down the angles go up diagonally even bigger beams – 64 ft long and of a scantling starting at 3 ft 4in. by 2 ft 8 in. and tapering to 12 in. at the place where, a little higher up, they meet the angles of the lantern.

The lantern, as will be noticed with delight both inside and out, does not stand angle above angle and side above side with the masonry octagon, but with a twist, so that each outer side faces an inner angle, and *vice versa*. It seems the *nec plus ultra* of that playing with spatial surprise which characterizes the Octagon altogether. But it has at the same time a sound functional reason. By means of that twist each of the reinforced angles of the masonry octagon shoots out diagonally two horizontal and two diagonally rising beams, and thereby the weight from each angle of the timber lantern is split at its foot and carried on diagonally by two pairs of principal beams. The whole, seen in a diagram, is much like a c 20 space frame. Standing inside, at the foot of the Octagon, however, one realizes nothing of all that and is simply thrilled and bewildered by the way in which eleven ribs sprout out of each angle-shaft and five of them carry one side of the lantern. The lantern has large windows and is gloriously light. The roof over the crossing is again of the tierceron kind, a splendid eight-cornered star with a boss in the centre adorned by a demi-figure of Christ. Above this is a chamber where originally bells were hung.

The name of the ingenious carpenter to whom we owe the timber work of the Octagon is in all probability known to us. In the Sacrist's Rolls for 1334–5 and 1336–7 appears the name of *William Hurley*, and he receives a salary quite out of proportion with all the others employed in the work. His £8 a year (plus board and lodging) compares with £2 for the resident master mason. In 1339–40, 1345–6 and 1349–50 he appears again, but with lesser sums. At that time he probably only paid occasional visits. Hurle (or de Hurlegh, or Hurley) was the most distinguished carpenter of his age. He can be followed through his career in London, from St Stephen's Chapel, that is the King's Chapel in the Palace of Westminster (1326), to the Guildhall Chapel (1332), and again to St Stephen's (1336, 1346, 1351–2) and to Windsor (1344, 1350). In 1336 he was appointed Chief Carpenter to the King's Works south of Trent. He died in 1354 or a little earlier. On his probable responsibility for the Ely choir stalls, see *Furnishings* below. (On Essex's and Scott's different treatments of the lantern later on, see *Exterior, Octagon,* above.)

There is one caveat about the great open floor space we see now (subject to the usually mobile furnishings of the late c 20). It was not meant to be so unencumbered. Immediately in the c 14, following Norman precedent, the choir stalls were placed there, screened against draughts, in an enclosure extending from the E crossing arch to the w crossing arch. This continued from the 1340s until the 1770s, when *Essex* moved the choir to the E end. As still today at Gloucester, Norwich, St Albans and Winchester, the crossing had been the accepted place for a Norman choir. Occasional orchestral concerts still prove the Octagon's heavenly acoustics. (On the present choir, see below; on the c 14 choir stalls, and former paintings of Saxon bishops on the former screen walls, see *Furnishings*.)

Immediately after – or perhaps before? – completion of the Octagon masonry, it seems that the three remaining

Norman bays E of the crossing were rebuilt, i.e. between Northwold's c 13 bays and the new crossing. These c 14 bays now hold the CHOIR. In the c 14 the altar w of the saint's shrine would seem to have been here. Between Essex's time and Scott's, these bays were w of the choir and contained *Essex*'s screen. The date of the three bays may be c. 1328–c. 1335. They are a little disappointing after the excitement of the Octagon. The capricious filigree of their gallery openings is, it is true, exceedingly pretty, and the arcade piers of Purbeck marble afford the most instructive comparison with those of the presbytery: the ones with the fine articulation of the E.E. style, the others with the less distinct play of light and shade of the Dec, the ones with each shaft finished by its own capital, the others with some of the shafts left without capitals. The vault is the earliest instance in East Anglia of a full-blown lierne vault (more elaborate than the N aisle vault, which must have been built first), and bosses emphasized the corners of the interlaced stars as much as their centres. But the system is that of the Norman and E.E. parts of the building unmodified, and thus the contribution of the new style seems only a matter of superficial adornment. As for details, the fleuron decoration of the orders of the arcade arches ought to be remembered, and the corbels and trefoils of the spandrels. The vaults of the choir aisles have (renewed) lierne vaults only in the N aisle, ridge ribs in both directions (which the presbytery aisles have not) in the s aisle. The octagon of lierne ribs in each N aisle vault occurs also in the Ethelbert Gate at Norwich.

The foundation stone of the LADY CHAPEL was laid in 1321, but work was perhaps interrupted for the sake of the more urgent reconstruction of the cathedral itself. So the building might have to be dated c. 1335–53. (Dr Coldstream, however, suggests continuous work by a separate crew of men and so earlier completion.) The exterior has been described. The interior is now reached from the N porch into the N transept. Originally a more important route of access led through a splendidly decorated DOORWAY in the N choir aisle into a two-bay-wide anteroom on the s side of the chapel. The doorway has as the principal motif of its decoration broad side niches placed diagonally – a position so much favoured by the designers of the early c 14. Damaged figures are in the spandrels of the doorway, and niches for more statuettes run all along the jambs and arch, with their own little brackets and canopies.

The Lady Chapel itself is basically no more than a plain parallelogram, and it might well be expected that what the early c 14 could do in that case would be no more than in the choir – the imaginative decoration of surfaces. But that is not so; the designer of the Lady Chapel, whose name we do not know for certain, has set the flat surfaces in an undulating motion, and it is from this that the great fascination of the room derives. The zone chiefly in ques-

50. ELY Looking east from the C14 choir
into the C13 presbytery

tion is that below the windows. Here seats have been placed
all along the walls, as if it were a chapter house. (But there
was a chapter house, now demolished, off the former
cloister, below.) From the level of the seats rise Purbeck
shafts, treated like thin buttresses. Then, however, almost
at once – perhaps in 1322 – this scheme was given up, and
the rest of the stonework is of a soft limestone, said to be
from Weldon or Clipsham. Each seat is treated as a deep
niche and has a canopy with that most characteristic Dec
motif, the nodding ogee arch or three-dimensional ogee
arch. The arches are cusped, gabled and thickly crocketed.
Underneath them and half hidden by them, the niches on
the N and S sides (not the E and W) each have a double arch
against their back walls. This increases the complexity of
the design considerably. Moreover, at intervals, corresponding to the strips of wall left standing between the

wide and high windows, is a wider niche projecting in its
arch further forward. In addition the corners are veiled by
niches placed diagonally. By these various means the
designer gives the vivid impression of a movement swinging and rocking forward and upward. The flowing tracery
of the windows takes up in two dimensions this feeling of
sensuous curves, but the wall between the windows, above
the broader niches, is given two tiers of blank arches and in
addition two tiers of minor arches in the jambs of the
windows. All these again have nodding ogee arches.

The vault is broad and not too steeply pointed. With its
star formations of liernes, its concealment of any division
into bays, and its innumerable comparatively small bosses it
spreads out easily across and harmonizes well with the
intricacies of the wall decoration.

The general impression of the room as we receive it now
is in one way quite false. The windows – the remaining
fragments prove that – had stained glass and the architectural details, also according to preserved traces, were all
painted. So there was not the clarity of today, but a rather

51. ELY Lady Chapel, begun 1321, roofed by 1345

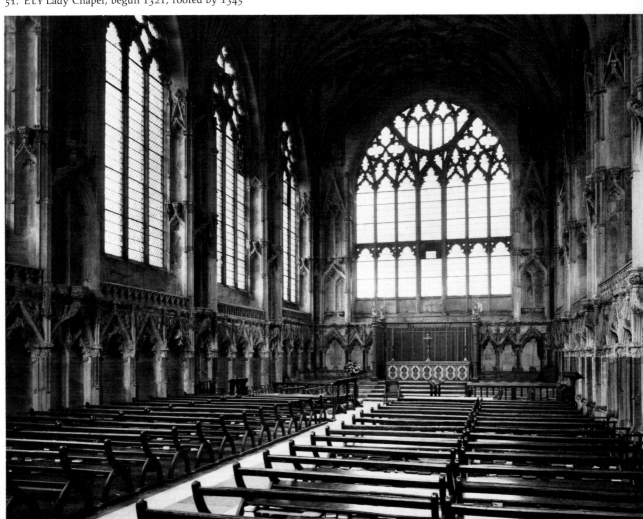

hotter and more exciting effect. (See *Stained glass* below.) With the present daylight glare from all sides, this is a difficult room to photograph.

The sculptural decoration of the Lady Chapel is of clunch. It is unfortunately far from intact. Not one figure, not one scene is as it should be, and what remains makes one feel sad about it. The decoration consists of figures of saints (?) in the small spandrels of the recessed sub-arches of each niche below the main nodding ogee arch, and of stories, usually comprised in two separate groups, in each spandrel to the l. and the r. of the gables of the nodding ogee arches. The iconography of the Lady Chapel was investigated by M. R. James. The scenes are from the life and the miracles of the Virgin, based mainly on the

so-called Evangelium Pseudo-Matthaei. The iconoclasm that smashed so many of these figures is thought to have been that of the C 16 rather than that of the C 17.

## FURNISHINGS, W TO E

Stained glass and monuments are described separately.

*West transept* FONT. By *Scott*, 1853, very E.E. with stiff-leaf capitals. (An exquisite late C 17 font, given to the cathedral in 1693 by Dean Spencer, is at Prickwillow, *c*. 3 miles away.) – ALTAR in the chapel. 1896 by *P. Thicknesse* of Liverpool. – PAINTINGS. Ceiling of the w tower by *H. S. Le Strange*, 1855. – Ceiling of the transept by *T. Gambier Parry*, 1878; cf. nave ceiling.

52. ELY Niches in the Lady Chapel, mid-1320s

*Nave and aisles*   The Norman stone pulpitum stood between what is now the first pair of piers of the nave (from the E). It was demolished by *Essex* in 1770, in consequence of the eastward move of the choir, but he recorded many of its details and re-used parts in his own screen, demolished by Scott (Cocke). – CROSS SHAFT AND BASE in the S aisle. Late C7, undecorated, but with an inscription in Roman capitals recording the cross as the gift of Ovin, steward of St Etheldreda. Bentham rescued it from use as a horse block at Haddenham (Cocke). – PAINTING. Remains of imitation masonry jointing in the vaults of the aisles; remains of scrolls and chevrons on nave piers, where the pulpitum once stood (see above). – Nave ceiling by *Le Strange*, continued by *Gambier Parry*; 1858–65, a scheme based on the ceiling of St Michael's, Hildesheim (Cobb).

*South transept*   MODEL for Octagon timber structure (see *Interior* above), said to be C18. – W wall, vestry DOOR, late C15. Of carved oak, similar to one in Alcock's chantry. It comes from Landbeach (Cobb), where there is a pulpit bearing Alcock's badges. – TILES, C14. Large reset pavement (usually covered), the centre in a circular pattern. Thought to have come from the passage between choir and Lady Chapel (Keen in B.A.A. 1979). Similar to a celebrated pavement in Prior Crauden's Chapel (see *Precinct* below). – PAINTING. Liberation of St Peter, Italian, C18? Originally bought by Lord Grantham; later formed part of the altar screen at Lincoln; given to Ely Cathedral by Dr Yorke, Dean of Lincoln and later Bishop of Ely. Placed on Essex's altarpiece at Ely in 1801, when it was thought to be C17 by Ribera (Cobb).

*North transept*   SCREEN, PANELLING, AND REREDOS of St George's Chapel, a memorial of the First World War, by *Sir Guy Dawber*, 1922. – SCREEN of St Edmund's Chapel, C15, much restored. – PAINTING in St George's Chapel. Remains of *c.* 1200 in the vault and on the walls. – In St Edmund's Chapel, also *c.* 1200, in the N lunette, the Martyrdom of St Edmund, restored in 1936, and below a curious bold ornamental design of vertical bars with crockets. On the facing wall an equally bold pattern of circles. The scene in the lunette can no longer be traced.

*Presbytery, choir and aisles*   Choir and sanctuary were refitted by *Scott*, 1848–52 and 1866–9. Wooden SCREEN with carving partly by *John Philip*, partly by *Rattee & Kett*, and brass gates and scrollwork by *Hardman*, with ornamental ironwork by *Potter* of London (cathedral handbook 1852); it was Scott's earliest major cathedral screen. – ORGAN CASE, 1851. Inspired by the medieval case at Strasbourg, *Scott* broke the rules by allowing pipes to project above the cornice, but it is nonetheless a most satisfying design, with excellent contemporary diaper on the pipes (Gillingham). – ORGAN STAIRS (N aisle), probably inspired by a pierced stone spiral staircase at Rouen. – ALTAR and REREDOS installed 1858, carvings by *Philip*,

1854 (Gunnis, Cobb). – PULPIT, 1866. Like all the above, designed by *Scott*. He also designed, for execution by *Skidmore*, a pair of aisle screens, one of which was shown at the 1862 Exhibition, and a pair of standing gasoliers, 1866–9 (one shown in the Victorian Church Art exhibition, 1971), for the choir. Next we see him to less advantage.

CHOIR STALLS. They are the most precious of the belongings of the cathedral, carefully repaired on removal eastward by *Essex* (Cocke), but sadly treated by *Scott*, who, beyond necessary repairs and justifiable restorations, chose to fill the graceful upper canopies with scenes sculptured heavily and sentimentally in terra cotta by *Abeloos* of Louvain. The stalls originally stood in the Octagon and can thus only have been started when the Octagon approached completion. They seem to have been finished in 1341–2. They were probably designed and supervised by *William Hurley* (see *Interior*, Octagon, above). The back stalls are placed in tall niches with cusped arches and ogee detail. Above these is a straight cornice running uninterrupted all the way through and perhaps a little tidied up by Scott to give better visibility to the Belgian reliefs. The canopies must of course have looked much lighter when there were no reliefs, but the whole can never have been as graceful and fanciful as for instance the Bishop's Throne at Exeter. That is partly explained by the stylistic development from *c.* 1315 to *c.* 1340. – MISERICORDS. All forty-seven back stalls have original misericords, and eighteen of the thirty-seven front stalls. This is not a number unique for so early a date: Winchester has as many, Salisbury more. Of representations the following may be singled out, numbered from the W. Back stalls N, 5, Huntsman with hare and dogs; 8, Woman looking through a forked tree; 10, Man picking grapes; 11, Confession; 12, Pelican in her piety; 13, Man with a hammer; 15, Wrestlers; 16, Man falling from a horse; 17, Virgin and Unicorn; 18, Two women; 19, Woman beating a fox; 20, Adam and Eve; 23, Two men throwing dice. – Front stalls N, 1, Beheading of St John, note the supporting scenes on the l. and r.; 2, Owl and mouse. – Back stalls S, 2, Two monks on a bench; 3, Noah's Ark; 5, Monkey; 6, Figure with monkeys; 8, Man with grotesque fishes; 10, Man and woman; 13, Seated king and queen; 14, King on canopied throne; 16, Samson and the lion; 17, Woman and child; 20, Bear and monkeys; 23, Two women. – Front stalls S, 1, Horseman; 2, Two women and Devil; 3, Grooming a horse; 4, Wrestlers; 16, Man and woman fighting; 18, St Giles and the hind. – Incidentally, the N screen wall behind the stalls, when they occupied the crossing, contained niches with painted 'portraits' of Saxon bishops and, it was found in 1771, their bones – part of a reverence for the pre-Conquest church, as at Winchester ('Fox's Boxes') and in posthumous effigies at Wells and Hereford.

Also in the eastern arm: REREDOS, Bishop West's Chapel, 1938, by *Sir Ninian Comper*. It makes one long for Gilbert Scott. This sentimental painting and these smooth gold grounds are as timid and genteel as Scott was robust. – Tristram found traces of PAINTING below the E window, kings in niches, C 14. – And finally a STONE SEAT, mid-C 13. Fragments of the arms shaped as an animal biting into a human head. Was this a bishop's throne, imitating a much earlier one?

STAINED GLASS, W TO E

Ely has little old glass. Some C 14 fragments remained in the Lady Chapel tracery (temporarily exhibited in the Stained Glass Museum; see below). Small-scale lively figures in niches, grisaille and yellow on a black ground, also groups of these with green and tan, all on a red ground. (Similar in design and colour to the Heraldic Window at York, N nave aisle, c. 1310–20, and in the early use of silver stain to obtain yellow.) While the dark grounds look stark to us, this glass must have paralleled the boldly undercut stone niches below it: with the flickering of candles and probably gilding on the carvings, the windows in daylight must have looked glowing and busy, and the whole chapel like a jewel-case instead of a greenhouse. (A challenge, perhaps, some day, for a new glass-designer?) Other medieval fragments have been assembled in the N window of the Alcock Chapel, the S window of the West Chapel, and a N chancel aisle window.

But in Victorian glass Ely is rich, as Lincoln is, and we have a better eye for it than we did. The most successful windows, it may be felt, are those – e.g. *Wailes*'s E lancets – full of small-scale detail in reds and blues like luminous textiles. In the N nave gallery is the admirable MUSEUM (stairs from N transept) of stained glass of all periods, rescued from redundant churches for preservation, exhibition and study. Mr Martin Harrison, the curator, has kindly given us the following list of Ely's Victorian glass artists.

WEST WINDOW. C 16 glass, possibly from St John Evangelist, Rouen, given by Bishop Yorke in 1807 and (very sensitively) restored and extended by *Charles Clutterbuck*, 1853. – SOUTH-WEST TRANSEPT. By *Wailes*, 1849. S W apse (St Catharine's Chapel): E window by *Hugh Easton*; S E window by *Thomas Wilmshurst*, 1856 (after Bassano's 'Baptism'). – SOUTH NAVE AISLE (from W to E). 1–2 by *Alfred Gérente*, 1849 and 1850; 3 by *Warrington*, 1850; 4 by *J. G. Howe*, 1850; 5 by *I. A. Gibbs*, 1850; 6 by *J. G. Howe*, 1850; 7 by *Wailes*, 1850; 8 by *A. Gérente*, 1851; 9 by *Clayton & Bell*, 1881; 10 by *Hardman*, 1853; 11 by *Rev. Arthur Moore*, 1850 (but a window at Thursford previously given to him is by Albert Moore the painter). NORTH NAVE AISLE (from W to E). 1 by *N. J. Cottingham*,

1852; 2–3 by *Frederick Preedy*, 1856 and 1866; 4 by *Ward & Hughes*, 1856; 5 by *T. Ward*, 1852; 6 by *F. W. Oliphant*, 1857, to a design by *W. Dyce*; 7–10 by *Wailes*; 11 by *George Hedgeland*, 1857; 12 by *A. Lusson*, c. 1860. – OCTAGON. All by *Wailes*. The S E window was the first window to be placed in the cathedral's C 19 reglazing (1845). – SOUTH TRANSEPT. S side. 1st and 2nd storeys by *Henri Gérente*, 1847–9. Gable window by *F. Preedy*. W side S by *Warrington*; centre by *A. Lusson*, 1853; N by *H. Gérente*. – NORTH TRANSEPT. N side N by *Wailes*, 1849; 1st storey l. by *Wailes*, 1846, r. by *Rev. A. Moore*, 1851; Perp 2nd storey window by *Henry Hughes*, 1862; W side N by *Rev. A. Moore*, 1853, centre and S by *A. Lusson* and *A. Lusson & Bourdant*. E side N by *Powell*, 1922; S by *Clayton & Bell*, 1880. – CHANCEL. All by *Wailes*, including the E window of 1857. – SOUTH CHANCEL AISLE (from W to E). 1 by *Henry Holiday*, 1893; 2 by *Powell*; 3–6 by *Clayton & Bell*, the best, 4, of 1860 ('Life of St Peter'). Bishop West's Chapel, E window, by *Comper*. – NORTH CHANCEL AISLE (from W to E). 1 by *Powell*; 2–3 by *Clayton & Bell*; 4–5 by *Ward & Hughes*, 1863. Bishop Alcock's Chantry E by *Clayton & Bell*, 1900.

MONUMENTS, W TO E

*Nave and aisles*    In the floor of the nave a large slab marks the entombment of Alan of Walsingham, begetter – one way or another – of the Octagon. No inscription or effigy records him (was this the trodden-down matrix of a brass?). – In the N aisle Dr Hodge-Mill † 1853, copper effigy (electro-plated) on a tomb-chest with alabaster and mosaic; designed by *Sir G. G. Scott*, executed by *Philip*. – Bishop Woodford † 1885, designed by *Bodley*; effigy recumbent on a tomb-chest below a canopy; no attempt at any originality.

*Transepts and crossing*    No monuments, except some minor tablets in the N porch which once belonged to the E aisle of the N transept (e.g. one by *R. Blore*, 1796).

*North chancel aisle (from W to E)*    Dean Caesar † 1636, standing wall-monument of alabaster with big kneeling figure. – Bishop Fleetwood † 1723, signed by *E. Stanton* and *C. Horsnaile*, a type which the bishops after the Restoration favoured at Ely, of moderate size and with no effigy. Inscription framed by two columns carrying an open scrolly pediment. – Bishop Nigellus(?) † 1169. Coffin-shaped slab of Tournai marble, the lower part broken off. The slab was found below the floor of St Mary's Church, but is earlier than the foundation of the church at the end of the C 12. The relief is considerably lower than in the C 13 tombs. The bishop is not the large figure, but the small naked soul held in a napkin by a large angel with beautifully, sharply, compactly and flatly modelled wings symmetrically rising behind his head. Bishop Nigellus's dates (1131–69) are the only ones which fit the style, although *c.* 1150 seems more likely than *c.* 1170. – Canon Fleetwood † 1737, signed by *P. Scheemakers.* A similar type to Bishop Fleetwood, but flatter. – Unknown bishop (headless). – Bishop Redman † 1506; large tomb-chest with panels decorated by cusped quatrefoils and similar motifs (the flamboyant wheel of four mouchettes, for example); recumbent effigy; large canopy; the whole the size of a chantry chapel; much renewed. – Bishop Kilkenny † 1257, a coffin-shaped slab of Purbeck marble with the recumbent effigy flanked by attenuated columns or shafts with stiff-leaf capitals; stiff-leaf crockets rise from the rim and bend across the shafts; the shafts carry a pointed trefoiled canopy; angels in the spandrels. – Shrine of St Etheldreda; a few remains of crocket capitals etc. These lie below a superstructure of unknown purpose. It is said to be part of a new C14 casing of the shrine or part of Bishop Hotham's monument (see s *chancel aisle* below). The ground stage is closed and has blank ogee arches. The monument is of no special merit and seems improbable as the contribution to the cult of the patron saint by those responsible for the Octagon and the Lady Chapel. – Bishop Hugh de Northwold † 1254. The type is the same as that of Kilkenny's tomb, but everything is more sumptuous – and rightly so, for the builder of the new retrochoir. The canopy has a more elaborately cusped arch, and along the sides canted down towards the tomb-chest are instead of shafts three tiers of small niches with figures of saints, again under cusped and thickly crocketed canopies. At the foot three minute figures illustrate the story of St Edmund (Northwold had been abbot of Bury St Edmunds). The monument is one of the finest of its date in England. – Bishop Patrick † 1707. Again white, again smallish and again no effigy. The front here curves forward, flanked by obelisks; segmental top with two putti: signed by *E. Stanton.* – Bishop Laney † 1675; the earliest of this modest type at Ely; black and white marble; inscription plate; achievement on top between the open scrolly fragments of a pediment. – Also in this aisle, brass to George Basevi, the architect, † 1845 in a fall from the w tower. Inscription with plan of his principal work, the Fitzwilliam Museum.

*East end*, NE *and* SE *chapels*   On the N, Bishop Alcock's; on the s, Bishop West's: chantries inserted at the E ends of the aisles. – Bishop Alcock † 1501. Begun in 1488, cf. the date-stone in a niche in the NW corner of the chapel. The fronts to w and s are mostly canopied, so closely and thickly that one is reminded of Spain more than of the reasonable English Perp. Equally bristly inside, even on the N wall, where the architecture of the chantry chapel is a screen in front of a window. Here is the monument to the bishop, high up, with the top of the tomb-chest below, left vacant, as if for an Easter Sepulchre. The chapel has a fan-vault, with an extremely pretty openwork pendant.

The wrought-iron GATES, with original lock, are of the same date as the chapel. – Bishop West † 1534. Made in 1525–33. This chapel is quieter in its external architecture. There is some blank space left, and the canopies do not crowd together quite so tightly. In the entrance from the w good contemporary iron GATES, more elaborate than the ones in Bishop Alcock's chapel, with tiers of tracery and scrollwork on top. The E window was replaced by one with Perp tracery. The vault is handsomely panelled, and it is in the infillings of this panelling that one can notice Early Renaissance motifs – the earliest at Ely. In other parts of the decoration also a few hints at the new Italian fashion can be detected. A study of the many bits of small-scale sculpture can be recommended. (West also gave a chapel to St Mary's, Putney, his birthplace, but it is wholly medieval in design.) – Inside the chapel on the floor, Bishop Sparke † 1836. Brass cross and thin brass surround, made probably in 1868, which is the date of the encaustic floor tiles. – Against the outer wall of the West Chantry facing N, Cardinal de Luxemburg † 1443. Tomb-chest with quatrefoils enclosing shields; recumbent effigy; the canopy much renewed.

*South chancel aisle (from* E *to* W)   Bishop Hotham † 1337. Tomb-chest only; for alleged canopy, see N *chancel aisle*, remains of shrine, above. The tomb-chest has blank broad ogee arcades, each subdivided by three-light blank windows with tracery to each individual light. Of the statuettes in the arcades only one survives, in a mutilated condition (w side, by one of the Lady Chapel sculptors; Coldstream 1979). The effigy was of alabaster – an early occurrence of the material (cf. Edward II † 1327, Gloucester Cathedral). – Canon Selwyn † 1875 (of the Selwyn Divinity School, Cambridge), recumbent effigy with praying hands; by *T. Nicholls,* 1879 (by him also the effigy of the canon's brother, Bishop Selwyn, at Lichfield). – John Tiptoft, Earl of Worcester, and wives. He was a humanist, had studied in Italy, was made Lord Treasurer of England, and was beheaded in 1470. Tall tomb-chest decorated with cusped 'saltire' quatrefoils with shields; recumbent effigies; canopy. – Bishop Gunning † 1684. Semi-reclining effigy, his head comfortably propped up on his hand; the figure placed without any back architecture (cf. Archbishop Dolben at York † 1688). The type comes from the monument to Richelieu in the Sorbonne in Paris. – Bishop Barnet † 1374; plain big tomb-chest with two tiers of small quatrefoils. – Bishop Goodrich † 1554; brass in the floor; largish figure; the thin arch surround only preserved as an indent. – Dean Tyndall † 1614; brass in the floor. – Bishop Heton † 1609; alabaster; recumbent effigy against a background of two black columns carrying heavy motifs. – Bishop William de Luda (of Louth) † 1299. There is no tomb-chest and the canopy serves as an entrance into the choir. It would be regrettable if the monument is damaged;

for it is so close in design to that of Edmund Crouchback, Earl of Lancaster, in Westminster Abbey (✝1296) that it comes no doubt from the same royal mason, and both have been attributed to *Michael of Canterbury* (cf. also Archbishop Peckham's tomb at Canterbury). Yet Draper (1979, n. 33) suggests that Luda's tomb was built as a gateway from the start (originally with a brass inset in the footpace). Tripartite canopy: the sides narrow, the centre wide and taller (a pattern soon used at Bristol: Berkeley Antechapel doorway, Lady Chapel reredos). The arches are cusped, with leaves in the spandrels. The leaves are already going knobbly and Dec, but there is no ogee motif yet anywhere. The tall gable in the middle has in the spandrel above the arch a blank pointed trefoil with a seated figure of Christ (?). Even the odd candle brackets l. and r. of the gable are as in the Crouchback monument. On the plinth seated angels, badly damaged on the s side, hopelessly restored on the N (choir) side. In the c 18 Luda's canopy served as model for James Essex's reredos at Lincoln and for garden gates at Strawberry Hill. – Sir Robert Stewart ✝1570; semi-reclining effigy in armour, cheek propped on hand, behind three short heavy Tuscan columns carrying a pediment with ribbon-work decoration. – Bishop Greene ✝1738; standing wall-monument, again without effigy. Two columns flanking an urn; segmental top. – Bishop Butts ✝1748. The 'anonymity' is here broken: portrait bust on top of a big monument of coloured marbles. – Sir Mark Steward ✝1603; heavy wall-six-poster with top obelisks and achievement; recumbent effigy. – Bishop Moore ✝1714; again the Ely type; no effigy, but two standing putti l. and r. of the inscription plate; top with urn between the scrolly parts of an open pediment. – Bishop Allen ✝1845; comfortably semi-reclining white marble effigy against a Gothic diapered background. By *I. Ternouth*.

*Choir*    On the floor a brass memorial to Prior Crauden ✝1341. The stone is original, the brasswork renewed. Large foliated cross, the head with ogee shapes; at the foot, small, the kneeling figure of the prior. – The similar slab to Bishop Hotham, apparently entirely c 19, marks the original site of his tomb.

### THE CLOISTER AND A SUMMARY OF THE PRECINCT

*Cloister*    The cloister at Ely is only partly preserved, and what there is has little of visual attraction. Of the Norman cloister no more can be seen than the bare and heavy blank arcade along the outer church wall. The w walk was rebuilt in the c 19, and the rest c. 1510. The design of the windows and the blank arcades of the surviving E and N walks are of no interest. The cloister was apparently not vaulted, except for the w walk, where the springers of the vault remain against the church wall. The bay in question, the N w angle of the cloister, is accessible

from the s aisle by a doorway the cloister side of which is elaborately decorated. It is the most important of the three remaining Norman doorways of the cathedral.

PRIOR'S DOOR. The doorway consists of a square outer order, one order of columns, and a square inner order. The lintel rests on two corbels, and on the lintel is a tympanum, surrounded by a roll moulding and a flat band corresponding to the outer pier below. All this is carved all over with foliage scrolls, and human and animal figures. The relief is

54. ELY Prior's Door, *c.* 1135

quite deep, but it does not intend to deny the existence of the surfaces into which the carver worked. That helps to date the Prior's Door. The Early Norman period would not have carved so lavishly, the Late Norman period would have done more undercutting and stressed the third dimension more. So Professor Zarnecki's date *c.* 1135 is more convincing than the late Sir Alfred Clapham's *c.* 1170. The tympanum contains a seated figure of Christ, beardless, in a vesica-shaped halo, supported by two angels. Each has one arm raised and bent at a sharp angle to reach the halo high up, and one of the two wings of each angel is also folded back so as to fill the space above the arm. The other wing fills the bottom corners of the tympanum. The angels seem to run away from the vesica, but look back. The tension between two contradictory movements in this attitude is familiar from France, and especially from the tympana of *c.* 1100–35 in Burgundy. The modelling of the figures is flat, drapery folds are often in the convention of two parallel incisions with a ridge between – a convention given up in France *c.* 1120. The lintel is made part of the tympanum, which is built up of separate layers of stone blocks, and the two corbels on which it rests are given the shape of heads with large staring eyes. The orders of the jambs will repay some attention. The outer order has medallions, filled by single figures or groups. It seems impossible to find any system in them. A man on the r. tending a vine indicates the popular theme of the labours of the months, the fishes on the l., the figures pouring out water from a vessel on the r., the crab or scorpion on the l. (foot) indicate the signs of the zodiac. But there are others which cannot be explained that way, and in any case there are fourteen each side and not twelve. The explanation is perhaps that the zodiac–labours-of-the-months pro-gramme was given to the carvers, but that it meant little to them and that they were left alone to do with it what they liked. It appears to us an odd way of treating church sculpture, but tallies with other cases in Norman England. There is in any case a great deal of naive playfulness in these figures and scenes (two men in a boat, a tumbler etc.), and also the animals hidden in the scrolls of the other orders, and that is perhaps what makes the carvings most enjoyable now. The middle order, i.e. the columns, gives another indication, beyond Burgundy, of the sources of the Prior's Door. The columns stand on shapeless lumps, but from engravings we know that each of these consisted of a human figure seated on the back of a lion, and animals or crouching humans carrying columns are staple motifs of Italy, especially of North Italian portals. There are the remains of two more lions at the top of the outer jambs. They are in an uncomfortably twisted position, with their heads below their hind legs.

The MONKS' DOOR also connects the s aisle with the cloister, but further E. The names are self-explanatory. A look at the plan of the monastic parts of the cathedral shows that the Prior's Door was close to the Prior's House, the Monks' Door to the dormitory and refectory. The Monks' Door is simpler in design, but of about the same date. It has two orders of columns and two of square piers. The inner order of the columns is spiral-grooved. This is continued in the roll moulding of the arch. At its apex is a small head. The capitals are decorated with foliage scrolls. So are the straight orders of piers and arch voussoirs. There is no tympanum. The door arch is trefoiled with cusps carrying chip-carved stars. Squeezed into the cusps of the foils are two figures of kneeling priors or monks(?), in style similar to the figures of the Prior's Door. Above them the voussoir of the arch ends in the meeting of two affronted monsters with intertwined necks – the same size as the kneeling monks. What can their meaning be? The doorway is cut into by *Grumbold*'s strengthening of the angle of aisle and transept aisle in 1696–8.

This strengthening also cuts into a third DOORWAY, which connects the E walk of the cloister with the transept aisle. It was originally of *c.* 1100–10 – cf. the flat chip-carved decoration – and was then reduced in size and enriched in decoration. The columns have beaded spiral bands and foliage scrolls. The capitals and the arch are also ornamented with scrolls. In the apex of the arch is the head of an angel.

To the w of the Monks' Door a large arched CUPBOARD was recessed into the cloister wall. Its forms date it to the late C13. The exit from the E walk of the cloister is by *Grumbold*'s modest C17 DOORWAY with a head in relief on the keystone.

In the cloister a window-head of timber from Prior Crauden's study (demolished; see *Precinct* summary be-low). Three lights, straight-headed, with ogee reticulation.

MONUMENTS. Humphrey Smith † 1743, designed by *John Sanderson*, carved by *Charles Stanley*. Bust in oval medallion; a putto leans elegantly on it; grey obelisk behind. – W. Pickering and R. Edger † 1845 in an accident which occurred on the Norwich to Ely railway line. Slab with a poem, called 'The Spiritual Railway' and eminently characteristic of the earnestness with which this new triumph of human ingenuity was still regarded. It begins 'The Line to heaven by Christ was made / With heavenly truth the Rails are laid' and ends 'If you'll repent and turn from sin / The Train will stop and take you in.'

*Buildings round the cloister*    The arrangement was the usual one with a passage called a slype immediately s of the s transept, and then the chapter house. The dormitory continued the E range to the s. The refectory ran along the s walk. The monks' kitchen lay s of it and not in line with it. On the w side were divers apartments including no doubt the cellar.

Of all these buildings very little remains. Into the Norman s wall of the s transept corbels of the early C13 have been set which correspond to the early C13 vaulting of the SLYPE. This passage gave access to the monks' cemetery E and SE of the chancel. The CHAPTER HOUSE was rectangular and about 76 by 34 ft in size. Of the

DORMITORY no more can be seen than two corners of its wall now w of the w entry into Infirmary Lane. Of the REFECTORY a little more remains – a goodly portion of its back, i.e. s, wall with a c 13 blank arcade on a bench-table and traces of the steps up to the lectern. Of the buildings to the w of the cloister not even traces have been found.

As for the rest of the PRECINCT, the monks' kitchen is now the bishop's rose garden. The former deanery, a house built into the great hall of the monastery, is now the bishop's house. The former Bishop's Palace, built *c.* 1500 w of the sw transept, had its gatehouse tower originally connected with the upper storey of the galilee by a gallery (hence the street name, The Gallery). The palace was much rebuilt *c.* 1670 and internally remodelled 1771; it has in its garden a startlingly huge plane-tree. Other monastic buildings s of the cathedral are part of the King's School, including that gem of the Dec style, Prior Crauden's Chapel, contemporary with the Octagon and Lady Chapel, and the former Queen's Hall, now the headmaster's house, also with evidences of the c 14, and Ely Porta, the great s gatehouse, begun 1397. s E of the cathedral, remains of the monks' infirmary indicate a date *c.* 1175–85.

Further on these buildings and the town, see the latest edition of B of E *Cambridgeshire*.

# Gloucester

## CATHEDRAL CHURCH OF THE HOLY AND INDIVISIBLE TRINITY *Anglican*

(Based on B of E *Gloucestershire: The Vale*, 1976, by David Verey, further revised, with information from Bernard Ashwell, Michael Gillingham and A. S. Brooks.)

Plan, Fig. 55, from the *Builder*, 1891, by F. S. Waller. There have been some changes since in the dedication of chapels.

Some references (see Recent Literature): B.A.A. conference papers (forthcoming); Harvey 1978 and forthcoming new edition of Harvey 1954; Verey and Welander 1979.

## INTRODUCTION

The cathedral stands in a small close formed by College Green on its s side and a complex of much rebuilt monastic buildings on the N side. Round the close are houses adapted from monastic to domestic use in the c 16–17 and mostly rebuilt in the c 18. College Green in monastic times was divided into an outer court at the w end of the abbey church, a lay cemetery to the s, and a monks' cemetery and garden either side of the E end, apparently linked by a tunnel under the Lady Chapel, which may then have had the precinct wall directly E of it. On the w the Great Gate, or St Mary's Gate, from St Mary's Square in the town, opens into the outer court of College Green before the cathedral's w front. Here there is no wide expanse as at Wells or Salisbury, but domestic-scaled enclosure at the feet of the great structure.

Gloucester was a Roman town. The Roman garrisons were generally withdrawn in A.D. 410; thereafter for nearly five hundred years there seems to have been only slight occupation. By the late c 9 Mercia had become a strong and active state controlling a wide area, and it is during this period that town life in Gloucester becomes apparent once more.

The foundation of St Peter's Abbey by the somewhat mythical King Osric in A.D. 681 must have been a stimulus to development. Timber buildings in the centre of the city have been dated by radiocarbon method to the c 8. In 909 Ethelflaed, the daughter of Alfred, and her husband Ethelred transferred the relics of St Oswald to Gloucester, and founded a monastery called St Oswald's Priory. The city at this time had a mint, and a royal palace at Kingsholm, and was evidently of particular significance to the rulers of Mercia. The Anglo-Saxon Chronicle states that Ethelflaed and Ethelred were buried in St Peter's Abbey; but the building of that date is not exactly on the site of our present cathedral. Aldred, Bishop of Worcester, began a new church in 1058, 'a little further from the place where it had stood, and nearer to the side of the city'. The original site seems to have been inside the Roman city wall; but the cathedral now stands fully over the NW corner of the Roman wall. In Saxon times the Roman walls still stood, and the E gate was still in use. The city had ten churches. A piece of Saxon sculpture, a roundel of Christ kept in the chapter house, according to the late Dame Joan Evans 'sets

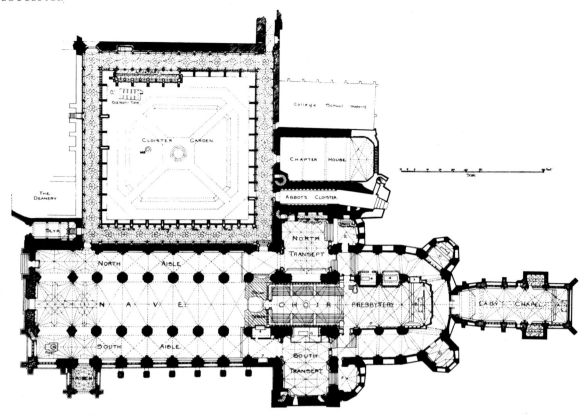

55. GLOUCESTER Plan from the *Builder*, 1891 (see p. 131)

Gloucestershire in the main current of European art some-where about 950'.

In 1022 the Bishop of Worcester introduced Benedictine rule to the monastery of St Peter. However, according to William of Malmesbury, 'zeal and religion had grown cold many years before the coming of the Normans'. In 1072, when the Norman Serlo was appointed abbot, the numbers were down to two monks and eight novices. The growth in wealth and importance of the religious houses in the first fifty years after the Conquest must have been remarkable; by 1100 Serlo had increased his numbers to 100 monks. William the Conqueror kept Christmas in Gloucester in 1085, and this was the occasion when he ordered the compilation of the Domesday Book; but whether he was staying with the Abbot or at the Saxon royal palace at Kingsholm has not yet been established.

The foundation stone of the new abbey church was laid on 29 June 1089, and the building was dedicated on 15 July 1100. This speed was a considerable achievement, and may represent only the eastern arm, along with the two E bays of the nave needed to buttress the intended tower. But in 1102 a fire partly destroyed the new work, only to be

followed by a more calamitous one in 1122. Why was it, we wonder, that Serlo got Robert, Bishop of Hereford, to lay the foundation stone in 1089 and not his Diocesan Bishop, Wulfstan of Worcester? The Bishop of Hereford, a French-man from Tournus, may have been involved in the choice of the large cylindrical columns for the nave, so like those of Tournus, and by then fashionable in the West Country abbeys like Tewkesbury and Pershore, and Hereford Cathedral. The nave westward of the first two bays was built after Serlo's death in 1104.

The abbot who followed immediately after Serlo was Peter (1107–13), who presented to the abbey the famous gold candlestick, made possibly by English goldsmiths in London and elaborately decorated in the style of the time with fabulous little men and beasts. It was unfortunately early lost to Gloucester; it must have been stolen (or sold? see below), because it was later given to Le Mans Cathedral in France, where it remained until the C19, when it was acquired by the Victoria and Albert Museum.

The fire in 1122 must have been a disaster. In the nave there are signs of calcination on the pillars due to falling rafters. The fire risk would have been enormously reduced

56. GLOUCESTER View from the north-east in 1828

by having a stone vaulted roof; but the nave roof was of wood. The nave aisles retained their c11–12 vaults, of which the northern set survives to this day, together with carved Romanesque capitals and pellet ornament. After such a disaster we would expect to find some account of repairs, but we do not. By contrast, the repairs of a hundred years later are carefully recorded. The nave roof, however, must surely have been patched up for the time being. Gloucester's individual circumstances as well as those affecting the whole country provide ample reason for the long delay in repairing the ravages of the disaster of 1122.

To understand the circumstances of the abbey in the c12, it must be kept in mind that it was situated next to a royal castle, one of the residences of whatever peripatetic monarch was in the ascendant, and consequently was near the centre of political strife. This was not the old palace at Kingsholm but a Norman castle built next to the abbey. It was the headquarters of Robert Earl of Gloucester, half-brother to the Empress Matilda, who when she was in power held her court there. On one occasion in 1142 she escaped from Oxford across the snow-bound Cotswolds to take refuge in Gloucester Castle. That most interesting

political character, Gilbert Foliot, abbot during 1139–48, was an open defender of Matilda's claims to the English throne. Foliot was a severe and masterful man, who had been Prior of Cluny, and was destined to become Bishop of Hereford and Bishop of London. He was Thomas à Becket's most formidable opponent. Abbot Hugh of Cluny, however, wrote of him as 'the mirror of religion and glory of the age, the luminary who shed lustre even on the great name of Cluny'.

In about 1170 the southern tower of the w front of the abbey church collapsed. In 1194 the monks had to sell their silver plate to ransom King Richard I, an episode which rings a familiar note in that century, and a third of their property was seized by King John in 1207; but abbey and castle were joined together in the political scene when the loyal barons assembled in the abbey church to swear allegiance to the boy king Henry III, who was hurriedly crowned there, traditionally with his mother's bracelet, in 1216.

The change of mood which came with the accession of the young king was electric. Hope and enterprise returned, exemplified in church life by an outburst of new building.

This was the springtime of Early English architecture. At Gloucester the urge was felt, though compared with other cathedrals little survives to show it. A new Lady Chapel was built in 1227. Was it inspired by the new Lady Chapel of 1220 at Westminster (on the site of the Henry VII Chapel)? Here it has not survived either, but the structure in the N transept through which one now enters the treasury belongs to that period, and could well have been (before removal to its present place) the entrance to the Lady Chapel. However, Dr Tudor-Craig thinks it is *in situ* and that it did enclose a reliquary, as marked on our C 19 plan; any irregularities about its construction would in that case be due to the Perp rebuilding around it.

In 1242 the new vault over the nave was finished, and this is the most significant feature of the period left us. Anything else was swept away in the Perp encasing of the presbytery and transepts and the rebuilding of the Lady Chapel.

In the margin of the verso of fo. 82 of the Royal M S. 13A III in the British Library, which is a C 13 copy of the *Historia Regum Britanniae* by Geoffrey of Monmouth, there is a drawing, made in the mid-C 14, showing St Peter's Abbey, Gloucester, from the W. We see a short stocky central tower, rather like the Norman tower at Tewkesbury, and this may well be Serlo's tower, which survived the fire in 1122. It carries a very tall spire which seems to have a lead covering and must be the spire Elias is said to have built in 1222. The nave roof has a steep pitch and is the one finished in 1242. The W front has a high gable, with a tall w window with reticular tracery, and this must be C 14, though no written record of it survives. The s w tower is shown with a little broach spire rebuilt *c.* 1245. The N side of the w front is masked by a building which may be the C 13 part of the old abbot's lodging (now Church House). This precious doodle confirms our opinion that a very considerable amount of work took place at Gloucester in the C 13.

Before the full effect of early C 14 innovations in English art were felt at Gloucester, Abbot John Thokey rebuilt the s aisle of the nave *c.* 1319–29, in the full-blown Dec style of the West of England encrusted with ballflower. This was where the original Norman wall had probably been overturned by the unbalanced thrusts from the vaulting. Bowtells (shaft-like mouldings) are treated as slender shafts with their own capitals and hexagonal miniature bases: these are the only details which look forward to the Perp style. In every other respect this work is unrelated to London developments and also unrelated to work in Bristol less than thirty-five miles away. The master of this s aisle must have been brought from Hereford or somewhere else within the region of most intense addiction to ballflower, which is peculiar to the w front of Lichfield Cathedral, Wells chapter house, Hereford central tower of *c.* 1315–18,

and Salisbury tower of 1320. Each window in the Gloucester aisle has about 1,500 ballflowers, and the new vault has ribs decorated with ballflower in the three eastern bays.

On 20 September 1327, King Edward II was horribly murdered in Berkeley Castle. His body had to be shown, and it had to look as if he had died of natural causes. It is probable that Abbot Thokey was ordered by the Court in London to bring the body in state to Gloucester, and at least some of the gear was sent down from London for the procession. The king's body was laid on the N side of the choir; but the funeral was delayed till 20 December 1327, when Queen Isabella and her son, the new King Edward III, were present at what was in fact a state funeral. It does not seem in these circumstances that Abbot Thokey was 'risking his life' by having the king buried in his abbey. It is also assumed by historians that immense sums in offerings at Edward II's tomb were provided by pilgrims.

This appears rather improbable, and the obvious source of money must of course be the new king, whose gifts *in piam memoriam* to Gloucester Abbey were the inspiration and provided most of the wherewithal for the rebuilding. The *Historia*, however, records that the offerings of the faithful were such that Abbot Wigmore rebuilt the s transept in six years. The door in the s transept traditionally called 'The Pilgrims' Door' certainly could not have been used for that purpose, and was perhaps an entrance from the transept into a sacristy rather than an entrance into the abbey from outside. Furthermore, later in the century the advowson of Holy Trinity Church, which was situated near the congested way into the abbey from Westgate Street, was given to the abbey 'in order to maintain the lights about the tomb of the king', which would hardly have been necessary had there been many pilgrims at that date.

The starting-point of the Perp style in England is the accession of Edward III, who did not assume full power until the autumn of 1330, and the specific marks of the new style appeared within the next year or so. The adoption of Perp details in royal work provided the badge of success. The royal taste set a fashion through the master masons to the Crown and their pupils. Gloucester played an important part in this development, partly with the Perp encasing of the choir in the mid-C 14: to the king, this dark Norman interior must have seemed an unsuitable shrine for his father. But first came changes in the s transept, where the four-centred arch, never adopted in other parts of Europe, suddenly appeared in the side windows of 1331–5. And the great s window of *c.* 1335, with mullions running straight up into the arch, is the first example still extant of that feature of the Perp style, since William Ramsey's work at St Paul's no longer exists. The formulation of the Perp style at St Paul's during 1332–5 preceded the appearance of definitely Perp detail at Gloucester Abbey. But a closer link seems to have existed between St Stephen's Chapel at the

Palace of Westminster and the Gloucester s transept. Big clerestory windows, four-centred arches, flowing tracery, prehensile cusps were all similar. Only the great s window has that minimal employment of the peculiarly Perp detail, the vertical mullions right up to the arch, and this design was not earlier than *c.* 1335, except in St Stephen's Chapel, a monument of the Kentish school and the work of Thomas of Canterbury. Dr Christopher Wilson now suggests that *Thomas of Canterbury* was the designer of the Gloucester s transept, where the shafts correspond with the vault ribs, as in the lierne vault in the crypt of St Stephen's. The source for St Stephen's was French, certainly not West Country. Edward III evidently made his mason, Thomas of Canterbury, available for Abbot Wigmore. But record of Thomas disappears in 1336, so he was not the architect of the eastern arm.

Another name emerges at this time, that of *John de Sponlee*, who succeeded Ramsey in charge of the royal works at Windsor Castle from 1350 onwards. His name suggests he came from Spoonley near Winchcombe and probably therefore worked at Winchcombe Abbey. He was born *c.* 1310 and trained between 1320 and 1335. John de Sponlee might well have been, as Howard Colvin indicates, the Master John the mason who carried out a survey of Gloucester Castle in 1336. Sponlee's shafting at Windsor, though nearly twenty years later, resembles the transept wall-shafts at Gloucester, which may indicate a possible involvement with work on the abbey. He was pensioned by 1364. Another master mason was called Thomas of Gloucester. He was warden of the masons at Westminster Palace in 1354–5 and in 1356 the principal mason working on St Stephen's Chapel.

Fan-vaulting, like the Perp style, is a peculiarity of England. In its earlier, c 14 phase it was centred on a small region round Hereford, Gloucester and Tewkesbury (see *Cloisters* below). As a mark of personal style it travelled with individual masters called from this area to work elsewhere, for instance with *Robert Lesyngham* from Gloucester to Exeter.

There are other signs of a regional style centred on a monastic works department at Gloucester, such as trefoil cusping as opposed to the more common cinquefoil. And from the beginning of the new work in the s transept, hexagonal rather than octagonal bases became a mark of the regional style. The s window tracery also has variants of hollow-sided hexagons inscribed in imaginary circles; and the regular hexagon is drawn out into an elongated form set vertically. The shape so formed was the basis of one great division of Perp tracery which Freeman, the influential Victorian architectural critic, called 'Alternate' in contradiction to the 'Supermullion', or what is called grid or panelled. The adaptation of the supermullion to tracery was foreshadowed in the eastern arm's great E window, where the canted plan demanded a central section separated from the lateral lights by two grand mullions. Supermullioned forms, however, are generally to be found E of Oxford, and our region w of Oxford favoured the alternate, which is also the earlier in date. (Alternate tracery lacks the supermullion continuing the vertical line of a main mullion; instead, such lines alternate. A counterpart, the supertransom, is formed by horizontal bands of crossed ogees linking the mullions; the less common lattice or X-transom also occurs in Oxfordshire and Gloucestershire.)

As a model for the future of the Perp style, the eastern arm of Gloucester was not available until much more than half the c 14 had gone by, and it is therefore not extraordinary to find that the style took time to catch on here. In the Cotswolds, however, emulation lasted for a very long time, and the nave of Cirencester church, which clearly emulates Gloucester presbytery, was not built till 1516–30. Owing to the proximity of Bristol to Gloucester, architectural historians have expected to find that there are stylistic similarities; but Harvey (1978) says not. None of the traceries at Bristol resemble those at Gloucester, nor do the mouldings. In the c 15 the Gloucester style moves E towards Oxford or N into the West Midlands, whereas Bristol masons 'colonized' Somerset, Dorset and the South-West. We may also mention the almost universal employment of the diagonal buttress on Gloucestershire church towers, including the cathedral, in contrast to the general Bristol use of paired buttresses set back from the angle as in Somerset and elsewhere in the West of England.

The c 15 produced a wave of tower building. The tower at Gloucester (*c.* 1450) was based on that of Worcester (1357–74), but converted its turreted outline to diagonal buttressing, finishing with the famous Gloucester coronet of filigree openwork pinnacles and battlements, so largely copied on a reduced scale for parochial towers like that at Chipping Campden. The towers of Gloucester and Great Malvern Priory, roughly contemporary, are so alike that they have to be attributed to a single designer.

The last alteration to the abbey, which was not finished till shortly before 1500, was the rebuilding of the Lady Chapel, also relating to reconstruction at Great Malvern while adhering closely to the mouldings and traceries of the previous century at Gloucester. The c 14 presbytery vault was echoed on a smaller scale. Here and at Great Malvern the independent school of vaulting that had begun with the nave at Tewkesbury retained its individuality to the end, preserving as its hallmark a pair of subsidiary longitudinal ribs on each side of the main ridge. The E window of the Lady Chapel has glass, now very fragmentary, which was made at Great Malvern.

After the dissolution of the monastery of St Peter's, Gloucester, Henry VIII secured an Act of Parliament under which he created the See of Gloucester, and the abbey church became the cathedral on 3 September 1541, 'considering the site of the late monastery in which the monument of our renowned ancestor the King of England is erected, is a very fit and proper place . . .'. We see, once again, the results of the murder of Edward II. If his tomb had not been here, it is quite likely that St Peter's Abbey might have been totally destroyed, as were the neighbouring abbeys of Winchcombe, Evesham, Hailes and Cirencester. The Abbot's Lodging became the Palace of the Bishop, the Prior's House became the Deanery, and the cloister garth the private garden of the Dean. At times of religious fanaticism statues of saints were smashed and reredoses hacked with axes, as in the Lady Chapel. The monks' refectory and dormitory were pulled down. The reign of Bishop Hooper helps to account for the empty niches in the cathedral. After Queen Mary Tudor's accession he was deprived of his bishopric, imprisoned for a year, tried for heresy, and condemned to be burnt at the stake, which took place at Gloucester, outside St Mary's Gate on 9 February 1555. The library has seven volumes of Hooper's works. He was not an original thinker, but absorbed the ideas of the more extreme Swiss reformers. He is often called the 'Father of English Puritanism'. He ordered all wooden screens to be removed in the Gloucester diocese, thus causing untold damage to our artistic heritage.

At the time of the Civil War the cathedral suffered less than might have been expected. It was, however, subsequently in grave danger of total destruction from the machinations of some people who are said to have 'agreed among themselves for their several proportions of the plunder expected out of it'. The Little Cloisters and the Lady Chapel began to be pulled down, and 'instruments and tackle [were] provided for to take down the tower'; but in 1657 the church was made over by grant to the mayor and burgesses at their request, and from this it is to be assumed that they wished to prevent it from possible ruin.

In the C 18 Bishop Benson (1734–52) spent vast sums of his own money on the cathedral; but most of his innovations were removed in the C 19, when taste changed. The taste of Bishop Benson's period is now very much admired again, and we can appreciate his choir stalls and other furnishings in the nave today. *William Kent*, the most fashionable of architects, was employed to erect a screen in 1741, and bits of this are preserved in the ambulatory triforium. It is said that he would have liked to have the Norman pillars fluted, but that would have been a shocking deviation from historicism and good sense, and we can hardly believe it was considered very seriously.

Considering what *Sir Gilbert Scott* and other C 19 architects are accused of doing to our cathedrals, Gloucester got off extremely lightly. Scott was here (1866–73 and as consultant after that), but he seems to have behaved with

great tact, which in fact was very often the case, as indeed with the *Wallers*, a local dynasty of architects who looked after the cathedral (especially, in the C 19, 1847–63 and 1873–90, and since). Victorian architects, it must be remembered, were faced frequently with enormous difficulties in restoration work because of neglect of the fabric in the previous century. It may indeed be to the credit of Bishop Benson and the like that Gloucester Cathedral was not falling down by the time the Victorians came on the scene, and so did not require to be largely rebuilt. In 1896–7 *J. L. Pearson* was consultant for restoration of the Lady Chapel.

A major scheme of repairs started in 1953, consisting of the reconstruction of the roofs of the nave, choir, N transept and cloisters. The cloister roof incorporates prestressed and light-weight concrete for decking to carry the re-cast lead outer covering. The S walk's pre-stressed concrete roof of 1956 was probably the first use of this material in the repair of a medieval cathedral in England. The architects were *N. H. Waller* and *B. J. Ashwell*.

Most of the cathedral is built of pale cream Cotswold stone (oolitic limestone) from Painswick, about 5 miles S E of Gloucester. But exposed battlements and pinnacles as well as the bottom courses of the walls are mostly of stone from Minchinhampton. Not one of the longer cathedrals, Gloucester is shorter than Salisbury, but slightly longer than Worcester, longer than Lichfield, considerably longer than Hereford.

EXTERIOR

The first view of the cathedral, as it opens before one's eyes on entering College Green from College Street, gives the impression that it is a Perp building. Closer inspection reveals its Norman bones in the rounded two-storey ambulatory with radiating chapels, and in the gabled ends of the transepts flanked in both cases by sturdy Norman turrets. The windows of the crypt, the ambulatory, and the ambulatory gallery also largely retain their round-headed Norman openings, though many are filled with later tracery. The radiating chapels are polygonal in plan, and E of either transept is a chapel too, of an oddly indistinct, rounded shape. Moreover, at gallery-level are two small bridges which have blank Norman arcading with zigzag. These are reset Norman work; internally they have blocked Norman windows. Such details, however, cannot at first be apparent to the eye, overwhelmed as it must be by the immense mid-C 15 Perp TOWER, which soars 225 ft, piercing the sky with its celebrated coronet of open parapet and airy pinnacles, and patterned all over with tier upon tier of blank arcading. The admirable effects of light and shade are produced by the bold projection of the diagonal buttresses, and the deep recessing of the windows and mouldings, and culminate in the openwork pinnacles at the top, each like the fantastic model of a church tower, and the openwork parapet and battlements.

Having returned to earth as it were, one finds oneself facing the SOUTH PORCH, which is the main entrance to the cathedral. This, like the rather similar porch at Northleach, was built *c.* 1420, but the niches are now filled with C 19 figures by *Redfern*. Inside it is beautiful, with stone panelling and lierne vault, and the inner DOORS have Norman hinge-work with trident-shaped iron strengtheners, thought to have been moved from the original Norman w door and adapted to fit the pointed doorway. The porch has an open parapet and pinnacles like the tower in miniature.

The SOUTH AISLE is buttressed, and some of the niches retain sculpture, notably of King Osric on the E, all much worn by the weather and contrasting, though recently cleaned, with the over-restoration of the porch. This aisle represents the only large extent of high Dec style of the West Country in the cathedral; all the windows which are early C 14 are profusely ornamented with thousands of ballflower. Ogee arches are entirely absent, a noteworthy sign of conservatism. The tracery in each window has a horizontal emphasis, and gives the impression of a large butterfly. There are seven bays altogether, and the easternmost window, although also decorated with ballflower, partakes of the Perp of the s transept. The clerestory windows above have ogee shapes and are placed under a C 15 embattled parapet. But between the windows are the shallow Norman buttresses with chevron at the angles. They stop two bays from the w front. These two bays are Perp, as the w end was rebuilt in 1420 by Abbot Morwent after the collapse of the Norman w end. What the latter looked like we do not exactly know. Most probably there were two towers. The front has two doorways, the main one set with its surrounding masonry in front of the plane of the nine-light w window. The projecting wall ends in a pierced parapet. Against the w window stand two thin flying buttresses, and l. and r. are two dainty turrets with flying buttresses. The second door enters the N aisle and is called the Dean's Door.

The Norman TRANSEPT FRONTS both have turrets ornamented with arcading in two tiers (one with intersecting arches, the other with zigzag), and in the s gable is a group of stepped, lancet-shaped, round-headed blank arches profusely provided with zigzag. Below, in spite of the Perp remodelling, are long vertical lines of chevron. These seem to be *in situ*, whereas the chevron round the great s window cannot be. Below this is the first existing Perp window, dating, as we have seen, from *c.* 1335. The tracery is awkward, but it is a turning-point in the history of English architecture, for here the mullion strikes the arch perpendicularly, a sign that the King's master mason

has arrived. The transept windows to the w must have been designed first, for in their tracery simple ogee motifs suffice, whereas the s window has strictly Perp panel tracery, with supermullions and vertical hexagons. In the s AMBULATORY TRIFORIUM is a Dec window with ballflower ornament, matched by a similar window in nearly the same position on the N. If the s nave aisle windows are *c.* 1318, these, because they use ogees as well as ballflower, may be called *c.* 1325–30.

Perhaps the *tour de force* of the whole edifice is the EAST WINDOW with its fourteen lights, its canted side-wings making the composition 4–6–4, with three transoms in the wings and five in the centre. This canting of the grid-frame, dictated by the Norman foundations in the crypt, gives strength against wind pressures. (The mason-in-charge at the time may have been *Thomas of Cambridge*; see *Cloisters* below.) At its date, this was the largest window in the world. The outer hoodmould turns into ogee shape and rises to the perforated parapet of the gable, flanked on either side by pierced pinnacles. (While the side-wings of the great window are canted back, the N and s walls of the E high bay are deflected outward to meet them: a unique treatment. Was it empirically worked out in mid-construction?) In order to give full light to the window, the LADY CHAPEL is almost detached. This, the last alteration to the monastery, was not finished till shortly before 1500. Though about a hundred years later than the choir, the Lady Chapel is stylistically indistinguishable from it. The tracery patterns are pretty well the same. Its E window has nine lights and three transoms, and an openwork parapet finishes the composition. Two identical chantry chapels project N and s, their fenestration in two tiers.

### INTERIOR

The NAVE is dominated by the huge cylindrical Norman columns of the arcades, which have narrow, round, convex capitals similar to those at Tewkesbury (consecrated 1121) and probably a regional invention. Seven bays with round Norman arches of three contrasting orders, a pair of strong soffit rolls, a straight edge, and chevron at r. angles to the wall; the arches are not wide, as the massive columns are comparatively close together. Above this is a narrow band of triforium (not a gallery, as in the eastern arm) on a string-course with chevron. The triforium is remarkably small (cf. Tewkesbury) and has two twin openings with short columnar piers and responds, scallop capitals, and chevron at r. angles to the wall. The Norman clerestory seems to have had chevron set vertically, but of the Norman clerestory only traces remain; for springing from the line of the triforium is the E.E. rib-vault added in 1242, an elegant and graceful hat that hardly fits the rugged face below.

58. GLOUCESTER The south transept of 1331–6 in 1828

The vault can be criticized as being too low. The probable reason for this is that much of the old Norman roof would have still been in existence in 1235, and to keep the weather out they built below it, a bay or two at a time. The first thing the builders had to do was to alter the walls of the Norman clerestory in order to reduce their height, because the new vault would be built against these walls, and the timber roof would eventually rest upon the wall-plate. It is supposed that the masons began from the w end, and as they approached the crossing they realized they had not calculated the spaces correctly. The statement in the *Historia* appears to say that the monks finished the work themselves without the assistance of the craftsmen they had at the beginning. As we look at the vault today, except for the two w bays altered later, the c 13 vault remains as it was in 1242. The first four of the remaining bays are identical in design, the last two are different. In the four bays the vault springs from a cluster of short Purbeck marble shafts standing on the floor of the triforium stage, which is divided from the arcade below by a string-course with a chevron moulding. Below this are extension vaulting-shafts which descend between the arches of the arcade and end in corbel heads. In the two eastern bays there are no clusters of Purbeck marble shafts, and the springing of the vault is dropped several feet down to the level of the triforium floor. At the same position the ridge member of the vault, which from the w has been of fairly broad proportions, is now greatly diminished in width. There is a steady rise in the apex of the vault from w to E, amounting to 18 in. in all and 3 in. in the two E bays. Perhaps it was at this point that the monks parted with their master mason, and had to finish the job as best they could, by stilting the vault from a lower position in order to make up the error. This was a clever solution to the problem; but we must admit that the somewhat unhappy relationship between the vault, beautiful though it is in itself, and the Norman work below, does provide grounds for aesthetic criticism.

In the early c 15 the Norman w end of the nave, the two most westerly bays, were altered in the Perp style and given lierne vaulting. The longitudinal ridge rib has two parallel subsidiaries l. and r., exactly as in the choir vault. The NORTH AISLE retains its Norman rib-vault with ribs of two rolls and a spur between, but the SOUTH AISLE was remodelled *c.* 1319 and has a vault of that period with ribs decorated with ballflower in the three E bays. The most easterly bay of the Norman nave is blocked with the PULPITUM and organ chambers. In monastic times there was a second screen in line with the present nave altar, and there were altars in the two aisles (see the piscina in the s wall), so that everything E of this line was, in the peculiarly English fashion, completely screened off from the nave. The existing stone screen with its rather dull Perp panelling is by *Smirke*, 1823, replacing *Kent*'s screen of 1741. On its

s side is the CHAPEL OF THE SALUTATION OF MARY, c 15 Perp. Above the chapel, on the s of the organ chamber, c 16 wood panelling. To the E, i.e. on the N side of the s transept, the CHAPEL OF ST JOHN, with a Late Perp stone REREDOS, restored in 1964 by *Stephen Dykes Bower*. This chapel is against the back of the choir stalls and is protected on the s by a fine wooden PARCLOSE SCREEN.

The SOUTH TRANSEPT – where, as has already been noted, the fully vertical mullion was first developed in the s window, and four-centred arches were used in the side windows, between 1331 and 1335 – is Norman with a skin of Perp panelling threaded by the great internal flying buttresses of the c 15 tower. A transept is isolated from the rest of the building, but the slight movement of the tower southwards must have caused concern: at the N E corner of the transept the vertical of the Perp panelling has had to be rebated into the tower in order to keep truly vertical, and

60. GLOUCESTER South transept steps to the south presbytery aisle in 1828

the huge internal flying buttresses, which penetrate the rectilinear system, must have been considered a necessity. The vault of the transept is a complicated and early example of a lierne vault, without the benefit of any boss to cover up the sometimes inexact meetings. It shows a direct relationship to the work in St Stephen's Chapel at Westminster of the 1320s. The transept's wide Norman bays and its galleries had to be kept because of the chapels, which were in use. The innovating treatment derived from France *via* Kent and *Thomas of Canterbury* is of great interest, although aesthetically disappointing. We can admire, however, the displays of virtuosity, the four-centred arches, the ogee shapes, the moon-like cusps, the hexagonal bases to the tall bowtells, the frilly tops of the twin entrances to crypt and ambulatory, and the figures set in trefoils above them which are carved detached from the wall. (On the bracket to the r. of the crypt entrance, see *Furnishings*.) Also on the E side of the transept and up eight steps (i.e. at ambulatory level), the CHAPEL OF ST ANDREW, Norman with an irregularly rounded or polygonal apse. In the s wall of the transept, a small doorway, with side pieces coming forward in a curve like the arms of a throne, is perhaps the entrance to a no-longer existing sacristy (rather than a 'pilgrims' door': there is no enrichment on the other side).

Next came rebuilding of the EASTERN ARM. In spite of the common factors between the s transept and the work which followed, there seems to have been a change of master mason. Thomas of Canterbury appears to have died in 1336, and the treatment of the presbytery seems to indicate second thoughts about the transept. Verticals are increased and the vaulting-shafts simplified. The vault is a mesh of liernes. The strainer arches at the crossing, described below, though different from Bristol's choir aisles, have the flavour of the West Country. After the s transept, Gloucester and London went their own ways. The dates within which this whole work on choir and presbytery was designed and executed cannot be made more precise than the thirty years between 1337 and 1367, and this includes the year of the Black Death in 1349, in which perhaps one-third of the population died. It used to be said that Perp was an economy-style, produced in the aftermath of the Black Death when labour was dear and simplification of detail was necessary: but this style already existed before the Black Death, both here and in London.

The Norman CROSSING, which still contains the choir, survives, although the w and E piers have been altered. To the N and s the piers have twin responds. The masons of the C 14 and C 15 did a marvellous conversion of the upper parts. It is as well to remember that what a building looked like was always as important to the medieval mason as was structure and function. In theory, in order to vault the crossing in his lierne manner, the master mason needed

points of support in the middle of the crossing arches; but this cannot have been so in fact, for he threw across the wide space four-centred arches so flat and so thin that they are hardly capable of carrying any weight, and look as if they were borrowed from a timber structure. On the not very pronounced apex of each of them he placed a vertical mullion accompanied on both sides by counter-curves. The result is a stone ogee arch in mid-air from which rise the seven ribs of the vault. This is a very original stylistic conceit which by contrast emphasizes the spatial unity of choir and presbytery, and isolates the transepts. The twin Norman respond mouldings at the crossing were joined together at the top (with a strange drain-pipe effect) and from them rise the mouldings of the mid-C 14 tower arches. The tower itself, it will be remembered, was rebuilt in the next century.

An examination of the EAST END must begin below ground in the CRYPT; for the crypt was naturally the part with which building began, i.e. it dates from 1089 and the following years (this and the next paragraph by NP). The crypt represents the Norman plan above, with ambulatory and three radiating chapels. England has six such crypts: St Augustine Canterbury, Winchester, Worcester, Canterbury Cathedral, Rochester, and Gloucester. At Worcester the centre part is four-naved; at Canterbury, in both buildings, and at Gloucester, three-naved. The Gloucester centre has columns with typical late C 11 volute capitals and groin-vaults. The wall-shafts have equally typical late C 11 two-scalloped capitals. In the ambulatory and the chapels are elements of the same date, but very shortly after completion of the ambulatory the masons must have realized that for their superstructure, with the sturdy round piers (of which more will be said presently), the ambulatory needed strengthening. So rounded responds were set below the upper piers and strong, elementary ribs were inserted, either of plain rectangular section or of one broad half-roll with two smaller quarter-hollows. There is no decoration, except somewhat later pieces of blank arcading in the s E and E chapels and some chevron at r. angles to the wall in the N E chapel. In the ambulatory is a piece of C 14 SCULPTURE, a small stone Crucifix.

What the Norman CHOIR AND PRESBYTERY looked like, one can see better in the ambulatory than in the centre. The elevational system was completely different from that later adopted in the nave, and in this respect it differs from Tewkesbury. It is the normal Norman system of arcade and gallery, both here with strong round piers. The piers have the same convex minimal capital bands as later in the nave. The transverse arches are of plain rectangular section. The wall-shafts have single-scallop capitals, and the vaults are groined. All this is still as in the crypt. The entries from the transept to the ambulatory have twin shafts. On the gallery the extremely interesting

feature is the half-tunnel vaults, a feature rare in England but frequent in France ever since Tournus of about the year 1000. The radiating chapels at the gallery-level have tunnel-vaults, but the Norman E chapel was of course twice replaced, by the C 13 and now by the C 15 Lady Chapel.

The guiding principle of the masons working on the choir and presbytery in the C 14 was to unify the space, and how well they succeeded. In the central space the Norman work is entirely masked by the Perp panelling begun after 1337. This stone panelling runs blank over Norman wall surfaces, and open where there were Norman openings. The Gloucester feature of close cusping is noticeable in the ogee panel-arches. The Norman piers have been partly sliced off to make room for the Perp shafts, which are anchored at the ground and gallery stage. From the floor by the choir stalls to the apex of the vault is about 92 ft. The vault with its longitudinal ridge rib is accompanied by two parallel ribs l. and r. – a motif invented here and then, as we shall see, taken over in the N transept (and the W bays of the nave). The vault shows such a multiplication of liernes and tiercerons that it is to be considered more textural than structural. Basically it is a double quadripartite vault. As the points of crossing increase, so do the bosses. They intensify the impression of texture, appearing to be heads of nails fixing a net to the vault. The vault was painted by *Clayton & Bell*, c. 1895. Note at the E end, centrally over the high altar, the figure of Christ in Glory, and on the surrounding bosses angels playing musical instruments, and carrying Passion emblems, an idea taken from the slightly earlier series at Tewkesbury, and much finer. The vertical lines of the shafts on the walls are nowhere cut by the horizontals, nor are the main mullions of the E window, so that the impression of soaring height is intensified. The E window is canted to place the foundations of the main mullions on the crypt walls below. A spin-off advantage was that it became canted against wind pressure; all the same the E bay of the vault looks as if it is held up by a glass wall. (Even more than Ely Lady Chapel, this space is hard to photograph against the inpouring light.)

The chronicle says it was not until the time of Abbot de Horton (or Houghton), 1351–77, that the work of the presbytery, with the high altar and second half of the stalls, was undertaken. Against this, the heraldry in the E window shows it to be largely a memorial to those who fought at Crécy in 1346. (But there will have been a pause for the Black Death and its aftermath.) If the dates of presbytery, clerestory and E window are 1352–67 (Harvey 1978), that tends to identify the master of the great E window, as well as the E cloister, hypothetically with *Thomas of Cambridge* – that is, to identify him as a structural innovator, here and also at Hereford (see *Cloisters* below).

The LADY CHAPEL is entered under the bridge which carries a small chapel and the upper passage running through the apse, which seems to have been three-sided rather than absolutely round. The Lady Chapel was finished c. 1500 with a lierne vault, and an E window very similar in design to that of the presbytery, though nearly a hundred and fifty years later. (The glass helps to date proceedings here; see *Stained glass* below.) N and S are CHANTRY CHAPELS with fan-vaults ingeniously adapted to an oblong plan. They support singing galleries which are held up by flying ogee arches across the open-panelled stone screens.

The SE ambulatory CHAPEL OF ST STEPHEN and the NE CHAPEL OF ST EDMUND AND ST EDWARD (formerly called Boteler's Chapel, after a C 15 abbot) are both entered through Perp stone screens. On the screen between the N ambulatory and the N transept a stone READING DESK is built-in, possibly for superintending the monks coming from the cloister into the choir. The screen openings here are similar to those corresponding on the S side. On the E side of the N transept, but part of the same building programme as the ambulatory (like the E chapel of the S transept), is the CHAPEL OF ST PAUL. See the twin responds with single-scallop capitals and the groin-vault. It looks as if the work of 1089–c. 1100 went as far as the lower parts of the transepts. In their upper parts chevron has arrived, and so it has in the nave.

The NORTH TRANSEPT, like the one on the S, was given a Perp veneer, but at a later date – between 1368 and 1373. The lierne vaulting is also later and more accomplished. The longitudinal ridge rib has a parallel rib either side, as in the choir, and the intersections of the ribs are covered by bosses. The entrance to the Treasury (given by the Goldsmiths' Company in 1977) in the Norman slype next to the chapter house is through the N wall of the N transept, so visitors pass through the C 13 SCREEN. It may not be *in situ* and may have been part of the narthex of the former Lady Chapel finished in 1227, i.e. the screen may date from c. 1230–40. On the other hand, this may be a reliquary chamber originally built in this position. The elevation is tripartite, with window-like openings l. and r. It is profusely enriched with Purbeck marble shafts, and the shaft capitals are of the most dramatic stiff-leaf types. The centre bay has the doorway with a trefoiled head set under a pointed gable, blank trefoils, and an eight-cornered star whose diagonal corners are pointed-trefoiled. The side arches have stiff-leaf covering the spandrels. Inside are three little rib-vaults with fillets on the ribs.

### FURNISHINGS, W TO E

Stained glass and monuments are described separately below.

*Nave* The early C 18 CHOIR STALLS and BISHOP'S THRONE here were turned out of the choir in the C 19 by

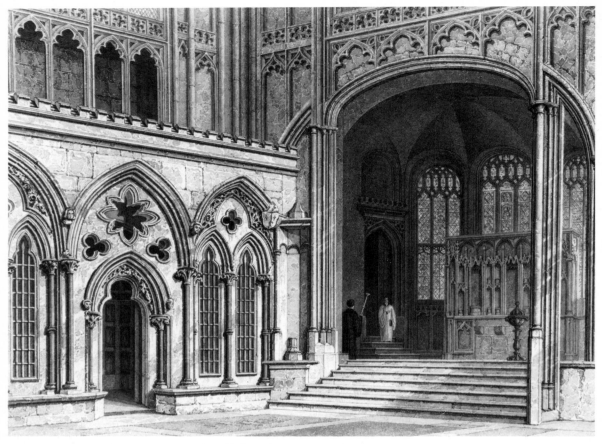

63. GLOUCESTER Screen, *c.* 1227?, north wall of north transept, in 1828

*Scott.* – PULPIT. C17, with stairs and sounding-board designed by *Stephen Dykes Bower, c.* 1946. – Nave ALTAR also by him. – LECTERN. First half of the C17; wood. – Scott's font is now in the crypt. – On the pulpitum (see *Interior*, nave, above) *Thomas Harris's* ORGAN (rebuilt 1920) in a fine case of 1665. *Chaire* case probably *c.* 1640 by *Thomas Dallam* (Gillingham). Harris's pipes were painted by *John Campion*, a local man, in heraldic designs; on the nave side, initials of Charles II on the tower caps (the W face, originally the back when the organ stood over the S stalls, has painting almost *trompe l'œil* in style instead of carving: Gillingham).

*North transept* (Screens: N wall, see *Interior*, N transept; between N ambulatory and N transept, see *Interior*, N ambulatory.) – The sumptuous Art Nouveau CLOCK CASE is by *Henry Wilson*, 1903. – E chapel. Reredos carved by *Redfern*, 1870.

*South transept* E wall at r. of crypt entrance: carved stone BRACKET, with dowel holes for an image which once

stood on it. It is L-shaped, i.e. of the form of the medieval equivalent of the architect's T-square, and so the bracket may have been the gift of the master mason. The little figures below the lierne-vaulted underside seem to suit that role: the master of the transept apparently seeing one of his masons fall from the vault. – E chapel. WALL PAINTINGS by *Thomas Gambier Parry*, 1866–8. Victorian encaustic floor TILES. Perp stone REREDOS with figures restored in the C19 (by *Roddis* of Birmingham) and recently redecorated.

*Crypt* Scott's nave FONT, carved by *Farmer & Brindley* of polished granite in Romanesque style.

*Choir* The STALLS, occupying the crossing, are of *c.* 1350 and very perfect with their three-dimensional ogee-carved canopies and a wonderful series of forty-four MISERICORDS (to which fourteen were added when the choir was restored by *Scott* in 1873). Subjects of the original set include boys playing ball, a knight slaying a giant, Samson and Delilah, Alexander's flight, bear-baiting, hawking, a mermaid, three shepherds beneath a star, a pelican in her piety, an elephant complete with howdah and with a horse's tail and hairy hoofs like a carthorse, and a king resembling Edward II's effigy in the presbytery (Remnant 1969). In time, the stalls date between those at Ely and Wells on the one hand and those at Lincoln on the other; misericords, though, were not necessarily all carved at once. – *Scott's* sub-stalls, 1869–73, carved by *Farmer & Brindley*, are very fine, with splendidly carved ends and finials. – Part of a C13 stall can be seen behind that of the vice-dean, N of the opening under the organ. (On the organ, see *Nave* above.) On the back of the N stalls (in the Dean's Vestry, S side of N transept) C14 PAINTING of Reynard the Fox.

*Presbytery*  C19 PAVEMENT of marbles and tiles with black and white sgraffito scenes, presumably designed by *Scott* and of very high quality. – But the sanctuary immediately before the high altar retains much of Abbot Seabroke's tiled PAVEMENT laid down in 1455. – REREDOS by *Scott*, 1873. Realistic groups of figures carved by *Redfern*. The three upper turrets have canopied statues of angels. Everywhere Scott has seen to it that the cusping is of the Gloucester variety, echoing Edward II's tomb on the N side of the presbytery. The reredos was painted in full colour in the 1890s at the same time as the C14 vault above. The recent polychroming of the figures on the reredos has pulled the whole composition together, with its new cross and candlesticks designed by *Dykes Bower*. – The quadruple SEDILIA, restored or recarved in the C19, are in detail much more commonplace, though the embattled parapet has three delightful angels, replacing those there before, sitting casually upon it and playing musical instruments. – The brass LECTERN of 1862 is an early design by *J. F. Bentley*, made by *Hart & Son* and shown at the 1862 Exhibition. A most spirited piece of Victorian craftsmanship, with eagle and dragon. – The light fittings were designed in *Bernard Ashwell's* office, and the Paschal candlestick, c. 1973, was designed by *Basil Comely* and made in the cathedral workshop.

*South-east ambulatory chapel*  Entered through a Perp stone screen. Panelled reredos. The vault was painted c. 1864 by *Burlison & Grylls*.

*North-east ambulatory chapel*  Also has a Perp screen. The C15 reredos is mutilated; it was coloured. Stone altar, restored. Medieval floor tiles.

*Lady Chapel*  Late C15 REREDOS, much mutilated. Unusual in preserving contemporary graffiti or scribbled memoranda of names of saints whose statues once adorned it. The restored triple SEDILIA are contemporary with it. – Medieval TILES on the sanctuary floor. – Dean (later Archbishop) Laud's COMMUNION RAILS. Square, tapering balusters. – FONT of lead, late C12. One of nine lead fonts in Gloucestershire, out of about thirty in the whole of England and Wales. This one, made from the same mould as five others, comes from St James Lancaut, a ruined church on the banks of the Wye. An arcade in low relief surrounds the bowl and contains alternately figures and scrolls.

## STAINED GLASS

### Medieval glass

PRESBYTERY EAST WINDOW. The great E window was probably finished by 1357. It was taken down and re-leaded by *Ward & Hughes*, c. 1862, under the superintendence of Charles Winston, with no new glass added. The stonework was repaired in 1914. With few exceptions the C14 glazier used white, blue, yellow and red glass. The white glass is full of bubbles, giving that silvery light which is so apparent in this window. The blue was pure pot-metal, so that it is blue throughout. The ruby glass would have been nearly opaque if it had been red all through; so a different process was invented to produce flashed ruby glass. A yellow stain

64. GLOUCESTER Lectern, 1862 (detail).
Designed by J. F. Bentley

was also used which was lighter than the pot-metal and varied in many shades. For line-shading a brown enamel, made from iron, was used, or copper, if a greenish-black was required. It is not so much the development of technique, however, which is remarkable in this window, as the development of design. The great Perp window determined the design of the glass. It is the first as well as the grandest example of the window filled with tiers of full-length figures which became characteristic of the following century. The drawing of the cartoons seems closely connected with contemporary French manuscripts; the face's lack of a bottom eyelid is characteristic. The canopies, flat-fronted, are often surmounted with lofty spires; the side piers from which the arch springs run up either side into pinnacles. The background behind the figures is quite flat and richly coloured, with no attempt to produce by shading the effect of its being a hollow niche.

In this window the largest possible area for glass has been obtained by deflecting outwards the side walls of the easternmost bays of the choir and by making the window a 'bow', so that it almost suggests a triptych. The subject of the window is the Coronation of the Virgin, who is attended by the apostles and saints as well as by the founders and representatives of the abbey. The subject and its treatment are somewhat similar to Orcagna's contemporary triptych in the National Gallery. Above the central group of Christ and Mary (the best and least damaged figure left) enthroned are three pairs of angels holding palms. The second from the l. has been lost and replaced by a C 15 Madonna from some other window. The figures on the same level as the central group represent the Twelve Apostles. The four outermost apostles on the s side have disappeared, with the exception of the feet of the last two, and have been replaced by four kings. The lower half of one of the apostles seems to have been used to replace the lower part of Christ; another may be found in the patched-up figure in the last light but one of the tier below. His large purple hat suggests St James the Greater, who was beginning to be represented as a pilgrim in the C 14, with a small picture of the face of Christ set in front of the hat. The much damaged figure, two to the l. of this, may also be an apostle. The others in this row are canonized saints, in pairs, turning towards each other; in the l. half, including the central pair, four virgin martyrs alternate with four male martyrs: St Cecilia and St George; a virgin whose emblem is lost and St Edmund; St Margaret of Antioch and St Lawrence; St Catherine without her wheel and St John the Baptist. On the r. there is too much confusion for certain identification. The lower tier has figures without haloes, which shows they are historical personages. The place of honour in the centre is occupied by two kings, but the one on the r. has been replaced by St Edmund, who is an intruder, as the scale of the figure shows; so is the one to

the r. of him. The other king (l. centre) may well be Edward II holding sceptre and orb, just like his recumbent effigy close by. His reputation as a quasi-saint was at its highest about this time. The inserted figure of the kings, on a larger scale but contemporary in style, may well have come from the clerestory windows. The quarries, a very large number of which survive, are ornamented with a star design or decorative insertions. The three principal tracery heads had gold flaming stars, though the central one has been replaced by a C 15 figure of St Clement as pope. The four corresponding openings of the two wings are relieved by ornamental roundels.

The quarry lights under the lowest tier of figures are varied by a series of roundels and heraldic shields which provide the chief evidence for dating the window shortly before 1357. The four shields on the l. and the four on the r. occupy their original positions, and their shape is the heater-shield of the C 14. From the l. the arms are as follows: (1) Arundel, a beautiful example of streaky ruby and of a lion drawn with a lead outline. Arundel fought at the Battle of Crécy. (2) Berkeley. The greenish chevron is much later glass. (3) Warwick. Exquisite diapering of the ruby field and the yellow fesse. Warwick fought at Crécy. (4) de Bohun, also at Crécy. On the r. (1) Pembroke, an early instance of the deplorable quartering. (2) Talbot, fought at Crécy. (3) Sir Maurice Berkeley, fought at Crécy, killed at Calais in 1347. (4) Thomas Lord Bradeston; note the single rose of the C 14. He fought at Crécy and is supposed to have given this window as a memorial to Sir Maurice Berkeley. The shields in the middle are (1) Ruyhale. (2) Edward I, but earlier than the rest. (3) Edward III, showing France quarterly, repaired in 1814. (4) The Black Prince, one of the original series. (5) Henry of Lancaster. (6) Instruments of the Passion; late C 15. Below are (1) England, late C 14. (2) Edmund Duke of York, late C 14. (3) Edward III, late C 14. (4) England, Henry of Lancaster, one of the original series.

LADY CHAPEL EAST WINDOW. The glass is now in such a confused and disordered state that we are hardly able to distinguish any definite subjects and carry away an impression of a mass of richly toned fragments, with here and there a face or a form dimly visible. The window generally contains work of the C 14 and C 15, and was reduced to this state early in the C 19, when alien glass was also introduced. The chapel was built under Abbots Hanley and Farley, i.e. between 1457 and 1499, and one would therefore expect the glass to be late C 15. As a rule, in cases of wholesale destruction, it is in the tracery openings and the cusped heads of lights that original glass has escaped and remains in situ, and that is so here. While the three central lights at the top of the window have been filled for the most part with imported glass, some at least of the contents of the smaller side lights immediately on both sides appear to be *in situ*. Both represent scenes in the open air, the blue sky or landscapes being continued into the cusped heads without any canopy or framework, a pictorial method characteristic of the late C15. The principal figure in the one on the l. is a crowned Madonna, and as there are remains of a similar figure in the small lights at both ends of the top tier, these four lights appear to be original, and illustrate miraculous stories about the Virgin. The nine main lights of the window, divided by two transoms into three tiers, again in the cusped heads, retain much original glass similar in character to that in the tracery lights. It seems likely that unframed scenes alternated with canopied figures, as in the E window of St Margaret, Westminster (before 1519): a compromise between the old and the new style. In the extreme right-hand light of the middle of the three tiers there are the substantial remains of a Madonna in a deep red mantle with jewelled border, standing on the crescent moon in the midst of a glory of gold rays. Her head has disappeared and the Child she carried has been replaced by a mass of alien fragments. At the bottom is an inscribed band of text reading 'S(an)c(t)a Ma(ria) cel(es)t(i) lumine'. This figure must have occupied a central light.

In the eighteen round openings set between the lower transom and the heads of the lights in the bottom tier, a comb alternates with a barrel or tun, preceded on the l. by an initial E and followed in the case of the comb by the syllable 'to' and in that of the tun by 'co'. Here is the rebus for Edmund Compton, the donor, who died in 1493. He was the father of Sir William Compton, a ward of Henry VII and friend of Henry VIII, and also Constable of Gloucester Castle in 1512 and of Sudeley in 1513, and Chief Steward of the abbeys of Gloucester and Cirencester. With these court connections of the Comptons, it is quite possible that this window was London work. This would account for the advanced form of some of the fragments, both pictorial and realistic, with their considerable infusion of foreign character, particularly in the physiognomy of the full faces and the deep, rich colours of the draperies.

The three central lights at the top of the window, however, are not later than the middle of the C15 and are obviously an insertion from another window. They are characteristic English work and similar to the original glass left in the windows of the N aisle of the nave. Bits of glass from side windows in the Lady Chapel, depicting the Passion, are also included, particularly the fairly well-preserved Precious Blood in the central light of the middle tier, which is said to be by *Richard Twygge*, who worked at Malvern and later at Westminster Abbey, 1507–10. His earliest recorded work was in 1476. Either side of this are soldier saints of the late C15. The Royal Arms of England is late C15 but of a different character. The bottom row of lights is mainly filled with C14 glass, from a Jesse Tree window, probably taken from the N transept. The kings,

however, must date from nearer the middle of the C14, and they resemble the figures in the great E window of the choir, though they do not belong to it; but the bearded face of an apostle in light one from the bottom r. probably does.

There are also fragments of medieval glass in the windows of the CHANTRY CHAPELS of the Lady Chapel. – On fragments of old glass elsewhere in the cathedral, see below.

*Victorian glass (W to E)*

SOUTH PORCH. E window by *Heaton, Butler & Bayne*. Angels ringing bells.

NAVE. Great W window by *Wailes*, to Bishop Monk † 1856, completed 1859. – SOUTH AISLE. W window by *Clayton & Bell*. – From W to E, first window by *Hardman*, 1864; second by *Bell* of Bristol, 1861; third by *Warrington*; fourth by *Clayton & Bell* (coronation of Henry III and heraldry); fifth by *Bell* of Bristol, 1860 (Brooks); sixth by *Clayton & Bell* (Edward II); seventh by *Warrington*, c. 1857; eighth by *Rogers* of Worcester, c. 1853. – NORTH AISLE. W window by *Hardman* (life of King Lucius). – From W to E, first window by *Clayton & Bell*; second by *Ward & Hughes*; third old glass restored by *Hardman*; fourth by *Clayton & Bell*; fifth old glass restored by *Hardman*; sixth by *Clayton & Bell* (Bishop Hooper); seventh by *Clayton & Bell*; eighth by *Preedy* of London, c. 1863. – CLERESTORY. Fragments of old glass, the third from the W on the N restored to the original design by *Hardman*.

NORTH TRANSEPT. W window by *Kempe*, 1894. – Great N window, Hicks-Beach memorial by *Hardman*, 1876 (life of St Paul). – EAST CHAPEL. Three windows by *Burlison & Grylls*, 1870: superb musician angels in the greens, brown and gold of their mature work (Harrison 1980).

SOUTH TRANSEPT. Great S window by *Hardman*. – W window by *Kempe*. – Some of the oldest glass in the cathedral is in the upper E windows of this transept: white scroll work of vine-leaves, on a ruby ground, in the heads, and plain quarries with simple borders below; restored by *Hardman*, c. 1865. – EAST CHAPEL. Three windows by *Hardman*.

SOUTH AMBULATORY. Three windows by *Kempe*. – SOUTH-EAST CHAPEL glass by *Clayton & Bell*.

NORTH AMBULATORY. Three windows by *Kempe*, the E one designed by *J. D. Sedding* (Brooks).

PRESBYTERY. N clerestory, five windows by *Clayton & Bell*. – S clerestory, windows in grisaille by *Hardman*.

LADY CHAPEL. Excellent side windows by *Christopher Whall* (1850–1924) working with his son and daughter, *Christopher* and *Veronica Whall*. – NORTH CHAPEL. Window by *Kempe*, 1895.

See also *Cloisters*, C16 and C19 glass, below.

There is no Norman figure sculpture, often to be found in the smallest local parish church, with the possible exceptions of one of the capitals in the crypt and the lead font (from a parish church) now housed in the Lady Chapel. There is, however, the elegant wooden effigy in the PRESBYTERY of Robert, Duke of Normandy, which must be earlier than 1219 and is possibly as early as 1160. He is not wearing poleyns on his knees, and his chain-mail suggests mid-C 12. The eldest son of William the Conqueror, he made war against his father. He went on the first Crusade in 1096, where he played quite a distinguished part; but he was greatly incensed that he was left Normandy and his younger brother William Rufus England. He had an engaging and likeable character but lacked the drive of his other brother, afterwards Henry I, who captured him in 1107. He died in prison in Cardiff in 1134 and desired to be buried in Gloucester Abbey. The effigy has a moustache. The body is protected by a hooded hauberk of mail reaching nearly to the knees, over which is a sleeveless surcoat. He wears a coronet of strawberry leaves and fleur-de-lys. The effigy rests on a chest-tomb of C 15 workmanship with an iron hearse framework for supporting a pall. Along the sides are the attributive shields of the Nine Worthies, part of a late C 15 cult, and facing E that of England quartered with France. The effigy is before the high altar, though he was probably buried in the chapter house. During the Second World War the effigy was put in the crypt with the Coronation Chair from Westminster, and, as Mr Bernard Ashwell has wryly pointed out, Duke Robert got nearer to the throne in the C 20 than ever he did in his lifetime.

*Presbytery (s side)* C 13 stone effigy thought to represent Abbot Serlo, the first Norman abbot and founder of the abbey church, supported on a cradle. The arch of the canopy over the head terminates in two diminutive heads. Below is a foliated boss representing maple leaves, naturalistic, not conventional. The monument cannot be earlier than *c.* 1280. The effigy was moved from the N side when the original position was given over to Osric. (On Osric and Edward II, see N *ambulatory* below.)

*South ambulatory* The Rev. John Kempthorne † 1838. Gothic tomb-chest with angels and rich canopy. No effigy. The style is '*c.* 1300'. – Bishop Ellicott † 1905. Alabaster tomb-chest and effigy, by *W. S. Frith*. – Brass to Rev. H. Haines, 1872, by *Heaton, Butler & Bayne*.

*Lady Chapel* Tomb-chest and effigy of Bishop Goldsborough † 1604. He wears a white rochet and black chimere, with lawn sleeves, scarf, ruff and black skull cap. – Elizabeth, wife of W. J. Williams and daughter of Bishop

65. GLOUCESTER Robert of Normandy, effigy *c.* 1160?, chest C 15. Pavement C 19, probably by Scott

66. GLOUCESTER Tomb of Edward II, *c.* 1330. North presbytery aisle. Detail of the effigy

67. GLOUCESTER Tomb of Edward II, *c.* 1330. North presbytery aisle

Miles Smith, † 1622. The effigy lies on its side, with an infant on the pillow. – Margery Clent † 1623, another daughter of Bishop Miles Smith. Tablet with frontally kneeling figure. Both by *Samuel Baldwin* of Stroud. – John Powell † 1713, signed by *Thomas Green* of Camberwell. Standing effigy of a judge, in marble, a noble figure by one of the outstanding statuaries of the first quarter of the c 18. – Dorothea Beale. Inscription by *Eric Gill*, c. 1907, on a bronze tablet by *Drury*.

*North ambulatory (i.e. under the N arcade)* At the E end, monument to Osric, which, however, only dates from c. 1530. Osric was honoured by Abbot Parker as the founder of the monastery, and his sister Kyneburg was the first abbess, at the end of the c 7. The effigy is rudely carved, perhaps in imitation of an earlier figure, and lies on a tomb-chest, above which is a Tudor canopy with a panelled soffit. In the spandrels on the N side, the arms of Abbot Parker and the attributed arms of Northumbria. – Tomb of Edward II. (Presumably at first kept elsewhere while the Perp encasing of the presbytery went on?) The effigy is of alabaster, London work of c. 1330. The canopy is fine-grained oolitic limestone from the Cotswolds, probably Painswick; plaster is used only for the joints. Restoration of the canopy was undertaken three times in the c 18 by Oriel College, Oxford. The tomb-chest on which the effigy rests is made of Purbeck marble, with ogee-arched recesses, cinquefoiled with crocketed heads. The canopy consists of two stages of ogee-headed arches with close cusping at the sides of the arches and ogee foils – the work of a genius – surmounted by finials with buttresses placed diagonally and terminating in pinnacles. It may well be called the most thrilling of all tomb canopies. Large ogee-headed niches have been cut away from the Norman piers at either end of the shrine. The capitals were painted brown with a motif of white harts after (or for?) the visit of Richard II in 1378. – The next monument is that of the last abbot, William Parker, the effigy carved of alabaster, c. 1535. It was prepared for him, but after the Dissolution he was not buried here; instead a Marian and an Elizabethan bishop lie below. Parker's effigy is vested in full pontificals, including his mitre (the abbots had been mitred since c. 1381). It lies on a high tomb with three panels on each side, the first and third bearing emblems of the Passion and the middle one the arms of Parker. In the frieze above are the Tudor rose, the pomegranate, a lion's head, oak-leaves, fleur-de-lys, and the initials W.M. for William Malvern (alias Parker). At the head, the Norman pier has been mutilated, and the abbot's arms are placed here surmounted by a mitre. The floor is paved with medieval tiles. The monument has close Perp screens to l. and r.

*North transept* On the W side is the large stone monument to John Bower † 1615, and Ann, his wife. The kneeling figures are painted.

*South transept* Tomb-chest with recumbent effigies of Alderman Abraham Blackleech † 1639, and his wife, Gertrude, according to Mrs Esdaile by either *Epiphanius Evesham* or *Edward Marshall*, with faces like those by Evesham and hands like Marshall's. The recumbent effigies are carved in alabaster with very perfect attention to the details of the clothing. His feet rest on an eagle and hers on a mailed fist holding a dagger. They lie on a black marble tomb-chest and are good examples of their period, whoever the sculptor was. – Next is the monument to Richard Pates, the founder of the Pates Grammar School in Cheltenham and builder of Matson House, † 1588. The effigies have disappeared, but the painted stone Elizabethan canopy remains. – Other monuments in the S transept are as follows. Marble bust of T. B. Lloyd-Baker † 1886 by *W. S. Frith*, the bust in relief in a medallion above a relief of Justice. – Small brass and marble tablet to Canon Evan Evans † 1891, by *Henry Wilson*. – Tablet to Benjamin Baylis † 1777, by *Bryan* of Gloucester. – Mary, wife of Thynne Gwynne, † 1808, by *Reeves* of Bath. – Canon Trotter † 1913, and Canon Scobell † 1917, nice, rich tablets of the period. – Chapel S of the pulpitum (Salutation of Mary). Abbot Seabroke † 1457. Tomb-chest and alabaster effigy of a mitred abbot. – Francis Baber † 1669. Large tablet with twisted columns and emblems of death. Open segmental pediment.

*Nave, south aisle* Near the S transept, the recumbent effigies of a knight and lady, in a c 14 canopied tomb which has an ogee arch with foliated crockets and finial. It is panelled at the sides and back and has a vaulted roof without bosses, like the roof of the S transept. On either side is a canopied niche. The ogee arches are three-dimensional with pinnacles. The cornice has a splendid single rose and double roses and leaves. The knight is said to be Sir John Brydges of Coberley, and he wears the S S collar, a Lancastrian badge instituted by Henry IV; therefore the effigy must be early c 15. The lady also has an S S collar. – In the S aisle the following tablets. Mary Clarke † 1792, by *W. Stephens* of Worcester, and Richard Clarke † 1796, by the same. – Prebendary William Adams † 1789, by *T. King* of Bath. – Jane Webb † 1811, by *Wood* of Gloucester. – John Webb of Norton Court † 1795, by *Bryan* of Gloucester in classical taste. – Mary Singleton † 1761, by *J. & J. Bryan*. Coloured marbles, Baroque style. – Sir George Onesiphorus Paul † 1820. Free-standing bust by *Sievier* on a large marble sarcophagus. – Sir John Guise of Higham † 1794, by *Millard* of Gloucester. A draped broken column. – Dame Mary Strachan † 1770, by *Ricketts* of Gloucester, who has produced a monument well above the usual provincial level; this one and the one to the Bishop of St David's nearby are outstanding even for their date. (Four generations of the Ricketts family, sculptors, flourished 1729–95: Gunnis 1953.) A cherub holds Lady

68. GLOUCESTER Monument to Canon Tinling † 1897.
By Henry Wilson

dated 1581–1630, for he was registrar to eight bishops. –
Sir Hubert Parry, composer ('Jerusalem'), † 1918. – Statue
of Dr Jenner, who first used vaccination, by *R. W. Sievier*,
London, 1825.

*Nave, north aisle*   w wall: Bishop Martin Benson
† 1752. – Bishop Warburton † 1779, by *King* of Bath. – N
wall: large monument to Charles Brandon Trye † 1811,
with bust in a medallion held by two life-size angels. –
Three pretty medallions to the bellmakers Abraham
Rudhall † 1798, Charles Rudhall † 1815, and Sarah Rudhall
† 1805. – Tablet to the Rudge family by *Millard*. – Col.
Edward Webb † 1839, by *H. Hopper* of London. Conventional mourning female; Gothic. – Samuel Hayward of
Wallsworth Hall † 1790, by *Bryan* of Gloucester. – Ralph
Bigland, Garter Principal King of Arms, † 1784. – Hester
Gardner † 1822, by *James Cooke*. The last three are good
classical monuments in a group together. – Sarah Morley
† 1784 at sea in passage from India. By *Flaxman* ('Impelled
by a tender and conscientious Solicitude to discharge her
parental Duties in person, she embarked . . .'). Three
angels receive her and her baby from the rolling waves.
Classical in style, Gothic in feeling. – Various tablets by
*Millard & Cooke* of Gloucester. – Alderman Thomas
Machen and his wife, Christian. Painted monument of
c. 1615 (perhaps by *Samuel Baldwin* of Stroud). He was
mayor of Gloucester and kneels opposite his wife. Above
them is a horizontal canopy supported by Corinthian
columns. The monuments in the cathedral have been
repainted at different times, for instance for the Three
Choirs Festival in 1797, but Machen the mayor has his
original red gown. – Canon E. D. Tinling † 1897. Bronze
figure kneeling and marble details; a fine example of the
period by *Henry Wilson*. – Ivor Gurney, poet and musician
of Gloucester, † 1937.

In the NORTH CHOIR GALLERY, a splendid monument
by *John Ricketts the Elder* of Gloucester with a bust of
William Little † 1723 and a panelled plinth with gadrooned
edge.

Strachan's portrait in a medallion, very elegant decoration,
and underneath are the Baronet's arms with delightful
little contemporary male supporters. – Richard Raikes
† 1823, by *Thomas Rickman*, Gothic. – Eli Dupree † 1707.
Bust on top in a broken pediment. – Gaoler Cunningham
† 1836. Erected by the magistrates, by the s door. – Bishop
William Nicholson † 1671. – Anthony Ellys, Bishop of St
David's, † 1761, by *Ricketts*; excellent detail. – Jane Fen-
dall † 1799, by *King* of Bath. – Alderman John Jones,
c. 1630. Painted, half-length upright effigy, by the Southwark workshops; a monument full of delightful details
such as the packets of deeds as though in pigeonholes and

## CLOISTERS AND RELATED BUILDINGS

CLOISTERS. About twenty-five miles away, at Hereford, one of the most vital buildings in the development of
the Perp style was completed in the years 1364–70: the
upper part, with vault and windows, of the decagonal
chapter house is only known to us from slight fragments
and from a drawing of 1721. There is a close link between
the Hereford chapter house, with its large single fan-vault,
and the smaller fan-vaults and traceries of the E cloister
walk at Gloucester. At Hereford the construction was
undertaken by Thomas de Cantebrugge, mason and citizen
of Hereford, during 1364–70. He probably came from the
hamlet of Cambridge on the Gloucester–Bristol road. The

six bays of Gloucester's E walk from the nave to the door of the chapter house were built under Abbot Horton, but this merely fixes the date between 1351 and 1377. In spite of their smaller scale the traceries and fan-vaults of this cloister correspond so exactly with the style and details used at Hereford there can be little doubt that the designer was one and the same man. As a working hypothesis it is suggested that *Thomas of Cambridge* was in charge at Gloucester for some time before 1364 and built the early bays of the E walk, and that he then left to take on the important contract at Hereford (having, Mr Harvey suggests, already drawn up the Hereford design *c.* 1359 while still in charge at Gloucester). He would then have set himself up at Hereford by investing in the freedom of the city, and *Robert Lesyngham* was thereupon appointed master mason at Gloucester. In this case Lesyngham would be the designer of the N transept and also of the remaining cloister walks, although they were not begun until 1381 and he was at Exeter by 1377. There is a subtle distinction between the E walk at Gloucester and the other three walks, the difference between the two architects Cambridge and Lesyngham. Indeed, the style of the N transept (1368–73) seems closer to the later cloister walks.

The E walk of the cloister therefore has the earliest surviving fan-vaulting known, dating from some time after 1351 and probably before 1364 (though not, perhaps, before the Hereford design was drawn out). The panelling of each window-bay is divided by two main pointed arches with a horizontal element at springing level, contrived by interlacing ogee archlets. This produces two pairs of elongated hexagons above, cusped equally top and bottom, and a third pair centrally at the top, all with supermullions and Y-tracery. The side to the garth is divided into ten bays, nine containing each a large Perp window of eight lights crossed by a broad transom projecting externally like a shelf as protection from the weather. The wall side has corresponding blank panelling. The other walks, vaulted between 1381 and 1412, are almost but not quite identical. This later work is slightly less pretty, and simpler, as the ogees do not interlace. And there are slight changes in the fans. But these are minor differences, and the whole is yet of unmatched harmony and conveys a sense of enclosure such as no other Gothic cloister does.

The N walk contains the fan-vaulted LAVATORIUM at its W end, lit by eight two-light windows towards the garth and by a similar window at each end. Half the width is taken up by a stone ledge and trough, which originally carried a lead tank from which the water came out of spigots where the monks could wash. There was an excellent drainage system, which survives in the garth. Opposite on the N wall of the cloister is a groined recess or almery where the towels were hung. Against the N wall a stone bench on which traces of scratchings survive indicat-

ing that the novices here played a game called 'Nine Men's Morris' or 'Fox and Geese'. The W walk closely resembles the E, and like it was a mere passage, but it has a stone bench along the wall. At its S end is the Processional Door into the nave. The S walk was probably shut off by screens. It has ten windows towards the garth, but below the transom the lights are replaced by twenty little recesses or carrels. Each carrel, used for study, is lighted by a small two-light window and is surmounted within by a rich embattled cornice.

STAINED GLASS. E walk, S to N: the first seven windows all by *Hardman*, eighth window by *Ballantine*, ninth by *Hardman*, tenth by *Clayton & Bell*. – The ten small two-light windows in the LAVATORIUM by *Hardman*. – A few other windows by *Hardman* in the other walks. – The best glass is in the S walk, but this is not C 19: it is mostly C 16 glass brought here in the C 19 from Prinknash Abbey, six panels having been given to Prinknash by Abbot Parker, the last abbot of Gloucester, and the rest by Lady Chandos of Sudeley. Woodforde writes: 'A much higher standard was maintained in the C 16 in drawing of heraldry than figures. Representations of Royal Arms and badges are particularly good.' Here are excellent examples, including the badge of Catherine of Aragon (pomegranate). Before *Scott* caused the reglazing of the cloisters, J. T. Niblett recorded seven examples of the Plantagenets' *planta genista* in the lavatorium window. – The encaustic TILES in the middle of the E walk are a memorial to the Rev. Sir W. L. Darell of Fretherne, 1865, by *J. W. Hugall*, who enlarged the parish church there for him.

From the E walk, between the N transept and the chapter house, a wide passage or SLYPE runs eastward to the monks' cemetery. It is chiefly of Early Norman date and was originally the same length as the width of the N transept against which it is built. It was entered from the cloister by a wide arch, later covered with Perp panelling, the doorway now *c.* 1870. Inside, Norman wall arcade on each side, with fifteen arches on the N, but only eleven on the S, the space between the flat transept buttresses admitting no more than that number. It is now the Treasury in which plate is exhibited, and is entered through the E.E. screen in the N transept. The roof is a plain tunnel-vault without transverse arches. The capitals are of two scallops. In the C 14, when the vestry and library over the passage were enlarged, the passage had to be extended to almost double its length. The original library stair was approached from this passage, but after the C 14 a new spiral stair from the cloister was made, intruding into the SW corner of the chapter house. The VESTRY communicates with the cathedral only through the chapel E of the N transept. The LIBRARY is C 14, retaining much of its original open roof, which springs from beautiful wooden corbels. Eleven windows on the N, each of two square-headed lights which lit

the bays or studies. The large end-windows are Late Perp. None of the old fittings now survive. For several hundred years the boys from King's School (founded by Henry VIII) did all their academic work here.

Next to the N off the E walk is the CHAPTER HOUSE. An earlier edition existed *c.* 1080. It is said that here William the Conqueror held 'deep speech' with his Witan at Christmas in 1085, and ordered the Domesday survey to be made. There was originally an apse, but this was replaced with a straight but canted end *c.* 1380. The roof is a tunnel-vault in three bays, carried by pointed transverse arches and so a second edition. The E bay is lierne-vaulted. The side walls have blank Late Norman arcades, the W end a central door flanked originally by windows and surmounted by three more. The lower part of this wall is part of Abbot Serlo's original chapter house, reddened by the flames which destroyed the wooden cloister in 1102. Inside the chapter house is preserved a piece of mid-C 10 SCULPTURE, of Christ Almighty or Pantocrator, from an age that was still linked with Carolingian art. It is a roundel with the classical motif of the running dog on its rim. – STAINED GLASS, E window, by *Christopher Whall*, 1903–5.

The next opening from the cloister led to the DORTER (dormitory), which no longer exists except for a fragment which can still be seen on the outside of the N E corner of the chapter house. It is a jamb of one of the windows built at the beginning of the C 14, with a small ballflower decoration round the capital of a slender shaft. It was there before the Norman apse of the chapter house was removed; for the later E end, which is square externally, has the corner cut off so as not to block the window. A Dec string-course also runs along the chapter-house wall. The building more or less in the dorter's place, built in 1850 as an extra schoolroom for the King's School, is now used as a gym.

In the N walk of the cloister there are two E.E. doorways, one at each end. The E one opens into a C 13 vaulted passage which led to the infirmary and at a later date the abbot's lodging. The passage is rib-vaulted in four bays with elegantly profiled arches and ribs. The W door now filled with a C 19 window was the entrance to the REFECTORY or FRATER. It has two orders of colonnettes and a richly moulded arch. This building, which was begun in 1246 on the site of the Norman one, has also disappeared, except the S wall, which is common to the cloister, parts of the E end and a fragment of the N wall.

For further description of the surviving monastic remains and subsequent alterations, see the latest edition of B of E *Gloucestershire: The Vale and the Forest of Dean.*

# Hereford

CATHEDRAL CHURCH OF THE BLESSED VIRGIN MARY AND ST ETHELBERT   *Anglican*

(Based on B of E *Herefordshire*, 1963, revised, with information from J. A. Finch, Michael Gillingham, Peter Howell, George McHardy and J. S. Whittingham.)

Plan, Fig. 71, from the *Builder*, 1892, by Roland Paul, showing the W front before and after Wyatt's rebuilding but not the early C 20 rebuilding. (Ridge ribs shown in the Lady Chapel vaults are, except for the E bay, erroneous.)

Some references (see Recent Literature): Bony 1979; Cocke 1973; P. Eames 1977; Harvey 1978; Morgan 1967; Morris 1974.

INTRODUCTION

Hereford Cathedral has been unlucky in a number of ways. Its W front is by *Oldrid Scott* and not one of his best, the nave is more than half *Wyatt*'s (from 1788, with, however, considerable restraint), the crossing and parts of nave and chancel are by *Cottingham* and son (from 1841, with considerable feeling for Gothic), and the E view is dominated by *Sir G. G. Scott*'s reconstruction (1856–63). Moreover, in distant views of Hereford the cathedral does not dominate the town as do those of Durham and Lincoln or Ely or Wells or Salisbury. The town of Hereford has three church towers, and the two with spires, i.e. those of All Saints and St Peter, are more prominent than the broad crossing tower of the cathedral; for the cathedral has lost its spire and moreover an additional W tower. Its collapse in 1786 started Wyatt on his alterations. And, finally, when one gets near, Hereford Cathedral suffers from the absence of a close proper. King Street and Broad Street run right

70. HEREFORD View from the north-east

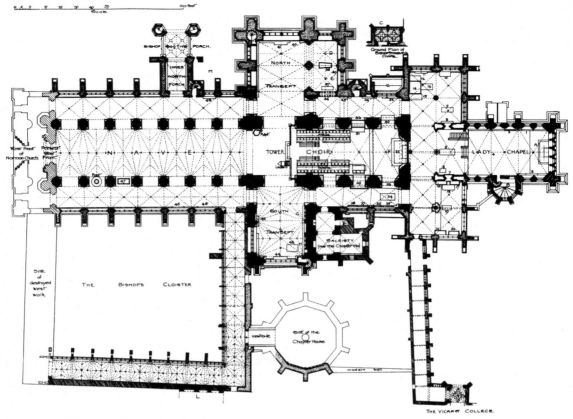

71. HEREFORD Plan from the *Builder*, 1892 (see p. 156)

towards the W front. There are no walls and gates between. Yet now that the approach from High Town and East Street along Church Street has been closed to traffic, one has the sense of approaching a close. And to W, N and E of the cathedral, lawns hold the town at bay. Yet again, the cathedral houses on the N side are part of the town, the Deanery is early C19, the Cathedral School with its busy new buildings faces the E end, the College of the Vicars Choral has a Georgian stone front towards the chancel, and it is only at the corner of the cloisters and the Bishop's Palace that a precinctual feeling can be evoked. If the S door from the E walk of the Bishop's Cloister happens to be open, there is a timeless view of episcopal lawn and elderly cedar of Lebanon, with the river hidden beyond, and Welsh mountains in the distance.

Hereford became a see in the late C7. A new cathedral was built in the first half of the C11 and burnt by the Welsh. There is no evidence that Robert de Losinga, Bishop of Hereford from 1079 to 1095 and brother of the Bishop of Norwich, began a new cathedral. Reynelm, Bishop in 1107–15, is called 'fundator ecclesie' in his obit. He will have begun the present church. A consecration took place between 1142 and 1148, and Bishop Robert of Bethune, who died in 1148, was buried in the cathedral, which, as the chronicle says, 'ipse multa impensa et sollicitudine consummavit'. Of this Norman church the E end is not preserved. Excavations have shown that it had three apses. It also has a chancel of three bays with aisles, and scanty but undeniable evidence brought forward by the late Sir Alfred Clapham points to towers above the E bays of these aisles – a German rather than a Norman or Anglo-Norman motif (cf. the destroyed St Maximinus at Trier, the remains of St Lucius at Werden, etc., and also, influenced by the Empire, Ivrea Cathedral and S. Abbondio at Como in North Italy, and, influenced by North Italy, S. Nicola at Bari and other South Italian cathedrals). To the W follow transept and crossing, the latter with a tower (now of later date), and a nave of eight bays ending in a front with no tower, but turrets to flank the aisles and flank the nave. There was a single large W portal and any amount of the blank arcading

72. HEREFORD West end after the collapse of 1786, drawing engraved 1830

which was such a passion among English masons. A w tower was put on in the early C14. Its collapse has already been referred to. Before that time the Norman E end had been replaced by a retrochoir widened into E transepts and by a straight-ended Lady Chapel on a crypt. There is no evidence of the date of this work. Style suggests *c.* 1190 to *c.* 1230 or 1240. Documents do not exist to confirm, but it has been suggested that the Interdict of 1208–14 explains the change of style between retrochoir and Lady Chapel. Immediately after the Lady Chapel had been completed, the clerestory of the chancel was rebuilt and vaulted. The mid-C13 seems a reasonable date to assume. Then Bishop Aquablanca (Peter of Savoy, 1240–68) began to rebuild the N transept about 1250 or 1255. Next the enshrining of the saintly Bishop Cantilupe's remains, first in the N transept in 1287 and later in the Lady Chapel, and the need for a ceremonial route for pilgrims to the shrine, inspired further rebuilding (Morris 1974). Much was done about 1290 and after, namely the inner N porch, the remodelling of the nave aisles and subsequently of the chancel aisles,

the completion or rebuilding of the E transepts, and the splendid crossing tower. After that only appendices were provided: two chantry chapels and the outer N porch. The date of the outer porch – 1519 – takes us close to the Reformation.

The cathedral is of greyish pink sandstone from Hollington, of better wearing quality than Worcester's red sandstone, for instance. The total length now is 360 ft, the height of the tower 165 ft.

EXTERIOR

The phases of the architectural history cannot be distinguished on the outside sufficiently clearly and separately to justify a chronological arrangement. This will be reserved for the interior. The outside is here described topographically from E to W.

We must thus start with the LADY CHAPEL. The E wall is much renewed by *Scott*, but not without guiding evidence. It is ornate and restless. The crypt appears only by its small pointed-trefoiled windows. The composition above is with turreted angle buttresses and a big E gable. Five widely-set stepped lancets shafted and with stiff-leaf capitals. Hoodmoulds on head-stops of which only few survive. Two tiers of pointed-trefoiled niches l. and r. and between the lancets. Above, blank wall decorated with eight moulded lozenges (a motif frequent at Lincoln c. 1240 etc.), the first and last with dragons on the top, and between the first and second and seventh and eighth an almond shape with dogtooth. Then a blank gallery with stiff-leaf capitals, hoodmoulds with dogtooth on head-stops. The middle niche is a little higher, and the dogtooth frieze rises there. Top wheel window with eight columnar spokes, entirely by Scott. L. and r. an arched niche, and at the top an almond shape, all by Gilbert Scott, as must also be the roof's iron cresting with the words 'Laudate Dominum' repeated.

The N and S sides are roughly identical. Three pairs of large shafted lancet windows with stiff-leaf capitals. Roundel in the spandrel of each pair. On the N side scenes, e.g. the Crucifixion, in the roundels. Then a frieze of interlaced arches with stiff-leaf capitals, the arches of different patterns. On the S side there are heads in the spandrels. On the N side a porch covers the outer stairway into the crypt. It has a steep gable containing a broad pointed-trefoiled niche. Entrance with shafts carrying stiff-leaf capitals. Arch with roll mouldings with fillets, but the inner order with a zigzag at r. angles to the wall, i.e. the only Late Norman or Transitional motif in an otherwise E.E. ensemble. It can only be re-used (see *Interior* below for the considerations regarding the interior of the re-trochoir and Lady Chapel). The porch has a quadripartite rib-vault with a stiff-leaf boss. The ribs stand on corbels with stiff-leaf capitals. Inner doorway with continuous roll moulding with a fillet. Hoodmould on head-stops.

On the S side the E.E. composition is broken by the AUDLEY CHAPEL, built before Bishop Audley was transferred to Salisbury in 1502. It is on a five-eighths plan with a lowish ground floor and a high, amply glazed upper floor. Panelled buttresses and pinnacles. To its W the CHOIR VESTRY, an insignificant C15 addition partly rebuilt c. 1860.

The architecture of the EAST TRANSEPTS and CHANCEL AISLES is almost uniform and has nothing to do with that of the Lady Chapel. Large four-light windows with tracery typical of c. 1300, e.g. on the N with three large pointed trefoils in the tracery of two of them and a pointed cinquefoil above. This work probably came after the remodelling of the nave aisles (the N aisle being the first leg of the pilgrim route from the N porch.) Morris suggests that remodelling of the second, eastern leg began c. 1307 when Cantilupe's canonization was being pressed. (Similar work at Dilwyn, a few miles away, was called 'new' in 1305.) The uniformity of c. 1300 is broken by another Perp chantry chapel, that of Bishop Stanbury, erected on the N side after his death in 1473: it is called 'newe bylded' in 1491.

Now the HIGH CHANCEL. The buttresses at the angles are of a different stone and a first hint at the Norman building. The rest is all of *Cottingham's* doing, i.e. c. 1842-3. The N and S sides have two-light windows with plate tracery (a quatrefoil) which stylistically precedes Aquablanca's bar tracery of the 1250s. The windows have shafts with shaft-rings and stiff-leaf capitals. Between them runs slender blank arcading. Above this there is on the S side a curious frieze of lozenges and quatrefoiled circles reminiscent of the upper E wall of the Lady Chapel. On the N side there is instead a blank arcade with pointed-trefoiled heads and paterae in the spandrels. The flying buttresses are clearly an afterthought.

One word on the externally visible traces of the Norman towers above the E bays of the chancel aisles, now mainly visible on the N. The buttresses on the E wall have already been mentioned. They mask the junction of towers and Norman E wall (above the apse). The E walls of the towers themselves are still in existence above the aisle roofs and now end with a diagonal. Moreover, from the roof of the N chancel aisle one can see the top of a tiny window in what was the S wall of the N tower. It has a stepped rounded top and a primitively carved tympanum. It must have looked down from an upper level of the tower towards the altar. Also the plinth of the S side of the tower exists (inside a new lavatory) and shows that this wall was as thick as the E wall.

The transepts are much more eloquent regarding the Norman building, or at least the SOUTH TRANSEPT. On the E side the upper windows are Norman and shafted. At ground-floor level is the present vestry, consisting of a utilitarian C15 E part and a Norman W part which was used as the Treasury. It looks from outside like a transept E aisle. It has a small, shafted window to the S (and one to the E only visible inside and with difficulty). At clerestory-level and hard to see five arches of Norman arcading immediately S of the junction with the chancel. The great S window is of c. 1400, large, of six lights, and of course Perp. In the gable above, a large oculus with thin ribbed trefoil, presumably Cottingham's (McHardy). In the W wall are two Perp windows, but between them a fragment of Norman interlace arcading and, below, a blocked Norman window with shafts and zigzag – the first we come across. The N transept is of a different period, and we shall turn to it with enthusiasm in a moment. Of the Norman transept no more is externally visible than one column of the same blind arcade at clerestory-level as we have seen (or not seen) on the S side. Maybe the transept was never continued or completed.

So to Peter of Savoy's, i.e. Bishop Aquablanca's, *chef d'œuvre*. The NORTH TRANSEPT was begun by him and

73. HEREFORD The north porch in 1830

sufficiently ready shortly after 1268 to receive his monument, a work as crisp, accomplished and *dernier cri* as the transept itself. That its source is Westminster Abbey is at once evident from the E clerestory windows, spherical triangles enclosing foiled circles. The same motif occurs at the Abbey in the gallery of the E parts.

Below them are circular windows under round arches on shafts (these windows belong to the library), and below them the aisle windows of three lights with three encircled trefoils in the bar tracery. To the N all is pulled together in an enormous six-light window, 50 ft tall. The E window of the Angel Choir at Lincoln, dating from the same period, is 59 ft in height. The N window of Aquablanca's transept has twice the three circles as before, and above them as a final achievement a large sexfoiled circle, taking up the figure six from the six lights. In the gable three cusped lights – below no cusping of lights occurred yet – and a final group of three quatrefoiled circles. To the w, even more impressive perhaps, two equally tall three-light windows. The transept has gabled buttresses with chamfered angles which in turn end in steep crocketed gables. At the bottom they have strange, steep, much-broken spurs such as castles use, but not churches. The E wall was begun before the rest; for the buttresses here on the set-off above the spurs have bases for shafts which were not continued with. They are to be seen also on the N E buttress facing N, and then stop.

The CROSSING TOWER is the only architectural feature of the exterior that can compete with the N transept. It must belong to the early C 14, as it is studded all over with ballflower, and it illustrates the change from 1260 to 1310 to perfection, a change from the Greek, i.e. classic, ideal of μηδὲν ἄγάν and the Gothic ideal of *masze*, as Wolfram von Eschenbach glorifies it, to profusion, excesses and so final exhaustion. The tower has cutwater angle buttresses all the way up and all the way panelled. They end in pinnacles just below the main pinnacles (which date from 1830). There are two tiers of tall two-light windows, but all are blank except two of the lower and two of the upper tier, on each side of which the upper are the bell-openings. The tracery is quatrefoils below, cinquefoils above. A band of cusped lozenges runs between the two stages. There was some remodelling of the tower by Wyatt (Colvin).

The WEST PARTS need less description. The aisle windows of *c.* 1290 have the unframed pointed trefoils we saw repeated farther E. On the N (the ceremonial route) the aisle windows have finely subdivided jambs and arch mouldings, where all the others are plainly chamfered. The clerestory windows by *Wyatt* are decent, self-effacing Perp, of two lights. The corbel table carries on from the transepts. On the N side in addition there is the NORTH PORCH, a piece of two dates and equally good in quality of both. The outer part is by Bishop Booth and dated 1519 on a little archway on its E side. It is open in large arches to N,

E and w. The N entrance has traceried spandrels and is flanked by hexagonal stair-turrets each with a glazed bay at the top, as entries to the upper chamber. Large three-light upper window. Low-pitched gable. The vault inside has diagonal ribs, ridge ribs and one set of liernes, making the square space into four squares. Square centre cusped. Lozenge bosses at the four main intersections. The inner part of the porch is earlier – of the time of the aisles, as entrance to the pilgrim route. It is two-storeyed, the top storey lit by no more than three small lancets. Below is an elongated quadripartite vault with ridge ribs and a leaf boss, no longer stiff-leaf, though the ribs stand on corbels still with stiff-leaf. The (former) outer doorway has a glorious surround with three orders of shafts and three orders of little figures and foliage in the arch. The system behind all the little figures will never be found, as there can be none. The middle order may be a Tree of Jesse, but why should, on the outer order, a bagpiper be followed first by a mermaid and then by the symbolic figure of the Synagogue? The inner doorway has five bold large cusps with openwork spandrels. The mouldings are set out with sprigs of stiff-leaf or fleurons. A stair-turret in the s E angle squeezes the adjoining window out of its regularity (as occurs – not in the corresponding position – E of the N transept, where there is a stair-turret of *c.* 1300).

Of the WEST FRONT little need be said. The Norman front was tall and barren, with much blank arcading, and not much else. A deep, probably impressive, w portal, two thin outer turrets, and two a little more substantial inner turrets – that was all. Rochester has been quoted as the best surviving comparison. A w tower was put on early in the C 14, when the crossing tower was built too. It was a little less mighty and a little lower, but had a great deal of ballflower too. This is the tower which collapsed in 1786 (a disaster long impending, according to Cocke 1973). The w front was taken back one bay, and *Wyatt* erected a non-committal w front. The one we see today, however, is by *John Oldrid Scott* and was built in 1904–8. He could be so good, so earnest and restrained. What made him choose the fullest-blown Dec to introduce to this cathedral? Moreover, why go so low with the side parts? The line of the aisle roofs is not even in an understandable relation to the line of the nave gable. And all the detail is so vociferous.

## INTERIOR

Major churches were usually built from E to w – for the obvious reason that it matters more to house altar and relics than to provide vast spaces for small numbers of monks or worshipping laymen.

At Hereford we do not know what the apses and the E towers were like, but we have the chancel, even if at its E end over-restored by *Cottingham*, and the s transept. Now

74. HEREFORD East side of the south transept, *c.* 1110

the embarrassing thing is that the SOUTH TRANSEPT, and especially its E wall, looks decidedly more archaic than the chancel. This is hard to explain, but special conditions connected with the Saxon cathedral and its altar space may have existed. The E wall has a tall blank arcade whose capitals are drastically re-cut, but clearly represent a state of carving not comfortably to be placed later than 1110. Above are three blank arches, the middle one shafted. There follows a triforium in three groups of arches, three, two, three, corresponding to the blank arches below. The triforium columns are very short and have scalloped and volute capitals. At sill-level runs a finely decorated string-course. Then again blank arcading, quite tall – that is a four-storey impression – and finally the wall-passage in front of the clerestory. It has the typically English stepped arrangement of low and very stilted high arches, and these were in a regular rhythm until the transept vault was put on about 1430. The stilted arches are set out with much zigzag, which allows this stage to be dated with some confidence as *c.* 1120 at the earliest. The N bay of the E wall differs in that it contains the opening to the s chancel aisle and the s chancel gallery. The details of the responds on the ground floor are all by *Cottingham* (but the arch is original – no zigzag), and the gallery corresponds to that in the chancel (see below). The s wall was entirely remodelled about 1400 (described after the C14 work on the crossing tower, below). The w wall also is much changed. The N bay belongs to the nave and largely to *Cottingham* (see below). The two Perp windows are of course an alteration, but there is one splay and shaft of a Norman window, decorated, as we have seen, externally with zigzag, and in the clerestory one of the low arches of the wall-passage. So the zigzag comes in at a lower stage in the w than the E wall, which tells us how building proceeded. (A recess still in the w wall is called 'ancient fireplace' on our plan of 1892, although with no flue shown.)

Immediately E of the transept is the former TREASURY, now part of the vestry. It was originally no more than a gangway and is vaulted in two groin-vaults, the oldest in the cathedral. It has (see *Exterior*, s transept, above) one s and one (hidden) E window, both shafted. The doorway to the chancel aisle is tall and completely unmoulded, but there are bits left of a finely ornamented string-course.

In the NORTH TRANSEPT nothing Norman remains visible, except of course the arch and gallery arch into the chancel aisle. On the C13 rebuilding, see below.

The CHANCEL comes next, or so it seems. Three bays of main arcading. Compound piers with (re-cut) decorated capitals: scallops, curly volutes, heads etc. An outer band of the arches has zigzags arranged to form lozenges. The shafts towards the nave ran up broad and sub-shafted to the ceiling. They were cut off when the new clerestory was built in the C13 (see chancel remodelling, below). Sill

course of the gallery also with geometrical decoration, much higher in relief than in the s transept. The gallery has one twin opening to each arch below. The responds are entirely out of keeping with those on the ground stage – halves of fat round piers, a *modus* which is in keeping with the liking for such piers in the West Country, even before 1100, notably at Tewkesbury and Gloucester. At Hereford they meant a change of plan, and the new motif was continued in the nave, as we shall see. Many-scalloped and otherwise ornamented capitals, zigzag in sub- and super-arches, tympana with various geometrical patterns in relief, a motif most closely paralleled at Peterborough, where rebuilding started in 1118. The E wall is opened in one big arch, reaching to the top of the gallery responds. It was entirely re-done by *Cottingham*. Originally it was the arch to the apse. Now the retrochoir appears behind it in the oddest way. This is also due to Cottingham; for when the retrochoir was built (see below), the arch was closed by a solid wall into which the w column of the retrochoir bonded. The wall served no doubt as a reredos. The capitals of the E arch and the adjoining N and s capitals are all Cottingham's. (But ORIGINAL CAPITALS preserved and displayed in the corridor to the Vicars' College off the SE transept ought to be mentioned here: they are decorated and include little, very primitively carved scenes such as the Annunciation and Christ in Limbo. Their style makes Dr Zarnecki's dating *c.* 1115 on the whole convincing, although the *fundatio* under Reynelm, i.e. a beginning of the whole rebuilding *c.* 1110, suggests 1120–5 rather. Dr Zarnecki's reference to relations back to Anglo-Saxon traditions is entirely sound.) The blank arcading above the E arch is by *Cottingham*.

Of the Norman CHANCEL AISLES little can be said. The E side of the N arch from the transept into the aisles indicates vaulting-shafts. The E arches of both aisles (into the E transept) are original. Above them, on the E face, is a blocked window, N as well as s. They must have led from the gallery to the roof above the apses, or rather from the first floor of the E towers. Of these E towers we have already heard. Evidence of their existence is scanty inside, but one can see against the E pier of the N arcade on the N side the chiselled-off remains of the arch respond which carried the w wall of the N tower. The evidence is clearer above the aisle vaults, and there exists for the s as well as the N tower.

Next in order of time came the CROSSING. Cottingham rebuilt the Norman piers entirely, but of the arches with their version of zigzag, which is like crenellation with triangular merlons, much is original. (On the C14 work, see below, after *Audley and Stanbury Chapels*.) The NAVE must for constructional reasons have been at least started at the same time. There is in fact a joint clearly visible. The E responds and the first two piers from the E (though again on

76. HEREFORD Retrochoir, *c.* 1200,
and east transepts, *c.* 1300, in 1831

the E end was too small. So the apses were pulled down, and a retrochoir, two bays deep to serve as an ambulatory too, and a Lady Chapel to its E were started. The dates are again entirely unknown. At Winchester a similar composition was begun by Bishop de Lucy (ruled 1189–1204), and Abbey Dore received its double ambulatory *c.* 1200–20. We can hardly go so late at Hereford; for the style is still Transitional, with some Late Norman motifs kept in an *ensemble* turning decisively Early English. The E transepts (see below, after remodelling of chancel and N transept) may have formed part of the scheme, but are in their architecture later. What remains is the space between the E arch of the chancel and the two walls of the vestibule to the Lady Chapel. The RETROCHOIR has two circular shafts with octagonal abaci, both perversely on the main axis of the building. Both were rebuilt by *Cottingham*, it is said correctly. One has a capital of upright stiff-leaf, the other of trumpet-shaped scallops, and the latter has a waterhold-ing base. That combination of capitals corresponds to the parts of *c.* 1200 at Abbey Dore. The ribs are set out with zigzag partly combined with chains of lozenges. They are pointed and were also rebuilt by Cottingham. It has already been said that the E arch of the chancel was blocked when the retrochoir was provided. Cottingham opened it, and filled the spandrel which now intrudes itself on our atten-tion, as we face (the rear of) the altar, with florid E.E. carving of stiff-leaf, the Virgin, angels and St Ethelbert in a little niche. (St Ethelbert was murdered *c.* 794, and his were the most valuable relics at Hereford, the cathedral being dedicated to the Virgin and to him.) The carving was

77. HEREFORD The crypt, *c.* 1200–20

the surface all Cottingham's) have capitals with interlaced trails etc. much like some of the crossing. Further w all is multi-scalloped capitals. The arcades have throughout heavy circular piers, a West Country preference, or at least piers nearly circular; for to the nave and the aisles they are a little widened by twin shafts. Those to the aisle were to carry the transverse arches of the aisles, those to the nave the tie-beams of the ceiling. The diameter of the piers is about 6 ft 8 in. by 7 ft 2 in. Arches with much zigzag, also meeting at r. angles. The Norman gallery which Wyatt removed was relatively low, of two twin openings to each arcade opening. This Norman nave may or may not have been completed at the time of the consecration of the 1140s. (For Wyatt's work on the nave, see below.)

Then nothing more happened for about fifty years. After that it was felt, as in so many other major churches, that done by *W. Boulton* of Lambeth. The retrochoir is separated from the E transepts by arches not decorated by zigzag, but the w responds still also have trumpet capitals (whereas there is stiff-leaf on the E responds). The windows or openings in the N and S walls of the vestibule to the Lady Chapel are also Late Norman in their details. The openings have keeled shafts, stiff-leaf capitals, and in the arches thick chains of elongated hexagons. The arches are pointed. The vault of the vestibule is quadripartite with an extra rib to run to the middle pier, which interferes so incomprehensibly with the view down the Lady Chapel.

A Lady Chapel was no doubt planned from the start. The entrance to the vestibule proves that. It was erected on a crypt. The CRYPT fills the space below the Lady Chapel, excluding the vestibule. It is aisled and has five bays with octagonal piers and single-chamfered arches. Against the walls they rest on tripartite corbels, the middle one filleted. That was the final moulding of the ribs at Abbey Dore. In the nave stiff-leaf bosses, the westernmost one a human bust.

The LADY CHAPEL itself is one of the two aesthetically most satisfying interiors in the cathedral. Judging by its style and the profusion of its detail, it must date from *c.* 1220–40. Its proportions give the feeling of a comfortable spreading, and the walls are so richly shafted as to convey luxuriance. In the end, however, the simple quadripartite rib-vaults leave one with a sense of repose. Three bays separated by tripartite vaulting-shafts with stiff-leaf capitals. Ribs and transverse arches all have the same slim mouldings. Stiff-leaf bosses. The E bay has an extra rib to the apex of the E wall, the only ridge rib in the chapel (here Paul's plan was mistaken). This wall is naturally the richest, and perhaps a little overdone. Shafted windows and detached shafts in front of them. Shaft-rings. Arches with much dogtooth decoration. The middle arch is moreover seven-foiled. Above, roundels and almond shapes with dogtooth. The side walls are more even in their richness. There are fewer motifs used. Each bay on either side has two windows. Their shafting is of five-nine-five in each bay. The shafts have shaft-rings too. Stiff-leaf capitals, hoodmoulds on head-stops, heads at the apexes, in fact a plethora of excellent heads. Also one whole figure of a bishop. In the spandrels roundels with cusped quatrefoils. (On the Audley Chapel of *c.* 1500, see below.)

Having now discussed retrochoir, vestibule, crypt and Lady Chapel, this is the moment to point out the small changes of detail which allow relative dating. Many of them have already been referred to, but a summing up may be useful. The bases are steeper in the retrochoir (but not the rebuilt detached piers) than in the crypt and Lady Chapel. The shafts adopt keeling in the retrochoir w responds and the window shafts and ribs of the vestibule, fillets in the crypt, crypt porch, and Lady Chapel ribs and E

shafts. As for capitals, trumpet-scallops are confined to the w responds of the retrochoir and the easternmost of the two detached piers. The stiff-leaf capitals, however, show a distinct line of development. They have big, single, upright crockets in the retrochoir w pier, the E responds, and the Lady Chapel vestibule, but go thick, lush and more confused in the Lady Chapel itself. The abaci are polygonal in the retrochoir, the windows of the vestibule, and the vestibule N E respond, but round in the S E respond. That must have been the last touch before work proceeded to the E; for in the crypt and the Lady Chapel all abaci are round. These details ought to be compared with those at Abbey Dore.

They can at Hereford also be watched in the upper parts of the CHANCEL, whose remodelling must have taken place before or just after the Lady Chapel was finished. The Norman clerestory was cut down or drastically remodelled. The vaulting-shafts were cut off and finished with twin gables with leaf motifs. Above them filleted tripartite vaulting-shafts with thick, 'disturbed' stiff-leaf capitals support a quadripartite rib-vault, also with stiff-leaf bosses. The clerestory carries on with the Norman motif of stepped arcading in front of a wall-passage. There are, however, two tall arches flanked by two low arches to each bay now. The tall arches have a kind of Y-tracery with stiff-leaf capitals. The windows corresponding to the paired tall arches have, it will be remembered, plate tracery. (On the remodelling of the aisles after *c.* 1300, see below.)

With the NORTH TRANSEPT we are once again on the highest level of architectural art. It was no doubt planned by Bishop Aquablanca, who died in 1268 and is buried in it, and the motifs so evidently derived from Westminster Abbey make a start before *c.* 1250 or 1255 all but impossible. (No wonder Aquablanca followed Henry III's favourite building so closely: the bishop was a close follower of the king, to the detriment of his relations with Hereford.) As for completion, we only know that Bishop Cantilupe's shrine (later transferred to the Lady Chapel) was set up in the N transept in 1287. (For the Aquablanca and Cantilupe tombs, see *Furnishings*, N transept, below.) The E arcade is of two bays with the astringent, almost straight-sided arches that resulted from imitating Westminster's arcade while unable fully to adapt the proportions of its greater height. (Did Lethaby at Brockhampton, a few miles off, have Hereford's N transept's steep arches in mind?) Here compound piers have stone shafts and also Purbeck shafts – again an import from Westminster Abbey. The Purbeck shafts have shaft-rings. Thick, rich stiff-leaf capital on the pier (which the Abbey has not), moulded capitals on the responds. Handsome little stiff-leaf sprigs on the bases. One big entirely under-cut dogtooth moulding in the arch. Hoodmoulds on head-stops. Vaulting-shafts on deliberately thin corbels. Blank gallery of two triple openings to each

78. HEREFORD Lady Chapel, *c.* 1220–40

79. HEREFORD North transept, east side, begun *c.* 1255

bay below. Thinly cusped, again almost straight-sided arches – all structural elements in this transept are thin. Three encircled quatrefoils in bar tracery above. The arches of course again nearly straight-sided. The diapering above, direct from Westminster Abbey, has been re-cut in the C19. The clerestory windows in the famous Westminster Abbey spherical-triangle form have very deep, stepped sills to the inside. (On slightly later and different use of the form, see Lichfield nave.) Quadripartite vaults with fillets on the ribs and bosses. The E aisle has windows shafted in Purbeck marble, some with stiff-leaf capitals, some moulded. Above the E aisle originally the Muniment Room, now the CHAINED LIBRARY (which was once in the cloisters; see *Furnishings*). That is why the gallery has always been blank. The only internal openings are small and paired and have shouldered lintels, typical of the later C13. The arch to the chancel aisle below which Aquablan-

ca's monument was set is essentially triple-chamfered and may be a later adjustment. The adjoining W bay of the N chancel aisle was re-vaulted at the same time, and it has at its E end a double-chamfered arch dying into the imposts. The transept's marvellous W windows and N window (see *Exterior*) are much shafted and much ringed.

The EAST TRANSEPTS pose a problem. There is evidence that they were begun at the time of the Lady Chapel campaign. A respond on the W wall of the N side has been chiselled off later, and on the E side there are two bases with attached bases for flat columns which were later not used. They correspond to the remains of a S doorway out of the SE transept preceding the present one. The bases of shafts are all flat. As it finally turned out, the transepts were built about 1300 – see their windows. They have each a central octagonal pier with a foliage capital already knobbly. The octagonal piers continue above it, and the ribs of the vault

80. HEREFORD Stanbury Chapel, *c.* 1480

die against this vertical piece. The vault has leaf bosses. The RCHM dates the NE transept with its vault to the early C14, the SE transept to the late C14. As we have seen, Morris suggests that remodelling of the pilgrims' route continued E of the main N transept from c. 1307, when Cantilupe's canonization was being pressed and removal of his shrine to the Lady Chapel contemplated. The E transepts were part of the same programme of improvements as the remodelling of the nave and chancel aisles. The work on the aisles (except for the W bay of the N chancel aisle, revaulted when the main N transept with its E aisle was rebuilt; see above) involved vaulting or revaulting on both N and S. On the S side, at least in the first bays from the E, the ribs and bosses are original, and the bosses have naturalistic foliage.

Two CHAPELS of the late C15 and early C16 can be taken in here, as they are E of the main crossing. Off the Lady Chapel to the S is the AUDLEY CHAPEL, built, as we have seen, before 1502 (see *Exterior*, Lady Chapel). It presents to the Lady Chapel a panelled wall with a low doorway and a small four-light window spared out of the panelling. The chapel is two-storeyed. The lower floor has a star-vault, hemmed in by the stair-turret. The upper floor has a lierne star-vault with cusped panels connected with the wall by fans. Off the N chancel aisle another chantry chapel had been added a little earlier, Bishop STANBURY'S CHAPEL. This has a fan-vault throughout. It was erected about 1480, and Mr Marshall in his book on the cathedral (1951) has found that Thomas Morton, Archdeacon of Salop and later of Hereford, an executor of the bishop, a brother of the Archbishop of Canterbury, and with another brother a lessee of the bishop's house at Bosbury, E of Hereford, can be connected with the fan-vault here as well as at Bosbury (Morton Chapel in the parish church), and the porch of the Vicars' College (between the passage from the SE transept and the Vicars' Cloister). The chapel is small and highly decorated. All walls have stone panelling with many shields displayed in the panels. The S wall has it too, except that the doorway cuts into it. Wide shafts with foliage bands l. and r. Instead of capitals two angels, mermaids and monsters. (For the bishop's tomb on the opposite side of the aisle, see *Furnishings*.)

When the crossing tower was rebuilt early in the C.14, the interior stage visible inside received a strange palisade of completely undecorated, chamfered stone piers very closely set and with one transom. The whole may be a device to reduce the weight of the wall. For the fan-vaults subsequently inserted to mask these, and removed in 1842, see the model in the N transept (*Furnishings*).

The SOUTH TRANSEPT received a new S wall apparently just before 1400. Such a date is supported partly by the fact that the monument of Bishop Trevenant (1389–1404) is clearly part of the new architecture of the wall. The monument with its three canopies is below the great Perp window. L. and r. of this there is panelling, and more and closer panelling above it. The vault (with the arms of the see, not the bishop) is of the tierceron type with one by two pairs of tiercerons and square bosses, and is supported by heads of king and bishop. Vault, wall and tomb might further be dated by a possible resemblance of the king's head to Richard II (J. S. Whittingham). In the C15 the Norman vestry (corresponding in position to an E aisle) was enlarged to the E by a two-storey bay. Its ground floor has a plain quadripartite rib-vault with single-chamfered ribs.

Now for the NAVE, after the collapse of the W tower in 1786. (For the Norman nave, see above, with the Norman crossing.) *Wyatt*'s work (1788–96) has been unjustly maligned. The decision to reduce the length of the nave by one bay was taken by dean and chapter in 1786, i.e. before Wyatt arrived on the scene. Although he could have saved the Norman gallery, his E.E. gallery with the simplest Y-tracery is not in the least offensive, and he repeated the Perp windows in an equally innocuous way. His vault is of timber, and the ribbing – one by one pair of tiercerons in each bay – is again self-effacing. The vaulting corbels, of which one cannot quite say that, are by *Cottingham*; before him, the shafts rose from the floor without break.

FURNISHINGS, E TO W

They are described as follows: Lady Chapel; Audley Chapel; crypt; vestibule; E transepts, N and S; chancel aisles, N and S; chancel; crossing; main transepts, N (with Chained Library) and S; nave; N aisle; N porch; S aisle. For every part monuments are placed at the end.

Hereford has many monuments, but only two of the first class (N transept), and it is unfortunate that those of the C17 and C18 have been all but wiped out.

*Lady Chapel* ALTARPIECE. By *W. H. R. Blacking*, c. 1950. Mixed Comper and Feibusch ingredients, and not a convincing mixture. – PAINTING. Painted figures under canopies, c. 1500, against the wooden screen of the Audley Chapel. Too dim to be judged. – STAINED GLASS. In the W bay on the S side the most beautiful glass in the cathedral. One light is patterns only; in the other, above Christ in Majesty, and below three quatrefoils. Of the late C13. – E window, the five lancets by *C. A. Gibbs*, 1852, and quite good; in the style of the C13, and designed, it is said, by *N. J. Cottingham*. Mosaic-like effect of very small pieces of clean colours. – SE and all N windows also by *Gibbs*, 1867. Influenced by the C13 glass. – MONUMENTS. Johanna de Bohun, Countess of Hereford, †1327. She is praying and wears a wimple. Over her head a nodding ogee canopy on two head-stops. Fleurons and little heads on the border. Arch on two head-stops. The top just ogee. – Peter de Grandisson †1352, brother of Bishop Grandisson of Exeter (they were great-nephews of Cantilupe). Tomb-chest with

panelling. The legs of the effigy no longer crossed. Rib-vaulted recess with straight top. Above an open screen with four figures of saints and the Coronation of the Virgin under arches (the last two figures recently given heads). The top again straight, with a cresting. All simple, large forms. An early case of a decidedly Perp feeling – Perp in that it stresses the horizontals so much.

*Audley Chapel* DOORS. Three original doors, one with four linenfold panels, carved with Bishop Audley's badge between 1492 and 1502, thought to be the first use of linenfold in England (P. Eames 1977). – RELIEF. Tuscan, C15, Virgin and Child, in an original frame. – STAINED GLASS. In the upper chapel shields and some small fragments.

*Crypt* ALTAR by *William Goscombe John*, 1920. – MONUMENTS. Incised slab to Andrew Jones † 1497, and wife. Large figures under a massive double canopy. – Four defaced stone effigies, one with fleurons and no doubt once good (McHardy).

*Vestibule* MONUMENT. A member of the Swinefield family; early C14. Beautiful long, slender recumbent figure with short beard. The hems of the gown fall nearly symmetrically and very melodiously. Arch with two hollow chamfers and a step. In the hollow chamfers a few ballflowers and many swine. At the foot also a few ballflowers. No ogee arches yet. Remains of PAINTING against the back wall. The recognizable head of one figure shows that this also was of high quality. – BRASS to Richard de la Barr † 1386. A 26-in. figure of a canon inside a handsome ogee-cusped cross-head.

*North-east transept* Effaced WALL PAINTINGS on the s wall, high up. – STAINED GLASS. In the SE window four early C14 figures under tall canopies that are almost entirely by *Warrington*, 1864. – The first window from the w on the N side is by *Heaton, Butler & Bayne*, 1877. – PULPIT. Oblong, of plain boards with a pierced quatrefoil, said to have been in use during the Civil War. – MONUMENTS. Coffin-lid of the C13, uncommonly densely foliated. – Parts of several others. – Recess with two orders of big ballflower. In it civilian, badly defaced; late C13. – Indents, not for brass, but for a composition or cement infilling: one priest, late C14; one knight and lady, early C15. – Dean Dawes, by *Matthew Noble*, 1869. Alabaster tomb-chest designed by *Scott*. White marble effigy on veined black marble slab. – Bishop Parfew † 1557, the effigy no more than a shapeless lump. Tomb-chest still entirely in the Gothic tradition. Four shields in quatrefoils. – Bishop Swinefield † 1317. Big recess. No effigy left. Arch with fine mouldings. Small ballflowers, also on the gable mouldings. The gable stands on two heads. In the gable an openwork pointed trefoil. Against the back wall a chiselled-off Crucifixion and a perfectly remaining all-over pattern of trailing vine, still treated quite naturalistically.

*South-east transept* WOODWORK. On the E wall frieze of ogee arches from a screen (cf. S chancel aisle). – STAINED GLASS. In the NE window, by *Warrington*, 1863. In Warrington's glass it can be observed that only the shapes of the medallions are inspired by the C13, but the groups are still three-dimensional and realistic in the Renaissance sense. – MONUMENTS. Brasses on the W wall, to Richard Rudhale † 1476, 4 ft 2 in. long, with parts of the buttress strips l. and r., on which figures of saints; and to a priest † 1434, 2 ft. – Brasses on the S wall, to Edmund Ryall † 1428, headless and now 20½ in.; to a bearded civilian † 1394, 19½ in.; to Dean Chaundler † 1490, headless, now 23 in.; and to a civilian said to be John Stockton, mayor of Hereford, † 1480, 25 in., plus fragments. – More fragments on the E wall, including William Porter † 1524. – Dean Harvey † 1500 (?). Tomb-chest with three shields in quatrefoils. Alabaster effigy, defaced. – Bishop Lindsell † 1634. Recumbent effigy. – James Thomas † 1757. White, marble bust attributed by Mrs Esdaile to *Roubiliac*. – Bishop Coke † 1646. Recumbent effigy. The architectural setting was destroyed by *Wyatt*, and now dates, with the group which crowns it, from 1875 (Howell). – Bishop Charlton † 1369. Recumbent effigy, the hands chiselled off. Tomb-chest with shields in cusped foiled fields. – On the floor Sir Richard de la Bere † 1514, and two wives; 19-in. figures. – Also two ledger-stones, dates of death 1669 and 1691. Two clasped hands tie the two together, and the inscription: 'In vita conjuncti, in morte non divisi'.

*North chancel aisle* DOOR to the Stanbury Chapel; original. – STAINED GLASS. NE window by *Warrington*, 1862. Comment as above. – To its w, Hunt memorial window by *Clayton & Bell*, death 1842 but allegedly made 1857. Charmingly humble busts in medallions. – MAPPA MUNDI. The work of *Richard de Bello*, treasurer of Lincoln Cathedral, later prebendary in Hereford Cathedral. Made shortly after 1280. (On the one hand he signs himself Richard of Holdingham and Sleaford, the prebend he held at Lincoln only until 1283. On the other hand Conway and Caernarvon appear on his map, and Edward I began those castles in 1283. Richard was at Hereford from 1305.) It is on vellum and the Orbis terrarum itself is 4 ft 4 in. in diameter. From the point of view of the history of art the most interesting facts are these. The geography is based more on Greek (Pliny), Roman (the Antonine Itinerary, the Physiologus), and Early Christian literature than on travels, the population on bestiaries, and the books on the Marvels of the East. The purpose is part-informative, part-religious. At the bottom l. Caesar with a papal tiara orders the world to be surveyed. Here also Richard himself is found kneeling. Geography includes the pillars of Hercules (two columns), the wall built by Alexander the Great to enclose the giants, the Colossus of Rhodes, the Garden of Eden, the Labyrinth of Minos, Mount Olympus, but also

Abraham at Ur, Lot's wife as a pillar of salt, the pyramid as Joseph's granary (a medieval barn), and a Norwegian on skis. True zoology is represented by elephant, lion, tiger, leopard, camel, crocodile, rhinoceros, bear, bull, ostrich and parrot. They mix freely with manticora, pelican, yale, sphinx, phoenix, and human monstrosities such as cynocephales, blemyae, gangines and monocoli.

MONUMENTS. A so-called Reynelm is the first of a distressingly uniform series of posthumous effigies of bishops made in the early C14 and placed under distressingly uniform arches. All provided to dignify the route to the Lady Chapel when Cantilupe's shrine was moved there (Morris 1974). If one has twenty-six fleurons on the inner arch moulding and twenty-five on the hoodmould and another has twenty-two and thirty-one, that is all that can be said. Only the little heads at the foot and apex of the hoodmoulds are rewarding. Most of the effigies are ponderous stuff too. – But that of Bishop Stanbury † 1473, is another matter. Alabaster monument, not in his chantry chapel but between aisle and altar, a place of honour. Tomb-chest with statuettes, still enjoyable. The effigy is quite powerful. – So-called Clive; see above under Reynelm. – So-called Mapenor. Again the same gesture, but shallow-relief and the plinth more tipped; better and perhaps a little earlier than the others. – Bishop Bennett † 1617. Only the alabaster effigy. The setting included two columns and a coffered arch. – So-called Braose, same gesture as Reynelm, but no arch, and one hand holds a tower. This is usually a symbol of prominent building activity. So perhaps he was meant to be Reynelm. – On Bishop Aquablanca's tomb, see main N *transept* below.

*South chancel aisle*  WOODWORK. Frieze of six plus six little blank ogee arches on colonnettes with shaft-ring. Probably from a C14 screen (cf. E wall of SE transept). – SCULPTURE. Statue of St John Baptist, about 4 ft tall, C15. From St Nicholas Bridge Street, demolished 1841. – STAINED GLASS. Four excellent early C14 figures under big canopies. Also much grisaille. – MONUMENTS. In the S wall four more of the repetitive recesses with posthumous effigies of bishops (presumably the S aisles formed the pilgrims' way out). The so-called Vere seems the earliest, a little lower in relief and with a little naturalistic foliage on the crozier. All recesses with ballflower. – Bishop Mayew † 1516. On a tall tomb-chest with eight saints. Recumbent effigy. The bold canopy, with crocketed ogee gables over pendant arches, the middle one wider, rib-vaulting inside, and pierced panelling above and behind the gables, is terribly re-cut. Stone screen towards the chancel. – So-called Losinga. Again the too familiar type. But he also holds a token-church. Low, almost straight-sided arch with big ballflowers to S and N.

*Chancel*  REREDOS. By N. J. Cottingham, 1852, executed by W. Boulton of Lambeth. – Communion RAIL by

*Lord Mottistone*, 1958. – CHAIR, *c.* 1200, i.e. something extremely rare (Eames: 'one of the most important pieces of medieval furniture in Britain'). Armchair, of wood, with all members turned. The lower front had a little arcade, of which two arches remain. – SCULPTURE. Statue of St Ethelbert. Stone, and to be assigned to the C14. – BISHOP'S THRONE (on its date, see *stalls* below). Three-seated, the side seats with nodding ogee arches like the stalls, but tall crowning crocketed pinnacles. The throne proper has a three-sided canopy with ogee arches instead, and above a thicket of thin shafts rising to the full height of the arcade. – STALLS. Early C14, probably later than the Exeter throne of 1313–16 with its very early use of nodding ogees. Of considerable interest, both historical and aesthetic. (The original stalls reduced in number and reset by *Sir Giles Scott*; see also stalls now in the S transept.) There are sixteen on the N side, fifteen plus the triple-throne of the bishop on the S side. The front rows are imitation, imitated from the original panelled front of the Bishop's Throne, but the back parts are fully original. They have nodding ogee canopies on detached shafts, with panelling going forward and backward above the canopies and a straight cornice or top-rail. The back panels have simple tracery. The ends are again panelled and have pairs of nodding ogee arches with pinnacles to finish them. The set of MISERICORDS is one of the best of its date in England, an early date, it must be remembered. They represent a variety of subjects, all secular, including woodwoses, a mermaid suckling a lion, a fox and geese, a stag and hound, a hunter and a boar, a lion and lioness, a griffin, a goat playing the lute, divers monsters, divers human heads, a domestic scene of husband and wife by a cauldron etc. Remnant (1969) says that, besides those on the original upper seats, old misericords are incorporated in modern seats as follows: two in the lower N row opposite upper Nos. 12 and 16 (numbered from the W), nine in the lower S row opposite upper Nos. 3–6 and 9–13 (numbered from the E). – ORGAN. An imposing Victorian 'functional' pipe-display with wrought-iron supports and excellent contemporary diaper decoration; by *Cray & Davison, c.* 1865, organ later rebuilt by *Willis* (Gillingham). – STAINED GLASS. Triple E window high up, by *Hardman*, 1870, as approved by *Gilbert Scott*, replacing glass by *Hardman*, 1851, to *Pugin*'s design, said to be too small-scale to be seen from below, the window itself having been rebuilt by the *Cottinghams* along with the whole E wall, previously containing a large five-light window with glass of the Last Supper designed by *Benjamin West* (Morgan 1967; McHardy). – The window over the organ is of 1889, by *Burlison & Grylls*. – PAVEMENT. Tiles designed by *Scott*, made by *William Godwin* of Lugwardine (near Hereford; see B of E volume on remains of his C19 brickworks). – MONUMENT. Brass to Bishop Trillek † 1360. A 5-ft figure

under a cusped and sub-cusped arch with an ogee gable. Above, round arch, flat top: the turn from Dec to Perp.

*Crossing* (The former S C R E E N, designed by *Scott* and made in 1862 by *Skidmore* of Coventry from wrought iron, brass, copper and cut stones, was in 1966 sent to Coventry – i.e. the basement of the museum there. Similar in type to Scott's screens at Lichfield and Worcester, but more elaborate, it was probably the second of his great series, after Ely's and before Lichfield's. It was shown in the International Exhibition of 1862, and is a High Victorian monument of the first order. A great loss to Hereford.) The fine brass eagle L E C T E R N, and the two pairs of metal G A T E S made by *Skidmore* in 1864 for the w entrances to the choir aisles from the transepts, survive from *Scott's* splendid ensemble. (Fragments of the medieval choir screen have been made into a door in the corridor from the S E transept to the Vicars' College; see *Cloisters* below.)

*North transept* S T A I N E D G L A S S. The N window is a Victorian piece to be proud of. It is by *Hardman*, of 1864. Two very large medallions going through three lights each, and twenty smaller medallions. – In the w windows C 15 figure fragments said to come from the nave w window, preserved after the disaster of 1786. – The circular clerestory windows are by *Clayton & Bell*, c. 1875–90. – Also by *Clayton & Bell* the transept aisle N, c. 1870. – By *Wailes*, c. 1865–70, the N window in the E wall. – M O D E L of the crossing, 1842 and probably by *Cottingham*, showing the fan-vaults he removed to lighten the load (see *Interior*, C 14 crossing, above).

M O N U M E N T S. The N transept holds the only two monuments at Hereford which are outstanding among any of their time in England: Bishop Aquablanca's and St Thomas de Cantilupe's. Bishop Aquablanca † 1268. Between the chancel aisle and the transept which he created. The architecture is more important now than the sculpture; for the effigy is defaced, and though the little heads on the border separated by slender blank two-light windows are charming, well preserved on the N side, and even exhibit some of their original colour, this cannot compete with the spare, incisive architecture of the canopy with its steeply erect gables. The head of the bishop lies on a diagonally placed pillow which in its turn lies on a cusped arch. The canopy stands on the most delicate Purbeck shafts or groups of them. (Exeter's sedilia canopy of half a century later with its Dec intricacies on equally slender shafts was to need metal for them.) It has exquisitely moulded arches with a quatrefoiled circle in each. In the gables a circle without foiling. All these details are in bar tracery, i.e. entirely transparent. Between the gables quatrefoil shafts rise and end in spires. The crockets and the small foliage at the top otherwise is all stiff-leaf, but of the bosses inside the little three-bay vault the E and w ones are naturalistic. Such foliage had been introduced at West-

minster Abbey between 1245 and c. 1250, but did not as a rule become much accepted outside until later in the century. In fact, the Crucifixus on the central finial on the s side hangs from a cross that is all stiff-leaf. – Shrine of Bishop (later St) Thomas de Cantilupe, surviving lower part. Erected probably for his burial in this place in 1287. The tomb-chest is of six bays. Knights as weepers (the possibility of their being Templars is doubtful) in a diversity of nimble attitudes, extremely well observed, stand under cinquefoiled pointed arches. The arches rest on short colonnettes with leaf capitals. Naturalistic, yet skilfully composed foliage in the spandrels. The effigy is missing. It was covered by an upper structure with open, pointed-trefoiled arches on shafts with moulded capitals but again naturalistically foliated spandrels. The top was no doubt to carry the *feretrum*, or shrine proper. – Defaced effigy of a priest, early C 14. – Brass to Dean Frowsetoure † 1529. The figure 4 ft 3 in.; side strips with saints. – Bishop Field † 1636, alabaster demi-figure, a type usual for dons and divines. – Bishop Charlton † 1343. Effigy with his head on a pillow stuffed into an ample canopy whose top projects as a semicircle. Cusped and sub-cusped arch. On two of the cusps censing angels, on the others large leaves. Crocketed gable with finial. No ogees. – Bishop Westphaling † 1601, an Elizabethan mandarin. The effigy is again deprived of its setting. – Bishop Atlay † 1894. Free-standing tomb-chest of white and red marble. Recumbent effigy by *Forsyth*.

C H A I N E D L I B R A R Y, over the N transept E aisle (staircase from N choir aisle). Late C 16 shelving, pews and folding desks inspired by the Bodleian's. (But some of the books, outside our scope, date from the C 12.) – Portable S H R I N E of St Thomas of Canterbury, early C 13, with Limoges enamel, 7 by 3½ in. On the front the martyrdom of St Thomas, on the roof his funeral, on the ends saints under arches.

*South transept* A L T A R P I E C E. A South German triptych, the centre a relief of about 1520–30, the painted wings mid-c 16 and of quite a different school. – Five S T A L L S from the choir; see above. They are built up of original parts in the canopies and some original bits below (e.g. figures on the end arm-rests). – S T A I N E D G L A S S. The great s window by *Kempe*, 1895. It is curious how parochial, i.e. un-cathedral, his glass is. Huntingford memorial window, 1862, by *Warrington*. – M O N U M E N T S. Bishop Trevenant † 1404, but his tomb and remodelling of the transept probably a few years earlier (see *Interior*, s transept, above). The effigy is deprived of its face, a special trick of the Hereford vandals. Fine triple canopy with a rib-vault inside represented almost in plan, i.e. almost vertically. Ogee gables, crocketed, and finials. Very well tied into the architecture of the whole wall. – Alexander Denton † 1577, and wife. Alabaster effigies, a baby lying by her leg. Pilasters on the tomb-chest.

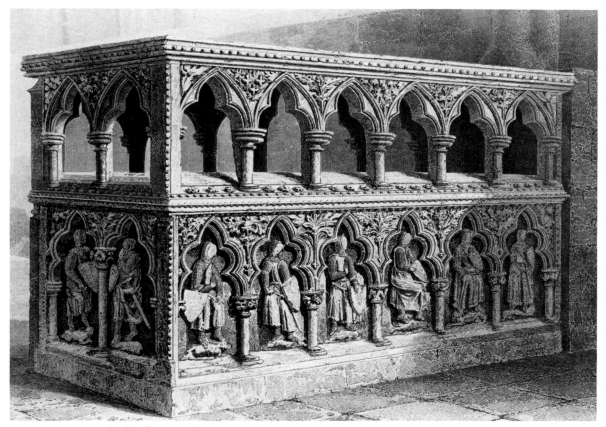

83. HEREFORD Tomb of Bishop Cantilupe, set up 1287

*Nave* PULPIT. Mid-c 17, with big panels separated by pairs of columns. Strapwork cartouches against the underside of the pulpit. c 18 tester, Gothick. – FONT. Norman, tub-shaped. Figures in an arcade. Greek key above, a motif rare in England. Against the foot four demi-figures of lions, said to be c 14 (of marble?). – MONUMENT. Sir Richard Pembridge † 1375. Alabaster knight, his head on his helmet. Tomb-chest with shields in quatrefoils.

*North aisle* STAINED GLASS. Above the Booth monument. By *Warrington*, 1862. – First window from E by *Heaton, Butler & Bayne*, 1888. – MONUMENT. Bishop Booth † 1535. Recumbent effigy. Ogee arch with five cusps. Crockets and finial. In front iron railing.

*North porch* DOORS. Small door to the stair-turret and large N door by *Potter* of London, c. 1854.

*South aisle* STAINED GLASS. In one window a jumble of old fragments. – MONUMENTS. Two of c. 1330–40, one under a septfoiled arch and with a good small head at the apex, the other faceless under an arch similar to that of Bishop Charlton in the N transept.

CLOISTERS, CHAPTER HOUSE REMAINS ETC.

*Bishop's Cloister* This is the normal cathedral cloister, although not normal in never having had a N walk (at Wells, where there is no N walk, one was intended in the late c 12). Hereford's is also unfortunate in having been deprived of half its W walk. The cloister was built in the c 15. A 'clericus novi claustri' is referred to in 1412–13, and the name of a man is inscribed in the vault of the E walk who became a canon in 1406. However, the E wall of the E walk is substantially earlier; see a Norman buttress. The chapter-house entrance is part of it, for the c 14 chapter house had a predecessor on the same site. The c 15 arcading towards the garth is, with one exception, the same all the way through. Four lights with an irregularly sexfoiled circle in an odd place in each light. Four-centred arches. The exception is the bay where the entry to the chapter house is placed. Here there is a taller opening with a two-centred arch, and an upper storey, known as the Lady's Arbour. The inside of this is very light, as the walls

84. HEREFORD Library over the north transept east aisle. Furniture late C16

are generously glazed: five lights w, four N, four s. Stair-turret at the SE corner. The cloister is entered from the s nave aisle by a doorway of *c.* 1300 (two orders of shafts with knobbly-leaf capitals, arch depressed – two-centred on vertical pieces). The vaults of the E range are partly of plaster, probably Georgian, and partly original. The original part begins in the bay with the entrance to the chapter house. The vaults – all except the SE corner – are tierceron stars, each cell arched towards the apex so that the main boss forms a concave-sided octagon. The bosses are figured, but of a comparatively elementary quality. The same design continues in the s walk, but this is now separated as the LOWER LIBRARY. The w range has nothing but two openings to the garth. The rest was rebuilt as a LIBRARY by *Sir Arthur Blomfield* in 1897. In the centre of the garth,

in former times, stood a preaching cross. – MONUMENTS. In the E walk Col. John Matthews † 1826. Of stone, local workmanship. An angel comforts a seated mourning woman. – Several pretty tablets. – In the Lower Library Richard James Powell † 1834. Inscription held by a seraph. Very Gothic surround. – Also an extremely fine chest of *c.* 1300. – On remains of a C11 Bishop's Chapel against the s wall of the s cloister, see below.

*Chapter house* Now a ruin in a pleasant garden E of the Bishop's Cloister. The chapter house was disgracefully pulled down in 1769, after the lead had been stripped from the roof in the Civil War and the building used as a quarry by the early C18. Fortunately William Stukeley drew its interior in 1721 (drawing in the Bodleian). Its uncommon architectural interest has recently been recognized, for it was fan-vaulted, with one of the earliest fan-vaults known, sharing this distinction, as well as details of design, with the E cloister walk at Gloucester. The first six bays at Gloucester are only known to have been begun during an abbacy of 1351–77, yet the three later walks there are closer in design to the N transept of 1368–73. For Hereford we have a contract of 1364 binding *Thomas de Cantebrugge* (or 'of Cambridge', a hamlet near Gloucester), by then citizen of Hereford, to continue and finish the new chapter house in the course of the next seven years: that is, in 1364 it was already begun. He is thought to have designed it in 1359, while still in charge at Gloucester (Harvey 1978).

What remains today is as follows. First the entrance from the cloister. Two orders of shafts and a *trumeau* in the middle. Knobbly capitals and arch mouldings with fillets. The two openings have shapely trefoiled heads. A pierced pointed quatrefoil over with a slight ogee curve at the foot. Gable with trefoil. All this is entirely Dec and has not a touch of Perp. Through this entrance one reaches a vestibule, which was rib-vaulted. The springers of the filleted ribs remain, and a fragment of the S jamb of the portal to the chapter house proper. The chapter house was decagonal. Three sides on the S stand up to a certain height and show their tall panelling with cusped blank arches and scanty remains of scenes in the spandrels. In the middle on the footing of the former central column lies what seems to be the defaced central springing stone, or fragment of the lower taper of the central conoid, as Norman Drinkwater put it (*Archaeological Journal*, 1955). The wall panelling stemmed from the very beginnings of Perp: Stukeley showed window mullions prolonged downward across the blank wall-face over the inner doorway, like the descending mullions of St Paul's chapter house and St Stephen's Chapel in London. In being ten-sided, Hereford's chapter house follows Lincoln's, or, nearer home, the ten severies or vault-cells of Worcester's then still round chapter house (made straight-sided in the late C14); yet the demands of a new form of vault must have been uppermost in Thomas's mind. This latest in the series of English cathedral polygonal chapter houses was perhaps the earliest result of a logical development from the cone of ribs (e.g. at Wells) to the fan-vault.

*Vicars' Cloister (College of Vicars Choral)* The vicars choral were a body of men in orders or minor orders who acted for absent prebendaries. The college was founded at Hereford in 1396. It was to have twenty-six vicars and a custos. Its original hall is partly preserved behind No. 29 Castle Street. They were given the present site in 1473 and built here four ranges round a not quite regular quadrangle as their living quarters, with hall and chapel, both since completely altered. The arrangement was much like that of e.g. the fellows of Eton College. The quadrangle was connected by a corridor with the SE transept of the cathedral, and had in addition a separate entrance with porch on the S side into which the corridor also runs. The premises are more complete than any of such an institution other than Wells and Windsor. The CORRIDOR is reached from the SE transept by a small doorway with a four-centred head, set in a rectangular frame. The corridor has simple three-light windows to the E only and a handsome tie-beam roof with cambered, traceried tie-beams and decorated principals. Kingposts with figures carved against them. Moulded purlins and rafters. Close to the doorway from the transept parts of the medieval CHOIR SCREEN of the cathedral have been assembled into a door. The dado had uncommonly fine six-light blank arcading in intersected arches – a Perp version of a motif of 1300. At the end of the corridor some original Norman capitals are kept (see Norman chancel above). By a turn to the E one gets to the PORCH, a pretty, fan-vaulted room open to the corridor and the N (on its vault, see *Stanbury Chapel* above). To the N a portal with two-centred arch and tracery in the spandrels. The porch has an upper storey which is too weathered to be recognizable in its carved details. Original DOOR. Oddly enough the porch doors connect with the Vicars' Cloister beyond only by a dog-legged corridor (anti-draughts?). The cloister has extremely simple two-light openings with very flat arches. The upper storey projects to above the walks and has only one-light windows. To the N, i.e. the close, the whole college was opened out in the C18 by giving it large sash windows on both storeys. The HALL lies in the centre of the S wing. It projects beyond the S range and is also entirely georgianized. Large windows, that to the S arched. Plain panelling on the walls. The CHAPEL (now chapter room) is in the E range projecting E. The projecting part is stone, the inner walls timber-framed. To the cloister walk the chapel originally opened in a screen. Its Jacobean balusters are *in situ*. The thin roof-timbers are C17 too. In addition, on the first floor in the SE corner is the LIBRARY (now Dean's private study), made Gothic in 1830.

The Bishop's Palace SW of the cathedral includes two ancient fragments. First, the late C12 GREAT HALL consisted of a nave and two aisles with monumental timber arcading and is still *c.* 75 ft long by *c.* 55 ft wide, encased in later work. How it was roofed is uncertain. It is one of the oldest secular timber structures in England. The other fragment, against the S walk (near its E end) of the Bishop's Cloister, was part of the N wall of the BISHOP'S CHAPEL built by Losinga before 1095, earlier than similar chapels in Germany. The type was square in shape and horizontally divided into a lower and an upper church. It stood until 1737 (when Stukeley drew it; see Drinkwater in *Archaeological Journal*, 1954).

Further on these and the rest of the Bishop's Palace, see the latest edition of B of E *Herefordshire*.

## Lancaster

CATHEDRAL CHURCH OF ST PETER *Roman Catholic*

(Based on B of E *North Lancashire*, 1969, and information from Roderick O'Donnell and John Martin Robinson.)

Cathedral since 1924. A fine, aspiring building in the style of *c.* 1300 by *E. J. Paley*, 1857–9. This and the church of St George at Barrow are his *magna opera*. Here the N W tower is 240 ft high and a prominent landmark in the varied scenery of Lancaster. High nave and chancel, with transepts and polygonal apse. Baptistery on the N side, octagonal and stone-vaulted like a chapter house, by *Paley & Austin*. The main apse has *Hardman* glass of 1859, and there is more *Hardman* glass of 1859 in the Lady Chapel and the two chapels of St Thomas and SS. James and John. The somewhat later, superb w window is by *Dunstan Powell* of *Hardman & Co.* Roofs of sanctuary and Lady Chapel painted by *Thomas Earley*, 1859. A partly dismantled reredos, now under the tower arch, is by *Giles Scott*, 1909, as also the tabernacle now in the baptistery. Stalls by *Paley & Austin* carved by *Boulton* of Cheltenham in the 1920s.

For surroundings, see the latest edition of B of E *North Lancashire*.

## Leeds

CATHEDRAL CHURCH OF ST ANNE *Roman Catholic*

(Based on B of E *Yorkshire: The West Riding*, 1967, and information from Peter Howell.)

Cathedral since 1878 when on another site, where the original church of 1837–8 was a replacement for a chapel of 1793. The present building of 1902–4, near the Town Hall, is by *John Henry Eastwood* (plan and structure) with free fresh detailing in Arts and Crafts Gothic by his assistant *S. K. Greenslade*. N tower with pyramid roof. Interesting plan with extremely wide nave, aisles, chancel, and upper galleries. Pointed tunnel-vaults of timber. The reredos in the Lady Chapel is by *Pugin*, 1842, with three large and six small figures and Dec cresting. Also from the previous cathedral the pulpit by *J. F. Bentley*, 1897. Since 1960 there has been reordering by *Weightman & Bullen*, with new marble floors, altar etc. Dr Howell adds: this fine church makes one regret that Eastwood did not build more; with Bentley and others he was in 1879 a founder-member of the Guild of SS. Gregory and Luke, which aimed to reform R.C. church art.

For the surrounding neighbourhood in central Leeds, see the latest edition of B of E *Yorkshire: The West Riding*.

## Leicester

CATHEDRAL CHURCH OF ST MARTIN *Anglican*

(Based on B of E *Leicestershire and Rutland*, 1983, as revised by Elizabeth Williamson, further revised, with information from George McHardy, Anthony New, Elizabeth Williamson, G. K. Brandwood and R. Keene.)

Cathedral since 1927. Still to the eye a large prosperous Perp parish church. Although externally Victorian, its building history goes far back, even, judging by one fragment of billet moulding *in situ* at the E end of the N aisle in its s wall, to the C 12. This frieze must have been on the outside of an aisleless Norman nave. The cathedral has nave and aisles, an outer s aisle, two porches, chancel and chancel chapels, and a tall crossing tower with a very tall spire. That tower and spire, loosely modelled on Ketton (Rutland), are the work of *Raphael Brandon*, 1861–2 (tower rebuilt) and 1867 (spire). The detail is all correct E.E. Three tall twin lancets on each face. The spire has tall broaches and three tiers of lucarnes. The tower replaced a Norman one and the spire an elegant later medieval structure. The N aisle was restored by *Street* in 1880, the outer s aisle by *Pearson* in 1897–8. *Pearson* added the ornate yet dignified s porch. The timber N porch retains its Perp wooden vaulting but was much renewed in 1862 (with the plaster panels with incised flowers etc. so typical of its date). The chancel chapels were rebuilt in 1865, again by *Brandon*. The tracery mostly C 19 designs, though the Perp work in the N chapel may be original. The large Perp w window is by *Brandon*, 1848. The Perp s w window originally had a transom. Song School and vestries, 1938–9, by *William Keay*.

Inside, the N and s arcades date from the mid-C 13. Five bays, piers with four main and four thin subsidiary shafts. The main shafts carry fillets which are continued into the moulded capitals. The arches have two chamfers and between them a thin filleted roll moulding between hollows. Perp clerestory rebuilt by *Brandon*. The outer s arcade (of six bays) is a generation later. The piers are taller but similar in section. The difference in date comes out clearly in a comparison of capitals and bases. The bases have three fine, even members instead of a contrast between one bold and one fine one. The capitals also have more and finer mouldings in addition, the piers are less pronounced in the contrast of shaft and hollow and in the contrast of major and minor shafts. Sedilia with trefoiled arches and piscina. Of the date of the aisle is also the N doorway, with many fine mouldings. The S E window is larger than the others, expressing the idea of a s transept. The nave was lengthened to the w by one bay in the C 15; see the Perp s w window, the slightly different piers and the wider w bay of the nave. Later still, perhaps about 1500, the arches into the chancel chapels with their semi-octagonal concave-sided responds. Concave mouldings also in the arches. The open timber roofs are all C19 but said to be copies of the originals: Brandon had published an influential book on medieval roofs. (Possibly from the original roof, three oaken figures now near the s door.)

### FURNISHINGS

Many of the C20, especially from the reordering by *Sir Charles Nicholson* upon the elevation to cathedral status. By him, *c.* 1927: BISHOP'S THRONE with tall canopy, STALLS, W GALLERY with concave front and ORGAN CASE. – SEDILIA. Three simple Perp stalls with heads on the arms. (The Provost's and Chapter Verger's stalls incorporate C15 traceried panels found in store in 1965.) – STAINED GLASS. E window by *Christopher Whall*, 1920, in an Expressionist style with many Pre-Raphaelite memories. He also did the w window in the inner s aisle. w window in outer s aisle. – PULPIT. Late C17 on a tall stem with curving stair. – N and W DOORS, Perp. – PAINTING. Resurrection of Christ, attributed to *Francesco Vanni*. Given in 1790 (s aisle, w end).

MONUMENTS. (Passage from sacristy entrance) Slab of Tournai marble, incised with figures of two civilians, once inlaid. Like a similar slab at Waltham-on-the-Wolds, it is foreign and early C14. – (N aisle) Enormous Ancaster stone slab, the earliest use in the C15, but re-used four times later. – John Whatton † 1656, and two wives. Signed by *Joshua Marshall*. Tripartite composition with three frontal busts in oval niches. The niches of the wives under flat draped curtains. – (Chancel) George Newton † 1746, a very fine Rococo monument, unsigned. Three free-standing busts on a big pedestal with a charming relief of little charity children. – (S chapel) John Johnson † 1780, designed by his son, the architect *John Johnson* † 1814, whose added tablet is below it (cf. Chelmsford). Beautifully carved by *Bacon*, standing figure of Hope with an anchor. – (Chancel) The Rev. E. T. Vaughan † 1829. Also a standing figure, but now frigidly Grecian. – Outside, incised slate HEADSTONES (uprooted), some signed, ring the churchyard on the s, and on the N also worthwhile, especially those set up against the N chancel chapel.

Reinforcing the proud civic-centredness of this former parish church, the timber-framed Guildhall stands next door on the w. Nearby some good Georgian houses. On these surroundings, see the latest edition of B of E *Leicestershire and Rutland*.

# Lichfield

CATHEDRAL CHURCH OF THE BLESSED VIRGIN MARY AND ST CHAD *Anglican*

(Based on B of E *Staffordshire*, 1974, revised, with information from Dean Emeritus Holderness, Charles Brown, Thomas Cocke, Michael Gillingham, Andor Gomme, George McHardy, John Maddison and Anthony Quiney.)

Some references (see Recent Literature): Bony 1979; Cobb 1980; Frew 1978; Kettle and Johnson 1970; Lockett 1980; Maddison 1978.

### INTRODUCTION

Lichfield is not one of the largest English medieval cathedrals (outer length 397 ft) but it has two features that single it out. It has its three spires – only the Victorian Truro also now has those – and it has its two pools below to southward and eastward, ensuring a picturesqueness of setting which none can emulate. The spires are echoed by *Street*'s spire on St Mary's just over the water, and there are memorable distant views from rising ground around the town, and indeed from the main railway line afar off. Moreover, this cathedral has a close, more complete than most, formed at the end of the C13 by Bishop Langton, though in part he may have been rebuilding Bishop Clinton's C12 walls. The close has the handsome late C17 Bishop's Palace (now a school) by *Edward Pierce* at the NE corner, the early C18 Deanery on the N, and the mid-C18 Selwyn House on the E. At the NE corner of the bishop's former garden, remains of a polygonal tower show that Langton's palace was fortified until blown up in the Civil War. The tower's surviving vault is like late C13 work at Caernarvon (Maddison). There seems never to have been a cloister, nor any room for one. The close is on rising ground, with the cathedral lying along a rock-shelf which forces its E–W axis to bend about 10° at the crossing, and the downward N-to-S slope is evident at the transept entrances. Visually the stone of the building itself has a wonderfully mellow range of tone, from coppery reds and lichened bronzes to old ivory, enhanced within by a mellow ensemble of Victorian fittings. But the local sandstone's poor wearing quality, as at Chester, has been a headache for deans and architects. That to the observant visitor Lichfield is largely a Victorian cathedral may, according to the visitor's awareness of the alternatives, be regarded as gain or loss.

The history of the see starts with Bishop Diuma in 656, and the fifth bishop was St Chad, Bishop of Mercia 669–72. The history of the cathedral on this site starts with a building consecrated in 700. The diocese in later Anglo-Saxon times stretched from Warwickshire to the Ribble. Under the Normans, in 1075, the see was transferred to Chester. It then went to Coventry, and to Coventry and Lichfield jointly. The chapter was reconstituted by Roger de Clinton in 1130. At that time much rebuilding took place or had taken place. A large apse has been excavated reaching from the central tower to about the middle of the fifth choir bay. This may have been of Clinton's time or earlier. To it, later in the C12, a narrower rectangular chapel was added. Then, c. 1200, a new choir was begun. Its E end was at the E end of the seventh bay of the choir of today, and straight-ended with an ambulatory as at Abbey Dore, Byland, Hereford Cathedral and Romsey. While the E part of that choir was replaced later, as we shall see, its w part is, at least at aisle- and arcade-level, preserved, and it is there (see *Interior* below) that the visible history begins. Unfortunately we have few fixed dates, even for the major building campaign of Bishop Walter Langton (1296–1321), although Maddison persuasively links the work to Langton's own political and financial fortunes: treasurer to Edward I, imprisoned by Edward II, temporalities restored 1312 (there will have been a gap between 1307, when Langton contributed lavishly to St Chad's shrine in the C13 choir, and 1312, when he was solvent again). The whole sequence must have gone like this: choir and sacristy c. 1200–20; transepts c. 1230–40; chapter house c. 1240 etc.; nave c. 1265 etc. and lower w front c. 1280 etc.; upper w front, great w window, and s w tower c. 1312 etc.; Lady Chapel begun between 1315 and 1321, central tower and N W tower contemporary with it; the three spires 1320s; rebuilding E bays of choir and presbytery begun late 1320s, completed late 1330s; followed by miscellaneous Perp work. Of masons we know a *Thomas*, c. 1230–50. *William*, his son, c. 1250–65, *Thomas Wallace*, c. 1265–80, and then *William of Eyton*, c. 1320–36 and, as a consultant, the royal architect *William Ramsey* from 1337.

In the Civil War this cathedral was damaged worse than any other. It was three times bombarded and the soldiery misbehaved inside. No medieval glass survived. In 1646 the central spire collapsed, in which direction is a question: in 1660 it was recorded that all the roofs were gone, though not whether that included vaults, nor is it recorded which vaults were rebuilt in the 1660s, but *Wyatt*'s mending of the second to sixth nave vaults w of the crossing may suggest old damage there (see *Interior*). The very considerable restoration of 1662–9 under Bishop John Hacket was a remarkable and dedicated achievement, much of it financed from his own pocket (*Dictionary of National Biography*; VCH III). Charles II gave timber for new roofs and his brother James gave a new w window, entirely different from the medieval one; and *Scott*'s replacement was to differ from either. But the Perp windows of the choir clerestory, nearly all rebuilt in Hacket's time, may have then retained their original design. When Horace Walpole visited the cathedral in 1760 he wrote: 'Nothing is left in the inside of ornament', though Lonsdale, writing in the 1850s, said much survived under successive layers of limewash. *James Wyatt* was consultant architect here 1787–93, his first cathedral task; the executant architect was *Joseph Potter*, who then became the cathedral architect 1794–1842, succeeded by *Sydney Smirke* 1842–57, and he by *Gilbert Scott*, and after him his son, *J. Oldrid Scott*, until 1908. The w choir arcade having been blocked against draughts in the C17, Wyatt blocked up the four E choir arches, and later Potter erected a traceried glass screen over the organ screen, then in the E crossing arch. The central spire, once again, had to be largely rebuilt under Wyatt. Much of the cathedral as we see it today is Gilbert Scott's, mouldings, capitals and statues as well as a good deal of window tracery. The question of how far it replaced accurately what had been there in the Middle Ages – or how far it could, considering the ruination of the 1640s and the nature of the stone – is only beginning to be seriously studied, so no definite answers can be attempted here.

## EXTERIOR

There is nothing Norman remaining on Lichfield Cathedral except two faint echoes inside (choir-aisles work of c. 1200). Outside the story begins with the transepts of c. 1230–40. Henry III's grant to Dean and Chapter in 1235 and 1238 to dig stone in the Royal Forest of Cannock will refer to them. Whether N or s came first is not certain, and in all stylistic considerations at Lichfield it must be remembered that the vast majority of the details are *Scott*'s. On balance s is more likely to be a little earlier.

The NORTH TRANSEPT has shafted buttresses and a twin portal encrusted with leaf decoration. The columns are in two tiers, attached and, in front of them, detached. In the arch are three orders of small figures in almond-shaped surrounds and three of square leaf slabs. Much dogtooth is used too. Two niches l. and r. Above is a tier of tall, slender

86. LICHFIELD View from the south-east in 1820

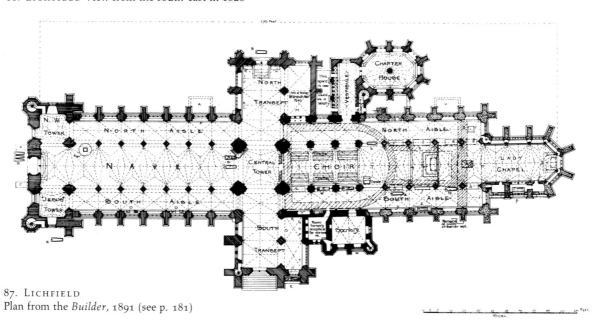

87. LICHFIELD
Plan from the *Builder*, 1891 (see p. 181)

lancets of even length, a reconstruction of 1892, it is said on safe evidence. In the gable are three openings with Y-tracery. The w wall of the transept has been altered: at low level shafts with moulded bases, and originally continuing up through the string-course to form the divisions between a row of blank windows with Y-tracery of which only the outer two remain, the rest replaced in the C19 by two four-light Perp windows (McHardy). The upper N windows are large and Perp. The E side is confused by the interference of chapter house and chapter-house vestibule. The CHAPTER HOUSE is an elongated octagon in two storeys, the upper now the library. The windows again have Y-tracery. On top of the buttresses are tabernacles with statues. The vestibule is two-storeyed too and has windows with Y-tracery to the upper storey on both N and W.

The SOUTH TRANSEPT has in its s wall another twin portal, also encrusted with leaf decoration. But there are here no figure panels in the arch. There is, or was, much dogtooth again. The capitals are of the crocket type, i.e. a type a little earlier. In the spandrels two oblong framed panels, one with a shield, the other with an inscription. The buttresses are very different from those on the N side. They are square, big, and without real set-offs, uncommonly impressive and, incidentally, by *Wyatt*. L. and r. of the portal is pointed-trefoiled and gabled wall-arcading. Above is a row of statues under trefoiled arches. In the gable are an elaborate rose-window (restored in 1758), and trefoiled niches l. and r. and a pointed quatrefoil at the top. But the centre windows are replaced by a large, nine-light, Late Perp window with a four-centred arch. To the E and a little older than the transept, a small treasury and the consistory court (former sacristy, with the later Chapel of St Chad's Head over it) project from the s choir aisle. Grouped lancet windows and angle-turrets, the w one shafted throughout its length. The w side of the s transept has good blank arcading and above two shafted lancets in each of the two bays. The top windows are Perp, as in the N transept. Just E of the steps to the s door, a tomb recess between buttresses with effigy of a deacon under a cusped arch. By the s w buttress a grotesque statue of Charles II as *restaurator* (contribution to Hacket's roofs), attributed to the young (*Sir*) *William Wilson* and made for the w gable where the great Christ figure had been (see below).

Next in the C13 followed the rebuilding of the NAVE. Here both sides are the same. Three-light shafted aisle windows with geometrical tracery (trefoils in circles), but the clerestory windows in the form of spherical triangles filled with three trefoiled circles. That is a motif from Westminster Abbey (combining aspects of gallery windows E and w of the crossing there), so c. 1265 or a bit earlier is reasonable for the beginning of Lichfield nave. The flying buttresses tell of stone vaulting. On the N side in the aisle wall is a shallow Late Perp recess with a four-centred arch and dainty foliage carving in the spandrels.

Work on the nave ended with the WEST FRONT, begun c. 1280. It is in many of its details *Scott's*, but the composition is mainly that illustrated by Britton in 1820 and indeed by Hollar before the Civil War (successive variations are shown in Cobb 1980). Scott's great w window replaced the 'debased' one of 1670 given by the future James II to replace the war-damaged medieval one known to us from Hollar's engraving. The original window, probably installed by Bishop Langton, resembled the windows of St Catherine's Chapel at Ledbury, Glos., that are also rife with ballflower as the Lichfield window and flanking towers are (Maddison). Lichfield w front is not wholly satisfactory. Hardly any English C13 front is. It is a screen in the first place, a little wider than nave and aisles, and, by the tiers of statues, stressing the screen character. (On the statuary itself, see the next paragraph.) But this front has two spires, and if spires are meant to aspire, these aspire too little, visible though they are from afar. Real two-tower façades in the Continental way (though unspired) are York and Beverley. Lichfield, like Wells, can't make up its mind; the screen is still partly in charge. The Lichfield w towers are not precisely alike (e.g. tracery of bell-openings), and the s w, probably earlier, tower is slightly higher. *Scott's* great w window picks up the ballflower motif from the bell-stage of the towers. The bell-openings are of only two lights, rather ungenerous. Also they don't appear central, because at the angles of the whole façade are big polygonal buttresses which go up higher than that. The sides of the towers incidentally continue the screen system. The tower pinnacles are square, and the parapets have saltire crosses. Four tiers of lucarnes in the spires. When the spires were set up is unknown, probably c. 1325 or so. They are noticeably lower than the central spire of about the same time. Between the towers the nave gable wall has flat pointed-trefoil decoration in odd directions (restored no doubt by *Scott*, but quite as Hollar showed before 1646). Infill decoration of the front consists of trefoils, quatrefoils and encircled cinquefoils. As for the other main element of a w front, the portals are too small to join in as separate voices. The middle one forms a little porch. The lowest tier of statues flanking the portals, like those flanking the great window and on the towers, suffer – despite their brackets and canopies – from standing against a smooth wall, as if floating on its surface. But the row of seated figures over the portals is anchored in trefoil-headed niches.

Now for the STATUARY itself. On the N W tower high up are five original statues. As for the row of figures under the great window, over the portals, the seated kings, some cross-legged, visible in a pre-Scott photograph and vaguely indicated in Hollar's view, might reflect C14 originals (cf. Exeter and Lincoln w fronts). But now, with the exception

of the above-mentioned five, the w front statues are all of 1876–84. (Some statues cemented in the 1820s, it is said over eroded medieval cores, are stored in one of the towers.) The Victorian figure of Christ now at the top of the w gable, by a *Miss Grant* (Cobb 1980), succeeded the image of Charles II there. But the original figure there is thought to have been the majestic late c 13 (or early c 14?) Seated Christ now at Swynnerton (B of E *Staffordshire*; Cobb 1980), where it probably arrived *via* the bishop's palace at Eccleshall after rescue from bombardment in the 1640s. It is *c*. 7 ft high, meant to be seen from below, and of sandstone lighter in tone, perhaps purposely, than its presumed setting.

The CROSSING TOWER has shafted polygonal buttresses, and the bell-stage pairs of two-light openings and narrower blank such openings l., r. and centre. The spire (rebuilt more than once as already explained) has five tiers of lucarnes and ballflowers up the angles. The tower is probably Langton's, from the same years as the Lady Chapel (Maddison), though the crossing below will have been rebuilt in the c 13 when the transepts and the nave were.

By 1325 progress had also been made on the rebuilding and lengthening of the EAST END. The LADY CHAPEL came first, begun probably between *c*. 1315 and 1321 (Maddison). The only definite date is that Bishop Langton († 1321) left money for its completion. It is as high as the chancel (which differentiates it from its contemporary at Wells) and it has a polygonal end, a form frequent on the Continent though rare in England. (But the then-existing Lady Chapel at Westminster Abbey had one; perhaps the c 13 Lady Chapel at Gloucester did too?) The apse windows are very tall, of three lights, and the tracery is unencircled trefoils, a motif that had become popular in England in the late c 13, though the interior will prove that too early a date here. The s windows of the chapel, and tomb recesses below, were much rebuilt by one of the *Scotts* (before-and-after photographs in Cobb 1980). Inside and part of the original structure on that side, three shallow chapels.

When *William Ramsey* was brought in to oversee the new PRESBYTERY and E extension of the CHOIR, he was bound both by the new Lady Chapel E of it and the surviving bays of the early c 13 choir w of it. (For his two-storey elevation, see *Interior*.) The aisles of the new extension seem to have continued the building campaign of the Lady Chapel, with windows partly Dec, partly arches upon arches, thought to be faithful copies of the originals (Maddison). The choir clerestory windows are more complicated. One at the SE is thought to be genuine Ramsey, with stonework probably renewed. Opposite at the NE, Perp with a five-pointed star, may or may not be original. And the rest, rebuilt though not necessarily redesigned for Hacket, are Perp, possibly of later c 14 type. Against one s

buttress stands the cathedral's best original statue *in situ* – a female figure, damaged. Flying buttresses, arched parapet, pierced battlements.

## INTERIOR

The rebuilding of the Norman cathedral seems to have started *c*. 1195. First came a new eastern arm, and what survives are the aisles and arcades of the three w bays of the choir of *c*. 1200. (Stepped lancet groups opening into the transept aisles from the westernmost choir-aisle bays were originally windows, so the Norman transepts had no E aisles.) This CHOIR WEST PART is unmistakably dated by the use of lush stiff-leaf still with a few Norman features, zigzag in the arch from the N aisle into the N transept, and

89. LICHFIELD The west porch (detail) in 1820

one trumpet-scallop capital in the wall-arcading of the same aisle. The rest at aisle-level indeed looks after rather than before 1200. The wall-arcading is pointed and cusped. The piers are shafted as richly as at Wells – groups of triplets with fillets. The arches are of many fine mouldings. The aisles have plain quadripartite rib-vaulting. In the N aisle the easternmost wall-shaft of this part of the choir and its opposite number towards the choir 'nave' are unrestored. But two building campaigns are represented in these bays of the choir: all above aisles and arcades is C 14, in tune with the bays to eastward. So further description of the choir has to be deferred (see below). First, however, the C 13 work S and N of this part of the choir.

Off the S choir aisle, first a small tunnel-vaulted chamber, probably a treasury, and then through a round-headed doorway the former sacristy, now CONSISTORY COURT (with the CHAPEL OF THE HEAD OF ST CHAD above it, reached by a staircase next to the doorway). Inside the consistory court, two orders of colonnettes and two bays of heavily single-chamfered rib-vaults. The vault of the chapel upstairs is not medieval, but the windows with their detached shafts are. From the chapel a handsome C 14 gallery on ribbed coving opens to the aisle, no doubt for showing the relic. This coving, in fact two bays of vaulting carried on delicately carved palms resting on cushion springers, is jettied out over the aisle. But the opening to the gallery was originally a window. So we have another aisle window of c. 1200–20. If the sacristy was indeed contemporaneous with the C 13 choir, then the chapel above must have been an afterthought. Maddison points out that the little gallery's carved fleuron frieze is quite different from Ramsey's fleuron friezes up in the clerestory (C 14 choir; see below), but identical in design to the cornice of the late C 14 pulpit at Nantwich, and probably relates to a record that Bishop Stretton (1360–86) paid for a new shrine for St Chad, i.e. probably for his separate head, the rest of him having been already richly enshrined before the entrance to Langton's Lady Chapel.

In the N choir aisle the entry to the CHAPTER-HOUSE VESTIBULE cuts into the wall-arcading. Above the entry a shafted lancet window. The vestibule has thick blank pointed-trefoiled wall-arcading, blank on the E side but on the W side detached to such a degree that a row of seats results. These were for the ceremonial washing of poor men's feet. The capitals of the colonnettes are original. Lancet windows in groups; stone vault in three bays with bosses. Above is another vaulted three-bay room. The CHAPTER HOUSE itself is approached by another double portal like those of the transepts, but less ornate. Stiff-leaf capitals, dogtooth. In the tympanum Seated Christ in a pointed quatrefoil recess. Thick pointed trefoiled wall-arcading with dogtooth and little heads. The dean's seat in the middle of the E wall is singled out by the doubling of the

colonnettes. Middle pier with ten shafts, with shaft-rings. Excellent capitals with lively leaf-carving, anticipating Southwell. The crowd of shafts was to be the motif of the Wells chapter house on a larger scale. Windows with deep reveals, shafted. Vault with bosses. Short vaulting-shafts on figure corbels, apparently unrestored.

The TRANSEPTS have an E aisle of two bays (which, as we have seen, the Norman transepts did not). The piers are developed from those of the choir, but differ a little and also have triple vaulting-shafts from the ground. The capitals are stiff-leaf. In the S transept the group of vaulting-shafts is accompanied by shafts with capitals at a lower level, continued in twins with shaft-rings. Moreover the main vaulting-shafts have above the abacus a Perp castellated second abacus. So there is some confusion here. The W and S side of the S transept has wall-arcading, the shafts with plain moulded capitals. The upper parts belong to the Perp

90. LICHFIELD Chapter house, c. 1240

91. LICHFIELD Chapter-house sculpture, mid-C13, in 1819

work of the choir and will be mentioned there. In the N transept on the E side the start from the S is two good capitals with small heads. (The E aisle, or St Stephen's Chapel, is now entered from the N choir aisle.) After that all is moulded capitals now, i.e. perhaps a reduction after the lavishness of choir and S transept. In the aisle and along the N wall, trefoiled wall-arcading. One boss has four radial heads. The N lancets are shafted. On the W side is pointed-trefoiled wall-arcading. The arch to the aisle also has moulded capitals as against the stiff-leaf of the corresponding S transept arch.

The CROSSING PIERS each have to the centre, i.e. set diagonally, four shafts with three rings, apart from the couples in the N, E and S, and the triples in the W. Many-moulded arches, and a C14 or C15 tierceron-star vault.

As externally, so internally, the NAVE is all one build. Even though drastically restored, it is one of the more important C13 structures in England, relating in its main features chiefly to Westminster Abbey and to the Lincoln Angel Choir. Westminster's eastern arm, with spherical-triangle gallery windows outside and paired gallery open-

ings inside, was up by the mid-1250s, and the first bays W of the crossing with slightly different gallery windows, by the early 1260s. The Lincoln Angel Choir version of the gallery openings, to which Lichfield nave is even closer, was rising between 1256 and 1280, about ten years ahead of the Lichfield work if that started c. 1265. Hereford N transept's version of Westminster was slightly earlier than Lichfield nave, but the only feature they shared was the spherical-triangle window, differently treated; to call Lichfield nave a sophisticated version of Hereford transept is to miss other differences.

The nave piers are still essentially of the W choir and transept type. The S arcade seems the earlier, six piers with stiff-leaf capitals, two more naturalistic, while the N arcade capitals have naturalistic leaf-carving throughout, e.g. oak-leaves on the third pier from the W (Gomme). Yet how much C19 renewal was there? In the spandrels thin encircled cinquefoils cut in two by the vaulting-shafts, a remarkably unclassic device at so classic a moment: Lincoln has paired trefoils here. Gallery of two two-light openings per bay, without windows in the outer wall. Bar tracery

92 and 93 (overleaf). LICHFIELD The nave, c. 1265, looking east and (right) elevation

and much dogtooth. And then the spherical triangles of the clerestory. Vault with ridge ribs and tiercerons. The easternmost and the two westernmost bays are still stone-vaulted, but the remaining five bays were re-done by *Wyatt* in cement and remain so: *Scott* refused to replace these with stone because of dangers in reintroducing the weight (Frew 1978). The aisles have pointed cusped wall-arcading with unrestored or little-restored capitals and shafted windows. Aisle vaults only scraped of plaster and pointed by *Scott* (J. B. Stone, 1870, *via* Dean Holderness), with longitudinal ridge ribs and no tiercerons. The w (tower) bay keeps the same system.

Then to the EAST END. The LADY CHAPEL has wall-arcading with nodding ogee arches and much crocketing. Now the nodding ogee arch is early when it is before 1315, and so in spite of windows of *c*. 1300 in style, the chapel cannot have been begun before 1310; Maddison suggests

94. LICHFIELD Presbytery, late 1320s to late 1330s

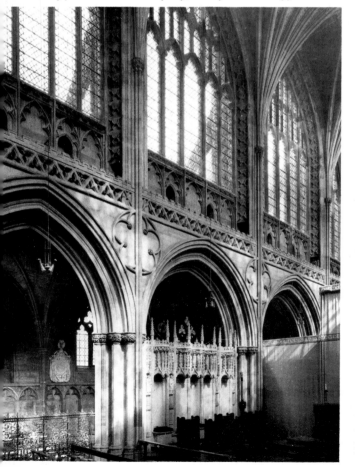

1315. So 1315–30 is perhaps the best date. Shafts for statues (designed by *Kempe*, carved by *Farmer & Brindley*, 1895) standing in the same position as e.g. in the Sainte Chapelle in Paris (which is also apsidal). The sill frieze to the windows with cusped zigzag, a West Country motif. Stone vault with ridge ribs and tiercerons, still in character with the main nave vaulting. On the s side three tiny chapels are included, the first two with two bays of vaulting and a longitudinal ridge rib. The third is more fanciful – the same scheme, but for one oblong bay only, is by four short additional ribs made to appear like four minute quadripartite rib-vaults. Crypts, i.e. boneholes, below may have been connected with the (much restored) tomb recesses outside.

The CHOIR, in conclusion, is the most complicated part of the cathedral. Its E part, the PRESBYTERY, was rebuilt to link the early C13 choir (above) to the new Lady Chapel, also to make room for St Chad's shrine behind the high altar, before the Lady Chapel entrance. The new bays continue topographically from the western work but stylistically from the eastern work. The E aisle walls are part of the Lady Chapel building campaign, as Harvey was first to notice, and so are the E responds of the arcade. All this could not be done without some interference with the three bays of the early C13. The junction is easy enough to see. There is no disguising the change from early C13 to early C14 foliage, especially on the (later?) N side, where the capitals become bands of knobbly leaf. The piers, even here, try to keep in a certain harmony with the old ones. However, there are of course vaulting-shafts now. For the old work they were added from the floor up, but now they stand on angel brackets and carry a statue each. The statues are by *Farmer & Brindley*, 1860: *Scott* is supposed to have had evidence for the brackets and the statues. In the new parts the motif of halved cinquefoils is taken over from the nave: some conscious historicism by *William Ramsey*, acting as consultant from 1337.

More important, either Ramsey or Langton's mason before him decided on a two-storey elevation for the choir. (Whether the C13 choir had a triforium, or like Pershore did not, is a question.) An open panelled passage was taken along below the new clerestory, using the same zigzag parapet as the Lady Chapel and also deriving the vault from there, in keeping with the nave vault too. Thus, between three-storey nave and one-storey E end was inserted a two-storey vessel, in a progression of elevations, yet with unvarying vaulting. So, within a century, Lichfield became a more unified assembly of parts than most. New and successful and typical of Ramsey are the blank quatrefoils framing the reveals of the upper windows. In the aisles the wall-arcading (pointed, cusped) now has heads and foliage in the spandrels, and most of that seems unrestored. One bay in the s aisle has a recess with two broad bands of

95. LICHFIELD Lady Chapel, *c.* 1315–21, as drawn in 1820

knobbly leaf again all the way round. The aisle vaults have longitudinal ridge ribs.

It now only remains to add that the system of the upper windows is continued into the transept E walls, but without the quatrefoil framing. The transept vaults are a later renewal, whether c. 1300 N and after 1350 s or both late C 15 does not seem certain (N transept vaults restored by *Potter*, 1795–7).

FURNISHINGS, E TO W

*Lady Chapel* The ALTARPIECE was carved at Oberammergau in 1895. – STAINED GLASS. Seven windows have glass brought in 1802 from the dissolved abbey of Herckenrode, near Hasselt, and made available to the cathedral by Sir Brooke Boothby. Restored and refitted here 1806–8 by *John Betton* of Shrewsbury (Harrison 1980), it dates from c. 1540, in style reminiscent of *Lambert Lombard*'s. Some of the glass went to St Mary's Shrewsbury, some is in other windows in Lichfield Cathedral (see below). – In the w bays, glass also said to be Flemish mid-c 16, acquired in the c 18 by a Marquess of Ely, and for the cathedral in 1895; also some *Kempe* glass. – MONUMENT in s chapel. Bishop Selwyn † 1878, by *Nicholls* (by whom also the bishop's brother's effigy at Ely). Recumbent effigy, surrounded by lavish wall decoration by *Clayton & Bell* and fine set of TILES by *William De Morgan*, inspired by Selwyn's New Zealand bishopric.

*North choir aisle* STAINED GLASS. Some from Herckenrode, some by *Kempe*. – MONUMENTS. Bishop Ryder † 1836. By *Chantrey*, 1841. A white kneeling figure without any setting. Chantrey liked that kind of isolation, which was a Victorian trait. – Bishop Woods † 1953. Lively bronze demi-figure, praying. By *Epstein*. – Bishop Lonsdale † 1867. Recumbent alabaster effigy by *G. F. Watts*, the Gothic setting by *Scott* and the present arrangement by *C. A. Nicholson*, 1914 (Dean Holderness).

*Chapter house* PAINTING, w wall. Remains of a c 15 Assumption with many figures.

*Choir* Low REREDOS and SCREEN of statues. The centre by *Gilbert Scott* with figures by *John Birnie Philip*, 1864; the side statues added by *Oldrid Scott*, twelve martyrs by *Kempe*, executed by *Farmer & Brindley*. – SEDILIA. The intricate canopies are largely original Perp work, supposed to have been part of the medieval stone altar screen covered up in the c 17 and later used by Wyatt for his Lady Chapel reredos that Oldrid Scott replaced. – GRILLES by *Atterton* of Lichfield. – STALLS and BISHOP'S THRONE. By *Scott*, carved by *Evans* of Ellaston, a cousin of George Eliot (Gordon Haight confirms that 'cousin' is likelier than 'uncle'). – PAVEMENT. Very fine, designed by *Scott*. Stone, inlaid, medallions with scenes from the history of the diocese, with kings and bishops.

*South choir aisle* PAINTING. In the E wall in a small niche a c 14 wall painting of the Crucifixion. – In the s wall under the third window from the E, a wall painting, c. 1400, of the Trinity flanked by censing angels. – STAINED GLASS. Some of the Herckenrode glass is here. – Also windows by *Kempe*, 1901, one to Bishop Hacket, restorer of 'this House of God overthrown by violent and wicked hands'. (Recent removal of Hacket's tomb (see below) from under this window revealed the above-mentioned painting of the Trinity.) – Also by *Kempe* the window above the entrance to the Chapel of the Head of St Chad and all the glass in the chapel (and its reredos). – The FURNITURE OF THE CONSISTORY COURT came from Bishop Hacket's choir. Triple SEAT, c. 1670, with twisted columns and Baroque back panels and front openwork panels, the canopies with deliberate Gothic overtones. – MONUMENTS, returning to the E. The Robinson children, 1817, by *Chantrey*. *Stothard* probably had a hand in it (Whinney). The white marble children are asleep. The sentiment already begins to turn Victorian, though the conceit of the sleeping child was taken over by Chantrey from Banks's Penelope Boothby (Brooke Boothby's daughter) at Ashbourne, of 1791. The Robinson monument is still the most popular in the cathedral. – Effigy of the type incarcerated in the wall, here with only the feet visible (see also two in the s nave aisle). – Dean Howard † 1868. White recumbent effigy by *H. H. Armstead*, dated 1872, the Gothic setting by *Scott*. – John Hutchinson † 1705. Tablet by *Edward Stanton*. – Col. Bagot † 1645 at Naseby. Purely classical tablet. – Purbeck effigy of a bishop (under the Trinity mural), called Langton's, but he died 1321 and this effigy is of the c 13; see folds of draperies and stiff-leaf decoration. – Archdeacon Moore † 1876. The white recumbent effigy, dead, not asleep, by *H. H. Armstead*. The design is by *Scott*. Dated 1879. – Purbeck effigy of a bishop, c. 1240–50 (presumably Patteshull † 1245), with a beautifully ascetic face. Shafts and a gabled pointed-trefoiled top. – Bishop Hacket † 1670. Recumbent effigy, coloured, on a high sarcophagus. – John Stanley of Pipe † 1515. Effigy on a tomb-chest. Defaced, alas. – Major Hodson † 1858 at the storming of Lucknow. Designed by *Street* and carved by *Earp*. Totally unlike the Street one knows. Showy, restless, with chunky forms heralding c 20 Brutalism. Busy scenes and allegorical figures. – Archdeacon Hodson † 1855, the monument of 1860–2 also designed by *Street*. Also with scenes of many figures. – Medallion of Erasmus Darwin, mid-c 19.

*North transept* STAINED GLASS. E aisle N by *Kempe*. – N lancets by *Clayton & Bell*, 1893. – MONUMENTS. Canon Lonsdale † 1907. Recumbent effigy of marble by *Farmer & Brindley*. – John Hodgson Iles † 1888. Signed *W. W. Ingram*, 1890. Recumbent effigy of stone. – Stephen Simpson † 1784. Large tablet of exquisite quality.

Oval medallion with bust in relief, signed by *T. Fisher* of York. – William Vyse † 1770. Another large tablet. – And to a later William Vyse † 1816, by *Samuel Hayward*. – In the N W corner, Dean Heywood † 1492. Only the cadaver remains of a large monument with the effigy on an upper tier and an elaborate canopy. – General Vyse † 1825, and Mary Madan † 1827. Companion pieces in white marble with profile medallions. – Sir Charles Oakley † 1826. By *Chantrey*. Also white, also with a profile medallion, so did he do the other two as well? – The E aisle of the N transept, now reached from the N choir aisle, contains an alabaster reredos by *Pearson* (Quiney).

*Crossing*  SCREEN, 1859–63. Designed by *Scott* and made by *Francis Skidmore* of Coventry, the figure work by *Birnie Philip*. Iron, brass and copper, light and transparent, of the highest craftsmanship and an ornament to any cathedral. Let Salisbury and Hereford be vandals and remove their Scott–Skidmore screens; Lichfield has held out till High Victorianism is at last appreciated in its best work. Part of a fine ensemble with the metalwork of the nave fittings.

*South transept*  In the E aisle the S window with Herckenrode glass. Other S wall glass, 1895, by *Kempe*. – Screen to St Michael's Chapel (Staffordshire regiments). Design based upon assegais and Zulu shields, commemorating the fallen in the campaigns of 1873–9. – MONUMENTS. 80th Regiment of Foot. 1846, by *Hollins*. In the Egyptian style, free-standing high black base and a white sphinx on top. Large white trophy below. – Andrew Newton. By *Westmacott*, 1808. Standing monument with a group of two children l., a standing woman r., and a second leaning over the central pedestal. – Sir William Parker † 1866, with good portrait medallion. – Bust of Dr Johnson. By *Westmacott*, 1793. – Bust of Garrick. By *Westmacott*, 1793, designed by *James Wyatt* (Colvin). – John Rawlins † 1685, good cartouche. – And nearby, to a later John Rawlins † 1741, still a cartouche. – On the S wall, three large tablets without figures: Lucy Grove † 1787, Jane Gastrell † 1798, Dean Proby † 1807.

*Nave*  PULPIT. Iron, all elaborate openwork. Two staircases. By *Scott* and *Skidmore*. – LECTERN. A brass eagle. By *Hardman* of Birmingham. – FONT. Designed by *Slater* and executed by *Forsyth*, c. 1862. – STAINED GLASS. The w window is by *Clayton & Bell*, 1869. – Brass to first Earl of Lichfield † 1854, of excellent quality. – WEST DOORS. Original iron scrolls, C 13 on original boards, restored internally (Brown). Thought to be by *Thomas of Leighton*, 1293, which would help date completion of the lower w front.

*North nave aisle*  STAINED GLASS. w by *Kempe*. – The westernmost N window by *Burlison & Grylls*, the next to the E by *Kempe*. – Then sixth from E again by *Burlison & Grylls*. – MONUMENTS (tower bay). Seward family

† 1764, 1780, 1790. By Bacon. Seated mourning woman under a weeping willow. The poem is by Anna Seward and includes herself. – Lady Mary Wortley Montagu († 1762), 1789 to commemorate her introduction of inoculation for smallpox. By *Thomas* (the lesser, later) *Scheemakers*. Run-of-the-mill figure by an urn. – Walmsley family † 1751, 1785, 1786, by *William Thompson* of Birmingham. Fine tablet in several marbles. Three putto heads at the foot.

*South nave aisle*  STAINED GLASS. The easternmost window by *Hardman*, 1870. Next *Clayton & Bell*, 1856, then *Ward & Hughes*, 1876, then *Clayton & Bell*, 1873, and under the tower *Burlison & Grylls*. (All these are dates of deaths commemorated, though the glass may all date from the period of *Scott*'s restoration.) – MONUMENTS. Two defaced effigies boxed in the wall, with busts and feet appearing (see also one in the S choir aisle). – Brass, 1850s, to Lt-Col. P. J. Petit by 'Waller, London'.

For the buildings of the close and surroundings, see the latest edition of B of E *Staffordshire*.

# Lincoln

CATHEDRAL CHURCH
OF THE BLESSED VIRGIN MARY  *Anglican*

(Based on B of E *Lincolnshire*, 1964, considerably revised, with information from the late Canon Binnall and John Cherry, Thomas Cocke, Peter Draper, Michael Gillingham, Anthony New, David O'Connor, David Palliser and Malcolm Seaborne.)

Plan, Fig. 98, from the *Builder*, 1891, drawn 1881 by A. Beresford Pite (on his rendering of the nave S W chapel vault, see the text).

Some references (see Recent Literature): Binnall 1966; Bony 1979; Clifton-Taylor 1972; Cocke 1975; Colvin 1978; Harvey 1974, 1978; Pevsner 1963, 1972; Quiney 1979; Remnant 1969; Singleton 1978; and forthcoming B.A.A. conference papers.

INTRODUCTION

Apart from Durham, no English cathedral is as spectacularly placed as Lincoln, on its 'vast hill . . . very perspicious and eminently in view a great many miles off' (Celia Fiennes). The street by which one most laboriously approaches it – on foot, as one should – is justly called Steep Hill. A less rigorous approach is by Greestone Steps. The hill rises so steeply only from the S. Once up there, one is on a plateau. The S view of the cathedral from a distance,

e.g. from the railway, is of singular evenness, the chancel about as long as the nave, two long horizontals, that of the nave ridge very slightly higher, and two verticals, the uncommonly slender crossing tower and the two also uncommonly slender W towers, appearing as one from this vantagepoint. The only lines not vertical or horizontal (besides the transept gables) are the diagonals of the pinnacles and of the spires of turrets on the W front. In the Middle Ages there were also, however, spires on all three towers. The silhouette is as unforgettable when it is a light grey in the early morning, or animated by the full midday sun, or changing in colour and seemingly in form when stormy clouds pass over.

Once up the hill, we find that the cathedral is not enclosed from the world; it has no close. Motor traffic, including heavy through traffic, passes all day and all night on all sides, the nearest on the S, the most obnoxious on the E. While there is no continuous space all round, there is lawn to the E and N W, a fenced-in piece to the N, and a piece with trees to the S E. But they are not read together. A hundred years ago a sense of precinct did exist. It is one of the most urgent planning problems of Lincoln (as Sir Nikolaus wrote in 1964) to restore dignity to the immediate surroundings of the monument that to most people means Lincoln. Worcester and St Paul's are similarly besieged, but on one side mainly.

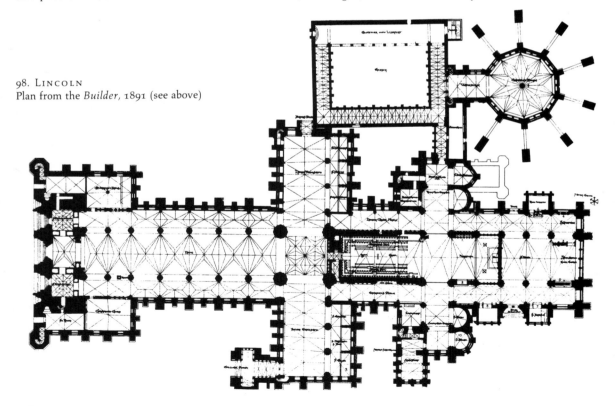

98. LINCOLN
Plan from the *Builder*, 1891 (see above)

99. LINCOLN View from the north-west

In the C 1 the Romans built a fortress and then a town on top of this hill. Tessellated pavements have been found in the cathedral precinct. In the early C 7, in the former forum in the heart of this upper town, St Paulinus, companion of St Augustine, founded the first Christian church in the kingdom of Lindsey: what appear to be its remains have been recently discovered in Bailgate, N W of the cathedral. After the Viking invasions Lincoln was a Danish *burh*. By the C 11, the vast diocese containing it stretched from Oxfordshire to the Humber, with the bishop's see at Dorchester as far from the Danes as possible. In 1068 William the Conqueror built the castle at Lincoln, W of the cathedral site. Then came the decision of 1072 that bishops should move their sees to fortified towns, and Bishop Remigius moved from Dorchester to Lincoln. By then the town within the old Roman wall contained many churches, but it is not clear whether a church already occupied Remigius's new site before he began to build.

The medieval cathedral is essentially of three periods, the first two divided into two phases: Norman, Early and High, the W front; E.E. the rest in one campaign from 1192 to *c.* 1250 and another from 1256 to *c.* 1280; C 14 to C 15 the towers and some additions. The C 17 brought the library and the cloister walk below it, directed by Wren. There was work in the early C 18 by *James Gibbs*, in the

later C 18 by *James Essex*, and in the mid-C 19 by *J. C. Buckler*. Scott was not here, except for a pulpit. But *Pearson,* as architect to the Dean and Chapter, carried out restoration during 1870–93 which included securing the W towers, restoring the N transept and chapter house, and investigating remains of St Hugh's apse (Quiney 1979). Fortunately proposals to remove Wren's library northward and re-medievalize the N cloister walk were still-born. The cathedral is 482 ft long inside. The crossing tower has a height of 271 ft. The chancel vault is 74 ft high, the nave vault 82 ft. The stone used is the brownish local oolitic limestone. On English marbles used internally, see E *transepts* below.

More in summary should be said. Wells and Lincoln are, Europeanly speaking, the earliest cases of a *national* Gothic. Any form of Gothic depended on knowledge of what France had done in the second half of the C 12. But in Spain, in Italy, in Germany the mid-C 13 had to come before Gothic was assimilated and a national idiom found. In England the moment for that came *c.* 1180 at Wells, *c.* 1190 at Lincoln, the French idiom having arrived at Canterbury *c.* 1175. Wells evolved by way of West Country influences. Lincoln's innovations took off from the work at Canterbury. *Geoffrey de Noiers*'s work that survives in Lincoln's E transepts and St Hugh's Choir is distinguished for its exquisite quality, its superb nobility and yet happy airiness and liveliness, and for the innovations it offered to England and ultimately to Europe. For a concentrated Victorian version of Lincoln, see Truro.

THE NORMAN CATHEDRAL

A council held at Windsor in 1072 decided that bishops' sees should be in walled towns rather than villages. So Remigius, first almoner of Fécamp and then bishop of Dorchester, moved to Lincoln. There, some time between 1072 and 1075, he began to build. His cathedral was consecrated in 1092. It was a cruciform building with an E end of a main apse and apses to the chancel aisles, flat-ended outside, i.e. the same arrangement as at Old Sarum in the same years and at Durham a little later. Its w front remains, though somewhat disguised. Its forms, however, can easily be disentangled from later ones, as they have the sturdy directness and the elementary details typical of the first decades of the Norman style in England.

The centre is a very tall and deep recess, though originally less tall than it is now. Its round arch must be reconstructed in one's mind's eye, where the plain Norman masonry is replaced by the decorated E.E. masonry. The recess steps inward in slight steps, and they are marked by shafts. To the l. and r. of this tall recess are two recesses of the same kind, but less tall. These are fully preserved. The elevation is the same as in the nave, but still in perfect order. The capitals of the shafts are of the most primitive volute type. The middle recess represents the nave, the side recesses the aisles. To the l. and r. of the side recesses are yet much lower niches, again of the same type. They are repeated round what were the corners at the time, and inside the present building niches of identical form and detail indeed exist and can be seen. The elevation with these five stepped, arched recesses is unique – exactly as if it were one of the most typical Early Norman plans stood on end, that of the staggered apses (main apse, two apses of the chancel aisles, two chapel apses reaching out from the transepts – the plan e.g. of Bernay and St-Nicholas at Caen, both in Normandy, and Blyth in Nottinghamshire). Tewkesbury has a tall single recess, a motif ultimately derived from Charlemagne's palace chapel at Aachen, but three, let alone five, are a very different matter. (Three, possibly five, such recesses on the w front of Bury St Edmunds abbey church – near, but not the same as, the former parish church in this book – were perhaps half a century later than Lincoln's, and Peterborough's three perhaps a century after Bury's.) What the original portals were like, there is no knowing. Another peculiar feature is the fact that w towers must have been planned from the start and that they are not flush with the front but lie back a little, also from the walls with the N and S niches. It is an odd arrangement to which the only parallels again are in the Empire rather than in Normandy: in buildings such as the collegiate church of St Patroclus at Soest. Inside the building, apart from the two extra niches only one Early Norman feature is visible: windows with roll mouldings looking from the towers into the space between the towers.

Under Bishop Alexander, nephew of Bishop Roger of Sarum who had much enlarged the late C 11 cathedral there, the w front was continued and altered. He ruled the diocese from 1123 to 1148 and was an ambitious and powerful man. Among his buildings the castles of Newark, Banbury and Sleaford ranked high. He began at the cathedral after a fire of perhaps 1141 and, we are told, vaulted the building – still a rare thing in England in the mid-c 12. We can see that he replaced the three portals by new, more sumptuous ones. The middle portal is surrounded by an outer frame of large crenellation, up the jambs and round the arch. There follow four shafts on the jambs on each side. They are much renewed, with shafts and jambs rearranged and recut in the c 18, probably under *Essex*, and in the c 19 under *Buckler* (Cocke), but it is comparatively easy to recognize what is old and what is not. The outer pairs of shafts have geometrical decoration, the inner pairs figured decoration. On the third on the r. are medallions with beasts, affronted beasts, birds, grotesques. On the l., on the other hand, the theme is different: continuous trails instead of medallions and in them, from bottom to top, a naked couple, snakes biting their vitals, then a beautifully composed, dramatic fight between two eagles, then a naked couple like the previous one, and two dressed men. The fourth (inner) pair of shafts has single figures climbing about in trails. One e.g. shoots an arm up against the next. The top figure on both sides is in expressive profile and holds two snakes. The meaning of the figures is not clear, though the naked *versus* the clothed, the biting *versus* the contained snakes indicate a programme. The innermost moulding in jambs and arch has the beakhead motif, i.e. animals biting into a roll moulding. The outer hoodmould ends in large dragons' heads. The side portals have no figures. Their three shafts on each side and their arches are decorated with lozenges, spiral-headed bands, etc., and also again beakhead. The l. and r. sides are not identical. Among the geometrical ornament used is the ubiquitous zigzag, also occurring at r. angles to the wall surface. These latter are all Norman motifs, but when it comes to the shafts of the central doorway, the stylistic sources are quite different. Professor Zarnecki has convincingly pointed to St-Denis, and his recent discovery that originally one large figure stood against the flat bare strip outside the outer shafts confirms this. They must have been 'figures-colonnes', to use Focillon's term, i.e. of the new, Gothic type apparently created at St-Denis and then taken over e.g. at Chartres. But the portal at St-Denis was only completed in 1140, and so Bishop Alexander was quick in adopting it and his master mason in adapting it to Anglo-Norman conventions. However, the stylistic position of the sculpture at Lincoln is much more complex and the matter of the column-figures is still conjectural. Dr Cocke says that Lumby, Essex's clerk of works, accused Essex of inserting them without evidence (plates and comments contributed anonymously to *Vetusta Monumenta*, 1781).

Above the low niches and running into the reveals of the side portal recesses is a frieze of sculptured scenes. They are from the Old Testament s of the main doorway, from the New Testament N. The choice is not inconsistent, more consistent in fact than any sequence of scenes in English Norman sculpture up to their date, at least as far as preserved material goes. The scenes on the s side consist of the following: the Expulsion from Paradise, Cain and Abel digging (with a border of foliage above), the Birth of Enoch (again with a foliage border above) and, below it, Lamech killing Cain, then two gaps, then scenes from the Deluge, God speaking to Noah, Noah building the Ark (with hammer and axe), then – evidently not *in situ* – Daniel in the Lions' Den, a scene in a box-frame, i.e. different from all others, and then back to the Deluge, Noah in the Ark, Noah leaving the Ark, and the Covenant, a long piece, and finally, round the corner, i.e. now inside the cathedral, the Deluge itself, badly preserved (and again with a leaf border above). (Professor Zarnecki convincingly suggests that the Deluge was meant for the gap where now Daniel is, and was found to be too wide and hence shifted. See also Norman fragments kept indoors: *Furnishings*, N E transept). On the N side starting from the middle: first a gap, then Dives and Lazarus, the Death of Lazarus, then a group of six of the Blessed in Heaven, then the Harrowing of Hell and, badly restored, the Torments of the Damned.

The motifs and the style of Bishop Alexander's sculptural and decorative work are remarkably mixed. The sculptured scenes arranged in a frieze along a façade are unmistakably North Italian. Modena is the most likely source. Here the sculpture of the w façade dates from some time after 1099, when the façade (the cathedral?) was begun. The short stocky figures also go with Modena. But other figures at Lincoln are quite different, especially the seated apostles. They are long, excessively slim, and wear mantles creased with close, parallel, agitated folds. That seems Burgundian more than anything, of about 1130 (Autun), and had an effect somewhat later at Malmesbury in Wiltshire. Beakhead is an initially West French motif, but by 1145 it had been fully acclimatized in England and in certain parts of the country indeed became very popular. The geometrical ornament used is Anglo-Norman in general, but for the shafts and climbing figures Professor Zarnecki has shown as the closest parallel the w portal of St-Denis, and that was only complete in 1140. Moreover,

we are told that Abbot Suger of St-Denis obtained workmen from many places, and so it is even possible that knowledge of Modena by the one, of Burgundy by the other principal carver had been transmitted through St-Denis. Anyway, what is certain is that Bishop Alexander was wholly up-to-date.

Norman also are the frieze of intersected arches above the aisle recesses, the gables exposed to the N and s with more ornate blank arcading and an attractive motif of chains of alternatingly large and small links in the top parts. The towers also were completed, again with blank arcading and again quite ornately. Polygonal angle buttresses with angle-shafts. (The two statues of bishops on the buttresses to l. and r. of the main portal seem to be early C 13 additions, although according to Dr Cocke their heads and feet are *c.* 1740 and the two statues, not originally of the same size or, necessarily, date, are not *in situ*.) Inside the cathedral, apart from the aforementioned niches that were really an external feature, the following can still be examined. Of the sides of the towers facing inward, wide blocked arches, still recognizable with their imposts, must have marked galleries, and above them, no doubt at clerestory height, is a single window on either side, with a continuous roll moulding and shafts with scallop capitals. Also inside the towers are curious small chambers, lit and unlit, especially one on the ground floor, very tall, very narrow, and tunnel-vaulted. (See also w *front*, C 13 remodelling and C 18 alterations inside, below.)

## ST HUGH'S CATHEDRAL AND ITS COMPLETION

St Hugh was born at Avalon, not the one in Burgundy but near Grenoble. He became treasurer of the Grande Chartreuse, then *c.* 1180 prior to the Carthusian house of Witham in Somerset, and in 1186 bishop of Lincoln. In 1185 a catastrophe befell the Norman cathedral. 'Scissa est', says Roger of Hovenden, 'from top to bottom.' In 1192 St Hugh began the rebuilding. The 'constructor' he commissioned is known to us by name. *Geoffrey de Noiers*, who began the new cathedral 'a fundamentis'. The name sounds French; whether a French architect is probable will be discussed later.

The cathedral has two pairs of transepts, on the pattern of the rebuilding of the e part of Canterbury in 1175–84. When in the Middle Ages churches were built, the start was usually at the e end, for understandable reasons. But of St Hugh's e end, that is the parts e of the eastern transepts, we know only from excavations. His plan, Geoffrey's plan, was the strangest hybrid. It was, one might say, one extremely long polygonal apse, with an ambulatory, i.e. to put it another way, the chancel aisles tapered or converged and the e wall of the high choir seems only to have been about half the width of the e crossing. Along the curious ambulatory thus formed there were seven radiating chapels, on the pattern which was one of the most usual in Romanesque France and England and in Gothic France: only owing to the odd shape of the high choir, the chapels were also arranged oddly. The E chapel was of three (or five?) sides of a hexagon, the side chapels one pair horseshoe-shaped, the next stilted semicircles, and the pair furthest W much smaller and of unknown shape. The English were great at inventing complicated variations on the simple theme of French radiating chapels. It must have been the strangest experience to wander through these unexpected spaces. But Geoffrey, as we shall see, throve on strangeness and the unexpected. The E end which has replaced St Hugh's is the Angel Choir, and this will be described below (following the *Summary 1192–1250*). St Hugh's E end is outlined in the floor of the Angel Choir, and Remigius's apse in the floor of St Hugh's Choir.

St Hugh died in 1200. It is said that King John helped to carry his coffin to burial 'a boreale ipsius aedis regione' by the altar of St John Baptist, where the bishop had hurried Geoffrey to finish his tomb: i.e. on the N side of the former E chapel dedicated to St John Baptist. There has been controversy as to whether this was the N chapel of the NE transept or simply the N part of the building, i.e. presumably the most desirable spot just N of the high altar. Browne Willis shows the position in the Angel Choir just N of the EW axis of the church, the tomb thus having remained in the same spot with the Angel Choir constructed around it (Draper). The NE chapel, which was lengthened soon after, was known at least from the C17 as the Lady Chapel, and indeed that was the position of Lady Chapels at Bristol (early C13), Peterborough (late C13), and Ely (early C14). The Lincoln chapel was partly rebuilt by *Essex* in 1772.

What remains of St Hugh's work now begins with the E transepts. Exactly how much was finished before his death is not known. The work of this special character continues up to the main crossing with the so-called St Hugh's Choir complete by c. 1210. Geoffrey's successors, modifying and altering this character, carried the rebuilding campaign through to the W end by c. 1250. First, the more extraordinary part of Geoffrey's design, the interior.

## St Hugh's interior

We have to start with one minute survival of the E end proper. Behind a wooden door on the S side in the angle between the E chapels of the SE transept and the Perp Longland Chapel added to the Angel Choir is a corbel with elementary stiff-leaf in one row and the springing of a wall arch and another arch. These, it would seem, must once have been inside the south-westernmost of St Hugh's ambulatory chapels.

For the rest of St Hugh's work, the start is the EAST TRANSEPTS. The E crossing piers belong to the Angel Choir and do not concern us yet. The E walls have three more bays, the first being chancel aisles, the others corresponding to the E chapels behind. The responds are at once of imaginative and delightful shapes. The first pair has a semi-octagonal core with five detached shafts alternately of Lincoln stone and Purbeck marble. The capitals have stiff-leaf, with two tiers of bold individual crockets. Even the shaft-rings have here a little leaf decoration. The second and third responds are half-cruciform with curved re-entrant angles and again five alternatingly detached limestone and Purbeck shafts. The passion for Purbeck shafting and for detached shafts, Geoffrey had caught at Canterbury. But he played on this theme with much greater resourcefulness than William of Sens, as we shall see presently. (It is now known that part of the English marble used at Lincoln is not Purbeck but Alwalton, longer-lasting and from a less distant quarry, near Peterborough: Clifton-Taylor 1972, quoting Donovan Purcell.)

Inside, the E transept chapels have blank arcading with round shafts, polygonal shafts, and polygonal shafts with concave sides, again a sign of Geoffrey's sense of play. Lively stiff-leaf capitals, deeply moulded arches, using fillets here and there. Also stiff-leaf hoodmould stops. The chapels are vaulted, and it is typical of Geoffrey that he uses irregular vaulting patterns of five or six or even seven ribs. Much very small dogtooth in the ribs. Stiff-leaf bosses. That the windows were shafted and the vaults rest on wall-shafts is a matter of course and need not be repeated. In the outer N chapel (NE transept) three especially fine corbel heads: a lady wearing a wimple, a man with an open mouth, a bearded man. From this chapel a doorway with deeply moulded arch leads to the N. (But it must be remembered that this chapel was at least partly rebuilt in the C18 by *Essex*.) In the SE transept S chapel a double piscina and opposite it a double aumbry. This has an Alwalton marble dividing post with a vertical semicircular projection to push the two bolts into. Above the chapels a gallery, again as at Canterbury, a clerestory and sexpartite vaults (with small dogtooth enrichment), except for the outer bays, which differ on the two sides and from the rest and must a little later be examined in detail. The gallery has two twin openings for each bay, much shafted. The sub-arches are low with a little dogtooth set under higher blank arches. In the tympana of the inner bays trefoils and quatrefoils pierced – a beginning of plate tracery. In the SE transept the inner bay has blank trefoils, the outer plain pierced circles. In the NE transept first a pierced quatrefoil and a pierced trefoil, then also circles; on the E side first a blank trefoil, then a pierced trefoil. Single clerestory lancets with narrow wall-passage. (Triangular openings mentioned in the old text are not visible from the floor, only in photographs taken from upper levels: they open into the back of the gallery.) The vaulting-shafts rise from the ground as part of the composite piers. The shafts for the intermediate ribs start in the gallery spandrels. They are on corbels in their turn supported by busts. The galleries are crossed by heavy pointed arches to help to buttress the high vault. This motif was continued throughout the cathedral.

Now the S E transept S wall, or at least its lower parts. Here for the first time an eminently important motif comes in, Geoffrey's most delightful invention: blank arcading in two planes set in a syncopated rhythm ('contrapuntal' may describe this better than 'syncopated': see Glossary), i.e. pointed blank arcading with detached limestone shafts close to the wall, and another row of arcading with Purbeck shafts and pointed-trefoiled arches set so that the shafts are in front of the apexes behind, and the apexes in front of the rear shafts. No one had quite done such a thing before, unless the turrets of the Norman W front of Ely qualify, where shafts run up in front of the arches of blind arcading. The ancestry of the motif is thus English, not French (even if it was imitated in France at Mont-St-Michel), and Geoffrey gloried in it. The system is applied to this particular wall with the most baffling little irregularities. The back arcading ends on the E with a half arch, the front arcading on the W with an embarrassed steep untrefoiled arch. Above the arcading two shafted lancets. The sill tallies with that of the gallery, the capitals tally with nothing.

Here we must abandon the S wall, and first turn to the W walls of both S E and N E transepts. In the S E transept the outer bay has the confusion of the access to the Song School (see below, after S E transept's outer bay). Then wall piers with polygonal cores and alternating Lincoln and Purbeck shafts. The inner bay has as its N pier, i.e. the pier where transept and chancel aisle meet, the most enterprising and surprising of all Geoffrey's piers – octagonal core, eight shafts around, alternating Purbeck and Lincoln, the latter concave-sided, but behind the E, S and N sides in both E transepts, the core sprouts out in monstrously big crockets forming a vertical row, as was done later up the edges of spires. The closest parallel to this is the crocketed cross for the Crucifixus in the Psalter of Robert of Lindseye, who was abbot of Peterborough from 1214 to 1222, and this is probably just a little later than the Lincoln piers. Similar too is, however, a Tree of Life in the St Albans Psalter of c. 1120–40, and so a tradition in illumination existed.

The W chapels, in the N E transept the TREASURY, have Geoffrey's syncopated (or contrapuntal) arcading, again with the painful corners. The muddle is worse in the S chapel. Six-ribbed vault on shafts which stand in front of the two-tier blank arcading. Richly shafted upper blank arcading. What is new now in the syncopated arcading is that busts of angels (and a demon peeping out of stiff-leaf) have arrived to enrich the spandrels. The N W chapel

underwent a change of purpose before it became the treasury. At some stage, probably in the C 18, it was horizontally divided. A floor was put in and, to light what was now the ground floor, oblong windows were put in too. What the upper floor was used for is unknown. Strange openings, oblong and triangular, like *arcosolia* were made for it. Recent conversion of the N W chapel into a treasury for the display of plate was done by *Louis Osman* in 1959–60 (see *Furnishings*, N choir aisle, below). The gallery on the W side of this N E transept is of course no real gallery but a wall-passage, but its front is treated exactly as on the E side, except that a slightly later date – as one would expect, if building went on from E to W – is indicated by the greater variety of pierced motifs in the tympana. They now include diagonally placed quatrefoils. The arches of the N W chapel, incidentally, are braced to E and S by wooden beams. This makeshift arrangement existed in other parts of Geoffrey's work as well, as the holes show. (Even at Westminster Abbey strengthening by iron ties was used.)

The N wall of the N E transept was treated completely differently and has no exact counterpart anywhere else. Here the whole outer bay was vaulted at ground-floor level. The vault has six ribs, as Geoffrey liked it; for they do not make a sexpartite vault. Above, a wide first-floor room was gained, for what purpose we do not know. It is the oddest room, extremely high now and decidedly behind the scenes; for from here one looks to the N at the back of the N front, to the S at the back of what one first assumed, standing in the transept, to be the N front. The latter has a gallery front just like the E side, and above two single clerestory lancets with wall-passage. But the real N front has nothing representing the gallery, just two tiers of tall lancets. There are plenty of putholes, but whether a ceiling was put in at once, we cannot say: the small doorway at clerestory-level makes one assume it, though it may have led to a wooden balcony. Aesthetically speaking, to make one see the real N front through this stone screen is Geoffrey's boldest experiment in vistas, but not his most successful. Or can there have been a functional reason? It is said to have a drain (New). But putting a garderobe into the vista seems unlikely. An intended tower has been suggested (by Canon Venables, historian of the cathedral in articles for *Archaeological Journal*, 1875, 1883, 1887), but that is not convincing.

The N wall ground floor, that is under the vault, has Geoffrey's syncopated arcading, stopped, however, by a somewhat later doorway to the cloisters and chapter house (for the passage to the cloisters, see *Chapter house and cloisters* below). The doorway has a segmental arch on short vertical pieces above the capitals, a motif of the second third rather than the first third of the C 13 (cf. Westminster Abbey and Salisbury in our companion volume).

In the SE transept the outer bay also must be taken separately; for on closer investigation this tells a strange story. The wall arches in the S and W walls prove that here too a vault was planned, and the roughness just S of the SE pier that something of the sort indeed existed, and a screen wall was started above. Then, however, the plan was abandoned, or perhaps what had been built fell down. In any case the S bay in its upper parts was remodelled or perhaps finally completed. This, it may be anticipated – for reasons of certain motifs – must have been done in the 1230s or a little later. What ought to be noted is this. The gallery bays to E and W have taller-looking arcading, four even arches for Geoffrey's twins. No Purbeck marble is used, but quite excessive amounts of dogtooth. The stiff-leaf capitals are much more disturbed. The change in the style of the capitals is most patent in the main vaulting-shafts. Here the diagonal ribs of the bay N of the outer one are Hugh's, the capitals of the broad transverse arches those of the later mason completing the bay. The S wall at this level is treated similarly. Above the clerestory windows, decoration with lattice work. The vault is quadripartite with a longitudinal N–S ridge rib.

Here we describe the SONG SCHOOL, because this addition to the outer W corner of the SE transept seems to have been an immediate afterthought. It is of two storeys, two by two bays, and severely plain in its details. The upper storey is thought to have been the cathedral choristers' song school continuously since before the Reformation (Seaborne, *The English School*, 1971). The lower storey is a vestry. It has a crypt underneath whose windows show outside. Chamfered buttresses. Shafted lancets, smaller above than below. All capitals moulded. Flat roof. That the Song School is an addition becomes perfectly clear from the way in which St Hugh's typical broad buttresses with their detached corner shafts are cut into. Originally there was only one W chapel, just as there is only one off the N transept. There this is continued to the N by a massive block with a staircase. Here there is a staircase too, but there are also at once three narrow quadripartite rib-vaults, one of them now divided from the others by a partition wall. Stiff-leaf bosses. The capitals are again heavily moulded. The windows have a continuous keeled roll moulding. A puzzle is the fact that the corbels for the first, i.e. northernmost, bay, the corbels which adjoin the wall of St Hugh's transept, are part of his work. Stiff-leaf on head corbels. Yet it is just here that St Hugh's buttress is covered by the annexe. So the building must be an afterthought, but it must have been started very soon after. The crypt is also rib-vaulted, the ribs being single-chamfered. There are here two narrow oblong bays with quadripartite vaults and then a large bay with a sexpartite vault. The top floor has the same kind of windows as below. Here even more of the S transept is blocked, including a two-light window at

the gallery level. The finest feature of the upper floor is a series of large head corbels, including a negro. They must have been meant for an upper vault or, more probably, for roof beams.

ST HUGH'S CHOIR. To the W of the E crossing St Hugh's Choir continues towards the main crossing. There are three main bays, and they would show Geoffrey's style at its purest if it were not for interference from the C14 choir stalls (see *Furnishings*); a fourth bay containing the pulpitum is less pure. But the stalls had predecessors and it is quite likely that Geoffrey's vaulting-shafts never went to the ground here. A more fatal interference was caused by the fall of Hugh's main crossing tower in 1237 or 1239 (see below). Strengthening was undertaken regardless of the aesthetic claims of Geoffrey's design. The strengthening is recognizable by the use of stubby Lincolnshire piers. mostly with fillets and an absence of the brittle Purbeck. So the E crossing NW pier already is not as Geoffrey had made it. The capital is flatter, more spread out than Geoffrey's. The SW pier on the other hand is Geoffrey's, except that the Purbeck shafts flanking the diagonal Lincoln shafts have been broken out. Their Purbeck capitals, however, are there. The other vaulting-shafts of the choir are of Purbeck and rise from simple cone-shaped brackets of Lincoln stone well above the arcade piers. These piers are Geoffrey's most elegant: square cores with chamfered angles and concave main sides, and in the concavities Purbeck shafts.

101. LINCOLN St Hugh's Choir, pier detail, *c.* 1200

102. LINCOLN St Hugh's Choir,
aisle wall arcades, *c.* 1200

The capitals are of Lincoln stone, twice the height for the core as for the shafts. Where the piers differ from this perfect scheme is due to the haphazard under-propping and the Lincoln stone thickenings. In the w arch of the N arcade the botching is most patent: an ornamental ring across the mouldings had to be carved to hide the fact that the voussoirs would not quite have fitted. (For C18 screening ornament on strainer beams at the E crossing, see *Furnishings*.)

The aisles have syncopated arcading along their outer walls (using Alwalton marble, not Purbeck, on the N side). The spandrels contain half-length angels (also prophets), eight on the N aisle, seven on the s aisle, and apparently a good deal earlier than the winged demi-angels on the Salisbury rood screen. Of the Lincoln figures a few have wings: out of three on the N, two might be original and one looks restored (John Cherry). On spandrel angels in gen-

eral, see *Angel Choir* below. The stiff-leaf capitals on this small scale are more abundant. The back arches now start using dogtooth. The vaults are quadripartite with an extra fifth rib to the centre of the outer wall of each bay. The ribs have the small dogtooth we have already found in the transepts.

Now the upper regions of the choir. The vaulting-shafts include Geoffrey's favourite concave-sided octagon section. The gallery remains unchanged, except that yet more forms come in in the tympana. Foils with leaf cusps e.g. appear. The clerestory has a new pattern, a group of three stepped lancets, and to its l. and r. absurdly small arches on absurdly short shafts. Above them, in the spandrels (except for the N E bay) assorted pierced foiled shapes, also upside down. The w bay shows the trouble after the fall of the tower as clearly in the gallery and higher up as on the arcade-level below. In the w bay gallery the separating pier between the two twins is a shapeless bundle of Lincoln stone shafts, a pound of candles, as Venables nicely called it. In the tympana a very small quatrefoil with fleur-de-lys cusps. Between the jamb shafts big dogtooth. Big dogtooth also in the clerestory.

And then the VAULT, which Paul Frankl so happily called the Crazy Vault of Lincoln. It is of European importance in that it is the first rib-vault with tiercerons, i.e. the first rib-vault with purely decorative intentions. It is true that subsidiary ribs are also a structural help in that they strengthen the skeleton and in that they reduce the size of cells. But the way it is done here is such that decorative enrichment clearly came first in its inventor's strange mind. To understand the vault one ought to start with an image in one's mind of a normal quadripartite vault. Geoffrey then added a momentous innovation for the English future, a longitudinal ridge rib. He then proceeded to open and shut one diagonal rib scissorwise so that it becomes tiercerons and touches the ridge at two points other than the centre. Finally he diverts the other diagonal rib accordingly so that one arm touches the one point of the scissor-tiercerons at its apex, the other the other. The result, as this arrangement is done in the same way throughout, is overwhelmingly lopsided. The vault starts over the E crossing and goes to one bay E of the main crossing, that is, four bays were treated in this way. (The bay over the pulpitum has a normal sexpartite vault.) But the most significant result of the Crazy Vault is that it invalidates the bay division which to French architecture had been and was going to be for nearly two centuries the basic fact of Gothic composition. The ridge rib runs all bays into one and stresses continuity. But the tiercerons do more. Geoffrey has no distinction in gauge between his transverse arches and his ribs; so one does not read his vault as bay after bay, but as a bunch of four ribs emanating from one springer and the bunch spreading palm-frond-wise, though not with opposite springers producing fronds in mirror-image. Instead there is once again the most convinced syncopation.

Many a reader has discovered that the above description of the Crazy Vault is easier to follow on the spot – and easier to criticize than improve (except perhaps with diagrams, as in Bony 1979, p. 44, and on our plan, p. 198).

Now the MAIN CROSSING (first phase, before Geoffrey's work ended). The piers have three Purbeck shafts to the crossing, two to the outside. The capitals have stiff-leaf in two rows. But above the capitals the style, i.e. the plan, changes, and we must stop. If we now turn to the MAIN TRANSEPTS we see the same. The E walls of the E aisle start to Geoffrey's plan. The front of the three chapels into which later low partition walls divide the aisle has syncopated arcading and the five-rib vault of the chancel aisles. But the two S ribs in the S transept, N ribs in the N transept,

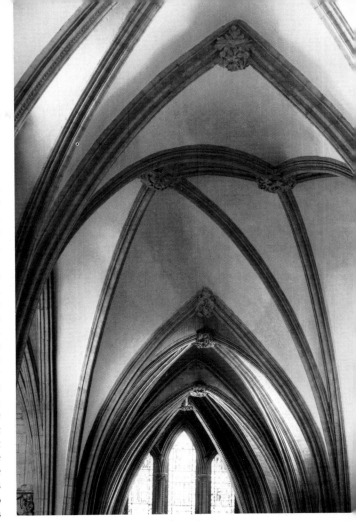

103. LINCOLN East crossing and south-east transept, c. 1192–1200, with 'crazy vault'

suddenly cease using the little dogtooth enrichment, and in the second chapel of the S transept the syncopated arcading is replaced by normal arcading. This return to normality marks the break. In the N transept it is even more abrupt. Here the syncopation stops midway down the second chapel. The last stage of Geoffrey's work otherwise differs only in small details, though one of them is significant enough. Geoffrey now decided to replace his tympana angels by arched holes without figures; for to peep through them at the apexes of the back arcading was a greater thrill. In the N transept he altered even more. For the sake of variety he let the back arcading be trefoiled and the front pointed. But the tympanum holes are here not pierced.

We now leave the interior of the main crossing and transepts, as it were, in mid-air. Before continuing with other masters' work on them, we must look at the outside of Geoffrey's work.

Much less need be said here. Again we must take the E transept first, St Hugh's Choir second, the transition to the main transept last. The E transept brings in at once Geoffrey's most characteristic and unexpected feature, main buttresses with a section of the front of a strong keeled shaft in the middle, two deep hollows l. and r., and then a chamfered corner in front of which stands another strong shaft, fully detached. Dragons, not always preserved, curl about the top of the base mouldings. The intermediate buttresses are just chamfered. In the NE transept front the middle buttress runs right to the third tier of lancet windows. The rhythm of fenestration is 1 + 1, then blank–1–blank, then the gable with five steeply stepped lancets, the outer ones blank. In the SE transept front the buttress goes up only into the first upper stage, but that is due to the alterations higher up of which we already know, and which express themselves externally by the prominent use of dogtooth. The pinnacles of the fronts differ. They differ throughout the building. Basically, however, the type remained that stated e.g. in the NE transept, i.e. polygonal, plain and crowned by a spire, with roll mouldings up the edges of the spire. The pinnacles at the corners of the SE transept add shafts up the octagon corners and eight gables. Also little angels stand on the tops. However, these are of course the pinnacles of the 1230s or 1240s.

The E sides of the transepts have the chapels attached. They state the elevational system of most of the rest. Shafted lancet windows with stiff-leaf capitals. Gallery with pairs of small lancets with a shaft between. Shafted lancets in the clerestory. The chapels differ in shape, the most curious being the NE chapel. (See above on the burial of St Hugh, and on the interior of the NE chapel.) Can this be the original shape? The elevational forms are perfectly convincing, but the obtusely pointed E wall looks dubious. The chapel is indeed the one which was lengthened fairly shortly after St Hugh's death. This C13 lengthening is still visible in the grass. Then *Essex* in 1772 rebuilt, it is said on Geoffrey's foundations, i.e. to the late-1190s length, and one must assume with the old materials. So the question remains: were they the old foundations? Essex, considering the time when he worked, was a careful archaeologist. The roof-line of the lengthened chapel can still be recognized: the clerestory had to be altered to accommodate it. The W walls, and indeed the walls of St Hugh's Choir, follow the same elevational system as the E sides of the transepts. In the SE transept at the SW corner the system is disturbed by the addition of what is now the Song School (see *Interior*, at end of SE transept, above). In the NE transept it is disturbed by a mighty staircase projection N of the W chapel. The clerestory alone has a new motif: a triple group of arches with windows in the outer arches. Flying

buttresses, the earliest ones at Lincoln and altogether before 1200 still a motif novel anywhere, even in France. The earliest examples there appear to belong to the 1170s, and so do those of William of Sens at Canterbury. In St Hugh's choir the clerestory has a different grouping. Each bay has five arches, four narrow, one wider. The middle three have the windows. The flying buttresses run up to this composition and cut into it. On the pinnacles of the two buttresses in the corner of the SE transept and the S aisle of St Hugh's choir two demi-figures of angels.

The same at the corner of the N aisle and the N main transept, i.e. a corner still, we assumed, built under Geoffrey. Indeed the joint between him and his successor which we could demonstrate inside the E aisle appears outside just as clearly. Geoffrey's broad buttresses with the detached angle-shafts disappear and are replaced by plain, normal chamfered buttresses. Also the pinnacles all go plain. In the S transept just one has a demon perching on it.

### Summary of Geoffrey's work
Here, where his span ended, we must stop for a few minutes and try to sum up in our minds what manner of man he was. His initial stimulus had come from Canterbury; that is certain. The detached shafts which he loved so much occurred there. But did William of Sens bring them from France or adopt them from England? It is not certain; Professor Bony has not been able to offer a firm answer. They do occur in the crypt at York and at Iffley just before Canterbury and in purely English contexts, but they also appear in Paris and Soissons at least in the 1180s. However that may be, Geoffrey was the most inventive user of this motif. He loved it because it made for transparency, for letting you see one thing behind the other, and that is what his syncopated arcading also does. Syncopation was his other passion. It is the mainspring of the design of the Crazy Vault. Was Geoffrey de Noiers then a Frenchman or an Englishman? (Noyers, incidentally, is not far from Sens.) Here again we shall never be able to say for certain. But the fact that matters is that the decorative vault which he had started became the chief English contribution to C13 and early C14 development. It became a field in which England kept far in advance of any other country. The same is true of the unexpected vista across a grille. So ought one not to attribute motifs in the event so English to an English designer? (A summary of the whole campaign to c. 1250 follows description of the C13 W end below.)

*The second and third masters*   And now to the second and third masters. We may even know their names; for about 1230 a *Michael* is called 'magister operis', and about 1235 an *Alexander* (possibly, according to Mr Harvey, the same Master Alexander who worked at Worcester; see also the Lincoln chapter house of these years, below). The second master continued the main transepts where Geoffrey had left them, the third master rebuilt the crossing tower after it had fallen in 1237 or 1239. The earlier date is recorded in the Chronicle of Peterborough, the later by Matthew Paris and in the Annals of Dunstable. Although chronologically wrong, we take this work first. The CROSSING TOWER starts at once using his typical motif, the typical motif of the 1240s at Lincoln: diagonal lattice decoration of flat surfaces. He uses it inside as well as outside the tower. Inside, in the corners a thin triple Purbeck shaft runs up to support what vaulting was projected. Tall wall-arcading in two tiers with wall-passages, grouped into threes below, fours above. Still limestone and Purbeck marble, still stiff-leaf capitals. The vault, as we see it now, is C 14 work; it will be discussed under that heading. Outside, the second stage has crockets up the jambs of the arcading between the shafts, a development from St Hugh's crocket piers, and one soon to be taken up in the Angel Choir (following w end and summary to c. 1250). The lattice in the spandrels has quatrefoils set in. Then the C 14 work starts also externally.

In the MAIN TRANSEPTS the second master replaced, as we have seen, the syncopated by plain blank arcading. Otherwise he did not change much. The low partition walls in the aisle could be his design in the s transept. They have blank arcading here with a pendant capital between two arches. In the N transept, where they are roofed like shrines and have Purbeck shafts, they cut across Geoffrey's and the second master's blank arcading. Also they have the big dogtooth we have so far only found in the completion of the outer bay of the S E transept, that is to say, work to be attributed to the third master. The second master's main piers of the aisle are inspired by Geoffrey's but lack appreciation of his detached shafts. The gallery does not change in essentials. Yet another new motif comes into the tympana: an elongated quatrefoil (E side s transept, second bay from the crossing). In the inner bays the fall of the tower must have caused damage, and repair work is as clearly discernible as in St Hugh's Choir. In the innermost single (not twin) arch of the N transept big dogtooth, as in the repaired bay of St Hugh's Choir. Nothing new in the clerestory. Vaults sexpartite, i.e. no craziness. The ribs with small dogtooth. The intermediate ribs on shafts starting at the sill height of the gallery.

The N and s walls differ. The N wall has a big doorway to the N, leading towards the former Deanery, the s wall a small doorway to a spiral stair. Above on the N follows the glorious composition of the DEAN'S EYE, i.e. a row of seven even lancets, not too high, with five of them pierced as windows, and then a rose of plate tracery. Its date can at least approximately be determined. The *Metrical Life of St Hugh*, written shortly after his canonization in 1220, mentions a s and a N window which it calls 'orbiculare'. The

pattern of the Dean's Eye is like this. A large quatrefoil in the middle, and its centre a concave-sided lozenge with a quatrefoil. In the outer spandrels a trefoil and two small circles and around the whole a band of sixteen circles. It is an original composition, just a little wilful perhaps, as are the contemporary rose-windows of the w front of Laon, the N transept of Chartres and the s transept of Lausanne Cathedrals, but not in the least imitated from any of them or, it seems, any other. The vault springs so low that from a distance it cuts into the rose. On the s side is the Bishop's Eye instead, a C 14 replacement to which we shall turn in due course (see below on C 14 work). The w walls also differ; for here, in the s transept, is the doorway to the galilee (second paragraph below). Otherwise the system is the same. Each sexpartite bay has two plus two steeply pointed blank arches at ground-level, then two lancets, then a wall-passage of two plus two with dogtooth, and then two clerestory windows.

Again the EXTERIOR of this part does not need much examination. The N transept front cannot be seen clearly, as it is interfered with by the cloister. It has in the middle a porch with a gable which has some dogtooth and is flanked by square pinnacles. The porch has a sexpartite vault, but all the details – shafts, vault, portal proper – are Victorian. Only the *trumeau* is old. In the tympanum an odd and scarcely believable triple blank arching. The date, if one can trust any of all this, must be that of the galilee porch to the s transept (an afterthought, as we shall see below). On the N side follows the row of lancets, and then the Dean's Eye. Of these we have reported. Externally the rose-window is surrounded by a kind of stiff-leaf fleurons and dogtooth. Dogtooth also in the gable. Three pinnacles, polygonal and shafted. On the s side the buttressing, especially towards the galilee, is more elaborate, and the Bishop's Eye fills a larger area. Of the C 14 also the window in the gable, and the bold frill of the gable. (This s gable rebuilt 1804 by *William Hayward*, the cathedral surveyor: Colvin 1978.) Differing C 13 pinnacles. That towards the galilee is the most highly decorated up to that date. It has crockets all up its spire. The w sides of the transepts offer nothing essentially new. The buttresses change from the chamfering Lincoln was accustomed to to a square shafted design similar to the s buttresses. The flying buttresses on the E side reach the clerestory in the same place as in St Hugh's Choir. The top in the s transept is a C 14 frieze of an undulating line cusped. The pinnacles of alternating size are of the C 14 too. They are the same in the N transept.

*The galilee*   This gratuitously large w porch into the s transept is an anomaly. It takes the place of normal N or s porches into naves. It is two-storeyed and cruciform. Entries from s and w, a tripartite large window-like opening to the N and the short passage to the portal to the E. Externally and internally blank arcading with very steep

arches, lush stiff-leaf capitals. Excessive dogtooth. To the s externally on the upper floor three lancet windows flanked by blank arches taller than they – a perverse motif. Along the top outside a Perp frieze of quatrefoils. Inside all terribly renewed. Rib-vaults, one narrow quadripartite bay to the w, two such bays N and s, two sexpartite bays and one quadripartite from the longer passage to the transepts. The angle-shafts of the cross are concave-sided polygons. Juicy stiff-leaf capitals and bosses. Overmuch dogtooth. The portal is physically all Victorian. Twin entry with *trumeau*. At the foot of the *trumeau* beasts with human heads looking up. In the tympanum a lozenge. The jambs double-shafted with exuberant foliage. The upper floor, now MUNIMENT ROOM, is very light. Three lancets to the w, three to the N, five to the s. Only to the E a blocked two-light window of the transept instead, final proof that the galilee was an afterthought too. But when was it built? The exuberance places it near the Angel Choir, the massing of dogtooth corresponds to the s bay of the s transept. So the date is most probably *c.* 1240–50.

*The nave*    There is no known date for the nave. The date usually given is 1233 for its roofing, and one assumes rightly that roofing means completed walls but not-yet-started vault. However, all that documents tell us is this. Hugh of Wells (Bishop of Lincoln 1209–35) made his will in 1233, leaving 100 marks to the fabric and all the felled timber that would be found on his estates at the time of his death. This special mention of much timber, it is argued, implies the need for much timber, and that points to a roofing job. But it can just as well point to the scaffolding and centering needed for a vaulting job. The nave is seven bays long plus the odd bay between the towers. The system is not drastically changed, and the second master may have expressed himself like this, where he had more freedom. The piers are still of Lincoln stone and Purbeck marble in various mixtures. And there is still a gallery and a clerestory with wall-passage. First the arcades. The arches have no dogtooth. The piers all have stiff-leaf capitals of Lincoln stone. The arches are wider than St Hugh's and make the piers seem slimmer. The second pair is Purbeck throughout. It has a square core set diagonally and hollow chamfers with shafts in the main directions. The third pier on the N side is octagonal with four Lincoln and four Purbeck shafts, all with fillets. The s pier is quite different. It has short straight projections in the main directions and three hollow chamfers in the diagonals. A total of eight Purbeck shafts and eight very thin Lincoln shafts. The nave master certainly did not suffer from any shortage of invention either. The fourth pair is like the second, the fifth like the third s pier, the sixth like the first.

The aisles have pointed-trefoiled arcading. A change in plan is very noticeable here, especially on the N side, where first twin arcading units still continue in the transept way,

and then the new design starts. The arches now – we are still on the N side – stand on detached triple Purbeck shafts. Each bay has two lancet windows. (The first wall-shaft differs from the others by having much dogtooth.) The vault continues the five-rib pattern of Geoffrey but adds a longitudinal ridge rib and one pair of tiercerons in the longitudinal direction. The vaulting-shafts cross in the best Geoffrey tradition in front of the apex of a wall-arcading unit. The intermediate shafts stand on moulded capitals as corbels. In the s aisle many details are more elaborate than in the N aisle, though the vaulting-shafts do not cross. They divide the wall-arcading into groups. The intermediate shafts stand on stiff-leaf, not on moulded, corbels. In the vault the ridge ribs are interrupted from the tiercerons of one bay to those of the next. Bosses are not only of foliage. Four are figured: three heads, Christ blessing with three heads grouped around, in both cases probably an allusion to the Trinity, a head tortured by beasts, the lamb. Also the wall-arcading of the new type does not start after two units of the old, but after some blank wall. But all that is minor.

The gallery is richer than that of the transepts. There are not two twins but two triplets per bay. In the sub-tympana are not one quatrefoil or trefoil but three, all cusped. The only exception is the first half-bay from the E, N as well as s, and that may be due to the repairs of *c.* 1240; for it stands to reason that the nave must at least have been carried up to the top for one bay to help support the earlier crossing tower. The two w bays are shorter than the others, and here the old system of one, not three, motifs in the tympana recurs. The calculation of units between crossing and Norman towers must have gone a little wrong. The shafting is mostly Purbeck. Stiff-leaf capitals. The clerestory wall-passage is of three arches of even height. The vaulting-shafts start on fine stiff-leaf corbels of moderate size.

The vault shows this master more conspicuously than anywhere else as the defender of normality. He adopted his predecessor's inventions, both ridge ribs and tiercerons, but he made a reasonable, easily-repeating pattern out of them. The pattern is that which we call the tierceron star. Longitudinal ridge rib, transverse ridge rib not of full length, one pair of tiercerons in each cell leading up to the ridge rib. It still reads palm-frond-wise and not bay-wise, indeed even more so than Geoffrey's, and for that very reason it made an epoch. It was at once taken over in the new E end at Ely, begun in 1234, i.e. perhaps even before, the vault of the Lincoln nave was actually executed. But at Westminster Abbey (first nave bay *c.* 1253) the transverse ridge rib was to go full length. The palm-frond effect was to be taken to its extreme at Exeter. (Meanwhile, the choir at Worcester was started in 1224 and has quadripartite rib-vaults like Salisbury of the same time, but with a longitudinal ridge rib. As for the so-called syncopated triforium arcading at Worcester, a comparable interplay between layers of arcading can be found at Chichester.)

Externally the nave brings little that is worth noting. The elevation after the transept appears two-storeyed. The gallery, instead of windows, has the smallest of slits. Alternating buttresses, plain pinnacles, flying buttresses. In the aisles each bay has one lancet window and one blank arch squeezed between it and the intermediate buttress. Why? Shafts and moulded capitals. The clerestory has a rhythm of three arches with windows and then three narrow blank ones. The flying buttress runs safely into the middle one of them, not as haphazardly as in St Hugh's Choir and, considering their width, more satisfactorily than in the transepts. Above this on the s side only a Perp quatrefoiled frieze and highly decorated canopied tabernacles for statuary. They alternate in their details. All have little monsters at their foot.

Towards the w end the aisle is covered by the w chapels. Their external architecture does not call for comment, but their existence does, and this cannot be made without first turning to the façade. The only thing about the external architecture that may be worth saying is that the E gable of the s w chapel has lancets with Y-tracery, a motif we have not so far met. There are small figures in the spandrels, a devil (?) and a pilgrim and a beggar.

*West front*    The w front was widened into a screen and thereby deprived of the logic of its Norman predecessor, which expressed at least more or less the nave and aisles behind. The English, ever since the Anglo-Norman style had established itself, had had a *faible* for screen façades. St Paul's had one e.g., and the thickness of the outer walls of the Norman w front of Lincoln was excessive too. But the architect who designed the c 13 front went the whole hog. He may have been the third master from the start, although it is certain only that the third master was busy on it higher up. Anyway, whoever he was, he spread his façade to the limits, and by decorating it with tier upon tier of blank arcading emphasized the horizontality of the screen yet more. Nor did he care about the discrepancy between his work and the Norman work which he left up. The result is curious rather than beautiful, and such an anticlimax after the nave that that alone may incline one to suppose a change in the lodge from the beginning. A functional justification of the lengthening of the façade, however, was attempted by placing behind it the spacious N W and S W chapels to which we have just referred. The idea may have come to the designer from the longest of all Norman w fronts, that of the abbey church at Bury St Edmunds, which also had such w chapels N and s of the aisles. Even Ely is similar to a certain extent, as it is in the angle-turrets. At Lincoln on these turrets – which have spires higher than the middle gable, and thus quite convin-

cingly call a halt to the horizontal spread of the screen – two statuettes are displayed, St Hugh (reset 1743: Cocke) and the Swineherd of Stow, who gave within his means gloriously generously to the fabric fund. The screen on the ground floor has small doorways into the w extensions of the chapels. Above them blank arcading and a small circular window, also flanked by blank lancets. Above the Norman front more blank arcading, exceedingly tall and with gabled canopies for images. Flat top with a c 14 cusped-triangle frieze, except for the nave gable, which has stepped arcading. Two windows to light the roof, two outer statues, in style with their stiff, short curves very much like some of those on the façade screen of Wells, which was begun, it can be assumed, about 1230–5. But the most interesting thing is what the architect did with the central Norman recess. The round arch it had came much too low for him. So he removed it, heightened the jambs, and put up a new pointed arch at a new level. In this heightening at once his *leitmotif* occurs, the lattice-work. Shallow sexpartite vault. Cinquefoiled circular window all encrusted with foliage. Small trefoils and quatrefoils opened out of the lattice. As for the dating of this stage, the lattice is equally prominent inside the crossing tower. This was no doubt rebuilt immediately after the catastrophe, say c. 1240. That makes sense for the upper part of the façade – especially if the roofing or, better still, the vaulting of the nave went on in 1233. So the motif may have come in already about that time and characterized Lincoln about 1235–45. For the large Perp w window, see the c 14 w front, below. In the spandrels of the big arch two more statues, a king and a queen, of the same style and date as those in the gable.

Behind this façade lie the w chapels and the complicated and not very satisfactory bay between the towers. The WEST CHAPELS are both of beautiful, erect yet reposeful proportions. They differ in one essential detail. The N or Morning Chapel has a slim central pier of Purbeck marble with eight keeled attached shafts and a Purbeck capital. The chapel thus is of four bays. They have quadripartite vaults with stiff-leaf bosses and plain ribs. The pier between N aisle and chapel is also all Purbeck. The screen wall which continues the aisle arcading has arches of a new kind towards the nave. They are pointed-cinquefoiled. Along the E and N walls blank arcading with moulded capitals. Double piscina in the E wall. The chapel extends to the w only one bay wide, but two bays long to the w façade. It is here that one can study the Early Norman N niche. The w doorway has a depressed two-centred arch on short vertical pieces – a Westminster Abbey motif, though here no doubt earlier than 1245. Hoodmould with dogtooth. The round window above is framed inside by shafting with stiff-leaf crockets. The tall, oddly shaped double-chamfered arch must be a remodelling.

The s w chapel or consistory court (now shop) is superficially the same, but it has no central pier – a bold decision to take, a challenge one is inclined to think which the architect made and answered. The vault is thus all one bay, a bay the size of one of the main nave bays (but not one of the adjacent w nave bays). The architect moreover, for the devilry of it, made his vault on paper the same as that of the n chapel – i.e. four quadripartite parts. But now they have to rise to an apex, and thus do not look regular in reality. So perhaps structurally one ought to define the vault as one of four diagonals and two ridge ribs and four additional diagonals connecting the middles of the sides. (Pite's plan, Fig. 98, does not make this clear.) Stiff-leaf bosses. Blank arcading as before. Screen wall to the aisle as before. The pier in the middle of that side all Purbeck as before. The other capitals of Lincoln stone and with stiff-leaf, not moulded as in the n w chapel. The w extension here was not open. It is separated by a screen wall with blank arcading like the rest. Only the bay to the w which stands against the tower, i.e. does not belong to the widening which the w chapels meant, is quite different. It has stiff-leaf capitals, one with a fine little head, steep arches, and in the spandrels deeply moulded blank lozenges. It looks as if this was a start of a more lavish system not continued when the provision of the wider chapels was decided on. In the w extension the ribs are not as simple as in the n w chapel. The doorway to the w is the same, but the inner framing of the circular window has a segmental arch instead of the later arch in the n w chapel.

The space under and between the TOWERS is awkward in its details. Between the towers is a full bay but one narrower than that of the nave, as Geoffrey from the beginning did not want his dimensions to be dictated by the Norman ones; but the vault repeats those of the nave. The ground stage is panelled and has side doorways clearly in the style of the early c 18. In fact all the w interior screen walls (N–S to the nave aisles, and E–W cutting off the central w bay) are by *James Gibbs*, c. 1728–30. Cocke also says *John James* gave a second opinion supporting Gibbs's structural alterations but saying the details should be Gothick, not classical. Above to N and S are blocked c 13 arches. To the E facing the nave a piece of seemingly Perp architecture: a remodelling by *James Essex* in 1775. It is a strainer arch forming a bridge. The arch hides the rise of c 13 shafts. In the side walls the blocked Gothic arches cut into Norman relieving arches and yet higher up the Norman windows already referred to. The broad arch between nave and tower hall is c 13 but confused in its details. The w wall, i.e. the back of the façade, again has some of the lattice decoration so prominent outside.

The rooms under the towers have stone panelling and doorways by *Gibbs* (with, on the nave side, only a minimum of remodelling by *Essex*) and also on two sides Dec

blank arcading, very different in mood from any of the c 13. The arches are trefoiled and end in ogees. There is plenty of ballflower (in the s, not the n room). The spandrels are filled with blank multi-cusped triangles. c 13 and Perp windows. Dec lierne vaults of an attractive design: a square in the middle, a star interlocked with it and projecting beyond it – all cusped.

*Summary of the campaign 1192–c. 1250*   We need now to sum up and trace the development of certain motifs which might help in the dating of the various parts. What we do not know at all is how far building had proceeded when, after only eight years, St Hugh died. We must not underestimate how much it can have been. At Canterbury the whole rebuilding and extending of the parts E of the main transepts took nine years. At Salisbury the Lady Chapel and retrochoir took five. Building certainly went on steadily after St Hugh's death; for in 1205 donors of money for the 'novum opus' were promised acceptance in the 'sodalitas' of those for whom prayers were said. The motifs which we can hang our tentative dating on to are the capitals, the lattice-work, the large and more sweepingly displayed dogtooth, and the lozenges.

Capitals, which seem at first the most promising, prove also the most intractable. What can be said after careful examination is very general. In St Hugh's work there certainly were at once, or almost at once, two designers, one who liked stiff-leaf more or less of a crocket kind, the other who preferred smaller, flatter, knobbly leaves, rather more spread out. What distinguishes St Hugh's capitals from later ones is only this. Even where he uses two tiers of stiff-leaf and even where the leaves are blown diagonally – a motif which appears remarkably early in Lincoln – there is also a zone below the leaves where the moulded shape of the capitals and the individual stalks are clearly seen. The opposite extreme is the Angel Choir – i.e. just beyond the date limit set for this summary – for there the lushest stiff-leaf covers the whole capital. In the nave the development from one to the other can be watched. In the galilee to the s transept, the later type is pretty well reached. But the development is not straight. Repairs introduce later types into earlier parts and conversely capitals of St Hugh's time could be re-used, where an event such as the fall of the tower had left them unused. Much clearer is the development in leaf corbels for vaulting-shafts. Again the end is the Angel Choir. The nave is halfway on. Now the nave was being roofed, or rather being vaulted, in 1233, and the style of the figures at the top of the w gable is similar to that of Wells in the 1240s. So perhaps one might venture the proposal that Geoffrey went on till say 1210–15, that immediately afterwards the main transepts were completed and the nave built by the second master, and that the nave was ready by c. 1230–5, whereupon the third master, starting about 1235, finished the w front and rebuilt the crossing tower.

The lattice motif is a further help. It is, as we have seen, all over the rebuilt crossing tower, i.e. a favourite of *c*. 1240. As it occurs also in the upper parts of the w front and of the rebuilt or very belatedly built s bay of the s e transept, these two parts can be tentatively dated *c*. 1240, or more safely *c*. 1230–50, which is what we have come to accept.

Then the big and demonstrative dogtooth. It is most conspicuous in the s bay of the s e transept and in the galilee to the s main transept. It also comes into the w bay of Hugh's choir rebuilt *c*. 1240, into the N transept inner bay also of *c*. 1240, and into the crossing arches of the same time. It also helps incidentally to date the partition walls in the N E transept E chapels.

## THE NEW EAST END: THE ANGEL CHOIR

In 1255 the cathedral authorities petitioned Henry III to allow them to take down part of the old town wall – the line was that of the Roman wall – to extend the cathedral. Licence was given. In 1280 the solemn translation of the Shrine of St Hugh took place, in the presence of King Edward and Queen Eleanor, the Archbishop of Canterbury, and eight bishops, including Bishop Quivil, the bishop-elect of Exeter, who must have had a good look at the nave vaults. So 1256–80 is the time it took to build the Angel Choir. The start must have been made soon after the nave was finished. But that was not an exception. More space for the clergy in their part of the church was a universal demand. In length actually the Angel Choir, with its five bays beyond the E transepts, goes beyond St Hugh's apse by only two bays, but in unimpeded space the difference was enormous; for the Angel Choir is an even oblong with a straight end, aisles and 'nave' ending flush. That was the plan of the new E end at Ely (called by Sir Nikolaus 'the missing link' between Lincoln nave and Angel Choir; see *Ely* on Northwold's E end of 1234–52).

The Angel Choir still follows the system of elevation laid down by Geoffrey. That means that a wide, not a high room was built. In France and even more in Germany one would have jumped up to a new height, regardless of what had gone before. The effect would have been sensational, but the harmony of the whole would have been destroyed. In that respect the Angel Choir is a compromise. But how much we owe it! However, while the system remained, in detail all is once again richer, i.e. richer than the nave. The piers alternate between a square core with strong filleted demi-shafts in the main directions and two slender detached Purbeck shafts in each diagonal, and all Purbeck squares with filleted demi-shafts and no detached shafts. All capitals are of Purbeck. The arches have big dogtooth.

Spandrels with blank cusped pointed trefoils (in the same position as the sunk trefoils at Ely). In the aisles once more the indispensable blank arcading. But the arches are cusped now, and above them is blank bar tracery, two twin lights with an encircled quatrefoil. Bar tracery is indeed, as we shall see, the principal innovation of the Angel Choir. It came from Westminster Abbey, where it had, in the design of 1245, been taken over from Reims. So Lincoln took to it after only ten or twelve years. It took about another ten years to appear in Lichfield nave and in Salisbury cloisters (though sooner on a small scale in Salisbury's Bridport tomb). The blank arcading has shafts and a vertical strip of thick leaf crockets. Spandrels with trefoils encircled and unencircled. The aisle windows are spacious, of three lights with bar tracery, two cinquefoiled circles, and a quatrefoiled circle over. Two strips of thick leaf crockets run up between the shafts. The vault continues the system laid down by the nave vault, but leaves out the lateral tiercerons and the transverse ridge ribs.

The B O S S E S are superb, the finest probably of their date, i.e. 1260, in England. The foliage bosses, side by side with the lushest stiff-leaf, display naturalistically leaves of the English countryside – oak, vine, maple, ranunculus and (according to Cave) the yellow water lily. There are also figured bosses, and their quality also is outstanding. One has a pair of wrestlers – one good, one evil? – their bodies modelled with supreme realism and the finest feeling for skin and muscle, and moreover an equally fine feeling for the *tondo* composition. Others show the Coronation of the Virgin, a lady with a page and a puppy, the Tree of Jesse with King David harping in the centre, a Prophet arguing with an Apostle, David and Nathan (?), a man fighting a monster, a monster with wings, two interlaced winged monsters, three interlaced lizard-like monsters, a man and a woman kissing and a third smaller head below with a very grim or worried expression, two elegant ladies' heads with wimples, a man battling with a merman. There are two types in the figures: some are fleshy and broad-faced, but others – especially the Coronation of the Virgin, the lady with the puppy, the apostles and prophets, and the Tree of Jesse – are extremely slender, their movements supple and their faces of that type which the so-called Joseph Master had established in France about 1240 and which the Westminster transept angels took over for England. All the scenes are in the s aisle; the N aisle has only foliage and some grotesques.

The 'nave' of the Angel Choir receives its light from the gorgeous eight-light E window, 59 ft high. The window is the perfectly logical extreme of the bar tracery started at Reims and in Westminster Abbey for two lights. The system is that each light has its own arch and the super-arch is independent of them. In the tympanum is a foiled circle. This the architect of the nave at Amiens in the 1230s

107. LINCOLN Angel Choir, spandrels with angels, c. 1260s–70s

and of the chapter house at Westminster about 1250 had
applied to four lights. There were now two super-arches
and one super-super-arch, all kept sharply separate from
each other. Lincoln has the earliest eight-light window
(c. 1275) preserved anywhere. The logic of the arches is
kept even here. There are seven circles, four quatrefoiled
below, two sexfoiled above, and at the top the large top
circle filled with a ring of six quatrefoils set alternately
upright and diagonally round one sexfoil. The composition
combines breadth and generosity with logic, and the sun
streaming in in the morning gives a heavenly clarity to all
forms. Three strips of thick leaf crockets up the jambs
between the shafts. The next step in large-window design
was to be the Joseph window of the late 1280s in the Nine
Altars Chapel at Durham.

The gallery openings are again two twins, as in St
Hugh's Choir. But they have bar tracery too, and that once

again adds breadth and richness. Encircled quatrefoils
above each two lights. The lights are cusped. The shafts are
of Purbeck, many of them, and with strips of crockets
between. Foliated hoodmoulds on head-stops. And in the
spandrels the ANGELS which have given the 'novum opus'
its name. There are twenty-eight angels plus the Virgin on
the s side, at the w end of bay one from the w, and Christ on
the N side, at the w end of bay one from the w. Christ is
displaying his wound and a censing angel is next to him.
The Virgin is giving her breast to the standing child, and
there is a censing angel next to her too. Of the angels only a
few can here be singled out. One basic stylistic distinction
appears at once. Christ and the Virgin belong to the style
derived from the Joseph Master and Westminster. So do
King David (E bay; s side) and two angels (with a book and
with a scroll – first and second bays from w; s side). But
most of the angels, and among them the most famous –

Angel with a little Soul, Angel of the Expulsion, Angel with scales (St Michael), Angels with hawk and gauntlet, with two crowns, with a scroll, with a viol – are heavier, with round faces and stronger limbs. In fact more than two hands can be distinguished, but only two masters. Below the brackets of the angels are exquisite little heads.

The use of angels in triangular fields such as these, especially along with the gallery tracery here, was no doubt inspired by the Westminster transept angels, probably finished by the mid-1250s and influenced by sculpture at Reims. The motif as such was of course not new at Lincoln, though in Geoffrey's choir aisles it had taken the form of small-scale self-enclosed half-figures. The Westminster censing angels are on a more monumental scale, being higher up, than the Angel Choir figures, but fragments of Angel Choir themes can also be found on a lesser scale in the Westminster ambulatory chapels. And music-making angels in Worcester choir (triforium s side), if their attributes are original, may precede Westminster's (Singleton 1978). For the type of small-scale winged demi-angels on Salisbury's former choir screen, N P suggests early manuscript sources (see the companion volume, Salisbury, *Furnishings*, N E transept). Ultimately, surely the Roman triumphal-arch composition with flying victories in the spandrels was behind some of this?

The clerestory carries the most conspicuous innovation. The windows are here of four lights. Each twin has an encircled trefoil, and the whole an encircled octofoil. But the wall-passage is placed between them and an open repetition towards the inside of the whole: mullions and tracery. This generous duplication – a waste of money for beauty's sake – creates the most wonderful sense of transparency, by seeing one layer through the other. Shades of Geoffrey even here, though it is true that the gallery at Westminster Abbey had done the same in a less conspicuous context.

The vault is the same as in the aisles, i.e. the nave system without the lateral tiercerons and transverse ridge ribs – not an improvement. The ridge rib has crockets l. and r. – shades of Geoffrey again. The infill-stones of the vault are blue lias (Clifton-Taylor 1972). The vaulting-shafts stand on long, fully crocketed leaf corbels. One of them at the foot (N E) has the Imp which has lured more people into Lincoln Cathedral than anything else.

As for the EXTERIOR, the E view of the cathedral is of course as much dominated by the great E window as is the interior. Otherwise the E front is restless. Three parts flanked and divided by buttresses. Blank trefoiled foliage above the base moulding. Stiff-leaf capitals. Mouldings with keels and fillets. Head and leaf stops. The outer reveals of the E window have two orders of crockets. To the l. and r. just one narrow blank arch – an unfortunate overdoing-it. The side parts have their three-light win-

dows also with two orders of crockets. Two cinquefoils and one quatrefoil over. To the outside, but painfully not to the inside, the windows are connected with the blank arcading on the buttresses by a normal blank arch. To the inside there is instead an abnormally narrow blank arch with continuous mouldings. It has not even thus enough space, and stands partly on the capital of the window shaft. On the buttresses, apart from blank arcading, places for statues with trefoil canopies coming forward like the head canopies of mid or later c 13 funeral monuments. Gablets (also as in monuments) with crockets and head-stops. The main gable of the E wall has a five-light window (into the space between vaults and roof, of course, invisible inside the Angel Choir). Its middle light is higher than the others – an end-of-the-century motif – and there are two trefoils in circles for the side parts, and for the middle an encircled octofoil of which each foil is again a trefoil. All mouldings are continuous rolls. To the l. and r. climbing blank arches. At the top of the gable small figure of the Virgin. Crockets on the gable sides. The side gables are of course entirely sham. They are quite small, with a blank window of two plus two lights and a cinquefoiled circle above. Flat continuous mouldings. The twins have above an unencircled trefoil – i.e. we are on the way out of the c 13 and towards the style of the cloister. Polygonal pinnacles of the usual type, but more richly appointed than any others. Even the buttresses have steep gables with crockets.

The N and s sides of the Angel Choir have three-light windows like the E walls of the aisles, buttresses with crocketed gables, and flying buttresses, i.e. the system is continued. It is interrupted by the three chantry chapels, two s flanking the Judgement Porch, one N; all Perp and basically similar, three bays each, with buttresses, friezes, parapets and pinnacles (for their insides, see *Furnishings*, Angel Choir aisles, below). The gallery windows – as in the nave – are so tiny that they can hardly be seen. Four-light clerestory windows. They have no shafts; all continuous rolls. The windows alternate with blank arches. The inner shaft of each of these arches is short, because it stands on the capital of the window shaft. To the l. and r. of each four-light window a tall blank arch. One curious piece of untidiness must be pointed out. On both sides the westernmost aisle window has the tracery left unmoulded. The buttress following borders on, and half hides, that of St Hugh's transept. In fact a fifth window was started, and of this one blocked light, one shaft capital, and the start of unmoulded tracery can be seen. It looks as if there had been a plan to demolish some of St Hugh's work.

The Angel Choir's two lateral portals open into the bay just E of the high altar. The more sumptuous s one is the so-called Judgement Porch. Unfortunately it is over-restored. It is so deep that it has a big gable over, decorated with blank trefoils, quatrefoils and a cinquefoil. Two en-

108. LINCOLN Judgement Porch, late C13,
south portal to Angel Choir

tries with a *trumeau* dividing them. Cinquecusped arches. The *trumeau* was renewed in the Perp style, as its section and leaves prove. That the Virgin is not medieval will be believed without proof. That it is of *c.* 1930 and not of the Victorian age is less easily believed. Tympanum with seated Christ in a pointed, elongated quatrefoil. Angels around and indications of the Blessed and the Damned l. and r. The hairy devils will be noticed at once. The Mouth of Hell curiously enough is below Christ. The jambs of the portal each have three thin shafts with stiff-leaf capitals, or rather had them. They carry nodding-trefoil canopies with gablets, just like mid or later C13 funeral monuments (and just as we have seen them in the E façade), but they are here completely detached, and behind all this the complete main shafting goes up to the capitals (shades of Geoffrey once more!). The voussoirs are of three orders, divided by very fine mouldings. The outer order has sixteen figures in

stiff-leaf foliage opening out to form almond-shaped niches for them. Eight are male, eight female. The latter represent the wise and foolish Virgins. The middle voussoir is all filigree foliage. The inner has twelve seated figures, six queens and six kings. The origin of all this, the tympanum with the quatrefoil and the composition of the voussoirs, is the work of *c.* 1250–60 at Westminster Abbey, just as the origin of the angels inside was there. In fact the style of the sculpture of the portal is more like the sharp, alabaster-like style of Westminster with its long parallel folds than like that of the angels. The Westminster connections come out even more patently in the large figures on the buttresses by the portal. Facing w and E, i.e. towards the portal, Ecclesia and Synagogue, both in very shallow niches. The brackets stand on three-quarter figures, an angel and Moses. To the outside, facing s two more female figures, also with the characteristic belts. Against the next buttress to the E (just above the E end of the Russell Chantry) the much discussed 'Queen Margaret'. Against the broader buttress after that (at the E end of the s choir aisle) a king and a queen. They may be original; see their proportions and drapery folds – those breaking at the queen's feet and the baggy ones along the king's side. But the heads and more must be completely redone.

The N portal is simpler. It also has a *trumeau*, and this also is a Perp remodelling. It carries the arms of Richard II. The C13 details are also all victorianized, except the head-stops of the blank arches to the l. and r. The tympanum has again a big pointed quatrefoil and a bracket for a figure. But there is no figure. The head beneath the bracket is unscathed.

### THE FOURTEENTH AND FIFTEENTH CENTURIES

This at Lincoln is a gleaning operation. Once the Angel Choir was complete, the cathedral was complete. What followed were improvements and replacements. They can be taken in chronological order.

CROSSING TOWER. In 1307–11 the tower was heightened, a daring thing to do. The dates are established by a letter of indulgence for gifts to the 'novum opus' in 1307 and a problem connected with the bell ropes in 1311. The master mason was *Richard of Stow*, whose contract for the 'novum opus' is of 1306. He had been master mason to the Lincoln Eleanor Cross in 1291–3. Externally the new work starts at the frieze of blank quatrefoils. The C13 buttresses are carried on, but their detail changes, of course. The bell-stage ('Great Thoms Nest' to Celia Fiennes, for its great bell) has two pairs of exceedingly tall twin openings. Elaborate, far-sticking-out leaf crockets. Each light is ogee-headed and has a pointed trefoil above the ogee. In the tympanum a pointed quatrefoil. Ballflower on the main

arches and the gables. The pretty openwork parapet and the four lead pinnacles were added in 1774 by *Essex*. The lead spire had been blown down in 1548 (never replaced, though that was contemplated by the Dean in 1774, only to be squashed by Essex, says Dr Cocke). Inside, the early C14 is not visible, as a vault is put in to hide it. It is a most ingenious lierne vault, assigned to the later C14. It is a development from the vault of the s w chapel. On paper it too seems to be a four-bay vault calling for a central support. Only where the four parts had been quadripartite they are now tierceron stars with ridge ribs in both directions. But owing to the rise of the vault towards the centre this simplicity of design on paper is not noticed. Instead one sees a middle square, set into a diagonally placed square, set into the square walls of the tower, and that is of course one of the ways of setting out proportional systems in the Middle Ages without getting into the arithmetic trouble of square roots.

The BISHOP'S EYE. Probably in the 1330s the huge circular window of c. 1220–30 in the main s transept was filled with the most elaborate flowing tracery – two lime-leaves side by side, as it were, and any number of mouchettes taking the place of the veining. To the transept the window is surrounded by a charming double band of filigree quatrefoils etc., one parallel to the wall, the other in the reveals, and all with ogee forms wherever possible. Outside below the window runs a curious frieze of completely flat, unmoulded interlocked lozenges, and above is a five-light window also with flowing tracery, but this of a more current pattern. It lights – very lavishly indeed – the roof of the transept. The gable at the same time, one assumes, was given its unique form of crocketing – a band of pierced double-curved forms.

WEST FRONT. Here, probably in the late C14, a large window with Perp tracery replaced the C13 windows, which, by the surviving shafting, cannot have been smaller. The aisle w windows are of the same time. They cut asymmetrically into the C11 system. Below the w window a Gallery of Kings was introduced, as Exeter had received one a little earlier. It cuts off the top of Bishop Alexander's portal. Eleven bearded, seated figures. The carver endeavoured to avoid uniformity. The position of the legs varies and achieves in the middle figure a high degree of artificiality. On this C14 motif of cross-legged kings, see Exeter w front; also, considerably restored, Lichfield w front.

Then, in the C15, at an unknown date, the w towers were heightened to take their place beside the crossing tower. The buttresses on the w side continue polygonal, as the Norman ones had been, and on the e side they turn polygonal. The bell-openings in pairs of two lights each were adopted from the crossing tower. They now have two transoms, but the part below the lower transom is blank.

The details also take the crossing tower into account; but all is less fancifully decorated. Originally the towers had recessed needle spires, but these were taken down as unsafe in 1807. Gibbs's and James's suggestion c. 1730 that the spires be removed provoked a riot (Cocke). Presumably the pinnacles were renewed or added to match the central tower's in 1807 too. Inside, the towers are lierne-vaulted, much like the crossing tower. The centre is a square, a star overlaps it and goes beyond it. All is cusped.

The WELL-HOUSE, NE of the e end. Small, hexagonal, shafts with fillets at the corners. Pyramid roofs with rolls up the edges. It all looks perfectly convincing, yet Dugdale shows only a wooden shed here. Dr Cocke has no evidence of Essex's involvement, but Lumby (†1804) could easily have made such a design.

FURNISHINGS, E TO W

Our source on the Victorian glass is the late Canon Binnall's excellent booklet on sale at the cathedral. Much of the quality of Lincoln's C19 glass was due to the interest of enlightened men, including Dean Ward (1846–60, who may or may not have been related to the Ward of Ward & Hughes) and the lawyer-connoisseur Charles Winston (who also advised at Norwich and Gloucester).

*Retrochoir (Angel Choir E of the reredos)* STAINED GLASS. Great e window by *Ward & Hughes*, 1855. Not at all bad. For more specific appreciation, see Binnall. The original C13 heraldic medallions were replaced 1762 by *Peckitt* of York. – Clerestory lights, Angel Choir and e side e transepts: sixteen single figures of apostles and other saints by the *Sutton* brothers (on whom see *Nave* below) inserted c. 1865–70. – ORGAN CASE. Small, with some rococo decoration. – MONUMENTS. N wall: Bartholomew Lord Burghersh †1355. Tomb-chest with ogee panels. Effigy, and at his head and feet standing pairs of angels, one holding a shield with his arms, the other his soul in a napkin. Hanging canopy of three stepped ogee arches. Tierceron-star vaulting inside. – Between N aisle and 'nave' two tomb-chests. Robert Burghersh and Bishop Burghersh †1340. On their N sides, pairs of standing or seated figures; on their s sides, shields in panels. On the second, effigy of the bishop. Of the canopies only odd pieces remain. – St Hugh. The special shrine made to contain his head was of course robbed and destroyed. What survives is part of the base, two bays by one, remade apparently in the early C14. Kneeling niches with nodding ogee canopies. Tiny apsidal vaults. Top encrusted with leaf, interspersed with faces. At each corner an angel, two mutilated, others of poor quality. On N and s sides shields bearing Instruments of the Passion (Palliser). – In the 'nave' Queen Eleanor. She was, with Edward I, present at the consecration in 1280 and died in 1291 at Harby, not far from Lincoln. The first halting-place of the funeral cortège was Lincoln. The effigy is a copy of that in Westminster Abbey, made by *William Torel* of London. The effigy and the canopy are of 1891. – Between 'nave' and s aisle Cantelupe Chantry, founded in 1355. Tall double canopy, cusped ogee arches and filigree gables. Typically Dec the idea of the buttresses set diagonally. The canopy is thin in depth, but it is vaulted inside all the same. There are now two tomb-chests beneath: Lord Cantelupe, only the trunk of a figure, and Prior Wymbysh † 1461, headless figure. The head lay on a helm. – In the n aisle Bishop Wordsworth † 1885. By *Bodley & Garner*. Recumbent effigy. Big canopy. – In the s aisle William Hilton R.A. † 1839 and Peter de Wint † 1849. 1864 by *Edward Blore*. Tomb-chest without effigies. But scenes carved by *I. Forsyth* after paintings by Hilton who, in the inscription, is called 'one of the most eminent historical painters this country has produced'. – Dean Butler † 1894. Alabaster, with recumbent effigy. By *Chavalliaud*, working for Farmer & Brindley's. – For chantry chapels to n and s, see *Aisles* below.

*Aisles, Angel Choir*    STAINED GLASS. To the l. of the great E window, E end n aisle, c 13 glass said to have come from the nave. Installed here in the c 18 by *Lumby* (Colvin). Jesse Tree figures and medallions with scenes from lives of saints, and magnificent borders. – To the r. of the great E window, E end s aisle, also c 13 and similar. – N aisle NE window († 1859) by *Ward & Hughes*. Nine medallions with life of Elijah. – Also on the n aisle, St Hugh window by *Henry Holiday*, inserted 1900, and a window by *Clayton & Bell*, inserted 1863. – Opposite, s aisle SE window († 1862), made in Nuremberg. Nine panels (worn) from the Old Testament. Tracery lights from the New Testament. – Also on the s aisle, a window of 1762 by *Peckitt*, intended to list chancellors of the cathedral since 1092. – STONE SCREENS. The first bays from the w are continuations of the screen at the w side of the retrochoir, and this is the reverse of the screens l. and r. and behind the reredos (see below). Their upper parts must be by *James Essex* (see below). But the screen in the next bay of the N aisle is original. It is the back of the Easter Sepulchre (N side of sanctuary, below). – MONUMENTS. A number of brass indents. Evelyn writes in 1654 that 'soldiers lately knocked off most of them'. – Between s aisle and sanctuary, chantry of Katharine Swynford, John of Gaunt's wife, † 1410, and her daughter, the Countess of Westmorland, † 1440. The monument is not complete. Four-centred arch panelled with cusped lozenges. Two tomb-chests, the western one of Purbeck marble with shields in plain roundels. On both lids there are indents for brasses. Iron GRILLE towards the aisle. The aspect towards the chancel has certain peculiar features which will be described presently. – For monuments farther E (except the following), see *Retrochoir* above.

CHANTRY CHAPELS. The FLEMING CHANTRY projects from the N aisle of the retrochoir. Earliest and externally plainest of the three (Bishop Fleming † 1431). The forms used are relatively few and big. Inside, the tomb-chest is between aisle and chapel. It has open arcading and behind it appears the corpse of the bishop in the winding sheet. It is the earliest example in England of this representation intended to shock. In France examples go back some thirty years further. On the tomb-chest recumbent effigy with two angels at the head. Canopy with hanging arches. Angels as pendants. Vault inside the canopy. Top as flat as if it were broken off. Doorway to the w of the monument. – The other two chapels flank the Judgement Porch on the s. RUSSELL CHANTRY (bishop † 1494). The front of the chapel to the s aisle is tripartite with a doorway balanced by a sham doorway with panelled back. In the middle the Purbeck tomb-chest. The arch is so flat that it is really a cambered lintel. It is panelled inside. In the chapel PAINTINGS round the walls by *Duncan Grant* (1958–9). They are curiously naive and out of touch, with a degree of naturalism, of idealism, and of stylization comparable to Puvis de Chavannes (or Augustus John or Hans Feibusch) rather than to mid-c 20 wall painters. – Perp GRILLE to the s of the tomb-chest. – LONGLAND CHANTRY (bishop † 1548). Externally a companion piece to Bishop Russell's, but more lavish in detail, especially inside. The front towards the aisle, while also tripartite and also provided with a false, panelled doorway, is extremely elaborate. The most interesting fact about this is that, when, at this very end of Gothic design in England, such elaboration was demanded, architects went to the French Flamboyant for inspiration rather than to the native Perp, and as the French Flamboyant is in its spirit, and even in such forms as ogee reticulation, so similar to the English early c 14 Dec, it is almost like a Dec revival. But there is another equally interesting aspect to this chapel. In closely examining the w wall inside, one discovers on the cornice below the ornate niches unmistakable, though small, Italian Renaissance details (shell-lunettes). Nothing else is Renaissance. The large punning inscription 'Longa terra Mensuram eius Dominus dedit' towards the aisle is e.g. still in black letter. – Original panelled ceiling with moulded beams and bosses. – DOOR original too, with iron handle. – All three chapels have heraldic glass by *Clayton & Bell*, end of c 19.

*Sanctuary, Angel Choir*    REREDOS, c 18. Stone, with partly open tracery. Designed by *James Essex*, 1769, made and signed by *James Pink*, 'the nonconformist mason who worked for decades on the most intricately carved and Catholic parts of the cathedral' (Cocke 1975). The design is fairly convincing archaeologically. Essex was indeed one of the first, if not the first, to take the reproduction of genuine motifs or pieces seriously. Here the triple gable was modelled (one is bound to say, not closely) on Bishop Luda's tomb canopy at Ely Cathedral, i.e. near to a style of *c.* 1300 that suited the Angel Choir. Tracery on the back added by *Buckler*, 1857, and more tracery inserted by *Pearson* (Cocke 1975; Quiney 1979); and at some stage none of the tracery was open (old photograph in Pevsner 1972, and see painting now in NE transept). – SCREEN WALLS l. and r. and returned one bay to the w (cf. *Aisles* above), the parts by the reredos indubitably by *Essex*, the others perhaps partly old (it has been suggested that the N bay is old, the S bay *Pink* on his own).

EASTER SEPULCHRE (N side of sanctuary). This charming piece is worth the closest study. It is of six bays, the three eastern ones being the sepulchre proper. The other three were intended to be a funeral monument and now contain the slab recording Remigius, the builder of the

Early Norman cathedral (but for his burial slab, see *Nave, Monuments,* below). The canopy stands on arches with pointed cusping. The small capitals of the shafts on which the arches stand have naturalistic foliage. Gables with crockets and finials, buttress shafts with pinnacles. Inside the two threes are divided by a cross wall, and this also and the E end walls have naturalistic leaves all over. Back wall with blank arches, two lights, trefoil-headed, a trefoil over, and an encircled trefoil in the tympanum. The tomb-chest or base of the E part carries three sleeping soldiers in relief. Finally the little vaults inside. They have flying ribs, i.e. no cells, the earliest example of this rare formation on record. For the Easter Sepulchre, judging by its details, tallies with the cloisters, which were being built by 1296. So *c.* 1290–1300 might be its most likely date. As we shall see, flying ribs also occur on the pulpitum (see main

110. LINCOLN Easter Sepulchre, *c.* 1290s–1300, north side of sanctuary

*Crossing* below), dated only 'early C 14'. Elsewhere they occur in the Berkeley Chapel vestibule at Bristol Cathedral, of the first decade after 1300, and then *c.* 1320–40 on the pulpitum at Southwell. (On possible links with the Eleanor crosses and London court style, and on the export of English influence to the Continent, see General Introduction.) Flying ribs, at least in England, never appeared on a large scale.

SEDILIA (?) (s side of sanctuary), a curious, not much noted detail to the l. of the Swynford Chantry (described under *Aisles*, Monuments, above). There are here two bays of a screen with diapers of stylized foliage, flanked by shafts with naturalistic foliage. The tops of the panels are identical with those on the back wall of the Easter Sepulchre. The upper part of the composition is broken off, and here runs a classical cornice said to be of *c.* 1670.

*North-east transept* SCREENS. Two Perp wooden screens to the E chapels, one with two-light divisions, the other including linenfold panels. – DOOR to the Treasury. C 13, its ironwork in long branches and scrolls. – SCULPTURE. Statue of a deacon, C 15, found on the site of the Hospital of St Giles. – Also two most valuable and beautiful fragments of Norman relief sculpture. Seated Christ and a Saint. One fragment contains Christ's halo and the dove above it, with scrollwork l. and r. Professor Zarnecki has proved that the seated Christ and the Saint fit together, but the halo and the dove with the scrolls do not fit the Christ. He suggests that the former two fragments belong to the S portal of the Norman W front, but the scrollwork with the dove was the top of a Tree of Jesse placed above the middle portal, aptly separating the New from the Old Testament scenes (see *Norman cathedral*, above). – PAINTING. Fresco paintings of four ancient bishops buried in the NE transept, where tombs were destroyed in the Civil War. By *Vincenzo Damini*, 1728, a curious intruder. (Dr Cocke suggests that they would look splendid if cleaned.) – Annunciation, by the *Rev. W. Peters*, 1799, oil on canvas. Formerly part of the reredos, after Essex's restoration. This picture would also deserve a good restorer's treatment. – STAINED GLASS, N wall. In the upper lights, geometrical patterns, one lancet signed and dated *W. Peckitt* of York, 1762. Lower lights by the *Suttons* (cf. *Retrochoir*, E clerestory lights).

*East crossing* IRON GRILLES, 1297 (sometimes partly hidden by hangings *versus* draughts). A very simple timeless pattern of affronted scrolls and one of the finest pieces of C 13 ironwork in England. The pattern is much the same as that of the iron grille of Queen Eleanor's monument in Westminster Abbey (q.v. in the companion volume, *Furnishings*, Feretory). – STRAINER BEAMS from the E to the W crossing piers, over the side gates to the choir. They were concealed in 1779 by Gothic canopy work designed by *Lumby* under *Essex* (Binnall, Colvin).

*South-east transept* SCREENS. Perp wooden screens to the NE chapel and the W chapel. – In the W chapel (Choristers' Vestry) a superb stone SCREEN of the early C 14, decorated with big leaf diaper of four-petalled flowers, also to the N, i.e. the choir aisle. In the flowers such unexpected little motifs as a bird's nest and a dog. Beneath a long stone LAVATORIUM, its front decorated with plain Perp panelling. Also, a plain FIREPLACE was at some time put into this chapel. – STAINED GLASS. Excellent imitation-C 13 glass in the three tiers of S windows by *George Hedgeland*, over the vestry on the W by the *Suttons*, and in the SE chapel grisaille-work which may well have been designed by *Winston*.

*North choir aisle* TREASURY (formerly NE transept W chapel). Converted 1959–60 by *Louis Osman*. It is the first in England of a kind handled with much more swagger in Italy. The main feature is a well-designed showcase for church plate, both the cathedral's and from parishes of the diocese. – The STAINED GLASS, abstract, coloured below but all in greys above, is by *Geoffrey Clarke*. – SCREENS to the choir. Of stone, with blank arcading. The first late C 13, as the leaves of the hoodmould stops turn naturalistic, the other with the big dogtooth of the 1240s or 1250s, i.e. after the fall of the adjoining tower. Whorls as hoodmould stops. – MONUMENTS. More brass indents.

*South choir aisle* SCREEN to the transept W chapel: see above. – SCREENS to the choir. The first like the first on the N side. The others of *c.* 1310, i.e. with tracery still of pre-ogee type, but ballflower. The capitals with the small naturalistic leaves of Easter Sepulchre and cloisters. – MONUMENTS. More brass indents. – Plain Purbeck base of the Shrine of Little St Hugh, the boy who disappeared in 1255, the supposed victim of a ritual murder by the Jews of Lincoln. It is a sinister story and ought to be pondered as one enjoys the purity and splendour of nave and Angel Choir. – In the CANONS' VESTRY a piece of very fine STAINED GLASS, a Presentation in the Temple, Austrian, 1544 (Binnall). The vestry still has its simple Gothick panelling of 1776 by *Essex* (Cocke). – Two windows on the aisle by *Clayton & Bell* were inserted in 1900.

*St Hugh's Choir* STALLS. There are three tiers and front desks on the N and S sides, two tiers and front desks in the return stalls, i.e. on the W side. They are for the canons, with below them the vicars choral and below these the choristers. The date of the stalls is fairly well known. John of Welbourn, treasurer of the cathedral from 1350 to his death in 1380, is called 'inceptor et consultor inceptionis stallorum novorum'. At the base of a stall close to the Dean's Stall (S 31, numbered according to the cathedral booklet) are moreover the arms of Dean Stretely, who was dean from 1361 to 1372. So the date must be *c.* 1365–70. Much restoration was done in the C 19, and especially of the lowest tier of N and S seats the majority is Victorian.

The system of decoration is as follows: The two top tiers have misericords and elbow-rests between the seats. Above the top tier are tall canopies with spires, the earliest enclosing tabernacles with little vaults inside. The statues in the tabernacles are all of 1892–3. The system of the canopies and a good many motifs of the misericords etc. were taken over about 1380 in the stalls at Chester Cathedral. (As Lincoln's stalls are partly restored, and York's were burned in the early C19, Chester has the best C14 set in the North of England: Harvey (1978) suggests the hand of *Hugh Herland* in all three.) On the N and S sides the third tier has backs with pierced quatrefoils enclosing figural motifs. The front desks have panel tracery with kings and angels in relief. In addition three standing saints on the front desk in the S W corner. The sculptural quality of the carving is not equal. The best work is in the MISERICORDS. Comments on a (necessarily limited) selection of them and also the SUPPORTERS l. and r. of the misericords and the ELBOW-RESTS between the seats follow.

s side, top tier. S1 Knight and Griffin; S4 a lion fighting a dragon; S5 an eagle in flight; S6 a king seated, part of an abbreviated Tree of Jesse to which the supporters also belong; S9 Siren; S15 two interlaced peacocks, and pairs of cranes as supporters, a very fine composition; S16 an ape on a unicorn facing an ape on a lion; S18 Sir Percival of Galles (?); S21 Judith and Holofernes; S23 Adoration of the Magi with, as the supporters, angels making music; S25 Alexander the Great raised to the sky by eagles (cf. Wells, Gloucester and Chester); S26 Tristan and Iseult and a squire and a lady-in-waiting as supporters; S27 a unicorn hiding in a virgin's lap; S28 the Coronation of the Virgin with angels making music on the supporters; S30 knight on a stumbling horse (the Fall of Pride) and on the elbow-rest the Pelican; S31 the Resurrection of Christ with the two figures of the Noli me tangere on the supporters. In the second tier the poppy-head by sa has Delilah with Samson's hair and Samson at her feet. The elbow-rest by sk shows a fine coiled dragon. sl has St George and the Dragon, sq a young man fighting a lion.

n side, top tier. N1 the Ascension of Christ (only his feet and the hem of his mantle are visible – which was a current medieval convention), censing angels on the supporters; N2 Assumption of the Virgin, Annunciation in the supporters; N9 lion's head, leaves sprouting out of its mouth; a beautiful swan on the elbow-rest; N10 ploughman with two horses and on the supporters a man harrowing and a man sowing; N12 a lion and a dragon fighting: N14 a mermaid; N16 St John in the cauldron; N17 on the elbow-rest a man's head, his tongue sticking out; N20 a boy on a crane; N24 Sir Yvain trying to enter the castle, the portcullis falling on his horse, heads of soldiers on the supporters; N27 a wild man shaking down acorns for the pigs on the supporters; N28 on the elbow-rest a naked figure

crouching; N31 a knight attacked by dragons, on the poppy-head monkeys playing and one monkey hanged. On the next tier note Nr with a pelican, Nw with a monkey on a bier, and Nx (the one in front of the Dean's Stall) with a naked child rising from a shell to face a dragon (cf. Chester and Manchester stalls). The animals in the quatrefoils of the backs of the third tier are mostly Victorian. Among the original ones are on the N side crouching lions, a fox carrying off geese, an owl, and, at the w end, the pelican, on the s side a bear, a squirrel, and, at the w end, three fables of the fox including his sermon to the geese.

BISHOP'S THRONE. 1778, by *William Lumby*, clerk of works under James Essex. According to Dr Cocke, 'fussed up by Benson' the C19 canon of Lincoln later Archbishop of Canterbury. – PULPIT. 1863–4, designed by *Sir G. G. Scott*. With apostles, scenes in relief, and a tall canopy. – CHANDELIER. Of brass, two tiers of arms. Dated 1698. – LECTERN. Brass, a spirited example of the traditional eagle type. Inscribed as the work of *William Burroughs* of London, 1667. Burroughs also cast the identical lectern in Canterbury Cathedral; see too his lectern at Wells.

*North transept* STONE GATEWAY to the N choir aisle. With its companion in the s transept, flanking the C14 pulpitum (see *Crossing* below). These gateways are C13, gorgeous pieces of the early Angel Choir years. Three Purbeck shafts in the jambs, big dogtooth and a chain of big flowers between. The richest stiff-leaf capitals. Arch with big dogtooth, then an order of openwork stiff-leaf foliage starting from a dragon at the bottom l. and r., and then again big dogtooth. Hoodmould with dogtooth on stiff-leaf stops. In the spandrels blank pointed trefoils with stiff-leaf cusps: these trefoils look C18 (Cocke) and indeed there was some work on 'arches at west end of choir aisles' by *Pink* under Essex (Colvin). – SCREENS. Two of the wooden screens to the chapels are Perp, with two-light divisions. It is rewarding to compare their differences. – STAINED GLASS. The rose-window (Dean's Eye) is the most complete piece of original glass in the cathedral (restored by *Ward & Hughes*, 1855). Its general effect of deep and rich glow and unity in variety needs no comment. What is represented is no easier of recognition than in French glass of the same C13 date. Why then is C20 abstraction – Mr Clarke's e.g. in the Treasury – yet not the same? It is a matter of depth, of layers of significance, which cannot be taken up here. In the centre of the rose God, in the top outer circle Christ. Around God worshipping figures. In one of the foils of the great quatrefoil a contemporary figure from a Tree of Jesse is inserted. Close to Christ the Evangelists and then Saints, Bishops, Angels. Inserted scenes e.g. the Death and Funeral of the Virgin, Jesus among the Doctors, the Foolish Virgins, the body of St Hugh, Joseph chosen as a husband for the Virgin, Adam and Eve. In the lancet windows below original grisaille glass. In the large lancet at ground-level to the l. of the doorway five c. 1360 angels from the great w window. In the lancet to the r. grisaille glass. – N chapel windows by *Harry Stammers*, 1953–8, *Christopher Webb*, 1955, and *A. K. Nicholson*. – PULPIT (mobile). A charming piece of mahogany, evidently of c. 1760–70. The body stands on Gothick ogee arches and carries Gothick quatrefoils. The stairs, however, are simple Georgian (slim turned balusters), except that the tread-ends are carved with tiny ogee arcading. – MONUMENT. In the s chapel to soldiers killed in the Indian wars. By *E. Richardson* of Melbury Terrace, London, 1851. With the two usual mourning soldiers. They lean on their guns as if they were extinguished torches.

*Crossing* PULPITUM. A gorgeous piece of early C 14 decoration, the finest in a county of many Dec splendours. It makes one understand how the Dec style came to be called Dec. (According to Dr Cocke it was extensively reworked by *Pink* under *Essex*, but except for some king figures it is hard to see what was done.) The pulpitum consists of four arches l. and r. of the portal. The four arches, really niches, have detached buttress shafts in front – making a depth of about 18 in. But the total depth is of course much more; for the pulpitum contains a vaulted chamber and staircase inside besides the passage through. The passage is vaulted in two bays with moulded diagonal and ridge ribs and bosses. Interestingly, these are flying ribs (kindly checked for me again by John Cherry) and on a slightly larger scale than the first miniature ones of the Easter Sepulchre in the sanctuary (above), more like those over the Bristol vestibule and perhaps contemporary with them or with those of the Southwell pulpitum. The chamber to the s (known as the Vergers' Arms) is also of two bays (N to S), but the ribs are here plainly single-chamfered. The staircase starts with a small vault too, and even here is a broad leaf frieze for the delectation of the eye. What delectations the front of the pulpitum has to offer can scarcely be described. The buttress shafts are covered with diapers and have three tiers of gablets. The back walls are all diaper, divided halfway up by a band of very large leaves. The arches are of course ogee. They are cusped and subcusped and have the customary crockets and finials. In the arch mouldings leaves, flowers and also tiny animals. At the springing of the arches grotesques. A little vault inside each niche. Spandrels with diaper. Flat parapet with another frieze of big leaves. The portal has two orders of shafts and a big ogee arch. To the l. and r. of the finial brackets for images. Two more in the diapered spandrels. (For stone gateways flanking the pulpitum, see N *transept* above and s *transept* below.) – ORGAN CASE. Gothic, 1826, by *E. J. Willson* (the Lincoln antiquary and collaborator with John Britton). If it looks rather spiky and busy under the medieval vaults, it does have a soaring quality rare for its date and is worth more respect than some writers give it

(Gillingham, who also says the polygonal *chaire* case on the E face is of 1851 by *Charles Allen*).

*South transept* STONE GATEWAY. Exactly like the N gateway, except that the band of capitals of the shafts has on the l. dragons (also owls), on the r. standing little men and dragons. – SCREENS. To the N chapel, known as the Works Chantry, a stone screen, over-restored. In the jambs of the doorway kneeling pairs of figures, benefactors of the building, as the inscription shows: 'Oremus pro benefactoribus istius ecclesie', in the gable seated bishop, in the finial royal coat of arms, datable to some time between 1358 and the early C 15. Inside the chapel a nicely decorated stone BRACKET. – To the second and third chapels the screens are of wood, Perp, and similar to those in the N transept. – STAINED GLASS. In the Bishop's Eye a gorgeous jumble of C 12–14 fragments, including substantial remains of the original Doom of c. 1330. He who examines it really closely can make thrilling discoveries. In the lancets below C 13 medallions. – In the s chapel, acceptable mid-C 19 imitation of C 13 medallions, signed by *H. Hughes* of London, 1862, in memory of Dean Ward † 1860. – w windows: N by *Ward & Hughes* († 1861 and 1875), middle and s by *Hardman* (a pair, c. 1884). – MONUMENTS. Bishop Edward King † 1910. By *W. B. Richmond*, 1913. An intruder from Rome, sculpturally speaking, but really a very excellent piece in the late C 19 tradition of bronze modelling, i.e. naturalistic and very lively. Inscription by *Eric Gill*, 1915. – Dean Fuller † 1699. Tablet with striking head, not *sympathique*, on a bad, flat bust. – Bishop John Dalderby † 1320. He was venerated as a saint and received a shrine. Of this only two brackets have survived, partly fixed to the vaulting-shafts, partly on octagonal shafts. One of them has some foliage. – In the s chapel Perp tomb-chest to Sir George Tailboys † 1538, with three big shields in quatrefoils. Back wall with panelling and five cows. In the spandrels two more. Cresting, and standing on it three shields.

*Nave and aisles* NAVE ALTAR and RAILINGS around. By *Sir Charles Nicholson*, C 20. – PULPIT. From St Mary, the English church of Rotterdam, built in 1708 (for other fittings from there, see Selwyn College, Cambridge). A fine big piece with a tester, not over-decorated. Curving stair with pierced feathery foliage panels. – FONT. Square, of Tournai marble, i.e. from the Norman cathedral. One of ten in England, the other in a cathedral being at Winchester. The base has enormous flat leaves on the corners, the bowl palmettes in the top corners. Against the sides of the bowl quadrupeds, mostly monstrous.

STAINED GLASS. Lincoln Cathedral, as we have already seen, has been extremely lucky with its Victorian glass. None is desperately bad, and some of the mid-C 19 is about the best of that time in England. It is that designed and made – *suis manibus*, they say in one brass inscription – by

111. LINCOLN Font, mid-C 12. South side of nave

the Revs. *Augustus* and *Frederick Sutton*, sons of Sir Richard Sutton. The glass is frankly in imitation of the C 13. It is successful, and it is never genteel, as so much copying is. By them the last four from the E in the S aisle, two of them dated 1861, the two others also complete by 1862. They also did the great W window, and this is in the C 14 style, with large figures under the right canopies and in some of the right colours. The tracery lights incorporate genuine parts of *c.* 1360. (cf. their work in the Angel Choir clerestory and in the S E transept.) – The rose-window above by *Heaton & Butler* from a design by *Crace*, 1858. – *Charles Winston* supervised some of the glass of this time. Artists whom he respected highly were *George Hedgeland* (S windows of S E transept, above; also W window at Norwich) and his father, *John P. Hedgeland*: by whom the fourth S aisle window from the E, commemorating Armstrong, before 1861. – Its r. neighbour by *Clayton & Bell*, inserted 1900, commemorates a death in 1860. – Farther E, the first window W of the crossing by *Frederick Preedy*, inserted *c.* 1860 (†1799); the second by *William Wailes*, given 1847; the third by *W. E. Chance*, inserted 1855 (†1854). – All on the N aisle by *Ward & Hughes*, *c.* 1860–73.

MONUMENTS. Black (Tournai?) slab found in the cloisters, probably of Bishop Remigius. It is in two parts, as Remigius's indeed was. Giraldus Cambrensis reports about 1200 that it was broken by the debris of a fire which occurred *c.* 1124. On the slab no effigy – a brief Tree of Jesse instead. The reclining figure of Jesse can only just be recognized. But Moses is above him, and Christ is at the top. More figures in the spaces l. and r. At the head two angels, their wings turned up and of a shape similar to those on the other oldest Tournai slab in England, the monument assigned to a bishop of *c.* 1150 at Ely (q.v., N choir aisle). Dating the so-called Remigius is hard, but if one goes by the angels and by the fact that these two are the only figured coffin-lids with no effigy but a different kind of representation, then one would have to assign a date *c.* 1140 to the Lincoln slab, and it cannot be the one broken in a fire *c.* 1124. The argument is of course not conclusive, as Giraldus's date may not be correct. – Bishop Kaye. 1857, by *Richard Westmacott Jr*. Tomb-chest and white-marble effigy, recumbent. – Dean Honywood † 1681. Tablet of good, restrained character. At the top open curly pediment. – In the room under the W tower Mrs Pownall † 1777. Plain white sarcophagus. The inscription is said to be by Horace Walpole.

CHAPTER HOUSE AND CLOISTERS

The chapter house must have been begun before 1220, but building must have taken quite some time. The initial date is given by the fact that the chapter house is mentioned in the *Metrical Life of St Hugh*, which was written between 1220 and 1230. The completing date is stylistic guesswork. The E walk of the cloister is contemporary with the chapter house although, alas, terribly restored. The rest of the cloisters, unnecessary really in a non-monastic cathedral, were started only about 1290. They are mentioned in a letter of Bishop Sutton, dated 1296.

There is a passage between the N E transept and the S E corner of the cloisters. The entry into this passage from the transept is by a doorway of the time of the chapter house. Three jamb-shafts with stiff-leaf capitals. Deep arch mouldings. The doorway does not fit the passage which follows. So, right in front of it, about 1300 another arch was placed, typical of its date in capitals and mouldings. Hoodmould with heads of a king and a bishop. The passage, like the S and W cloister walks, is extremely characteristic of *c.* 1300, like them having four-light openings with Geometrical tracery, already with cusped arches and unencircled pointed quatrefoils, and the top circle (which is not yet given up) filled with alternating rounded and pointed trefoils – all of course in bar tracery and all, incidentally, on a small, almost miniature scale. Also all nicely and busily shafted inside and outside. (The passage openings to the W,

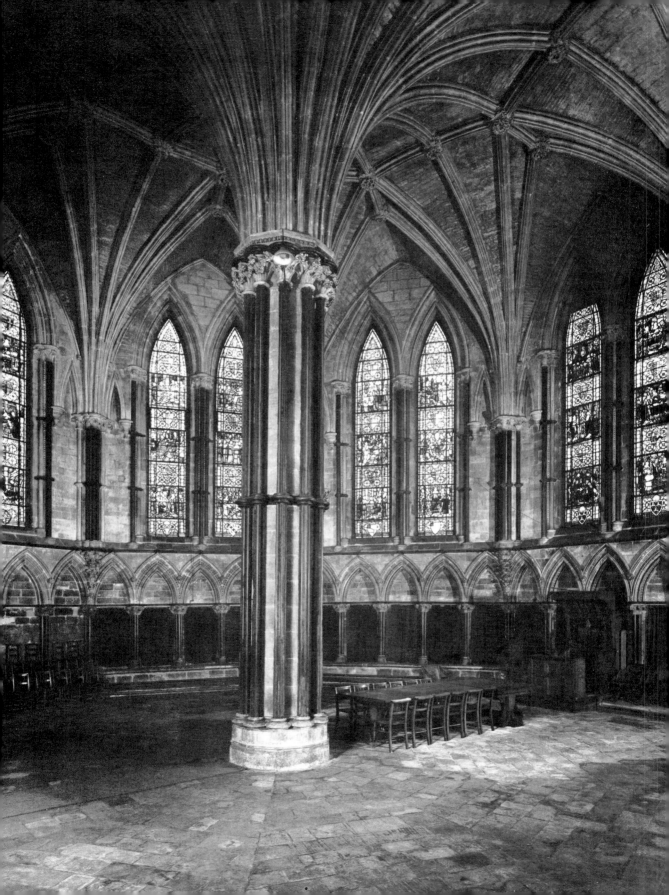

an enclosed open space behind the scenes, are left unde-
tailed.) The capitals in the passage are still naturalistic,
though just turning bossy, and they are bossy or knobbly
or sea-weedy in the cloisters. The passage has a stone vault
with longitudinal ridge ribs and no tiercerons, the cloister
wooden vaults, though the E walk has stone vault-
springers. (To the E of the passage small rooms with much
renewed straight-headed Perp windows on two floors. The
best preserved has four cusped lights. Behind this a room
with moulded beams. The inner walls of this addition to the
passage are timber-framed.) Further description of the
cloisters follows that of the chapter house.

## Chapter house

The chapter-house entrance is, like most of the others at
Lincoln, double. Quatrefoil *trumeau*. Arches with openwork foliage, all Victorian, i.e. *Pearson's*. Cusped quatrefoil in the tympanum. The chapter house is a decagon.
Centrally planned chapter houses became an English speciality. Early examples (usefully summed up by Stratford
1978) began with Worcester's originally circular one with
its ten bays and central pier, and included a twelve-sided
one at Abbey Dore, both of the C 12. But Lincoln's ten-
sided one is the first prominent example of a polygonal
chapter house (with Beverley and Westminster shortly
after, and then the undercroft at Wells, all octagons).
Whether the fact that Worcester and Lincoln in the early-
mid-C13 both had a master mason named Alexander means
some direct connection, as Mr Harvey (1974) suggests, is a
question.

The Lincoln chapter house has a pyramid roof (lowered
in pitch by *Essex*, re-restored 1800 to its present form,
according to Dr Cocke). Each bay has two shafted lancets
with a blank lozenge above. Blank arches l. and r. of the
lancets and on the buttresses. The lancets have continuous
inner mouldings (a keeled roll). All shafts are keeled or
filleted and have shaft-rings, all capitals are moulded. The
top of the chapter house is Perp. Shallow blank arches with
fleurons, quatrefoil frieze. Small corner pinnacles. Eight
flying buttresses to enormous outer buttresses far distant.
The exterior of the passage towards the cloister has the
same system. Impressive w front of the chapter house
visible above the E range of the cloister. Bare wall. Big
circular window without tracery. Gable with three stepped
lancets. Side gables or turrets with saddleback roofs. All
the capitals again plainly moulded.

The INTERIOR consists of a passage of access and the
chapter house proper. The passage is of two bays with
sexpartite vault. Blank arcading with stiff-leaf capitals and
dogtooth. Two windows per bay on each side. The vaulting-shafts start at the level of the sill of the windows. Small
stiff-leaf corbels, as in the nave. To the w a tier of seven

steep arches, all new, and then the circular window which is
set inside between two shafts carrying a wide round arch.
The chapter house itself has a central pier, decagonal like
the building, with ten concave-sided Purbeck shafts.
Shaft-rings, crocket capitals. The walls continue the blank
arcading, with dogtooth more conspicuous in the E parts.
Vaulting-shafts on much bigger stiff-leaf corbels, more
like the Angel Choir now. Two windows per bay plus l. and
r. narrow blank arches, so narrow that the inner shank
stands on a pendant. Vault of twenty ribs emanating from
the pier. The ten intermediate ones correspond to transverse ridge ribs in a longitudinal building. Ridge rib (as it
were longitudinal) around the ridge. Above each bay of the
outer walls one pair of tiercerons. – Canopied CHAIR, said
to be c. 1300; canopy, lions and book-rest much restored.

How should we date this chapter house? The *Metrical
Life of St Hugh* († 1200) tells us that he started it and that
Hugh of Wells, the bishop of Lincoln who died in 1235,
completed it. That is surprising. The upper parts certainly
look 1235 at the very earliest, namely the lozenges outside
which recur at the very w end of the nave (in the s w chapel)
and in the tympanum of the galilee, if they can be trusted
there, and the galilee is pretty certainly later than 1235.
Also the leaf corbels for the vault seem post-nave even if
pre-Angel Choir, i.e. after 1230 and before 1260.

## Cloister

The exterior of the cloister is quite bare. There were no
rooms needed along it as there were in monastic cathedrals.
Inside, wooden tierceron vaults with many bosses, those of
the E range earlier and best. In front of the chapter house
e.g. Christ blessing, also the Coronation of the Virgin. In
the s and w ranges much foliage, also monsters, also a lady
with a wimple, a man's face with his tongue out, a man's
face pulling his mouth open, pulling one side of the mouth,
blowing two horns, etc. The bosses at the N end of the E
range have been interpreted as Occupations of the Months.
At the s end of the w range two bosses seem to be C 15
replacements (Cave). In the E walk blank arcading with
stiff-leaf capitals and arches with dogtooth; and, as has
been said, stone vault-springers and all in this walk much
restored. In the N wall doorway of the C 13, one order of
shafts, stiff-leaf. This led to the deanery. Larger archway at
the E end of the N range, perhaps not original. The staircase
behind it certainly is not, and the fine REREDOS
architecture of the early C 18 with a segmental pediment
below a bigger triangular one, with garlands down the
pilasters and fine detailing, is not *in situ*. It is not recorded
where it came from. This bay, i.e. the bay projecting E from
the N end of the E range, is incidentally timber-framed, as
one can see from the N outside, where it is gabled. It
represents all that is left of the OLD LIBRARY, built in or

113. LINCOLN The C13 cloisters from the C17 north walk

about 1422, on top of the E cloister range. Inside the roof is preserved, low-pitched, with tie-beams alternating with horizontal demi-figures of angels as if there were hammer-beams, which there are not. Moulded beams, purlins with bosses. – Three of the original PRESSES also still exist, really long double lecterns with poppy-heads and a dividing rail decorated with pierced quatrefoils. The library was mostly burnt in 1609, and in 1674 Dean Honywood presented a new one.

The N range of the cloister was in decay and the HONY-WOOD LIBRARY, above a new cloister walk, went up in its stead. Honywood obtained the services of *Wren* to design it. The builder was called *Evison*, and he was to build it 'according to Sir Christopher Wren's directions and Mr Tompson's model'. *Tompson* was probably the Thompson who was one of the busiest masons on Wren's City churches. Arcade with Tuscan columns. (Viewing the

cathedral from this walk is like standing in the Renaissance looking back at the Middle Ages.) Upper floor of eleven bays. Simple well-set windows with wooden crosses. The centre window is discreetly emphasized by a straight entablature and a garland. The main doorway is from the deanery, i.e. the W. Two Tuscan columns, a pulvinated frieze, and a segmental pediment. The window above it has volutes at the foot and a straight entablature. Inside one long room, just like a college library. Book-shelves along both walls (the first in England so arranged, according to Canon Binnall); originally only low ones between the windows. Cornice with projections and recessions. Ceiling on coving entirely plain. The only adornments are the E doorway and the W window, both large, with a surround of leaf and then vertically halved composite demi-columns. Segmental pediment. (The library is temporarily closed for repair of damage by death-watch beetle.)

Adjoining the Honywood Library is an annexe in Tudor style, the DEAN WICKHAM LIBRARY. It is by *C. Hodgson Fowler* of Durham and was built in 1909–14 (now coffee-shop).

FURNISHINGS in the cloisters. SCULPTURE. In the N walk all kinds of fragments. The three-quarter figure blowing a horn is the Swineherd of Stow who contributed generously to the building fund and was perpetuated, a companion to St Hugh himself, on top of one of the turrets of the W front (see *St Hugh's cathedral* above). – MONUMENTS. Stone coffin-lids with large interlocked circles, Anglo-Saxon rather than Norman. – In the s range monument to *Richard of Gainsborough*, 'olim cementarius istius ecclesie', who died in 1300. Large incised slab. The slab in the floor is a copy. The damaged original is on the wall. Triple canopy with ogee arches and angel pendants. He is shown in his professional dress, praying. By the side of him his L-square. Greenhill considers the slab foreign – not a likely suggestion, because of the ogee arches, which were unknown abroad at the time. – To its l. incised slab to Thomas Lovedon, *c.* 1400.

For the precinct, gates, walls and buildings generally, see the latest edition of B of E *Lincolnshire*.

# Liverpool

## CATHEDRAL CHURCH OF CHRIST *Anglican*

(Based on B of E *South Lancashire*, 1969, revised.)

Liverpool's skyline is dominated by its C20 cathedrals, emblems at opposite ends of Hope Street. The Anglican cathedral, near the s end, is oriented N–S. (Although our description uses the ritual directions, the 'E end' lies to the s, and the 'w front' faces N.) This hugely dignified apparition stands high on St James's Mount above a picturesque cemetery in an old quarry on one side, the remaining terrace houses of the Georgian merchants' quarter round about, and the man-made ruins of Toxteth beyond. It was an ideal site to choose so far as placing the cathedral above city and river was concerned, although it made nonsense of the domestic scale of this neighbourhood.

The diocese of Liverpool was established in 1880. At first the church of St Peter did service for a cathedral. A competition for the site of St John was held in 1887, but abandoned in 1888. The final site was selected in 1901, and architects were asked to submit portfolios of work. At first it was stipulated that the new design must be Gothic, but after objections, raised particularly by the *Architectural Review*, this condition was removed. (Already in 1881, Canon Venables of Lincoln recommended in the *Nineteenth Century* that Liverpool should turn to the style of Wren's 'Great Model' for St Paul's, an idea that lay dormant until Lutyens revived it for the Catholics of Liverpool; see below.) The assessors were Bodley and Norman Shaw. They chose five out of 103: Austin & Paley, C. A. Nicholson, Giles Gilbert Scott, Malcolm Stark, and W. J. Tapper. Among those not selected were, e.g., Lethaby, Mackintosh and Reilly. The winner was (*Sir*) *Giles Gilbert Scott* (1880–1960), son of George Gilbert Scott Jr (see the Catholic cathedral at Norwich below), and so of the third distinguished generation of that family. The design he submitted in 1903 differed in many ways from that executed. It was cruciform with a six-bay nave and twin towers over the transepts. Scott was not quite twenty-three at this date, and Bodley was nominated joint architect. This did not work well, and when Bodley died in 1907 Scott took over as sole architect. Work started in 1904, after certain alterations had been made in the design, and work on the superstructure started in 1906.

The Lady Chapel came first, in 1906–10. Then, in 1909–10, Scott made sweeping changes in his design. A central tower replaced the twin towers, two sets of transepts were designed to frame it, and the nave was shortened drastically to match the choir. It became an entirely different, but spatially equally convincing composition. Liturgically this is hardly so. The transepts, the major portals between them, and the tower space are useless, functionally speaking – except when harbouring unusually large crowds – and that has remained a worrying fact about this cathedral. Under the new scheme, choir and E transepts were built in 1910–24. The tower to a once again revised design was begun in 1924. Bombs fell near the s E corner of the cathedral in 1940, yet during both wars building went on. The w transepts were completed in 1941, the tower in 1942, and the nave was begun in 1948. Scott made a revised design for the w front in 1942, an elaborate affair with an angular prow-like w porch, but in 1967, at the last stage in the building's history, the w front was redesigned by *Frederick G. Thomas* of Scott's firm. When Scott died in 1960, he had been concerned with the cathedral for fifty-nine years, against Wren's thirty-five years at St Paul's (yet, though 1675–1710 are the years usually given, Wren was involved there even before 1666). But Scott, though younger than Wren, was more tired towards the end, and the style of his building has worn worse than Wren's. In 1710 there were few who would have had a right to call St Paul's old-fashioned. Liverpool Cathedral is desperately of a past that can never be recovered (the desperation perhaps now in the eye of the critic). Goodhart-Rendel in 1953 called it a scenic prodigy aloof from architectural reality, 'either a great engine of emotion or nothing', and predicted that its tremendous tower might become the venerated last resting-place of romantic architecture.

114 and 115. LIVERPOOL (ANGL.) (*below*) 1903–78. Designed by Sir Giles Scott. (*right*) Interior view to the high altar

The cathedral is built of dull red Woolton sandstone. It is about 600 ft long – longer than Winchester is and longer than Old St Paul's was – and the tower is 331 ft high, 80 ft more than Canterbury's Bell Harry. It is this height which remains in one's memory and which succeeds in 'sending' one. (Sir Nikolaus here explained in 1969 that he used this term because he had used it in describing Coventry Cathedral for the *Buildings of England* in 1966; yet, oddly enough, it appears nowhere in that description, although doubtless he used it of Coventry elsewhere; he did use it in 1963 of the Brighton Pavilion – so varied are the vehicles of architectural transport.)

## EXTERIOR

The earliest part is the LADY CHAPEL on the SE, and that is still conventionally, though very competently, Gothic of the Late Bodley kind, high, with buttresses with many set-offs, and tall two-light Dec windows. Only the Lady Chapel's s porch is freer in the details, with Arts and Crafts touches. On the NE the CHAPTER HOUSE was begun in 1906. It is octagonal and connected with the choir by a passage which continues as an ambulatory behind the sanctuary, and also by a bridge higher up, the sort of romantic feature one can find in Beresford Pite's or F. L. Griggs's dream drawings. The CHOIR was started in 1910. The E wall with its single large window is flanked by two turrets with oddly short spires or polygonal pyramid roofs. What distinguishes the choir, and especially its N and S sides, from the Lady Chapel is what distinguishes the whole of the rest of the building – a style no longer dependent on Bodley. Scott now uses very large, bare, smooth surfaces, and contrasts them with small, prettily detailed and highly ornamental areas, all Gothic, mostly Dec, but tending to the Flamboyant rather than the English Dec. The choir has a smaller outer gallery of little arches right at the top, a motif inspired by, e.g., Albi. The windows are not Dec, but on N and s a rather bald late C13 Geometrical, while the great E window has stiff plant-forms more Arts and Crafts than Dec.

Highly original and bold is the composition of two pairs of TRANSEPTS flanking the tower and main portal – Scott was partial to such dualities. The Rankin Porch of the main portal is matched by the Welsford Porch, utterly useless, because leading straight into the abyss of the cemetery. But it had to be there, because N must match S. The portals themselves are preceded by a deep niche or porch opening to outside by a large round arch. The whole is powerfully framed by the transepts. Low entrances outside the transept fronts to w and E lead into the undercroft. The arches die into the imposts. This is another of Scott's favourite motifs derived from the best Gothicists of the late C19. Inside the porch are three identical portals, their details in an ornate Late Gothic evidently influenced by the Spanish style of the Reyes Catolicos, i.e. the period about 1500. Spain altogether must have impressed Scott most. The TOWER is magnificently seen at a distance from anywhere. The slightly leaning four angle-turrets are most sensitively detailed; again there is much bare wall and much busy little decoration, especially at the top. The pinnacles seem tiny. Finally the exterior of the NAVE. The nave was not curtailed, as threatened in the 1960s, and its three bays balance the choir as intended in 1910. With *Thomas's* w window of three equal lights under a glazed untraceried tympanum, much plainer than the distant E window, the w end is nobly finished.

## INTERIOR

Entering by the Rankin Porch one finds oneself in a narrowly confined space, with another set of two identical Spanish portals and a figured rib-vault. Then straight into the space of the TOWER, a height which seems immense. Its figured rib-vault seems far away. Height is the greatest asset of this cathedral interior, though the management of the spaces is exciting too, and much of the older detail convinces in the historical setting of 1900–10.

The LADY CHAPEL interior (reached from the s choir aisle) is impressive, very Bodleyish, with elongatedly polygonal piers, their arches dying into the imposts, and a transparent triforium or passage halfway below the clerestory windows. The triforium has a florid Arts and Crafts cresting and at its sill an equally florid inscription. The vault has curved ribs such as occur in Spain, but hardly in England. Triple-arcaded w gallery with organ above. The black and white marble flooring has asymmetrical patterns. The CHOIR has a much simpler vault, just two narrow quadripartite bays for each bay below. The choir aisles are really not aisles but ample passages through side spaces with transverse ribbed vaults, the type of Albi and Catalonia. The aisles are continued behind the altar by the low passage which continues to the N as the passage to the chapter house. The TRANSEPTS have neither gallery nor triforium, just a long balcony. Construction of the chancel and E transepts had begun before Scott's redesigning of 1909–10, and this explains the enormous transept piers (which, when started, were intended to carry the twin towers) and the curious vaulting devised to overcome the difficulty of the central space being wider than the chancel. For the sake of balance these features were repeated westwards. Scott constantly continued to revise his designs in minor as well as in more fundamental ways – see e.g. the varying designs of balcony balustrades throughout or the mouldings and treatment of the piers in the E and w transepts. Even the pier shafts of the E and w tower arches are different.

The NAVE, comparatively short and at a lower level, like a vestibule to the great central space, is partly cut off from it by a bridge, or semicircular arch carrying steps to a centred floating balcony, a strange device and again a romantic illustrator's stratagem. (Its nearest forebear actually built in England would be Waterhouse's staircase-bridge across the central hall of his Natural History Museum at South Kensington.) This piece of scenery does seem to anchor the vast piers – and doubtless affords vast views of great occasions for 'the media'.

FURNISHINGS

Much of the decoration suffers from an easy sentimentality – what the French call *bondieuserie*. – FONT. Marble, with relief figures by *E. Carter Preston*, and canopy designed by *Scott*, square with flamboyant top. – REREDOS. A *retablo*, Spanish in style, designed by *Scott* and made by *Walter Gilbert & L. Weingartner*. – COMMUNION RAIL, by *Gilbert & Weingartner* too, with few widely spaced uprights. – CHOIR STALLS, by *Waring & Gillow*. Feeble. – ORGAN CASE, designed by *Scott*. – Lady Chapel ALTAR-PIECE designed by *Bodley* and *Scott*. Again entirely un-English. – SCULPTURE. Pietà by *E. Carter Preston*. – Holy Family by *Josephine Vasconcellos*. A fibreglass moulding after the original in St Martin-in-the-Fields in London. – MONUMENTS. In the Lady Chapel Mrs Neilson † 1945 by *E. Carter Preston*. – Also Nurses' Memorial by *David Evans*. – In the s choir aisle Bishop Chavasse † 1933, by *Evans*. Kneeling, with a model of the cathedral as then completed. – Bishop Ryle † 1900, by *Carter Preston*. – Dean Dwelly † 1957. By the same. – In the SE transept, sixteenth Earl of Derby † 1908. Designed by *Scott* and made by *Farmer & Brindley*. – STAINED GLASS. Mostly by *Powell & Sons*. All the Lady Chapel glass replaced after the last war. In the chapter house, four by *Morris & Co.*, 1916–23, examples of the firm's decay before its liquidation. – On the chapter-house staircase, windows by *Kempe & Co.*, 1916, and also too late to be good. – But the glass of the great w window, designed by *Carl Edwards* and installed at the close of construction, has a fine swirl of forms and brilliant colour. The cathedral organist is reported to have said it reminds him of Messiaen.

Now for the cathedral at the other end of Hope Street.

# Liverpool

## METROPOLITAN CATHEDRAL CHURCH OF CHRIST THE KING   *Roman Catholic*

(Based on B of E *South Lancashire*, 1969, revised.)

Cathedral since 1967. If the Anglican cathedral on Liverpool's skyline seems an engine of past emotion, the Catholic cathedral may at first seem a cross between cooling tower and circus tent, part power station, part fairground. It stands at the N end of Hope Street, the Anglican one near the s end, both on high ground, so a relation was bound to be set up between them. The Catholic orientation 1930–60 was N–S with the ritual 'E end' at the N, so Lutyens's and Scott's ritual 'w fronts' were to face one another, half a mile apart, like two cats. The new cathedral's lantern is a recognition of that special relation. It does not compete, yet it responds. It is with its pinnacles of the same tribe, but where the Anglican lantern is solid, the Catholic lantern's details are thin and delicate. The Liverpool skyline has at once taken to the newcomer visible over river and city.

Liverpool became a Catholic diocese in 1850. In 1853 a cathedral was begun in the grounds of St Domingo House at Everton, the northern suburb where the bishop lived. The architect was E. W. Pugin, and no more was built than the Lady Chapel (in St Domingo Road, 1856, 1885; his greater father A. W. N. Pugin is said to have submitted designs in 1845, according to Edward Hubbard). Then, nearly eighty years later, in 1930, the diocese, impelled by the strong and lively Irish-Catholic contingent on Merseyside, decided to build a cathedral such as Britain had never seen and such as few churches in the world would emulate.

*Sir Edwin Lutyens* was commissioned. The design was exhibited at the Royal Academy in 1932. Christopher Hussey called it 'English renaissance of Wren, but with his baroque idiom modified by what may be termed a fusion of Roman precedent with twentieth-century austerity'. The area to be covered by the cathedral was 233,000 sq. ft; the length was to be 680 ft, the width 400 ft, the height to the top of the dome 510 ft (dimensions that would have outdone those then taking shape at the other end of Hope Street). These figures compare with 715, 450, and 450 for St Peter's in Rome, 510, 250, and 366 for St Paul's in London; and Lutyens's central dome was to have a diameter of 168 ft, larger than existed anywhere (St Peter's 137, St Paul's 112). The plan was for a longitudinal but very compact building. It was to consist of a short nave and double aisles, the dome to the diameter of nave and inner aisles, transepts of nave and double aisles, and a short chancel with an apse and the circular chapter house behind it. But that was not all. The nave was to start at its 'w' (i.e. s) end with a narthex and 'N' and 's' chapels, the 's'

chapel being the baptistery. The transept ends were to have angle chapels too, four of them. Moreover, the apse was to be flanked by large apsed chapels, and 'N' and 'S' of these were to be sacristies. (As with other modern cathedrals sited for secular rather than religious reasons, the old ritual directions are not the actual ones.)

The exterior was to be of buff brick with much of granite dressings. The walls, in the model, look severe, with small, arbitrarily placed windows. The 'w' (i.e. S) front was to have four huge piers, sheer, except for decorative aedicules high up. The piers were to carry three arches, the middle one wider and much higher, forming three deep recesses, a Lincoln motif much enlarged. The stonework, all detailed meticulously by Lutyens, was to be the supreme example of his late passion for modular relations between all ashlar blocks. The major proportions were equally rationalized into simple relations. A huge wooden model of the design, made for Lutyens by John B. Thorp and shown in the Lutyens Exhibition of 1981, suggests a cluster of Lutyens war memorials with a dome on top. But Sir John Summerson's sophisticated and intricate analysis in that exhibition's catalogue demonstrates the design's successful synthesis of elements of the Roman arch of triumph and bold response to the challenge of Wren's St Paul's.

Work began in 1933 but was abandoned in 1940 (continued for a while after the war to a modified design by *Adrian G. Scott*). Only the CRYPT was built, but what a crypt! For comparison one can only think of that of St Peter's, and in addition of the substructures of such a Roman palace as that on the Palatine, or better still Diocletian's at Spalato. The crypt covers no more than the choir area of the cathedral, i.e. its 'E' (=N) end. The plan is very complex and hard to understand, under vaults which seem to stretch into infinity. (The crypt is usually closed to sightseers, though open for services.) One enters a Chapel of Our Lady of Dolours, which has aisles, really double aisles of different widths. The chapel ends in three apses. They are scooped into the mighty substructures of the organ wall and chapter house above. To them correspond two circular rooms below. But outside the aisles of the Chapel of the Dolours are a further aisle to the N ('E') and the S ('W'). They run all the length of the crypt, i.e. the width of the sanctuary. They differ in details: one has the two amply-scaled circular staircases and a narthex between, the other has the two ends with columns so as to create three-naved fragments of the type which Romanesque crypts favoured. Moreover, 'N' of the two circular rooms, the whole of the Chapel of the Dolours repeats as the Chapel of the Crucifixion, and 'w' of the two circular rooms, beneath the future high altar, is the large Archbishops' Chapel.

The crypt was built to a height of 12 ft above ground. It is entered from the South Crypt Court (i.e. the E) by two doorways. These and the large window between have all the exasperating whimsy of late Lutyens, exasperating not *per se*, but in such a building and on this monumental scale. No one can afford to be a joker when it comes to a cathedral and its colossal architectural members. Take the leaning blocking of a large part of the tapering doorway pillars, or the hole through to expose a circular motif. However, once this shock is got over, the internal spatial effects are superb. There are more shocks inside. A 'Rolling Stone' (with a presumption both aesthetic and theological) was made to form the entry to the archbishops' burial chapel: a circular piece weighing six tons and swinging round. The brickwork is superb too – exposed by *Sir Frederick Gibberd*, against Lutyens's intention – especially in the tunnel-vaults and groin-vaults without transverse arches. The staircases are wide and of the newel type, with wide flights interrupted by intermediate landings and a wide open well. Each flight has steps carefully detailed so as to start with convex and end with concave steps. The balustrade was to have no raised posts or knobs of any kind which would have prevented choristers from sliding down it – a typical Lutyens touch (not apparently apocryphal). Where columns appear in the crypt they are of the Tuscan order and have *no* entasis.

The Lutyens cathedral, being obviously far too large ever to be completed, even in its scaled-down postwar version, was finally abandoned when a competition was held in 1959. The greatest problem was what to do with the crypt. *Sir Frederick Gibberd* won the competition in 1960, and the stroke of genius which alone made him deserve his victory was to finish the crypt off with a large platform for open-air services, continue that platform to the S, and build his cathedral on that S half of the site, which was unimpeded by Lutyens. It was the stroke of genius corresponding to Sir Basil Spence's keeping the Perp walls of St Michael's as the forecourt to his Coventry Cathedral.

Otherwise the change of architectural mood, from 1951, the year of the Coventry competition, to 1959 is overwhelming. In 1951 it was a matter of course that the winning design would be longitudinal and that a central design with the altar in the middle such as the growing Liturgical Movement demanded would have no chance of prize and execution. So Sir Basil Spence had to work to this traditional scheme, and believed in it. The Liverpool competition insisted on a close association of the congregation with the celebrant, i.e. the central importance of the high altar, and on perfect visibility for all 2,000 for whom accommodation had to be found. This clearly meant that only a central plan could win. That there is no such thing as complete visibility, with part of the congregation following mass from behind the priest's back, is at present too easily forgotten. Acoustic problems of course also arise. A centralized priest has yet to be invented.

116. LIVERPOOL (R.C.) 1960–7. Designed by Sir Frederick Gibberd. On crypt by Sir Edwin Lutyens designed 1932

237

Sir Frederick Gibberd's plan is convincingly simple. (He gave it a dress rehearsal in his chapel for Hopwood Training College, purer and smaller; see B of E *South Lancashire*.) Here it is a circle surrounded by thirteen chapels, the main entrance hall, and two side porches. The entrance is from the s ('w'); the N ('E') chapel projects further than the others. So an axial system is firmly established. The structure is sixteen reinforced concrete trusses of boomerang shape held together by a concrete ring at the height of the bend of the boomerang members and again at their top. On the upper ring stands the high, fully glazed, tapering lantern, weighing 2,000 tons. It ends in pinnacles and is to their tops 290 ft high (only 40 ft less than the Anglican cathedral tower, but 40 ft more than Bell Harry at Canterbury). The concrete boomerangs are helped in their function by flying buttresses which reach them at the lower ring. They alone, though they were an afterthought, are extremely prominent. The special relation of the lantern to the Anglican one has been pointed out. The newcomer holds its own.

For the rest of the exterior, doubts cannot be silenced. The chapels and porches surrounding the cylinder are each different in shape from the next, and nearly all deliberately uncouth (Nicholas Taylor, of a different generation, calls it 'appealing clumsiness'). The source of this uncouthness is of course late Le Corbusier, and the skylight funnels on some of them, round and square, are only too clearly derivative. Their aggressiveness, and especially that of the jagged main portal, contradicts the serene simplicity of the main space, and the barbaric concrete relief above the main entrance (by *William Mitchell*) is even more aggressive. The symbolism of the three crosses can just be detected, but the forms are of a painful primeval cruelty. To whom will, or can, this appeal among those who visit the cathedral to pray or for services? Professor Gardner Medwin in *The Times* called it 'a striking artefact which could be taken for some obscure symbol of an ancient cult'. The bell-holes above the relief are equally blunt and ruthless. The nearest architectural parallel is Breuer's St John Collegeville as the nearest parallel of the whole scheme of the cathedral is Niemeyer's Brasilia Cathedral.

Sir Frederick denied that there was direct inspiration. He pronounced himself 'infuriated' by that comparison and pointed out that it is only superficial, because his structural members are vertical below the lower band, or if you include the flying buttresses, delta-shaped, whereas Niemeyer's trusses slant from the start. But the flying buttresses of Liverpool, even if they are only additional support, are the most prominent feature, especially as they are distinguished by white mosaic facing set against the greyish-white Portland stone of the rest and the truncated cone of the aluminium roof. (It should be added that this part of the structure is not wearing well.)

The interior is easier on the eye and the mind. The entrance hall is low, and beyond it there is at once the wide, single space under the funnel-shaped roof. It is splendidly spacious and appeared even more so before the benches and the altar canopy were *in situ*. Its diameter is 194 ft. (The longer diameter of the ellipsoid Royal Albert Hall is more but with its banks of boxes not comparable; Aia Sophia Istanbul is only 107 ft across.) The structural members appear here in full clarity. They are of exposed concrete poured into smooth shuttering. The chapels and porches are – a brilliant conceit – treated as independent buildings not only because they are of brick, stone-faced, but visually even more convincingly, because they are framed l., r., and top by small strips of dark blue glass, by *Piper* and *Reyntiens* (see *Lantern* below). The danger of the dark blue is that in certain lights it makes the altar look all blue, not white as surely intended: an effect that has been compared to the psychedelic violet light in Californian funeral chapels.

The irregularity of the shapes of the chapels is much more easily accepted inside than outside. What they have in common is that they are all very high in relation especially to their depth. Lighting is diverse too, and so are the wall surfaces. Some are wide open to the centre, others are all but closed, and the small arched entrance of one is a clear indication that Sir Frederick is not lacking in sympathy with the Lutyens of the crypt. As for shapes of chapels, the baptistery for instance is horseshoe-shaped to the inside, the 'E' chapel (of the Blessed Sacrament) is oblong with tapering sides and has a monopitch roof rising to the 'E' wall. The 'E' wall is of pitted stone. The 'N' and 's' chapels with the subsidiary entrances have balconies low down. The chapel following clockwise after the 'N' chapel (St Joseph) has wood slatting and a steep pyramid ceiling. The chapels l. and r. of the 'E' chapel are the only ones treated symmetrically. Following after the chapel to the r. of the 'E' chapel is the one with the Lutyens arch. The chapel r. of the 's' chapel receives light through an oculus in the roof of a kind of tight, high apse. But on the whole the variety of shapes appears less dominant inside than outside. Instead it is the fenestration and the colouring of the glass which tell, e.g. red in the chapel immediately l. of the main entrance, white and light brown in the Lady Chapel, green and yellow in that with the bishop's throne, etc.

The HIGH ALTAR stands right in the centre of the rotunda. It is a slab of pure white marble quarried at Skoplje, 10 ft by 3 ft 6 in. by 3 ft 6 in. in size and weighing nineteen tons. Above is a circular CANOPY, designed by *Sir Frederick Gibberd* and consisting of vertical tubes of various lengths. It is a doubtful blessing. From some viewpoints it links the altar to the lantern, from others it confuses the s–N ('w'–'E') axis. – The CRUCIFIX high up is

by *Elisabeth Frink*, the ALTAR CROSS and CANDLESTICKS by *R. Y. Goodden*. – The FLOOR pattern (and also the BAPTISTERY GATES) are designed by *David Atkins*. – The BENCHES are by *Frank Knight*. They are low and simple and do not detract from the spatial unity. – In the Chapel of the Blessed Sacrament REREDOS and STAINED GLASS are by *Ceri Richards*, in the Lady Chapel and the Chapel of St Paul the glass is by *Margaret Trahearne*. – The STATUE of the Virgin is by *Robert Brumby*. – By *R. D. Russell* is the BISHOP'S THRONE with its simple canopy, by *William Mitchell* the main DOOR, again decidedly frightening. It might be the introduction to some cruel Mexican ritual: and it is no good trying to justify this ferocity by saying that Romanesque sculpture can be ferocious; for the C 20 just isn't the C 12 (a remark added in the 1960s). – The climax of the interior is the STAINED GLASS of the lantern. It is abstract and moves from yellow (N, i.e. 'E') to red (SW) and blue (SE). It was designed by *John Piper* and made by *Patrick Reyntiens*. – Bronze figure of Christ by *Elisabeth Frink*.

Gibberd's cathedral stands on a podium that continues the top of the Lutyens crypt. The Lutyens part he simply made into an area for open-air services. The N ('E') end of the church has an open-air altar, and the Lutyens staircases are delightfully finished by concrete pyramids, as Gibberd as they are Lutyens. The podium part of the Gibberd building is used for car parking, sacristies, storage, lavatories and even a tearoom, accessible directly from the entrance hall. Finally, E of the podium are some accessory buildings, all ashlar-faced, extremely well scaled, and prettily landscaped. Their simplicity is the right foil for the main building.

Consecration took place in May 1967, five years after building had begun – a short span that was an accommodation of cathedral-making to a late C 20 budget (something like £1½ million). Gibberd's incorporation of Lutyens's crypt, without letting it dictate his own design, his care for the shape on the skyline, and his powerful central space are visually highly successful, although liturgically the space is proving much less flexible than traditional cathedral spaces. As for certain excrescent features, their brutal aggressiveness is a trait from which church architects in the 1960s seemed incapable of escaping, and which must have had social consequences. Liverpool of the 1980s contains a major monument to the expressionism of the 1960s.

For the surroundings of these two cathedrals, see the latest edition of B of E *South Lancashire* and, with care, the newspapers.

# Manchester

## CATHEDRAL CHURCH OF ST MARY, ST DENYS AND ST GEORGE  *Anglican*

(Based on B of E *South Lancashire*, 1969, revised.)

Plan, Fig. 119, from the *Builder*, 1893, by F. P. Oakley, drawn before *Champneys'* additions on W and SE, and before war damage removed the Ely Chapel.

When in the C 15 this newly refounded parish church took up its position in a more commanding manner above the E bank of the River Irwell, it was the third on its site. Manchester itself was an old town on the site of a Roman fort. In 1698 Celia Fiennes noted the 'very large Church all stone and stands high so that walking round the Church yard you see the whole town'. A century later the Industrial Revolution born in Manchester was already smoking the view. By the 1840s Victoria Station was going up across the river from the church. Today the inky Irwell, slotted through roads and rails and bridges W of the cathedral, is hard to find. On the cathedral's N side, motor traffic separates it from its original priests' houses that became the celebrated C 17 school called Chetham's Hospital, now Chetham's School of Music. On the cathedral's E and S sides, a few Victorian buildings still give some sense of a close, acting as hedges against the inflation of the Arndale Centre to southward. To someone walking up Deansgate's new ramp from Market Street, only the cathedral tower ahead looks pre-*Nineteen Eighty-four*. But reaction has set in; a conservation area has been declared around cathedral and school, Victoria Station has been cleansed of soot, and there is even hope for the Irwell.

The old collegiate church became a cathedral in 1847. Briefly in the 1870s the diocese in this centre of Nonconformity considered plans for impressive rebuilding on a larger site. R. H. Carpenter (architect of Lancing School Chapel) prepared drawings in gigantic Gothic for the open space of Piccadilly Garden. There were to be a very long and tall nave, two sets of transepts, and an octagonal lantern tower. One wonders if this published but unbuilt design of 1876 was of any interest to Pearson when designing Truro three years later, or even to the Liverpool competitors twenty-five years later (see Truro in the companion volume and Liverpool Anglican above).

Now for actual building history. In 1421 Henry V granted a licence to Thomas de la Warre, rector of Manchester, to refound his parish church as a collegiate establishment with a warden, eight priests, four clerks and six lay choristers. It was essentially a chantry college with daily masses for Henry V, the Bishop of Coventry and Lichfield, the rector, and their progenitors. The domestic premises to northward are by good fortune preserved as the

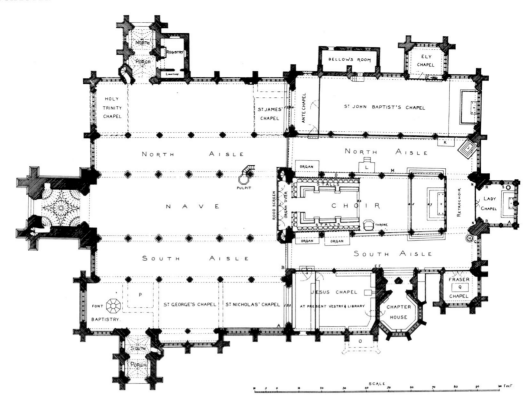

119. MANCHESTER Plan from the *Builder*, 1893 (see p. 240)

aforementioned school. The first warden (1422–58), John Huntington, rebuilt the choir of the church, and the third warden (1465–81) the nave. The most generous was the fifth warden (1485–1509), James Stanley, who was Bishop of Ely 1506–15 and a son of the Thomas Stanley who after Bosworth Field became first Earl of Derby (so Bishop Stanley was stepson to Thomas's second wife, Margaret Beaufort, mother of Henry VII). The Bishop himself had children, of whom the eldest, Sir John Stanley, fought at Flodden in 1513, an event said to be commemorated in the adding of the Derby Chapel to the church. A little Ely Chapel was built off it on the N side for the Bishop's tomb. In a period when Ely's other bishops made themselves elaborate burial chapels within their cathedral (cf. the Alcock and West Chapels at Ely), a Stanley – and step-brother to the king – preferred his family church. He also gave the fine choir stalls and rood screen. It was the century ending with his death that determined the commodious-ness of the church.

Save for one small piece of Saxon sculpture, possibly from the first church on the site, nothing in the church is pre-Perp, and there is no stylistic case for placing one detail before another. (The VCH seems too confident in its report on the building history c. 1420–c. 1520.) This applies also to the chantry chapels which grew around the core of nave aisles and choir aisles and gave the church its present character. Externally they create the impression of outer aisles: on the N the Derby Chapel (or St John Baptist Chapel, now Regimental Chapel) begun by Bishop Stanley c. 1513; on the S the Jesus Chapel of 1506 and the Fraser Chapel of 1886. Between the latter two is the tiny octag-onal chapter house, c 15 (formerly with a Victorian conical roof, not apparently original). The Lady Chapel at the E end is small too, projecting to the E only a little, and had E windows before the last war.

In the C19 there were restorations, first a disastrous one in 1814–15 by a *John Palmer* from Co. Durham, then much refacing and the rebuilding of the tower by *J. P. Holden* in 1862–8. The unfulfilled project of 1876 (above) was followed by more scholarly restoration in 1885–6 and after by *J. S. Crowther*. The Victorian restorers determined much of the external appearance of the building. Thus

Holden heightened the w tower by nearly 20 ft, while keeping its general profile, and entirely rebuilt the Jesus Chapel. Crowther put on all the pretty pierced parapets, and built the N and S porches. Internally he rebuilt both the inner and outer arcades, apparently respecting the original details. (Donald Buttress says most of the inner part of the choir is medieval; the inner faces of the N and S tower walls still retain Palmer's plastering of c. 1815.) The exterior was refaced in harder-wearing Derbyshire stone, while the original variety of red sandstone was used inside.

At the end of the Victorian period came extensions by *Basil Champneys*: w porch and vestries (one now an exhibition room), 1898, and the large SE annexe 1902–3. As we would expect, they are excellent, the porch as ornate as the church, the annexes subdued yet charmingly varied in grouping and with felicitous decorative passages such as the two oriels to the S. War damage in 1940 included a direct hit on the Derby Chapel and much destruction in the Lady Chapel. Rebuilding and repair by *Sir Hubert Worthington*. The Ely Chapel, formerly N of the Derby Chapel, was not rebuilt.

The church is 172 ft long, i.e. the length of a parish church of the first order. Ornament was lavished on its exterior more by the C19 than the C15. The w tower is sheer below but richly appointed at the top. On each side are two two-light bell-openings with transom, and there is panelling over. The battlements are openwork, as all battlements of the church now are. Buttresses recessed and decorated with a niche. The two porches are two-storeyed. The outer S aisle has four-light windows of two different designs, and the Jesus Chapel has again a different design. The E view is impressive, thanks chiefly to Worthington's bare E wall. Above it is the seven-light choir E window. The N outer aisle has four-light windows, but to the E five and to the w seven. The clerestory windows are of five lights. Here and everywhere, below the open battlements is a frieze of square fleurons. At the junction of nave and choir are two prominent rood-stair turrets, differing in details.

The interior is of six bays w of the choir arch and six bays E of it. Upon entering the nave there appears the peculiarity, resulting from C15 provision of extra chantry chapels, of greater width than length: the nave inside is c. 115 ft N–S by c. 82 ft E–W. Piers and arches throughout the church are of seven different designs, but it must be said once again that no sequence of building can be deduced from them. (The VCH e.g. dates the choir E responds and the Lady Chapel arch c. 1330, but bases and capitals are polygonal, and so the date seems too early.) The pattern of the choir and nave arcades with enriched spandrels under a crested frieze may owe something to the Winchester nave (Harvey 1978). All the various arcades, and the chapter-house entrance, are worth some study and record. There certainly was no endeavour to keep in keeping. Points of

special interest are the portal to the chapter house, with its panelled arch and panelling above the doorway, the very high tower arch, and the excellent roofs, that of the nave with bosses and with demi-angels holding musical instruments, and that of the choir with tracery enrichment. The w beam of the choir roof has Huntington's rebus in the spandrels, witnessing his responsibility for the choir. The choir arch with its traceried spandrels and cresting is attributed to Stanley's patronage (with his rood screen, below).

## FURNISHINGS, E TO W

*Lady Chapel* TAPESTRIES designed by *Austin Wright* and made by *Theo Moorman* in 1957, with attractive figures and scenes. – The SCREEN is partly original, and the statuettes are a specially welcome survival. The strip below the canopies has entertaining grotesques. – Engraved glass by *David Peace*.

*Choir* STAINED GLASS. No prewar glass remains in the cathedral. The main E window is signed by *Gerald Smith*, who worked for A. K. Nicholson Studios (information from David O'Connor). – The choir E part has wrought-iron SCREENS, with Gothick pinnacles, and a wrought-iron COMMUNION RAIL, both delightful. They date from 1750–1. – Above the screens the upper parts of Perp wooden screens, just one large ogee arch per bay and very big panel tracery. – The STALLS are of course the most famous thing in the cathedral. They are without any doubt the finest in the North of England: only Chester's and Carlisle's can compare. These were installed by Bishop Stanley c. 1508, probably made by *William Brownfleet* of Ripon, who also made stalls for Ripon and Beverley (Harvey 1974). Above the exquisite canopies is another tier of simpler canopies and then a cresting with segmental arches on pendants. The return stalls are backed up by the rood screen. The stalls have a full set of thirty MISERICORDS, on the S side with the Stanley badge, on the N side with the merchant's mark of Richard Beswicke. The N side is a little later than the S side. On the N side, from E to W: rabbit cooking the hunter, unicorn, cock and cockatrice fighting, venerer and stag, stag and hound, the fox's triumph, men playing backgammon, child fighting dragon, winged lion, man having broken his wife's cooking pot, dragon, two monsters fighting, pelican, angel bust. On the S side, E to W: gryphon, antelope, sow playing bagpipes and pigs dancing, wild men and dragon fighting, lion passant, bear-baiting, man robbed by monkeys, fox stealing goose, men on camel fighting unicorn, elephant and castle, shield, dragon, eagle, eagle and child. The front stalls have poppy-heads, and animals and grotesques on the front curve up to the poppy-heads. – The BISHOP'S THRONE is of 1905 and in keeping. – ORGAN CASE, 1952, to replace Gilbert Scott's

120. MANCHESTER View through the C 16 choir screen

case, destroyed in 1940. – Brass CHANDELIERS, given in 1690 and 1715. – In the floor, BRASS to Warden Huntington † 1458. The figure is 3 ft 3 in. long and has a canopy surround. The brass w of it is of 1890. (For screen, see *Nave*.)

*South chapels and chapter house* Fraser Chapel. MONUMENT to Bishop Fraser † 1885 by *Forsyth*. White marble recumbent effigy. – The screen to the chapel is partly original. – So is the N screen of the Jesus Chapel. – PAINTINGS over the entrance to the chapter house: The Teachings of Christ, with predella of Beatitudes, by *Carel Weight*, R.A. 1963, with still another panel on the inner side of the *trumeau*. Parables in C20 dress yet like Gothic miniatures in this setting. – MONUMENTS. Hugh Birley, M.P., alabaster effigy recumbent, 1886, by whom? – Thomas Ogden † 1766, tablet with an obelisk on top.

*North chapel* In the Derby Chapel, BRASS to Bishop Stanley † 1515 (on the N side, until 1940 near his tomb in the Ely Chapel), fragmentary and now 29 in. long. – Against the w wall, MONUMENT to Charles Lawson, 1810, by the younger *Bacon*. Tablet with the headmaster and two boys, a bust of Homer on the ground. – Also in the Derby Chapel (formerly in the Lady Chapel, earlier in the nave) is the C18 FONT, a partly fluted octagonal bowl on a baluster stem. – The SCREEN to the choir aisle is only very partly original. – STAINED GLASS. E window by *Margaret Traherne*, 1966, in memory of the war and the rebuilding architect Worthington, its mass of lurid reds not wholly successful in evoking the fires of 1940.

*Nave* The ROOD SCREEN is a broadly treated piece with a four-light opening l. and r. of the doorway. It was erected by Bishop Stanley. The lower parts in their present form are made up of old fragments. The screen was restored and altered by *Scott*, to whom the parapet is due. – In the E respond of the N nave arcade is a re-set piece of Anglo-Saxon SCULPTURE, the small relief figure of an angel with the wings spread in different directions. Said to be from the first church on this site. – In the s aisle, STATUE of Thomas Fleming, by *Baily*, 1851. – At the w end of the aisle, MONUMENT to Dauntesy Hulme † 1828, tablet with the Good Samaritan. – At the w end of the N aisle, seated figure of Humphrey Chetham, the school founder, by *W. Theed*, 1853, a schoolboy at the foot of the base. – STAINED GLASS. At the w end, three windows by *Antony Holloway*, 1972–80: to St George on the s and St Denys on the N, both with rich reds, and to the Virgin in the tower window, with blues and yellows. Semi-abstract and true to the character of stained glass in their use of small design elements.

*South-east annexe* SCULPTURE. A beautiful relief panel of the Christ Child with St Mary, St Denys and St George, by *Eric Gill*, 1933, is over the entrance.

Further on the cathedral's changing surroundings, see the latest edition of B of E *South Lancashire*.

# Middlesbrough

CATHEDRAL CHURCH OF ST MARY    *Roman Catholic*

(Based on B of E *Yorkshire: The North Riding*, 1966, revised.)

Cathedral since 1878. Gaunt red brick, with details of c. 1300, by *George Goldie*, 1872–8, replacing a church of 1848. No tower. Additions of 1902 by *Edward Goldie*. Long nave arcades, wide shallow transepts giving effect of outer aisles, no chancel arch. Tall dark hammerbeam roof. Reredos: painting of Virgin and Saints by *Girolamo Cotignola*, 1528, given by the great ironmaster Henry Bolckow, one of the makers of Middlesbrough and its first M.P., not himself a Catholic but civic-minded towards the new diocese. There are intentions to replace this cathedral with a new one.

For its present surroundings, see the latest edition of B of E *Yorkshire: The North Riding*.

# Newcastle

CATHEDRAL CHURCH OF ST NICHOLAS    *Anglican*

(Based on B of E *Northumberland*, 1957, revised, with information from David O'Connor, S. E. Dykes Bower, Ronald Sims, George McHardy and J. A. Finch.)

Cathedral since 1882. Until then a parish church, and a proud parish church in character it has remained. Its architecture, with small exceptions from the C12 and early C13, belongs entirely to the C14 and C15 – a very rare thing among the churches of Northumberland. The exceptions are a blocked window in the NW crossing pier which the late Herbert Honeyman assigned to the Norman predecessor of the present church, fragments of ribs found and preserved of a vaulted late C12 chancel, and the E respond of the N arcade, together with the masonry above the N arcade. This is E.E. work of probably the early C13, after the Norman church was destroyed by fire. Mr Finch also points out that part of the E respond of the s arcade survives with a keeled shaft and rough shape of a capital, i.e. a counterpart to the E.E. respond on the N; also that, by the s respond, a shallow worn stone with lozenge ornament suggests remains of a Norman w crossing arch. One can reconstruct in one's mind a church with N and s aisles and piers of square core and four big semicircular keeled shafts, something similar to Newminster (the Cistercian abbey near Morpeth, founded 1137, a daughter of Fountains and mother of Roche). The crossing externally is not now marked by tower, lantern or flèche.

As for the later Middle Ages, the c14 dominates inside, the c15 outside, the latter thanks chiefly to the remarkable design of the w tower and its spire (total height 193½ ft). The tower is said to have been completed in 1448. (In the tall lierne-vaulted bay under the tower the central boss bears the arms of Robert Rhodes, M.P., †1474, who also endowed other church fabrics in Newcastle and whose family's arms are on the font standing in that bay; see *Furnishings*). The tower rises on a sturdy square base with diagonally placed polygonal buttresses. w doorway, large w window of five lights with panel tracery. On the next stage small two-light windows and much solid masonry. The bell-openings after that are tall, of two lights with a transom and coupled on each side. Above this there are pierced battlements and big polygonal pinnacles. These pinnacles keep in position the so-called crown: four mass-ive flying buttresses which hold up a square spire. The buttresses are concave below, ogee-shaped, and crocketed on top. The spire consists of an open lantern with panel tracery carrying four pinnacles and a recessed spire again held in position by miniature flying buttresses. The design of this structurally most ingenious crown seems related to that of the pre-Fire St Mary-le-Bow in London. Although the crown burnt there in 1666 was apparently early c16, its c14 predecessor was probably similar. A possible crown succession, apart from Continental precedents, might be: St Mary-le-Bow I c. 1357 or after; St Nicholas Newcastle c. 1448 or at any rate by c. 1474; St Giles Edinburgh c. 1495; King's College Aberdeen c. 1500; St Mary-le-Bow II by 1512. It has to be said that the crown at St Nicholas was twice rebuilt, in 1608 and in the c19 by *Gilbert Scott*, and at least twice repaired in the c18. (A threat of bombardment by Scots in the Civil War was robustly averted by filling the tower with Scottish prisoners.) The tower is flanked by low w transepts added in 1834–44 by *John* and *Benjamin Green*.

The c14 work at St Nicholas can be dated with some certainty. Mayors of 1348, 1350, 1361, etc., are recorded as amongst those who helped in the building. An indulgence of 1359 was offered to those who would help in the founding and endowing of new chapels. Money was left in 1369 for the fabric of one chancel window. The heraldry of roof bosses refers to the years 1390 to 1412. It seems likely that nave and transept were complete by about 1350 and that the chancel followed about 1360 etc. The Chapel of St Margaret attached to the s aisle was established in 1394. It is clearly later than the aisle wall – inside it breaks the uniform run of curious low arched recesses (on which see *Interior* below). The design of the windows does not help much in defining phases more precisely than this. It is partly Dec with flowing tracery, partly Perp and partly c19 imitation of Dec and Perp. *Benjamin Green* in 1834–6 rebuilt the n aisle we do not know how correctly and St

Margaret's Chapel apparently quite different from what he found (H. L. Honeyman). *Dobson* in 1824 rebuilt the n end of the n transept, and in 1859 the e wall, and in both cases altered the windows. Of original windows the following are Dec: n and s transepts, s aisle and clerestory. They are probably not all of the same date and can be sorted out as follows. Cusped intersected, that is early c14, s aisle (renewed), and n chancel chapel n and e. On the n side the neighbouring window has flowing tracery, so that perhaps intersecting was still used as late as 1335 or so. Flowing tracery also in one w window of the w aisle of the transept. On the other hand the upper w windows of the n transept are of the Late Dec type with three ogee-headed lights under one shallow segmental arch. The same design all along the clerestory and in the w transept s aisle. In the s transept e wall there are side by side a window with flowing tracery and one that is straight-headed with reticulated tracery. The rest of the windows are Perp. To complete the exterior it must be added that, at the expense of Sir Walter Blackett of Wallington, a LIBRARY was built on the s side in 1736 with a vestry under. This is in a pure Palladian style, attributed to *Daniel Garret* (Colvin), with rusticated ground floor and giant Ionic pilasters and alternating window pediments on the first floor. In 1832 and 1834 the n and s porches were provided.

The INTERIOR impression is mellow if not elating (there was cleaning and restoration in the 1970s). The church is not high, that is the arches do not start high up from the piers and the clerestory is small. Also, although the total length is 245 ft, it is so cut up that it is never quite felt. The nave has only four bays, the crossing breaks the axial vista, and the chancel with another four bays remains a separate unit. Yet the design is remarkably unified. It is characterized by the use of octagonal piers with chamfered arches dying into them without any capitals. Even the chancel arch dies into the wall. The crossing piers are the only element of something like cathedral scale. Moreover they are very uncommon in design: triple-chamfered with no capitals at all. In the s transept double-chamfered arches and a chamfered hoodmould on head-stops, in the n transept triple-chamfered arches instead, in the nave as in the n transept, and in the slightly lower chancel also identically. Of other features the graceful little oculus with a wheel of five mouchettes low down in the w wall of the n chancel chapel (St George's) must be mentioned first of all. It is typical of 1330 or 1340 and gives some borrowed light to an oblong CRYPT below part of the n transept. The crypt is vaulted with five heavy, single-chamfered transverse arches.

In the s transept s wall a low arched recess. The similar low recesses all along both nave aisle walls, already referred to – four a side before St Margaret's Chapel was added on the s – are thought to have been tomb recesses hopefully inserted in the C13 for 'founders' tombs' to make money for rebuilding. Their presumed C13 date means that the nave aisle walls were not again rebuilt in the C14 (see above, however, on *Green*'s rebuilding in 1834–6). The series of repetitive recesses at Hereford (N chancel aisle) is comparable. Finally, the C15 tower opens into the nave with one arch in which the disregard for capitals at St Nicholas is carried to the extreme of a six-fold chamfering. The timber roofs of the church are mostly original, but of no aesthetic interest. Only the W tower bay is vaulted (on its central boss, see dating of tower, above).

## FURNISHINGS

FONT. Of Frosterley marble, octagonal, with concave sides and shields on them. Six of the eight refer to the Rhodes family. The same type of font also in other Newcastle and Northumberland churches. – FONT COVER. *c.* 1500. With elaborate Gothic tracery, gables, pinnacles, foliage, and crockets. Inside a tiny rib-vault, with an exceedingly pretty boss of the Coronation of the Virgin. The C17 must have repaired some of the woodwork; see the brackets in the first tier of openings. It may well have done more. Again such elaborate font covers occur also in other Newcastle churches. – LECTERN. Eagle lectern of brass of *c.* 1500, the same type as more than twenty others in England, e.g. at Southwell (Oman, *Archaeological Journal*, 87, 1930). – ORGAN CASE. For the *Renatus Harris* organ of 1676, enlarged 1891. Excellent carving in the classical style, no doubt London work. – Carved ROYAL ARMS of Charles II, S transept W wall.

Cathedral fittings sensitively designed *c.* 1882 by the cathedral architect *R. J. Johnson* include the ROOD SCREEN and STALLS, with woodcarving by *Ralph Hedley*, and the PULPIT of Uttoxeter marble (the lion on its staircase like Stevens's lions then in front of the British Museum, now on Wellington tomb railings in St Paul's, q.v. in the companion volume, *Furnishings*, Nave). – Also designed by *Johnson* the alabaster REREDOS (side screens of Caen stone) with statues by *J. S. Westmacott*, and accompanying sedilia etc. The reredos is of the St Albans-Winchester-Southwark type: cf. Bodley's formerly at St Paul's and Pearson's for Truro.

STAINED GLASS (these notes contributed by David O'Connor). The only medieval glass is a fine C15 fragment of the upper half of a Virgin and Child in the E window of St Margaret's Chapel. – The rest of the glazing is mainly Victorian. E window by *William Wailes* of Newcastle, 1860 (Crucifixion and Last Supper with the Four Evangelists), in an oddly eclectic mixture of medieval and Renaissance styles. – NORTH CHOIR AISLE. E window, *Clayton and Bell*, 1901. – Easternmost in N wall, *L. C. Evetts*, 1962, simple design with Passion Symbols set mainly in white

glass. – Second window, *Caroline Townshend*, 1907. – Fourth window, *Kempe*, 1902. – Fifth window, *H. W. Bryans*, 1902. – SOUTH CHOIR AISLE. E window, *L. C. Evetts*, 1962. Easternmost in S wall and second window, *Wailes*, 1861 and † 1851. – Fourth window, Corporal Acts of Mercy, depicting the local chemist Joseph Garnett † 1861, by *Wailes*. – CHOIR CLERESTORY. Series of windows by *Kempe*. – ST GEORGE'S CHAPEL. Windows by *A. K. Nicholson*, 1934–6. – NORTH TRANSEPT. Abstract design by *S. M. Scott*, 1971. – CLERESTORY. Windows by *Kempe*. In the crypt below, four interesting little pictorial panels, *c.* 1931, the easternmost showing a shipyard's travelling crane. – SOUTH TRANSEPT. E wall, two windows by *Powell* of Leeds, 1880. – S wall, *Powell* of Leeds, 1877, and *Kempe*. – CLERESTORY. Three windows in E wall by *Kempe*. – NAVE NORTH AISLE. Easternmost, *P. C. Bacon*, 1921. – Second window, Indian Mutiny, *Wailes*, 1859. – Third and fourth, Boer War, *H. W. Bryans*, 1903. – NAVE SOUTH AISLE. Fourth window (St Margaret's Chapel S), *Mayer & Co.* and bad. – Fifth window (St Margaret's Chapel W), *Kempe*, 1896. – Sixth window, *Kempe*, † 1897. – SOUTH-WEST TRANSEPT. S window, *Wailes*, the figures of SS. John the Baptist and Evangelist copied from C15 glass in All Saints, North Street, York. – WEST WINDOW. Jesse by *Clayton and Bell*, 1866.

MONUMENTS, W to E. S aisle W wall. James Archbold † 1849, with portrait bust. – Robert Hopper Williamson † 1835, by *Dunbar*. Seated figure on a comfortably padded chair; well characterized lawyer's face. – Matthew White Ridley † 1813, by *Flaxman*. Standing figure in toga against the conventional obelisk. – S aisle, St Margaret's Chapel. Several coffin-lids with crosses, one of them of the rare type where at the top the head of the effigy appears in a sunk panel and at the bottom the feet in another sunk panel. Head and feet are exceedingly small, and if one reconstructs the whole figure hidden by the slab with its cross, sword, hammer and axe one obtains quite preposterous proportions. – N aisle W wall. Admiral Lord Collingwood † 1810, designed, 1819, by *C. R. Cockerell*, who was not entirely pleased with its execution by *Rossi* (D. Watkin, *Cockerell*, 1974). It has the somewhat coarse and sensational character that Rossi's monuments in St Paul's Cathedral also tend to display. Bust on high pedestal placed against ample stone drapery. – N aisle. Calverley Bewicke † 1815, by *E. H. Baily* from a design supplied by *Theed*, exhibited at the Royal Academy in 1819. The dying man sits on a chair supported by his daughter and faced by a standing allegorical female. The figures are in the round against a simple Gothic background with a long slender flying angel. – N transept. J. Bainbridge † 1823, also by *Baily*. Portrait in roundel and urn at the top. – S transept. Effigy of a cross-legged knight, early C14 (S wall recess). – Maddison monument, probably *c.* 1635. Six kneeling effigies (the six dates of death are 1611, 1624, 1633, 1634, 1646 and 1653), two facing each other across a prayer-desk in the usual way, two kneeling frontally behind their backs, and two at the sides. Below, again as usual, the children, sixteen in all. The monument stands on a bracket with vastly oversized leaves and does not keep parallel to the wall but comes out with canted sides to a bevelled edge in the middle, because it stood formerly against one of the piers of the crossing. – Hugo Moises † 1806, by *Flaxman*. A rather uninspired allegorical female looking up to heaven and leaning on a pedestal with a portrait and a severely undecorated urn. Very much less attractive and sensitive than the best of the contemporary monuments in the s chancel aisle.

In the s chancel aisle, however, the most interesting monument is medieval. High on the wall, giant double BRASS, originally in All Saints' Church. To Roger Thornton † 1429, and wife † 1411. Made soon after her death (Norris 1978). Its length of 89 in. almost that of Wyville's at Salisbury. An oblong plate with incised design, not cut-out figures on a stone slab – i.e. the Continental, not the English way of treating a brass. The origin may be North German; Norris (1978) says Flemish. The two figures have to l. and r. and between them buttresses with seven tiers of saints. On the l. of the l. and the r. of the r. buttresses, additional figures in profile and only half visible: an early case of a trick of perspective. Below the two main figures seven sons and seven daughters. More figures in the canopies.

Also in the s chancel aisle, several nice unsigned tablets of the late c 18. – Henry Askew by *Henry Webber*, 1801, with a big group of allegorical figures by an urn, this rare sculptor's best work. – Matthew Ridley by *John Bacon*, 1787, the best monument in the cathedral. Large seated figure against an obelisk, very tenderly felt and delicately carved. – Hannah Mosely † 1784, with portrait medallion, signed by *Fisher* of York. – John Collingwood Bruce † 1892, by *George Simonds*. Recumbent marble figure on sarcophagus. At his feet an open book. It is Bruce's *Roman Wall*; the page displayed contains the acknowledgements. – N chancel aisle. Bishop Lloyd, by *Oliver & Leeson*, 1908, with the recumbent marble effigy by *F. W. Pomeroy*. Elaborate tomb-chest and canopy; all Gothic. – N chancel chapel. Tablet to Thomas Surteis † 1629, with short columns and coat of arms and a French inscription. – William Hall † 1631, with the usual two kneelers and the children in relief below.

SURROUNDINGS

On the s side of the church a slip of a close, Amen Corner. On the N side, *Gilbert*'s statue of Queen Victoria presides over St Nicholas Square. On the w the cathedral tower confronts the traffic. To the s w the Castle and the railway. For travellers across the Tyne bridges the Anglican cathedral's lantern tower, though lower than other spires (see the R.C. cathedral below), crowns Newcastle's spectacular skyline. On all this, see the latest edition of B of E *Northumberland*.

# Newcastle

CATHEDRAL CHURCH OF ST MARY    *Roman Catholic*

(Based on B of E *Northumberland*, 1957, and information from Peter Howell and Roderick O'Donnell.)

Cathedral since 1850. Designed by *A. W. N. Pugin* in 1841 to replace a c 18 chapel. The body of the church built 1842–4 is notable for the separately roofed aisles, producing the three-gabled E end, so effective externally with its big Dec windows. Originally hemmed in by other buildings but now almost free-standing. *Archibald Dunn* designed the noble s w tower with needle spire (completed 1872), an important addition to Newcastle's skyline. The tower contains the entrance porch (as of 1981) reached through a bit of green churchyard (partly surrounded by cathedral offices by *E. W. Pugin*, 1858, and by *Dunn*, including round tower, c. 1870). The whole forms a most successful group, varied yet without levity. It remains to be seen what reordering of the entrance may do.

Inside, nave, aisles and sanctuary form one open space (from which *Goldie*'s stone rood screen of 1853 was removed some years ago, and his low side screens from the sanctuary in 1980). No clerestory. – Original FITTINGS designed by *Pugin* include: high ALTAR of Caen stone (TABERNACLE added by *Dunn*), now with the former Lady Altar, also by *Pugin*, placed in front of it; Lady Chapel REREDOS, now moved forward; TILES now moved about with changes in floor-level; and the PULPIT, now used as an ambo (lectern). – STAINED GLASS: the Jesse (main E) window designed by *Pugin* and made by *Wailes*, as probably the E side windows too. In the aisles some windows by *Barnett* remain (1980). – Also by *Pugin* the FONT, now moved up to the sanctuary. As for the polygonal s w baptistery, added 1902 by *Dunn, Hansom & Fenwicke* with ostentatious Boer War memorial in the middle, there are plans to find a new home for the war memorial and convert the space into a new porch. Reordering 1980–1 by *Napper Collerton Partnership*.

On the rest of the Newcastle skyline, see the Anglican cathedral above and the latest edition of B of E *Northumberland*.

# Northampton

CATHEDRAL CHURCH OF OUR LADY
AND ST THOMAS OF CANTERBURY   *Roman Catholic*

(Based on B of E *Northamptonshire*, 1973, and information
from George McHardy and Roderick O'Donnell.)

Cathedral since 1850. A small church of St Felix was built
to a design by *A. W. N. Pugin* in 1844, part of which is now
the sacristy: it stands to the r. of the cathedral (as seen from
the road), and to the r. again a narrow gabled bay was once
the chapel added to the Georgian house next r. again when
that became the residence of the vicar apostolic. Of the
cathedral built 1862–4 to *E. W. Pugin*'s design with reverse
orientation, there now remain the nave and aisles with w
polygonal apse. His intended w tower was not built. The
present eastern arm, with straight E end, transepts and low
crossing tower, was built 1948–60 to designs by *Albert
Herbert*, replacing some A. W. N. Pugin work.

   The Victorian nave has lowish arcades with squat
quatrefoiled piers on high plinths, typical Edward Pugin.
Tall clerestory with Geometrical tracery and a curious roof,
also typical of him, with a first stage of coving carrying a
second open stage of thin timbers. *Hardman* glass, *c.* 1865,
in the w apse and also in two clerestory windows nearest to
it on N and s. Apse corbels by *R. L. Boulton*. No furnishings by either Pugin survive here, but some glass of
1845 from St Felix's is now in the Catholic Church of St
John Baptist, Bridge Street. The cathedral's C 20 E window
contains glass from Ashby St Ledgers (New).

   Further on Northampton, see the latest edition of B of E
*Northamptonshire*.

# Norwich

CATHEDRAL CHURCH OF THE HOLY
AND UNDIVIDED TRINITY   *Anglican*

(Based on B of E *North-East Norfolk and Norwich*, 1962,
revised, with information from A. B. Whittingham, Eric
Fernie, Keith Darby of Feilden & Mawson, Thomas Cocke,
Michael Gillingham and Nicholas Penny.)

Plan, Fig. 123, from the *Builder*, 1891, by Roland Paul after
plan by John Adey Repton, *c.* 1800; so the E chapel of 1930
and the Saxon throne as restored in 1959 are not shown.

Some references (see Recent Literature): Borg *et al.* 1980;
Cherry 1978; Fernie 1974, 1977; Harvey 1978 and forthcoming; Whittingham 1980, 1981.

INTRODUCTION

Norwich Cathedral lies low, and if it were not for the spire
which rises above its crossing, it would not be more
prominent in the picture of its city than is Winchester
Cathedral. The spire makes the cathedral, as one
approaches Norwich. When one is nearer and happens to
have found a good vantagepoint, the other distinguishing
features enter the picture: the exceedingly long nave and
the strange geometrical richness of the decoration of the
crossing tower. The interior is at its most powerful when
one first sits down in the nave. The E part, as so often,
cannot address us clearly, owing to the many ritual partitions interrupting the view. The styles contributing are
the Norman and the Perpendicular, but both speak the
same language. The palisade of closely crowding masts in
the Norman walls, in spite of the arches between them, is as
relentless as the bundles of closely crowding staffs that
make the ribs, and the three parallel lines of bosses along
the ridge shoot into the distance with the same straightness
and the same never-halting tempo as the arcades. Rarely
does the unity of English architecture from the C 11 to the
C 16 carry so much conviction. And this is the case because
the periods in between the Norman and the Perpendicular
are not strongly represented here.

   The cathedral in its original parts is built of Barnack and
Caen stone. Clipsham stone has been used in restoration.
It is 481 ft long, about the same as Peterborough, slightly
less than Lincoln and York, considerably exceeded by
Canterbury, St Albans, Ely and Winchester.

   Of the masons who designed and built it we know only
some of the post-Norman men, indeed nothing certain
before *c.* 1300. The first known names concern the rebuilding of the Norman cloisters. The E walk, begun *c.* 1297,
is thought to have been carried on by members of the
*Ramsey* family, two of whom are known to have built the s
walk from 1324 into the 1330s, and then the w walk from
1335. The handsome doorway into the nave at the N end of
the E walk is thought to be by the great *William Ramsey*.

123. NORWICH
Plan from the *Builder*, 1891 (see p. 250)

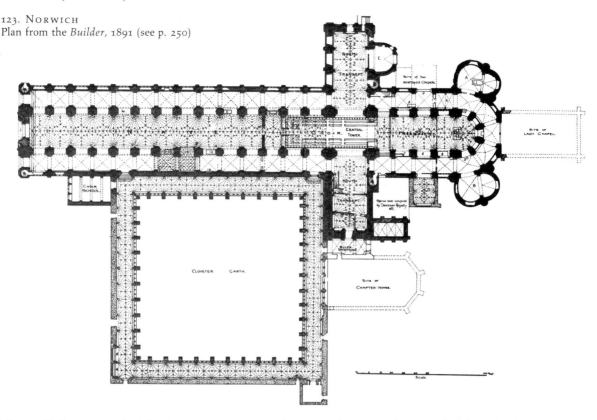

The N walk, begun 1356 by *John Attegrene Jr*, was carried on 1385–1415 by *Robert Wodehirst* or *Wadhurst*, who had rebuilt the presbytery clerestory 1362–9, and the same walk was vaulted 1416–30 by *James Woderofe* or *Woodruff*, who may also have been responsible for the great nave w window. *Robert Everard*, master in charge at the cathedral 1451–85, rebuilt the spire after it was hit by lightning in 1463, and presumably he was in charge of vaulting the nave from *c.* 1464 and the presbytery from *c.* 1472. Mr Harvey and Mr Whittingham have uncovered much about the Norwich masons in relation to their work at other centres, e.g. London and Ely.

In the beginning, there was Bishop Herbert de Losinga. He was born in Normandy, where he reached high office, and in 1091 was raised from being prior of Fécamp to being Bishop of East Anglia. The Saxon bishops' seat had been from *c.* 800 or earlier at North Elmham, *c.* 20 miles N w of Norwich; the see lapsed in the mid-C 9, was revived *c.* 955, and in *c.* 1075 moved briefly to Thetford, *c.* 27 miles s w of Norwich. Apparently in accordance with Archbishop Lanfranc's order that sees should be transferred to bigger and more fortifiable towns, the see was moved to Norwich in 1094. Yet, more likely, the move from Elmham to Thetford was in response to that order, for the move to

Norwich seems to have resulted from the defeat of one of Losinga's predecessors in an attempt to gain control of Bury St Edmunds Abbey too. At any rate the new cathedral was begun at Norwich in 1096. We know little of how it progressed. According to the late C 13 *Registrum Primum*, repeating what its author had known 'ex relatione antiquorum', Losinga began the building on the future site of the C 13 Lady Chapel, i.e. at the E end, and built it to the Holy Cross altar, i.e. to one bay w of the pulpitum or four bays w of the crossing. He died in 1119 and was buried in the middle of the presbytery, and his successor Eborardus (1121–45) 'ecclesiam integraliter consummavit'. However, a fire broke out in 1171, the damage was repaired in 1173, and, according to another late C 13 source, Bartholomew of Cotton, Bishop John of Oxford (1175–1200), 'consummavit ecclesiam'. The final consecration, however, did not take place till 1278. The question whether the Norman church, as we know it, was completed before 1145 or after 1175, allows of only one answer. Its style is emphatically not that of 1180. The only confusing detail is the signs of a fire which are evident on the first and second piers from the E of the nave on the s side and about the same part of the arcade on the N side, where the stone is coloured a faint pink. But there were two other fires after that of 1171: one after riots in 1272 and one after the lightning struck in 1463. (On signs of fire see end of *Interior*, gallery, eastern arm, and nave, third pier N side W of the crossing.)

Dating can be further summarized (see also the masons above). In 1362 the spire fell, and money spent on the presbytery in 1364 and 1369 must refer to repair of damage there and to the making of a new clerestory. Money was left for the new W window in 1449, the lower W front having been remodelled 1426–36. The vaults were put up by Bishop Lyhart (1464–72) in the nave, by Bishop Goldwell (1472–99) in the presbytery, and by Bishop Nykke (after 1509) in the transepts. There was again rebuilding of the spire after 1463. From the C17 on, restorations were frequent (Colvin, Cocke). In the 1670s much money was spent on the N aisle and transepts, in the 1740s there were extensive repairs to the tower, the N side of the church, and the W front under *Matthew Brettingham* (then busy at Holkham), and the spire was repaired in the 1750s by *Parsons*. *Wilkins* did restoration work in 1806–7. The W front was repaired by *Francis Stone* in 1815, by *Salvin* in the 1830s, and by *Blore* c. 1840. *John Brown* restored the tower in 1842. Scott was not here. As with other cathedrals, surviving drawings and engravings show how extremities most exposed to weather, e.g. the W front turret tops, changed shape with changing tastes down the centuries: doubtless after a series of medieval caps and pinnacles, C16 ogee-domical caps or 'tips' can be surmised, though by 1656 a view shows slim lead-covered spirelets, yet by 1794 a view shows ogee caps (Brettingham reverting to the C16 type?), next rebuilt in the 1830s as tall polygonal candle-snuffers, and in 1974 as ogee caps again – at any rate offering least surface to weathering. The presbytery roof was renewed in 1955 with steel trusses by *Stephen Dykes Bower*, and other roofs since with reinforced concrete trusses, and tower and spire reinforced, by *Bernard Feilden*.

## EXTERIOR

As Bishop Losinga began at the E end, we are deprived of his earliest work. The present St Saviour's Chapel, by *Sir Charles Nicholson*, 1930–2, is on part of the site of a C13 Lady Chapel (pulled down in the C16) of which the straight E end is exposed on the lawn E of the present chapel. The C13 chapel was an enlargement of Losinga's E chapel, of which the horseshoe plan is known from excavations. It was the E chapel of a church planned on the principle of an ambulatory round the apse with radiating chapels, and additional chapels E of the transepts, a principle established for cathedrals and abbey churches in France from the early C11 onwards or even earlier. Rouen Cathedral as begun before 1037 is an early example in Normandy. And Norwich presbytery is thought to have been built by

masons who had just finished Bury Abbey presbytery, as a smaller edition of Bury (Whittingham 1981).

Except for the E chapel, the arrangement survives uncommonly completely at Norwich, and this is one of the church's architectural distinctions. Moreover, there seems no change of plan for quite a distance, and one is thus entitled to regard the whole E part and probably more as representing the plan laid down by Losinga's unknown master mason. It is a straightforward plan and elevation, a standard plan and elevation, one would be tempted to say, if it were not for the extremely curious shape of the SE and NE chapels. They consist of two parts each, both parts curved, the apse facing almost due E and an antechapel, as it were, facing almost due N and S. The E part is semicircular, the W part of a horseshoe shape. The parts are moreover connected with one another and with the walls of the chancel aisles to their W and of the E bays of the ambulatory to their N (the S chapel) and S (the N chapel) so that a composition of five curved surfaces results, undulating and somewhat ill-defined. The French did not mind their SE and NE chapels unambiguously facing SE and NE. It might seem as if this architectural impurity at Norwich were a half-hearted attempt to improve what English masons and clergy felt to be a ritual impurity. But Eric Fernie points out that the two chapels clearly face 10° S and N of E respectively, so their shape cannot be explained as an attempt to orientate; and the same applies at Canterbury, though at Lincoln excavated evidence is unclear.

Now for the system of the external elevation. What distinguishes it from most other Norman and, indeed, Europeanly speaking, Romanesque churches is that it has a gallery not only over both nave and presbytery aisles but also covering the E chapels of the transepts, the NE and SE radiating chapels, and no doubt Losinga's E chapel. Elevational details that can still be gathered, partly from the S and partly from the N side, are as follows. Large shafted ambulatory windows, chapel windows, and presbytery aisle windows all with billet mouldings. Big frieze of blank arcading on a nutmeg course. Small shafted single gallery windows. All the shafts have simple scallop or simple volute capitals. Above the original tier of gallery windows was added, to improve lighting, an upper tier of straight-headed four-light windows of alternating designs (one has a row of reticulation units). The roof of the raised gallery wall, of which the straight-headed windows form part, is pierced by the footings of flying buttresses with complex soffit mouldings which form a most unhappy junction with the gallery roof timbers. These soffit mouldings begin at the point where the buttress would have emerged from the original gallery roof. It therefore seems likely that the raised gallery roof post-dates the flying buttresses, and as these must go with Goldwell's high vault, the new upper gallery windows must be late C15 or early C16 (Fernie).

124. NORWICH North transept front, *c.* 1120, in 1816

125. NORWICH West front, C12, C15 etc., in 1816

For the Norman clerestory we must go farther w. The whole part of the cathedral E of the crossing was given a new, much taller clerestory in the 1360s. This has tall four-light windows of typical Early Perp character: two-centred arches, and in the head still a motif reminiscent of the four-petalled flower. The flying buttresses are steep and vigorous. On them seated figures of prophets (as at Peterborough), though these are Victorian; some of the original (c 16?) figures are in a near-by garden and near the Visitors' Centre. Panelled battlements, with odd inconsistencies of design. On the N side, traces of a former Relic Chamber (see *Interior*, platform over N presbytery aisle) and to its w the arch of a chapel.

The TRANSEPTS help to finish the visual picture of the Norman E parts. The N transept is more helpful than the s transept, for the s front of the latter, abutting on the E range of cloisters, was at some time heavily restored in its lower parts (Mr Dykes Bower says this was part of *John Brown*'s restoration). Also, to the E of the s transept is a group of later structures: namely the Bauchun Chapel of c. 1330, but with a late c 15/early c 16 window, running s off the presbytery aisle, and the former Chapel of St Catharine (now Dean's Vestry) of c. 1250–75, running E off the transept and having small lancets to the s on two storeys and Victorian windows to the E. The original arrangement was, as has been said, an apse off the E side of the transept. On the N side this survives in its lower storey only (now St Andrew's Chapel, used in Elizabethan times as a house, later as a furnace room; restored 1920). On both sides of the building, traces of the upper storey can be seen. The lower arch on the s side is best examined from the staircase of the present E attachment.

The elevational system of the N front of the N transept is this. On the ground floor a small doorway to the Bishop's Palace. Two orders of shafts. One single-scallop, one volute capital. The effigy of a bishop above this doorway is a fibre-glass replica; for the very interesting original, see *Furnishings*, SE ambulatory, below. To l. and r. of the image shafted windows. Above them tall shafted windows. Then a new motif which we shall not meet again for some time. Instead of the normal blank arcading of the presbytery and the s transept there are here big intersected arch-heads. (These, and the intersected arches on the retaining wall for the bishop's throne (see *Interior*, E end, below) suggest that this N front was being completed and the effigy installed over the bishop's door at the same time that the old bishop's throne was installed behind the high altar: c. 1120.) Then again tall shafted windows, and two more tiers in the gable. Square angle-turrets. All the buttresses are flat and shafted too.

The w sides of the transepts show another sign of progress, and it comes only at clerestory level, i.e. at the end of operations. The clerestory is tripartite throughout with the big central window part raised – the usual English arrangement. Traces indicate that this was the way with the former clerestory of the E end too. But in the w walls of the transepts the minor arches have zigzag, the first in the cathedral, and the main arch has billet in the s but a kind of barrel or bobbin motif in the N transept. In the s transept w wall these minor arches have the whole of the field below diapered – but it is not certain how far the motif was accurately renewed. Anyway, it must be remembered that at this stage a desire for ornamental enrichment made itself felt.

The CROSSING TOWER is more boldly decorated than that. In fact it is the only boldly decorated work of the Norman period at Norwich and, even so, not with any of the luxuriance which one is accustomed to in the Late Norman style. There is no abundance of motifs. The motifs employed are unusual and, if anything, austere: blank arcading, now also with intersected arches, and in addition between the bell-openings vertical strings of alternating lozenges and circles, and above the windows, very big and provocative, two tiers of again vertically connected circles or port-holes, as the upper ones served as bell-openings. The angle buttresses are square and over-closely shafted, almost reeded, but have on top polygonal turrets, also Norman. Only their crocketed spirelets belong to the c 15 work, when the present fine needle-spire was put on, with crockets up the edges and lucarnes in three tiers in alternating directions. The spire is recessed behind battlements decorated with shields.

On the Norman NAVE there are no external changes of any significance from the system of the E parts. The N aisle windows are of the early c 14 (cusped intersected tracery). The original gallery windows are part of a blank arcading of three even arches; above that tier an upper tier of larger, Perp windows was introduced to give more light to the gallery. The clerestory is still tripartite as it was, but the decorative enrichments of the transepts were not continued. The only change to be noted on the nave is on the s side, three w bays, where the blind arcading below the gallery has intersected arches: these are c 19, like those on the w front s side (below).

The w front, it must be admitted, is a disappointment. Is this because a w transept was intended to be added as they existed at Ely and Bury St Edmunds (as Clapham, on scanty evidence, regarded as possible)? But excavations in front of the façade have revealed no foundations and no suggestion of any intention to carry walls farther w (Fernie 1974). So is it because the English were rarely at their best in Norman and E.E. façades? As it is, the effect is lowered yet more by the admixture of c 15 work, in itself of a high standard. The Norman façade had three portals, the remaining aisle portals being lower than the central one. Above them is again blank arcading (intersected on the s side, which is not borne out by the view published by Britton in 1816; cf. also the s side of the nave around the corner) with a window over, flanked by blank arches. There are polygonal angle-turrets, of which the outer pair since 1974 have been crowned by Tudor-like ogee caps (as in the c 18–early c 19 and presumably the c 16, but with Gothic spirelets in the c 17, and in the c 19–20 tall polygonal caps; see *Introduction*, restorations, above), with the inner pair now capped by lead flats. As for the nave front, this has its ambitious Perp portal with diagonally set niches and a shallow vault, pairs of outer niches with small seated and kneeling figures above, and then the nine-light w window. Bishop Alnwick built the w portal 1426–36 and in 1449 left money for the great w window. The clusters of Norman shafting on either side were only added in the c 19, but remains of early shafts were found when the porch was narrowed late in the century.

## INTERIOR

We must again start at the EAST END, but we can now take it for granted that the system was never changed to the very w front. This system was one almost uniformly adopted in England (except in the w), namely a nave (or chancel) with groin-vaulted aisles, a gallery, a clerestory, a flat timber ceiling. The latter we can only presume from the shafts which ran right up to it to support the main beams. The clerestory has the arrangement with a stepped tripartite wall-passage in front of the window, as it was introduced at Winchester and taken over at Ely and everywhere in England. The gallery has unsubdivided openings, as had been done at St-Étienne in Caen, designed c. 1065, and then in England, e.g. at Old St Paul's in London. It is an impressive system, more uncompromising somehow than the twin openings under one arch at Winchester, Ely and Durham.

The details, once this has been established, are as follows. At the E end of the ambulatory the tall twin arch with dogtooth decoration, now leading into the Lady Chapel of 1930, may well belong to the preceding Lady Chapel built by Bishop Walter de Suffield (1245–57; pulled down in the c 16), although the dividing clustered shaft and the responds can be no earlier than the later c 14. The Norman ambulatory has broad unmoulded transverse arches on strong coupled shafts between its groin-vaults. Wall-arcading, that motif the English never tired of, runs along

126. NORWICH South ambulatory, 1096–1119, with c15 font

127. NORWICH North ambulatory, 1096–1119, with c15 lectern, in 1816

the outer walls. The windows, where they survive, are shafted. Capitals are of one or two scallops or have primitive volutes. (See also the paragraph on the gallery, end of *Interior* section.) Facing the entry to the Lady Chapel is what seems a screen wall but is the retaining wall for the Bishop's Throne. The wall has a deep niche with shafts carrying capitals later than the surrounding ones. The adjoining bays continue this retaining wall, and they have intersected arches. So the very early throne (see *Furnishings*, Presbytery, below), was not installed at once, but only at the time when intersected arches became the fashion at Norwich – say about 1120 – and in fact the first enthronement in the cathedral took place in 1121.

The S E and N E chapels look as weird from inside as they do from outside. The relation between their groined vaults and their plans ought to be observed particularly. The blank arcading runs round the chapels as it does round the ambulatory. In the N E (Jesus) Chapel are five brackets for images, one of them bigger than the others. They are probably Perp. There is no change when it comes to the chancel aisles. Off the s aisle the Bauchun Chapel runs s. The arch with semicircular responds and semicircular capitals is typically Dec. An identical arch opened into a corresponding chapel on the N side, but that arch is blocked and the chapel has disappeared (traces of an arch outside). The Bauchun Chapel extended further E, as a blocked arch, not visible from outside, proves. The Perp s window and the vault prove also that the whole chapel was remodelled in the C 15 or early C 16. The vault has exactly the same pattern as the nave and presbytery vaults (see below) and the same abundance of bosses. Here the bosses illustrate Chaucer's *Man of Law's Tale* of an Early Christian queen wrongly accused: the remodelling of the chapel is said to have been done by *William Sekynton*, Corrector General of Crimes who held consistory courts here and is buried here. In the E wall is an uncommonly big niche with a tall pedestal for an image, in the s wall a low tomb recess.

Over the N aisle a platform connects with the former Relic Chamber (see *Exterior*), with a spiral stair down to the aisle and other steps to the presbytery. It served no doubt also as a watching point. The underside of the platform has heavy, single-chamfered ribs, rising on responds characteristic of the early C 14. The platform is now a treasury for the exhibition of diocesan plate (cf. e.g. the one in Winchester nave).

The PRESBYTERY strikes one at once, as one enters, by its height. This is of course due to the altered clerestory, but the Norman wall treatment with its many sturdy shafts contributes much. The actual height is 83 ft. The apse piers have three shafts in steps to the inner side, but the sides to the aisle openings are treated as if they were part of a circular pier hidden by the shafts and steps. The design is the same in the nave at Ely, and seems also to have existed

at the crossing there, perhaps even in the E arm. Whether Ely or Norwich is earlier in use of the motif one cannot say (an uncertainty borne out by analysis of eastern English pier-forms in Cherry 1978). The arches have two roll mouldings and a billet moulding. The gallery is large and undivided, with stilted arches. The clerestory is that of the C 14. The system must have continued into the straight part of the presbytery. The gallery is intact but the arcade-level was completely recast in the Perp style, probably by Bishop Goldwell. The only indication of the Norman arcade still existing is the E respond of the N E bay of the presbytery aisle and part of the base of the w respond. The arches are made four-centred by Goldwell, and the thickness of the wall which they pierce made the occasion for a display of tracery inside. Tracery in the spandrels too. Tall blank ogee arches between them with crockets. The new design just laps over into the gallery by means of a parapet of cusped lozenges, a pretty motif. On the gallery-level traces remain between the arches which, in conjunction with what the nave will show, can be defined as the remains of shafts up to the roof. The traces make it certain that there was an alternation of twin shafts and single shafts. The Gothic clerestory keeps the stepped rhythm of the Norman tradition but simplifies it into low-high-low-high-low etc. The lower unit has an ogee head, and from this the lush palm-fronds of Bishop Goldwell's vault spread. The harmony between the clerestory of 1362–9 and the vault of c. 1472–99 is perfect; how the clerestory harmonized with the old timber roof during the intervening century we cannot tell. That roof was there, above the vault, till 1955. The vault, if one analyses it, is a rib-vault with diagonal and ridge ribs and three pairs of tiercerons in the N and s, one pair in the E and w walls. That far it is the system invented for Exeter two hundred years before. But the Norwich vault has a pattern (already introduced in the nave) formed by lierne ribs along the middle as well. The forms are a lozenge, an irregular, elongated eight-pointed star, a lozenge, etc. This in itself also was not a new idea. The Ethelbert Gate, mainly of 1308–17, and a few years after it the Ely Lady Chapel and Ely choir, had done very much the same well over a hundred years before, and it remains noteworthy that the Perp style could so successfully take over a Dec motif. The lierne part is studded with bosses. A few of them have figural subjects (Assumption, Trinity). In quite a number appears Bishop Goldwell's rebus.

The TRANSEPTS can be treated as one, for they do not differ in essentials. (Direct passage between them was originally blocked at the crossing by the choir stalls, as in other Norman monastic cathedrals, e.g. St Albans, Winchester, Gloucester.) The E walls are of necessity more varied than the others. Arcade and gallery (i.e. the arches from the presbytery aisle) are as before. The clerestory

now appears for the first time of a type no doubt also retained. It is the familiar stepped tripartite arcading in front of a wall-passage. Some of the shafts of the N transept are decorated, the only ones in the cathedral if one excepts those of Losinga's effigy on the outside, N front (now in replica; see *Furnishings*, S E *ambulatory*, below). The bay following that of the presbytery aisle is virtually blank, as the staircases to the crossing tower go up behind it. On the N side the small doorway has a tympanum with a diaper pattern. Above the ground stage is tall blank arcading with billet and then a tall area of blank wall. On the S side this area is covered with more, very tall blank arcading, and that arcading is intersected. The fact may not be without significance. The level is almost the same as that of the intersected arch-heads noted outside the N transept. So – to say it once more – perhaps, when that level was reached, there was a tendency to decorate a little more freely. The clerestory here has a single and a twin opening to the transept. Above this and above the lower arches of the stepped tripartite arrangement ran yet another band (an interrupted band) of blank arcading, a unique motif, almost resulting in the impression of a four-tier elevation. The last bay to the N is unpardonably irregular, with only two parts of the tripartite arrangement fitted in. In the S transept, although there was restoration in the C 19 by *Brown* or by *Salvin* (blind arch at aisle-level), Mr Fernie thinks most of the end bay is original. The end walls of the transepts have large windows in two tiers. On the ground floor of the N wall an anomaly occurs – corresponding to the effigy outside. There are two lengths of billet moulding arranged like twin Saxon triangle-headed arches, and a carved head is placed between them, again with a little billet triangle over. The feature looks very odd. For the W walls the S transept is more helpful. The lower windows are flanked by arched niches on the l. and r. The clerestory level is in the W wall normal in the N transept as well as the S. The squeeze of the E wall does not recur. The transept vaults were only put up after 1509. Yet they continue the presbytery (and indeed the earlier nave) vaults without change. The bosses here represent the early life of Christ, and there are about 150 of them. Off the S transept is the former Chapel of St Catharine, now Dean's Vestry. This has E.E. rib-vaulting in three bays, the ribs with one hollow chamfer. One boss has a beautiful (albeit Victorian) bishop's head in a wreath of stiff-leaf foliage. On St Andrew's, the N transept's E chapel, restored 1920, see *Exterior* above.

The CROSSING TOWER could of course be built only when the transepts and indeed the first bay or bays of the nave had reached full height. Its upper parts are thus appreciably later in style than the rest. This has already been emphasized when the exterior was described. The crossing piers have three shafts side by side in the E and W, two in the N and S arches. Scallop and volute capitals still go

on. The lantern is open. The first tier is an arched wall-passage, the second blank arcading in pairs with near the angles a circle instead – the motif famous from the outside. On the stage above the designer of this outside motif has done something equally surprising. The windows, which externally form minor incidents in a band of arcading, are internally given the tripartite treatment, but with absurdly narrow side-parts. The window itself is flanked by fat shafts on which stand finer shafts, a motif which the clerestory of the transepts had already established.

The NAVE continues the same system entirely, except for one attempt at a break. The system is no doubt still that of the presbytery, and it can now at last be fully summed up. In the aisles there is no change at all. The arcade has piers with the slightest alternation of supports. The major pier has triple shafts on the arch faces and double shafts on the nave face (these latter, originally carried right up to the Norman ceiling beams, are obscured by the C 15 vaulting shafts). The minor pier has a circular core expressed on the arch faces and a single shaft on the nave face. Large unsubdivided gallery, clerestory with wall-passage and tripartite arcading. The gallery alone shows a change in decoration. Up to now no decorative friezes other than of billets and nutmeg have been found. Now zigzag occurs, a motif favoured in England from about 1115 or 1120 onwards. We have seen it arrive at Norwich very unobtrusively outside the clerestory of the transept on the W side. That stage in building may well have been reached at the same time as the first gallery arches of the nave. But the introduction of such a motif can hardly be called a break.

A real break occurs a little farther W at ground-level, in a place which may well have been begun when the gallery arches and the transept clerestories were built. At first it seems that the break occurs at the fifth pier from the E. Instead of the minor pier described above, here is a very strong circular pier, vigorously spiral-grooved. It is short, yet its diameter is about 7 ft 6 in. Does this magnificent motif represent a change of system? Farther E, in the third pier of the N side, just such a round spiral-grooved pier has been partly exposed, encased in the present standard shape, and just W of the point where the future crossing tower had to be buttressed by enough nave construction (two bays) to be safe until the nave could be continued. There are signs of (probably C 12 or C 15) fire on this pier. Losinga, we are told, built as far as the nave altar of the Holy Cross. That altar customarily stood W of the pulpitum, which ran across between piers there. In fact excavations have shown a rubble foundation wall running right across the church in that place. This must have marked the end of Losinga's work, at any rate by the year of his death, 1119. For what we now see to have been two pairs of special piers, Mr Fernie (1977) has the convincing explanation that they were meant from the start to define the nave sanctuary.

Their centres do not lie in line with the centres of the cores of other minor piers, but a few inches in towards the nave, making them stand out. Spirally tooled pier shafts occurred in Ernulf's crypt at Canterbury and in the York crypt, but the great originals in England of spiral grooving on a huge scale must have been the two pairs in Durham choir, begun 1093. Spiral columns defining shrines have a history going back to those of the c 4 in Old St Peter's, Rome. (In Rome it came to be alleged that those were from Solomon's Temple in Jerusalem, hence the present term 'salomonic'. Small-scale use of the motif on St Edward's Shrine at Westminster in the c 13 came with Cosmati craftsmen direct from Rome.) The mason here is unknown entirely, but if he was also responsible for the various zigzags, he was perhaps a new man starting about 1115. The stopping short of the grooving on the s w pier may have occurred at the end of Losinga's work, Mr Whittingham suggests, the rest of the decoration of that pier being done in paint in the absence of a craftsman capable of carving a spiral on a curved surface.

The break between Bishop Losinga's and Bishop Eborard's work is not everywhere clear higher up. It has been noticed that the abaci change very slightly between piers and shafts two and piers and shafts three. To the E there is a slight convex member between the vertical and the sloping part. To the w it is notched instead and then chamfered. So everything points to a break at pier three, and – we may add – at bay one in the gallery and at the w clerestory in the transepts. The only snag is that the rubble wall rises w of that line. It can, however, perhaps be suggested that in spite of Losinga having marked the w termination of his project the changes in the abaci and piers mark the start of a new build. This could then be dated fairly securely to 1120. The only minor change is that the capitals of the wall-arcading on the N side, after pier five, are much busier and livelier. The same is not true of the s aisle, but the wall of this may well have been built first, since it was needed for building the cloister. In spite of these more varied capitals, the style remains essentially as it had been before, and a post-fire date is out of the question. Right up to the w front nothing can be later than the deposition of Eborard in 1145. The w wall of the nave shows the outline of the Norman central portal, flanked by pairs of blank arches.

Of later contributions to the nave the most important is the vault. This was built for Bishop Lyhart c. 1464–72 and it inaugurated the lierne-star pattern of vaulting in the cathedral. (The chronological sequence over about fifty years was to be: nave, presbytery, Bauchun Chapel, transepts; as happened at Exeter and Lichfield, an unchanging pattern of vaulting unified the interior from one end to the other.) The number of bosses is again prodigious (over 270), and they represent scenes from the Old and New Testaments, from the Creation to the Last Judgement.

Altogether well over 800 bosses have been counted in Norwich Cathedral (including the cloister). Otherwise there is a very fine portal into the cloister in the E bay. This has shafts carrying a depressed two-centred arch; for the beautiful work on its other side, see *Cloisters* below. It may date from c. 1310 and must be the work of one of the *Ramsey* family. In two bays of the s aisle remodelled by Bishop Nykke (†1536) are wall seats with cusped lozenges along the fronts; on his monument and its setting, see *Furnishings* below. One of the s windows has pretty fleurons in jambs and arch.

As a final confirmation of the findings so far expounded, a visit to the GALLERY is to be recommended. This is what

131. NORWICH Pier, c. 1115–19,
originally one of four defining the nave sanctuary

it will show. The gallery was not vaulted. The only transverse arches were at the E end of the presbytery aisles, i.e. the start of the ambulatory. The lean-to roof, still marked in the transept walls, made it necessary to run the twin shafts to much less in height against the walls than against the gallery piers. In fact, the twin shafts carried Norman (internal) flying buttresses below the aisle roofs; a few voussoirs survive. The whole of the E parts of the gallery, starting from the ambulatory, has far more volute capitals, also of quite playful shapes, than were used further w. The Norman gallery windows were shafted and set in a severe blank arcading of arches on broad pilasters, not colonnettes. This is specially impressive in the NE and SE chapels. Signs of fire are evident on piers one and two from the E in the S aisle gallery. From here, looking at the N wall of the arcade opposite, the discolouring of the stone is equally evident. The fires of both 1272 and 1463 affected the presbytery (Whittingham 1980).

FURNISHINGS, E TO W

*St Saviour's (the E) Chapel*    Several PAINTINGS of the Norwich School, of the highest value. They should be seen and described together with the retable in St Luke's (the SE) Chapel, as comparisons will prove illuminating. In St Luke's Chapel: five-part retable given by, or at the time of, Bishop Despenser, i.e. c. 1380–90, and the finest piece of East Anglian painting of its time. In St Saviour's Chapel: five-part, similar retable, but later and not originally a retable, made up of panels from the parish church of St Michael-at-Plea (Annunciation and Crucifixion from a chancel screen and two saints from a parclose screen, these four of c. 1410–20, and a Resurrection of c. 1430–40 that once formed part of a retable); also two very good fragmentary scenes, Betrayal and Crucifixion, from the retable of St Michael-at-Plea, of the same date as the Despenser retable. The differences between the earlier and later pieces are evident. In the 1380s the colours are softer and subtler, the draperies have a gradual shading inspired by Italian Trecento painting, and the facial types are close to those of the same years in North Germany, especially the work of Master Bertram in Hamburg. Also, in the 1380s a patterned gilded background is all that sets the figures off. The Christ of the Resurrection is strictly frontal and his gesture conventional and hieratic, the sarcophagus appears as a diagonal on the picture plane rather than in depth. Fifty years later the scene of the Resurrection has become a scene indeed, placed in space and in landscape, with the sarcophagus unmistakably leading into depth, and Christ standing on it in a gently demonstrating pose. Yet conventions are certainly not yet discarded as they were to be in all painting influenced by the Flemish discoveries of the 1420s and 1430s, i.e. by the van Eycks, Robert Campin and Roger van

der Weyden. Thus e.g. the little structure in which the Annunciation takes place is just as fantastical as that of the Scourging of Christ of the earlier retable. Yet here again the figures certainly have more weight and substance, and also more charm. These child-like heads with large round foreheads and small features were an international fashion of the ending C14 and early C15. The bonier and perhaps uglier heads of 1380 allow for a more convincing presentation of tragedy and suffering.

*Ambulatory from the E to the NW, including the NE (Jesus) Chapel*    Of WALL PAINTING (of the C13 – probably largely after the fire of 1272) many traces survive here and especially in the chapel, where they are no doubt renewed. They appear, however, with their dark green columns and the red, light blue and yellow of the capitals etc., quite convincing and in accordance with illuminated manuscripts. Even more important are the twelve Saints arranged around Christ in the vault of the bay converted into the bridge in front of the Relic Chamber. The conversion belongs to c. 1275 (after the fire), but most of the figures, which must once have been very good indeed, are of the early C14. But the accusing angel on the transverse arch must be of c. 1275, and the same is true of the bishop's head on a capital below and some neighbouring ornament. – STAINED GLASS. In the E window of the Jesus Chapel, designed by *Sir T. G. Jackson* and made by *Powell's*. – PAINTING on the altar, Adoration of the Magi, C15, by *Martin Schwarz*. – MONUMENTS. Between the presbytery and the N aisle, base of a monument to an unknown person, C15, with ogee-headed panels. – In the same bay against the wall, Elizabeth Calthropp † 1582. Tomb-chest with tapering pilasters. No effigy. Semicircular top with shell fluting. – In the arch towards the presbytery, next bay, Dr Thomas Moore † 1779. Signed by *Thomas* (or his nephew *John*) *Ivory* and *J. de Carle*. Weeping putto under a medallion with palm-fronds. – Under the same arch but on the E respond WALL PAINTING with many figures and many scrolls and, according to Mr Whittingham, the Virgin and St John to the l. and r. of a cross, and, above, the Fathers of the Church, the Evangelists, and God the Father surrounded by angels. – In the second bay from the w of the N presbytery aisle, the Erpingham window with fragments of medieval STAINED GLASS assembled by Dennis King.

*Ambulatory from the E to the SW, including the SE (St Luke's) Chapel*    First, one of the chief treasures. WALL-MONUMENT to a bishop, beardless, standing with crozier tightly between two spiral-fluted columns under an arch, the sides tapering slightly towards the foot. The tapered sides have suggested, not only to Clapham but to C18 and probably earlier scholars (Cocke), that what we have here is the lid of the monument to Losinga placed in the middle of the presbytery after his death in 1119. As such it could be the most ancient of English funeral monuments. There is reason to suppose that when it was set over the bishop's entrance to the N transept (where there is now a replica) it pre-dated that part of the building. Although slightly cut down (with gabling cut away from the head and a dragon from the foot), the slab with the effigy fits the niche too well to have been inserted in the C17, the earliest time at which Losinga's grave-slab would have been removed from the presbytery. It may even have been brought from elsewhere to the niche specially provided in the original design of the N transept front. Eric Fernie very tentatively suggests it might represent one of the bishops who converted East Anglia, Felix or Fursa. Possibly the spiral colonnettes on the slab echo the great spiral-grooved piers just set up in the nave? – but probably here more simply stress the memory of a holy person.

Also in the S E ambulatory, STAINED GLASS. Window of St Brice, a large figure of the C16, probably French, from Langley Park (cf. in Langley parish church, B of E *North-West and South Norfolk*, C16 E window glass brought from Rouen Cathedral 1787). – In the S E Chapel of St Luke (now parish church to the Close), E window medallions, 1868, by *Hardman*, W window medallions, 1881, by *Clayton & Bell*, a typical change of style. – On the very fine late C14 Despenser RETABLE in the chapel, see under *St Saviour's Chapel* above. – FONT in the chapel, from the former church of St Mary-in-the-Marsh. A sumptuous piece of the East Anglian type, with eight seated figurines on the foot, eight standing figurines against the stem, and the Seven Sacraments separated by eight angels against the bowl. – MONUMENTS. Richard Brome, c. 1500. Wall panel with ogee arch and panelling over. – Prior Bozoun. Low chantry chapel with a four-centred canopy, tracery-panelled inside. To the w of the chapel, long tomb-chest to Bishop Wakering † 1425, with small standing figures and shields in cusped circles.

In the Bauchun Chapel (former consistory court, now chapel for Friends of the Cathedral). PAINTINGS. Adoration of the Magi, French C17, good. – On the w wall, Presentation of Christ in the Temple, by *John Opie*, 1791. – MONUMENTS. William Rolfe † 1754, by *Thomas Rawlins*. Varied marbles. The carving of putto and skull before an obelisk is worthy of, say, Cheere (Dr Penny). – Thomas Batchelor † 1729, signed *Singleton & Bottomley*. A Gibbs pattern provincially treated: pediment on scrolls, putti with skulls and trumpets (Dr Penny). – Recent additions: STAINED GLASS S window, 1964, by *Moira Forsyth*, SCULPTURE of Virgin and Child, 1968, by *John Skelton*, IRONWORK screen and gates designed by *Bernard Feilden* and made by *Eric Stevenson*. – MONUMENTS between S aisle and presbytery. Bishop Goldwell † 1499. Accessible from the presbytery, where it forms a chantry chapel. Its composition is part of Goldwell's remodelling of the pres-

bytery arcading. From the lower level of the ambulatory the tomb-chest seems excessively tall. Alabaster effigy. Big canopy, its underside a shallow traceried tunnel-vault. – Bishop Overall † 1619, but erected 1669 by Bishop Cosin of Durham, whose mentor and patron Overall had been. Still a Jacobean classical tablet, surmounted by a broken pediment, with a small frontal relief of Overall. An eagle, Cosin's emblem, jammed in on top (Cocke).

*Presbytery* In the apse BISHOP'S THRONE, now thought to be of c. 630–47, with ornament added c. 680–90. Probably originally made for a stone cathedral built at Dommoc in Suffolk, abandoned in the C9, and the throne presumably transferred to North Elmham and then to Thetford before it was brought to Norwich. Installed here c. 1120, its setting restored 1959. (The most recent analysis is that of Whittingham 1980.) It faces w and is thus in the traditional Early Christian position, familiar from Parenzo (c 6) and Torcello but also to be found north of the Alps (e.g. at Vaison; and probably also originally at Hexham, cf. B of E *Northumberland*; and see also recent restoration of the original position at Canterbury). This throne is a stone chair with arms and low back, and originally set in the centre of a semicircular stone bench for attendant clergy: a plan exactly as at Parenzo etc. Dr Ralegh Radford established in 1959 that the two arms of the throne do not belong together. The original s arm is lost and the present smaller one was apparently originally part of the flanking bench (another former arm of that bench was dug up in 1975). Naturalistic carving, in an early Pictish punched and pecked technique, can barely be made out. Subjects seem to relate to the Revelation of St John: a dove attacked by dragons, a star fallen to earth, a serpent breathing fire etc. It has been suggested that Abbot Benedict Biscop sent a craftsman down from his own church at Monkwearmouth, founded 674. A shaft below the bishop's feet communicated with a relic-hole below, i.e. the niche in the retaining wall facing the ambulatory (cf. Winchester Cathedral, remains of Norman 'Holy Hole' on w side of retrochoir). – DEAN'S CHAIR, presented in 1922. In the middle of the back, painted relief medallion of the Emperor Maximilian, dated 1512. The rest C17 engraved ivory panels, perhaps also German. – Goldwell monument: see *Ambulatory* above. – On a column, aedicule MONUMENT to John Moore † 1725, and his brother Thomas, signed *Robert Page*. Columns of porto venere marble and a cluster of putti (Dr Penny). – In the E clerestory windows STAINED GLASS, 1847, many small figures. D. King attributes the start of the E clerestory window scheme to *Yarrington* of Norwich.

*Choir* The STALLS formed one continuous row at the raised level with their canopies blocking off the transepts. Now divided between the presbytery, crossing and nave portions of the choir. Traceried fronts, canopied backs, straight cresting, arms with human figures and heads, animals and monsters. Mostly of the C15 but not of one date. The division between those of c. 1420 and those of c. 1480 is complicated, but e.g. the difference between the canopies w (1420) and E (1480) of Nos. 16 s and N is easily seen. For the sixty-one surviving MISERICORDS, the accepted dates are c. 1420 for the western stalls, c. 1480 for those below the tower, and c. 1515 for a few at the E (Remnant 1969; also booklet by Whittingham at the cathedral).

*Crossing*   The wooden PULPIT here was designed by *Seddon* in 1889 and made by *Hems* of Exeter. – BISHOP'S THRONE, designed by *Pearson* in 1893 and unveiled in 1895. – LECTERN. Of brass, Flemish, late C15. A pelican instead of the usual eagle. The three statuettes between the thin flying buttresses were called new in 1841 and do not appear in Britton's view of 1816. – SWORD AND MACE RESTS. Wrought iron, C18, symbols of Norwich civic pride and not more sumptuous than those in the parish churches.

*South transept*   SCREEN with doorway to the presbytery aisle. Of stone, filling the Norman arch. Perp, with plenty of close panel tracery. In the jambs and arch of the doorway pedestals for statuettes. – CHEST. Of sandalwood. North Italian, late C16. In the lid Crucifixion, Scourging and Resurrection, drawn in pokerwork. – CLOCK JACKS. Small, probably C17.

*North transept*   SCREEN, a Victorian paraphrase of the s transept screen. – SCREEN to the E chapel, neo-Jacobean, 1920. STAINED GLASS in chapel, C16, from the deanery. Angels with coats of arms, including Wolsey's: he stayed there in 1524. – w window of the transept, designed by *Burne-Jones* and made by *Morris & Co.*, 1904. Three lights, commemorating an officer dead in the Boer War. – MONUMENTS. Bishop Bathurst, by *Chantrey*, 1841. White marble. Seated peacefully with folded hands. – Bishop Pelham, by *James Forsyth*, 1896. White recumbent effigy on an alabaster tomb-chest. – Violet Morgan, by *Derwent Wood*, 1921. White kneeling maiden.

*Nave and aisles*   PULPITUM. Rebuilt by Bishop Lyhart after the fire of 1463, but completely remodelled by *Salvin* in 1833. On it ORGAN, the case by *S. E. Dykes Bower*, designed 1939, completed 1950, with scholarly use of C17 detail inspired by such cases as Exeter's or Gloucester's (Gillingham). – Against the N side of the pulpitum are parts of the Perp stone SCREEN formerly between ambulatory and Jesus Chapel. – Against the s pier by the pulpitum MONUMENT to William Inglott, organist, † 1621. Painted. Inscription with strapwork surround. – In the s aisle at that point MONUMENT to Thomas Gooding; Elizabethan. Painted skeleton with inscription including the familar 'As you are now Even so was I'. – Then CEILING PAINTING in the vault, good but very faded work of c. 1175. Professor Tristram refers to an Adoration of the Magi with shepherds

in the w compartment and three medallions with stories of Bishop Losinga in the w arch. – Then in the N aisle MONUMENT to Sir John Hobart † 1507. Tomb-chest with the brasses missing. – In the next bay STAINED GLASS window († 1849) by *Warrington*. – Back into the s aisle for the MONUMENT to Dean Gardiner † 1589. Illegible inscription. Tomb-chest with two shields; pediment on pilasters; no effigy. – MONUMENT to Bishop Parkhurst † 1575. Plain, with brown lid. The brass is missing. Back panel to the E with curly top-gable. – In the nave stone PULPIT of 1889, designed by *Carpenter & Ingelow*. – Then the MONUMENT and its surround which Bishop Nykke erected for himself. He died in 1536. It consists of two bays, though the tomb-chest in the w bay of the two is not his but that of Chancellor Spencer. The whole of the two vaults in the aisle was faced with shallow rising tunnel-vaults decorated with panel tracery. In the E bay a low base with panel tracery and shields, and against the E pier three niches with pedestals for images. Chancellor Spencer's tomb-chest is low. – Between N aisle and nave, tomb of Osbert Parsley † 1585, composer of sacred music and lay-clerk in the cathedral. – STAINED GLASS. Five-light window signed by *O'Connor*, 1864. – Three-light window by *Wailes*, 1859. – MONUMENT. Dean Fairfax † 1702, by *William Stanton*. Inscription with flanking columns and outside them piles of books with oil-lamps burning on them. Good quality all round. – Again into the N aisle. Blocked DOORWAY with a four-centred arch, and in the spandrels centaurs and leaf; very pretty. – Then MONUMENT to Sir Thomas Wyndham † 1521. This is between N aisle and nave. Tomb-chest of Purbeck marble. Three shields in quatrefoils. Three brasses missing. – Finally in the w window an enormous expanse of STAINED GLASS. Six large scenes still treated completely pictorially. It is signed by *Hedgeland* and dates from 1854, a date surprisingly late for this interpretation of the art of the glass-painter. On George Hedgeland (according to Mr Sewter, supervised here by Charles Winston, the Victorian connoisseur of stained glass, which makes the style all the more surprising), see also Lincoln, *Furnishings*.

*Gallery*   MONUMENT. Thomas Ivory, the sculptor-architect, † 1779, by *John Ivory*, his nephew. Simple tablet with urn at the top.

## CLOISTERS AND SURROUNDINGS

Nothing can actually be seen of the Norman cloister, although its existence is clear from the one small window above the later doorway from the E bay of the s aisle and also from the position of the refectory and its windows. The pretty mid-C12 capitals now displayed at the Visitors' Centre (over the w wall of the cloister) come probably from the cloister: fragments of exceedingly fine work of c. 1140 in a style quite unlike anything else in Norwich Cathedral, with nimble figures in various actions and entwined in foliage trails. When these were exhibited at the University's Sainsbury Centre in 1980, it was suggested that they were by the same shop as the C12 sculpture at Ely (Borg *et al.* 1980).

The cloister was rebuilt from 1297 onwards. First came the three bays of the chapter-house entrance, then, it seems from the bosses, the bays S of these, and after that the bays N of them. Progress was slow (see *Introduction* above on the masons), with completion only *c.* 1430. Yet the system never changed, though the tracery of the openings and the style of the sculptured bosses did. The system is a two-storeyed elevation (only on the N side the upper storey is a dummy), a most unusual thing, the lower part vaulted on wall-shafts of three detached shafts clustering round a stronger one. Round capitals and tierceron vaults with delicately moulded ribs and an unparalleled wealth of BOSSES. There are nearly 400 of them. In the S and W ranges they illustrate scenes from the Apocalypse, in

132. NORWICH Boss, Apocalypse series, C14, south cloister walk

the N and part of the E ranges from the Life of Christ. But there is also a bay of the N walk with the Life of the Virgin and another with the story of St Thomas à Becket. The TRACERY of the openings in the E range is of trefoiled arches with a tiny ogee flip at the top and in the head

spherical triangles and trefoils upside down. In the S range there are three cusped ogee arches and in the heads an alternation of two motifs of the four-petalled flower with two cinquecusped quatrefoils. The outer arch mouldings are different too. The W range is similar, though the motifs in the heads are different. The N range clearly came last. It starts from the W with flowing tracery and continues with Perp motifs. The last bay before the N E corner is the junction of 1300 and 1430. The tracery is of the type of the early E walk, though not quite the same, but the outer arch moulding is as in the rest of the N and in the W and S walks, and the bosses belong to the late not the early style of sculpture.

To this we must now turn: for in the corner bay is the PRIOR'S DOOR, one of the most beautiful portals of the budding Dec style, erected probably about the year 1310 or a little later. (Whittingham assigns the portal and adjoining book cupboards to the great *William Ramsey*.) Four detached shafts, and in the arch figures under crocketed ogee gables arranged radially and applied 'metalwork-fashion' (Bony): Christ seated in the middle, between angels, and then four more figures. Against the E wall three deep niches with crocketed ogee gables on head corbels. In the vault Christ in Limbo, a praying bishop and a praying monk, and foliage still naturalistic. There are also very fine bosses immediately against the wall, notably the four Evangelists. They are, like the ones just mentioned, perfect examples on a small scale of the style of sculpture in the early C14. In the E wall further on the blocked doorway to the slype, again with a crocketed ogee gable. The arch here is both cusped and subcusped.

After that comes the chapter-house entrance, tripartite as usual, with two wide twin windows and a twin entrance (i.e. with *trumeau*) and iron gates. The room itself, a rectangle with polygonal E end, has unfortunately disappeared, as has indeed the whole E range. It is now simply a lane leading to the S transept. But the chapter-house entrance can best be seen from that side. All arches are ogee-headed and the motifs in the spandrels between them have ogee tops too. From the same vantagepoint one can also observe what remains of the W wall of the dormitory, which was on the upper floor of this range. From the S E corner to the S another doorway with an ogee gable, cusped and subcusped. It leads into the DARK ENTRY. This is Norman and tunnel-vaulted and has in its E wall a doorway with a finely moulded early C14 arch. In the W range of the cloister, close to the former refectory entrance two bays converted into a lavabo with the fronts decorated with a delightful trail pattern. Arches with quatrefoils behind and three canopied niches per bay for sculpture. In the N W corner the other usual entrance into the aisle. Niches with nodding ogee canopies up one moulding of jambs and arch, six niches in all.

The s and w ranges round the cloister must also be studied principally from outside, i.e. the close. The s range contained, as was customary, the REFECTORY. Of this the N wall stands to full height, with twenty-three shafted windows, closely set, then to the E one on its own, and then, marking the wall between the refectory and the Dark Entry, a broad, flat buttress and after that the doorway to the Dark Entry. Above this is another Norman window. s of the refectory some remains of the INFIRMARY, enough to confirm the late c 12 date of which the *Registrum Primum* tells us. John of Oxford, according to the *Registrum*, built it, and he ruled from 1175 to 1200.

The w range is now less articulate. Only the N chamber, adjoining the w front of the cathedral, exists in full. It was the Outer Parlour and is now the Song School. Norman, remodelled in the later c 13. To the s the Guest Hall, of which nothing remains except the E wall and the w doorway inside a porch added in the c 13. In what was the E wall of the w range (i.e. the w wall of the cloister), close to the c 13 stair-turret of the Song School, is a small circular double-splayed window, of a type, not in towers, always

133–5. NORWICH Tracery. (*left*) East cloister walk, *c.* 1297–*c.* 1324. (*below left*) South cloister walk, 1324–*c.* 1335. (*below right*) North cloister walk, 1356–1430

136. NORWICH Prior's Door, *c.* 1310, from east cloister to the nave

considered Saxon in Norfolk churches (e.g. St Julian, Norwich, and Coltishall and Witton-next-the-Sea). Traces of five more such windows are also visible. The wall is 180 ft long and has on its E side, superimposed, the interlaced Norman arches characteristic of the parts of the cathedral near the W end (though those, as we have seen, seem now of the C 19). What this wall may have belonged to (according to Mr Fernie) can be most easily explained as the cloister's W wall built early in the building programme, even before 1096, before stone and perhaps masons had arrived from Caen. Its 180-ft length, as one side of the square cloister that entirely conditioned the Norman layout, would have been on an unprecedented scale for a Saxon building and need not be explained by the prior existence of a Saxon establishment here.

For the Bishop's Palace (a distressing building of 1858–9 perpetrated by *Ewan Christian*), the Deanery (former Prior's Lodgings), the early C 14 chapel of Carnary College just W of the cathedral's W front (now Norwich School), the various gates to the Close including St Ethelbert's Gate, the Erpingham Gate and the Bishop's Gate, and the houses of the Close and Norwich itself, see the latest edition of B of E *North-East Norfolk and Norwich*.

# Norwich

CATHEDRAL CHURCH OF ST JOHN BAPTIST
*Roman Catholic*

(Based on B of E *North-East Norfolk and Norwich*, 1962; Anon. [J. W. Picton], *A Great Gothic Fane*, 1913; Rossi 1981; and information from Peter Howell, Roderick O'Donnell and John Martin Robinson.)

Cathedral since 1976. The site is on high ground (the floor said to be level with the foot of the Anglican cathedral spire) just outside the old St Giles gate of the medieval city wall, where there was a prison 1827–81. An amazing church, proof of Victorian generosity and optimism for the future of Catholicism in England, and of regard for its past, the Dukes of Norfolk having supported a Catholic mission in Norwich since the C 17. The church was given by the fifteenth Duke of Norfolk, who had already built Arundel (q.v. in the companion volume; and compare also the earlier generosity of the Earls of Shrewsbury at Nottingham and Shrewsbury). Begun 1882, completed 1910, the whole designed originally by *George Gilbert Scott Jr*, and continued during his illness and after his early death by his brother, *John Oldrid Scott*.

The church was to be, from the beginning, of cathedral size, 275 ft long and over 80 ft high inside the chancel, and all ashlar-faced. The nave is of ten bays, the chancel of four, the transepts of three with an E aisle, and there is a tall crossing tower. (The polygonal former Walsingham Chapel, now Lady Chapel, off the E side of the N transept was designed by *Oldrid Scott*.) The style is E.E., with all windows lancets and fine if conventional combinations of them, with flying buttresses for the clerestory, a triforium inside, and stone vaulting throughout, quadripartite in the nave (built first and finished 1894), with ridge ribs and tiercerons in the chancel. Sumptuous portals with marble shafting of deep grey Frosterley marble, the same in the wall-arcading, and more in the E parts, and stiff-leaf capitals everywhere. The church is of course an end, not a beginning. It has nothing of the new Arts and Crafts freedoms of its time. It is in the realm of Pearson's self-effacing historicism (cf. Truro); yet surely it relates more nearly to the senior G. G. Scott's late masterpiece, St Mary's (Episcopal) Cathedral, Edinburgh.

The feature that gives the interior its peculiar holiness is the STAINED GLASS by *John Powell* of Hardman & Powell and, for the E parts, his son *Dunstan Powell*. The colours are dark and glowing, the composition designed on C 13 cathedral principles: historicism here too, supremely well done. Glass in the N transept N window, also Clayton & Bell glass in the Lady Chapel, had to be replaced after war damage. – The original IRONWORK all designed by *Oldrid Scott* and made by *Skidmore*. Splendid original bronze gates have recently been disposed of. – Part of the former high altar by *Adrian Gilbert Scott*, 1957, now stands under the crossing tower.

Further on this part of Norwich, see the latest edition of B of E *North-East Norfolk and Norwich*.

# Nottingham

CATHEDRAL CHURCH OF ST BARNABAS
*Roman Catholic*

(Based on B of E *Nottinghamshire*, 1979, as revised by Elizabeth Williamson; further revision contributed by Andor Gomme and Roderick O'Donnell.)

Cathedral since 1850. In Derby Road west of the old centre of the town. Built 1841–4 to the design of *A. W. N. Pugin* and financed largely by the sixteenth Earl of Shrewsbury with the help of the bishop and congregation. Though begun ten years before the restoration of the hierarchy, it was designed (like St Chad's Birmingham) with cathedral status in mind. It is 190 ft long: Pugin had to fight to get something this big. The church is cruciform with single-bay transepts and a square-ended E ambulatory. The exterior style is E.E., and it was less cheaply executed than most of Pugin's churches, though in gritstone which is now very grimy and must always have been severe. The proud crossing steeple, 150 ft high, dominates the building. The spire, of a south Midland type, is solid rather than elegant, based closely on the original (and later discarded) design for St Giles Cheadle, Staffs (by Pugin, 1840–6), with a cluster of lucarnes and pinnacles half-hiding the broaches (a simpler version of that designed but never executed for St George's Cathedral Southwark: see under London in the companion volume). From N and s the tower, which has excessively cut-back buttresses at the E angles only, is asymmetrical; the transepts too are buttressed only at their E angles – presumably because of the fall of the land to the E, of which Pugin took advantage to work in a vaulted undercroft below the sanctuary but partly above ground. There is a fine rhythm of breaks in height between the various parts, although individually the façades are rather papery. The church looks its best from the lower ground to the E, where a family of gables clusters below the motherly-looking steeple in a satisfyingly complex pattern.

The interior is nothing like so impressive as Pugin's higher and bolder Killarney, in Co. Kerry, Ireland, of 1842. It is now impossible to appreciate Pugin's original intentions at Nottingham, since so much of his furnishing and decoration has been eliminated. The nave has five-bay arcades of rather coarse octagonal columns and double-chamfered arches. The clerestory throughout has two windows per bay in the standard Nottinghamshire Perp manner, the deeply splayed reveals with flat two-centred heads. The roof, as usual starved-looking, is double-framed with collar purlin and crown-posts on widely spaced principals (that in the chancel a bit richer, with arched trusses and one tier of arched wind-braces). The low Perp-type arch profile appears again in the middle of the three high lancets in each transept, in the aisle windows, in the side arches of the Lady Chapel where they have no springers, in the tower staircase openings and even in the openings between the transepts and the ambulatory. More startling is the tough treatment of the lantern stage of the tower: each side has a miniature arcade of four unmoulded lancets in a wall jettied on machicolations. Pugin's toughness here, the quality Butterfield so admired, strikes an odd note against the fastidious elegance of the chancel piers. Other detail in the E chapels includes wall arcades of two-light blank arches with ballflower. The choir E wall under the rose-window is pierced with a two-bay arcade with its central column behind the site of the original high altar; this, with the undercroft and square-ended ambulatory, suggests Glasgow Cathedral as the model.

FURNISHINGS

The choir was designed to be wholly enclosed but now only the parclose screens to N, s and E are left. Chancel screen,

rood and high altar were removed in the late C19. *F. A. Walters's* restoration of some Pugin features in 1927 was undone in 1961–2. All that remain are the original Crucifix, now hanging from the chancel arch, and some of the twenty-six STAINED GLASS windows designed by *Pugin* and made by *Wailes*, of which only the aisle windows survive. Those in the transepts are by *Nuttgens* and of the early 1940s. The altar is now under the crossing, to suit the new fashion. The modern decoration is harsh and crude. The whole effect could hardly be farther from the enclosed richness Pugin intended. But the chapels have some Pugin decoration. The Blessed Sacrament Chapel (s of s chancel aisle) with red, gold and green STENCILLED PATTERNS on walls and columns looks typically Pugin and splendid. The chapel was painted and restored by *Alphege Pippet* in 1933. Its culminating feature is an outsize CIBORIUM similar in form but not detail to that in the chapel at Grace Dieu in Leicestershire, with a saddleback tiled roof on thin columns.

Further on surroundings, see the latest edition of B of E *Nottinghamshire*.

# Peterborough

CATHEDRAL CHURCH OF ST PETER, ST PAUL AND ST ANDREW  *Anglican*

(Based on B of E *Northamptonshire*, 1961, and B of E *Bedfordshire and the County of Huntingdon and Peterborough*, 1968, further revised, with information from Thomas Cocke, Michael Gillingham, R. N. Hadcock, Anthony Quiney, Alan Rome and A. C. Sewter.)

Plan, Fig. 138, from the *Builder*, 1891, by Roland Paul.

Some references (see Recent Literature): Cherry 1978; Cobb 1980; Quiney 1979.

INTRODUCTION

Celia Fiennes in 1698 after visiting Ely drove on to Peterborough and found the town neat and the cathedral 'a

magnificent building standing in the midst on advanced ground'. She noted the '3 great arches' of the w front; and these in the c 18 impressed Horace Walpole as 'noble & in great taste'. The triply-beetling cliff-face still stands out above the expanding town that originally grew up before the gates of the monastery. Now the old market-place that used to hustle before these gates has been cleared of stalls and named Cathedral Square. The developers of Peterborough have so far respected the cathedral's pre-eminence on their skyline. And so it still heads the proud parade of great churches that alert travellers watch for alongside the main railway line from King's Cross to the North.

Henry VIII raised Peterborough to cathedral rank in 1541. Before the Reformation it had been a Benedictine abbey from c. 673, having been originally founded c. 655–6 by a monk, Saxulf, aided by Paeda king of Mercia (Haddock). The monastery was sacked by the Danes in 870, re-colonized and rebuilt c. 965, and sacked again by Hereward in 1070. The church was, however, spared. It was burnt in the great fire of 1116. Rebuilding started in 1118 under Abbot John de Séez. He died in 1125, and little can have been done between 1125 and 1132. In 1143 at the latest services were held in the new building. One can assume therefore that by then the chancel was usable. The nave probably dates from c. 1150 etc. Its w end cannot have

been reached before 1177; for the Chronicle tells us that Abbot Benedict built (i.e. probably completed) the whole nave 'usque ad frontem', and he ruled the monastery from 1177 to 1194. Finally, after many changes of mind the present w front was complete by the time of the great consecration in 1238. After that a Lady Chapel was built E of the N transept in 1272 etc. and consecrated 1290 (in type and position probably influencing Ely's a generation later). This chapel was destroyed during the Commonwealth and only a crude view of 1656 survives. Shortly after 1290 a chapel between the Lady Chapel and the presbytery aisle was built (see *St Thomas's Chapel* below). The Norman crossing tower was replaced c. 1325 by a lower and less ambitious one, with an octagonal lantern. A porch was inserted in the w front in the late c 14, windows were renewed almost entirely in the c 14 and c 15, and the retrochoir was erected E of the Norman E end between 1496 and 1508.

In the late c 18 new screens were designed by *John Carter*. These were replaced after 1827 by *Edward Blore*, whose fittings were in turn removed by *J. L. Pearson* (except for stone apse screens which survived till the 1920s). The principal restoration was Pearson's, 1883–97, twice bedevilled by public controversy. What he actually did was rebuild the crossing and its tower in replica,

138. PETERBOROUGH
Plan from the *Builder*, 1891 (see p. 271)

137. PETERBOROUGH Apse begun 1118, and retrochoir begun c. 1500

1884–90 (except for omitting tall corner turrets of 1813, when the c14 octagonal lantern was removed), design new fittings completed in 1894, including the baldacchino (or ciborium, or, in plain Anglican, altar canopy) to house the high altar, and superb marble pavements; finally, after a gale blew down a pinnacle in 1895, he rebuilt part of the w front. To sum up the rows (as culled by Quiney and Cobb): (1) When in 1882 the central tower was found to be dangerous, the e and w crossing arches were c14 pointed, the other two Norman; in the c14, the tower had been lowered and lightened, a stage of arcading above the main arches removed and used as rubble, and the Norman capitals recut. Pearson proposed restoring the Norman design all round and building a taller tower with a rein-stated arcade and a c13-type spire. Uproar. Settled by Archbishop Benson, the c14 work to be rebuilt as found, all four crossing arches to look as before, continuity of tradition to be maintained. (2) When in 1895 the w gables proved unsafe, Pearson recommended taking down the entire upper w front and rebuilding. In furious opposition the S.P.A.B. recommended strengthening *in situ*. This time Pearson won, rebuilding with most of the old stones. These celebrated causes occurred just when the preservation of ancient buildings had become a fierce issue. We also owe to Pearson the first opening up of the choir (removal of w return stalls, 1935). The R.I.B.A. has his drawings for the (splendid) unexecuted spire and for the altar canopy, floors, screens etc. In the 1920s there was much repair of roofs etc. by *Leslie T. Moore*. Major repairs now proceed.

The church consists of nave and aisles, a w porch, a crossing with tower, transepts with e aisles, a presbytery with aisles (the choir occupying the crossing and two e bays of the nave), and the retrochoir. The Norman work survives exceptionally complete. Only the ground floor of the main apse and the two side apses at the end of the presbytery aisles have disappeared. The cathedral is built of Barnack limestone from a quarry owned by the monks c. 8 miles N of Peterborough. It is 481 ft long and 81 ft high inside. The tower rises to a height of 143 ft.

The only Roman remains were a number of fragmentary inscribed slabs of Barnack rag found during Pearson's restoration. As the site of Durobrivae (at Water Newton, c. 4 miles s w) belonged to the medieval monastery, that may have been their source. Of the SAXON CHURCH the wide transepts and the straight-ended chancel have been excavated and can be seen below the floor of the present s transept and part of the crossing. The Saxon church had a w steeple which was consecrated in 1059.

## EXTERIOR

The NORMAN CHURCH was begun in 1118. Its e end largely remains. It had three apses, one wide one still forming the e end of the presbytery but altered on the ground floor, and two smaller at the ends of the aisles. Those side apses do not survive, but the line of the s apse is marked in the floor inside. Of the EXTERIOR of the ground floor of the main APSE all that can now be seen is a stretch of wall e of the former aisle chapels with a zigzag course on the level of the windowsills. It is always said that such zigzag decoration, which became the main stand-by of the Anglo-Norman style when it came to enrichments, was introduced c. 1110. At Peterborough it occurs, as this course shows, from the very beginning, i.e. from 1118. Above the ground floor there are windows in two tiers with a frieze of intersecting blank arcading between the two tiers. (Intersecting arches are found at Durham as early as 1093, though at Norwich they appear first in work of c. 1120: ambulatory wall under throne, upper N transept front.) The windows have Dec tracery, the upper ones under segmental heads. The bays are separated by demi-shafts. The parapet has medallions with busts. These belong to the c13 (and stem of course from much older, Roman tradition). Norman spirelets stress the point where the presbytery adjoins the apse.

The PRESBYTERY is four bays long. Its aisles have a zigzag course at the sill-level of their windows. One N window alone has its original shape preserved, with a zigzag and a billet surround. The others on the s side are of the late c13 (five stepped lancet lights under a segmental arch). On the N side they are Perp. A second zigzag frieze runs above the top of the windows. The gallery windows have flowing tracery on the N side and simpler Dec tracery on the s. The bays are separated by broad Norman buttresses with shafts at the angles. On the N side they are strengthened by small c14 buttresses. On the N side the blocked arch in the style of c. 1300 belongs to the CHAPEL OF ST THOMAS, erected shortly before 1298 (not the same as St Thomas's Chapel by the precinct w gate). The two lower blank arches to the e of it with the springers of a vault belong to the same. The chapel formed the link between the presbytery and the former Lady Chapel (see below). The clerestory of the presbytery has tripartite bays, the side pieces being blank arches. The bays are separated by demi-shafts. The windows are now Perp. Norman corbel table and Perp parapet with blank quatrefoils.

Norman evidence about the TRANSEPTS must be pieced together from the s as well as the N arm. The transepts have e aisles. Their e windows were probably like the presbytery N and s windows, with zigzag and billet surrounds. A zigzag ran at sill-level, as is indicated by remains in the s transept. The windows have all been replaced, on the s by larger ones of c. 1260–75 with three stepped lights and three foiled circles over, on the N by one of the same type and the two former entrance arches into the late c13 Lady Chapel. The present Perp-looking windows here are c19.

The gable of the Lady Chapel can still be seen. The gallery windows are Norman in the N transept (with blank lower coupled arches l. and r.), except that one (and the aisle gallery window to the N) is replaced by late C 13 windows with a large pointed trefoil above three stepped lights. The S transept has Dec gallery windows. The sill course of the gallery has zigzag on the N as in the presbytery, but no longer any zigzag on the S clerestory and parapet as in the presbytery.

The transept end walls have on the ground floor windows like those in the aisles, i.e. with zigzag and billet surrounds (on the S wall, but only partially on the N wall). A doorway to the S also has zigzag in the arch. It has three orders of colonnettes. The upper windows are all Perp in Norman surrounds. Much blank arcading, especially small arched friezes above the first and the second upper windows. The walls end in gables flanked by polygonal turrets. In the W wall, which is exposed only on the N side, the windows are all Perp, but the surrounds remain in their Norman form. There is again much blank arcading of the same system as on the S and N sides. At the clerestory-level the shafted buttresses change into demi-shafts to comply with the aisled presbytery and the aisled E side of the transepts. The W wall of the S transept is in its lower parts hidden by the VESTRY built in the second half of the C 12.

The CROSSING TOWER was originally work of c. 1160–70 and higher than now (see *Introduction* above on restorations). The present tower is *Pearson*'s careful rebuilding of 1884–90 of a replacement of c. 1325, crowned until 1813 by a wooden octagon somewhat like the lantern at Ely (though at Peterborough only the lantern was octagonal). The tower has polygonal panelled buttresses, two three-light bell-openings with transom, and, flanking them, blank two-light and four-light windows. The parapet is panelled. Whether we should regret Pearson's unrealized spire is doubtless more a question for those dealing with the cathedral's structure today, than it is any longer a question of historical rightness or environmental propriety.

The NAVE continues the Norman system of the E part for two bays, though certain changes in various points show that work proceeded gradually and slowly. Such changes are that the zigzag frieze at the sill-level of the aisle windows goes on for three bays on the N side but is discontinued on the S side at once. Also the buttresses drop their shafts at the level of the windowsills of the gallery on the N side, but at the level of the sills of the ground-floor windows on the S side. Moreover in the clerestory the rhythm of the bays of the transept W wall is continued for two bays on the N side, for only one on the S. All this, and the former remarks about the zigzag at gallery-level in the transepts, proves that work on the N side preceded that on the S. Of details the following ought to be noted. Near the middle of the N aisle is a doorway with three orders of colonnettes and capitals with decorated scallops. The arches have exceptionally much zigzag, both on the front and at r. angles to it. The details look mid-C 12. On the S side there are two doorways which originally led into the cloister. The Canons' Door is in the first bay from the E. It has four orders with block capitals. In the inner arch moulding fleur-de-lys foliage is set in the triangles of a beaded zigzag – the only occurrence of Norman foliage at Peterborough (cf. Ely). The Bishop's Door to the W walk of the former cloister is a C 13 insertion. Four orders of colonnettes, big dogtooth between. Finely moulded arch. The ground-floor windows of the aisles with their five stepped lancet lights under depressed arches are typical work of the late C 13. The gallery windows are Dec (segmental heads) but still flanked by small blank Norman arches. Clerestory and corbel table carry on the system of the E parts. The windows are Perp, the parapet now has cusped wavy decoration. The continuation of the exterior to the W will be described in the section on the W end below.

INTERIOR

Generally speaking, the impression, as one enters from the W, is strong and consistent, thanks to the survival of Norman work all the way from W to E and the absence of any obstacle to the eye in trying to penetrate to the apse. The architecture is robust and determined, reiterating its simple statement with conviction. In detail the bays of the APSE are separated by triple shafts. The ground floor is altered (see the section on the *New Building* below), but some capitals of former blank arcading remain. The wall-passage at first-floor level round the apse has against the back wall blank intersecting arcading, at the same height as the same motif occurs outside. The upper storeys of the straight bay between the former apse arch and the apse proper continue the system of the original chancel, but in a painfully lopsided way. On both levels the bay has only two-thirds of a tripartite arrangement. It is remarkable how little C 12 and C 13 masons worried about such incongruities. The former arch between apse and chancel has triple responds too. The arch itself has disappeared, and the verticals of the piers are continued instead by ogee-headed niches. There are many small discrepancies on the top level of the apse indicating that it may originally have had a vault leaning against the former apse arch. The date of the alteration (C 14? c. 1500?) is not certain.

The PRESBYTERY is four bays long. The piers are octagonal, circular and dodecagonal. The apparently planned variety of pier-forms at Peterborough, at ground and gallery level and with intentional not random placing of angles and attached shafts, was unprecedented in 1118, forming a series not of changes of mind but of deliberate

139 (*overleaf*). PETERBOROUGH Presbytery, begun 1118. Altar canopy, 1894, by Pearson

experiments improving on the octagon-circle alternation already existing at Canterbury (Cherry 1978). The responds are triple groups like the shafts of the apse. The aisles are rib-vaulted, an early occurrence for England and indeed Europe. The earliest rib-vaults in existence are at Durham of c. 1095–1100. In France they appear c. 1100–20. The date of the design at Peterborough is, as we have seen, 1118. The transverse arches have a rectangular section with rolls along the angles, the ribs have a demi-roll on a rectangle. The mouldings are big and bold. The outer walls have large intersecting arcading. The capitals are of the block type, or varieties of heavy scallops. They are all big and bold, as far as the piers are concerned, but more playful in the wall-shafts of the aisles (where of course they might well be the result of re-carving). The arches have heavy roll mouldings and billet frieze round the outer edge. On the side towards the sanctuary shafts rise in front of the piers to the ceiling. They were probably originally meant to carry transverse arches. There is no indication that a rib-vault was ever intended. The original ceiling was replaced in the C 15 by a complicated wooden ceiling-cum-vault, i.e. a panelled ceiling, four square cross-ribbed panels wide, on a deep coving with tierceron ribs. The ceiling has many bosses. Among them are the Crucifixion, the Assumption, Christ in Majesty, the Annunciation. The flat painted ceiling over the apse has a Christ in Majesty, renewed in the C 19 as existing in a description of the early C 17, though painted over in the C 18–early C 19 (Cobb).

The gallery has large arched openings subdivided by a tall shaft helping to carry two sub-arches. The piers alternate between a compound shape and a circular one with demi-shafts on rectangular projections. The capitals are busier than below. The tympana have different fillings, starting on the N side with a pierced circle and a group of four pierced circles, on the S side with one plain tympanum. The others have diapering in relief and no piercing. A frieze at the floor-level of the gallery has zigzag coming forward at r. angles to the wall plane. The outer moulding of the arch has the same motif. Horizontal zigzag or zigzag at r. angles to the wall plane is usually regarded as a Late Norman motif. Here it can hardly be later than c. 1135. At the floor-level of the clerestory zigzag was begun at the E end on the S and the w end on the N side, but was soon discontinued and replaced by an undecorated course. The clerestory has a wall-passage with the tripartite stepped arcading familiar in English Norman buildings (e.g. Winchester, Ely, Durham transepts).

The CROSSING piers (renewed by *Pearson*) differ. Those to the E and w have responds with three shafts in a line and arches altered in the C 14, those to the N and S triple responds as we have found them in other places and arches with zigzag at r. angles to the wall plane. The tower has a lierne vault of timber. The central boss shows Christ in

Majesty, the other bosses the Signs of the four Evangelists and the Instruments of the Passion.

The E sides of the TRANSEPTS are aisled and continue the design of the presbytery, though with significant changes. The alternation of round and octagonal piers is simpler, and the shafts up to the ceiling are no longer in front of the piers, but start above them. The arcade responds are segments of circular piers. The billets of the arches are coarser. Above the arcade runs a course with horizontal zigzag just as in the chancel. The gallery piers alternate as in the presbytery. The gallery tympana have on the S side the same relief diapering as in the presbytery (except that the southernmost tympanum is left plain). On the N side the first bay has diapering in the flat, the second in relief, the others again in the flat. Below the clerestory the string-course has a little zigzag in the N transept and none in the S. In the clerestory there is no change from the presbytery. Between the aisle bays of the S transept low separating walls are inserted to divide them into chapels. Towards the presbytery aisle is a low arched recess on short Norman columns. Above this, at the top of the wall, runs a small frieze which seems zigzag at first, but is in fact nutmeg (as is also the frieze in one bay of the presbytery N aisle). In the middle chapel is flat intersecting arcading. The S chapel has normal blank arcading like the rest of the transepts. The N wall of the aisle in the N transept contains a small doorway with fish-scale decoration in the tympanum (on such ornament, see also e.g. Chichester in the companion volume). The other walls of the transepts have tall blank arcading on the ground floor, shafted windows in two tiers, and the familiar tripartite stepped arcading of the wall-passage on the clerestory level. The bays are divided by tall demi-shafts. In the blank arcading of the S transept S wall one capital is a big monster head. The string-course above the blank arcading again has nutmeg instead of zigzag decoration. This applies to the end and w walls of both transepts. The S transept has a doorway in its S wall. The transepts both have original CEILINGS. They are flat, of wood, and have bold lozenge patterns.

Adjoining the w wall of the S transept is the VESTRY. This dates from the late C 12. It is entered by a Dec doorway with an ogee arch. The vestry is of three bays, with low cinquepartite rib-vaults (quadripartite plus a spare rib towards the main wall). The ribs have a slight chamfer, the transverse arches a rectangular projection and keeled rolls at the angles. The arches and ribs rest on short piers with scalloped capitals.

The NAVE goes on without change of system, though changes of detail are as noticeable inside as they are outside. The blank arcading resumes the intersecting of the

141. PETERBOROUGH
North transept east arcade, c. 1125–30

140 (*previous page*). PETERBOROUGH Choir and crossing, looking west. Pavement by Pearson

142. PETERBOROUGH
Painted ceiling, nave (detail), before 1238

demi-roll. The capitals are busier. Small changes in the details of the bases within the nave are noted in the V C H. The arch mouldings change at once E of the crossing. They contain one more roll moulding to the nave. The gallery tympana have relief diapering only in the first two bays from the E. After that they are plain. An odd, unexplained anomaly is the crocket capitals of the third gallery pier from the crossing on the N side. They must be an alteration of *c.* 1200 or later. Perhaps the capitals had at first been left uncarved. On the W end of the nave, see separate section below.

The NAVE CEILING is a very precious survival. It must date from *c.* 1220, or, at any rate, before the consecration of 1238. It is canted, decorated with lozenge patterns like those of the transept ceilings, and retains its original colouring. In the lozenges are figures of kings and queens and saints, a Janus head, a monster feeding on the bleeding limbs of a man, figures with musical instruments including an animal playing the harp, an architect with L-square and dividers, a monkey on a goat etc. A chromolithograph of 1857 shown in the N choir aisle was done from a drawing 'made from the clerestory' in 1830.

THE WEST END

This is an area of so many changes and problems that a separate section must be dedicated to it. What is certain is that the Norman nave was intended to be nine bays long with W towers over the ninth aisle bays. This appears from the greater width of the piers between the eighth and ninth bays, which is specially noticeable on the gallery-level. The outer wall of the bay in question is thicker too, and a buttress on the S side is much wider. On the gallery one can also see that a transverse arch ran across, of which the N respond survives and a lump of stone where the S respond was. Close to this there is a spiral staircase whose W wall was clearly bonded originally against a cross wall. In spite of this, when the decision was taken to continue the nave to the W, the system was still not changed. Yet by then 1175 must have been reached.

The history of the existing W end with its W transepts and its deep niches is complicated. Sir Charles Peers has tried to elucidate it in the V C H, and the following account follows his explanations. He distinguishes four stages. The first has been discussed. It is the beginning of Norman W towers over the ninth aisle bay from the E. The second stage was a lengthening by one more bay plus a W transept, on the lines of Ely and Bury St Edmunds, though with two towers instead of one. These towers were thus two bays W of those first planned. The third stage was the addition of giant niches one bay deep and as wide as the transept. They were to be divided into seven bays with the middle one widest and to have three openings just like Lincoln. The

eastern arm. The capitals on the S side are as simple as those of the E arm and transepts, which indicates that the S aisle wall was carried up very early, probably in connection with work on the claustral parts. On the N side the capitals are more decorated and clearly later. They play on forms of scalloping, of little volutes etc., and beasts' heads with wide open mouths. The aisle vaults occasionally have very small bosses at the intersection of the ribs. The arcade piers resume the shafts towards the nave. In shape the piers differ from those in eastern arm and transepts. They begin from the E with a respond with clustered shafts; then follows a circular form with attached shafts on flat projections in all four directions – a form developed from the piers of the gallery in eastern arm and transepts – then the clustered pier is repeated, i.e. the principle of alternation continued. After that, however, this principle is abandoned and all piers are like the second, i.e. they are circular with projections on all four sides consisting of a rectangle with a last stage was a revision in the design of the three niches by which they received their present rather unfortunate form, that is five bays in width instead of seven, with the outer openings consequently wider than the middle one, and with two angle-turrets to project beyond the line of the transept and give the effect of a wider screen, comparable e.g. to Salisbury. The flanking square turrets thus oblique-ly upstaged the intended w transept towers, of which only one was completed. The great consecration of the cathedral took place in 1238 when the w front was finished.

In detail the following can be seen. When it was decided to lengthen the nave – a decision which must have been taken c. 1180 – the Norman system was still not given up. So bay ten and even the openings from the aisles into the w transept keep to the elements already described. The wall-arcading on the s side now at last takes up the lively forms of capitals which had been used on the N side from the E end of the nave onwards; on the N side the tenth bay has for the first time waterleaf capitals. Peers pointed out many more small changes, but they are not of great relevance. The first major change is the fact that the arches across the transepts are pointed. Their details are typical Latest Norman with

big, rich zigzag and similar more complicated and even bigger motifs set at an angle. The vaults are quadripartite with the much finer details and more delicate members of the E.E. style. In the aisle bays below the towers bell-holes are left, that under the N tower being surrounded by playful ribs. The centre bay has a boss with stiff-leaf foliage. To the E springers can be seen in the first nave bay, proving that the intention existed of vaulting the nave in the new style. The w wall is purely E.E. in its motifs, except that the three doorways are still round-headed. But they have finely moulded arches and stiff-leaf capitals (the leaves at the centre arch semi-naturalistic), and there is pointed blank arcading at the ground-level, and the upper windows (altered Perp) are set in tall blank E.E. arcading too. In the projecting bays of the transept the change is also made to E.E. forms and proportions, but even here the windows behind the gables follow the system of the Nor-man clerestory. One must assume that the E, N and s walls of the transept were completed first, and that the w wall and the vaulting followed.

To the outside, i.e. the niches, which will be described presently, the middle portal has a *trumeau* or middle post

143. PETERBOROUGH West front, c. 1180–1238

of, probably, the local Alwalton marble with a beautifully carved relief round the circular base, which is also of such marble. This represents a man upside down and tormented by devils. He has been interpreted as Simon Magus. The portal had five or six orders of colonnettes, the side portals have five orders. The w wall (before the addition of the giant niches and the Perp porch) had in addition tall blank arcading with sub-arches sharing their outer mouldings with the super-arch, then a frieze of small trefoil-headed arches, and then again tall arcading broken by the windows. Here the rhythm goes restless owing to the necessities created by the altered design of the front.

The exterior of the w transept essentially continues the system of the w wall. But the windows with their cusped intersected tracery are a late c 13 alteration of former windows which must have been lancets. Inside the s arm, a double piscina of that date. The tall, narrow E windows have Perp tracery. The gables have a many-foiled circular window each and up the slope of the gable a frieze of lunettes. The gables are flanked by polygonal turrets. On their top storey zigzag still occurs. Of the w towers only that on the N side was fully built (there is a stump of a s w one). The N W one as bell-tower was emphasized from at least the c 17 (?) by a curious, waisted spire, removed c. 1812 (views of 1656 and c. 1727). The tower lies awkwardly behind the later porch, and can only be seen and appreciated in its original meaning if one stands far enough away from the cathedral. The tower has lancet windows on two storeys and blank arches to their l. and r. The pinnacles are polygonal.

Of the plans for the giant niches before the idea of the projecting turrets was accepted we can see only one indication. Immediately w of the start of the w buttresses of the transepts on their N and S sides the wall projects a little and has a shaft at the angle just like those of the transept buttresses. The projection reaches up only a few feet and is then discontinued.

The GIANT NICHES in their final form are an unhappy addition, though they proceeded from a grand conception. This conception was no doubt based on Norman Lincoln, where three deep niches, the central one wider and taller than the others, receive the faithful, and the three or possibly five niches at the abbey of Bury St Edmunds of about half a century after Lincoln's and about a century before Peterborough's. At Peterborough this motif was developed into recesses which were to be a full bay deep and endowed with quadripartite vaults in seven bays of which the outer corresponded to the transept projections, three of the others to the portals, and the remaining two to the spaces between the portals. In execution, however, all this was changed. Turrets were added outside the area of the original composition. The seven vaulting bays were reduced to five, with the outer bays much wider than the

central one, and the outer arch openings or portal niches consequently much wider than the middle niche. A worrying rhythm is thus created for the front proper, and nonsense is made of the former w wall with its details. Nonsense is incidentally also made of the three gables above the entrance arches. The details must be seen to judge of the truth of this indictment. The most painful thing is the way in which the wide side openings lead to side portals appearing out of axis. In detail the three truly monumental giant portals have six orders of shafts each with three shaft-rings. The centre arch has tufts of stiff-leaf rising in subsidiary orders between them (a Lincoln motif). The arches are decorated with a bobbin motif, foliage and dogtooth. The turrets have the usual blank arcading, including a frieze of trefoil-headed arches such as had occurred on the w wall behind the niches. Higher up there is an interesting motif of blank intersection with zigzag decoration set in front of blank arcading. This motif may well be inspired by the angle-turrets of the façade of Ely Cathedral.

The tops of the turrets were completed only in the c 14 – not to the benefit of the former conception of the whole w end; for they compete with the N W tower diagonally behind them, and the general effect from far enough away is one of profusion – it is true – but also of confusion. The top of the s turret is the more elaborate of the two. The angle-shafts turn into square pinnacles set diagonally, and behind these rises an octagonal spire with one set of lucarnes and four spirelets accompanying it and linking it to the angle pinnacles. These spirelets have an open bottom stage and are crocketed. The N turret is simpler. The angle-shafts here end with taller pinnacles, and the spirelets are missing. The gables above the portals have the most haphazard assembly of motifs, quatrefoil in circles, trefoil pointed arch-heads, niches with statues (gradually being replaced by work of *Alan Durst*), foiled circles with heads, wheels with six or eight spokes etc. Moreover, the strong shafts which are set between the three portals are suddenly replaced by turrets. All this shows the disastrous effects of the change of plan from the narrow–wide–narrow to the wide–narrow–wide rhythm for these portals. Inside the niches the top storey of the w wall of the church is affected equally disastrously by this change. Because he had reduced them from seven to five and widened the outer ones, the designer chose to give these quadripartite vaults an additional w–E rib running against the façade wall of the church. This plays havoc with the blank arcading and fenestration at that stage.

Finally, to do yet more damage to the w view, a little Perp PORCH like a little house was tucked into the middle opening of the c 13 porch, filling it in width but not in height (perhaps inserted to buttress it?). This work was done in the later c 14. It is two bays deep and two storeys

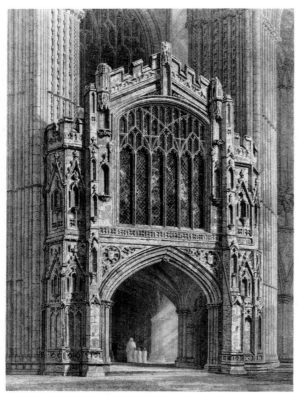

145. PETERBOROUGH
C 14 porch in the west front, in 1827

main Norman apse shows inside the new building. The apse windows were continued to the ground and these new openings linked up by arches and new triangular spaces to the retrochoir. There is plenty of enjoyable tracery here to conceal the awkward junction. The apse arches have cusped four-centred arches with tracery over, and the triangles are also marked by four-centred arches with tracery over. Moreover, the beginning of the retrochoir proper is marked by a broad arch with big, heavy fleurons in the deep main moulding both to the W and E. The retrochoir has four-light and three-light windows with panel tracery, separated by buttresses. The set-offs of these are decorated with fleurons. The work is crowned by an openwork parapet very similar to that of King's College Chapel, Cambridge, and seated figures on the tops of the buttresses which must have been of good quality when they were newly made and still have a fine architectonic effect (cf. similar figures at Norwich). Inside, the windows are continued by blank panelling with stone benches. The vault is a very handsome fan-vault carried on slender shafts. The new building is internally slightly higher than the aisles, and the closely panelled vaulting at that height gives it a sense of comfortable as well as rich enclosure. Mr Harvey has suggested that *John Wastell*, before he began in 1508 at King's College, Cambridge and built the fan-vaults there, may have been the designer. (And Wastell will have observed the fan-vaulted Lady Chapel, of the years after 1468, at Canterbury, where he was working in the 1490s.)

FURNISHINGS, E TO W

*Retrochoir or New Building*    Approached from here, in the apse space behind the high altar, the so-called HEDDA STONE (although, as Abbot Hedda was killed by Danes in 870, it can have nothing to do with him). An extremely important piece of Anglo-Saxon sculpture to be dated c. 800 by comparison with illuminated manuscripts, High Crosses, and also such work as is preserved at Breedon-on-the-Hill in Leicestershire. Grey stone with a pitched roof. Against the long sides standing figures of the apostles in close-fitting arcading. The short sides are defaced. The roof is pitched like that of a metal shrine and has scrollwork with interlace, affronted pairs of animals, and also what has been called an 'inhabited scroll', i.e. a vine scroll with an animal inside. The figures are stiff, mostly frontal, and have the fluffy carving and the deeply drilled eyes characteristic of their date. Comparable work is also to be found at Castor and at Fletton. – In the retrochoir, three bays of a BASE, Perp, with a quatrefoil frieze at the foot, panels and canopied niches, and a cresting with a frieze of little beasts, belong probably to the Shrine of Hedda. – Ironwork apse SCREENS by *Pearson*. – STAINED GLASS. Southernmost E window by *Clayton & Bell*. – MONU-

high. It has tierceron vaults with ridge ribs (star-vaults) on the ground floor (the Coronation of the Virgin and the Trinity on the two main bosses), and an upper floor with a large Perp window. The upper floor is reached by two spiral staircases which project in front of the C 13 jambs. (On one of these a fireplace with flue has been built in.) The doorway has a depressed arch. The spandrels have blank tracery decoration. The gable above the Perp window is of low pitch and embattled.

THE 'NEW BUILDING' AT THE EAST END

Abbot Robert Kirkton, whose rebus, initials and other signets appear all over it, erected a new retrochoir. He ruled the monastery from 1496 to 1528. The retrochoir is two bays deep and as wide as the church nave and aisles. The new work links up with the old in the following way. The aisle apses of the Norman church (which must have been remodelled in the C 13 – see their elegant quadripartite rib-vaults and the handsome DOUBLE PISCINA in each bay N and S) were removed and the aisles connected by two new bays with the retrochoir. It is here that the exterior of the

MENTS. Abbot, probably R. Kirkton †1528. Recumbent effigy of stone; defaced. Two angels by the pillow. – Orme family, early C17. Hanging monument almost completely ruined. Of the figures only one small group survives. – Bishop Cumberland †1718. Signed by *Thomas Green* of Camberwell. Hanging monument with open segmental pediment above the inscription plate and standing putti to its l. and r. – Thomas Deacon †1721. Signed by *Robert Taylor (Sr)*. Standing monument. White and greyish marble. Semi-reclining, well-carved effigy with wig. Reredos background with Corinthian pilasters and an open segmental pediment. – Dean Ingram. Recumbent effigy of white marble by *H. R. Ingram*, 1903.

*Presbytery* BALDACCHINO or CIBORIUM, 1894, designed by *Pearson*. Made by *Robert Davison* of Derbyshire alabaster (of the same hue as the surrounding Barnack stone of the building), enriched with mosaic. A most architectural yet transparent altar canopy, it is as successful an addition to its setting as the very different one now in St Paul's. (A gilded aluminium Epiphany Star applied to the underside of the canopy vault by *Pace* in the 1970s is not an addition.) – Fine inlaid MARBLE PAVEMENTS from apse to crossing, also designed by *Pearson* (cf. e.g. Bristol, Truro). – Big standard CANDLESTICKS designed by *S. E. Dykes Bower*. – In the apse (for the HEDDA STONE, see *Retrochoir* above), two TAPESTRIES, late C16, probably Flemish. – STAINED GLASS. Perp fragments assembled in the latter C18 by Dean Tarrant (Cocke). – The graves of Catherine of Aragon †1537 (under the N arcade) and Mary Queen of Scots †1587 (opposite in the s aisle till translated to Westminster Abbey by James I) are marked by banners.

*South presbytery aisle* MONUMENTS. Four abbots, all of local Alwalton marble varying in hue from light tan to nearly black. All made within the thirty years from *c.* 1195 to *c.* 1225. Of only one, the first from the E and in date the latest (supposed to be Alexander of Holderness †1226), the tomb-chest is preserved. It has short columns and quatrefoil panels (cf. the Marshall monument in Exeter Cathedral). The effigy is flanked by shafts carrying a projecting pointed trefoiled canopy. Stiff-leaf ornament. The third of the series alone has a rounded-trefoiled canopy over his head, also carried on shafts. It is much defaced. The second has a rounded cinquecusped canopy which is very depressed and carries bits of buildings. The curly hair and beard are a sign of an early date. The fourth is in higher relief. It has no flanking shafts. Two angels at his head, a dragon at his feet. – Also of the C13 a coffin-lid with foliated cross. – Joseph Stamford †1683. Pretty cartouche with cherubs' heads. – Archbishop Magee of York, former Bishop of Peterborough †1891. By *J. Forsyth*. White recumbent effigy on a chest, classical Elizabethan forms.

*North presbytery aisle* CHEST. C15, with elaborate tracery. – STAINED GLASS. One window (†1856) by

146. PETERBOROUGH
Tomb slab of Abbot Benedict, *c.* 1195

*Wailes*. – MONUMENTS. Another early abbot of the same material and date as those in the s aisle. Beardless head under a rounded-trefoiled arch. Shafts by his sides with capitals clearly still of the C12. A dragon at his feet. – Dean Duport †1679. Very classical, with open pediment with curly ends and garlands. Small. – Constance May †1681. Cartouche with fine flower carving.

*Crossing* THRONE and PULPIT, 1892 by *Pearson*. – Farther W, large brass LECTERN, late C15, English. With inscription referring to Abbot William de Ramsey (1471–96). The same pattern as at St Nicholas King's Lynn, Christ's College, Cambridge, St Mark's Venice, etc.

*South transept* SCREENS. Late C15. – SCULPTURE. In the W wall a small C13(?) panel with two figures under arches. – In the low excavated space of the Saxon s transept several Saxon stones with interlace ornament. – STAINED GLASS. s wall, lowest tier, easternmost. By *Morris, Marshall & Faulkner*, 1862, i.e. a very early work of the firm. Two scenes, predominantly red and brown, by *D. G. Rossetti* (who only designed glass 1861–4): Sacrifice of Abraham and Joseph Lifted from the Pit, with four small figures above by *William Morris* and shields below by *Philip Webb* (Sewter). – Next to this to the W by *A. Gibbs*, 1861. – Agony and Betrayal window, 1864, by *Heaton, Butler & Bayne* (Harrison 1980).

*North transept* SCREENS. Perp with much tracery. Not *in situ*. – STALLS. Fragments of two units of the original choir stalls of some time between 1233 and 1245. Slender double shafts with stiff-leaf capitals. Remodelled in the late C16 or early C17. – STAINED GLASS. N wall, lowest tier, first and second from E: *Clayton & Bell*, 1860, 1863; tier above this from E to W: *Cox & Son*, c. 1849, *O'Connor*, 1865, *Heaton, Butler & Bayne*, c. 1852; top tier 1865. – Former nave altar and other fittings, Neo-Georgian, by *Leslie T. Moore*.

*Nave*   Choir bays. STALLS by *Pearson*. – ORGAN CASE. By the organ-builder and antiquary *Dr Arthur Hill*, 1904. It acts as a screen to the instrument (by the Hill firm, 1868 etc., rebuilt by *Harrison*, 1980) which stands in the gallery, and so it is rather less architecturally successful than Hill's earlier Chichester case (which completely contains the instrument), while forming an excellent composition (Gillingham). – Large hanging ROOD, 1975, by *George Pace*, with aluminium figure by *Frank Roper*, gold against red. Amazingly effective in this austere Norman place. (More so than Edward Barry's Neo-Norman huge stone pulpit of 1873 must have been; see Cobb 1980.) – Mobile nave altar and portable organ by *Pace*. – Against the W wall, high up, PAINTINGS of Old Scarlett the gravedigger (†1594) who buried two queens (see *Presbytery*) in 1537 and 1587: N of the central door painted on the wall and found under the copy of 1747 on panel now hanging S of the door; Celia Fiennes saw the original in 1698. – Three W doors, possibly C12 strengthened by C13 saltire-ledging. – WEST TRANSEPT CHAPELS. N chapel, FONT. C13 bowl, possibly of Alwalton marble, on C19 supports. The bowl has twelve shallow projections or undulations decorated with stiff-leaf. (For many years used as a flower-pot in a prebendal garden.) – In the S chapel, three C14 MISERICORDS oddly affixed to three stall-backs by *Pace*.

*Porch*   Fine and elaborate IRON GATES (are they by Pearson?).

SUMMARY OF THE PRECINCT

The precinct is entered from Cathedral Square, the former market-place by the Outer Gate, built by Abbot Benedict (1177–94) and considerably altered in 1302–7. N E of it is St Thomas's Chapel (a separate matter from the one once standing N of the N presbytery aisle). This is the chancel only of a church of c. 1330 whose nave was pulled down. To the S of the Outer Gate some C12 vaults connected with the King's Lodging and the Abbot's Prison. The range continues with Victorian building and then the Abbot's Gate, of the early C13. To the N as well as the S are original figures, deserving to be better known than they are. The upper windows (Knights' Chamber) altered in the Jacobean style. Then two more bays much as the N bay. More Victorian building, and at the end of this range a blocked single-chamfered C14 arch and a vaulting-shaft. So the range continued towards the SW angle of the church. Through the Abbot's Gate one reaches the Bishop's Palace,

once the Abbot's House of the monastery. Now mostly Victorian Gothic, but in it survive two mid-C13 undercrofts.

The remains of the cloister can be reached from the E end of the range containing the Abbot's Gate by a passage along the S side of the W parts of the church, or direct from the church by the two portals already described. The cloister walks survive nowhere, and against the church there are not even any traces of the bays and their vaults left. The existing W wall was the E wall of the cellars. In it there are some blocked early to mid-C12 doorways, and also, at the N end, one well-preserved one with one order of columns and one continuous roll moulding. The arch has a big outer billet moulding, similar to those of the transepts. There is also a small C14 doorway with flowing tracery, one Perp doorway with a four-centred arch, and one doorway with Late Norman arch fragments (crenellation, frieze of lobes – cf. the gables of the cathedral). The remains of the arcading are superimposed on all this. They are Perp.

The S range has remains partly E.E., partly Perp. E.E. the blank arcading with sub-arches, whose outer mouldings are those of the super-arch as well, and also two doorways, at the E and W ends. The W doorway is round-arched. It has four orders of colonnettes and a beautiful arch with extremely fine, deeply cut stiff-leaf. Tympanum with a quatrefoil and two dragons. This doorway leads into the refectory, of which no more stands than the very wall we have just looked at. Towards the interior, i.e. the S, it has blank arcading with very varied paterae in and above the spandrels. They contain much stiff-leaf. Of the refectory E wall the N springer of some taller blank arcading is the only sign of decoration. The C13 arcading of the S wall of the S range was replaced in the five bays next to the refectory doorway during the C15 by a renewed lavatorium of very rich Perp panelling. The E doorway of the S range of the cloister has a segmental arch and a quatrefoil above this. Fine mouldings; stiff-leaf detail. The doorway led into the Hostry Passage. Of the E range nothing at all survives. Part of its place is taken by two Georgian stone houses of three storeys. Doorway with pediment on Tuscan columns. The Hostry Passage ran along the E wall of the dormitory wing, which exists no longer. From the S end of the passage one turns E to visit the impressive remains of the C13 infirmary.

More fully on the precinct, and on the surrounding town, see the latest edition of B of E *Bedfordshire and the County of Huntingdon and Peterborough*.

# Ripon

CATHEDRAL CHURCH OF ST PETER
AND ST WILFRID *Anglican*

(Based on B of E *Yorkshire: The West Riding*, 1967, revised, mainly by John Hutchinson, and with information from S. E. Dykes Bower, Michael Gillingham, Anthony New and David Palliser.)

Plan, Fig. 147, from the *Builder*, 1893, by Roland Paul.

Some references (see Recent Literature): Bony 1979; Kidson 1962; Remnant 1969.

## INTRODUCTION

The town of Ripon has narrow winding streets, and near the cathedral are brick-built C 17 and C 18 houses, but also trees and gardens. The best views of the cathedral are from High St Agnesgate to the S E, from the racecourse and the road to Sharow. Ripon is near the northern edge of the West Riding, not far from Fountains Abbey.

Ripon became a cathedral in 1836, after having been one for five years in the C 7 under Bishop Eadhead, 681–6. The first church belonged to a monastery founded by Scottish monks *c*. 660. Wilfrid became abbot shortly after. He replaced the Scottish customs by the Benedictine rule and rebuilt the establishment on a different site. It is the present one, and the crypt belongs to his church. Of the church itself Eddius says that Wilfrid built it of smoothed stone with many columns and porticus ('politis lapidibus a fundamentis in summum aedificatam variis columnis et porticibus suffultam erexit'). Wilfrid's church (above ground) and the monastery were destroyed by King Eadred of Northumberland in 950. After that the establishment became collegiate, and the church was no more than the parish church of a very large parish, although regarded by the Archbishop of York as a kind of sub-cathedral for the N part of his big diocese. The present church has one adjunct, S of the chancel aisle, which seems completely Norman externally. The date of this part is controversial. A rebuilding of the whole church was begun 'de novo' by Archbishop Roger of Pont-l'Évêque, but not completed by him. He ruled from 1154 to 1181, and as the forms of his work at Ripon are exceedingly progressive, that is entirely Gothic, even a date about 1175–80 would be very early for England. The details are Cistercian in character. Roger of Pont-l'Évêque's surviving crypt at York Minster is still in a sumptuously decorated Late Romanesque, though surviving elements of the choir there suggest that that may have been more advanced stylistically. So Ripon can no doubt be placed towards the end of his career and represents a change of programme and taste similar to that of Bishop Hugh le Puiset of Durham at about the same time. We do not know how fast work proceeded at Ripon, but the W front was clearly not reached until *c*. 1220–30. There was rebuilding of the E end between 1286–8 and *c*. 1330, and

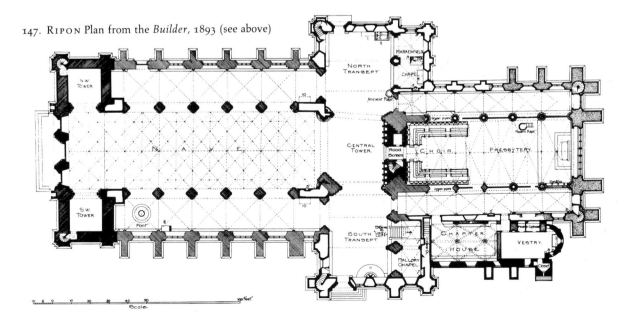

147. RIPON Plan from the *Builder*, 1893 (see above)

the E wall itself was apparently built between 1286–8 and 1296 (Bony 1979, citing Lehmann-Brockhaus 1956). Towards the end of the Middle Ages a number of substantial additions and alterations were made. The early C16 mason in charge was probably *Christopher Scune*, master mason of Durham Cathedral, who is mentioned at Ripon in 1514 and again, this time as supervising the masons, in 1520–1.

The college was dissolved by Edward VI and the chapter re-established by James I. (The church was in the care of the Duchy of Lancaster 1547–1605: Colvin 1975.) Restorations were carried out by *Blore* (c. 1830), *Railton* (c. 1845) and *Scott* (1862 etc.).

Ripon Cathedral is not impressive in size. It is only 270 ft long, and the screen divides its length. Moreover its internal appearance is more a mixture of styles than can please the eye. Everywhere a later time has interfered with an earlier without effacing its architectural elements completely. However, Ripon possesses one of the noblest E.E. west fronts in England, and that alone deserves a visit. In addition, the archaeological interest of its late C7 crypt is considerable. And the late C13 great E window is of that northern series which includes Lincoln's Angel Choir E window of c. 1275 and Durham's Nine Altars N window of the late 1280s.

EXTERIOR

Medieval churches were usually built from E to W. The altar and the chancel space were more important than the parts serving the laity. At Ripon, however, as is also usual, the original E end is no longer in existence, having been reconstructed, though probably not greatly lengthened, between c. 1286–8 and c. 1330. Roger's choir probably had an eastern cross-aisle. The splendid E window must date between 1286 and 1296, according to Bony's reference cited above. It is of seven lights with Geometric tracery just going, in certain details, a little restless. Flanking three-light groups with their own tracery, the higher central light spiking a large circle of unenclosed trefoils – a grander and more advanced disposition of elements of the chapter-house vestibule windows at York. The gable above is entirely by *Scott*. The N and S sides of the chancel clerestory also have Geometric tracery. There are flying buttresses here too. But on the S side, attached to the chancel aisle, is an apsed Norman-looking structure with two simple wall-shafts up the apse. It has irregular S windows, those to the crypt narrow, deeply splayed externally and fitted with tiny tympana; while the circular windows of the chapter house above have moulded surrounds, like picture frames, largely renewed. After 1300 a Lady Chapel (now Library) was built on top of the chapter house. This has tall straight-headed windows with intersected tracery, cusped. A much later date has been proposed for this, but the

windows of Roger's S choir aisle were left unaltered when those of the N choir aisle were recast early in the C14; and this really only makes sense if the chapel was already built. Massive buttressing added to support it makes dating of the substructure all the more difficult. See *South Annexe* below.

What the original CHANCEL and its aisles looked like externally can only partly be reconstructed. The aisles had plain lancet windows (see S aisle, inside). The clerestory arrangement was of one tall round-headed window per bay flanked by a blank lancet l. and r. (see the three W bays on the N side). The aisle windows here have near the E end two-light and simple tracery of c. 1300, near to the W end remodelled two-light Dec windows.

The TRANSEPTS give the most vivid impression of the C12 work. They have an E aisle but no W aisle. The E aisle E side has tall shafted round-headed windows and, above, the same clerestory arrangement as in the chancel – see *Interior*, N transept; in the S transept these upper windows are Perp. W walls with plain tall round-headed windows only. The end walls, close to their W ends, have a doorway with three orders of shafts and round arches, plain tympanum on the S and a 'cusped' sub-arch on the N; three even, tall, shafted round-headed windows above (with their two-light tracery of c. 1300), and again three even, tall double-chamfered windows above. Plain gable on the N side, tall turrets with twin openings under a round arch near the top. Perp window in the S gable.

The CROSSING TOWER is not high. Roger's tower was trapezoidal in plan, but this does not tell externally. Late C15 reconstruction modified this, but the agonized pile-up of corbelling and squinching needed to bring the S E corner out to a right angle can only properly be appreciated from the library roof. The tower has on the N and W sides plain Norman windows l. and r. of the steep former roof-line, on the S and E sides two-light Perp windows, a replacement which will be understandable inside. A spire said to have been 120 ft high collapsed in 1615.

Now the NAVE. This is in its appearance entirely Perp, of the early C16. Aisles buttressed with three straight gabled set-offs on the S, two concave-sided on the N side. Three-light windows, battlements. Clerestory with five-light windows and battlements.

Finally the WEST FRONT. It is E.E., and entirely composed of lancets. Also it is flat, without projections and recessions. Both these facts give it a nobility not achieved in the busy display of a variety of motifs often overlapping or left without *rapport* with each other at Salisbury or Wells. Two W towers originally with spires, taken down in 1664 and replaced by ill-fitting battlements. Centre gabled. The towers have no entrance, for a reason to be discussed later. So the three-portal composition in the French manner is compressed in miniature into the centre bay. Shafted jambs, much dogtooth decoration, gables over the arches.

149. RIPON West front, *c.* 1220–50

Above the portals (much restored by *Scott*) five tall, even lancets, shafted and with dogtooth decoration. They had tracery of two lights each with spherical quadrangles above the cusped lights; in the quadrangles, rounded quatrefoils. However, it seems that this tracery must have been an addition; at any rate, *Scott* swept it away. Mr Dykes Bower points out that it was probably badly decayed and, however attractive in old prints, not part of the original design. So we owe to Scott a return to the E.E. front. Above these windows five stepped lancets, also formerly of two lights and traceried, and then three in the centre of the gable. That is all. The towers have first a band of pointed-trefoiled blank arcading and then three storeys of stepped lancets, some blank, some with windows. Nothing could be simpler. (Though there is the usual stepping of the sill-strings this is more discreetly managed than usual in E.E. compositions.) The façade has been blamed for appearing cold. That may be due a little to Scott (and be comparable to some people's taste for old varnish on pictures). But largely it confirms the truth that classicity can easily be mistaken for coldness.

## INTERIOR

Here we must, of course, start with Wilfrid's CRYPT. (This and the next paragraph rewritten by John Hutchinson.) One of the earliest Christian survivals in England, built probably *c.* 670, it is very similar to the crypt at Hexham, also founded by Wilfrid. It is now approached from the s w by a passage which is not part of the original design. The crypt consisted, originally, of the oblong, tunnel-vaulted relic chamber, about 11 ft long (with five small recesses in the walls, and a larger one in the E wall, possibly for a window), a second half-tunnel-vaulted chamber to the w, and narrow, flat-roofed passages to N and S. The N passage certainly had stepped access at the E end, but there is no evidence for corresponding access to the shorter S passage, though this could have been lost when the tower piers were reconstructed and enlarged. The walls are covered with a cement of Roman strength and lastingness. The crypt lies below the central tower of the present church and must have been below Wilfrid's high altar. The crypt has recently been converted into a Treasury for the display and safekeeping of diocesan plate. The loss – aesthetically, archaeologically and emotionally – cannot be measured against convenience and security. Glass screens in heavy metal clips fail in their presumed aim to be inconspicuous.

Next in time comes perhaps the SOUTH ANNEXE. This has a low vaulted crypt five and a half bays long (divided early in its history by a thick wall) with an eastern apse. Square piers with chamfered corners, moulded abaci, and chamfered vaulting-ribs are nowhere inconsistent with the plainer parts of Roger's work. The external architecture

looks earlier than the internal, and a later alteration of a late C 11 or early C 12 structure has been assumed. However, Bilson did not believe in a date earlier than the second half of the C 12. Above is the CHAPTER HOUSE: circular piers with spreading moulded bases and a rib-vaulted roof, all clearly of the late C 12-early C 13. The bullseye windows relate to this vault, but only two and a half bays survive, the eastern part having a flat panelled ceiling dating in its present form from *Scott*'s restoration after 1862, as does the splendid wooden spiral staircase leading up to the LIBRARY: absolutely straight and functional with no decorative excrescences. The early C 14 library, formerly the Lady Chapel, has flat-topped windows with acutely intersecting tracery. The flat ceiling is again by *Scott*, the carved corner pieces said to be C 14, though this is difficult to assess as they are painted over. Roger's choir aisle elevation can be studied at close quarters. Waterleaf capitals to the window shafts, stark pilasters with chamfered tops beneath a moulded cornice with adventurously carved gargoyles. The arch above the entrance from the transept is part of another of Roger's windows.

150. RIPON Crypt, *c.* 670

The CHANCEL is architecturally the most important part of the church, though because of later interference not aesthetically the most rewarding. The design of Archbishop Roger's mason was noble and remarkably up-to-date, as it was begun before, or is at least contemporary with, William of Sens's French work of 1175 at Canterbury. But the source of Ripon is rather the Cistercian Gothic of Roche than the Cathedral Gothic of Sens or Noyon and Laon. (Kidson (1962) said the masons came to Ripon from Byland, begun not before 1177, and so assumed that Ripon was begun after the rebuilding of Canterbury choir started in 1175; at any rate, Bony confirms Bilson's date for Roche of c. 1170. On Byland, see B of E *Yorkshire: The North Riding*, on Roche B of E *The West Riding*.) The design is now only recognizable in the w bays of the N side. Arcades of strong piers with four major and four minor shafts. Simplest moulded capitals. Resolutely pointed arches. Cinquepartite vaulting-shafts standing right on the abaci of the piers, but what do they support? Blank triforium, tripartite with the centre arch round, the flanking arches pointed. Twin lights below the centre, now glazed, following the lowering of the aisle roof. Plate tracery quatrefoils above them and below the centre arch. Tall clerestory with wall-passage and the window wall with apparently the same tripartite rhythm, a round arch between two pointed ones (but Scott said he found evidence for a third, narrower pointed arch centrally over the piers below with a single, slender shaft set in front). This system is that of St-Denis and Sens, i.e. of France c. 1140–50.

The E bays on the N as well as on the S side were reconstructed in or before c. 1300, though most of the piers seem Roger's work and also the E responds; on the date of the great E window, see *Exterior* above. Sumptuous SEDILIA in the Lincoln–Southwell–Selby style of c. 1320–30. Heavily crocketed nodding ogee arches, crocketed steep gables. Plenty of delightfully fanciful detail, all much restored. Triforium design different from Roger's (also different on the N from the S side), and clerestory lush with Geometrical tracery in two layers, one for the windows, the other enclosing the wall-passage. The effect was taken over probably from the Angel Choir at Lincoln. The vaulting-shafts are thinner too, and they stand on head-stops. At the junction of the old and the new work on the N side a gay display of heads to hide the awkward junction and especially the difference in the thickness of the wall. On the S side the stops for the vaulting-shafts are a little more elaborate, and there are tiny sprays of stiff-leaf foliage at the meeting points of the arcade arches. The four w bays on the S side were reconstructed in the C15 into a more up-to-date Perp. This was perhaps due to damage which had occurred in the crossing tower (see the Perp outer S and E windows of the tower).

The piers are Perp, the spandrels panelled, and triforium as well as clerestory have Perp windows.

The chancel has a wooden VAULT with a series of excellent C14 bosses, showing e.g. the Creation of Adam, God speaking to Eve, the Expulsion from Paradise, the Annunciation, Christ in Glory, two bishops, a king and a bishop etc. The vault is by *Scott* and replaces a plaster vault, but the bosses prove the existence of a C14 vault. The C12 never, it seems, proceeded to stone vaulting.

In the CHANCEL AISLES more of Roger's work can be pieced together. On the S side, behind the Perp arcades, the windows survive, and the quadripartite rib-vaults resting against the wall on vaulting-shafts which stand on corbels still with waterleaf capitals. On the N side the windows are Dec, otherwise the arrangement is the same. The westernmost bay was strengthened with heavy single-chamfered ribs, probably after the trouble with the crossing tower had arisen. The E bays of the aisles are of c. 1300. The shafts and ribs are all thinner. At the E end in both aisles Dec wall panelling.

The CROSSING is in a curious state, as implied above (*Exterior*, though not noticeable outside). The tower seems always to have had a trapezoidal plan. The N w pier and the finely moulded arches springing from it are in the state of Roger's time. The others have to varying degrees been remodelled in the C15. All this work was of course connected with the collapse of the tower. Seen from the w end this lopsidedness of the piers and arches is a serious fault. Inside the tower the N and w sides have a low slightly corbelled-out triforium with twin pointed openings. The intermediate support is square and chamfered. Above this on either side three tall round-headed openings, the centre ones blocked by the gable behind. On the S and E sides two Perp windows instead and no triforium below. Lattice-girders were inserted in the tower by *Scott*.

The TRANSEPTS have an E aisle of two bays, and a third bay giving entrance to the choir aisles, but these were interfered with, and the whole of the E side of the s transept rebuilt, when the tower was reconstructed. The original dividing pier on the N side has tripartite shafts on three sides and pointed arches. The aisle rib-vaults have thinner ridge ribs (N only) and transverse ridge ribs, an enrichment supposed to have been invented at Lincoln c. 1210–15. The windows are round-headed, as are all other original windows in the transepts. Triforium and clerestory as in the chancel, but with tripartite instead of cinquepartite vaulting-shafts. (Dr Palliser notes that the end walls, also one window in the N transept w wall, have an odd system of a round arch flanked by thin pointed openings, all embraced under one super-round arch; cf. *Chancel* above.) The w walls have one tier of three tall windows, and then one tier of thin twin openings corresponding with the triforium, with a quatrefoil pierced in the spandrel, then again a tier of

three windows. In the S transept the chapels were converted into the Perp style of the crossing, and the triforium has simple single openings with Y-tracery. The arches into the chancel aisles are blocked. They differ, however, in detail. That in the N transept is chamfered, too early to be connected with the trouble over the crossing tower, though the additional ribs in the first N bay might well be contemporary with the doorway. The door in the S transept has finer mouldings and three niches over. The flat medieval roofs with slightly cambered tie-beams were rescued by *Scott* from behind *Blore's* papier-mâché vault.

The NAVE raises interesting problems. It appears at first sight Perp. Five bays with piers of an enriched form of the characteristic section with four big shafts and four big hollows. Moulded arches, finely divided vaulting-shafts. Five-light clerestory windows. Wooden lierne ceiling of 1868, which *Scott* based on those of the York transepts. Quadripartite stone vaults and three-light windows in the aisles. However, the time of Roger (or his successors?) survives in parts, and what these parts show is highly puzzling. The remaining fragments are near the W and the E ends, as follows.

The first bay from the E has a high piece of solid wall, then a tall stone triforium of one lancet with coupled lights on a detached shaft (quatrefoil pierced in the spandrel) and then Perp interference which makes it impossible to make a guess about the upper windows. What is certain, however, is that the C 12 nave had no aisles, and can only have been lit from the clerestory windows. The W bays confirm this, although there the presence of the towers may modify the system. The large arches into the tower walls in any case would not be repeated farther E and may represent a reconstruction since the tower arches have proper E.E. mouldings consistent with those of the W front. Above these two bays are preserved, one wide and then one narrow bay like that at the E end. The wide one has four stepped openings, low side ones, high centre ones with the string very oddly carried across at the springing, again with the quatrefoil in the spandrel, all under a round arch. The clerestory above is tripartite as in the chancel near the transepts, but with dividing shafts square and chamfered as in the gallery in the crossing tower. The clerestory above the narrow bays has three panelled lancet lights with the same piers. All the detailing of Roger's corbelling and bracketing is highly individual. Scott in his drawings reconstructed a nave in which this alternating rhythm would go all the way through. That cannot be accepted as certain. It is possible that the broad W bay was an exception and the rest had a repetition of narrow bays only. In any case here also is the same consistent handling of Gothic detail as in the chancel. There are single shafts between the bays, though as they run almost to the roof they can scarcely have carried a vault.

The TOWERS were originally completely clear of this nave: an English tradition which lacks the logic of the French two-tower façade in front of nave and aisles. It converts what seems such a clear statement externally into a purely decorative screen. The outer E walls of the towers are indeed visible inside the aisles. The rooms inside the towers have a shafted lancet decoration with some nailhead.

FURNISHINGS, W TO E

*Nave*    PULPIT. 1913 by *Henry Wilson* (known especially for his fittings for St Bartholomew's Brighton). On marble shafts. The body with heavy bronze and silver decoration in florid Arts and Crafts style. — STAINED

152. RIPON Pulpit by Henry Wilson, 1913

GLASS. W window by *Burlison & Grylls*. – MONUMENT. Hugh Ripley †1637. Defaced in the Civil War and re-erected in 1730. By *Daniel Harvey*. With a preposterous frontally kneeling figure and an architectural surround.

*South aisle* Under the tower FONT, C12, big circular trough with eight spurs or ribs. – In the aisle second FONT, Perp, of blue marble, octagonal; concave sides with shields and lozenges. – MONUMENTS. Plain TABLE TOMB with massively chamfered marble slab carved at one end with a scene in relief of a lion and a kneeling lady in a wood. – Under the tower, Sir Edward Blackett †1718 (the coalmining tycoon of Newby Hall, later owned by Weddell; see S transept below). According to Gunnis by *John Hancock*: other works by him are at Blyth, Nottinghamshire, and Stainton, North Riding. Grotesque semi-reclining figure with big wig. Flanked by large standing figures. Tall reredos background with segmental top. Two putti under. – STAINED GLASS. One window with excellent medallions of *c.* 1320–30, re-set, another (No. 4 from W) by *Clayton & Bell*, Nos. 2, 3 and 5 by *Heaton, Butler & Bayne*.

*North aisle* At the W end, DRUM of a big circular column attributed to the Saxon C10 rebuilding of the church (diameter *c.* 3 ft 6 in.). – Base of a stone SCREEN; Perp. – STAINED GLASS (from the E) No. 1 by *Comper*; No. 2 a fine heraldic window of 1840 by *Willement*; No. 4 by *Burlison & Grylls*; Nos. 5 and 6 by *Ward & Hughes*.

*Crossing* SCREEN. Perp, and probably late C15, but with recent statuary. Wide doorway with ogee gable. Four large niches l., four r., tier of small canopied niches for twenty-four figures above, very wayward tracery between. Much restored, but still impressive. Original traceried DOOR in the doorway. – ORGAN CASE, 1878, by *Scott*, a late design and not his best (Gillingham).

*North transept* SCULPTURE. Small statue of James I. Made in 1603 for the southernmost niche of the York pulpitum. Of no sculptural value, but standing on a strange extension of Roger's pier. – STAINED GLASS. Two windows by *Ward & Hughes*, one each by *Wailes* and *Barnett*. The latter a restoration of 1815 of some medieval glass. – Also a window in the E aisle by *Harry Harvey*, 1977. – MONUMENTS. Sir Thomas Markenfield, later C14. Knight and lady on a tomb-chest (E wall). – Sir Thomas Markenfield †1497, and wife. Tall tomb-chest with panels of unusual shape, with shields on them. – Recumbent effigies, N wall. – C15 panelled stone PULPIT. – C15 'EASTER SEPULCHRE' from Cowthorpe: a strange and delightful canopied chest.

*South transept* Traces of PAINTING on wall behind library staircase. – STAINED GLASS. All by *Wailes*. – MONUMENTS. Sir John Mallorie of Studley Royal, 1678, pretty tablet without figures. – Aislabie family also of Studley Royal, also without figures. – William Weddell, 1789, by *Nollekens*, a delightful design. Bust of great

elegance on a pedestal, the whole in what purports to be a rotunda, as they were built in gardens at the time. Tall semicircle of four fluted columns with composite capitals; modelled on the Choragic Monument of Lysicrates. (This was Weddell of Newby Hall, early member of the Society of Dilettanti, collector of marbles, and patron of Robert Adam.)

*Library* Alabaster panels of the Resurrection, the Coronation of the Virgin, and St Wilfrid; early C15?

*Crypt* Fragment of Anglo-Saxon CROSS-HEAD, dated *c.* 750–850 by Collingwood.

*Chancel* HIGH ALTAR and REREDOS by *Sir Ninian Comper*. – STALLS. Of the gloriously rich canopy work the E parts are by *Scott*, the W parts much restored by him. The style corresponds to that of the stalls at Manchester and Beverley (all three sets probably by *William Brownfleet* of Ripon: Harvey 1974). The Ripon stalls are dated on a misericord 1489 and on a bench-end 1494. This bench-end carries a representation of the Elephant and Castle. Others

153. RIPON Choir stall, bench-end, 1490s, probably by William Brownfleet

have poppy-heads. An outstanding series of thirty-four MISERICORDS, with e.g. (s from E) Samson with the gates of Gaza, Jonah leaving the whale, pelican, fox and goose, pigs dancing and making music, mermaid, owl, angel with a shield carrying the date 1489; (N from E) green man, fox caught by hounds, fox and geese, fox preaching etc. – Another MISERICORD, probably late C 13 and said to come from the preceding stalls, with two armed men in combat (Remnant 1969). – STAINED GLASS. E window by *Wailes*, 1854, remodelled 1896.

*South chancel aisle* SCREEN. Wrought iron, C 20, by *Leslie Durbin*, reprehensible. MONUMENT. Moysis Fowler, first dean of Ripon, † 1608. With bad figure stiffly reclining on one side.

*North chancel aisle* STAINED GLASS. Third window from E by *O'Connor*, 1868, fourth by *Barnett* of Newcastle 1869.

Further on surroundings and the town of Ripon, see the latest edition of B of E *Yorkshire: The West Riding*.

# Salford

## CATHEDRAL CHURCH OF ST JOHN EVANGELIST
*Roman Catholic*

(Based on B of E *South Lancashire*, 1969, and contributions from Andor Gomme, Peter Howell and Roderick O'Donnell.)

Cathedral since 1850. On Chapel Street, the long spinal street of Salford (named not for a Catholic predecessor but for an Independent chapel). Built 1844–8 to the design of *Matthew Hadfield* of Weightman & Hadfield. Pugin had made plans in 1842 but they were not used, there being some point of principle on which he would not give way. But Eastlake says Pugin admired the building by his close follower Hadfield. Poorly sited, as many C 19 Catholic cathedrals were, but an altogether stately and, more surprisingly, coherent design, based as it was on three medieval churches, Newark, Howden and Selby, reduced somewhat in scale but faithfully reproducing details. All three were soon to be included in Edmund Sharpe's *Architectural Parallels* of 1848 (though whether the engravings were issued singly earlier is not clear), and the *Builder* was severe upon Salford, suggesting that the architect would have done better to consult Sharpe more widely and pick his details from a larger choice of models. Such simplistic reproduction was of course common in the 1840s.

It is a cruciform design with a dominating crossing steeple which comes from Newark with one storey missed out and the spire slightly squatter; otherwise all is copied exactly, including the idiosyncratic triangular mouldings

which link the windows. Much the same is true of the w front, after that of Howden, its proportions decidedly stubbier than the real Howden, closer to those of Sharpe's engraving. The only omission of note is the transom of the main w window. The nave takes over Howden's arcade and roof, shortening the piers somewhat, but Hadfield hadn't the nerve (or the money?) to put a real passage through the bare stretches of wall at clerestory-level. (The eastern limb of the actual Selby has details so close to those of Howden that it is virtually certain that the same team of medieval masons worked on both; perhaps that determined the choice of Selby as model for the chancel here.) The gorgeous flowing tracery of Selby's E window is reproduced exactly, but the arcade is reduced in length and in richness of moulding.

DECORATION AND FURNISHING of the E parts was by *Weightman, Hadfield & Goldie* (as the firm became) in 1853–5, including the high altar, screens infilling the choir arcade, Lady Altar (heightened 1882), the Leeming Chantry on the s and the Lee Chantry on the N. Stone and wood carving by *Lane & Lewis*, including bosses (choir vault 1854) and stalls. Brasses on tombs (Lee Chantry) by *Hardman*, E window by *Wailes*, 1856. – The Blessed Sacrament Chapel (s transept) is part of the original building, but the fittings are of 1884 by *P. P. Pugin*, including altar, iron screen, wall and ceiling decoration; with painting by *Pippet*, stone carving by *Boulton*, and metalwork by *Hardman Powell & Co.* – One memorable WINDOW in the s choir aisle. It shows St Matthew with Hadfield holding a plan of the cathedral, St John with a model of it, and St George with Goldie holding an elevation of the reredos. – Also, at the N wall of the N transept, tomb of Bishop Sharples † 1850, his recumbent effigy holding a model of the cathedral. (For Hadfield's other chief work, also with portrait, see Sheffield R.C.) – The reordering of 1972, by *Cassidy & Ashton* of Preston, made a new sanctuary at the crossing, leaving the old sanctuary intact.

On surrounding Salford, see the latest edition of B of E *South Lancashire*.

# Sheffield

## CATHEDRAL CHURCH
## OF ST PETER AND ST PAUL *Anglican*

(Based on B of E *Yorkshire: The West Riding*, 1967, revised, with information from David O'Connor, Rev. G. C. White and Anthony New.)

Cathedral since 1914. Formerly the parish church of Sheffield, it stands at the centre of the old city, with some streets of C 18 houses around. The original church plan was cruciform and therefore probably earlier than the visible forms, which are all Perp or later, except for chevron-ornament incorporated in the E interior wall (White). Crossing arches early C 15. Crossing tower with crocketed spire of about the same time. Bell-openings of four lights with transom. The spire rises behind a parapet. Only a few of the shafts of the many-moulded jambs and arches have capitals. Note s springer of the old N aisle. Chancel internally C 15 (but see E walls below). The Shrewsbury (SE) Chapel was added by the fourth Earl † 1538 (see *Monuments* below): slender and tall octagonal piers, embattled abaci.

There was later work by *John Carr* (s and E sides of chancel, 1773–5), *Thomas Atkinson* (chancel N chapel, 1777), and other alterations by *William Lindley* (Carr's former assistant) 1791–1802, *Charles Watson* (Lindley's former partner), 1802 etc., and *Robert Potter*, 1841, much of their work being altered or replaced by a restoration of 1880 conducted by *W. Flockton*. The exterior E wall of the chancel and chancel chapels is still essentially late C 18 in character: the details must be studied to recognize this. Of Flockton's restoration, the transepts, W front and W part of the nave (but see below on *Bailey*'s work), nave arcade etc., and the E windows. But the main E window may be a C 18 version of its medieval predecessor (White).

In 1919 it was decided to build a new larger cathedral to a design by *Sir Charles Nicholson*. He changed his plans in 1936, and from that time date the offices N of the old E end and the Chapel of the Holy Spirit W of these and N W of the old building. This chapel, dedicated only in 1948, was meant to be the ritual 'E' end of a newly oriented plan that was to run N–S with the old parts as a kind of transept. The chapel is tall and aisleless and in a conventional Gothic. After the Second World War a new large nave in the direction of Nicholson's was designed by *G. G. Pace*, but this has in its turn been given up. Now there has been a return to the old orientation, with the old E choir and chapels still the functioning E end, and the latest new parts extending to the W, leaving Nicholson's N-pointing parts as an appendix. The new W parts, with new W crossing, are by *Arthur Bailey* of Ansell & Bailey, in a depressingly traditional style, a kind of free Gothic with minimal tracery and close-set buttresses ending squarely above the roof-line in the fashion of 1960. Bailey's towered porch over the entrance from Church Street tries at once 'not to be Gothic and not to be not Gothic' (as Anthony New has put it) while harmonizing with the older work. Altogether, a different kind of architectural tangle from those of the great medieval cathedrals.

FURNISHINGS

STAINED GLASS. The N transept N window was designed by *H. Gérente* in 1847 and completed by *A. Gérente* for the w window of All Saints Margaret Street in London, but disliked by Butterfield and replaced, coming eventually to Sheffield Cathedral *via* St Luke's Hollis Croft. It is a copy of part of the C 14 Jesse window at Wells (choir E). Figures under canopies. (Provenance *per* Brian Sprake, relayed by Dr O'Connor.) – E and w windows by *W. E. Dixon*, 1880 and 1881. – N chancel chapel E window, 1935, by *Christopher Webb*: sentimental. – Chapel of the Holy Spirit, 'E' window, 1940, by *Webb*.

MONUMENTS. In the Shrewsbury Chapel monuments to the fourth and sixth Earls. The former († 1538) with alabaster effigies of the Earl and his two wives under a flat-topped panelled arch with a heavy pendant. Straight cresting. Tomb-chest with twisted shafts at the corners and shields in quatrefoils. – The monument to the sixth Earl († 1590) is against the s wall. Recumbent effigy in armour, the head on the rolled-up end of a straw mat. Very large, but not very imaginative architectural surround with big top achievement. – Formerly in the s transept, large sarcophagus made 1584–5 for the same earl, perhaps for his first wife. (Recently moved to a space near the vestries.) No effigies. Tomb-chest with fluted Ionic pilasters and shields in bold strapwork panels. – In the s chapel, monument to George Bamforth † 1739, with bust against the foot of a tall obelisk in relief. – J. Wilkinson (chancel N side) with bust, 1805 (*Chantrey*'s first work). – A. Mackenzie † 1816 (from the former church of St Paul), with two standing allegorical figures l. and r. of the inscription and a bust on top; and Thomas Harrison and Mrs Harrison (s aisle) with allegorical figure seated by two urns, 1823. – Thomas Watson (N aisle), 1835, by *Edward Law*, with bust. – Archdeacon Blakeney (sacristy), 1896, by *Onslow Ford*, with bust. – More recent monuments: Bishop Burrows by *G. G. Pace* and *David Kindersley*, Bishop Heaslett by *G. G. Pace*.

Other furnishings include the BISHOP'S THRONE by *Sir Charles Nicholson*. – In Nicholson's Chapel of the Holy Spirit: REREDOS by *Temple Moore*, SCREEN and STALLS by *Comper*. – In the N chapel (St Katherine's): C 15 wooden SEDILIA, canopied, simple panelling with cusped arcading behind, one seat smaller; sub-deacons were evidently presumed to be thin (White). – Pretty SCREEN, 1935, by *W. H. Randoll Blacking*.

For an account of surrounding buildings in this largest city of Yorkshire, see the latest edition of B of E *Yorkshire: The West Riding*.

# Sheffield

CATHEDRAL CHURCH OF ST MARIE
*Roman Catholic*

(Based on B of E *Yorkshire: The West Riding*, 1967, and information from Peter Howell, Roderick O'Donnell and John Martin Robinson.)

Cathedral since 1980. In Norfolk Row, in an area laid out *c.* 1770 for the Dukes of Norfolk, and on the site of their local agent's house, from which a C18 Catholic mission operated. The church was built 1846–50 to the design of *Weightman & Hadfield*, in fact the work of *Matthew Hadfield* and, with St John Salford (see above), one of his two most effective works. Proud S W tower with spire, the spire with three tiers of dormers. The style of the church, based on study of the C14 St Andrew Heckington in Lincolnshire, can be described as Geometrical to Decorated. The Munster Lady Chapel, an addition of 1878–9 by *M. E. Hadfield & Son*, is sited attractively over sacristies, up a spiral stair.

The REREDOS designed by *A. W. N. Pugin*, 1850, and carved by *Theodore Phyffers* still survives (1980). – ORGAN CASE, 1875, designed by *J. F. Bentley* and carved in Austrian oak by *J. E. Knox* for the organ built by *T. C. Lewis*. – STAINED GLASS. *Pugin* designed the W window, made by *Hardman*. The E window, designed by *George Goldie* (who joined the firm of Weightman & Hadfield in 1850), includes a portrait of the architect Matthew Hadfield (see also at Salford). Both E and W windows show sacred events in several tiers, but the superior quality of Pugin's design is patent. S transept S window by *Wailes*. Lady Chapel glass by *Hardman*. Two windows on the Lady Chapel stairs designed by *Bentley*, made by *Lavers, Barraud & Westlake*, Annunciation 1878, St Joseph 1884. – MONUMENT, now mutilated and absurdly placed under an altar on the N side of the nave: Fr Charles Pratt, 1850, effigy holding a model of the church. By *Thomas Earp*, carver to George Myers, the firm of church-builders. – In the N transept, alabaster TABLET to the architect of the church († 1885), designed by his son, *Charles Hadfield*, and carved by *Frank Tory*. Figure of Our Lady of Pity after a cast given to Matthew Hadfield by his old friend Pugin.

Until reordering in or before 1976, i.e. before it became a cathedral, this was one of the most completely and artistically furnished and decorated Catholic churches in the country (Howell). Much still survives, statues and shrines, stained glass, memorials, and a considerable quantity of painted ceramic wall decoration etc. But much has gone. Whereas the architectural history of Sheffield's Anglican cathedral has been a matter of additions and extensions, the decorative history of the Catholic cathedral has been mainly a matter of subtraction.

For the architectural surroundings of Sheffield's two cathedrals, see the latest edition of B of E *Yorkshire: The West Riding*.

# Shrewsbury

CATHEDRAL CHURCH OF OUR LADY
HELP OF CHRISTIANS
AND ST PETER OF ALCANTARA *Roman Catholic*

(Based on B of E *Shropshire*, 1958, and information from Peter Howell, George McHardy and Roderick O'Donnell.)

Cathedral authorized 1850. Picturesquely placed partway uphill from the river on the road called Town Walls after the former medieval fortifications. Shrewsbury was designated one of the first new Roman Catholic sees in 1850 and a cathedral design was discussed by A. W. N. Pugin with the new bishop and the sixteenth Earl of Shrewsbury in 1851, not long before both Pugin and the Earl died. *E. W. Pugin* then made a further design for the seventeenth Earl, grander than the one actually built 1853–6. As built, impressive, though without a tower. The impact is created by very tall proportions of nave and aisles, a short high chancel, and a steep gable with big bell-cote. Sand-coloured stone going grey. Dec tracery. Entrance up steps within S W porch. Inside, thin octagonal piers with lushly carved capitals. Fine open nave roof trusses, less eccentric than Edward Pugin's later work and more like his father's. Sumptuous St Winefride's Chapel on the S E, 1891, possibly by *Edmund Kirby*.

Good mid- and late Victorian fittings. High altar and font by *Lane & Lewis* to E. *Pugin*'s design. Fine pulpit with sculpture and coloured marbles, also by him? – In Blessed Sacrament Chapel, altar and reredos probably by *Alphege Pippet*. – Stations of the Cross in the manner of Gill (cf. Westminster R.C.) by *Philip Lindsay Clarke*. – STAINED GLASS. E window, 1856, by *Hardman*, with kneeling figure of the seventeenth Earl. Much later *Hardman & Co.* glass. – Six windows, 1906–21, by the Arts and Crafts artist *Margaret Rope*: baptistery, 1906; W window, *c.* 1910; chancel S, 1915; chancel N, 1921.

# Southwell

(Based on B of E *Nottinghamshire*, 1979, as revised by Elizabeth Williamson, further revised, with information from Ronald Sims and George McHardy, and *The Leaves of Southwell*, 1945.)

Plan, Fig. 157, from the *Builder*, 1892, after a plan by Ewan Christian.

A recent reference (see Recent Literature) is Summers 1974.

## INTRODUCTION

Southwell is a country town like Sherborne or Selby in the overpowering presence of a large medieval church. Although the minster has always had a *cathedra*, it was raised to be head of a see only in 1884. Plenty of legends about the foundation and earliest history of the minster exist. The first date which can be accepted as probable is 956 for the grant of the Manor of Southwell with much land around by Eadwig, King of the English, to Oskytel, Archbishop of York, although the original charter has been lost. (According to a report of 1853, some late Saxon carved stones were re-used in rebuilding the central piers.) By the early C 11 St Eadburh, daughter of the Anglian King and Abbess of Repton, had been buried here. Then, between 1050 and 1060, we hear, Archbishop Kinsius gave bells to the *monasterium*. In spite of this designation the establishment at Southwell was apparently never monastic: it seems always to have been collegiate, that is, a church to which a college of secular canons, priests not monks, was attached. In 1108–14 it became the mother church of the county and was obviously one of the major churches in the province of York; just like the chapters of Ripon and Beverley, its chapter was after 1171, except for occasional visitation, entirely independent of York. It owned or con-trolled about one-quarter of Notts and had certainly all the regional influence of a cathedral (without incidentally possessing either a Dean or a Provost). The buildings, as we see them, belong chiefly to three periods: (*a*) from 1108 onwards, (*b*) from 1234 onwards, and (*c*) about 1288. These periods refer respectively to (*a*) façade, nave, crossing, crossing tower and transepts, (*b*) E arm, and (*c*) chapter house.

The stone used throughout was 'white' (yellowish or greyish) Mansfield sandstone, fine-grained and at its best in interior work protected from weather, such as the famous leaf-carvings in the chapter house (Clifton-Taylor 1972). Traces of painted colour have been found on choir arcade columns and aisle walls, mostly red, blue and black, with remains of gold on the carving in the N E transept, and the chapter-house vault was in the past heavily lime-washed in red. But the chapter-house 'leaves' show no signs of paint whatever (Sims). So the medieval habit of painting architectural sculpture was not invariable. There was restoration work on the building in the C 19 by *Ewan Christian*, and there has been recent work on recladding of roofs, cleaning of choir and chapter house, and restoration of outer N porch with new inner entrance porch under *Ronald Sims*.

A large Roman villa lies beneath the minster and its cemetery. This may have been a courtyard house. Part of one wing, containing a suite of baths, was excavated in 1959. A reconstruction of the painted plaster from one of the rooms in the baths hangs on the S choir aisle in the minster. After the Roman building had fallen into ruins, at least one Saxon hut was erected on the site.

## THE NORMAN CATHEDRAL

Building began about 1108 under Archbishop Thomas of York. Usually work started from the E, and of the E end of Norman Southwell we know only from excavations. It had a straight-ended chancel, not an apse, an arrangement then almost unique in England, chancel aisles with apses, and little apses attached to the transepts, that is (save for the chancel ending) the same composition as many a major Romanesque church in England and France (in Notts, for example, Blyth). Whether a change of plan occurred between the chancel and the surviving parts farther w, we cannot say, but it is a fact that the decoration of all that exists now is of one kind, with the exception of the historiated capitals of the E CROSSING PIERS. Each of those capitals, with strong volutes and more old-fashioned than the scallop capitals in the rest of the minster, is carved with one scene. With one exception the iconography is quite simple but without continuity from one scene to the next. The scenes are the Last Supper, an unidentified scene including an Annunciation, a procession relating to the

156. SOUTHWELL View from the north-west

Entry of Jerusalem on the next capital, the Agnus Dei, and the Washing of Feet. They are among the most important examples of such capitals in England, comparable with those at Hereford (perhaps the first *c.* 1115), Westminster Abbey and Reading. The technique of these, based on manuscript-drawing technique, is extremely linear, a criss-cross of folds in the draperies without any comprehension or system, and faces with large, staring eyes, consistent with a date of *c.* 1120.

Most impressive of all are perhaps the N and S CROSS-ING ARCHES, on enormously tall semicircular piers. The capitals consist of such tiny scallops and so many of them that they are only a fringe, not independent members of

the structure (mass-effects rather than effects of articulation). The two stages of the central tower which appear inside have cable and wave decoration on the lower stage (the earliest in England, according to Sir Alfred Clapham), and zigzag on the upper stage. The composition of the TRANSEPTS is very strong and simple too: blank arcading the whole height of the ground floor, carrying a narrow gallery on the N side of the N transept and the S side of the S transept. Clerestory with wall-passage (cf. nave). The windows with one order and a roll moulding in the arch or with big cable mouldings or billet friezes on the labels as their only ornaments. The W and E walls have the plainest entries into the aisles and chancel aisles, but on the E there was, farther away from the crossing, a larger opening into a chapel, both in the N and S transepts. In the N transept this was redone about 1260, and in the S transept it is blocked and was besides, before it was blocked, altered, for it now has zigzag decoration for the large arch and in addition a smaller doorway again with zigzag (and billet in its outer order). Zigzag does not seem to occur at Southwell before about 1140 or 1150 (cf. the top storey of the crossing tower mentioned above), and so one must presume some later adjustment. (When the two acutely pointed and uneven arches with which the S transept's E chapel arch had been filled were removed in the C 19, the incomplete detail was invented. And see the N transept's E chapel arch, as filled in the C 13, below.) Above the larger openings on the ground floor is a triple arch with a wall-passage behind which led from the S and N galleries to the galleries above the chancel aisles – a handsome motif, though a little out of keeping with the rest of the composition at Southwell. (For the carved lintel in the N W corner of the N transept (not *in situ*), see *Furnishings*.)

The NAVE is 318 ft long, 137 ft wide, and 50 ft high, with towers 105 ft high. It has seven bays plus the bay farthest W between the two W towers which is separated from the others by some solid wall carried up to the ceiling as pilasters towards the nave, necessary to help in abutting the towers. The slightly narrower W bay is different only in details from the others. Their system is as follows. The arcade has short circular piers, very short if compared with those at the crossing (S and N; for E and W are composite), and again insignificantly small many-scalloped capitals, some with a very minimum of decoration in the scallops.

The arches have a billet frieze outside and then straight steps with a thin angle roll and a double soffit roll. The aisles are rib-vaulted, the technique of the vaulting still awkward, but the rib profile no longer of the most elementary: two ridges between two rolls (roll-ridge-ridge-roll). The aisle windows are quite large (but only the one farthest N W is original). To continue now with the elevation of the nave, the gallery above the ground-floor arcade appears to have the same undivided seven (or eight) openings on each side. But they were not originally meant to be like that. Corbels on the sides and an odd stump of a shaft downwards from the apex of the arch show that the intention was to subdivide the opening by twin arches on a colonnette (as, for example, at Peterborough and in many other places) and then leave the tympanum above these arches open and divide it only by another colonnette standing on the first and connecting it with the apex of the main arch. It seems an odd, uncalled-for idea, but it would not have been unique; for at Romsey in Hampshire it can actually still be seen as executed about 1150, probably under immediate influence from Southwell (cf. the straight end to the chancel and at the beginning of the nave the very tall circular piers with small, many-scalloped capitals). The clerestory has much plain wall. The round-headed inner openings have one order of short scalloped shafts. As we shall see outside, the actual windows are circular. The wagon roof was only put in in 1880, but finishes the composition quite successfully.

It is a composition which combines in a remarkable way the robust with the lively. Although the piers of the nave are short and thick, the impression is not overpowering.

157. SOUTHWELL
Plan from the *Builder*, 1892 (see p. 301)

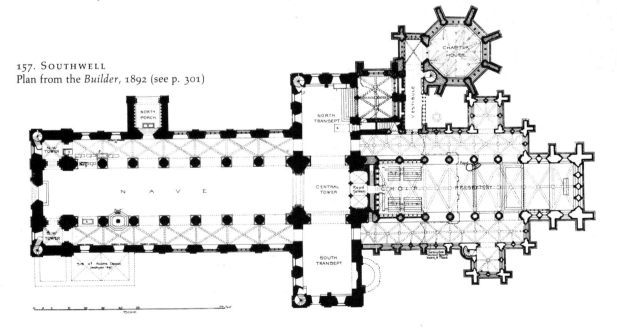

The gallery is so proportioned as to let its arches appear to skip elastically to the E instead of weighing down on the ground-floor arcade. With the twin openings as projected the effect would of course have been even more agile. The same can be seen in the aisles, where the ribs create a busy shuttling forward and backward, very different from the inert masses of the groined vaults at Blyth. Altogether a comparison of Blyth and Southwell will elucidate the difference between the C 11 and the more vivacious early C 12.

Strangely, the clerestory windows are circular outside. Otherwise the side elevations are very plain, the aisle windows with a zigzag surround and then an order of colonnettes, the roof on a wavy corbel table. The N side has in addition a large, sumptuously zigzag-decorated NORTH PORCH, tunnel-vaulted (rare in England, cf. Tewkesbury). Its lower storey is decorated by blank arcades inside with intersected arches and its upper storey by little windows facing N and again plenty of zigzag. The circular chimneys with conical tops are restored but based on original work. The transept gables have large horizontal zigzag bands with bands of dots between, slightly different on the N from the S. The central crossing tower has two orders, arcades with intersected and above with plain arches. To visualize its original appearance it should be imagined with a pyramidal roof.

The FAÇADE is unique in having pyramidal roofs to its towers. They were rebuilt in 1880 by *Ewan Christian*, the Ecclesiastical Commissioners' architect, on the pattern which they had until a fire of 1711. The date of their construction is unknown. They are shown in Hollar's engraving in Dugdale's *Monasticon* after a drawing by Hall, not correct in all details. They were rebuilt after the 1711 fire, and again in 1802 with flat roofs by *Richard Ingleman*, surveyor to the fabric 1801–8. To reconstruct in one's mind the original appearance of Norman churches it is essential to forget about the flat tops of the towers which we now see nearly everywhere, or indeed the needle-sharp spires of the type of, say, Norwich. Southwell comes much nearer to the ideal of the C 12 and, indeed, the towers are the only ones besides Worksop surviving in full. In other ways the façade can now hardly be used to re-evoke Norman ideals, for the large central window belongs of course to the C 15. The towers, slightly different from each other in detail, climb up with flat buttresses, without set-offs, but with six string-courses crossing them, the lowest two continued from the aisle elevation. On the sixth stage, blank arcading carried all round, even over the buttresses. All the capitals are of cushion type, and decoration here and in the central portal is again chiefly zigzag. There are five orders of columns to the portal, the capitals scalloped with little bits of ornament in the scallops. Inside it is of two orders, the outer one with pleated capitals and

more zigzag, the inner one a continuous roll curiously broken at the haunches. Aisle-end windows C 19, copied from the other aisle windows. They were three-light Dec before.

## THE C 13 CATHEDRAL

In 1234 Walter de Gray, Archbishop of York (who rebuilt the transepts there), decided to pull down the Norman E end here and replace it by a larger new one in an up-to-date style. The E ARM was lengthened by four bays and the new EAST CHAPEL and a pair of EAST TRANSEPTS were finished c. 1241. (A slight break in level will be noticed in the sill of the upper storey where replacement of the old meets the entirely new. A similar break in level farther E is unexplained.) The ensuing plan pattern is identical, for example, with Beverley and also Salisbury, that is, quite a usual pattern of the E.E. style, if quite impossible in any other country but Britain. Neither the double transepts (so long after Cluny) nor the straight-headed chancel and E chapel found favour anywhere on the Continent. The elevation of the Southwell E arm is unusual for its date in England. It is two-storeyed, not three-storeyed, that is it has no middle storey in the sense in which Lincoln and Salisbury and Westminster Abbey have them. Instead, the whole height of the nave wall is pulled together into two stages, the ground-floor arcade with piers consisting of four major and four minor filleted shafts and deep hollows between (cf. Lincoln, St Hugh's Choir), moulded capitals, and finely profiled multiform arches, and the upper floor with a tall order of twin lancets for each bay, so tall that in it there are small insignificant openings from the existing gallery behind and, above them, clerestory windows with a wall-passage in front. The idea may have come from Ripon, where c. 1175 an aisleless nave was for the eye divided in two instead of three storeys in a comparable way. Pershore in Worcestershire (1223–39) is more similar to Southwell, which also has aisles in the main portion, but Pershore is probably independent. The two E bays at Southwell, however, are aisleless and also two-storeyed. We might recall that Rochester's aisleless and two-storeyed E end is thought to have been vaulted by 1214. (Bony 1979, p. 73, n. 26, lists other English variations on the two-storey theme with clerestory wall-passage c. 1140–c. 1240: Southwell is not unique.)

This E end has two tiers of lancet windows. The shafts are mostly filleted, the capitals mostly moulded. Stiff-leaf capitals, however, also occur, especially close to the E end, and on the S more than the N. Otherwise there is dogtooth and nailhead decoration and no other ornamental motif. Both the E bays and the 'nave' as well as the aisles of the main E arm are rib-vaulted, with slim, resilient ribs springing from shafts which rest on corbels, that is are not carried down into the ground-floor piers. The vaults have ridge ribs everywhere, an innovation of Lincoln of *c.* 1210, very un-French, but accepted almost at once everywhere in England. At the crossings of the ribs fine foliage bosses. With the exception of this motif the style of Southwell points clearly to Yorkshire. The designer's predilection for lancets and a rapid succession of upward-shooting lines is North English and different from the happy breadth of Lincoln. It is this emphasis on fine perpendicular lines which one remembers in thinking of the Southwell E arm. All shafts are duplicated or triplicated. All main mouldings are cut up into thin stringy lines. Even the consistent use of fillets on shafts acts that way: the eye perceives three lines instead of one. The appreciation of the solid drum-shape of a pier or shaft, which the Norman masons of the nave had so obviously possessed, has gone completely. Instead of it

the love of the C 13 belongs to the line, the line tensely stretched and carrying currents of energy. However, the general shape of the space is not as excessively tall as in contemporary French work; it is rather broad and shows, specially at the E end, a very clear horizontal division. So there is no excess either way. And the E transepts are low.

The E arm stands as a monument to this style, the classic English Early Gothic style. To it also belongs the N transept chapel of two bays, opening towards the transept in two exceedingly steep arches, both within a single Norman arch and one much more acute than the other. (As mentioned above, there was until the C 19 a similar arrangement in the S transept.) The detail inside, such as shafts (keeled), capitals, and vaults with ridge ribs and foliated bosses, also dates this chapel as *c.* 1250 or 1260. Originally a pulpitum or stone screen between chancel and crossing of the same

159. SOUTHWELL East end, begun 1234, and chapter house, *c.* 1290

160. SOUTHWELL East end, begun 1234

161. SOUTHWELL Chapter house, *c.* 1290, vault

style may have existed (see the concealed stairs by the SE pier of the crossing). Stairs from the N choir aisle lead to the library over the N transept chapel.

By *c.* 1260, we can assume, the building was once again complete. Nothing then happened to it until about 1288, when Archbishop John de la Romaine gave the decree to build a new CHAPTER HOUSE. On the N side it was to be connected with the E arm by a corridor looking with a few cloistral openings on to a little courtyard W of the E transept. The courtyard is now alas taken up by vestries. A double doorway opened out of the chancel aisle into the corridor. The corridor leads to a vestibule, and the entrance to the chapter house itself is at right angles to this. The chapter house is polygonal, as English examples often are,

but it differs from most others in that it is built without a central pier. That gives it a delicious feeling of airiness and breadth, although its size is not great. (The domical ribbed vault over Wells Lady Chapel, designed before 1310, comes of the same family, Mr Harvey has pointed out. The other pier-less chapter house, the one at York dated probably just before Southwell's, has a timber vault over its wider span, but Southwell's is stone-vaulted.) However, the glory of the chapter house, vestibule, corridor and doorway from the N choir aisle is their carved decoration, exquisite and by no means excessive (and, as reported above, never painted as e.g. the contemporary leaf corbels at Exeter apparently were). It consists almost entirely of foliage carved with supreme skill to emulate nature. This realism was the new

162. SOUTHWELL Chapter house, *c.* 1290, foliage r. of door

ambition of the late C13, inspired by French mid-C13 innovations which English masons must have known. The plants represented are chiefly maple, oak, hawthorn, ranunculus and potentilla, vine, ivy and hop. It will never be possible to determine how far they were copied from sketches in notebooks made during French apprenticeship or journeys, and how far from nature. Both methods were no doubt used. That the result is classic Gothic and not Victorian, that it has a soul and does not only please the senses, is due to the fact that the carvers were never satisfied with mere imitation but succeeded in keeping stone as stone, in preserving intact the smoothness and firmness of surfaces; in short, they achieved a synthesis of nature and style.

To quote from the now rare King Penguin of 1945, Pevsner's *Leaves of Southwell*: 'And is not the balance of Southwell something deeper too than a balance of nature and style or of the imitative and the decorative? Is it not perhaps also a balance of God and the World, the invisible and the visible? . . . The inexhaustible delight in live form that can be touched with worshipping fingers and felt with all senses is ennobled . . . by the conviction that so much beauty can exist only because God is in every man and beast, in every herb and stone . . . Seen in this light, the leaves of Southwell assume a new significance as one of the purest symbols surviving in Britain of Western thought, our thought, in its loftiest mood.' A noble thing to say in 1945.

The climax of the whole is the chapter-house portal. Here alone Purbeck marble is used of which the Lincoln architects were so fond. The contrast between the slim spare quality of the chancel with its majority of purely moulded capitals and minority of stylized stiff-leaf and the ease with which the whole chapter house and each capital spread themselves out is remarkable, a contrast which characterizes 1275–1300 as against 1200–50 (see the Angel Choir in comparison with St Hugh's Choir and nave at Lincoln). The development of the windows and their tracery deserves attention too. Instead of the exclusive use of lancets, there are now three lights grouped together with, above, two circles containing trefoils, the topmost one a quatrefoil. That is in principle what the chapter houses at Westminster and Salisbury also do, and most richly the Angel Choir at Lincoln. But in a few details Southwell goes beyond the smiling classicity of these buildings of 1250–75. The designer places a pointed trefoil above the middle light of the three into its top, thereby breaking the perfect harmony. Similarly in the vestibule

163. SOUTHWELL
Chapter house, c. 1290, doorway

(upper N window) there are trefoils not surrounded by circles. Evidently the faith in perfection was wavering, and indeed only ten or fifteen years after the completion of the chapter house the clarity of the Early English style had finally given way to the intricacies of the Decorated.

## THE FOURTEENTH AND FIFTEENTH CENTURIES

Of the Dec style Southwell possesses an outstanding example, the PULPITUM or stone rood screen erected c. 1320–40 (stone for it being carried in 1337). It replaced an existing one assumed above to date from c. 1250. There was restoration in 1820 by the *Bernasconi* brothers, who renewed the heads etc. The pulpitum is of the 'veranda type', that is open-fronted, with vaults under a porch roof. These little vaults possess flying ribs, like those of the Easter Sepulchre and the pulpitum at Lincoln, and the vestibule at Bristol, but otherwise rare in English architecture. The N and S walls have blank tracery with plenty of ogee, that is double-curved forms, the chief innovation of c. 1300 in tracery design. The W façade has two blank bays and three large openings with openwork ogee cusping. The E side is even richer, a two-storeyed composition with niches on the ground floor (one of them adorned with a diaper pattern of large undulating leaves, again very similar to Lincoln) and gables with blank flowing tracery on the upper floor. In the centre are much restored figures. Apart from these there are masses of small heads used in the same way as the C 13 had already profusely used them. The crocketing of the gables of the pulpitum is prodigious, perhaps even more luxuriant than in the Lincoln pulpitum but very similar to the Percy tomb at Beverley on the one hand, the Lady Chapel at Ely on the other. It was evidently an East Anglian School which was called to do decorative work from Yorkshire to Cambridgeshire. Its genius is unquestioned, even if one cannot fail to realize how licentious 1320 was as compared with the nobler and more disciplined C 13.

The SEDILIA must be by the same masons. The seats (unusual because there are five of them) are separated by free-standing buttress-shaped shafts connected with the wall by little embattled bridges. The stories told in many figures in the spandrels were so freely restored by the *Bernasconis* in 1820 that little remains of their original character. (Excellent plaster choir stalls by the Bernasconis were removed by *Ewan Christian*.) Besides pulpitum and sedilia the early C 14 contributed only the three windows of the N transept chapel. Their restless shapes need only be compared with the windows of the aisles added more than a hundred years later to understand the difference between the age of Edward II and the matter-of-fact, prosperous, this-worldly C 15.

The Perpendicular style, however, did more than that to the church. By knocking out nearly the whole of the centre

164. SOUTHWELL Pulpitum, c. 1320–40, west face, and C 12 crossing arch

165. SOUTHWELL Pulpitum, *c.* 1320–40, east face (detail)

of the Norman front and replacing it by one gigantic seven-light window with a broad, but still two-centred pointed arch, floods of light were admitted into the dark interior, but its original character was ruthlessly disturbed. The window is of a curious design. It has two transoms, the lower running through as usual, but the upper at alternating heights in the seven lights. A castellated pattern is thus formed, and the tracery details continue this up-and-down rhythm. It is entertaining, if somewhat hard. In addition, the C15 built a large chapel along the s aisle which was pulled down in 1784, and a pretty doorway in the s chancel aisle with good heads of a king and queen as label stops.

### FURNISHINGS

FURNISHINGS. Tessellated PAVEMENT, found (and now visible through a trapdoor) on the w side of the s transept. Saxon, according to Dr Ralegh Radford, possibly part of the transept paving of the pre-Norman church. – TYMPANUM in the N transept. Too wide for its present position, it seems to have been a triangular-headed lintel tympanum. Carved with St Michael and the dragon and, to the l., David rescuing his flock from the lion, the latter scene rare in sculpture but not in manuscripts and metalwork. Early C12 in style, with traces of the Anglo-Saxon Urnes style, e.g. in the entwined tail of the dragon. Underside unusually carved with bands of rich ornament. Not like the crossing capitals and possibly slightly earlier (from the previous church?), but very close indeed to the tympanum at Hoveringham, about 5 miles away. – FONT. 1661;

166. SOUTHWELL Pulpitum, *c.* 1320–40, flying ribs in 'veranda' vault

octagonal; one of many put up in Notts immediately after the Restoration (the same type at East Bridgford, Walkeringham, Newark, Orston, Scarrington, Shelford, Sibthorpe, Tythby, Whatton). Their plain panels with bands forming diagonal crosses with roses, fleurs-de-lys, and often cherubs' heads are easily recognized. The cover belongs to the font. – EAGLE LECTERN. Brass, *c.* 1510, found *c.* 1780 in the lake at Newstead Abbey and given to Southwell in 1805, presumably by Lord Byron. One of a series made in the late C15 and early C16, probably in East Anglia, which includes those at Oxburgh, Norfolk, St Gregory Norwich, Holy Trinity Coventry, Lowestoft, Dundee, Newcastle Cathedral, St Michael Southampton, and Urbino Cathedral. – Also from the lake, brass CANDLESTICKS, *c.* 1500. – BENCH-ENDS. The usual poppy-head type; s transept. – MISERICORDS. Six of the C14 on the E side of the choir screen, part of the original stalls and all with human figures. – WEST DOOR. A superb example of an original C 12 door with extensive large and simple scrolls developing out of the iron hinges. – NORTH DOOR to the porch, C 14, with a pattern of ogee reticulation all over. – ORGAN CASE. One by *W. D. Caröe.* – SCULPTURE. Large wooden Virgin and Child by *Alan Coleman,* 1952, by the S E crossing pier. Brought from the chapel at Kelham Hall in 1974.

STAINED GLASS. The medieval glass gathered together in a S chancel aisle window is just a jumble, visually enjoyable for reasons quite independent of the original composition of the pieces. – E window. The four lower lights contain important C 16 French glass given in 1818 by Henry Gally Knight, who bought it in Paris with a provenance from the Temple Church, demolished in 1795, when the windows went to Lenoir's museum broken up in 1814. The scenes, with large figures in Mannerist attitudes, are, from l. to r., the Baptism of Christ, the Resurrection of Lazarus, the Entry into Jerusalem, and the Mocking of Christ. (Restored and adapted for their present position by *Joseph Hale Miller.*) Upper lights 1876 by *Clayton & Bell.* – E arm. Heraldic glass in the three N lancets possibly by *Miller.* – Chapter house. Many small fragments without much interest arranged symmetrically in the large windows. Mostly Flemish C 16–17, but in windows one and two fragments of English C 13–15 glass and in window three C 13 and C 14 fragments including a large incomplete panel of the Betrayal of Christ and an Adoration of the Magi of c. 1300 from Gonalston. – VICTORIAN GLASS. In the nave aisles much brightly coloured glass by *O'Connor,* providing an excellent review of the firm's work. Healing the Sick, Raising the Dead, and Preaching to the Poor were shown at the 1851 Exhibition. – By *Kempe,* N and s aisle E windows, 1875 and 1880, good early work; S side sanctuary, 1898; westernmost N transept, 1907; N chapel, three windows.

MONUMENTS. Slab with a foliated cross in a round-arched recess in the N aisle. – Two incomplete incised slabs of c. 1300. – Headless alabaster figure of an archbishop (c. 1450) in the S aisle of the E arm. – Archbishop Sandys † 1588. Alabaster, very lifelike, with the four small angels at his head and feet, on a richly moulded tomb-chest against the front of which small figures of the members of his family kneel. The composition is nothing unusual, but the execution is better than most of the Elizabethan alabaster-work in Notts. There is (no wonder, one should probably say) nothing provincial about it. Repaired in 1852 by *Joseph Hall* the younger of Derby. – Bishop Ridding † 1904. Large bronze figure with a finely characterized head, by *F. W. Pomeroy,* 1907, kneeling at an alabaster prie-dieu on a tomb-chest; an altogether striking composition devised by *Caröe.* – Bishop Hoskyns † 1925. Bronze bust by *W. Reynolds Stephens.*

167. SOUTHWELL Effigy of Bishop Ridding, 1907, by F. W. Pomeroy

Finally, the buildings that surround the minster reflect its medieval origins and collegiate status (cf. Lichfield). To the S, the remains of the medieval Archbishop of York's Palace, round the minster yard the prebendal houses of the non-resident canons who held livings from the minster, and to the N E the houses of the Vicars Choral who did the church offices of those non-resident canons. For more details on surroundings, see the latest edition of B of E *Nottinghamshire.*

# Wakefield

## CATHEDRAL CHURCH OF ALL SAINTS *Anglican*

(Based on B of E *Yorkshire: The West Riding,* 1967, revised with information from Michael Gillingham, Peter Howell, Anthony New and Anthony Quiney.)

Cathedral since 1888. In spite of extension at the E end this has remained, like the cathedrals of e.g. Bradford and Chelmsford, a large and proud parish church. Standing in the centre of this spacious county town, it has recently been isolated from traffic. The exterior is wholly Perp, while owing much to *Gilbert Scott's* restoration of 1858–74. But there was enough evidence of medieval work left after C 18 restorations (S side rebuilt 1724 and much of the N side in the late C 18) to make Scott's work generally reliable. At the end of the C 19, for the purposes of the newly created cathedral, *F. L. Pearson* between 1897 and 1904 added a transept and a new chancel with retrochapel (according to the late George Pace, perhaps actually designed by *W. D. Caröe*, who had been a pupil of Pearson Sr).

The chief external feature is the w tower, with angle buttresses, two tall two-light bell-openings on each side, and a tall much crocketed spire set back behind a parapet and crocketed pinnacles. The spire is 247 ft high, the highest in Yorkshire. It was under construction in 1420, when money was bequeathed for the 'nova fabrica campanilis'; *Scott* had to rebuild it. Aisles and clerestory have decorated battlements and pinnacles. The aisle windows are of four lights under segmental arches with some panel tracery. The clerestory has four-light windows in the nave, three-light windows in the chancel. The aisled chancel was building in 1458 and probably complete by 1475, when glass for the E windows was given. The only older feature outside is the N doorway, with continuous mouldings, including a keeled one.

The interior is less easily understood. The arcades seem at first sight uniform, if not in shape, at least in style. In fact they are far from it. As Micklethwaite has worked out convincingly, the N arcade contains two round piers which were originally shorter and made for the building of an aisle in the mid-C 12. Then in *c.* 1220 the piers of the s arcade were made, alternately circular and octagonal. About a century later, the N arcade received new piers of a typically Dec section, quatrefoil, but the four shafts connected by a continuous wave. The Norman piers were at the same time heightened and given capitals which must have been made beforehand, when it was intended to replace the old piers by two more of the new design. The arches have double-quadrant mouldings throughout on both sides, that is, all belong to the early C 14. A chapel in the church was consecrated in 1329, and one can assume that the work was then complete. Then, after about a hundred years, the w tower was added a little to the w of the former w wall. This was in course of building in 1420. To this time belongs the w bay (without hoodmoulds). The chancel arch belongs to the early C 14 and resembles the early parts of the N arcade. The chancel arcades are Perp – as we have seen, of *c.* 1450–75. They have five bays, with octagonal piers and arches with hollow chamfers. Late Perp also the nave clerestory and the panelled ceiling with carved bosses. *Pearson's* (or *Caröe's*) retrochapel has very thin long shafts separating narrow aisles from its nave and a complicated lierne vault of stone.

FURNISHINGS

FONT. Dated 1661, one of many of the years immediately after the Restoration. Octagonal, with initials etc. in a kind of beaded lettering and some coarse foliage. The cover is new. – ROOD SCREEN. An excellent piece of 1635, with thin long tapering pillars and elaborate carving (cf. Slaidburn and St John Leeds). The rood of 1950 by *Sir Ninian Comper*, of no sculptural interest. – PULPIT. Made in 1708 as a three-decker. – CHANCEL STALLS. No high backs, but instead simple Perp screens behind them. The stall-ends have poppy-heads, also some decoration with animals, and on one the arms of Thomas Savile of Lupset and his wife, married 1482. Ten seats have original late C 15 MISERICORDS (Nos. 1–3 N and 2–8 s), one with the Percy badge of crescent and fetterlock; fifteen other misericords are not medieval (Remnant). – ORGAN CASE in aisle given 1743; the chancel case by *F. L. Pearson*. – BENCH-END, s chancel aisle, with tracery in two tiers. – IRONWORK. Fine entrance gate, s porch, C 18. – STAINED GLASS. Nearly all by *Kempe*, starting in the 1870s. E window by *Lavers & Barraud*. w window by *Hardman*. s w window by *Barnett* of Newcastle. – MONUMENTS. Sir Lyon Pilkington † 1714. Semi-reclining in an easy posture. Putti l. and r. Big reredos background with segmental pediment on which recline two allegorical figures. – John Ingram † 1780, and family, signed *J. Wilton*. A delightful and very original tablet set against one of the octagonal piers of the chancel. Seated woman in an elegant, well-studied attitude. – Mrs Maude † 1824, by *J. Kendrick* to the design of Mrs Maude's husband. Tablet with the usual female figure bent over an urn.

For surrounding buildings, see the latest edition of B of E *Yorkshire: The West Riding*.

# Worcester

CATHEDRAL CHURCH OF CHRIST
AND THE BLESSED VIRGIN MARY *Anglican*

(Based on B of E *Worcestershire*, 1968, revised, with information from Bernard Ashwell, G. K. Brandwood, Michael Gillingham, George McHardy and Neil Stratford.)

choir. C 14: rest of nave, main crossing, transept w
windows, s transept vaulting

Plan, Fig. 169, from the *Builder*, 1892, by Harold Brakspear.

Some references (see Recent Literature): Cobb 1980; Gem,
Zarnecki, Stratford, Wilson, Singleton, Morris, Lockett,
Keen *et al.* in B.A.A. *Worcester* 1978; Lockett 1978b.

INTRODUCTION

Worcester Cathedral from the w, from across the Severn, is
a superb sight, the tower in its proportions one of the
noblest of its kind. A view from the E is out of the question,
now that the new road and roundabout have removed all
peace – the cathedral stands as in a vice between road and
river. The site of the city at a bend in the River Severn has
been occupied for more than 2,000 years: the first, Early
Iron Age settlement overlooked an ancient ford close to the
present cathedral. There is evidence of a Roman fort s of
the cathedral. The history of the cathedral itself goes back

168. WORCESTER View from the south-west

to the late C7. In the C10 Oswald, who introduced (or re-introduced) the Benedictine rule when he was made bishop in 961, rebuilt it. There were apparently then two churches, one dedicated to St Peter and one 'almost contiguous' to it dedicated to St Mary (is it not likely that this stood E of St Peter's as a separate Lady Chapel, as in the Saxon layout recently discovered at Wells?). There was damage by the Danes in 1041. Wulfstan, bishop at the time of the Conquest, rebuilt St Mary's. He was the only Saxon bishop to remain in office, and the reason was that he supported William. He began the present building in 1084. The monks re-entered the choir in 1089, and a synod took place in the crypt in 1092 (i.e. there was then no chapter house, but that may date from only ten or twenty years later). The next relevant dates are the fall of a tower in 1175 (now thought to have been a W tower rather than the crossing tower, and the cause of rebuilding at the W end of the nave), the canonization of Wulfstan in 1203, a fire in the same year, the death of King John in 1216 and his burial before the Norman high altar between St Oswald and St Wulfstan, a solemn rededication in 1218 in the presence of Henry III (probably to affirm the importance of the previous event), and then in 1224 under Bishop William of Blois the beginning of a new E end ('novum opus frontis', for *frons* could mean E end), perhaps partly complete by the time John was reburied in his new tomb in 1232. Harvey

(1974) suggests that a mason *Alexander*, known to have worked here from 1224, was the Alexander who went to work at Lincoln in 1235. Worcester's geographical position made it a likely point of interchange for the comings and goings of masons. The name of *John Clyve* occurs here in the late C14. Individual C14 dates will be referred to, largely affecting the crossing tower and the nave. Work in the late C18 included a new E window, already rebuilt in 1660–2 (Colvin), and a new W window, both again replaced in the C19. There was structural restoration at the E end by *Abraham Perkins* (cathedral architect 1845–73) and much refurnishing by *Scott*, 1863–74: the records of these operations convey the flavour and complexity of direction by Victorian committee, lay and ecclesiastical (Lockett 1978a, 1978b).

As at Chester, Lichfield and Carlisle certain sandstones of the western counties have made trouble. Worcester's Norman parts include oolitic limestone from the Cotswolds and grey-green Highley sandstone, the latter used also in the W nave bays and in some of the C14 work: the Highley stone has worn best of all (Ashwell). The webs of the late C12 vaults at the W end of the nave and the C13 vaults of the eastern arm are filled with local tufa, chosen for its lightness as in the choir vaults at Canterbury in the rebuilding after 1174. But the exterior is largely of the so-called New Red Sandstones, which are soft and crumbly

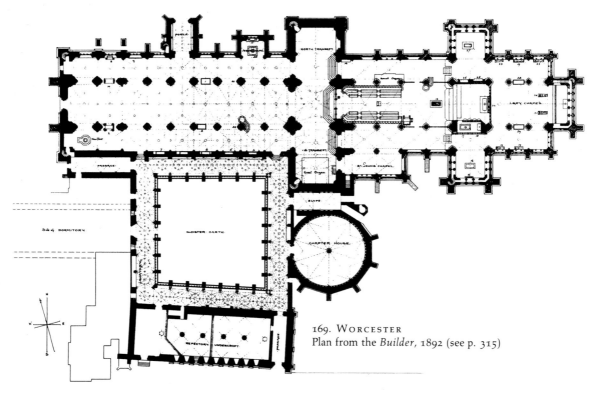

169. WORCESTER
Plan from the *Builder*, 1892 (see p. 315)

170. WORCESTER View from the north-east in 1832

and weather badly. There has had to be incessant refacing, which explains the new-looking surfaces and absence of patina (a problem further described by Clifton-Taylor 1972). Renewed researches to find a stone that is more lasting while still visually suited to the old work have so far failed. Nevertheless, views of the cathedral during the past three centuries published by Cobb (1980) show that its outstanding feature, the tower, though altered in details, has suffered no drastic alteration in those years. The cathedral is 425 ft long (Salisbury 473 ft, Lichfield 397 ft).

EXTERIOR

The shape of the E end of Wulfstan's cathedral can be guessed from that of the crypt, 'quam ego a fundamentis aedicavi', said Wulfstan. It must have had a chancel with apse and ambulatory. Excavations at crypt-level have revealed a pentagonal S W chapel, which assumes the existence of central and N W chapels. And transept chapels flanked the choir aisles. However, the part E of the transepts has been replaced by the E.E. work. So the examin-

ation should start at the TRANSEPTS. The N transept has its flat buttresses. They have nook-shafts with fillets, i.e. are not of Wulfstan's time, but Late Norman or Transitional. The angles carry octagonal shafted turrets. The N end of the N transept was virtually rebuilt 1748–51 by *Nathaniel Wilkinson* (Colvin). The great N window is Victorian. The E and W sides are blank, except for Perp windows high up. In the S transept the S window is also Victorian. The very long Perp window in the W wall is impressive.

Next the CHANCEL, begun in 1224. It consists of four bays, then an E transept, on the pattern of Canterbury, Lincoln and Salisbury, and then three bays of retrochoir with a Lady Chapel only projecting by one narrow bay. The new E end has a total length which places the crossing tower just halfway between W and E wall. The fenestration of the E parts is very beautiful and harmonious, but it is nearly all by *Perkins*, who replaced a large 'Perp' window of 1792 (by *Thomas Johnson*, who in his turn had replaced a rebuilding of 1660–2). Perkins's correct E.E. was guided by the existing E transept lancets, long and slender. The big flying buttress on the N side dates from the C 18. The early buttresses are still flat. On the s side of the chancel at its w end projects a two-bay chapel of the same style and period as the rest, i.e. the s transept's rebuilt E chapel.

Rebuilding of the NAVE was probably begun about 1320 and it was not vaulted until 1377 (further on dating, see *Interior* below; the two w bays had already been rebuilt, as we shall see). Its s side one cannot see in its totality, because of the cloister. But in the cloister it is patent that the lower parts of the walls with the flat buttresses are Norman. For the entrances to the cloister, see *Cloisters* below. The upper parts are all Victorian. Flowing tracery in the aisle windows. Then small, two-light, straight-headed windows marking the Library, i.e. a room made in the c 15 above the s aisle in the former aisle roof and outside the triforium. The clerestory has three-light windows with straight shanks. The w end, i.e. the last two bays, introduce to a different phase. There is Norman walling here, and flat buttresses and a Norman corbel table. Two round-arched aisle windows are outlined inside (see below). More of nave details is to be seen on the N side. Here the aisle windows are of three lights, with the five-petal-flower motif in the tracery. The projecting Jesus Chapel has a more florid Dec design. The clerestory windows are Dec too. So is the NORTH PORCH, dated by Dr Hopkins 1386 (c 17 notebooks of Prebendary Dr Hopkins, presumably based on rolls now lost). It is two-storeyed. Its façade is all Victorian, with its many corny statues (by *Hardman*). The walls are panelled and have a top quatrefoil frieze. The sides are completely blank. The interior is of two bays, vaulted with oblong tierceron stars on Purbeck marble shafts. The shafts carry sparse knobbly capitals. But look at the inner portal and you see two long thin Norman columns with block capitals – part of the Norman N portal or porch. At Tewkesbury there is just such a portal still fully preserved. The Tewkesbury porch in front of it is tunnel-vaulted. Above the Worcester doorway is the re-used head of a Dec five-petal window. The westernmost two bays of the nave prove to be Late Norman; see the clerestory windows (later filled in with two-light reticulation tracery) and the flat buttresses. Also the wall is thicker here.

The WEST FRONT is almost entirely Victorian. The w window is of 1865. But traces of the N and s doorways, part of the arch of the middle doorway and fragmentary bases either side of that door, show that the w front was always here. The arch has zigzag and thin roll mouldings. The sculpture is by *Boulton*.

Rebuilding of the CROSSING TOWER was finished in 1374, after seventeen years' work, therefore begun 1357. It is in two stages, the lower of seven very slim bays with transom. Only two contain windows; the rest is blank. The sills climb up the roof-lines of the adjoining parts. All the bays carry crocketed gables. The upper stage, above a band of quatrefoils, has two-light bell-openings with transom

and bays for statuary under canopies l., r. and between. The tracery of the upper windows is Dec, that of the lower, however, Perp, and it seems likely, especially if one considers the interior, that there has been interference. The details, however, are all shown already in Britton's *Cathedral Antiquities*, i.e. in 1836.

INTERIOR

The great asset of Worcester is the unity of its interior. Although the c 13 and the c 14 have contributed about evenly, the c 14 designers were so conformist that the century and a half hardly tells until one begins to study the detail. Chronologically, however, the evidence starts of course with Wulfstan's time, and for this one must go first into the CRYPT. Here is Early Norman work at its most impressive. The crypt consists of a centre of four vessels separated by columns, and seven bays long plus the *corona* or semicircle of apse columns. Around this space went an outer ambulatory, now walled off. It was separated from the centre by thick square piers about 6½ ft thick. The straight ambulatory part is divided into two vessels, nine bays long. Moreover there is the crypt under the Norman s chancel chapel, again in two vessels. It has an E.E. continuation, and the rib-vault of this seems to indicate the existence of an apse above. It is a straightforward quadripartite vault, but in the middle of the w side, from the Norman middle column spring three radiating ribs to touch the centre of the E.E. vault and the middles of the two diagonal ribs up to it from the angles. All the Early Norman columns have plain capitals, mostly block type and single-scallop type, but also one of the rare form of a single-trumpet-scallop (a form nonexistent either in Germany, whence the block capital was imported, or in France). Some abaci have billet enrichment. The vaults are plainly groined, and there are no transverse arches at all.

Chronologically next one ought to inspect the TRANSEPTS, and the very w end of the chancel, though Early Norman evidence is rare here. It consists of the following: One strong shaft of the w respond on the s side of the chancel, with a block capital and a base like many in the crypt. In the first bay of the chancel N side is the start of a gallery or triforium arch. In the aisle roofs one can see on the s as well as the N side the jambs of the triforium arches. On the s side there is also the jamb to the transept. Standing in the s transept one sees more plainly the whole arch into the former transept E chapel (not now communicating, but once, like the E chapel of Gloucester's s transept, eight steps up). The capitals are of block type but with foliage trails, and they are drastically re-done. Mr Stratford convincingly connects them with the early c 12 crypt at Canterbury and also with the work of c. 1120 etc. at Romsey (chancel E bays and s transept). Note their profuse

171. WORCESTER Crypt, begun 1084

decoration of acanthus foliage of the Winchester type, a dragon, and an angel (Zarnecki 1978 discusses the manuscript sources). The arch has big rolls and square mouldings. Above are the traces of an upper chapel arch. Such upper chapels were not rare in England (see e.g. Canterbury). There is no reason to date the capitals later than *c.* 1130, but what else there is of Norman evidence in the transept is definitely Late Norman. The S transept S wall, Mr Stratford thinks, was begun at the same time as the slype S of it (see *Cloisters*), i.e. immediately after 1084, but while still at a low level work must have been stopped until *c.* 1120–40, when the E arch just discussed was built (or sooner if the chapter house beyond the slype dates from *c.* 1100–15?). At that time stone courses in two alternating colours were favoured (S W turret stair, E arch, and indeed the chapter house; John Maddison remarks that the striping of stone should be compared with Speyer crypt and other German work). Delay in the construction of the transept is reasonable from the functional point of view, as completion of the chancel was so much more important in the 1080s. There is, to continue with the S transept, a shafted window

with zigzag at r. angles and a kind of outer stylized beakhead. The crocket capitals make a date before *c.* 1190 impossible. In the W wall is the start of blank trefoiled arcading. In the S wall is a much larger window with the same details and with keeled shafts. The keeling links this up with the major vaulting-shafts of the transept. They were, as Willis said, 'engrafted' into the walls. The buttresses outside (see above) were provided at the same time. (It should be added that blind windows in the S wall are obscured by a Victorian organ.) The shafts are tripartite and show clearly that they were intended for rib-vaults different from the present ones. They survive up to their stiff-leaf capitals, but the present vault standing on them dates from *c.* 1375 and has liernes. (Brakspear's plan, Fig. 169, is not very clear.) Of that time also the following Perp elements. Very impressive the three-tier W window of four lights with detached mullions to the inside and some openwork cusping. Impressive also the seven-light and five-light stone grilles in the E wall at triforium level. Other bays have blank panelling. The S window is Victorian. The arches to the chancel and nave aisles are C 14 again.

But what is the date of the s transept's Late Norman work? If it was the crossing tower that fell in 1175, it seems quite likely that vaulting was introduced in the damaged transepts and that the new windows came in at the same time. However, the repairs cannot have been done at once. The w bays of the nave, to which we shall turn presently, are a little earlier in their details and yet seem to be of c. 1185. The upper parts of the s transepts (Mr Stratford comments), with their sophisticated varieties of zigzag seem to go with the w bays of the nave, but they have also, as we have seen, stiff-leaf capitals and in the hood of the triforium dogtooth as well. It is true that in the Canterbury choir of 1174–85 dogtooth and zigzag appear side by side, but in the West Country the earliest occurrence of both motifs together is in the retrochoir of Hereford Cathedral c. 1190–1200. A further question is whether a development can be recognized between the e and the w walls. In favour of a later date for the w than the e is the fact that the triforium opening in the w walls has a trefoiled head. That would be surprising before 1200 (cf. Lichfield, choir aisles, w bays, c. 1200–10).

The N transept differs in many ways. The arch to the (demolished) Norman e chapel is here all Victorian and without telling details. The vaulting-shafts, though very similar to those on the s, are not quite the same; Willis says the remodelling of c. 1180–90 was done first on the N: the shafts there resemble those of the w bays of the nave (see below), those of the s transept have deeper hollows between the shafts. The N transept's vault is simpler, no liernes, just diagonal and ridge ribs. If this is really of 1376, it would be surprising. It looks c 13, not c 14. Can the donation in 1281 of a Bishop of Ely towards the rebuilding of the tower have anything to do with it? The arch to the chancel aisle is like the one in the s transept, but the arch to the nave aisle is early c 14, not late. We shall come back to that. The Perp wall treatment differs from that in the s transept. It is much less enterprising. The N window is again Victorian.

Now, before going into the chancel one ought to see what is inside those two WEST BAYS OF THE NAVE which had promised Norman work outside. They are treated like this: The e piers were begun with demi-shafts on a flat surface but continued at triforium-level with five vaulting-shafts. The w piers have the vaulting-shafts from the start. So here is Early v. Late Norman. To the arcade arches there are a continuous quarter roll and thin shafts, some of them keeled. The arch continues the quarter roll and then has steps. The arches are pointed. The treatment of the triforium is idiosyncratic. Three stepped round arches with a continuous quarter roll. Attached shafts with trumpet and

crocket capitals. Arches with zigzag at r. angles and three paterae in relief above them. The whole is set in a pointed arch with a continuous quarter roll. Tripartite stepped clerestory, pointed–round–pointed. Again continuous quarter rolls, again zigzag. The vaulting-shafts are arranged for wall arches, transverse arches and diagonal ribs. The Perp vault put in in the c 14 contradicts them. In the s aisle the original vault is preserved, the earliest rib-vault in the cathedral. The wall-shafts are as in the nave, and the capitals are trumpet-scallop. In the N aisle the vault is Perp, as in the bays further E. This work at the w end of the then Norman nave is neither dated nor datable, but should, except for the lower parts of the E piers, be of c. 1185. (Wilson (1978) shows that it must indeed have been a w tower that fell in 1175.) Stratford points to diagonally set zigzag in the triforium arches and its reflection at Bredon and Bricklehampton, and to the parallels with the leaf paterae in the Glastonbury Lady Chapel, the nave and N porch of Wells, the nave of St David's, and the w front of Llandaff. The Lady Chapel of Glastonbury, datable to 1184–6, has crocket capitals just like the w bays at Worcester, i.e. a French type of capital. Another, especially French, is in the w chancel bay of Abbey Dore.

The EASTERN ARM is the architecturally most rewarding part of the building. It is uniform in style and almost a building in itself, with its own transepts to the full height of the chancel, and with four bays w and four bays E of the transepts. It is most thrilling in the Lady Chapel bay and the transepts, where verticalism is unchecked, especially as the latter have no aisles. Unlike other cathedrals with full-height E transepts (Canterbury, Lincoln, Salisbury) this has its high altar at the E crossing. The sanctuary is raised above the flanking transepts, and higher than the choir, which stands above the Norman crypt. One descends from the choir aisles to retrochoir and Lady Chapel. The fact that the E crossing piers rise from the latter floor-level, even though the crossing contains the raised sanctuary, increases the sense of verticality. That is further increased by the double tiers of long lancet windows. The whole 'novum opus' belongs to a more sumptuous period than that preceding it. Purbeck marble was lavished over it, on the pattern of Canterbury and Lincoln. Work proceeded from E to w, and there is – though hardly noticeable – a joint w of the E transept. E of the joint the aisles have blank pointed-trefoiled arcading. The shafts are Purbeck in the Lady Chapel, stone otherwise. The capitals are all leaf crockets. In the spandrels is sculpture, foliage, and genre (i.e. little animals and monsters) and figure scenes, many religious. The majority are Victorian (by *Boulton*) but some, especially in the Lady Chapel, in the s aisle E wall, the N aisle N wall, and most especially in the s E transept, are well preserved. The figures are thin and agile. (Where original, they must pre-date the spandrel sculpture in the

172. WORCESTER Nave west bays, c. 1185

173 (*overleaf*). WORCESTER
Lady Chapel and retrochoir, begun 1224

radiating chapels at Westminster Abbey.) You find a knight fighting a centaur (Lady Chapel), the Angel with the Last Trump, the dead clambering out of their graves, the Expulsion from Paradise, St Michael with the Scales, the Tortures of Hell, a knight and a lion, Sagittarius (all SE

175. WORCESTER Wall arcade,
south-east transept, before 1232?

transept), and (on the N side) the Annunciation, the Nativity, the Visitation. What conveys that irresistible *excelsior* to the Lady Chapel and the transepts is that, though windows are in two tiers, Purbeck shafts run up all the way. In the retrochoir aisles are also detached Purbeck shafts in front of the windows. The aisles are rib-vaulted with small bosses. The piers of the retrochoir have eight Purbeck and eight subsidiary stone shafts and crocket capitals. Only one N capital shows mature stiff-leaf. The arches have many mouldings. The triforium is very odd and very English. There are two layers of arcading. In the front are for each bay two-light openings with much Purbeck marble and with sculpture in the spandrels. (For a similar triforium with spandrel sculpture, see the Chichester retrochoir; also the choir aisles at Lincoln.) The sub-arches grow out of the super-arches in anticipation of what was to be Y-tracery, i.e. the sub-arches have only their inner shank entirely to themselves. Behind that detached arcading runs an even blank stone arcade which keeps to its own rhythm. Tripartite stepped clerestory with detached Purbeck shafts. The vaulting-shafts in the Lady Chapel rise from the ground, in the retrochoir from the arcade spandrels. They have head corbels here, and capitals first at triforium sill-level and then again at clerestory sill. Quadripartite vault, just with a longitudinal ridge rib. In the E transepts triforium, clerestory, and vault are the same. The E crossing piers have to

the inside four Purbeck and three stone shafts, and yet there is no space for the diagonal ribs. The vault has of course ridge ribs longitudinally as well as transversely. (It will be remembered that the E window-wall was much rebuilt – in 1662, in 1792, in 1857, and very likely already in the late Middle Ages – but its original C13 form was probably approximated by *Perkins*.)

The chancel W of the E transepts is to all intents and purposes the same. If differences are sought out, it is at once visible that the blank aisle arcading ceases and that capitals are getting richer in their displays of stiff-leaf. There is also the fact that head-stops on hoodmoulds only come into the interior now. Moreover, the arch soffits differ. W of the E transepts there is a hollow in the arch, where E of them there was a roll. That the chancel should be a little later than the retrochoir stands to reason. The new work was of course started outside the Norman chancel, and this was pulled down only when the new work reached that far W. Triforium sculpture on the S side of the choir, suitably enough, includes music-making angels: if their attributes are original, they must be precursors of those in the Lincoln Angel Choir. The S chapel or vestry (which replaced the Norman S transept's E chapel) has two bays with quadripartite vaults. The capitals are of the rich type, the windows Purbeck-shafted, except for parts of the E window, which is played down for some unknown reason. In the N chancel aisle is a pretty little oriel. This belonged to the Sacrist's Lodging, and the small Perp doorway in the aisle led to it.

At the main CROSSING the display of Purbeck marble is over. The known date of completion of the tower, 1374, is said to have been seventeen years after it was begun. The Perp piers are therefore a recasing of *c.* 1357, with broad hollows between the shafts and small individual capitals. The upper stages of the tower are not visible from inside. Odd lierne vault of 1376. Work on the nave vault was going on in 1377, but the crossing piers are in the style of the nave S arcade (see below).

With the crossing we have anticipated. Rebuilding of the NAVE started between 1317 and 1327. It was not a start from scratch. Apart from the two W bays (above), we have seen that the N porch contains part of a Norman portal, evidently early, and that the W wall is Norman. (It is a question, however, whether the S wall is Norman too. The deep niches along the S aisle, completely unmoulded and undecorated, if this were a Norman wall would be unique in England. But scholars, e.g. R. D. H. Gem and G. K. Brandwood, now feel these were C14 and meant to hold tombs.) As for the post-Norman work in the nave, the arch between N aisle and N transept must be early C14, and

176. WORCESTER Nave, begun *c.* 1320.
Choir screen, 1864–73, by Scott

indeed Bishop Cobham (1317–27) vaulted the N aisle. That probably refers just to the beginning; for the arcade E respond is already like the rest of the N aisle. That the Jesus Chapel has the most elaborate window tracery has already been said. The N aisle is of seven bays to the start of the Norman W bays. The arcade piers are very complex, but still starting out from the triple vaulting-shaft. The centre one has a fillet now. In the diagonals are two keels. The arches of course are as complex. The capitals are treated as one band with thick knobbly leaves. The triforium is based on that of the C13, though without the subtle background arcading, and the clerestory is stepped tripartite. That is, the nave was designed in a purposely conservative way to carry on from the eastern arm – with a sense of the whole building as at Lichfield, though in a different sequence.

The S arcade is clearly later. There are different bases and thin leaf capitals instead of the band of leaf, the triforium has smaller capitals too, and the clerestory is generally thinner in its forms. So N went up before S, perhaps to leave the monastic side alone as long as possible. But the last two C14 bays on the N side before the Late Norman bays are reached, change to the thinner clerestory details too, though they are not quite like those on the S side. Then finally vaulting took place. The vault preceded those of crossing and S transept; for it has only diagonal and ridge ribs and single tiercerons, but no liernes. This vault extends over the Late Norman W bays. The E bay of the nave is in its upper details disturbed by flying buttresses for the crossing tower, which was begun in 1357. The N aisle and the Jesus Chapel have vaults like the nave, the S aisle more elaborate lierne vaults. That confirms the sequence postulated for the arcades.

Finally, the view E from the nave takes note of the rise in floor-level between cross-arm and eastern arm, to allow for the Norman crypt under the choir: unlike Lichfield or Lincoln or Salisbury, but exceeded by Winchester and even more by Canterbury in this rise to the E.

FURNISHINGS, E TO W

*Lady Chapel and retrochoir* ORGAN CASE. Small and partly early C18. – PAINTING. The vaults of the whole E vessel were painted by *Hardman*. – STAINED GLASS. The E window with scenes in medallions is by *Hardman*, designed by *John Hardman Powell*, 1862, and shown at the Exhibition of 1862. – MONUMENTS. Bishop Walter de Cantelupe † 1266. Purbeck marble, his feet against stiff-leaf, and stiff-leaf by the sides of his head. The head is in quite high relief. – Bishop, said to be William of Blois † 1236; flatter than the former. – Mrs Digby. By *Chantrey*, 1825. White marble. Seated figure on a couch. On the short sides of the base praying angels in shallow relief. – Earl of Dudley (the most overwhelming member

of the Joint Restoration Committee). White marble effigy, 1888, by *James Forsyth*, sculptor of the Perseus Fountain at Witley Court for him. Alabaster base, designed by *Scott*, with open arcading. – Lord Lyttelton (chairman of the committee), also by *Forsyth*, 1878. White marble effigy on an alabaster tomb-chest by *Scott*. – Prior Moore (?). He made preparation for his tomb c. 1525. This is in a niche behind the high altar, below the back of the reredos (see below), here filled by memorial to Dean Peel, 1877. Alabaster surface with incised cross and symbols of the Evangelists.

*South retrochoir aisle and south-east transept* TRIPTYCH. C15 with small alabaster Virgin and Child in centre and painted wings, the whole on a domestic scale and apparently in its original housing. – STAINED GLASS. By *Hardman*. – MONUMENTS. Cross-legged knight, mid-C13. Perhaps Robert de Harcourt. – Tomb-chest of Sir Gryffyth Ryce † 1523. With its shields in cusped quatrefoils still pre-Renaissance. On it two brasses by *Hardman*. – The following two tombs in the substructure of Prince Arthur's Chantry (see below). Bishop Giffard † 1302. Canopy over his head. Against the tomb-chest exquisite scenes and figures (Weighing of Souls, Christ Showing His Wound, St Andrew and St Peter). – Lady, probably of the Giffard family, c. 1300.

*North retrochoir aisle and north-east transept* SCREEN. Stone, of three-light divisions and with a dainty quatrefoil frieze. This is genuine C15 work, though re-set. – STAINED GLASS. The E window by *Hardman*; good. – MONUMENTS. Bishop, Purbeck marble, c. 1300. – Lady, mid-C13, very fine. The lid of the tomb-chest is raised a little above a base with a stiff-leaf border. The lady stands on a stiff-leaf corbel. – Cross-legged knight, early C14. – Bishop de Braunsford † 1349 (?). The recess has plenty of ballflower decoration. – Bishop de Cobham † 1327. The modelling of the face is remarkably sensitive. The recess fits an early C14 date.

*Chancel* REREDOS (see also the back in the retrochoir). Designed by *Scott*, and made by *Farmer & Brindley* for £1,500. Shrine with five figures, very opulent. (On the chantry S of it, see below.) – PULPIT. By *Stephen Baldwin*, 1642 (so recognized by Mr Philip Styles). Octagonal, of stone, with Signs of the Evangelists, Tables of the Law, the Eye of God etc. Altered and restored 1874, with steps by *Scott*. Both Pugin and Scott mistook the pulpit's 'Gothic survival' for work of c. 1500 (Lockett 1978b). Said to have been made for nave sermons after troops destroyed old fittings in 1642 (Cobb 1980). Originally with a very idiosyncratic carved wooden sounding-board (now lost) held by disembodied hands; its support bore a relief now in the N choir aisle (below). Cobb shows Britton's drawing of the whole thing. – LECTERN. Made by *Hardman* to *Scott*'s design, 1873. Brass, with eagle, and three figures of saints on the base. – SCREENS. All of *Scott's* restoration. Wood and metal as well as stone. – The brass COMMUNION RAIL, the THRONE, and the ORGAN CASE (see also S *transept* below) are *Scott's*. – Some of the STALLS contain bits of old work, much renewed by *Farmer & Brindley* to *Scott's* design. But they do incorporate the MISERICORDS from the stalls of 1379. There are forty-two in all. They represent e.g. an old man stirring a pot, a man playing a flute, an angel playing a viol, a knight holding a dagger, a butcher slaughtering an ox, the Circumcision, Presentation of Samuel, a woman writing, a sower, knights tilting, an angel playing a lute, a huntsman blowing a horn, a knight fighting two griffins, three reapers, three ploughmen, three mowers, Abraham and Isaac, the Temptation of Eve, the Expulsion from Paradise, Moses descending from Sinai, the Judgement of Solomon, Samson and the Lion,

a man beating down acorns, a lion and a dragon fighting, a sow with piglets, a knight hawking, a monster, a sphinx, a cockatrice, a naked woman riding on a goat, Adam delving and Eve spinning, a stag beneath a tree, a dragon. Some of these scenes clearly mean Labours of the Months, others may belong to the Bestiary. – The LIGHTS on the stalls are by *Jack Penton* and recent. – The elaborate gilt iron SCREENS in the two W bays are by *Skidmore* of Coventry. – MONUMENT. King John † 1216. Effigy of Purbeck marble, probably *c.* 1230 (reburied 1232). One of the finest of its time in England. Drapery as good as on any contemporary French effigy. Two bishops by his head (St Oswald and St Wulfstan). Tomb-chest of *c.* 1529, still with no Renaissance detail. Shields in enriched quatrefoils. (Neither for this royal monument nor for the following one do any records of carvers survive, Mr Colvin says.)

177. WORCESTER Effigy of King John, *c.* 1230

178. WORCESTER Prince Arthur's Chantry
from the south-east

On the s side of the sanctuary, between the s piers of the
E crossing, PRINCE ARTHUR'S CHANTRY. In its sculpture
an immediate though little documented forerunner of the
Henry VII Chapel sculpture at Westminster. Prince
Arthur, Henry VIII's elder brother, died in 1502, but work
started only in 1504. To the sanctuary the chantry has six
bays, the E bay of two lights, the next of three, the third
again of two both rising higher, then two of three, the
second with the ogee-headed entrance, and the last blank,
of two, and again rising higher. The two higher bays are
enriched by small statuary, and there is plenty of small
statuary inside. In many cases the heads were spared by the
Reformers. The high openings have instead of transoms
cusped arches, and on them cusped arches reversed. It is a
controlled, not at all haphazard composition. The interior

has a lierne vault in two bays with two pendants oddly
buttressed or shored. Reredos filling the E wall, crowded
with figures and canopies. The tomb-chest of the prince,
with no effigy, stands in the middle. It is quite simple, with
shields in quatrefoils. From the S E transept, the chantry is
one storey higher over a basement, where the two Giffard
monuments are incorporated (see above). There is above
them a broad band of Tudor roses, portcullis, other flowers,
and angels.

*South chancel aisle* STAINED GLASS. The kneeling
prince is a copy of a representation at Malvern Priory and
said to be early C 19. – MONUMENTS. Mrs Rae † 1770, by
*I. F. Moore*. Of coloured marbles. Sarcophagus with a curly
top on which two putti. Above, against an obelisk, the
portrait medallion flanked by palm-fronds. – William

*Main crossing* The medieval pulpitum was replaced in 1556. The C16 replacement was altered in 1613 and again in 1818, with misericords fixed to it. Finally replaced by *Scott*'s handsome open SCREEN, of his Lichfield–Hereford type. His first designs for this one 1864. Set up 1873. Made by *Skidmore* of metalwork, woodwork and marble, it is the centrepiece of what is now the most complete surviving set of Scott furnishings.

*South transept* STAINED GLASS. S window by *G. Rogers*, designed by *Preedy*, 1853. – MONUMENT. Mrs Hall (of Jamaica and Bevere) †1794. Standing white monument with pensive seated woman by a wreathed urn. Good. – Huge ORGAN CASE by *Scott*. A fine Victorian case, now mostly empty, with good stencilling on the display pipes (Gillingham). Overwhelming like Lord Dudley, who insisted on having a nave organ as well as a choir organ.

*North transept* STAINED GLASS. The great N window by *Lavers & Barraud*, 1866. – MONUMENTS. Bishop Hough. By *Roubiliac*, 1746. A Rococo composition, i.e. one in which symmetry is artfully avoided. On the l. a standing female figure raising a piece of drapery to reveal a relief on the sarcophagus which shows the scene of the eviction of Hough from Magdalen College after he had

179. WORCESTER Prince Arthur's Chantry, begun 1504, interior

Burslem † 1820. By *Westmacott Jr*. White tablet with a seated angel in profile.

*North chancel aisle* SCULPTURE (on windowsill). Canopied stone relief of a fortified city, i.e. the New Jerusalem. It decorated the support of the sounding-board of the choir pulpit of 1642 (see above). Removed by Perkins (Scott's *Recollections*, quoted by Lockett 1978b). Was it a late C14 or C15 fragment reset in 1642? – MONUMENTS. Bishop Maddox † 1759. By *Prince Hoare*. Standing monument of black and white marble. Sarcophagus with relief of the Good Samaritan. On the r. a decently draped female with an upturned torch. Very staid – no doubt in deliberate contrast to Bishop Hough's monument of 1746. – Randolph Marriott † 1807. By *T. King* of Bath. Pretty tablet with an altar and a weeping willow.

180. WORCESTER Monument to Bishop Hough, 1746, by L. F. Roubiliac

been elected president. James II wanted a Catholic president. On the r. a small seated cherub holding a medallion with the portrait of Mrs Hough. Above, on the sarcophagus, the bishop rises in a diagonal, or rather serpentine movement. Obelisk at the back. – Bishop Fleetwood † 1683. The very reverse. No figures at all. Just a reredos or aedicule. Two columns and an open segmental pediment. Black and white marble. – Bishop Stillingfleet † 1699. Also of the reredos type. Two putto heads rather unconvincingly lift a drapery from the inscription. – Sir Thomas Street † 1695, but done by *Wilton c.* 1775–80. An exquisitely chaste reredos and an Adamish urn like a wine-cooler. A putto hovering above.

*Nave* PULPIT. Designed by *Scott* and carved by *Forsyth.* – LECTERN. A gilt angel, 1894, by *Jones & Willis* (No. G57, *Victorian Church Art* 1971). – STAINED GLASS. The great w window 1874 by *Hardman*, designed by *Scott.* – PAVEMENT of Sicilian white and Kilkenny black marble. Here *Scott* is said to have been inspired by Amiens, yet it is far more like Burlington and Kent's floors at York. – MONUMENTS. Robert Wilde † 1608. Two recumbent effigies. Tomb-chest with decorated strips instead of pilasters. Various inscriptions have been removed. – A Beauchamp and his wife, *c.* 1400. Tomb-chest with shields in ogee-headed panels. The effigies are impressive. Her head rests against a swan. – Dean Eedes † 1596. Effigy on a high tomb-chest with garish leaf decoration. Canopy of four incorrectly detailed columns. Cambered heads, vault inside with diagonal and ridge ribs. – Bishop Thornborough † 1641, but erected in 1627. The monument is not at all complete, but even what remains shows that this was a much more correctly classical job.

*South nave aisle, from* E STAINED GLASS rather tame. In some of the windows fragments of C14 glass. In the window above the cloister doorway glass by *Lavers & Westlake*, 1893. Not very good. – FONT. By *Bodley*. With tall cover reaching to the vault; cf. his font at Southwark (Anglican). – MONUMENTS. Bishop Thomas † 1689. Not large and very simple. No figures, no display, not even twisted columns or garlands. – Thomas James † 1804. A pair of urns. – A prior; C14. In a late C13 recess. – Bishop Parrie † 1616. Recumbent effigy. In another such recess. – Sir Thomas Lyttelton † 1481. Tomb-chest, badly retooled. The brass is missing. – Mrs Warren † 1792. By *Ricketts*. Weeping putto by an urn. – John Bromley † 1674. Signed by *William Stanton*. Standing monument, narrow. With an urn on top. – Sir Thomas Lyttelton † 1650, and his wife † 1666. By *Thomas Stanton*. Also standing, also narrow. Black and white marble; classical. – Bishop Freake † 1591. Signed by *Anthony Tolly*. High tomb-chest with caryatids, shields and strapwork. Arch and back tablet. Has this never had an effigy? – Bishop Blandford † 1675. Standing monument, of noble simplicity. High Tuscan columns and an open curly pediment. No figures at all. – Col. Sir Henry Walton Ellis † 1815 at Waterloo. Large, white, standing monument. He sinks from his horse and is received by an angel. A kneeling soldier on the r. By *Bacon Jr.* – FONT. Of the *Scott* time, with high cover. – MONUMENTS. Richard Woolfe † 1877. Sgraffito plate of very good design. – Richard Solly † 1803. White standing monument by *Bacon Jr.* Mother and three children weeping at the sarcophagus. Of very fine quality, as Bacon could be. – Bishop Gauden † 1662. Black and white. Demi-figure in an oval recess. Segmental pediment at the top. A little heavy, but the decoration is nicely done. This was originally at the back of the high altar. – Bishop Johnson † 1774. By *Nollekens* the bust, by *Robert Adam* the composition. – STAINED GLASS. The w window typical *Clayton & Bell*; 1872.

*North nave aisle* In the E bay STAINED GLASS with 1862 as the date of commemoration. It is by *Lavers & Barraud*, and the best Victorian glass in the cathedral. Slender stylized figures in a very intense style. – MONUMENTS. Bishop Bullingham † 1576. The base is Perp and has probably nothing to do with the effigy. He is lying on his back supporting with his belly and thighs the weight of the quite large block with the inscription etc. He was, we read among other things, 'a painful preacher of the truthe'. – SCREEN to the Jesus Chapel. Of stone, in two tiers. Probably by *R. A. Briggs*, *c.* 1895. – STAINED GLASS in the Jesus Chapel, 1849 by *Wailes*. Individual ogee-headed panels in two tiers. – SCULPTURE. A fine C13 corbel with two tumblers. – Above, big ROYAL ARMS, later C17, probably brought in from outside. – MONUMENTS. John Moore † 1613, and members of his family. Three large kneeling men and behind them, in a fan-vaulted recess, three large kneeling women. Coupled columns. The urns must be an C18 addition. – Mrs Godfreye † 1613. Standing monument. She kneels, quite small, in a recess with two columns and an arch. – Monument to those who fell in 1845 and 1846 by the Sutlej River. By *Westmacott Jr*, 1849. Standing monument of white marble. A soldier stands, hand on breast, by the side of a large flag. Classical style. – Tablet of *c.* 1640. Corpse in a winding-sheet, yet propped up on the elbow. Oval medallion surrounded by a wreath. The commemorative inscription was no doubt painted on. Two putti on the open segmental top pediment. Inscription: Μακάριοι οἱ νεκροί etc. – Bishop Hurd † 1808. By *W. H. Stephens*. Simple and without figures. Classical and a little dry. – Bishop Philpott † 1892. By *Sir Thomas Brock*. Seated white figure, one hand raised.

SCULPTURE. In the gallery over the w bays of the SOUTH AISLE are nineteen pieces of stone diapered with rows of small arches, further evidence of the decoration of the Early Norman structure. Such wall areas exist also at Christchurch (Hants) and Castor (Soke of Peterborough; before 1124).

CLOISTERS, CHAPTER HOUSE ETC.

The Norman cloisters were rebuilt in the C14 and C15, starting with the E walk and ending with the W walk. Rebuilding of the N walk presumably began in conjunction with the rebuilding of the S nave aisle. The time taken overall was about a century. One enters from the church by a doorway at the E end of the N cloister which, with its capitals and fine arch mouldings, looks *c.* 1300 at the latest. The doorway from the church at the W end of the N cloister is smaller and Perp. The most striking motifs, the chains of reticulation units in the window embrasures and some transverse arches and the squints between each bay, are applied to all walks but the western. The window tracery is Victorian, part of *Perkins*'s restoration completed 1868, replacing C18 tracery illustrated by Britton. The vault in all four walks is of the same type with a central octagon of lierne ribs, but there again the W is different in details. It is the bosses which distinguish walk from walk. In the E walk there are not over-many, and they are small and nearly all leaves and heads. The S has the finest bosses, all figures and scenes. The centre bay shows the Coronation of the Virgin. The W range again has small leaf bosses. The N bosses are quite different, with applied figures of angels instead of real bosses. It must be assumed that, though W was actually last in its walk, N was vaulted last, probably held up by the new work in the nave.

However, basically the cloister is Norman, as a closer and more extensive examination of the ranges around will at once show. The E wall has clearly Norman masonry, and as one enters the SLYPE, the first room in the E range, one is back in Wulfstan's time. (Now called the chapter parlour, it had a treasury above.) One enters through a doorway of the C14 with a niche l. and r., but the blind arcading in two bays of three arches each has columns with block capitals, single-scallop and single trumpet capitals just like the

181. WORCESTER Cloisters, C14 east walk with former C18 tracery, in 1831

182. WORCESTER Chapter house, early C12, C13 and late C14, in 1831

crypt, and there are among the capitals even bulbous Anglo-Saxon ones, probably re-used, although an 'overlap' is not impossible. After all, Wulfstan was an Anglo-Saxon, not a Norman. The bulbous capitals are similar to C10 capitals in the Wipertus Crypt at Quedlinburg and also the C11 capitals at Great Paxton in Huntingdonshire. One bulbous base also survives, but on the opposite side. After the slype the cloister E range continues with two large rectangular recesses, probably the receptacles for the Norman library. The chapter-house entrance belongs to the C14 again. There are here two niches l. and two r. Perp panel tracery above, quite possibly the earliest in the cathedral.

But the CHAPTER HOUSE itself (now Song School) is Norman again, and no later than say 1120–5: or even c. 1100–15 (Stratford 1978, a most helpful reconsideration of this earliest surviving example of that solely British speciality, the centrally planned chapter house). Worcester's is particularly memorable for being, originally, round (in ten sections) inside and out, as the lower inside wall still is; in the late C14, when the large four-light Perp windows

were made, the upper walls inside and the outer walls entirely (where externally visible) were rebuilt straight-sided with Norman stones to form a decagon. The banding of green and white stones inside and use of both red and white stones outside probably date from the original building. With its middle column supporting semicircular radial ribs, this building shared with Durham choir a willingness to experiment with a major stone vault over a broad span (over 55 ft here). The central column, despite its most elementary capital (re-used?), is almost certainly a C13 reconstruction (Stratford). The work of the C13 and C14 suggests that the original structural solution here was imperfect. But, although the vault too may have been interfered with since c. 1115, essentially such a vault on such a column must have been there from the first. The lower wall zone above the niched seats has intersecting blank arcading, with a billet frieze running above but otherwise not enriched as later Norman work would have been.

Continuing along the cloister, one passes a plain single-chamfered doorway and then, turning the corner, the C13

183. WORCESTER Christ in Majesty, *c.* 1220–30, refectory

doorway which leads into the usual tunnel-vaulted passage to the S. In the passage is a low doorway with a segmental arch to the refectory undercroft. The S exit has a portal of *c.* 1200. There are four orders of colonnettes, and in the round arch one order of pellets and one of individual affronted small leaves.

The main room on the S side is, again as usual, the REFECTORY (now part of the King's School, with access only from the S). It stands upon an Early Norman undercroft but, above, the refectory is of the mid-C14. At the E end of the refectory is a magnificently bold carved composition unfortunately largely chopped off. Its centre is an over-life-size Christ in Majesty in an elongated quatrefoil glory surrounded by the Signs of the Evangelists. The date of this must be *c.* 1220–30, as the drapery demonstrates. The composition is French in type. If it were complete, this piece would be among the two or three best of their date in England. The C14 must have appreciated it, or else it would not have been re-used. The friezes below, with heads and beasts, and above, as well as the thinly vaulted niches l. and r., are a C14 addition.

The cloister wall towards the refectory is not to be deciphered with certainty. The main C14 doorway was near the W end. Hoodmould with leaf and three small animals. But before that one passes two large blocked Norman arches and another doorway to the undercroft.

The W range of the cloister is completely exceptional among English monastic cathedrals in that it had the DORMITORY running E–W to a line far forward of the cathedral front. The normal position for the dormitory is of course in the E range on the upper floor, but the arrangement here puts the reredorter close to the river for the drains' sake (cf. Durham). The infirmary is also here, a separate building S W of the cathedral, although its normal place would have been somewhere E of the E range; but there was more peace and quiet near the river. In the W cloister, meanwhile, coming from the S walk, one sees first the wide two-bay LAVATORIUM of the monks, C14 of course, and then a deep Perp niche with a four-centred arch and a Perp doorway. This was the main dormitory entrance. But it replaced a Norman one of which a high arch with a big roll moulding is still visible. The smaller round-headed doorway belongs to the Late Norman work, with its continuous filleted roll. This Late Norman work appears once more in the portal to the PASSAGE in the N bay of this range. It is reasonable to presume that the passage was built at the same time as the immediately adjoining W bays of the nave. Just inside the passage is the doorway to the LIBRARY, which is in the roof space over the S aisle. It was prepared for this or some other purpose in the C15, by adding to the height of the outer wall and introducing the small paired windows already observed. It is known that Bishop Carpenter founded a library about the middle of the C15.

Finally, E of the E range and chapter house are the ruins of the GUESTEN HALL (demolished 1859). This was built probably near the end of Braunsford's priorate, i.e. c. 1338–9 (Morris 1978). The remaining windows indeed exhibit flowing tracery of the first order, the best in the cathedral. The hall was of five bays. Three had large transomed windows; the two on the r. were higher up and had a small doorway under. Here another building adjoined the hall. On the opposite side were four bays of windows plus a porch. The fine roof has been removed to the Avoncroft Museum at Stoke Prior near Bromsgrove.

Worcester Cathedral has little real PRECINCT. Ever since in 1794 a road was cut through its NE angle, it has lost its seclusion, and the new channelling of all the through traffic along just that corner has made things infinitely worse. In spite of C19 industrial growth, C20 Worcester *was* a cathedral town first and foremost, and that makes it totally incomprehensible that the City Council should have permitted that act of self-mutilation.

The former Bishop's Palace, N of the cathedral on the Severn bank, no longer has anything to do with the cathedral. It seems just a large Georgian house next to the very C20 Technical College and near the ferocious traffic route, but inside are C13 remains. Between this house and the cathedral is College Yard with Georgian houses and trees. N of the chancel originally stood a large octagonal bell-tower, one of the free-standing ones as Chichester's still is, but with a steep conical roof or spire. Immediately E of it, and close to the cathedral's E end, was the now demolished parish church of St Michael. On the S side of the cathedral is a bit of real precinct, College Green, entered from the outside world by the C14 great gate called the Edgar Tower. Further on these surroundings, see the latest edition of B of E *Worcestershire*.

# York

## CATHEDRAL CHURCH OF ST PETER (YORK MINSTER) *Anglican*

(Based on B of E *Yorkshire: York and the East Riding*, 1972, by NP with John Hutchinson, revised mainly by John Hutchinson, with contributions by Derek Phillips, David O'Connor, Ben Johnson and Bernard Barr, and information from Thomas Cocke and Michael Gillingham.)

Plans: Fig. 184 from the *Builder*, 1893, by Roland Paul. (It is important to realize that the medieval high altar stood one bay W of the present one, i.e. in the E transept bay, which on plan can only be detected by the transepts' more elaborate vaulting-plan. Thus the retrochoir included the medieval feretory bay, where the high altar now is, as well as the Lady Chapel bays. Structurally, the presbytery was only indicated by the E transepts, which are clearer in elevation than on plan.) Fig. 185 is an outline plan of the recent excavations (Aylmer and Cant 1977).

Some references (see Recent Literature): Bony 1979; Coldstream 1972; Gee and Harvey in Aylmer and Cant 1977.

**Late note**: our description, inevitably, was completed before the fire of 1984.

### INTRODUCTION

The Minster in its great length and with its keep-like central tower continues to be the main element in the unparalleled view from York's medieval city walls. So far as overall size goes, York is one of the hugest churches in Europe. In architectural interest and in its very different way, the ancient seat of the Archbishops of York is as marvellous a monument as that of the Archbishops of Canterbury.

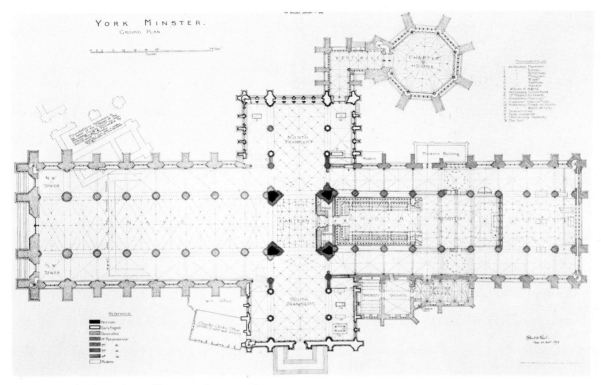

184. YORK Plan from the *Builder*, 1893 (see p. 334)

York Minster was founded on the site of a Roman fortress by Edwin, King of Northumbria, in 627, after he had been converted to Christianity by Paulinus. His was a wooden oratory. It was rebuilt of stone shortly after, completed by King Oswald and repaired by Archbishop Wilfrid in the late C 7. Archbishop Aethelbert's church of *c.* 780 may have been a rebuilding, or adjacent, or somewhere else entirely. Whatever form the Saxon church took, it was burnt in 1069, repaired, again damaged in 1079, then rebuilt by Archbishop Thomas of Bayeux shortly after. Archbishop Roger of Pont-l'Évêque (1154–81) rebuilt the choir.

But of this early history the building above ground tells almost nothing, giving no more than a few hints to the knowing. York Minster is a cathedral almost exclusively Gothic, and for the Gothic style or rather styles in England it tells us a more consistent and complete story than any other cathedral. Between about 1230 and about 1475 every stage is represented, so much so that the following description has to be chronological by parts: Archbishop Thomas's, Archbishop Roger's, the C 13 transepts, the chapter house of the late C 13, the nave of 1291 to *c.* 1350, the retrochoir and choir of *c.* 1361–1420, and the three towers built *c.* 1407–*c.* 1475. Especially for the C 13, phase after phase can be followed and all of the highest quality. York Minster consists of nave with aisles, transepts with aisles, and aisled choir and retrochoir separated by E transepts that project only in elevation. Only a few low additions on the S side break the grand rectangularity of the whole. There has never been a cloister.

The Minster is built of magnesian limestone from Tadcaster. It is 486 ft long inside, the nave only a little shorter than the eastern arm (measuring both from the centre of the crossing), the transepts together a little shorter than the nave. The nave is 99 ft high inside, the choir 102 ft, the transepts only 92 ft. (The choir is exceeded in England only by the nave of Westminster Abbey at 103 ft.) The central tower is 198 ft high externally, the W towers are 196 ft. That is a pity; for equality of height does not make for a perfect composition from afar. *William Kent* and *Lord Burlington* redesigned the floor, 1731–5. The Minster was restored by *William Shout* in 1802–28, by *Sir Robert Smirke* in 1832 etc. after a fire, the nave by *Sydney Smirke* in 1840 after another fire. There was further restoration under *Street*, 1868–81, and *Bodley*, 1882–1907. Recent restorations culminated in the massive programme under *Dr Bernard Feilden*, 1967–72.

Robert Willis's account of the Minster (in a paper delivered in 1846, published 1848 and recently reprinted, see Recent Literature) still seems remarkably perceptive, though now knowledge of the Norman cathedral involves a reassessment of the building's development, which is set out to some extent in Aylmer and Cant (1977). John Browne's majestic *York Minster* (1847) remains invaluable.

### THE EXCAVATIONS
(Contributed by John Hutchinson and Derek Phillips)

The 1967–72 programme for strengthening the foundations of the Minster provided a unique opportunity to explore the early history of the building and site. Almost the whole of the transept and crossing area, together with the E and W ends of the nave, was excavated to a depth of 14 ft. Other excavation was possible in the choir aisles, Lady Chapel and outside the E and W ends. Excavation in Dean's Park and S of the choir followed in 1972–3.

### Roman

The alignment of the legionary fortress is intersected by the E–W axis of the Minster at approximately 48°; this at least makes the Roman remains readily identifiable among the work of later builders. Enough of the plan of the *principia* emerged to show that it had a width N W–S E of 230 ft. Drums and bases from the *basilica principiorum*

185. YORK
Plan of excavations 1967–72 (after Aylmer and Cant 1977)

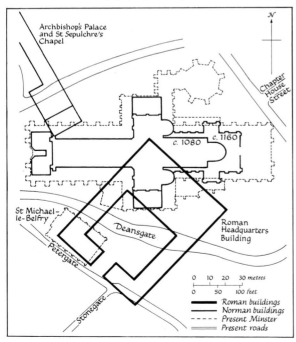

were found beneath the S transept, including one complete fallen column 22 ft high and 3 ft in diameter, of no known order but approximating to Tuscan. This rather alien object has been re-erected opposite the S door of the Minster. Another base remains *in situ* in the undercroft. (The column base beneath a trapdoor in the crypt is Roman, but possibly not in its original position.)

The remains of the N W and N E walls of the *principia* date originally from the early C 2. An addition to the N W, of the late C 4, had a room decorated with painted plaster. The remains of this have been remounted, and are typical of late Roman-British wall decoration; the design is in three horizontal zones, a dado of imitation marbling, subject panels divided by pilasters supporting an entablature, all effectively shaded, then a frieze with the shallow reveal of a horizontal window, an exceptionally rare discovery.

### Saxon

Nothing has been found that can be accepted with certainty as part of the Saxon cathedral, though traces were found of post-Roman buildings on approximately the Roman alignment. Such elucidation as is possible must await the publication of the full account of the excavation. Perhaps the most striking discovery was a cemetery of the C 9–11 below the S transept. Many of the later graves were marked with stone slabs, head and foot stones, and their decoration – mainly animal ornament of the beast-chain type – shows that a strong English artistic tradition persisted in York despite Scandinavian settlement.

Significantly, these burials also followed the Roman alignment, the graves having been cut into the rubble of the destroyed *principia*. Other Saxon material including decorated slabs was re-used in the foundations of the Norman church.

### The crypt and undercroft

The crypt is a very confusing place. Archbishop Thomas's work is encased in Archbishop Roger's (on which see below), and this in turn was partly reconstructed, partly abandoned when the present choir was built, and the rough footings of the Perp arcades obstruct Roger's aisles. All of this is surrounded by the brick arched and vaulted structure contrived after the 1829 fire to support the choir floor, leaving the Norman work free for inspection by the agile, and showing the restoring architect's archaeological sense. Recent work has added to the confusion. Most of what remains of Archbishop Thomas's church is in the vast 'new' undercroft, beneath the central tower, the transepts and the E end of the nave, but there massive concrete foundations liberally dotted with steel bolts encase much of the Norman work. On the C 12–14 choir crypt see p. 348.

186. YORK C 12 choir crypt as rebuilt under the late C 14 sanctuary

## Norman

If Saxon evidence is slight, Norman evidence is copious and sensational. Archbishop Thomas's church was both architecturally and technologically remarkable. The nave, over 45 ft wide internally, was aisleless; the transepts had single E apses, and there was a third somewhat larger apse at the end of the unusually long E arm. Between the transept apses and the choir were stair-turrets whose presence and long survival are critical to an understanding of the building's development. The central tower was the same size as at present, but the arches were somewhat narrower. Externally, the church was 362 ft long; 160 ft across the transept. The w end was one and a half bays to the E of the present one, and had boldly projecting buttresses at the angles.

The foundations were reinforced with massive timbers laid in a regular grillage. Those of the E arm were wider than the rest, and may imply, among other things, that the church had a small crypt (paired walls running E–W stood on these foundations). The walls were of mortared rubble faced with rubble largely of Roman origin, and some herringbone masonry. The walls were covered with plaster painted with red lines to simulate ashlar.

Part of Thomas's E apse can be seen below a trapdoor in the crypt. The treasury is housed between the footings of the w part of the choir, but the herringbone masonry illustrated in Browne's *York Minster* (1847) is now hidden behind display cases. The tower footings are largely encased in concrete, but the arch leading to the choir can still be traced. The s transept is the area clearest of later (and earlier) intrusions, and the entrances to the E apses of both transepts are clearly visible. The privileged and intrepid can visit the s transept apse down a ladder at the s w corner of Roger's crypt. In the boiler house, traces remain of the N transept apse, together with the barrel-vaulted chamber at the foot of the N stair-turret. This has a one-step arch absolutely plain. Traces of the spiral staircases remain above the vaults at the W ends of the choir aisles. Of the exterior of Thomas's church the painted plaster and chamfered Millstone Grit plinths are best seen near the entrance to the undercroft. The inner step of the apparently twice-stepped pilasters supported a wall arch.

Thomas's crossing piers form the core of the present piers, and behind the E spandrel on the N side of the nave, one shaft with steep base mouldings remains *in situ*, the base 43 ft above the Norman nave floor. The one visible piece of Thomas's superstructure which the visitor is likely to see was discovered in 1974. This is the remains of a fat shaft with a voluted and foliated capital, from the N jamb of the S transept apse, and can be seen in the N spandrel of the entrance to the S choir aisle. Similar but more ornate capitals for paired shafts (possibly from the entrance to the E apse) are displayed in the undercroft. They have no parallels in England; crypt capitals at Bayeux offer the closest analogies.

### Late Norman

Of Archbishop Roger of Pont-l'Évêque's choir nothing remains above ground, but for his crypt we have plenty of evidence. This choir must have been a building of great magnificence, and when fifty years later the new transepts were built, there can have been no intention of demolishing it. This led to difficulties, as we shall see, but Roger's choir may properly be considered the start of the present Minster.

The choir floor-level was higher than at present, thus giving greater headroom in the crypt. It was of eight bays, of which the third bay from the E was an eastern transept with small square projections N and S. (Such an extra transept had a source in Conrad's choir at Canterbury and in the late C 11 rebuilding at Cluny.)

The three W bays of the crypt were built around the W end of Thomas's choir, Roger's ashlar encasing Thomas's herringbone. The W bays were entrances, but how? Take the N aisle. The crypt was below the five eastern bays with the outer aisles continuing to the W outside Thomas's inner walls and ending in canted 'quadrant' porches to which access was gained by steps which probably began in the C 12 pulpitum. These porches had triple shafts in the canted corners. The doors were in the E walls. They had enterprising geometrical decoration and spiral shafts. The closest local analogy to this is the refectory door at Kirkham Priory. These arrangements may be traced with difficulty at the W end of the S aisle. (Much more remained in the N aisle but this was dismantled during the 1967–72 restoration, and is piled up in Roger's N crypt transept.) Beyond

this two bays of aisle only with half-round wall-shafts until one cleared the remains of Thomas's work. The exterior had twice-stepped buttresses with nook-shafts and a moulded plinth.

The E part of the crypt had five aisles and was biaxially symmetrical – i.e. the transepts occupied the double middle bay N and S – though there were some anomalies in the setting out. The bays E to W were arranged A A B–B A B, B–B leading to the transepts, which were entered through double arches. The outer arcades have massive round piers with attached or detached shafts, lozenge patterns or spiral zigzags to the piers, and many-scalloped capitals. Tiny pellets are also a feature. Responds with three half-shafts and again scalloped capitals. The arches had more zigzag, the vaulting-ribs a half-round between two hollows. The middle arcades had single round shafts, moulded bases, and square plinths with nicely carved spurs with leaf decoration. The bases remain *in situ*, but the columns and seven of the capitals and much other material were used (see p. 348) to build the crypt below the later sanctuary. The capitals have scallops, primitive leaf designs in beaded bands, shells, and a row of figures holding up the abacus. At the transept entrances were four round shafts arranged in a lozenge shape. Many of the forms are still barbaric, but they are carried out with a precision and skill far in advance of their forebears at Durham.

Of Roger's choir we know little, but it is significant that Browne illustrates waterleaf capitals found among the remains. Waterleaf was introduced *c.* 1170 and Roger died in 1181. The huge foundations of the Perp choir piers are rockeries of re-used Norman material including W-shaped zigzags and pelleted bobbin ornament.

Plenty of problems remain unsolved. Why was Thomas's work allowed to survive in the crypt? Was the W part of Roger's choir walled in, as still at Rochester? More important, how did one get into Roger's aisles, blocked at the W end partly by the turrets, partly by the crypt aisles? And finally, how was the sharp change in floor-level from Thomas's transepts to Roger's choir negotiated?

Prior to the building of the present nave a new 'westwork' was added, a porch 11 ft wide, flanked by towers 22 ft wide – both measured internally – and built just W of Thomas's front touching the buttresses, its W wall immediately under the present W wall. Some sculptural elements which may be associated with this structure will be discussed with the W front.

The Norman church was thus far removed from our accepted Norman ideal as exemplified by, say, Durham or Peterborough, but it was by no means unique. The Durham–Peterborough plans approximated more closely to the ideas of the Gothic builders, who contented themselves with propping them up and adapting them. Kirkham

Priory retained something very like the Thomas–Roger plan until the Dissolution, and Roger's church at Ripon also approximated to the Thomas–Roger plan, even to having the chancel narrower than the aisleless nave. So presumably Archbishop Roger was satisfied with his composite cathedral. Even the c13 w end at Ripon with its projecting towers may have continued the York idea.

## THE TRANSEPTS

The transepts were built *c.* 1220–55. The s transept came first, built by Archbishop de Gray, who was buried there in 1255. The N transept was built by John le Romeyn (Romanus), who is also associated with the c13 central tower. The style is later than that of the s transept, and as Romeyn also died in 1255 that may be a completion date.

The transepts are externally similar though not identical on the E and w sides, but completely different on the s and N. On the E and w sides the most notable motif is the clerestory with arched windows and blank arches. In the s

transept these are in sets of five (a triplet of windows with an arch each end) divided by shallow canted buttresses, but in the N they appear all in a row without any bay division. The aisle walls of the s transept have large buttresses between the bays and smaller ones mid-bay, all with gabled tops breaking the parapet. Windows and blank arches are awkwardly hemmed in by a string run right across below the top stage of the buttresses. This is abandoned in the N transept, and the gable tops of the buttresses are kept level with the window heads – a less restless effect.

The s front has a middle porch. This projects slightly, and has shafts with lush stiff-leaf capitals, a rib-vault inside with a boss, and an inner arch of sumptuous, though sadly damaged, undercut stiff-leaf. Above are three ugly gables by *Street*, who also added the rather pedestrian, octagonal turrets. To l. and r. are pairs of lancets, above them three singles, the middle one with Y-tracery. The outer jambs show signs of a change in design. In the gable is a splendid rose-window of two circles of centrifugal arches on columns. The centre is a sexfoiled circle.

187. YORK View from the north in 1819

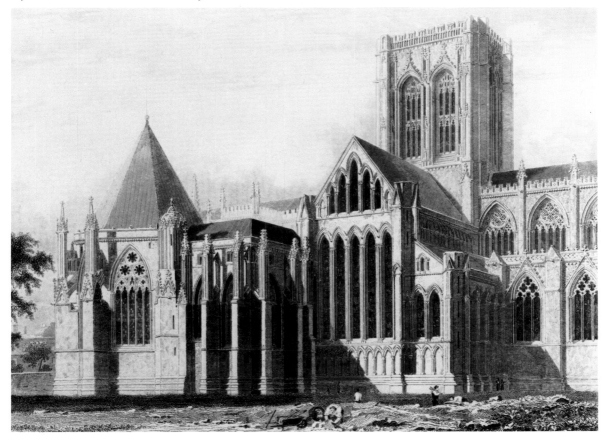

The N transept has one tier of lancets, but they are the celebrated Five Sisters, five lancets of an equal height of 55 ft. In the gable are seven stepped lancets, the first and last blank. Below, a wall arcade on shafts of alternating section. To the E in the N bay is an ornate doorway with stiff-leaf capitals. The arch is cinquecusped (cf. Byland). To the W in the S bay is a small doorway, overlapped by the N aisle of the nave. For the N doorway to the chapter-house passage, see below.

The interiors are similar. They are aisled, the S transept W aisle being narrower than the others. Dr Gee suggests that the outer walls of this were the first part built, and a change in plan involved moving the arcade westwards of its originally intended position. The piers stand on waterholding bases and are compound with shafts alternatingly attached of limestone and detached of Purbeck marble. The main shafts have fillets, and the capitals are of the stiff-leaf kind. The arches are finely moulded with some small dogtooth decoration, different in detail N from S, and some billet on the E arcade. The aisles are rib-vaulted, quadripartite, but with a fifth rib in the middle of the cell towards the outer wall which makes five and in the outer corner bays six. The S transept W aisle has the ribs single-chamfered, the other ribs are nicely moulded. An odd anomaly is that the innermost bays of the projecting parts of the transepts have much narrower arches, and that they are blocked, but the reasons for this are best discussed when dealing with the tower. The gallery above the arcades has three bays of twice twin openings per bay with what might be called coinciding arches (again with limestone and Purbeck shafts). That is: the four sub-arches are lancet-shaped, each twin is under an arch whose outer shanks run exactly parallel to those of a super-arch for all four, and this is semicircular. (Or it seems so at first sight; but in the S transept only the centre bay is round-headed, the outer bay being pointed because slightly narrower; the other details conform. Was this an error in setting out, or is it too far-fetched to see it as an attempt to give greater prominence to the centre bay, where Walter de Gray planned to erect his own monument?) In the tympanum of each twin is a quatrefoiled circle, and the tympanum of the super-arch has a large cinquefoiled circle. There are again stiff-leaf capitals and dogtooth enrichments.

In small details the N transept differs from the S, and the W side of the S 'nave' from its E side. As to the latter, the W triforium e.g. has leaf paterae, and the E has not. As to the forms, the clerestory has large dogtooth to the shafting in the N transept, where also the strings above the clerestory and below the triforium have what Browne refers to as 'laurel-leaf zigzag'. The rere arches of the N transept aisle windows are much more richly treated, set between acutely pointed blind arches and filling the whole space below the wall rib of the vault, but this means that the intermediate

ribs have to spring at a different level to the others. That the capitals of the N transept are richer, with some beasts among the stiff-leaf, goes with the later date. On the other hand, the Purbeck vaulting-shafts which start above the pier capitals stand on gorgeously big leaf corbels in the S transept; in the N transept the corbels are insignificant, but the arcade piers have figured hoodmould stops instead. In the S transept at the top of the vaulting-shafts, springers of wall arches appear, though the form of the original transept roof remains enigmatic. In fact, the whole of the HIGH VAULTING of York Minster is of wood. Though ribbed, the transept vaults are tunnel-vaults. That of the N transept is of c. 1400, rebuilt 1934–51; that of the S transept is by *Street*, recently restored. Square panels and some original early C 15 bosses.

## THE CHAPTER HOUSE AND VESTIBULE

There is no documentation for the date of the chapter house and vestibule. Speculation ranges from Dr Gee's starting date of c. 1260 to Professor Bony's completion date well into the C 14. However, the glass in both suggests a completion date well before the end of the C 13, and there is a general development of tracery, with some aberrations, from chapter house to nave *via* the vestibule, marked by the gradual freeing of the cusped elements from their more formally Geometrical surrounds. It seems probable that the work started c. 1275 and was complete when the nave was commenced in 1291. The chapter house is an octagon and, except for the smaller one at Southwell, it is the only polygonal one without a middle pier. But then, the tierceron vault here is of wood – the oldest of the wooden roofs of the Minster. But Dr Gee also suggests that there was a change in plan from an intended stone vault with a central pillar to the present wooden dome (on which see below). The windows are of five lights with three circles over, and that appears at first to imply a harmony such as that of the Westminster and Salisbury chapter houses. But there is one element which breaks that harmony, and it is characteristic of the short phase of unrest before, with the coming of the ogee arch, the licence of the Decorated set in: the middle light is higher and steeper than the others, and stabs up into the zone of the nine-foiled circles. The chapter seats have a delightful enrichment: instead of blank arcading behind as at Southwell, each seat is in a shallow niche and has a canopy. The canopy is octagonal, slightly squashed or broadened, and carried on Purbeck shafts with a mixture of stiff-leaf and naturalistic caps; the front three sides, however, are pendant on little leaf cones. Thus all along the wall below the windows there is a gentle undulation, again heralding the curvaceous style to come. The canopies have on their canted front five gablets alternately wide and narrow, all with tiny head-stops, and finials of

189. YORK Chapter-house sculpture, *c.* 1290, in 1818

equal size, leaves curling and blowing upwards. Above the gables and below the windows runs a leaf frieze of naturalistic foliage. The entrance has a *trumeau*, and against this stands an exquisite statue of the Virgin, typical late C 13, much restored. The canopy may have formed the base of a Crucifixion in the quatrefoil above. Above, towards the interior, is an odd row of thirteen niches, eleven under a shallow arch (angels above the outer ones). They no doubt contained Christ and the Twelve Apostles.

The exterior has big buttresses with gablets, turning into cruciform pinnacles, and flying buttresses in two tiers, the lower normal (associated by Dr Gee with the stone vault), the upper simply a block, with horizontal top and bottom, closely traceried and gableted like the pinnacles, connected with the wooden vault. These closely traceried elements are repeated on the stair-turret. The window jambs and arches have deep, flat faces at r. angles to the wall face, with thin mouldings and shafts at the edge. This proves to be developmentally important. The whole structure is topped by the vast octo-pyramidal roof, whose ingenious construction is explained by a model in the chapter house.

The cells of the wooden vault were originally boarded and painted with over-life-size figures of considerable grandeur. One of them and substantial fragments of two others are preserved in the undercroft museum. In 1798

*John Carr* supervised the replacement of the boarding by lath and plaster. This new vault was decorated by *Willement* in 1844–5, a scheme partially reinstated recently.

The VESTIBULE, i.e. the L-shaped passage between the N transept and the chapter house, was begun rather later than the chapter house, but not much. The chapter-house buttress adjoining on the E is arrested in the stage before the addition of the upper flyers. The blank arcading is of twin cusped arches and in the circle above alternating leaf bosses and head bosses like paterae. The leaf decoration is mainly naturalistic, with a few stiff-leaf survivors, and there are small figure subjects on some of the capitals (e.g. the one s of the chapter-house door). The passage is rib-vaulted, with big leaf bosses, and in this vault for the first time at York (though late – nationally speaking) a longitudinal ridge rib appears. Outside, the buttresses turn halfway up to square, detached pinnacles with tall blank arcading, linked to the wall by open traceried elements. The blank window over the chapter-house door keeps to the chapter-house pattern. L. and r. are very tall blank windows of four lights paired under painfully acute arches. The rest of the tracery is just a little later than the chapter house: large circular elements appear subdivided with round enclosed trefoils and pointed, unenclosed, ones. The tracery plane is close to the inner face of the wall so that the flat right-

190. YORK Chapter-house ceiling, completed *c.* 1290

angled arch soffits of the chapter house are retained, but here they are sprung direct from the face of the buttresses on which the jamb shafts appear as a thin applied line. This is the first English building whose design aimed at the total substition of window for wall. Though few of its successors managed the job so thoroughly, ambition certainly outran technique, so that outside it is an intellectual rather than an aesthetic exercise, some of the window arches taking on the oddest shapes in order to reach their buttresses. Inside, however, it is a triumphant success, and one hardly notices the blocked lights and odd tracery in the sheer spatial splendour.

The design was badly set out, and the windows adjoining the transept are a sign of embarrassment, the southernmost absurdly narrow, yet of two lights, the next a little wider but with very odd tracery including vertical mullions threaded through the apexes of gables. A related motif occurs in the portal of the N transept. The details are even odder there. It is a twin portal with a super-arch and a gable over. At the apex of the gable is a transom, and on this stand two more sub-arches and a central mullion reaching right up to the apex of another super-arch. There are still encircled quatrefoils and a cinquefoil with big leaf cusps. All this cuts into two E. E. windows whose heads survive above. To the vestibule, over the door is a four-light blank window, with a big cinquefoil (the door enclosed, in effect, in descending mullions). On this, and elsewhere in the vestibule, there survived till the recent cleaning considerable traces of late C 14 painted heraldry. The enclosing arch is the E. E. hoodmould with stiff-leaf stops of the two former windows, part *in situ*, part re-used. Between this and the vault, bits of the N E transept wall can be recognized and compared with those of the w aisle.

The upper storey of the vestibule was a mason's design shop or TRACING HOUSE (cf. Wells). It was provided with a fireplace and a garderobe which can still be seen ingeniously spanning between the E vestibule wall and the detached pinnacle. The floor of gypsum has the setting out of full-size mouldings and tracery designs, the earliest belonging to a presbytery window. The original timber scissors roof survives.

## THE NAVE

The nave was begun at its S E corner in 1291. The master mason was *Simon*, according to Harvey. Externally the aisles have buttresses with niches and high pinnacles. Those on the N and all the flying buttresses are *Bodley's* work of 1905–7, though the rough stumps of the flyers were there before. Probably they were left incomplete when the intention to vault the nave in stone was abandoned. On the parapet of blank quatrefoils stand, or stood, small figures. The windows are just a little later in motifs than those of the chapter house and passage. They are of three trefoiled lights with three unencircled quatrefoils over, all rather big and bald. Above the windows are crocketed gables cutting into the parapet. The clerestory is high, the windows are still pre-ogee, large circular elements again, with a diagonal cross pattern of short lights with quatrefoils in squares, and the flat, right-angled jambs with edge mouldings reappear, this time with a passage outside the windows instead of inside, as was more usual.

However, when one goes on to the w front, it will be seen at once that its upper parts are no longer pre-ogee, but display the full panoply of flowing tracery in the second tower-stage windows and in the splendid middle window of eight lights 55 ft high. This is in fact datable to 1338 (contract for glazing) and *Ivo de Raughton* may have been the mason (Harvey). Below, i.e. around and above the doorways, all is still late Geometrical, a sumptuous version of the aisle design. Against the wall are niches for statues. They have crocketed gables and run round the buttresses and continue in the centre l. and r. of the twin portal. Above this is a glazed circle with three pointed trefoils, and one order of the arch voussoirs has scenes from the story of the Creation. Above are three statuettes all over-restored by *Michael Taylor* in 1801–16, when the foliage was also restored, much of this now sadly crumbling. The change from 1300 to the full Dec is most obvious where in the blank arcading simple arches change to nodding ogee arches. The w window tracery has four pairs of lights, paired again under ogees, their points carried up, then turned into the centre to form a large heart-shape, all sumptuously subdivided. Above is a steep gable decorated with flowing tracery partly blank, partly open where it cuts above the horizontal parapet. Above again the low nave gable has more flowing tracery, stepped battlements, and an open pinnacle. The w tower windows have large reticulation units subdivided into small ones, while others have mouchettes spiralling round quatrefoils. (See further on the w towers and the w front below.)

The two evangelical symbols on the w face of the S W tower are part of the surround of a late C 12 aureole, the others being inside, flanking the extreme apex of the w window. Some C 12 statues are re-used on the tower buttresses and there are more in the undercroft. Though terribly worn they can be related to the superb series of statues at St Mary's Abbey. This sculpture may relate to the C 12 westwork.

The interior has piers somewhat different from those of the transepts; only the upper parts are entirely novel, though following a French C 13 trend. The arcading is 51 ft high. The piers have big attached shafts without any use of Purbeck marble. The three shafts towards the nave run right up to the vault, the minor shafts interrupted at the level of the arch springing not by capitals but by heads. To the arch openings the shafts are triple and have capitals,

192. YORK Nave capitals, *c.* 1300 (detail)

and these now have naturalistic foliage. Shields of donors occupy the spandrels both here and in the choir. The W bays, planned from the start for two towers, have stronger piers and arches across nave and aisles. The aisles have quadripartite rib-vaults and wall-arcading with trefoils and pointed trefoils (cf. the chapter-house passage), but now all under crocketed gables and separated by pinnacles. Triforium and clerestory are made into one by way of descending mullions, the triforium defined by a row of gablets and quatrefoils. The elevation therefore does not appear any longer to be of three tiers, as in the transepts, but of two, triforium and clerestory amounting to a height of 43 ft. The general resemblance of the nave design to that at Troyes has often been remarked, and Bony adds Clermont-Ferrand. The windows are of five lights, and the triforium has no more than a wall-passage. The vault was made in 1354, but burnt in 1840. It was then replaced by *Sydney Smirke*. It is probable that the original intention was for a quadripartite stone vault.

The W wall shows inside – just as it does outside – where the blank arcading changes from the design of 1291 to that of *c.* 1330. Nodding ogee arches again indicate the later stage. Above the aisle doorways is some figure sculpture of apparently genre motifs (Samson and the foxes?). In the N aisle is a doorway to a former chapel, with above it a standing female saint (the Virgin?) and two angels, very fine, early C 14.

THE EASTERN ARM

This consists of the four-bay choir, the one-bay E transepts, projecting only at clerestory level, and the four-bay retro-choir. The original arrangements are important here. The high altar stood in the E transept bay backed by a high wooden screen behind which was the Shrine of St William. (Fragments of the Frosterley marble shrine base are in the Yorkshire Museum, with fragments of St William's gorgeous tomb which stood in the nave.) So the original

193. YORK View from the south-east

high altar stood one bay w of the present high altar. Willis has proved that the retrochoir and presbytery bays were built before the choir, i.e. as an extension outside the Norman choir, starting as usual with the outer wall. This enabled Roger's choir to remain in use for as long as possible. In 1394 services began to be said in the new vestry, and this probably marked the demolition of the last parts of Roger's choir. The retrochoir can be dated 1361 to c. 1370, though it was left incomplete; the choir followed c. 1390–1420. The design deliberately continues that of the nave, an unusual procedure in the Middle Ages, though also done, and with a pattern even less up to date, in continuing the naves at Beverley and Westminster Abbey. The details of course are adjusted – the capitals e.g. have the sea-weedy character of the late C 14. On the other hand the vaulting-shafts have even the small figures in the same places as in the nave. The arch mouldings are not like those of the nave, but not essentially different. The triforium, however, now has blank arches below the parapet and Perp panelling above the arches. Even subtler are the differences between presbytery and choir, and they are telling developmentally. Yet the whole is essentially Perp from the start, and 1361 is an early date for the Perp style in the North. The aisle windows remain basically unchanged – but those of the retrochoir have a taller tracery format. They are (like those of the nave aisles) a little bald. Crocketed hoodmoulds. The great nine-light E window shows the survival of a certain sympathy for the Dec past even into the early C 15. The frieze of heads below is a charming, lively feature. L. and r. of the window are three tiers of niches. Above the three E windows all is blank panelling. Parapet of open arches with gables. High crocketed pinnacles, especially at the outer corners of the aisles.

John Harvey gives three master masons for the eastern arm: *William Hoton* for the retrochoir aisle walls; *Robert de Patrington* for the arcades and clerestory; and *Hugh de Hedon* for the work in the choir.

The main external difference between eastern bays and choir is in the clerestory: that of the retrochoir has in front of the five-light windows an arcade of three bays with cusped arches and a low transom – i.e. the external passage of the nave clerestory is retained. The choir abandons this, returning the passage to the inside, and besides has tracery less attached to the ogee past. The interior is affected by the change, for where in the retrochoir triforium and clerestory are read as one plane, in the choir the clerestory is set back and the unity destroyed. The foliage carving changes from vertical leaves to horizontal trails.

The boldest Perp windows are those of the E transept facing S and N, the St Cuthbert and St William windows, but they are simply the choir clerestory windows projected downwards, through three tiers of transoms. The buttresses and pinnacles of the E bays are larger than those of the choir, a discrepancy which resolves itself as best it may at the sides of the E transept windows.

Inside, the aisles of both the retrochoir and the choir have blank arcading and panels with statue niches l. and r. of the windows. The aisle vaults have longitudinal as well as transverse ridge ribs. To the l. and r. of the E window are tiers of twin niches. The window itself up to its second transom has a grille in front to the inside like the external grille of the clerestory. The same was done in the E transept N and S windows. These transepts incidentally are not pronounced internally. The arcade runs through in front of them carrying a bridge, even if above the bridge all is open. The high vaults with liernes are again of wood. They are by *Sir Robert Smirke*, 1829–32. At the W end of the choir aisles are Perp screens with traceried spandrels to the arches and tiers of niches on one side only.

Part of Roger's choir remained in use until 1394. When the choir was rebuilt at the end of the C14 much of the Norman work was re-used in foundations, but part of the crypt was reconstructed to provide the platform for the high altar and feretory. Seven out of the available ten Norman capitals are re-used (see *Late Norman crypt* above), and the reconstructed work is built against the completed bases of the retrochoir piers, both facts indicating that this is part of the choir scheme, rather than the retrochoir scheme. There are four bays in width, and two and two-thirds in depth. The piers are round, with octagonal abaci; the capitals (described p. 338) are re-used Norman material of c. 1160, like the vaulting-ribs. The springing of the crypt vault is above the floor-level of the retrochoir aisles, and the N and S ends of the vault open into those upper aisles through re-used Norman arches with zigzag. Towards the aisles the arches have stops with delightful little scenes. The two arches where the present entrances are have re-used Norman arches with zigzag.

By the early C15, work on the choir was far enough advanced for it to be necessary to do something about the C13 tower arches, which were still related to Thomas's nave, Roger's choir and whatever form was originally taken by the transept roofs. Moreover, Thomas's turrets were still blocking the W ends of the aisles. Presumably it was intended to retain the tower itself. An ambitious scheme was started to raise the arches, recase the piers, remove the turrets and create new entrances to the aisles. If spectral arches in the E walls of each transept are to be trusted this last was to be done by making the innermost bays of the transept half as wide again as before. Not surprisingly, in 1407 there was a collapse, and *William Colchester* was sent to supervise the works. New arches were constructed to the choir and nave aisles and solid walls faced with blank arches were built to fill up the gap between these and the nearest transept pier, providing a sort of flying buttress, and the rather flimsy screens were added across the choir aisles. (See also *Furnishings*, Crossing, on the pulpitum.) The remaining pier of the N transept W arcade was also replaced.

### THE TOWERS

The CROSSING TOWER was started soon after the collapse in the early C15. It was paid for in great part by Bishop Skirlaw of Durham. Its piers are still those of Archbishop Thomas, as we have seen, but they are encased. The weight of the tower has done much harm. (The following is contributed by the cathedral librarian.) The fabric accounts show that in 1470, when work on the rebuilt central tower was at last drawing towards a close, forty-six oaks were purchased from Ulleskelf and brought down the River Wharfe and up the Ouse to York, and *James Dam*, woodcarver, and his man were paid 45s. for nine weeks' work. In the following year the number of joiners employed jumped from four to seventeen (while masons fell from twenty-one to eight), divers men of Deighton were paid 7s. 4d. for carrying timber for bosses from Deighton Wood to the Minster Close, three men were paid 6s. for working at Cawood on the cutting of wood bought for bosses, and *David Carver* was paid 17s. 4d. for carving bosses and given a bonus of 10s. by the spontaneous will and grace of the Chapter. In 1472 the tower, including the bosses, was painted inside, using, 3,100 leaves of beaten gold, two casks of linseed oil, blue 'ynde', vermilion, red lead, white lead, ochre, varnish etc. Of the carvers, James Dam, probably a Fleming from Damme near Bruges, became a freeman of York as a carver in 1456–7, and in 1479 was carving stone at the Minster. His son *John*, a goldsmith, became a freeman in 1482. David 'Carver' is probably a relative, the same *David Dam* who was paid as a carver in 1485. The master carpenter from 1457 to about 1472 was *John Forster* or Foster, who became a freeman in 1457–8; in about 1473 he was succeeded by *James Whinfield*, until at least 1485.

194. YORK Crossing, timber ceiling and bosses, 1470s

The tower is of course fully Perp. The design is very spare – just two three-light openings to each side and a flat top with openwork battlements. Thin set-back angle buttresses. The original design may well have included a belfry above the lantern, abandoned when the inadequacies of the foundations became apparent, or at least pinnacles; it would be a good thing for all distant views if they were there. The mason of the tower was *William Colchester* (sent to York by Henry IV from Westminster Abbey: Harvey.) The timber roof inside is original, completed in the 1470s.

The WEST TOWERS completed the Minster, as a substitute for the projected central belfry, but there is no documentation. They must have been complete by the final consecration of the building on 3 July 1472. The towers are very different in character from the crossing tower – decorated all over as against the sobriety of a generation or two before. The buttresses have many set-offs, there is crocketed panelling above the windows, and the crowning is open-work battlements with eight pinnacles. The buttresses do not continue into the pinnacles, which results in a piquant pulling-in just below the battlements.

### THE WEST FRONT SUMMED UP

The W front as it presented itself in the late C 15 is in general outline the most French of all English cathedral façades, and it is curious that a type created in France in the C 13 caught on in England so late. The English C 13 type is the screen façade of Lincoln and Wells, and indeed, if one examines the York façade a little more attentively, one will notice that the designer of 1291 still believed in the English screen effect. The walls have, as has been said before, four tiers of gabled niches going right round the buttresses as well. English also and not French are the small portals and the huge mid-window. The screen effect disappears only with the work of the 1330s. There is tall, tight blank panelling above the mid-window and blank wall round the tower windows of the same level, and only then, round the bell-openings of the towers, is rich display taken up, whereas at Beverley Minster the verticalism of the towers is stressed from ground-level on.

### THE SOUTH ADDITIONS

S of the E end of the nave is the MINSTER BOOKSHOP, a two-storey building of 1418–20 (Barr), of four bays, built to house the library.

S of the S choir aisle is a range of controversial date. It is supposed to comprise, at the E end, the chantry chapel founded by Archbishop Zouche, known as the ZOUCHE CHAPEL, started in 1350, and further w the VESTRY and the CONSISTORY COURT, formerly the TREASURY (on

our plan called sacristies), both belonging to the last decade of the C 14. There is no architectural evidence of a break externally. Moreover, when the retrochoir was started in 1361 its aisle buttresses were set out just beyond the transepts of Roger's choir so that it could remain in use for as long as possible, and the E wall of the range is built against one of the 1361 buttresses, with the chapel over part of the site of the transept: both arguments for a late date. The presence of cupboards and a well in the 'chapel' make it much more probable that it is the vestry to which services were transferred in 1394, and that the whole range dates from the early 1390s. (Further on dating the cupboards, see *Furnishings*.) The 'chapel' is an extremely refined bit of work, with tierceron vaults, Purbeck wall-shafts and leaf caps and bosses. The windows have heavy mullions and transoms. In the SW corner the building is canted-out to accommodate the pretty well. The VESTRY has two bays of quadripartite rib-vaulting separated by one narrow tunnel-vaulted bay. The CONSISTORY COURT has a pointed tunnel vault with ribs or arches of Late Norman material from Roger's choir.

### FURNISHINGS

They are described from E to W, and central space before N aisle before S aisle. Much of the information is derived from Dean Addleshaw's 'Architects, painters, sculptors, craftsmen 1660–1960, whose work is to be seen in York Minster', *Architectural History*, 10, 1967. Monuments and stained glass are described separately below.

#### Lady Chapel
'Nave'. REREDOS. With three reliefs designed by *Bodley*, 1905, carved by *Lawrence A. Turner*. – RAILINGS to the S aisle and in this to the W. By *Bainbridge Reynolds* to a design by *Sir Walter Tapper* imitated from a railing in the Siena Town Hall. The date is 1930. – North aisle. REREDOS, with crucifixion. Partly designed by *Street*. The terracotta work by *Tinworth*, 1879. – Iron SCREEN to the S. Scrolls of c. 1686 (from the Dolben monument) on a screen of c. 1724 (from the Watson-Wentworth monument).

#### Crypt
FONT COVER. By *Comper*, 1946. – SCULPTURE. Relief of the Virgin, c. 1150 (and not Anglo-Saxon). A beautifully disciplined piece of work, wholly characteristic of its date. – Large relief of Hell etc. Late Norman. The damned in a cauldron, devils stoking. Confused in composition, indeed wildly agitated. It cannot be part of a tympanum, as the carving goes round the r. corner. Mr Brooks puts forward the attractive idea that it may have belonged to an external frieze like that of the w front of Lincoln Cathedral. – The Virgin as a child and St Anne. Early C 15, probably French.

– Simple iron GRILLES to the choir aisles; C 15. Segmental rococo grille round the Hell relief.

*Choir*

HIGH ALTAR. Behind it a STONE SCREEN of eight bays, by *Sir Robert Smirke*, after the 1829 fire; a fairly faithful copy of the original C 15 screen, a fragment of which is in the gardens of Moreby Hall, Naburn. – GOSPEL AMBO. Free Georgian. 1951, by *Sir Albert Richardson*. – STALLS, EPISTLE STAND, CANDLESTICKS, with leafy Arts and Crafts motifs. The first and third by *Sir Charles Peers*, 1944 and 1939, the second by a yet unknown designer. – CHOIR STALLS, ARCHBISHOP'S THRONE, PULPIT. All by *Smirke*, after the fire of 1829. Gothic, and successfully trying to keep in the spirit of what was burnt. Ornate decoration and canopies. – ORGAN. 1832, by *Elliot and Hill*. – North aisle. SCULPTURE. On the S side, relief of the Conversion of St Paul. Small and long; wood; Flemish, *c.* 1600. – Cast-iron SCREENS round the organ pipes designed by *Heindrick Franz de Cort* for the de Gray monument, 1804.

ZOUCHE CHAPEL, S of the S choir aisle. Two STALLS, preserved when the choir stalls were burnt. Decorated arm-rests. One MISERICORD with an eagle, the other with an atlas. – Two Flemish (?) statues of the C 16 and two small Flemish reliefs of *c.* 1600, evidently belonging to the relief in the N choir aisle. – CUPBOARDS. Late C 14, with delightful ironwork, their doors flush with the N wall. (P. Eames (1977) dates them, and the room, '*c.* 1500' with the walls 'built to contain them'. The wall is the aisle wall of the late C 14 SE transept and choir. While it is just structurally possible that the wall was refaced to incorporate the cupboards and the new vault put in at that late date, it is surely not very probable stylistically, and the carcass must certainly be late C 14, the same as the rest of the range because of the availability of Norman stonework for re-use in the other room: Hutchinson.)

*Crossing*

PULPITUM. Doorway with ogee gable, on the l. seven statue niches with figures of English kings, and eight on the r. (On the asymmetry, see below.) Very high, closely detailed canopies. Straight top. The kings go from William the Conqueror to Henry VI. All except Henry VI (by *Michael Taylor*, 1810) are original. (Henry VI's image presumably removed after 1461, returned after 1485, and again removed at the Reformation as an object of special piety; his niche later occupied by James I's statue, now at Ripon.) The style is lively and sometimes verges on caricature. The statues were restored by *Bernasconi* in 1814–18, and he also did the plaster angels above the canopies. The doorway leads to a small space with panelled walls and a tierceron vault with bosses. Wrought-iron gates of *c.* 1702.

196. YORK Pulpitum, mid-C 15, boss in passage vault

There is an inner porch with a fan-vault, scarcely visible in the gloom. There has long been a tradition that the screen was the work of *William Hyndeley* in the last quarter of the C 15. However, as Henry VI was deposed in 1461, the House of York would surely have been included after that date. A mid-c 15 construction seems likely as part of the works in support of the new tower. Harvey (in Aylmer and Cant 1977) suggests that the pulpitum was already begun by 1420 (at any rate, its E wall behind the return stalls), with seven niches intended either side on the W face, and subsequently altered, before 1461, to include Henry VI. (Cf. the also debatably dated pulpitum of kings at Canterbury.) – ORGAN CASE. Designed by *Sir Robert Smirke*, 1832, originally with an ungainly 'crown-work' in the centre, later removed; good diaper decoration on the display pipes (Gillingham).

### North transept

IRON GATES to the choir aisle, c. 1710. – PAINTING. By *Tristram*, 1932, in imitation of Crivelli. – ASTRONOMICAL CLOCK. 1955, by *Sir Albert Richardson* and *H. J. Stammers*, frieze by *Maurice Lambert*. C 15 wooden screen with tall traceried panels behind the Greenfield monument. – CLOCK FACE by *Bodley*, 1883 (Dean Addleshaw). The two men-at-arms date from 1528. STATUE of Christ with the Cross by *Fisher*, c. 1761. – K.O.Y.L.I. Chapel, fittings by *Tapper*. – IRON SCREEN (E side). 1925, by *Walter Tapper* and *Bainbridge Reynolds*, after one in the Capilla Real at Granada (Dean Addleshaw). – Iron SCREEN (s side). Late C 17 ironwork from the Lamplugh monument.

### Chapter house and vestibule

DOORS. Late C 13, with splendid, not overdone iron scrolls. – Similar scrollwork on two COPE CHESTS. – SCULPTURE. Against entrance *trumeau*, Virgin, late C 13; see *Chapter house* interior, above.

### South transept

The SOUTH DOOR has blank tracery; Perp. C 18 Gothick inner face by *Kent* (Cocke). – The iron GATES to the choir aisle are like those in the N transept. – In the W aisle, iron SCREENS by *Walter Tapper* and *Bainbridge Reynolds*, 1926–9. They are designed on a scale with their surroundings.

### Nave

PULPIT. 1948, by *Comper* in a late C 17 style. – LECTERN. A big brass eagle, presented in 1686. Almost identical with that of 1683 in St Mary-le-Port at Bristol. – SWORD-REST, close to the lectern, C 18; nothing special. – DRAGON BRACKET in N triforium a copy of one which formerly supported a font cover. – PAVEMENT. 1731–5, to a design by *Lord Burlington* and *William Kent*, extending also into the transepts (and originally in the choir). A major work costing £4,000, using black marble and local Yorkstone, for a vast geometrical design with Greek key patterns up the aisles, all sadly obscured by seating, and never fully re-

instated at the W end after the recent restoration. (Incidentally, Gilbert Scott's fine black-and-white pavement at Worcester (q.v.), said to have been inspired by Amiens, is more like this at York, which itself may relate to Amiens.)

### MONUMENTS, E TO W

### Lady Chapel

On the E wall Archbishop Frewen †1664. Recumbent effigy. The reredos back with a broken pediment with scrolly top, typical of about that date. – Frances Matthew †1629. Small kneeling figure between columns and under looped drapery. Two statuettes l. and r. – Archbishop Sharp †1714. By *Bird*. Black and white. Semi-reclining figure on a black sarcophagus. Reredos of four pilasters. Drapery looped back from the inscription. – In the N arcade Archbishop le Scrope †1405. Tomb-chest with four shields in quatrefoils. – Archbishop Markham, 1844, to *Salvin's* design, brass by *T. Willement*. – In the s arcade Archbishop Bowet †1423. High canopy; no effigy. Panelled E and W walls and four-centred arch inside. Top with pendant vaultlets and tall open niches with figures. – Archbishop Matthew †1628. The recumbent effigy only.

NORTH AISLE. A telling contrast between the inscription tablets of Lionel Ingram † c. 1623–4 and Samuel Brearey †1735. – Other C 18 tablets, charming cartouches to the Gibson family. – Dr John Dealtry †1773. Signed *Fishers*, i.e. John I and II. Standing figure by an urn. Good, if rather cold, but the architectural detail exquisite. – Admiral Medley †1747. Bust with naval trophies l. and r. On the sarcophagus a naval battle. Weeping putti l. and r. on the sarcophagus. The monument is by *Sir Henry Cheere*, who was paid £262 10s. od. for it.

SOUTH AISLE. John Piers †1594. Inscription tablet with two columns and strapwork. – Anne Benet, 1616, by *Nicholas Stone*. Small, of alabaster; excellent. Frontal demi-figure with two harpies l. and r. and two more below. – William Wentworth, Earl of Strafford, †1695, attributed to *J. Nost*. Large, standing monument of a type fashionable about 1700. Two standing figures and an urn between. Reredos back wall. – William Burgh †1808. By *Sir R. Westmacott*. Standing white Faith with a black wooden cross. – Elizabeth Eynnes †1585. Brass bust.

### North choir aisle

Lady Mary Fenwick †1708. Standing monument. Black and white marble. Bust at the top. – Sir William Ingram †1623. Two frontal demi-figures and two allegorical caryatids. – Henry Swinburne †1623. Standing monument. Kneeling figure. Three small allegories l. and r. and above. – Opposite: Thomas Watson-Wentworth †1723. By *Guelfi* to a design of *William Kent*. White standing monument. Standing figure leaning on an urn. His wife seated lower down on the r. There is now no back panel. – Archbishop Savage † 1507. Recumbent effigy in a heavy Perp surround with shallow panelled niches l. and r. Recess with four-centred arch all panelled. The wooden super-structure, 1949, by *Richardson*. – Again opposite, Henry Belassis, by *Nicholas Stone*, 1615–16. Rather conventional for him. Standing monument with two large kneeling figures, both facing E. – Several attractive Georgian tablets. – Archbishop Sterne † 1683. Standing monument. Reclining figure in a square recess. Drapes, pretty garlands and a semicircular pediment. Putti l. and r. – Archbishop Musgrave. Recumbent effigy by *Matthew Noble*; 1864, on a plinth by *J. R. Brandon*. – Dr Beckwith † 1843, effigy by *J. B. Leyland*. – Archbishop Vernon Harcourt, also recumbent, again by *Noble*; 1863. – Prince William of Hatfield, son of Edward III, † 1344 aged eight. Small alabaster effigy, recumbent with a long mantle, worn but of beautiful quality. Set in a shrine-like arrangement running the full height of the aisle; three tiers of tripartite, vaulted canopies above a tomb-chest with tracery of squares and other odd shapes, not at all flowing. – Sir George Savile, 1789, by *John Fisher*. White statue in contemporary dress, but with a toga. He is holding the 'petition of the freeholders'. Elegant pose and impeccable craftsmanship, but stylistically still mid-century.

### South choir aisle

Archbishop Lamplugh † 1691. By *Grinling Gibbons*, who was paid £100 for it. Like most of Gibbons's stone sculpture, stiff and awkward. Standing figure in a heavy surround. The top is a segmental pediment. – Edmund Bunny † 1617. Painted tablet with kneeling figure. – Nicholas Wanton † 1617. Tablet with a frontal kneeler. No space for legs, of course. – Opposite, Archbishop Dolben † 1686. White marble. Semi-reclining effigy. Reredos with a pretty group of putti on a cloud. – Again opposite, Henry and Edward Finch, 1729, by *Rysbrack*. White, with a convex front. Two busts and an urn between. – Archbishop Hutton † 1605. Standing monument, the effigy lying stiffly on his side. Three kneeling figures below. Back panel with strapwork. – William Gee, dated 1611. Large and bad. Three kneeling figures, the middle one frontal. Small kneeling figures below. – John Hodson † 1636. Simple tablet with columns and a pediment. Two putti on it. – William Wickham † 1840, by *J. E. Hinchliff*, a chaste contrast in pediments. – *Europa* troopship memorial, by *John Birnie Philip*, 1858. With a small scene. – William Mason (Horace Walpole's friend) † 1797, and his nephew William Dixon † 1854, made in 1862 by *F. A. Skidmore*. Gothic tablet of metal with a prickly gable and alabaster statuettes. – Nineteenth Regiment, 1855. Large brass plate with incised figures. By *John Hardman Powell*.

### North transept

Rear-Admiral Sir Christopher Cradock † 1914. By *Pomeroy*. Alabaster tablet, tripartite. Portrait medallion and two bronze statuettes. – WEST AISLE. War Memorial of the King's Own Yorkshire Light Infantry by *Voysey*, 1920. – Thomas de Haxey, *c.* 1424. Grim. A cadaver behind a grating. – EAST AISLE. Archbishop Greenfield † 1316. Brass, 4 ft 2 in. long, the brass surround missing, but a sumptuous architectural surround. Tomb-chest with heavily crocketed arches. Canopy of the type of Aymer de Valence in Westminster Abbey. Cusped and subcusped arch, a blank trefoil in the gable. Crockets and finial. Tall, multiple flanking pinnacles. Longitudinal wall above disguised as a gable. No ogee at all yet, which is instructive for York chronology. – The ALTAR next to this monument is the tomb-chest of Archbishop Rotherham † 1500.

### South transept

Archbishop Thompson. By *Bodley*, 1896. Recumbent effigy by *Sir Hamo Thornycroft*. Angels on the tomb-chest. Gothic triple canopy. – Archbishop Walter de Gray † 1255. The finest of the monuments in the Minster. Tomb-chest with Purbeck effigy. L. and r. shafts with stiff-leaf sprays. The shafts carry a gable. Angels in the spandrels. Over the tomb-chest a canopy of three by two bays on originally ten Purbeck shafts (now nine). They carry pointed-trefoiled arches. Stiff-leaf capitals, stiff-leaf in the spandrels. Roof with three by one blank gabled arches, also pointed-trefoiled. The big finials are by *Bernasconi*, 1803–5 (Barr). In 1968 it was discovered that the lid of the Archbishop's coffin carried a life-size painting of the deceased, an effigy presumably done to commemorate him before the coffin went into the tomb-chest of the monument. The archbishop is represented frontal, his staff in one raised hand, blessing with the other. The colours are those of C 13 illuminated manuscripts – red, blue, green, all mild rather than faded. Unfortunately little survives of the face. – Archbishop Ludham † 1265. Purbeck marble slab on trefoil arcade. – Dean Duncombe † 1880. Designed by *Street*, the recumbent effigy by *Boehm*. At his feet three choristers. Gothic canopy.

### Nave

NORTH AISLE. Much restored Late Perp. monument with quatrefoil panelling and a four-centred arch. – SOUTH AISLE. Brass tablet to John Coteril † 1595.

STAINED GLASS

Introduction by Ben Johnson, revised, pp. 355–8. Description by David O'Connor, pp. 358–66. (See also O'Connor and Haselock, 'The Stained and Painted Glass', in Aylmer and Cant 1977.)

The pulling down of Archbishop Roger's church to make way for the rebuilding of York Minster between c. 1230 and c. 1475 entailed glazing in new styles and consequent loss of nearly all the c 12 glass. Some panels and fragments do survive, although their precise origins are not clear. But from the c 13 on, no single building in England can approach York Minster for sheer quantity of medieval glass, and few churches in Europe have retained their original glazing on such a scale.

York glass may not have suffered as much as other places at the hands of over-zealous Protestant reformers, but it was certainly at risk during the siege of the city by Parliamentary forces under Lord Fairfax, prior to the Battle of Marston Moor (1644). An eye-witness records that cannon balls damaged some of the Minster windows, but excessive destruction was avoided when Fairfax accepted as a condition of York's surrender that no harm should come to the Minster or to the parish churches. More recently, during the Second World War, many windows were removed to safety. Perhaps more damage has been caused by neglect and lack of maintenance in the past.

Medieval York fulfilled all the requirements for becoming a centre of glass painting in having wealthy patrons and access to raw materials. Glass, the heavy basic commodity, was readily imported through Hull and transported up river to York. Little or no coloured glass was manufactured in England and that evidently of poor quality. The chief sources for coloured and white glass were areas along the Rhine, Burgundy, Lorraine, Flanders and France. Lists of ships' cargoes consigned to Hull describe glass as 'Renysshe' and 'Hessian' or as coming from Burgundy.

York, it must be remembered, was a prosperous commercial centre during the c 14 and c 15, trading in locally produced wool and other commodities with the Low Countries through the York Merchant Venturers and the German Hanse, which had depots in the city and at Hull. Consequently there was no shortage of wealth to support the glass painters. Many patrons' names are known. Their social status varies from mercantile middle class to ecclesiastics and nobility. St William's Window in the Minster was paid for by members of the Ros family. One must have gained a certain prestige from giving things seen publicly, and one's name lived on after death. What is more, gifts to religious establishments weighed well in the balance. No doubt there were less exalted motives: Walter Skirlaw in arranging to pay for the great E window in York Minster may have been trying to gain favour as a possible candidate for the archbishopric, which fell vacant in 1405.

As well as donors', many York glaziers' names are known, mostly from the Rolls of Freemen. Twenty-two names of undoubted glaziers are recorded for the c 14, the earliest being 'Laurentius de Stok, verrour' and 'Walterus le verrour', made freemen of York in 1313. During the c 15

recorded names more than double to some fifty-two, which is a measure of both increased production and increased patronage. Numbers in the Freemen's Rolls fall off in the c 16 to thirty-seven, but after the Reformation few of these are likely to have been glass painters. In the c 17 Henry Gyles is the only glass painter for whom there is firm evidence. J. A. Knowles has shown that the craft of glazing in York was frequently handed down within families. During the c 14 the craft was practised by a number of Prestons, who may have been related, and during the c 15 a number of recognizable families are recorded: the Chamber family working from c. 1400–50, the Inglishes from c. 1450 till after 1503, the Shirleys 1439 till after 1463, the Shirwyns at the end of the c 15, the Pettys from c. 1470 to c. 1528, and the Thompsons from 1492 till after 1613. But while many names are known from the c 14 and c 15 (and it is c 14 and c 15 glass that York has most of), in only a few instances do we have documentary evidence for the glazier of a particular window. A Master Robert (Ketelbarn?) and Thomas de Bouesdun glazed the three w windows of the Minster, c. 1339; John Thornton was brought from Coventry to supervise the glazing of the great E window (1405–8); and Matthew Petty and others were paid in 1471 for painting the crossed keys emblem of the Dean and Chapter forty-eight times in the central tower.

York glaziers were organized as a guild, from what date is not clear. Of the two sets of ordinances, the earlier is c. 1380 and the other 1463–4. By the early c 14 the craft was in the hands of local people, and there is justification in referring to a York school of glass painters. Just what and when were the school's beginnings the paucity of extant glass prior to 1300 and the lack of documentation prevent one from knowing, but subsequent developments are fairly clear in broad outline, although a great many details are still to be filled in.

Amongst the earliest stained glass in York is a single panel from a Jesse window (now in the bottom row, second window from the w, nave N aisle). Whether it marks the beginning of glass painting in York it is not possible to say. In design it resembles Jesse windows at St-Denis (c. 1142–4) and Chartres (c. 1150–5), but the painting style suggests a date of c. 1170–80, and it probably once adorned Archbishop Roger's choir. From the same series comes the St Nicholas panel (easternmost window, s nave aisle) and various panels re-used in the nave clerestory. Another c 12 panel, of different type, is at the foot of the Five Sisters Window in the N transept, and represents Habakkuk giving relief to Daniel in the Lions' Den. These panels represent the kind of glass and colour effect which, multiplied many times, one would have found in Archbishop Roger's choir (1151–81). Such narrative panels were probably parts of medallion windows, the type where narrative scenes from the Old and New Testaments or saints' legends were

197. YORK Stained glass, c. 1170–80 for Roger's choir (?), now south nave aisle. Miracle of St Nicholas

adjoining sides of each piece of glass to give an effect when leaded together of trellis-work supporting foliage. The finished effect was a subtle interplay of various layers (rigid geometry, trellis, and curling leaf stems) against a whitish-grey ground.

Possibly because grisaille glass was too subtle and a little uninteresting, it was, before the end of the C 13, relieved by coloured panels. The drawing of foliage on grisaille glass had become more naturalistic; individual species are recognizable and leaves spring more realistically from central stems. The earliest York examples of these characteristics are in the chapter house. These windows (c. 1285) have narrative scenes from the lives of Christ and a number of saints in geometric medallions set in a grisaille glass ground patterned with leaves that spring from a central stem running the length of each window and curling over trellis-work. A subsequent development can be seen in the nave aisle windows (c. 1310–20). They continue the use of naturalistic foliage and trellis painted on grisaille glass, but narrative scenes are now set beneath canopies in rectangular panels in a horizontal double row running the length of each aisle. Strips of coloured glass alternate with strips of white to counteract the architecture's vertical lines.

Several features of Dec glass can be noted in the nave aisle windows: borders as a decorative aid, donor figures, heraldry, canopies and the use of yellow stain (also called silver stain, being derived from a compound of silver). York glaziers are amongst the earliest users of yellow stain. Medieval glass was coloured in manufacture, which meant that coloured areas had always to be cut to shape and leaded into a design. Yellow stain, on the other hand, could be applied wherever required and was most frequently used for hair, crowns, drapery patterns. The nave aisle windows provide examples of its early use.

Borders of these windows are very distinctive. They carry various devices, sometimes heraldic, occasionally a donor's initials, quite often figures in niches – the Bell-founders' Window not surprisingly has bells. That glass painters were not ignorant of developments in manuscript painting is clear from the borders of the fifth window from the W in the N aisle (sometimes called Pilgrimage Window). Along the bases are illustrations from fables, a satirical monkey funeral, and a hunting scene, while at the sides monkeys and squirrels clamber among vine stems. Similar subjects in profusion can be found in the borders of East Anglian manuscripts, e.g. the Peterborough Psalter of c. 1300 and Queen Mary's Psalter of the early C 14. The developments in naturalism mentioned earlier also reflect contemporary trends in other media, e.g. the East Anglian manuscripts again and the leaf capitals of Southwell Minster (q.v.).

Heraldry, increasingly important, appears in traceries and borders and quite often as the subject of a window, e.g.

enclosed in a geometric frame (circles, quatrefoils etc.) and disposed symmetrically to fill the window space. Spandrels and areas between scenes were filled with foliage decoration or with plain or diapered glass. This type of design was in general use, examples being found in Chartres, Bourges and Canterbury. Other types of window were also favoured, such as figure windows and rose-windows.

In contrast to the colourful brilliance of the medallion and figured windows, the introduction of 'grisaille' during the C 13 struck a note of restraint. It has been suggested that the plain white windows of the Cistercians were influential in this respect. In York's case there were nearby foundations at Kirkstall, Fountains, Byland and Rievaulx. In general Cistercian interiors were light and airy, while coloured glass tended to make interiors dark. It may have been this factor, rather than the Cistercians' prohibition against windows with figures and crosses, that accounts for the use of grisaille glass in York and for its introduction generally. Grisaille windows were also much cheaper and more easily produced than coloured, a consideration no doubt appreciated by the Dean and Chapter when confronted with filling the larger E.E. windows in the Minster's N transept.

The best example of grisaille glass in York is the Five Sisters Window in the N transept. Its original overall design has been lost, but enough glass remains to suggest some of its original appearance. Several rows of geometric shapes were each filled with a regular pattern of leaves and stems painted on white glass. A line was painted along two the nave clerestory lights. Donors are included, usually at the bases of windows – e.g. the nave N aisle window, fourth from the W, where the donor presents the window he has paid for – but sometimes in tracery or tops of lights. Architecturally windows have again changed shape. Glaziers now have to contend with several lights in a single window and have a number of difficult tracery openings to fill.

Canopies are a special feature of windows from the late C 13 to the early C 16. The changes in design are legion and not readily condensed. In general they reflect contemporary architectural styles and decoration, at the same time increasing in complexity. An approximate line of development for the York school may be traced from the late C 13 canopies in the chapter house and vestibule, through the early C 14 nave aisle windows, to the W windows of c. 1339, which have taller canopies and a three-dimensional hint in the side shaftings. Figures are introduced too. A transitional window in the Minster (third from E, S choir aisle E) of c. 1375 has spires, hexagonal shafts and turrets with figures. Close to the work of Thomas of Oxford (c. 1385) in New College Chapel, Oxford, are remnants of a Creed series (choir clerestory N, second and third from E, and S, third from E) which have been attributed to *John Burgh*. *John Thornton*'s complex, elegant canopies in the great E window (1405–8) vary in design. They show interior vaulting and have a great many pinnacles and mounting gables, sometimes with figures, together with seated and standing figures in the side shaftings. There is more to be said about Thornton.

When the rebuilding of the Minster's E end was completed, it presented windows to be filled on a scale unprecedented in York. Were the York glaziers up to the task? Such seems not to have been the opinion of the Dean and Chapter, for the plum job of filling the great E window went to *John Thornton*, specially brought in from Coventry. To judge from the Freemen's Roll, most York glaziers were either natives of York or from nearby villages and towns. Strangers were rare; two are recorded, *Johannes de Ireland* (1352) and of course John Thornton. A number of outbreaks of plague between 1349 and 1390 may have reduced the number of York glaziers and provided a few openings for outsiders. Some decline in quality is certainly apparent towards the end of the C 14, although whether this is due to the untimely demise of some York masters through plague or to other reasons is not clear.

It is most unlikely that John Thornton would have been employed without having proved his abilities to someone connected with York. Most probably this was Richard Scrope, Bishop of Lichfield and Coventry from 1386 till he became Archbishop of York in 1398. Thornton's origins are unknown. He may have had some connection with Thomas of Oxford, but this has yet to be established. One may surmise, however, that reports of the new style of glass painting practised by Thomas of Oxford under the patronage of William of Wykeham in Winchester and Oxford reached York, and that the Dean and Chapter were after some comparable work for the new building. Thornton's work has all the characteristics of the then fashionable International style.

Without doubt Thornton revitalized the York school with his command of scale, draughtsmanship and dramatic narrative. Several changes took place. Narrative expanded enormously in the much enlarged Perp windows; eighty-one scenes illustrate the Apocalypse in the Minster E window; 105 relate St William's life in St William's Window. There are changes in background designs from diapers to fernleaf, and of course changes in figure styles. Colour counterchange, usually alternate red and blue, between picture and canopy grounds, and from light to light, is adopted as a regular feature. Painted white glass is more extensively used for figures and canopies, while the range of coloured glass is less. Colours are less subtle, but brighter, which may be due to improved manufacture allowing fewer impurities into the pot metal. Changes in tonality that occur between the C 14 and the C 15 are readily apparent if one contrasts the mid-C 14 windows in the S choir clerestory E and the great E window. Not all of these changes are directly attributable to Thornton.

Just how much work Thornton did in York has yet to be established; only the Minster E window is documented as by him. Made a freeman in 1410, he was still alive in 1433. He had a number of assistants working under him on the E window and it is likely that these subsequently formed a nucleus of glass painters working in his style. St William's Window may have been supervised by Thornton. It is clear that York glass painting after 1408 bears the unmistakable stamp of his influence, although, as in the N choir clerestory W windows, the effect is sometimes stereotyped.

Existing types of painted window, such as the Jesse Tree, or canopied single figures, continued in use during the late C 14 and C 15, but with the addition of the costly large-scale narrative windows already mentioned and a much cheaper new type. This was the single figure in painted white and coloured glass standing in a token landscape setting or set on plain quarries with no other adornments except perhaps a heraldic device. A series of these fills the S transept E wall windows. Cost of windows was usually estimated by the square foot, and prices varied with the type of window required, the amount of coloured glass used, and the complexity of design. As in other areas of medieval craftsmanship, the patron got what he paid for.

The rose-window and upper lancets of the S transept S wall were the last major work by the medieval glass painters in the Minster. Radiating pairs of white and red roses commemorate the union of York and Lancaster.

From the end of the C 15 glass painters from the Low Countries are found working in England. The change in religious climate with the Reformation depressed the market for picture windows, although heraldic windows maintained their popularity. We have already remarked on the decreasing numbers of glass painters resident in York in the C 16–17. The work of *Henry Gyles* (1645–1709) is largely heraldic and executed in enamelled glass. Production of coloured glass seriously declined when Lorraine, the primary source, was ravaged by Louis XIII in 1636 and glass works were demolished along with castles and other buildings. While glass painters had used enamelled and coloured glass together, they were now limited to yellow stain and enamelling to obtain colours. Enamelling involved the application of small quantities of ground coloured glass in a medium to white glass. This in turn introduced new design principles. The medieval mosaic principle of leading pieces of coloured and white glass into a design was frequently unsuitable, especially as heraldic devices became more and more complex. Enamels, on the other hand, could be disposed freely and accurately whenever required on a single piece of white glass resulting in fewer lead lines. Consequently windows tended to be made up from square or other regular shaped panels. An example of these by *Henry Gyles* is the arms of Archbishop Lamplugh (c. 1690) in the s choir aisle.

There is no definite record of any glass painter in York between the death of Henry Gyles in 1709 and 1753, when *William Peckitt* (1731–95) produced his first sample piece for the Guildhall's Old Council Chamber. Peckitt reintroduced colour in large areas in his windows and took out a patent (1780) for his own method of manufacturing sheets of coloured glass from white. The method seems to have been the medieval process of flashing, but results tended to be lurid and uneven. These he leaded together in characteristic abstract regular patterns. He provided the Minster with much coloured glass, undertook a number of restorations, and supplied windows as far afield as Lincoln (1762), New College, Oxford (1764–74), and Exeter Cathedral (1766). For the New College work he received, as part payment, a portion of the Jesse Tree by *Thomas of Oxford*, now in the Minster s choir aisle.

The C 17 and C 18 saw considerable neglect of English medieval glass. However, interest in the medieval mosaic principle of design revived during the C 19 and stained-glass windows were again manufactured in quantity. In general the Gothic Revival led to much restoration of ancient glass and to many new windows, pseudo-medieval in style. At the beginning of the century there had been little glass production at York. When the Rouen Visitation was given to the Minster in 1804 (easternmost s choir aisle), *James Pearson* of London extended the glass and painted new armorials. In 1809 *Jacob Wright* of Leeds

made the large armorial window in the Archbishops' Chapel (Minster Library). But c. 1820 the Barnett family began to produce windows at York. *John Barnett*'s 'restoration' of the chapter-house E window (1845), praised by the *Ecclesiologist*, was a virtual facsimile of the original (and can now be seen in the nave clerestory). At the end of the century, between 1899 and 1903, *Kempe & Co.* in the transepts followed closely the C 15 scheme while attempting to add their own touches of splendour, not aggressively out of sympathy with the overall concept of the transept glazing. Of more recent glass, an armorial by *Harcourt Doyle* and three panels by *Harry Stammers* have fitted in. But a window of 1944 by *Ervin Bossanyi*, inserted in the Zouche Chapel in 1975, is aggressive in style and colour.

Here begins detailed description of the stained glass.

### Eastern arm

(From N W choir aisle to E end to S W choir aisle, including E transepts, and followed by clerestories.)

### North-west choir aisle, W to E

Three stylistically related windows of c. 1420–35 perhaps by glaziers trained in John Thornton's workshop. In the first, the gift of Henry Bowet, Archbishop of York in 1407–23 (from l. to r., the subjects reading from top to bottom): St Paul, St Paul's conversion, preaching, and martyrdom; Virgin and Child, Annunciation, Adoration of the Magi, Archbishop Bowet kneeling before an altar bearing his arms (cf. the similar panel of Walter Skirlaw in Thornton's E window); St Peter, St Peter walking on the sea, in prison, and his crucifixion. – In the second, the gift of Thomas Parker, canon in 1410–23: St John of Beverley, the saint celebrating mass, King Athelstan placing a sword on an altar, donor; St Thomas of Canterbury, Thomas as Chancellor with Henry II, the saint's enthronement, his martyrdom; St William of York, collapse of the Ouse bridge, the saint's enthronement, healing at his shrine. – In the last, the gift of Robert Wolveden, canon and treasurer in 1426–32: St Chad, St Chad saving a hart, Wulfhere king of Mercia killing his son, death of St Chad; St Paulinus, St Paulinus's enthronement, preaching before King Edwin, donor; St Nicholas, St Nicholas's steward dispensing alms, miracle of Jewish money-lender, the saint resurrecting three boys.

### North-east transept

ST WILLIAM'S WINDOW. 1422, given by members of the de Ros family of Helmsley Castle, who appear in the bottom row. The other hundred panels show episodes and miracles from the life of St William. The illustration of medieval dress and customs is characteristic of the new large-scale narrative windows – cf. the great E window and St Cuthbert's Window in the S E transept. In the tracery Christ and the Virgin in the apex with archbishops, kings and angels.

### North-east choir aisle, W to E

Composite St Edward the Confessor, mid-C 14 St Vincent, C 15 St Peter, above composite panels of the resurrected Christ appearing to St Mary Magdalene and to St Peter (the initials R.S. in the border refer to Archbishop Richard Scrope †1405). – Alternate rows of Passion scenes and prophets, mid-C 14: Tribute Money, Garden of Gethsemane, Disciples; Zechariah, David, Malachi; Entry into Jerusalem, Christ washing the Disciples' feet, the Last Supper; Jeremiah, unidentified prophet, Joel. At the bottom three mid-C 14 panels, an archbishop, tracery light with lion's mask, St John the Baptist. – Impressive figures of St Stephen, St Christopher and St Lawrence by the *Master Robert Workshop*, c. 1340: below a mid-C 15 Coronation of Virgin between two mid-C 14 tracery lights; at bottom, made-up Annunciation, a C 14 tracery light, and made-up Noli Me Tangere. Armorials in the tracery, 1971, by *King & Son* of Norwich. – Seven scenes from the legend of St James the Great told from bottom l. to top r.; North French Renaissance glass of mid-C 16; at top r. C 18 Nativity. Armorial in tracery, *King & Son*, 1971.

### East end

ST STEPHEN'S CHAPEL, E window, of uneven quality, c. 1420. Crucifixion with the Virgin and St John above a mid-C 14 St James the Great flanked by four scenes from the life of St Stephen: martyrdom, trial, preaching, pilgrims at the saint's shrine. In the tracery Virgin and Child, St Stephen, St Lawrence, six angels making music.

GREAT EAST WINDOW. *John Thornton* of Coventry contracted in 1405 to execute the window within three years; this he duly did, and the completion date of 1408 appears together with his monogram in the apex of the traceries. Thornton was to provide glass, lead and workmen, paid for by the Dean and Chapter, and to receive 4s. for every week he worked, plus £5 after each year and an extra £10 if the work was completed on time. He set new standards in draughtsmanship and dramatic narrative and revitalized the York school of glass painters – a fact to which the St William and St Cuthbert windows bear witness. The donor, Walter Skirlaw, Bishop of Durham, † 1408, appears at the centre of the bottom row of kings and ecclesiastics connected with the history of York. The theme of the window is symbolized in the tracery apex by God enthroned, holding the text 'Ego sum Alpha et Omega'. Below him are Old Testament figures, saints and the nine orders of angels. The narrative part consists of twenty-seven panels in three rows illustrating the Old Testament

from the Creation to the death of Absalom, and eighty-one panels in nine rows illustrating the legend of St John and his Revelation – one of the most extensive Apocalypse series in medieval art and unique in glass painting.

ALL SAINTS' CHAPEL, E window. In the centre a mid-C 14 St James the Great, from the same series as windows two and three from the E in the S E clerestory, surrounded by fragmentary and crudely restored panels of c. 1375 illustrating the legend of St Edward the Confessor, the pilgrims and St John. In the tracery, Massacre of Innocents; St John boiled in oil and drinking poisoned cup; at top C 17 armorial.

### South-east choir aisle, E to W

Two panels with the Fall of Man, part of a Triumph of the Virgin window from Rouen, after Engrand le Prince, c. 1530; also from Rouen, imposing Visitation of 1625 after Raphael Sadeler. It was presented to the Minster in 1804 and set up with the armorials above and below by *James Pearson*, 1805–11. – Mid-C 15 Isaiah, Trinity, King Edwin, with two panels of St Catherine and Marriage scene below. In the tracery armorials by *King & Son*, 1971. – A window of c. 1375 with St James the Great, St Edward the Confessor, St John the Evangelist; Massacre of the Innocents, Christ and the Doctors, Baptism of Christ; Virgin and Child between two patched armorials. – Renaissance style Crucifixion from Rouen, c. 1530, with armorials by *Harry Stammers*, 1952. Beneath are armorials of Princess Elizabeth, daughter of James I, 1613; Archbishop Thomas Lamplugh, by *Henry Gyles*, c. 1691; Archbishop John Williams but as Bishop of Lincoln, 1626 (on whom see also our other volume: London, Westminster Abbey, Jerusalem Chamber).

### South-east transept

ST CUTHBERT'S WINDOW. The gift of Thomas Langley †1437, Bishop of Durham and formerly canon and dean of York. He can be seen in a panel at the bottom r. next to John Kemp with his cardinal's hat; since Kemp became a cardinal in 1443, the window can probably be dated after that year. In the lowest division St Cuthbert holding the head of King Oswald, surrounded by kneeling members of the Lancastrian dynasty and ecclesiastics. Above are seventy-five episodes from the life of St Cuthbert. Ten of the main scenes and the tracery lights are by *J. W. Knowles*, who restored the window in 1887.

### South-west choir aisle, E to W

Part of a Jesse Tree by *Thomas of Oxford*, c. 1385, formerly part of the W window in New College Chapel, Oxford, given to William Peckitt in part payment for a replacement W window which he completed in 1765. The figures from the Doom in the tracery lights are stylistically less ad-

198. YORK Stained glass, 1405–8, great east window (detail).
Four scenes from Revelation Chapters 14 and 16, by John Thornton

vanced than the 'soft-style' kings and prophets above and beneath. Peckitt's own additions are obvious. – Holy Family window of c. 1420 celebrating three marriages. Salome and Zebedee with St John the Evangelist and St James the Great above the marriage of Joachim and Anna and Joachim and Anna at the Golden Gate; Joachim and Anna with the Virgin and Child above the rejection of Joachim's offering and the Birth of the Virgin; St Mary Cleophas, her husband Alphaeus, and their four children, and St Simon, St Jude, St James the Less and St Joseph the Just above the Annunciation to Joachim and the Presentation of the Virgin in the Temple. – In the tracery modern armorials by *King & Son*, 1971. – Reconstructed window of c. 1420 with l. three scenes from martyrdom of St John the Baptist; centre, two scenes from the Passion above Symbols of the Passion by *Harry Stammers*, 1956; r. Martyrdoms of St Ursula, St Edmund and St Thomas of Canterbury; lower down are the Mass of St Gregory and the Mass of St John of Beverley, c. 1420, flanked by two rather composite mid-c 15 panels from the Te Deum series in the N transept. In the tracery, armorials by *King & Son*, 1971.

Off the sw choir aisle, the glass in the ZOUCHE CHAPEL. E window, a pleasing kaleidoscope of fragments including several early c 14 pieces from the Mauley Window in the nave. Below are three panels of a bishop, Henry VI, and Cardinal John Kemp, Archbishop of York 1426–52; late c 15 and not original to the Minster. In the s wall easternmost, St Francis freeing birds and healing a leper, *Ervin Bossanyi*, 1944, but presented to the Minster and inserted in 1975. – Next two windows, mainly small-scale c 14–16 quarries and fragments with birds, animals and amusing genre scenes.

*Clerestories, eastern arm (w to E, N before s)*

NORTH-WEST. Four windows of c. 1410–30 with a series of single figures of kings and ecclesiastics under canopies with armorials beneath. They illustrate the history of Christianity in the North. From w to E: St Edwin, St Gregory the Great(?), King Edward III, St Paulinus; in the lower tracery, Prophets. – St Aidan(?), St Oswald, St Honorius, St Oswin, St Finan; in the tracery, Old Testament kings and apostles. – St Bosa, King Oswy, St Agatho, King Alfrid of Northumbria, St Wilfrid; in the tracery Coronation of the Virgin, female saints, male saints, prophets and angels. – St John of Beverley, St Ceolwulf, Pope J(ohn IV?), King Eadbert, St Wilfrid II; ecclesiastical saints, Old Testament prophets and kings.

SOUTH-WEST. Four windows continuing the series opposite. From w to E: archbishop, king, St Eleutherius, King Lucius; in the tracery the Coronation of the Virgin and fragmentary figures of saints, apostles and ecclesiastics. – Archbishop Thadiocus(?), King Cadwallader, Pope Vigilius, King Arthur, St Sampson; in the tracery mainly

popes. – Archbishop, king, pope, king, St Sigfrid of Wearmouth; in the tracery fragmentary figures of popes and female saints. – Mutilated figures of archbishop, king, pope, king, archbishop; in the tracery remnants of saints and prophets.

EAST TRANSEPT (i.e. flanking each main window). (N) Four armorials in the top tracery lights. (s) Two windows of the second quarter of the c 15: the unofficial saint Archbishop Richard Scrope and the kneeling figure of his brother Stephen with armorials (E) and St William of York and Robert Wolveden with armorials (w).

NORTH-EAST. From w to E. Two windows with apostles and prophets from a Creed series, c. 1385. St Peter, St Andrew, St James the Great, St John, St Thomas. – St James the Less, King David, Amos, Daniel, St Philip (the latter by *John Barnett*, 1831). – Two plain windows.

SOUTH-EAST. From w to E. Prophets from same series as those opposite, c. 1385. Zephaniah, Haggai, Joel, Hosea, Jeremiah. – Two windows with exceptionally fine mid-c 14 narrative panels above figures of saints under canopies: Death of Virgin, Funeral of Virgin, Coronation of Virgin, Pentecost, Noli Me Tangere, above St Matthew, St Thomas, St Jude, St Margaret, St Helen. – Adoration of the Magi, Massacre of the Innocents, Presentation, Flight into Egypt, Annunciation of the Death of Virgin, above St Matthias, St Paul, St John the Evangelist, St Andrew, St Bartholomew. – Glass from St Paul's Middlesbrough, by *Victor Milner*, 1909; St Peter, the Virgin Mary, St John the Evangelist, St James the Great, above St Augustine, St Alban, St Stephen, St Ambrose.

*Crossing, main transepts, chapter house*

*Crossing tower*

A double row of forty-eight shields with the arms of the Minster by *Matthew Petty* and others, 1471.

*South transept*

EAST WALL. Five lancets with single figures of c. 1434 set on quarries (a popular and inexpensive type of c 15 window): St William of York, St Michael, St Gabriel, St John the Baptist with donors, Virgin and Child. Original armorials above, those below by *King & Son*, 1978.

SOUTH WALL. Rose-window with roses of York and Lancaster (c. 1515) and central sunflower (1793). Four lancets below, early c 16: St William of York, St Peter, St Paul, St Wilfrid, with corresponding armorials. Below again Abraham (1780), Solomon (1780), Moses (1793), St Peter (1768) above armorials, all by *Peckitt*. In the two easternmost lancets St George and St Oswald by *Kempe*, 1890, in the two westernmost St Sampson and St William of York by *Kempe & Co.*, 1907, with grisaille of c. 1240 in the heads of the lights.

199. YORK Stained glass, 1780, south transept. Solomon, by William Peckitt

WEST WALL (ST GEORGE'S CHAPEL). Two lancets with high-quality mid-c15 glass, from St Martin, Coney Street, York (?). Series of Te Deum panels with a reconstructed Trinity in the second window.

*North transept*

WEST WALL (ST JOHN'S CHAPEL). Four single lancets with glass from St John Micklegate, York. In the first, four scenes from the life of St John the Baptist and two donor panels, mid-c14, workshop of *Master Robert*; grisaille below *c.* 1300. In the second, incomplete St John the Baptist and donor panel, mid-c14; Coronation of Virgin, mid-c15; grisaille, *c.* 1300. The next two lancets contain remains of a window commemorating Sir Richard Yorke, Lord Mayor, † 1498. Above are tracery-light angels with shields of arms; beneath are Trinity, incomplete St George, fragment panels, St Christopher; then the donor and family with inserted Trinity; more mid-c14 donors, and at the bottom St Barbara and St Christopher, another donor and two heraldic panels by *Harry Stammers*, 1946.

NORTH WALL. In the N window of St John's Chapel twin lancets with c19 grisaille incorporating medallions with the arms of City of York (from St John Micklegate), an early c16 rose; St George and St Michael (from St John Micklegate), two armorials by *Reginald Bell*, 1933. In the transept N wall itself the FIVE SISTERS WINDOW, five lancets with grisaille glass of *c.* 1250, the outstanding example of glass of this type. Some traces of the original foliate pattern remain. The austere effect is only slightly relieved by the *c.* 1200 panel inserted in the bottom centre light of Habakkuk visiting Daniel in the Lions' Den. The grisaille in the upper lancets is modern.

EAST WALL. Five lancets of *c.* 1434 like those in the S transept. Three of the figures and the five armorials beneath are replacements by *Kempe*. St Peter (1902) with early c14 arms of Latimer above; St Paul (1899); St Lawrence (1902); St Stephen; St Nicholas.

*Chapter-house vestibule*

The glazing was done after that of the chapter house and before the nave aisles, *c.* 1290. – NORTH WALL, E to W. Single figures of saints under canopies; above, Christ between apostles; below, Virgin and Child between apostles. In the tracery re-used late c12 border fragments. – Second window, above, St John the Baptist, Coronation of the Virgin between censing angels, and crowned saint; below, St Peter, Crucifixion flanked by Virgin Mary and St John, St Paul. Tracery: mainly re-used late c12 glass.

WEST WALL, N to S. Above, St Mary (Cleophas?), St Elizabeth, Virgin and Child, St Mary Salome, St Anne?; below, crowned saint (Margaret?), St Catherine, St Mary of Egypt, St Mary (Magdalene?), St Martha?; at the bottom armorials. In the tracery mainly re-used late c12 borders. – Second window. Four pairs of kings and queens without inscriptions. Probably Edward I and Eleanor of Castile and their predecessors. In the tracery mainly re-used 'stiff-leaf' grisaille with some late c12 fragments. – Third window. Probably four saintly kings of England;

above, St Edward (Confessor or Martyr), St Oswald; below, two unidentified kings; bottom row, armorials; tracery, re-used C 12 and C 13 fragments.

SOUTH WALL. Above, St Robert (Grosseteste?), archbishop, St Edmund of Abingdon, bishop; below, St Stephen, St Lawrence, deacon, St Vincent; tracery, mainly re-used C 13 grisaille.

EAST WALL, N to S. Above, Doubting Thomas (over two lights), Ecclesia triumphant; below, Noli Me Tangere (over two lights), the fall of Synagogia; medieval fragments in the tracery. – Old Testament prophets; above, Jeremiah, Abraham, Isaiah; below, David, Moses, Daniel; armorials beneath. In the tracery some re-used C 13 grisaille.

*Chapter house*
In the chapter house itself, seven five-light windows, originally glazed *c.* 1285, of the type with narrative medallions on grisaille, here patterned with more naturalistic foliage than the Five Sisters Window in the N transept: leaves and branches spring from a central stem and individual species such as ivy and oak are readily identifiable (though the overall effect of the design is, alas, barely apparent because much of the original glass has been lost). Armorials in the tracery lights. The glass is described from l. to r. on entry. First, episodes from the life of St Catherine; tracery glass by *William Peckitt*, 1768. – Then scenes from the life of St William of York with the saint under a canopy at bottom centre. Not original to the Minster are two large circular medallions of the Coronation of the Virgin and the Virgin and Child and in the bottom row the drunkenness of Noah and an angel. – Scenes from the Infancy of Christ and the life of the Virgin Mary, from the Annunciation at bottom l. to the Assumption at top r. – E window. Of the original scheme of Passion and Resurrection scenes only the Ascension, bottom centre, survives. The window was severely 'restored' by *John Barnett*, 1845 (his borders and tracery lights remain), but his facsimiles were removed in 1959 and are now in the nave clerestory. The window now contains in the top two rows a series of *c.* 1430, Coronation of the Virgin, Ascension, Doubting Thomas, Supper at Emmaus, Road to Emmaus; Annunciation, Nativity, Harrowing of Hell, Resurrection, Noli Me Tangere; in the bottom two rows besides the original panel, nine scenes from a life of St Thomas of Canterbury, *c.* 1530, from St Michael-le-Belfrey Church, York, where others in the series survive. – Scenes from the life of St Peter. – Scenes from the life of St Paul. – Scenes from the lives of SS. Thomas of Canterbury (under canopies), Margaret, Nicholas, John the Baptist and Edmund.

*Nave*
The windows in both aisles once formed a unified decorative scheme in which alternate bands of grisaille and

coloured glass ran the length of the aisles acting as a counterpoint to the vertical lines of the architecture. Three windows do not fit this scheme: the Jesse window in the S aisle and the westernmost windows in both aisles. All the aisle windows are of *c.* 1310–20 unless otherwise indicated. The emphasis given to canopies and borders within the overall design is an important new feature of early C 14 windows. Narrative scenes are set beneath canopies in two rows across three main lights and each light is defined by a broad border. Heraldry, leaf stems and drolleries feature in these borders. Some windows contain yellow stain and are among the earliest known examples of its use. The grisaille glass is patterned with naturalistic foliage running over trellis-work, although the design is not often clear. The nave clerestory windows also form an early C 14 scheme, with two bands of colour on plain patterned glazing. Upper row of figure panels, including re-used late C 12 glass and later replacements. Lower row of mainly early C 14 armorials of royalty and northern magnates. Tracery lights recently replaced with modern glass.

*Nave south aisle,* E to W
Memorial to Archbishop William Greenfield † 1315. Mass scene, archbishop healing cripples, archbishop blessing layman; St Nicholas resuscitates three boys, archbishop protecting cleric from king, layman kneeling before cleric; at the bottom, fine late C 12 panel of the Conversion of the Jew (Christian thief caught by a cart) from a St Nicholas window, between fragmentary C 15 ecclesiastics. In the tracery glass of 1782 by *W. Peckitt*. Bishops and kings in the centre of the borders, flanked by the tower and cup of Eleanor of Castile. – Second window. Very reconstructed panels of Annunciation, Nativity, Baptism of Christ, Noli Me Tangere, donor, Christ appearing to the Virgin Mary; at the bottom, arms of the Worshipful Company of Glaziers, by *Harcourt Doyle*, 1949, between two C 16 Flemish roundels. In the tracery *Peckitt* glass of 1782, including at the top a fragment of Eve and the serpent. In the borders saints, and bishops in the centre flanked by white falcons on sprigs of oak. – The third window was given by Robert de Riplyngham, canon 1297–1322, who is seen teaching boys of St Peter's School in the reconstructed panel of the bottom row. In the main lights, much restored and with a number of inserted C 15 heads, scenes from the story of St John: converting the idolaters of Ephesus, in a vat of boiling oil, condemned by the Emperor Domitian to exile on Patmos, standing on the seven churches, raising Drusiana, unharmed after drinking poison. In the tracery St Catherine, a censing angel, St Margaret; in the borders vine stems on either side of green falcons and oak leaves. – In the fourth window, given by Canon Stephen de Mauley († 1315) but heavily restored by *Burlison & Grylls* in 1903 and virtually of that date, the martyrdoms of St Stephen,

St Andrew and St John the Baptist, with six members of the de Mauley family below. In the tracery, Crucifixion with the Virgin and two women and St John with the centurion and a Jew. In the borders white falcons and oak leaves flanking kings and bishops. – Fifth window. Jesse Tree, c. 1310–20, but restored in 1950 and much added to; none of the heads is original. Oak leaves and vine stems in the borders, glass of 1789 by W. Peckitt in the tracery. – In the sixth window, made up, but fitting the general decorative scheme, St Edmund, made-up St William crossing the Ouse bridge, St Edward the Confessor; St Michael and a composite figure, made-up Annunciation, Mass of St John of Beverley(?). Three armorials in bottom row, King & Son, 1973. – The seventh window was made up in 1951 with mainly mid-c 14 glass removed from other windows. Under reconstructed canopies St Lawrence, St John boiled in oil, St Stephen, St Cuthbert(?), crucifixion of St Peter, four of them against squared diaper grounds. The three lower panels in the central light represent Joachim in the wilderness, Joachim and Anna before the Golden Gate, Annunciation. In the l. light bottom panel made-up Presentation, on the r. arms of Thomas Dalby, c. 1520. Three foliage panels of c. 1340 in the tracery.

*South aisle, west end of nave*

This window and its companion in the N aisle were ordered together in 1339 from the glass painter *Thomas de Bouesdun*. The canopy designs and general layout are identical. In the main lights Crucifixion with the Virgin and St John beneath very fine buttressed and pinnacled canopies inhabited by two little figures; bottom centre, St John the Evangelist by *Peckitt*, who restored the window in 1758. In the tracery St John the Baptist (c 15 head), St Mary Magdalene (restored head), and St Clare with a monstrance.

*Great west window*

Commissioned 1339 by Archbishop William Melton from *Robert (Ketelbarn?)*; one of the finest medieval stained-glass windows in the country. At the bottom above a row of foliage panels stand eight saintly archbishops of York (most of the heads from *Peckitt*'s restoration of 1757). In the middle the twelve apostles; at the top the Annunciation, Nativity, Resurrection and Ascension, each spread over two lights, and the Coronation of the Virgin in the apex of the two central lights. At the bottom of the tracery, pelican and Agnus Dei, with the original foliage filling the tracery lights.

WEST DOOR (tracery over). In the circular central section, top l. St Edmund with other fire-crazed fragments of kings and angels, mainly from the choir clerestory, c. 1430. Triangular openings at the sides, Gothick motifs by *Peckitt*, probably c. 1757.

*North aisle, west end of nave*

Ordered 1339 (cf. companion at w end of s aisle, above). Virgin and Child flanked by SS. Catherine and Margaret. At the bottom, centre of main lights, St Peter, by *Peckitt*, 1758. In the top tracery Christ in Majesty, with crucifixions of St Peter and St Andrew below.

*Nave north aisle, w to e*

In the first window a collection of mainly early c 16 glass: large St Christopher combining upper half of French c 16 figure with c 15 lower half with donor from the Minster, flanked by scenes of Pentecost and the Ascension (the canopies do not belong); three composite late c 14 figures below, St Michael in the middle the best-preserved; a French Renaissance canopy and French panels of Nativity, Annunciation to shepherds and the Annunciation to the Virgin; bottom centre, Call of St Peter.

The second window is of c. 1335, with some earlier and later insertions. In the tracery the Coronation of the Virgin with angels either side. The top three scenes represent the Annunciation, Nativity and Adoration of the Magi. In the bottom row Virgin and Child, king from Jesse Tree (c. 1170–80, from an earlier church on the site), donor(?) with a later head. In the central row, three Ingram armorials, 1623. c 15 angel with the Minster shield in the bottom central light.

Third, or Penancers' Window: martyrdom of St Paul, inserted Coronation of the Virgin, martyrdom of St Peter, above three scenes of a penitentiary scourging and absolving sinners. In the borders, penitentiaries holding keys and counting coins and remnants of masons and carpenters at work. In the tracery *Peckitt* glass of 1779.

In the tracery of the fourth window Christ in Majesty between St Peter and St Paul. Below, martyrdoms of St Lawrence, St Denis and St Vincent(?), and in the bottom row the Virgin and Child between donors, one of whom presents a window. In the small medallions in the centre the stoning of St Stephen, in those at the base the martyrdom of St Edmund. Heraldic borders.

Fifth window. Christ between two angels with Passion Emblems in the tracery: above, a Crucifixion scene spread across three lights. In the lower row a knight and lady robed as pilgrims flanking St Peter. Borders: in the central light the alternating arms of England and France with a fox stealing a goose at the base; in the outer lights monkeys and squirrels along a vine stem above a satirical funeral procession of monkeys and a hunting scene. In the small medallions grotesques and diverting scenes such as a woman beating her husband and a wrestling match.

Sixth, or Bellfounders' Window, given by Richard Tunnoc, goldsmith and bellfounder. In the tracery St Peter between St Andrew and St Paul. Three panels of the miracle of the Ouse bridge with St William of York on

200. YORK Stained glass, *c.* 1339, great west window.
Archbishops, apostles, New Testament scenes, by Robert (Ketelbarn?)

horseback above; below, Tunnoc presenting the window to St William, flanked by scenes of tuning and casting bells. The canopy work and outer borders consist of bells in niched arcades and single niches; in the centre border monkeys playing musical instruments.

The seventh, or Heraldic Window (nearest the crossing) was given c. 1310 by Canon Peter de Dene, who kneels at the foot of the central light. The main lights and tracery tell the story of St Catherine, beginning at the bottom l.: St Catherine before Maxentius, converting philosophers, the philosophers executed, St Catherine in prison, tortured on the wheel, beheaded; in the tracery her burial by angels. Equally important is the heraldry; eight royal shields of arms on grisaille; in the outer borders heraldic eagles and lions, and in the central borders armed knights and members of the royal families of England and France wearing heraldic coats.

*Clerestory, south side of nave,* E *to* W
In the first window, figure panels by *John Barnett & Sons*, 1845, from their restoration of the former E window of the chapter house; Temptation of Christ, Entry into Jerusalem, Arrest of Christ, Conspiracy of Judas, Christ led away captive. – Second window, from the same series, Flagellation, Carrying Cross, Crucifixion, Deposition, Entombment. – Third window, late C12 panels with SS. Peter and Paul, flanked by apostles and trumpeting angels, from a Doom window. – Fourth window, five scenes with devils tormenting damned souls in Hell, from same series but much restored. – Fifth window, five restored late C12 panels from the life of St Benedict. – Sixth window, five much restored late C12 panels with scenes after Christ's Resurrection, three women at tomb, Noli Me Tangere, Supper at Emmaus, Miraculous Draught of Fishes, Christ appearing to Apostles. – Seventh window, at present only the early C14 armorials are in the window. – Eighth window, at present plain.

*Clerestory, north side of nave,* E *to* W
Four panels by *John Barnett*, 1845, from same series as those opposite: Pentecost, Christ with Passion Emblems, Coronation of the Virgin, Doom. – Second window from same series, Harrowing of Hell, women at the tomb, Resurrection, Noli Me Tangere, Doubting Thomas. – Third window, early C14 St James the Great, with kneeling donors and wine-trade scenes. At present, windows 4 to 7 have only armorials and window 8 is plain.

As for the surroundings of the Minster, one can speak of a precinct only with reservations, and of a close in the Salisbury or Wells sense even less. On W and S, normal traffic runs along. On the E is an intricate group of small streets, with only some parts looking to the Minster. The feeling of a close is just conveyed on the N. On these surroundings, see the latest edition of B of E *Yorkshire: York and the East Riding*.

# Glossary

For abbreviations of institutions (e.g. S.P.A.B.), see below; for abbreviations of publications and publishing bodies (e.g. RCHM and VCH), see Recent Literature below.

For further references, some with diagrams, the following can be consulted: *Recording a Church, an Illustrated Glossary* (T. Cocke, D. Findlay, R. Halsey, E. Williamson, 1982); *A Dictionary of Architecture* (J. Fleming, H. Honour, N. Pevsner, 1966, 1975 etc.); *The Dictionary of Ornament* (M. Stafford and D. Ware, 1974); *A Pattern of English Building* (A. Clifton-Taylor, 1972); *Building in England down to 1540* (L. Salzman, 1967); *The Illustrated Glossary of Architecture* (J. Harris and J. Lever, 1966); *The Classical Language of Architecture* (J. Summerson, 1964); also glossaries in B of E volumes revised since 1979. The *A.P.S.D.* (*Architectural Publications Society Dictionary*, 1853–92, mainly by Wyatt Papworth) is still useful.

ABACUS (*lit.* tablet): flat slab forming the top of a capital (plural: abaci).

ABUTMENT: the meeting of an arch or vault with its solid lateral support, or the support itself.

ACANTHUS: formalized leaf ornament with thick veins and frilled edge, e.g. on a Corinthian capital.

ACHIEVEMENT OF ARMS: in heraldry, a complete display of armorial bearings.

ACROTERION (*lit.* peak): plinth for a statue or ornament placed at the apex or ends of a pediment; also, loosely and more usually, both the plinths and what stands on them.

ADDORSED: description of two figures placed symmetrically back to back.

AEDICULE (*lit.* little building): architectural surround, consisting usually of two columns or pilasters supporting a pediment, framing a niche or opening. See also *tabernacle*.

AFFRONTED: description of two figures placed symmetrically face to face.

AGGREGATE: small stones added to a binding material, e.g. in concrete. In modern architecture, used alone to describe concrete with an aggregate of stone chippings, e.g. granite, quartz etc.

AISLE (*lit.* wing): passage alongside the nave, choir or transept of a church, or the main body of some other building, separated from it by columns, piers or posts.

AMBO: originally a raised reading-stand in Italian medieval churches, replaced after the C14 by the pulpit.

AMBULATORY (*lit.* walkway): aisle at the E end of a chancel, sometimes surrounding an apse and therefore semicircular or polygonal in plan.

AMORINO: see *putto*.

ANGLE ROLL: roll moulding in the angle between two planes, e.g. between the orders of an arch.

ANNULET (*lit.* ring): shaftring (see *shaft*).

ANTAE: flat pilasters with capitals different from the order they accompany, placed at the ends of the short projecting walls of a portico or of a colonnade, which is then called *in antis*.

ANTEFIXAE: ornaments projecting at regular intervals above a classical cornice, originally to conceal the ends of roof tiles.

ANTEPENDIUM: see *frontal*.

ANTHEMION (*lit.* honeysuckle): classical ornament like a honeysuckle flower.

APRON: raised panel below a windowsill, sometimes shaped and decorated.

APSE: semicircular (i.e. apsidal) extension of an apartment: see also *exedra*. A term first used of the magistrate's end of a Roman basilica, and thence especially of the vaulted semicircular or polygonal end of a chancel or a chapel.

ARABESQUE: type of painted or carved surface decoration consisting of flowing lines and intertwined foliage scrolls etc., generally based on geometrical patterns. Cf. *grotesque*.

ARCADE: Series of arches supported by piers or columns. *Blind arcade*: the same applied to the surface of a wall. *Wall arcade*: in medieval churches, a blind arcade forming a dado below windows.

ARCH: The *round*, i.e. semicircular, *arch* characterizes the Romanesque (in England, Norman) style. The *pointed arch*, with equal curves meeting in a point, characterizes the Gothic style. Other traits: *chancel arch*: E opening from the crossing into the chancel. A *depressed arch* is composed of curves from three centres. *Diaphragm arch*: transverse arch carrying a masonry gable and dividing sections of a wooden roof, probably to prevent fire from spreading. An *ogee arch* is composed of two double curves. *Relieving* (or *discharging*) *arch*: incorporated in a wall, to carry some of its weight, some way above an opening. A *segmental arch* is composed of a segment of a circle. A *stilted arch* has sections of straight jamb between the imposts and the spring of the arch. *Strainer arch*: inserted across an opening to resist any inward pressure of the side members. A *transverse arch* runs across the main axis of an interior space. *Triumphal arch*: Imperial Roman monument (e.g. of Constantine) whose elevation supplied a motif for later classical compositions. *Westminster arch*: a stilted segmental arch used especially by C13 English royal masons.

ARCHITRAVE: (1) formalized lintel, the lowest member of the classical entablature (see *orders*); (2) moulded frame of a door or window (often borrowing the profile of an architrave in the strict sense). Also *lugged architrave*, where the top is prolonged into *lugs* (*lit.* ears) at the sides; *shouldered*, where the frame rises vertically at the top angles and returns horizontally at the sides, forming shoulders (shrugged, one might say).

ARCHIVOLT: architrave moulding when it follows the line of an arch.

ARCUATED: dependent structurally on the use of arches or the arch principle. cf. *trabeated*.

ARRIS (*lit.* stop): sharp edge at the meeting of two surfaces.

ASHLAR: masonry of large blocks wrought to even faces and square edges.

ASTRAGAL (*lit.* knuckle): moulding of semicircular section, often with bead-and-reel enrichment.

ASTYLAR: term used to describe an elevation that has no columns or similar vertical features.

ATLANTES (*lit.* Atlas figures, from the god Atlas carrying the globe): male counterparts of caryatids (q.v.), often in a more demonstrative attitude of support.

ATRIUM: inner court of a Roman house; also open court in front of a church.

ATTACHED: see *engaged column*.

ATTIC: (1) small top storey, especially within a sloping roof; (2) in classical architecture, a storey above the main entablature of the façade, as in a triumphal arch.

AUMBRY: recess or cupboard to hold sacred vessels for the Mass.

BALDACCHINO: free-standing canopy over an altar, supported by columns. Also called *ciborium* (q.v.).

BALLFLOWER: globular flower of three petals enclosing a small ball. A decoration used in the first quarter of the C 14.

BALUSTER (*lit.* pomegranate): a pillar or pedestal of bellied form. *Balusters*: vertical supports, of this or any other form, for a handrail or coping, the whole being called a *balustrade*. *Blind balustrade*: the same with a wall behind.

BASE: moulded foot of a column or other order; pedestal of a shrine.

BASEMENT: lowest, subordinate storey of a building, and hence the lowest part of an elevation, below the main floor.

BASILICA (*lit.* royal building): a Roman public hall; hence an aisled building with a clerestory, usually a church.

BATTER: inward inclination of a wall.

BATTLEMENT: fortified parapet, indented or crenellated so that archers could shoot through the indentations (crenels or embrasures) between the projecting solid portions (merlons).

BAYS: divisions of an elevation or interior space as defined by any regular vertical features such as arches, columns, windows etc.

BAY-WINDOW: window of one or more storeys projecting from the face of a building at ground-level, and either rectangular or polygonal on plan. A *canted bay-window* has a straight front and angled sides. A *bow window* is curved. An *oriel window* projects on corbels or brackets and does not start from the ground.

BEAKHEAD: Norman ornamental motif consisting of a row of bird or beast heads with beaks, usually biting into a roll moulding.

BELFRY: (1) bell-turret set on a roof or gable (see also *bellcote*); (2) room or stage in a tower where bells are hung; (3) bell-tower in a general sense.

BELLCOTE: belfry as (1) above, sometimes with the character of a small house for the bell(s).

BILLET (*lit.* log or block) FRIEZE: Norman ornament consisting of small half-cylindrical or rectangular blocks placed at regular intervals.

BLIND: see *arcade*; *baluster*; *portico*.

BLOCKED: term applied to columns or architraves that are interrupted by regular projecting blocks. See also *Gibbs surround*.

BLOCKING COURSE: plain course of stones, or equivalent, on top of a cornice and crowning the wall.

BOLECTION MOULDING: convex moulding covering the joint between two different planes and overlapping the higher as well as the lower one, used especially in the late C 17 and early C 18.

BOSS: knob or projection usually placed at the intersection of ribs in a vault.

BOX PEW: pew enclosed by a high wooden back and ends, the latter having doors.

BRACE: subsidiary timber set diagonally to strengthen a timber frame. It can be curved or straight. See also *roofs*.

BRACKET: small supporting piece of stone etc. to carry a projecting horizontal member. See also *console*; *corbel*.

BRASS: a memorial engraved on a sheet of brass often inset in a stone slab.

BRATTISHING: ornamental cresting on a wall, usually formed of leaves or Tudor flowers or miniature battlements.

BROACH: see *spire*.

BUCRANIUM: ox skull used decoratively in classical friezes.

BULLSEYE WINDOW: small circular or oval window, e.g. in the tympanum of a pediment. Also called *œil de bœuf* or oculus.

BUTTRESS: vertical member projecting from a wall to stabilize it or to resist the lateral thrust of an arch, roof or vault. Different types used at the corners of a building, especially a tower, include angle, diagonal, clasping, and setback buttresses. A *flying buttress* transmits the thrust to a heavy abutment by means of an arch or half-arch.

CABLE MOULDING: originally a Norman moulding, imitating the twisted strands of a rope. Also called *rope moulding*.

CALEFACTORY: room in a monastery where a fire burned for the comfort of the monks. Also called *warming room*.

CAMBER: slight rise or upward curve in place of a horizontal line or plane.

CAMES: see *quarries*.

CAMPANILE: free-standing bell-tower.

CANOPY: projection or hood, usually over an altar, pulpit, niche, statue, seat etc.

CANTED: tilted, generally on a vertical axis to produce an obtuse angle on plan, e.g. of a canted bay-window.

CANTILEVER: horizontal projection (e.g. step, canopy) supported by a downward force behind the fulcrum. It is without external bracing and thus appears to be self-supporting.

CAPITAL: head or crowning feature of a column or pilaster.

CARREL: niche in a cloister where a monk could sit to work or read.

CARTOUCHE: tablet with ornate frame, usually of elliptical shape and bearing a coat of arms or inscription.

CARYATIDS (*lit.* daughters of the village of Caryae): female figures supporting an entablature, counterparts of Atlantes (q.v.).

CASEMENT: (1) window hinged at the side; (2) in Gothic architecture, a concave moulding framing a window.

CASTELLATED: battlemented.

CAVETTO: concave moulding of quarter-round section.

CELURE or CEILURE: panelled and adorned part of a wagon roof above the rood or the altar.

CENOTAPH (*lit.* empty tomb): funerary monument which is not a burying-place.

CENTERING: wooden support for the building of an arch or vault, removed after completion.

CHAIRE ORGAN: in old organs, the second organ added to the great organ, possibly so named because it was placed below and in front of the main organ, so forming the back of the player's seat.

CHAMFER (*lit.* corner-break): surface formed by cutting off a square edge, usually at an angle of forty-five degrees.

CHANCEL (*lit.* enclosure): that part of the E end of a church in which the main altar is placed. Sometimes applied to the whole continuation of the main vessel E of the crossing. See also *choir* (2).

CHANTRY CHAPEL: chapel, often attached to or inside a church, endowed for the celebration of masses for the soul of the founder or others.

CHEVET (*lit.* head): French term for the E end of a church (chancel and ambulatory with radiating chapels).

CHEVRON: zigzag Norman ornament.

CHOIR: (1) the part of a church where services are sung; in monastic churches this can occupy the crossing and/or the easternmost bays of the nave; (2) the E arm of a cruciform church (a usage of long standing, though liturgically anomalous).

CIBORIUM: canopied shrine for the reserved sacrament or a baldacchino (q.v.).

CINQUEFOIL: see *foil*.

CLASSIC: term for the moment of highest achievement of a style.

CLASSICAL: term for Greek and Roman architecture and any subsequent styles inspired by it.

CLERESTORY: upper storey of the nave walls of a church, pierced by windows.

CLOISTERS: quadrangle surrounded by roofed or vaulted passages connecting a monastic church with the domestic parts of the monastery. Usually, but not always, S of the nave and W of the transept.

CLUNCH: in some areas a term for one of the harder varieties of chalk when used for building.

COADE STONE: artificial (cast) stone made from *c.* 1769 by Coade and Sealy in London.

COFFERING: arrangement of sunken panels (*coffers*), square or polygonal, decorating a ceiling, vault or arch.

COGGING: a decorative course of bricks laid diagonally as an alternative to dentilation (q.v.). Also called *dogtooth brickwork*.

COLLAR BEAM or COLLAR PURLIN: see *roofs*.

COLLEGIATE CHURCH: church endowed for the support of a college of priests and therefore with numerous altars and a sizeable choir.

COLONNADE: range of columns supporting an entablature or arches.

COLONNETTE: in medieval architecture, a small column or shaft.

COLOSSAL ORDER: see *order*.

COLUMN: in classical architecture, an upright structural member of round section with a shaft, a capital, and usually a base. See *orders*.

COLUMN FIGURE: in medieval architecture, carved figure attached to a column or shaft flanking a doorway.

COMPOUND PIER: a pier consisting of a bundle of shafts (q.v.), or of a solid core surrounded by attached or detached shafts.

CONSOLE: ornamental bracket of compound curved outline.

COPING (*lit.* capping): course of stones, or equivalent, on top of a wall.

CORBEL: block of stone projecting from a wall, supporting some feature on its horizontal top surface. *Corbel course*: continuous projecting course of stones or bricks fulfilling the same function. *Corbel table*: series of corbels to carry a parapet or a wall-plate (for the latter, see *roofs*). *Corbelling*: brick or masonry courses built out beyond one another like a series of corbels to support a chimneystack, window etc.

CORNICE: (1) moulded ledge, projecting along the top of a building or feature, especially as the highest member of the classical entablature (q.v.; see also *orders*); (2) decorative moulding in the angle between wall and ceiling.

COSMATI WORK: Italian C12–13 decorative work in marble inlaid with coloured stones, mosaic, glass, gilding etc. by craftsmen known as the Cosmati.

COURSE: continuous layer of stones etc. in a wall.

COVE: a concave moulding on a large scale, e.g. in a *coved ceiling*, which has a pronounced cove joining the walls to a flat central area.

CRADLE ROOF: see *wagon roof*.

CREDENCE: in a church or chapel, a side table, or often a recess, for the sacramental elements before consecration.

CRENELLATION: see *battlement*.

CREST, CRESTING: ornamental finish along the top of a screen etc.

CROCKETS (*lit.* hooks), CROCKETING: in Gothic architecture, leafy knobs on the edges of any sloping feature.

CROSSING: in a church, central space at the junction of the nave, chancel and transepts. *Crossing tower*: tower above a crossing.

CROWN-POST: see *roofs*.

CRYPT: underground or half-underground room usually below the E end of a church. *Ring crypt*: early medieval semicircular or polygonal corridor crypt surrounding the apse of a church, often associated with chambers for relics. See also *undercroft*.

CUPOLA (*lit.* dome): especially a small dome on a circular or polygonal base crowning a larger dome, roof or turret. Sometimes denotes any dome between drum and lantern.

CUSP: projecting point formed by the foils within the divisions of Gothic tracery, also used as a decorative edging to the soffits of the Gothic arches of tomb recesses, sedilia etc.

DADO: the finishing of the lower part of an interior wall (sometimes used to support an applied order). *Dado rail*: the moulding along the top of the dado.

DAGGER: see *tracery*.

DAIS: raised platform at one end of a room.

DEC (DECORATED): historical division of English Gothic architecture covering the period from *c.* 1290 to *c.* 1350. The name is derived from the type of window tracery used during the period (see also *tracery*).

DEMI-COLUMNS: engaged columns (q.v.) only half of whose circumference projects from the wall. Also called *half-columns*.

DENTIL: small square block used in series in classical cornices, rarely in Doric. In brickwork, *dentilation* is produced by the projection of alternating headers or blocks along cornices or string-courses.

DIAPER (*lit.* figured cloth): repetitive surface decoration of lozenges or squares, either flat or in relief. Achieved in brickwork with bricks of two colours.

DOGTOOTH: typical E.E. decoration of a moulding, consisting of a series of squares, their centres raised like pyramids and their edges indented. See also *cogging*.

DOME: vault of even curvature erected on a circular base. The section can be segmental (e.g. saucer dome), semicircular, pointed, bulbous (onion dome) or compound (curves from more than one centre).

DORMER WINDOW: window standing up vertically from the slope of a roof and lighting a room within it. *Dormer head*: gable above this window, often formed as a pediment.

DORTER: dormitory; sleeping quarters of a monastery.

DRESSINGS: smoothly worked stones, used e.g. for quoins or string-courses, projecting from the wall and sometimes of different material, colour or texture.

DRIPSTONE: moulded stone projecting from a wall to protect the lower parts from water. See also *hood-mould*.

DRUM: (1) circular or polygonal wall supporting a dome or cupola; (2) one of the stones forming the shaft of a column.

EARLY ENGLISH: see *E.E.*

EASTER SEPULCHRE: recess, usually in the wall of a chancel, with a tomb-chest to receive an effigy of Christ for Easter celebrations.

EAVES: overhanging edge of a roof; hence *eaves cornice* in this position.

ECHINUS (*lit.* sea-urchin): ovolo moulding (q.v.) below the abacus of a Greek Doric capital.

E.E. (EARLY ENGLISH): historical division of English Gothic architecture covering the period *c.* 1190–1250.

ELEVATION: (1) any side of a building, inside or out; (2) in a drawing, the same or any part of it, accurately represented in two dimensions.

EMBATTLED: furnished with battlements.

EMBRASURE (*lit.* splay): small splayed opening in the wall or battlement of a fortified building.

ENCAUSTIC TILES: glazed and decorated earthenware tiles used for paving.

EN DÉLIT (*lit.* in error): term used in Gothic architecture to describe stone shafts whose grain runs vertically, instead of horizontally (as in the stone's original bed), against normal building practice.

ENGAGED COLUMN: one that is partly merged into a wall or pier. Also called *attached column*.

ENTABLATURE: in classical architecture, collective name for the three horizontal members (architrave, frieze and cornice) above a column.

ENTASIS: very slight convex deviation from a straight line; used on classical columns and sometimes on spires to prevent an optical illusion of concavity.

ENTRESOL: mezzanine storey within or above the ground storey.

EPITAPH (*lit.* on a tomb): inscription in that position.

ESCUTCHEON: shield for armorial bearings.

EXEDRA: apsidal end of an apartment; see *apse*.

FASCIA: plain horizontal band, e.g. in an architrave.

FENESTRATION: the arrangement of windows in a building.

FERETORY: (1) place behind the high altar where the chief shrine of a church is kept; (2) wooden or metal container for relics.

FESTOON: ornament, usually in high or low relief, in the form of a garland of flowers and/or fruit, hung up at both ends; see also *swag*.

FIBREGLASS (or glass-reinforced polyester (GRP)): synthetic resin reinforced with glass fibre, formed in moulds, often simulating the outward appearance of traditional materials.

FIELDED: see *raised and fielded*.

FILLET: in medieval architecture, a narrow flat band running down a shaft or along a roll moulding. In classical architecture it separates larger curved mouldings in cornices or bases.

FINIAL: decorative topmost feature, e.g. above a gable, spire or cupola.

FLAMBOYANT: properly the latest phase of French Gothic architecture, where the window tracery takes on undulating lines, based on the use of flowing curves.

FLÈCHE (*lit.* arrow): slender spire on the centre of a roof. Also called *spirelet*.

FLEUR-DE-LYS: in heraldry, a formalized lily, as in the royal arms of France.

FLEURON: decorative carved flower or leaf.

FLOWING: curvilinear, as of tracery.

FLUSHWORK: flint used decoratively in conjunction with dressed stone so as to form patterns: tracery, initials etc.

FLUTING: series of concave grooves, their common edges sharp (arris) or blunt (fillet).

FOIL: (*lit.* leaf): lobe formed by the cusping of a circular or other shape in tracery. *Trefoil* (three), *quatrefoil* (four), *cinquefoil* (five) and *multifoil* refer to the number of lobes in a shape. See also *tracery*.

FOLIATED: decorated, especially carved, with leaves.

FRATER: see *refectory*.

FREESTONE: stone that is cut, or can be cut, in all directions, usually fine-grained sandstone or limestone.

FRESCO: *al fresco*: painting executed on wet plaster. *Fresco secco*: painting executed on dry plaster, more common in Britain.

FRET: see *key pattern*.

FRIEZE: horizontal band of ornament, especially the middle member of the classical entablature (q.v.). *Pulvinated frieze* (*lit.* cushioned): frieze of bold convex profile.

FRONTAL: covering for the front of an altar. Also called *antependium*.

GABLE: area of wall, often triangular, at the end of a double-pitched roof. *Gablet*: small gable. See also *roofs*.

GADROONING: ribbed ornament, e.g. on the lid or base of an urn, flowing into a lobed edge.

GALILEE: chapel or vestibule enclosing the porch at one of the main entrances to a church. See also *narthex*.

GALLERY: balcony or passage, but with certain special meanings, e.g. (1) upper storey above the aisle of a church, looking through arches to the nave and generally with outer windows; also called tribune and often (erroneously) triforium; (2) balcony or mezzanine, often with seats, overlooking the main interior space of a building; (3) external walkway, often projecting from a wall.

GARDEROBE (*lit.* wardrobe): medieval privy. See also *reredorter*.

GARGOYLE: water-spout projecting from the parapet of a wall or tower, often carved into human or animal shape.

GEOMETRIC: historical division of English Gothic architecture covering the period c. 1250–90. See also *tracery*.

GIANT ORDER: see *order*.

GIBBS SURROUND: intermittently blocked door- or window-frame as used e.g. in c16 Italy by Vignola, in c17 England by so-called artisan mannerists, and in c18 England by James Gibbs.

GISANT: effigy depicted as a naked corpse.

GOTHIC: the period of medieval architecture characterized by the use of the pointed arch. For its subdivisions, see *E.E.*; *Geometric*; *Dec*; *Perp*; *Flamboyant*.

GROIN: sharp edge at the meeting of two cells of a cross-vault; see *vault*.

GROTESQUE (*lit.* grotto-esque): classical wall decoration in paint or stucco adopted from Roman examples, particularly by Raphael. Its foliage scrolls, unlike arabesque, incorporate ornaments and human figures.

GROTTO: artificial cavern usually decorated with rock- or shellwork, especially popular in the late c17 and c18.

GUILLOCHE: running classical ornament of interlaced bands forming a plait.

GUTTAE: small peg-like elements of the Doric order, below the triglyphs.

HAGIOSCOPE: see *squint*.

HALF-COLUMNS: see *demi-columns*.

HALL-CHURCH: medieval or Gothic Revival church whose nave and aisles are of equal height or approximately so.

HAMMERBEAM: see *roofs*.

HEAD-STOP: see *label stop* (under *label*).

HERRINGBONE WORK: masonry or brickwork in zigzag courses.

HEXASTYLE: see *portico*.

HOODMOULD: projecting moulding above an arch or lintel to throw off water. When the moulding is horizontal it is often called a label; see also *label stop* (under *label*).

HUSK GARLAND: festoon of nutshells diminishing towards the ends.

ICONOGRAPHY: description of the subject-matter of works of the visual arts.

IMPOST (*lit.* imposition): horizontal moulding at the springing of an arch.

IMPOST BLOCK: block with splayed sides between abacus and capital.

IN ANTIS: see *antae*.

INDENT: (1) shape chiselled out of a stone to fit and hold a brass; (2) in restoration, a section of new stone inserted as a patch into older work.

INTARSIA: see *marquetry*.

INTERCOLUMNIATION: interval between columns.

INTRADOS: see *soffit*.

JAMB (*lit.* leg): one of the straight sides of an opening.

JOGGLE: mason's term for joining two stones to prevent them from slipping by means of a notch in one and a corresponding projection in the other.

KEEL MOULDING: moulding whose outline is in section like that of the keel of a ship.

KEY or FRET PATTERN: classical running ornament of interlocking right angles.

KEYSTONE: middle and topmost stone in an arch or vault.

KINGPOST: see *roofs*.

KNEELER: (1) kneeling figure; (2) horizontal projection at the base of a gable; (3) hassock or kneeling-cushion in a church.

LABEL: horizontal hoodmould (q.v.). *Label stop*: ornamental boss or head at the end of a hoodmould.

LADY CHAPEL: chapel dedicated to the Virgin Mary (Our Lady).

LANCET WINDOW: slender pointed-arched window.

LANTERN: windowed turret crowning a roof, tower or dome.

LANTERN CROSS: churchyard cross with lantern-shaped top, usually with sculptured representations on the sides of the top.

LAVATORIUM: in a monastery, a washing place adjacent to the refectory.

LECTERN: reading-desk, usually of metalwork, for reading from the Scriptures.

LESENE (*lit.* a mean thing): pilaster without base or capital. Also called *pilaster strip*.

LIERNE: see *vault*.

LIGHT: compartment of a window.

LINENFOLD: Tudor panelling where each panel is ornamented with a conventional representation of a piece of linen laid in vertical folds.

LINTEL: horizontal beam or stone bridging an opening.

LOZENGE: diamond shape.

LUCARNE (*lit.* dormer): small window in a roof or spire.

LUGGED: see *architrave*.

LUNETTE (*lit.* little or crescent moon): (1) semicircular window; (2) semicircular or crescent-shaped surface.

LYCHGATE (*lit.* corpse-gate): roofed wooden gateway at the entrance to a churchyard where the coffin rests to await the clergyman.

MANDORLA: almond-shaped oval around figure as an aureole.

MERLON: see *battlement*.

MISERICORD (*lit.* mercy): shelf placed on the underside of a hinged choir-stall seat which, when turned up, supported the occupant during long periods of standing. Also called *miserere*.

MODILLIONS: small consoles (q.v.) at regular intervals along the underside of the cornice of the Corinthian or Composite orders.

MOUCHETTE: see *tracery*.

MOULDING: ornament of continuous section: see, e.g., *cavetto*; *ogee*; *ovolo*; *roll*.

MOURNERS: see *weepers*.

MULLION: vertical member between the lights in a window opening.

MUNIMENTS: title deeds and other documents kept in a Muniment Room.

MUNTIN: vertical part in the framing of a door, screen, panelling etc., butting into or topped by the horizontal rails.

NAILHEAD MOULDING: E.E. ornamental motif consisting of small pyramids regularly repeated.

NARTHEX: enclosed vestibule or covered porch at the main entrance to a church. See also *galilee*; *westwork*.

NAVE: the middle vessel of the limb of a church w of the crossing or chancel and flanked by the aisles. Occasionally also used of the central space of a transept, Lady Chapel etc.

NECESSARIUM: see *reredorter*.

NEWEL: central post in a circular or winding staircase; also the principal post where a flight of stairs meets a landing.

NICHE (*lit.* shell): vertical recess in a wall, sometimes for a statue.

NIGHT STAIR: stair by which monks entered the transept of their church from their dormitory to celebrate night services.

NODDING OGEE: three-dimensional S-curved arch, as of a canopy.

NOOK-SHAFT: shaft set in the angle of a pier or respond or wall, or the angle of the jamb of a window or doorway.

NORMAN: see *Romanesque*.

NOSING: projection of the tread of a step. A *bottle nosing* is half-round in section.

NUTMEG MOULDING: consisting of a chain of tiny triangles placed obliquely.

OBELISK: lofty pillar of square section, tapering at the top and ending pyramidally.

OCULUS: see *bullseye window*.

OGEE: double curve, S-curve, bending first one way and then the other. Applied to mouldings: *cyma recta*; or with a reverse curve: *cyma reversa*. See also *nodding ogee*.

OPUS ALEXANDRINUM: ornamental paving of coloured marbles in geometrical patterns.

OPUS SECTILE: inlaid work with the design formed from cut marbles, like a jigsaw puzzle.

OPUS SIGNINUM: floor concrete of Roman origin, made from crushed brick, pottery and lime.

ORATORY: (1) small private chapel in a church or a house; (2) church of the Oratorian Order.

ORDER: (1) upright structural member formally related to others, e.g. in classical architecture a column, pilaster or anta; (2) especially in medieval architecture, one of a series of recessed arches and jambs forming a splayed opening. *Giant* or *colossal order*: classical order whose height is that of two or more storeys of a building.

ORDERS: in classical architecture, the differently formalized versions of the basic post-and-lintel (column and entablature) structure, each having its own rules for design and proportion. *Superimposed orders*: term for the use of orders on successive levels, usually in the upward sequence of Doric, Ionic, Corinthian.

ORIEL: see *bay-window*.

OVERTHROW: decorative fixed arch between two gatepiers or above a wrought-iron gate.

OVOLO MOULDING: wide convex moulding.

PALIMPSEST (*lit.* erased work): re-use of a surface. (1) of a brass: where a metal plate has been re-used by turning over and engraving on the back; (2) of a wall painting: where one overlaps and partly obscures an earlier one.

PALMETTE: classical ornament like a symmetrical palm-shoot.

PANELLING: wooden lining to interior walls, made up of vertical members (muntins, q.v.) and horizontals (rails) framing panels (see *linenfold*; *raised and fielded*).

PARAPET: wall for protection at any sudden drop, with a walk behind it, e.g. at the wall-head of a church.

PARCLOSE: see *screen*.

PARGETING (*lit.* plastering): in timber-framed buildings, plasterwork with patterns and ornaments either moulded in relief or incised on it.

PARLOUR: in a monastery, room where monks were permitted to talk to visitors.

PATERA (*lit.* plate): round or oval ornament in shallow relief, especially in classical architecture (plural: paterae).

PAVILION: (1) ornamental building for occasional use in a garden, park, sports ground etc.; (2) projecting subdivision of some larger building, often at an angle or terminating wings.

PEDESTAL: in classical architecture, a tall base sometimes used to support an order; also the base for a statue, vase, shrine etc.

PEDIMENT: in classical architecture, a formalized gable derived from that of a temple; also used over doors, windows etc. Called *open* if its frame is interrupted at the bottom, *broken* if at the top.

PENDANT: feature hanging down from a vault or ceiling, usually ends in a boss.

PENDENTIVE: spandrel formed as part of a hemisphere between arches meeting at an angle, supporting a drum or dome.

PERISTYLE: in classical architecture, a range of columns all round a building, e.g. a temple, or an interior space, e.g. a courtyard.

PERP (PERPENDICULAR): historical division of English Gothic architecture covering the period from *c.*1335–50 to *c.*1530. The name is derived from the upright tracery panels used during the period (see *tracery*).

PIER: strong, solid support, usually round or square in section. See also *compound pier*.

PIETRA DURA: ornamental or scenic inlay by means of thin slabs of stone.

PILASTER: representation of a classical column in flat relief against a wall. *Pilastrade*: series of pilasters, equivalent to a colonnade. *Pilaster strip*: see *lesene*.

PILLAR: free-standing upright member of any section, not conforming to one of the classical orders.

PILLAR PISCINA: free-standing piscina on a pillar.

PINNACLE: tapering finial, e.g. on a buttress or the corner of a tower, sometimes decorated with crockets.

PISCINA: basin for washing the communion or Mass vessels, provided with a drain; generally set in or against the wall to the s of an altar.

PLINTH: projecting base beneath a wall or column, generally chamfered or moulded at the top.

PODIUM: continuous raised platform supporting a building.

POPPY-HEAD: carved ornament of leaves and flowers as a finial for the end of a bench or stall.

PORCH: covered projecting entrance to a building.

PORTICO: a porch, open on one side at least, and enclosed by a row of columns which also support the roof and frequently a pediment. When the front of it is ranged with the front of the building, it is described as a *portico in antis* (see *antae*). Porticoes are described by the number of frontal columns, e.g. tetrastyle (four), hexastyle (six). *Blind portico*: the front features of a portico attached to a wall so that it is no longer a proper porch.

PREDELLA: (1) step or platform on which an altar stands; hence (2) in an altarpiece, the horizontal strip below the main representation, often used for a number of subsidiary representations in a row.

PRESBYTERY: (1) part of a church lying E of the choir where the main altar is placed; (2) a priest's residence. See also *sanctuary*.

PRINCIPALS: see *roofs*.

PRIORY: monastic house whose head is a prior or prioress, not an abbot or abbess.

PULPIT: an elevated stand of stone or wood for a preacher which first became general in the later Middle Ages, replacing the ambo (q.v.). Sometimes with an acoustic canopy called a *sounding-board*.

PULPITUM: stone screen, usually one bay deep, in a major church, provided to shut off the choir from the nave, also as a backing for the return choir stalls. Sometimes carries the organ.

PULVINATED: see *frieze*.

PURLIN: see *roofs*.

PUTHOLES or PUTLOCK HOLES: holes in the wall to receive putlocks (or putlogs), the short horizontal timbers which scaffolding boards rest on. They are often not filled in after construction is complete.

PUTTO: small naked boy (plural: putti). Also called *amorino*.

QUADRANGLE: rectangular inner courtyard in a large building.

QUARRIES (*lit.* squares): (1) square (or diamond-shaped) panes of glass supported by lead strips called *cames*; (2) square floorslabs or tiles.

QUATREFOIL: see *foil*.

QUOINS: dressed stones at the angles of a building. They may be alternately long and short, especially when rusticated.

RADIATING CHAPELS: chapels projecting radially from an ambulatory or an apse: see *chevet*.

RAGGLE: groove cut in masonry, especially to receive the edge of glass or roof-covering.

RAIL: see *muntin*.

RAISED AND FIELDED: of a wooden panel with a raised square or rectangular central area (*field*) surrounded by a narrow moulding.

RAKE: slope or pitch.

REBATE: rectangular section cut out of a masonry edge to receive a shutter, door, window etc.

REBUS: a heraldic pun, e.g. a fiery cock as a badge for Cockburn.

REEDING: series of convex mouldings; the reverse of fluting.

REFECTORY: dining hall of a monastery or similar establishment. Also called *frater*.

REPOUSSÉ: decoration of metalwork by relief designs, formed by beating the metal from the back.

REREDORTER: (*lit.* behind the dormitory): medieval euphemism for latrines in a monastery. Also called *necessarium*; see also *garderobe*.

REREDOS: painted and/or sculptured screen behind and above an altar.

RESPOND: half-pier bonded into a wall and carrying one end of an arch.

RETABLE: altarpiece, a picture or piece of carving standing behind and attached to an altar.

RETROCHOIR: in a major church, the space between the high altar and an E chapel, like a square ambulatory.

REVEAL: the inward plane of a jamb, between the edge of an external wall and the frame of a door or window that is set in it.

R.I.B.A.: Royal Institute of British Architects.

RIB-VAULT: see *vault*.

RIDGE: see *roofs*.

RIDGE RIB: see *vault*.

RINCEAU (*lit.* little branch) or ANTIQUE FOLIAGE: classical ornament, usually on a frieze, of leafy scrolls branching alternately to left and right.

RISER: vertical face of a step.

ROCK-FACED: term used to describe masonry which is cleft to produce a natural rugged appearance.

ROCOCO (*lit.* rocky): latest phase of the Baroque style, current in most Continental countries between *c.* 1720 and *c.* 1760, and showing itself in Britain mainly in playful, scrolled decoration, especially plasterwork.

ROLL MOULDING: moulding of curved section used in medieval architecture.

ROMANESQUE: that style in architecture (in England often called Norman) which was current in the C11 and C12 and preceded the Gothic style. (Some scholars extend the use of the term Romanesque back to the C10 or C9.) See also *Saxo-Norman*.

ROMANO-BRITISH: general term applied to the period and cultural features of Britain affected by the Roman occupation of the C1–5 A.D.

ROOD: cross or crucifix, usually over the entry into the chancel. The *rood screen* beneath it may have a *rood loft* along the top, reached by a *rood stair*.

ROOFS: timber roofs are generally called after the principal structural component, e.g. crown-post, hammerbeam, kingpost etc. Some elements are the following. *Braces*: subsidiary timbers set diagonally to strengthen a frame. *Collar beam*: horizontal transverse timber connecting a pair of rafters or principals at a height between the apex and the wall-plate. *Crown-post*: stands on a tie-beam to support the collar purlin (see below), usually with four-way struts; i.e. its particular character is three-dimensional. *Hammerbeams*: horizontal brackets on opposite sides at wall-plate level, like a tie-beam with the centre cut away. *Hammerpost*: a vertical timber set on the inner end of a hammerbeam to support a purlin, and braced to a collar beam above. *Kingpost*: a vertical timber standing centrally on a tie- or collar beam and rising to the apex of the roof, where it supports a ridge. *Principals*: pair of inclined lateral timbers of a truss which carry common rafters. *Purlin*: horizontal longitudinal timber (*collar purlin*: single central purlin carrying collar beams and itself supported by a crown-post). *Queenposts*: pair of vertical, or near-vertical, timbers placed symmetrically on a tie-beam and supporting side purlins. *Rafters*: inclined lateral timbers sloping from wall-top to apex and supporting the roof covering. *Ridge, ridgepiece*: horizontal longitudinal timber at the apex of a roof supporting the ends of the rafters. *Tie-beam*: the main horizontal transverse timber which carries the feet of the principals at wall-plate level. *Wallplate*: longitudinal timber on the top of a wall to receive the ends of the rafters. See also *wagon roof*.

ROPE MOULDING: see *cable moulding*.

ROSE-WINDOW: circular window with patterned tracery about the centre. See also *wheel window*.

ROTUNDA: building or interior space circular on plan.

RUBBLE: masonry whose stones are wholly or partly in a rough state.

RUSTICATION: treatment of joints and/or faces of masonry to give an effect of strength.

SACRISTY: room in a church for sacred vessels and vestments.

SALOMONIC COLUMNS: with spirally grooved or 'twisted' shafts originally inspired by those, allegedly from Solomon's temple, at the saint's shrine in Old St Peter's, Rome.

SALTIRE CROSS (ST ANDREW'S CROSS): with diagonal limbs.

SANCTUARY: area around the main altar of a church. See also *presbytery*.

SARCOPHAGUS (*lit.* flesh-consuming): coffin of stone or other durable material.

SAUCER DOME: see *dome*.

SAXO-NORMAN: transitional Romanesque style combining Anglo-Saxon and Norman features, current *c.* 1060–1100.

SCAGLIOLA: composition imitating marble.

SCREEN: in a church, structure usually at the entry to the chancel: see *rood* (*screen*) and *pulpitum*. A *parclose screen* separates a chapel from the rest of the church.

SECTION: two-dimensional representation of a building, moulding etc., revealed by cutting across it.

SEDILIA: seats for the priests (usually three) on the s side of a chancel; a plural word that has become a singular, collective one. One such seat: sedile.

SET-OFF: see *weathering*.

SEVERY: cell or compartment of a vault.

SGRAFFITO: scratched pattern, often in plaster.

SHAFT: upright member of round section, (1) the main part of a classical column, or (2) component of a Gothic compound pier or of a series flanking Gothic openings. *Shaft-ring*: ring like a bolt round a circular pier or a circular shaft attached to a pier, characteristic of the C12 and C13. *Wall-shaft*: partly attached to a wall.

SILL: horizontal member at the bottom of an opening.

SLYPE: covered way or passage, especially in a cathedral or monastic church, leading E from the cloisters between transept and chapter house.

SOFFIT (*lit.* ceiling): underside of an arch (also called *intrados*), lintel etc. *Soffit roll*: roll moulding on a soffit.

SOUNDING-BOARD: horizontal board or canopy over a pulpit. Also called *tester*.

S.P.A.B.: Society for the Protection of Ancient Buildings.

SPANDRELS: roughly triangular spaces between an arch and its containing rectangle, or between adjacent arches.

SPHERICAL TRIANGLE: accepted but unsatisfactory term (three-dimensional adjective, two-dimensional noun) for a triangular window-frame with convex-curved sides.

SPIRE: tall pyramidal or conical feature built on a tower or turret. *Broach spire*: starting from a square base, then carried into an octagonal section by means of triangular faces. *Needle spire*: thin spire rising from the centre of a tower roof, well inside the parapet.

SPIRELET: see *flèche*.

SPLAY: chamfer, usually of a reveal.

SPRING or SPRINGING: level at which an arch or vault rises from its supports. *Springers*: the first stones of an arch or vaulting-rib above the spring.

SQUINCH: arch or series of arches thrown across an angle between two walls to support a superstructure of polygonal or round plan over a rectangular space, e.g. a dome.

SQUINT: hole cut in a wall or through a pier to allow a view of the main altar of a church from places whence it could not otherwise be seen. Also called *hagioscope*.

STAIR: for elements, see *newel*; *nosing*; *riser*; *strings*; *tread*. In churches the commonest stairs are spiral stairs in turrets or in the thickness of the wall; also pulpit steps.

STALL: seat for clergy, choir etc., distinctively treated in its own right or as one of a row.

STANCHION: upright structural member, of iron or steel or reinforced concrete.

STEEPLE: tower together with a spire or other tall feature on top of it.

STIFF-LEAF: late C12 and C13 type of carved foliage found chiefly on capitals and bosses, a mainly English development from crocketing.

STILTED ARCH: see *arch*.

STOUP: vessel for the reception of holy water, usually placed near a door.

STRAINER: see *arch*.

STRAPWORK: C16 and C17 decoration, used also in the C19 Jacobean revival, resembling interlaced bands of cut leather.

STRING-COURSE: intermediate stone course or moulding projecting from the surface of a wall.

STRINGS: two sloping members which carry the ends of the treads and risers of a staircase. Closed strings enclose the treads and risers; in the later open string staircase the steps project above the strings.

STUCCO (*lit.* plaster): a fine lime plaster worked to a smooth surface, and often painted.

SWAG (*lit.* bundle): like a festoon (q.v.), but also a cloth bundle in relief, hung up at both ends.

SYNCOPATED ARCADING: double layers of blank arcading set so that apexes of arches lie in front of shafts and *vice versa* (with an effect better described as counterpoint than syncopation).

TABERNACLE (*lit.* tent): (1) canopied structure, especially on a small scale, to contain the reserved sacrament or a relic; (2) architectural frame, e.g. of a statue on a wall or free-standing, with flanking orders. In classical architecture also called an *aedicule*. See also *throne* (2).

TABLET FLOWER: medieval ornament of a four-leaved flower with a raised or sunk centre.

TABLE TOMB: memorial slab raised on free-standing legs.

TAS-DE-CHARGE: stone(s) forming the springers of more than one vaulting-rib.

TERMINAL FIGURE: pedestal or pilaster which tapers towards the bottom, usually with the upper part of a human figure growing out of it. Also called *term*.

TERRACOTTA: moulded and fired clay ornament or cladding, usually unglazed.

TESSELLATED PAVEMENT: mosaic flooring, particularly Roman, consisting of small *tesserae*, i.e. cubes of glass, stone or brick.

TESTER (*lit.* head): bracketed canopy over a tomb and especially over a pulpit, where it is also called a *sounding-board*.

TETRASTYLE: see *portico*.

THREE-DECKER PULPIT: pulpit with reading-desk below and clerk's stall below that.

THRONE: (1) the bishop's seat in the choir; (2) stand for a vessel displaying the Host or relics.

TIE-BEAM: see *roofs*.

TIERCERON: see *vault*.

TOMB-CHEST: an oblong chest, usually stone, meant to contain or appear to contain the coffin of the deceased, often with carved effigy and/or canopy on top. See also *table tomb*.

TOUCH: soft black marble quarried near Tournai.

TOURELLE: turret corbelled out from the wall.

TRABEATED: dependent structurally on the use of the post and lintel. cf. *arcuated*.

TRACERY: intersecting rib-work in the upper part of a window, or used decoratively in blank arches, on vaults etc. *Plate tracery*: early form of tracery where decoratively shaped openings are cut through the solid stone infilling in a window head. *Bar tracery*: a form introduced into England *c.* 1250. Intersecting ribwork made up of slender shafts, continuing the lines of the mullions of windows up to a decorative mesh in the head of the window. *Geometrical tracery*: characteristic of *c.*

1250–1310 consisting chiefly of circles or foiled circles. *Y-tracery*: consisting of a mullion which branches into two forming a Y-shape; typical of *c.* 1300. *Intersecting tracery*: in which each mullion of a window branches out into two curved bars in such a way that every one of them is drawn with the same radius from a different centre. The result is that every light of the window is a lancet and every two, three, four etc. lights together form a pointed arch. This treatment also is typical of *c.* 1300. *Reticulated tracery*: typical of the early C14, consisting entirely of circles drawn into ogee shapes so that a net-like appearance results. *Panel tracery*: Perp tracery formed of upright straight-sided panels above lights of a window. *Dagger*: lozenge-like Dec tracery motif. *Mouchette*: curved version of the dagger form, especially popular in the early C14.

TRANSEPTS (*lit.* cross-enclosures): transverse portions of a cross-shaped church, i.e. arms flanking the crossing to N and S.

TRANSITIONAL: transitional phase between two styles, used most often for the phase between Romanesque and Early English (*c.* 1175–*c.* 1200).

TRANSOM: horizontal member between the lights in a window opening.

TREAD: horizontal part of the step of a staircase. The *tread end* may be carved.

TREFOIL: see *foil*.

TRIBUNE: see *gallery* (1).

TRIFORIUM (*lit.* three openings): middle storey of a church treated as an arcaded wall-passage or blind arcade, its height corresponding to that of the aisle roof. Unlike a gallery, has no outer windows. See also *gallery* (1).

TRIGLYPHS (*lit.* three-grooved tablets): stylized beam-ends in the Doric frieze, with metopes between.

TRIUMPHAL ARCH: see *arch*.

TROPHY: sculptured group of arms or armour as a memorial of victory.

TRUMEAU: central stone mullion supporting the tympanum of a wide doorway. *Trumeau figure*: carved figure attached to a *trumeau*; cf. *column figure*.

TUDOR FLOWER: late Gothic ornament of a flower with square flat petals or foliage.

TURRET: small tower, usually attached to a building.

TYMPANUM (*lit.* drum): as of a drum-skin, the surface between a lintel and the arch above it or within a pediment.

UNDERCROFT: vaulted room, sometimes underground, below the main upper room. See also *crypt*.

VAULT: ceiling of stone formed like arches (sometimes imitated in timber or plaster). *Tunnel-* or *barrel-vault*: the simplest kind of vault, in effect a continuous semicircular arch. *Groin-vaults* (usually called *cross-vaults* in classical architecture) have four curving triangular surfaces produced by the intersection of two tunnel-vaults at right angles. The curved lines at the intersections are called *groins*. In *quadripartite rib-vaults* the four sections are divided by their arches or ribs springing from the corners of the bay. *Sexpartite rib-vaults*, most often used over paired bays, have an extra pair of ribs which spring from between the bays and meet the other four ribs at the crown of the vault.

The main types of rib are: *diagonal ribs, ridge ribs* (along the longitudinal or transverse ridge of a vault), *transverse ribs* (between bays) and *wall ribs* (between vault and wall). *Tiercerons* are extra, decorative ribs springing from the corners of a bay. *Liernes* are decorative ribs in the crown of a vault which are not linked to any of the springing points. In a *stellar vault* the liernes are arranged in a star formation. *Fan-vaults* are peculiar to English Perp architecture in consisting not of ribs and infilling but of halved concave cones with decorative blind tracery carved on their surfaces.

VAULTING-SHAFT: shaft leading up to the springer of a vault.

VENETIAN WINDOW: a form derived from an invention by Serlio, also called a *Serlian* or *Palladian window*.

VERANDA(H): shelter or gallery against a building (or as part of a pulpitum), its roof supported by thin vertical members.

VERMICULATION: stylized surface treatment as if worm-eaten.

VESICA: oval with pointed head and foot, usually of a window or tracery.

VESTIBULE: anteroom or entrance hall, e.g. to a chapel or chapter house.

VITRUVIAN SCROLL: running ornament of curly waves, on a classical frieze. See also *wave moulding*.

VOLUTES: spiral scrolls on the front and back of a Greek Ionic capital, also on the sides of a Roman one. *Angle volute*: pair of volutes turned outwards to meet at the corner of a capital. Volutes were also used individually as dec-oration in C17 and C18 ornament.

VOUSSOIRS: wedge-shaped stones forming an arch.

WAGON ROOF: roof in which closely set rafters with arched braces give the appearance of the inside of a canvas tilt over a wagon. Wagon roofs can be panelled or plastered (ceiled) or left uncovered. Also called *cradle roof*.

WAINSCOT: see *panelling*.

WALL-PLATE: see *roofs*.

WALL-SHAFT: see *shaft*.

WARMING ROOM: see *calefactory*.

WATERHOLDING BASE: type of early Gothic base in which the upper and lower mouldings are separated by a hollow so deep as to be capable of retaining water.

WATERLEAF: a leaf-shape used in late C12 capitals, in form broad, unribbed and tapering, curving out towards the angle of the aba-cus and turned in at the top.

WAVE MOULDING: a compound ornament formed by a convex curve between two concave curves, used especially in the early C14. See also *Vitruvian scroll*.

WEATHERING: inclined, projecting surface to keep water away from wall and joints below. Also called *set-off*; and see *dripstone*.

WEEPERS: small figures placed in niches along the sides of some medieval tombs. Also called *mourners*.

WESTWORK: the w end of a Carolingian or Romanesque church, consisting of a low entrance hall and above it a room open to the nave, the whole crowned by one broad tower, sometimes flanked by w transepts.

WHEEL WINDOW: circular window with tracery of radiating shafts like the spokes of a wheel. See also *rose-window*.

# Recent Literature

A thorough bibliography of the English cathedral – starting, say, before the Norman Conquest – could fill a book by itself. This is a selective list of recent books and articles. Fuller lists appear in Harvey 1978, Bony 1979, Morris 1979 (both main bibliography and individual lists), and British Archaeological Association conference transactions since 1978 (all, below). For books by c18–19 architectural writers, see Pevsner 1972 (to which one must add the name of John Browne (1847) on York) and Cobb 1980, also Crook's latest edition of Eastlake 1872. Professor Willis's papers on cathedrals (1842–63), so often mentioned in our text, have lately been reprinted (see below). 'Colvin' undated refers to Colvin 1978. A series recently begun, the Courtauld Institute Illustration Archives, includes *Cathedrals and Monastic Buildings in the British Isles*, Archive 1, 1980. New surveys are being made, of medieval English stained glass under the auspices of the British Academy (see Caviness, below) and of medieval English wall painting under the auspices of the Courtauld

Institute of Art (meanwhile see E. W. Tristram's books of 1950, 1955). The National Monuments Record library holds full collections of new and old photographs of the English cathedrals. The Royal Institute of British Architects Drawings Collection's rich holdings include drawings for cathedral works by e.g. the great Victorians, Scott, Pearson and Bentley, and its published catalogue has been gradually appearing (see Fisher *et al.* below). Useful background reading on cathedral history, with bibliographies, can be found in the Ecclesiastical History of England volumes, e.g. Professor Owen Chadwick's two on *The Victorian Church*, 1966–70. Inexpensive well-illustrated booklets, often with texts by specialists, and showing details of work such as roof bosses and misericords not easy for visitors to see, are increasingly available at cathedral bookstalls, and a number are cited below. See also the Glossary for a list of books containing illustrated glossaries of architectural terms.

Addleshaw 1967. G. W. O. Addleshaw, 'Architects, painters, sculptors, craftsmen 1660–1960, whose work is to be seen in York Minster', *Architectural History*, Vol. 10, 1967.

Addleshaw 1971. G. W. O. Addleshaw, 'Architects, sculptors, designers and craftsmen 1770–1970 whose work is to be seen in Chester Cathedral', *Architectural History*, Vol. 14, 1971.

Aylmer and Cant 1977. G. E. Aylmer and Reginald Cant (eds.), *A History of York Minster*, 1977 (especially chapters by Gee, Harvey and O'Connor).

B.A.A. *Worcester* 1978. British Archaeological Association Transactions, *Medieval Art and Architecture at Worcester Cathedral* (conference 1975), 1978. Series continued with *Ely* (1976), 1979; *Durham* (1977), 1980; *Wells* (1978), 1981; *Canterbury* (1979), 1982; *Winchester* (1980), 1983; *Gloucester* (1981), *Lincoln* (1982) *et al.* in preparation.

Beard 1981. Geoffrey Beard, *Craftsmen and Interior Decoration in England 1660–1820*, 1981.

Belcher 1970. John T. Belcher, *The Organs of Chester Cathedral*, 1970.

Bennett n.d. B. T. N. Bennett, *The Choir Stalls of Chester Cathedral*, n.d.

Binnall 1966. Peter B. G. Binnall, *The Nineteenth Century Stained Glass in Lincoln Minster*, 1966.

Bock 1961. Henning Bock, 'Exeter Rood Screen', *Architectural Review*, Vol. 130, 1961.

Bock 1965. Henning Bock, 'Bristol Cathedral and its Place in European Architecture', Bristol Cathedral 800th Anniversary Booklet, 1965.

B of E. Nikolaus Pevsner *et al.*, the *Buildings of England* series: original volumes 1951–74; revisions in progress.

Bony 1979. Jean Bony, *The English Decorated Style, Gothic Architecture Transformed 1250–1350*, 1979.

Borg *et al.* 1980. Alan Borg *et al.*, *Medieval Sculpture from Norwich Cathedral* (catalogue, Sainsbury Centre for Visual Arts, University of East Anglia), 1980.

Britton. See Crook 1968.

Cave (1935) 1976. C. J. P. Cave, *The Roof Bosses of Winchester Cathedral* (1935), reprint 1976; and other publications by Cave on bosses, e.g. at Canterbury, Exeter, Gloucester and Lincoln.

Caviness 1977. Madeline H. Caviness, *The Early Stained Glass of Canterbury Cathedral, c. 1175–1220*, 1977.

Caviness 1981. Madeline H. Caviness, *The Windows of Christ Church Cathedral, Canterbury*, 1981.

Cherry 1978. Bridget Cherry, 'Romanesque Architecture in Eastern England', *British Archaeological Association Journal*, Vol. 41, 1978.

Clifton-Taylor 1972. Alec Clifton-Taylor, *The Pattern of English Building*, 1972.

Cobb 1980. Gerald Cobb, *English Cathedrals, The Forgotten Centuries, Restoration and Change from 1530 to the Present Day*, 1980.

Cocke 1973. Thomas H. Cocke, 'Pre-Nineteenth Century Attitudes in England to Romanesque Architecture', *British Archaeological Association Journal*, Vol. 36, 1973.

Cocke 1975. Thomas H. Cocke, 'James Essex, Cathedral Restorer', *Architectural History*, Vol. 18, 1975.

Cocke 1979. Thomas H. Cocke, 'The Architectural History of Ely Cathedral 1540–1840'; see B.A.A. *Ely* 1979.

Colchester 1977. L. S. Colchester, *Stained Glass in Wells Cathedral*, 1977.

Colchester 1978. L. S. Colchester, *The West Front of Wells Cathedral*, 1978.

Colchester 1982. L. S. Colchester (ed.), *Wells Cathedral, A History*, 1982.

Colchester and Harvey 1974. L. S. Colchester and J. H. Harvey, 'Wells Cathedral', *Archaeological Journal*, Vol. 131, 1974.

Coldstream 1972. Nicola Coldstream, 'York Chapter House', *British Archaeological Association Journal*, Vol. 35, 1972.

Coldstream 1976. Nicola Coldstream, 'English Decorated Shrine Bases', *British Archaeological Association Journal*, Vol. 39, 1976.

Coldstream 1979. Nicola Coldstream, 'Ely Cathedral: the Fourteenth Century Work'; see B.A.A. *Ely* 1979.

Colvin 1963, 1975. H. M. Colvin on Westminster Abbey in Colvin (ed.), *The History of the King's Works*, Vol. I, 1963, and Vol. IV, Pt 1, 1975.

Colvin 1966. H. M. Colvin, *Views of the Old Palace of Westminster* (*Architectural History* Vol. 9), 1966.

Colvin 1971. H. M. Colvin, *Building Accounts of King Henry III*, 1971.

Colvin 1975. See Colvin 1963.

Colvin 1978. H. M. Colvin, *A Biographical Dictionary of British Architects 1600–1840*, 1978.

Croft-Murray 1962, 1970. E. G. Croft-Murray, *Decorative Painting in England, 1537–1837*, 2 vols., 1962, 1970.

Crook 1968. J. M. Crook, 'John Britton and the Genesis of the Gothic Revival', in J. Summerson (ed.), *Concerning Architecture*, 1968.

Crook 1970. See Eastlake.

Crook 1980. J. M. Crook, 'William Burges and the Completion of St Paul's', *Antiquaries Journal*, Vol. 60, Pt 2, 1980.

Crook 1981. J. M. Crook, *William Burges and the High Victorian Dream*, 1981.

Dickinson 1976. J. C. Dickinson, 'The Origins of St Augustine's, Bristol', in P. McGrath and J. Cannon (eds.), *Essays in Bristol and Gloucestershire History*, 1976.

Downes 1969. Kerry Downes, *Hawksmoor*, 1969.

Downes 1971. Kerry Downes, *Christopher Wren*, 1971.

Draper 1978. Peter Draper, 'The Retrochoir of Winchester Cathedral', *Architectural History*, Vol. 21, 1978.

Draper 1979. Peter Draper, 'Bishop Northwold and the Cult of St Etheldreda': see B.A.A. *Ely* 1979.

Eames (E.) 1980. Elizabeth S. Eames, *Catalogue of Medieval Lead-Glazed Earthenware Tiles in the . . . British Museum*, 1980.

Eames (P.) 1977. Penelope Eames, *Furniture in England, France and the Netherlands, Twelfth to Fifteenth Centuries* (special number of *Medieval Furniture*), 1977.

Eastlake (1872) 1970. C. L. Eastlake, *A History of the Gothic Revival* (1872), revised by J. M. Crook, 1970.

Erskine 1981–2. Audrey Erskine (ed.), *The Fabric Rolls of Exeter Cathedral*, 2 vols., 1981–2.

Fernie 1974. Eric Fernie, 'Excavations at the Façade of Norwich Cathedral', *Norfolk Archaeology*, Vol. 36, Pt 1, 1974.

Fernie 1976. Eric Fernie, 'The Ground Plan of Norwich Cathedral and the Square Root of Two', *British Archaeological Association Journal*, Vol. 39, 1976.

Fernie 1977. Eric Fernie, 'The Romanesque Piers of Norwich Cathedral', *Norfolk Archaeology*, Vol. 36, Pt 4, 1977.

Fernie 1980. Eric Fernie, 'Norwich Cathedral', *Archaeological Journal*, Vol. 137, 1980.

Fisher, Stamp *et al.* 1981. Geoffrey Fisher, Gavin Stamp and others (ed. Joanna Heseltine), *Catalogue of the Drawings Collection of the R.I.B.A., The Scott Family*, 1981.

Fitchen 1961. John Fitchen, *The Construction of Gothic Cathedrals*, 1961; and review by Pevsner in *Architectural Review*, Vol. 129, 1961. Also see Robert Mark, *Experiments in Gothic Structure*, 1982.

Fletcher 1979. John Fletcher, 'Medieval Timberwork at Ely': see B.A.A. *Ely* 1979.

Frew 1978. J. M. Frew, 'Improvements: James Wyatt at Lichfield Cathedral 1787–92', *Lichfield Archaeological and Historical Society Transactions*, Vol. 19 (1977–8), 1979.

Gem 1978. R. D. H. Gem, 'Bishop Wulfstan II and the Romanesque Cathedral Church of Worcester': see B.A.A. *Worcester* 1978.

Glasscoe and Swanton 1978. Marion Glasscoe and Michael Swanton, *Medieval Woodwork in Exeter Cathedral*, 1978.

Gomme 1979. A. Gomme, M. Jenner and B. Little, *Bristol, An Architectural History*, 1979.

Gunnis 1953. Rupert Gunnis, *Dictionary of British Sculptors 1660–1851*, 1953.

Harrison 1980. Martin Harrison, *Victorian Stained Glass*, 1980.

Harvey 1954. John H. Harvey, *English Medieval Architects, a Biographical Dictionary down to 1550*, 1954 (new ed. forthcoming).

Harvey 1972. John H. Harvey, *The Mediaeval Architect*, 1972.

Harvey 1974. John H. Harvey, *The Cathedrals of England and Wales*, 1974.

Harvey 1978. John H. Harvey, *The Perpendicular Style 1330–1485*, 1978.

Harvey. See also Colchester and Harvey.

Hewett 1974. Cecil A. Hewett, *English Cathedral Carpentry*, 1974; and see review by Quentin Hughes and D. T. Yeomans in *Times Literary Supplement*, 29 August 1975.

Hope and Lloyd 1973. Vyvyan Hope and John Lloyd, *Exeter Cathedral, A Short History and Description*, 1973.

Hunting 1981. Penelope Hunting, *Royal Westminster* (exhibition catalogue), 1981.

Jervis 1976. Simon Jervis, *Woodwork of Winchester Cathedral*, 1976.

Jordan 1980. William J. Jordan, 'Sir George Gilbert Scott R.A., Surveyor to Westminster Abbey 1849–1878', *Architectural History*, Vol. 23, 1980.

Kettle and Johnson 1970. Ann J. Kettle and D. A. Johnson, 'The Cathedral of Lichfield', *Staffordshire*, Vol. III, ed. M. W. Greenslade, *Victoria County History*, 1970.

Kidson 1962. Peter Kidson in P. Kidson, P. Murray, and P. Thompson, *A History of English Architecture*, 1962.

Knowles and Hadcock 1971. David Knowles and R. N. Hadcock, *Medieval Religious Houses*, rev. ed. 1971.

Leedy 1975. Walter C. Leedy, 'The Design of the Vaulting of Henry VII's Chapel, Westminster: a Reappraisal', *Architectural History*, Vol. 18, 1975.

Little 1979. See Gomme 1979.

Lockett 1978a. R. B. Lockett, 'The Victorian Restoration of Worcester Cathedral': see B.A.A. *Worcester* 1978.

Lockett 1978b. R. B. Lockett, 'George Gilbert Scott, the Joint

Restoration Committee, and the Refurnishing of Worcester Cathedral 1863–74', *Transactions of Worcester Archaeological Society*, 3rd series, Vol. 6, 1978.

Lockett 1980. R. B. Lockett, 'Joseph Potter, Cathedral Architect at Lichfield 1794–1842', *Lichfield Archaeological and Historical Society Transactions*, Vol. 21 (1979–80), 1980.

McLees 1973. A. David McLees, 'Henry Yevele: Disposer of the King's Works of Masonry', *British Archaeological Association Journal*, Vol. 36, 1973.

Maddison 1978. John Maddison, *Decorated Architecture in the North-West Midlands* (University of Manchester PhD dissertation), 1978.

Mark 1982. See Fitchen.

Matthews 1975. Betty Matthews, *The Organs and Organists of Winchester Cathedral*, 1975.

Matthews n.d. Betty Matthews, *The Organs and Organists of Exeter Cathedral*, n.d.

Morgan 1967. F. C. Morgan, *Hereford Cathedral Church Glass*, 1967.

Morris 1974. R. K. Morris, 'The Remodelling of the Hereford Aisles', *British Archaeological Association Journal*, Vol. 37, 1974.

Morris 1978. R. K. Morris, 'Worcester Nave from Decorated to Perpendicular': see B.A.A. *Worcester 1978*.

Morris 1979. R. K. Morris, *The Cathedrals and Abbeys of England and Wales: the Building Church, 600–1540*, 1979.

Munby 1981. Julian Munby, 'The Chichester Roofs, Thirteenth-Century Roofs of the Cathedral and Bishop's Palace', *Chichester Excavations*, Vol. 5, ed. A. Down, 1981.

Norris 1978. Malcolm Norris, *Monumental Brasses*, 3 vols., 1978.

Pevsner 1961. Nikolaus Pevsner, 'A Note on the East End of Winchester Cathedral', *Archaeological Journal*, Vol. 116, 1961.

Pevsner 1963. Nikolaus Pevsner, *The Choir of Lincoln Cathedral*, 1963.

Pevsner 1972. Nikolaus Pevsner, *Some Architectural Writers of the Nineteenth Century*, 1972.

Pevsner. See also B of E.

Physick 1970. John Physick, *The Wellington Monument*, 1970.

Pierce 1965. William Wilkins and John Adey Repton, *Norwich Cathedral (c. 1798–1800)*, ed. S. Rowland Pierce, 1965.

Quiney 1979. Anthony P. Quiney, *John Loughborough Pearson*, 1979.

RCHM. Royal Commission on Historical Monuments, England, *An Inventory of the Historical Monuments*, 1908–, in progress.

Remnant 1969. G. L. Remnant, *A Catalogue of Misericords in Great Britain*, 1969.

Rigold 1976. S. E. Rigold, *The Chapter House and the Pyx Chamber, Westminster*, 1976.

Roberts 1971. Eileen Roberts, *A Guide to the Abbey Murals* (St Albans), 1971.

Rodwell 1980a. Warwick Rodwell, *Wells Cathedral, Excavations and Discoveries*, rev. ed. 1980.

Rodwell 1980b. Warwick Rodwell, 'The Cloisters of Wells Reconsidered', Annual Report to Friends of the Cathedral, 1980.

Rodwell 1981. Warwick Rodwell, 'The Lady Chapel by the Cloister at Wells and the Site of the Anglo-Saxon Cathedral': see B.A.A. *Wells 1981*.

Rossi 1981. Anthony Rossi, 'The Cathedral of St John the Baptist at Norwich', *Archaeological Journal*, Vol. 137 (1980), 1981.

Runcie 1977. Robert Runcie, then Bishop of St Albans (ed.), *Cathedral and City, St Albans Ancient and Modern*, 1977; includes articles by Martin Biddle and Christopher Brooke.

Salzman 1967. L. F. Salzman, *Building in England down to 1540*, rev. ed. 1967.

Sewter 1974–5. A. C. Sewter, *The Stained Glass of William Morris and His Circle*, 2 vols., 1974–5.

Singleton 1978. Barrie Singleton, 'The Remodelling of the East End of Worcester Cathedral in the Earlier Part of the Thirteenth Century': see B.A.A. *Worcester 1978*.

Skeat 1977. F. J. Skeat, *The Stained Glass of St Albans Cathedral*, 1977.

Smith 1977. M. Q. Smith, 'The Harrowing of Hell Relief in Bristol Cathedral', *Transactions of the Bristol and Gloucestershire Archaeological Society*, Vol. 94, 1977.

Stanton 1972. Phoebe Stanton, *Pugin*, 1972.

Steer 1973. Francis W. Steer, *The Catholic Church of Our Lady and St Philip Arundel*, 1973.

Stratford 1978. Neil Stratford, 'Notes on the Norman Chapter House at Worcester': see B.A.A. *Worcester 1978*.

Summers 1974. Norman Summers, *Prospect of Southwell*, 1974.

Summerson 1964. John Summerson, 'Inigo Jones', *Proceedings of the British Academy*, Vol. 50, 1964.

Summerson 1975. John Summerson on Old St Paul's and on Exeter cloisters, in H. M. Colvin (ed.), *The History of the King's Works*, Vol. IV, Pt 1, 1975.

Swanton 1979. Michael Swanton, *Roof-Bosses and Corbels of Exeter Cathedral*, 1979; see also Glasscoe and Swanton.

Swanton 1980. Michael Swanton, 'A Mural Palimpsest from Rochester Cathedral', *Archaeological Journal*, Vol. 136 (1979), 1980.

Tudor-Craig 1976. P. Tudor-Craig, *One Half Our Noblest Art* (booklet on Wells west front), 1976.

VCH. *Victoria History of the Counties of England*, 1900–, in progress.

Verey and Welander 1979. David Verey and David Welander, *Gloucester Cathedral*, 1979.

*Victorian Church Art 1971*. *Victorian Church Art*, exhibition catalogue, Victoria and Albert Museum, 1971.

Whinney 1964. Margaret Whinney, *Sculpture in Britain, 1530–1830*, 1964.

Whinney 1971. Margaret Whinney, *Wren*, 1971.

Whittingham 1980. A. B. Whittingham, 'Norwich Saxon Throne', *Archaeological Journal*, Vol. 136 (1979), 1980.

Whittingham 1981. A. B. Whittingham, 'The Ramsey Family of Norwich', 'The Foundation of Norwich Cathedral', 'Gates of the Cathedral Close' etc., *Archaeological Journal*, Vol. 137 (1980), 1981.

Willis (1842–63) 1972–3. Robert Willis, *Architectural History of some English Cathedrals . . .*, 2 vols., 1972–3; dates first read and/or published: Hereford 1842, Canterbury 1844, Winchester 1845, Norwich 1847, York 1848, Salisbury 1849, Oxford 1850, Wells 1851, Chichester 1853(61), Gloucester 1860, Lichfield 1861, Peterborough 1861, Worcester 1863, Rochester 1863.

Wilson 1978. Christopher Wilson, 'The Sources of the Late Twelfth-Century Work at Worcester Cathedral': see B.A.A. *Worcester* 1978. See him also in B.A.A. *Durham* 1980 on C 14 work at Durham.

Woodman 1981. Francis Woodman, *The Architectural History of Canterbury Cathedral*, 1981.

Zarnecki 1978. George Zarnecki, 'The Romanesque Capitals in the South Transept of Worcester Cathedral': see B.A.A. *Worcester* 1978. See also his standard works on English Romanesque sculpture, 1951, 1953.

# Illustration Acknowledgements

James Austin 68, 96, 183; Courtauld Institute 10, 17, 30, 47, 93–4, 103, 126, 131, 137, 141, 148, 166, 192; Jack Farley 64; George Hall 31–2, 34, 77–8, 80, 128, 195; Sonia Halliday and Laura Lushington 197–9, 200; A. F. Kersting 1 (by permission of the Provost and Chapter of Birmingham Cathedral), 2, 6, 12–13, 16, 18, 21–5, 27–9, 33, 35–40, 43–5, 49–50, 52, 57, 59, 62, 65–7, 69–70, 74–5, 79, 81–2, 84, 88, 92, 97, 100, 102, 104–18, 122, 130, 136, 139–40, 143–4, 146, 149, 151–4, 158, 161–2, 164–5. 167–8, 171–80, 186, 188, 190, 191, 193–4, 196; National Monuments Record 3–4, 20, 101, 121, 150, 155–6, 159–60, 163; Sefton Samuels 120; Walter Scott 15, 19, 46–7, 51, 53–4, 61, 85, 90, 99, 129; University of East Anglia 132–5; Bill Walker 7–9, 11; Jeffery Whitelaw 142.

The map and Figure 185 were drawn by Reginald Piggott. Engravings were taken from John Britton's *Cathedral Antiquities* 1813–32, and plans are acknowledged in their captions.

# Index

This is an index to names and places: to architects, artists and craftsmen, to churchmen, to people commemorated by monuments, and to cathedrals and churches.

Pages including illustrations are shown in *italic* type.